Across Cultures

A READER FOR WRITERS

Sheena Gillespie
Robert Singleton

Queensborough Community College
City University of New York

ALLYN and BACON

BOSTON   LONDON   TORONTO   SYDNEY   TOKYO   SINGAPORE

To Ruth, Flo, and Helen; to Jay Ford; and to the Memory of
Rachel Maria Asrelsky, a Victim of Pan Am Flight 103,
December 21, 1988—Advocates of Crossing Cultures

Copyright © 1991 by Allyn and Bacon
A Division of Simon & Schuster, Inc.
160 Gould Street
Needham Heights, Massachusetts 02194

Library of Congress Cataloging-in-Publication Data

Across cultures : a reader for writers / [selected by] Sheena Gillespie, Robert Singleton.
      p.   cm.
  ISBN 0-205-13065-8
    1. College readers. 2. English language—Rhetoric. 3. Readers—
Culture. 4. Culture. I. Gillespie, Sheena.
II. Singleton, Robert.
PE1417.A27 1991
808'.0427—dc20
                                       90-21641
                                             CIP

This textbook is printed on
recycled, acid-free paper.

Credits

Pages 5–6   From *The Beginning: Creation Myths Around the World* by Maria Leach. Copyright 1956 by Funk & Wagnalls Company; permission of Harper & Row, Publishers, Inc.

Credits continued on page 487, which constitutes an extension of the copyright page.

Printed in the United States of America

10 9 8 7 6 5 4 3 2 1   95 94 93 92 91 90

CONTENTS

CHAPTER 3.   Education

CHAPTER 5.   Interactions   287

CHAPTER 6. Choices

RHETORICAL CONTENTS

DESCRIPTION

DEFINITION

COMPARISON AND CONTRAST

CAUSE AND EFFECT

PERSUASION

PREFACE FOR THE TEACHER

Across Cultures is a reader that invites students to look beyond their own society and culture. The title embodies our guiding image of a reaching out—moving beyond the immediate and the parochial to an acknowledgement and acceptance of pluralism and diversity within and among cultures. In our usage, such reaching out does not mean blending or blurring or assimilating (or hybridizing, in the biological sense). The outreach we mean may be found first, in the selection of readings by authors from and about many countries: by North Americans writing about other cultures and about United States culture and subcultures; by members of ethnic subcultures in the United States, such as immigrants or their children, African-Americans, or American Indians, writing about the United States; and by persons from other cultures writing about those cultures. Second, this reaching out is encouraged by the text's apparatus, in aids to the student. "Perspectives" (quotations); chapter introductions; selection headnotes; the end-of-lesson trio "Interpretations," "Correspondences," "Applications;" and "Additional Writing Topics" are found in every chapter.

The outreach implied by the title *Across Cultures* is an outgrowth of our understanding of the term *culture.* To define culture is a task not to be limited to a mere dictionary definition. Distinguished anthropologists A. L. Kroeber and Clyde Kluckhohn have devoted a sizable volume, *Culture: A Critical Review of Concepts and Definitions,* to this topic. Their effort continues whenever anthropologists communicate. In assembling this textbook, we have found Bronislaw Malinowski's essay on culture in the *Encyclopedia of the Social Sciences* (vol. IV), and Kluckhohn's 1962 essay, "The Concept of Culture," particularly useful. In those works these definitions appear: Culture is the "artificial, secondary environment" that human beings superimpose on the natural, and (from Kluckhohn)

Culture, then, is . . . that part [of human life] which is learned by people as the result of belonging to some particular group, and is that part of learned behavior which is shared with others. It is our social legacy, as contrasted with our organic heredity. It is the main factor which permits us to live together in a society, giving us ready-made solutions to our problems, helping us to predict the behavior of others, and permitting others to know what to expect of us.

From these definitions, then, these characteristics of culture follow: Culture is social, it is a human achievement, and human achievements are designed to serve an end or good; that is, the good of human beings. The world of culture is a world of values. Although the good may be immaterial—truth, beauty, honor, glory—cultural good must be realized in temporal and material form. Culture consists as much of conserving values as of realizing them. And finally, culture is pluralistic. It is society's attempt to realize a large number of values, some of them highly complex.

Today, travel across boundaries and continents—physical meeting of people from different cultures—is going on at a rapid rate. The rate of immigration to America approaches that at the turn of the century. "With an annual influx of 90,000 or more legal immigrants and an additional 40,000 or so undocumented aliens arriving each year, the proportion of foreign-born New Yorkers may pass the historic 1910 high of 40 percent within a decade," writes Sam Roberts in *The New York Times* of July 22, 1989. "The latest group of immigrants is considerably more diverse nationally," he says. These numbers and this diversity are reflected in our schools, especially those in New York, Los Angeles, Miami, San Antonio, and other cities, but also in smaller towns across the country.

When we look up from our daily newspapers and around at the faces of our students, we can see that this immigration is reflected in our students' diverse racial, ethnic, national, and cultural backgrounds—blacks, whites, Native Americans, Asians, Africans, and Hispanics. If ever a group of people faced the world's variety, it is today's teachers and students. As Mike Rose, associate director of Writing Programs at the University of California at Los Angeles and author of *Lives on the Boundary: The Struggles and Achievements of America's Underprepared* (1989), writes:

> Diversity. A word much in the news. A single word used to represent many kinds of students who are not from mainstream America: ethnic minority students, immigrant students, older students, students from the white working class. Both the popular media and our professional literature tell us about the problems and challenges a diverse student population presents to colleges—to our professional training, our curricula, our institutional procedures.*

And Ronald Takaki, professor of ethnic studies at the University of California at Berkeley, writes in the same *Chronicle* (March 8, 1989, p. 15):

---

*Non-Traditional Students Often Excel in College and Can Offer Many Benefits to Their Institutions," *Chronicle of Higher Education* (Oct. 11, 1989), p. B2.

The need to open the American mind to greater cultural diversity will not go away. We can resist it by ignoring the changing ethnic composition of our student bodies and the larger society, or we can realize how it offers colleges and universities a timely and exciting opportunity to revitalize the social sciences and humanities, giving both a new sense of purpose and a more inclusive definition of knowledge.

In the last few years we have heard much about cultural literacy. Without engaging in the debate about whether E. D. Hirsch overemphasizes education as information, we simply point out that Hirsch sees no conflict in cultural literacy and *multi*cultural literacy: a large percentage of the items in Hirsch's own "Appendix: What Literate Americans Should Know"† relate to non-American or American minority cultures. Abraham and Isaac, Achilles, Africa, Afghanistan, the Alamo, Algiers, Allah, Ankara, Apaches, apartheid, and Aztecs are just a few of the A items.

Advocates of both cultural and multicultural literacy may complain that Hirsch's list is arbitrary, but who would wish it monocultural? The goal of this volume is to provide a sampler of today's vast cultural diversity. In doing so, we hope to promote an attitude of acceptance, even celebration, of that diversity and to suggest ways of probing correspondences, relationships, and mutual benefits therein. We do not attempt to—we cannot—hide the difficulties and suffering sometimes caused by cultural diversity, but we do believe these difficulties can be reduced when people know more about others and therefore are more accepting of them.

The selections we offer in *Across Cultures* cover a much greater variety of cultural trends than the table of contents indicates. For example, traditions, the subject of Chapter 1, naturally leads to questions of family life, the roles of women and men, the influence of feminism, class differences, and rituals and ceremonies of all kinds. Work, the subject of Chapter 4, leads to such related subjects as affirmative action, immigration, cultural displacement, family narratives, and definitions of success. The chapter on aspirations (Chapter 7) deals with many of these same subtopics, but seen from a different angle; it also focuses on the relationship between the individual and the group, mentors, and role models. The chapters are also interconnected in ways that the table of contents cannot indicate. For example, "work" exists within a matrix of traditions, relationships, education, choices, and aspirations. Hence our inclusion of "Correspondences" throughout the book. These questions ask students to make connections and draw comparisons between the "Perspectives" (brief quotations at the beginning of each chapter) and the selections in that chapter, between the selections within the chapter, and between the selections in different chapters.

Each chapter begins, as we have said, with "Perspectives," brief pro-

†*Cultural Literacy* (1987), pp. 152–215.

vocative quotations that stimulate thought and discussion on the chapter topic. Next come the selections—myths, folktales, essays, and short stories. Whereas many of the essays and stories reflect the seemingly endless—often tumultuous—changes in current events, our rationale for including myths and folktales is to show culture in its conserving role. Although *Across Cultures* probably pays more attention to shifts in population and to political and economic changes around the world, these changes occur against backgrounds of centuries of history and tradition, of treasured stories of origins and beginnings that give direction to the current shifting allegiances. Such stories may actually revive and sustain some cultures.

The opening selections of each chapter are myths or folktales that remind us of how culture sustains us. These stories are regarded as holy, as scripture, as culturally indispensable; they link time and the timeless. As N. Scott Momaday says of the storyteller in American Indian tradition: "[He] creates himself and his listeners through the power of his perception, his imagination, his expression, his devotion to important details. He is a holy man; his function is sacred."

Helen Vendler, distinguished critic, professor of English at Harvard University, and past president of the Modern Language Association, pleads in her Presidential Address of 1980 for the implicit value of studying "myth, legend, and parable":

> It is not within our power to reform the primary and secondary schools, even if we have a sense of how that reform might begin. We do have it within our power, I believe, to reform ourselves, to make it our own first task to give, especially to our beginning students, that rich web of associations, lodged in the tales of majority and minority culture alike, by which they could begin to understand themselves as individuals and as social beings. We must give them some examples of literature, suited to their level of reading, in which these tales have an indisputable literary embodiment. All freshman English courses, to my mind, should devote at least half their time to the reading of myth, legend, and parable; and beginning language courses should do the same. [*PMLA*, Vol. 96, no. 3, p. 350]

Cultural commentary in our text is direct and explicit. Each chapter includes one selection on general American culture by an American writer, two or three selections by writers from diverse ethnic groups within the United States writing either on the experience of those groups or on individuals within them, and about five selections by writers from cultures elsewhere in the world.

A "Geographical Index" at the back of the book indicates the worldwide scope of these selections, the better to place American culture and its own diversity in a world context for comparison. Comparison or cross-examination is the purpose of the questions called Correspondences, which follow each selection. The Applications section provides writing and discussion topics and follows each group of "Perspectives" and each selection.

These activities call on the student to analyze cross-cultural similarities and differences and sometimes to place themselves at crossroads. Each selection is preceded by a biographical/cultural headnote and is followed by questions—Interpretations—which provoke thinking and discussion, probe comprehension, call attention to important rhetorical features, and help the reader relate the selection to the chapter topic.

We are grateful to Joe Opiela, our editor, who initiated and shaped this project. Our especial thanks to Margaret Cavanaugh, Kathy Howard, Marge Caronna, and Bibi Hussain for their generous assistance in the preparation of yet another manuscript.

We would like to thank the following reviewers for their helpful comments and suggestions: Margot Banks, Kean College of New Jersey; Vivian R. Brown, Laredo Junior College; Kathleen Shine Cain, Merrimack College; Barbara Carr, Stephen F. Austin State University; Ian Cruikshank, Florrisant Valley Community College; Jean English, Tallahassee Community College; Sallyanne H. Fitzgerald, University of Missouri–St. Louis; Christopher Gould, University of North Carolina; Alan Heineman, University of San Francisco; Carol Hovanec, Ramapo College; Keith Miller, Arizona State University; Joyce M. Pair, Dekalb College; Victor Villanueva, Northern Arizona University; Gary Waller, Carnegie-Mellon University; John R. Williams, Southeastern Louisiana University.

PREFACE FOR THE STUDENT

This book points toward possibilities hardly imagined in the world of your parents. Through business travel, tourism, governmental foreign aid, immigration, and an explosion in all kinds of communication, cultural interactions are occurring at a greater rate than ever before.

Old cultures, and even some not so old, like that of the United States, like to think, "We are the world." But once cultures cross— whether such meetings add to or subtract from the sum of their parts—they are never again the same: they can never again claim absoluteness, exclusivity, or monopoly. To promote such meetings, or crossings, is the purpose of *Across Cultures: A Reader for Writers*.

Whenever you read a newspaper or watch television, you are reminded that every aspect of your life—from politics and economics to music, the movies, fashion, sports, and education—is affected by developments around the globe. A tunnel is built under the English Channel from Dover to Calais and people in Gloucestershire pubs feel less like islanders. The Berlin Wall falls and Washington talks of a peace dividend. Gorbachev institutes *glasnost* in the U.S.S.R. and Cuba suddenly finds itself criticized in the usually friendly Soviet press. The NATO and Common Market countries must adapt to a non-Communist Eastern Europe and a united Germany. Tiananmen Square explodes and London steps up its attempts to evacuate a shaky Hong Kong. Only thirty-five years after the Civil Rights sit-ins in Montgomery, Alabama, approximately 7,000 African Americans hold public office in the United States, one of them the first black governor. The New World reverberates in the Old. Nelson Mandela walks out of prison in Capetown and credits world-wide sanctions with bringing hope to antiapartheid forces in South Africa. Change begets change. Immigration to New York City approaches again its historic 1910 high of 40 percent. How do we meet such changes? Preparation for the redefinition of globalism in the approaching new century requires a new definition of an educated person: An educated person is one who is culturally literate and appreciates, understands, and is tolerant of intercultural relationships.

Cultural meetings can occur in many ways. By culture we mean that "artificial, secondary environment" (Malinowski) which human beings superimpose on the natural environment. Wherever people make their mark on nature, they are creating a culture; a great deal of effort goes into a "creative conversation" about the value of these marks. A society expends a great deal of effort in attempting to conserve what it deems to be most valuable. Our first chapter, "Traditions," deals with such efforts. The remaining six chapters suggest some of the many ways in which cultural meetings can occur: in the family and other relationships, in education, in our work, interactions, choices, and aspirations.

At the center of each chapter are readings on a common subject or meeting ground, but you are introduced to the chapter through a group of brief quotations ("Perspectives") to stimulate personal responses in journal entries and collaborative explorations in group projects. Each selection is introduced with a biographical headnote that places the author in a particular historical-geographical context. After each selection are two sets of questions: "Interpretations," to provoke thinking and discussion and to call attention to specific rhetorical features, and "Correspondences," to encourage comparisons of cultures. Accordingly, you will often be asked to compare selections within, between, and among chapters.

The first one or two selections in each chapter are myths or folktales. These stories show culture in its conserving role. The stories purport to explain a people's origin or trace their values to earliest times. Each chapter also has selections by authors from and about a variety of countries: by North Americans writing on other cultures or about United States culture and subcultures; by members of ethnic subcultures within the United States, writing about themselves (often as outsiders); and by foreigners writing about their native cultures. At least two selections in each chapter are short stories.

Several features of the book will help you to apply the readings to your study of writing. The "Perspectives" section can be used to stimulate journal writing. "Applications" questions provide structured opportunities for you to convey what you have learned to a wider audience than just your peers through more structured writing and discussion activities. The "Additional Writing Topics" at the end of each chapter require you to conduct interviews, engage in debate, take positions, or reach conclusions. And a "Rhetorical Glossary" defines terminology essential to any writing class.

When you look around your classes and your campus, you probably see a student body diverse in its many countries, classes, and ages. When *this* inclusive group says, or sings, "We are the world," they are right. This is the world of *Across Cultures*.

CHAPTER 1

Traditions

The idea of tradition or heritage is inherent in most definitions of culture. For example, the anthropologist Edward Sapir says that "culture is . . . the socially inherited assemblage of practices and beliefs that determines the texture of our lives" (*Language,* 1921, p. 221). J. L. Myers asserts, "culture, then, is what remains of men's past, working on their present, to shape their future" (*Political Ideas of the Greeks,* 1927, p. 16).

Although conservation of traditional values is characteristic of all cultures, some honor it more than do others. "Rejection of tradition," writes Paula Gunn Allen in *Who is Your Mother? Red Roots of White Feminism* (p. 14), a leading Native American writer and anthologist, "constitutes one of the major features of American life." Americans, continues Allen, can and should learn from Native Americans to value tradition: "The Native-American view, which highly values maintenance of traditional customs, values, and perspectives . . . has the advantage of providing a solid sense of identity and lowered levels of psychological and interpersonal conflict."

Robert Bellah qualifies this line of argument. He feels that the tendency of Americans to reject tradition does not necessarily eliminate its influence: "In our forward-facing society, we are more apt to talk about the future than the past. . . . yet even in the debate about our future, our cultural tradition in its several strands, is still very much present, . . ." (*Habits of the Heart: Individualism and Commitment in American Life,* 1985, p. 27). Thus it is no surprise that our attitude toward tradition is ambivalent. (We want it, but we want to be free of it; we love part of the tradition but also hate part of it.) Tradition is both past and future, both history and destiny:

1

"So long as it is vital, the cultural tradition of a people—its symbols, ideas, and ways of feeling—is always *an argument about the meaning of the destiny its members share. Cultures are dramatic conversations* about things that matter to their participants, and American culture is no exception" (italics ours). Americans need to learn to participate in such conversations about our own traditions and those of other, older cultures. It is no accident that almost every selection in this chapter comes out of a very old culture—Bantu, Mayan, Native American, Egyptian, Persian (Iranian), Chinese, and Polish.

Our purpose in this chapter is to explore the significance of these traditions—both our own and those of others. These opening selections demonstrate the universal importance of traditions but also celebrate their diversity. They show that the "dramatic conversations about things that matter" are continuous and may lead to a number of conclusions. They suggest an astonishing variety of tradition in its "several strands": rituals, ceremonies, customs, "symbols, ideals, and ways of feeling." Little wonder, then, that *intra*cultural (and, less wonder, *inter*cultural) conversation is sometimes argument.

We can see such argument variously in progress, whether in Russell Baker's and N. Scott Momaday's reflections on the importance of their family origins or in Jehan Sadat's visit back in time to her husband's village and her subsequent reassessment of her assumption "How miserable the [traditional Egyptian] women must be." On a lighter note, Michael Kaufman explains and defends handkissing's contribution to Polish morale.

In "The Water-Faucet Vision," Gish Jen gives a spirited child's-eye view of Chinese-Americans in California, juxtaposing childhood encounters with Catholic Christians and adult encounters with fundamentalist Christians. In "The Wedding," Shusha Guppy shows the happy side of arranged marriage in the pre-Iran Persia of her parents' generation.

When "dramatic conversation" stops—when tradition is unquestioningly accepted or revered—it can stifle, maim, or kill. So, at least, suggests John King Fairbank as he looks at footbinding, a thousand-year-old custom that ended only in this century. In "The Lottery," a cautionary tale set in a New England village, Shirley Jackson also suggests that blind adherence to custom can be deadly.

Let us hope that the overheard conversations in this chapter will convince you that "answering" our heritage(s) is preferable to silence.

PERSPECTIVES

I was born a thousand years ago, born in the culture of bows and arrows . . . born in an age when people loved the things of nature, and spoke to it as though it had a soul.

Chief Dan George

When you are in the presence of sorrow, you are in a holy place.

George Santayana

But in order to speak about all to all, one has to speak of what all know and the reality common to all. The sea, the rain, necessity, desire, and the struggle against death—these are the things that unite us all.

Albert Camus

I have found that life persists in the midst of destruction, and therefore, there must be a higher law than that of destruction.

Mohandas K. (Mahatma) Gandhi

When there is pain, there are no words; all pain is the same.

Toni Morrison

The position of women in a society provides an exact measure of the development of that society.

Gustav Geiger

Memory is the diary that we all carry about with us.

Oscar Wilde

Tradition is a guide and not a jailor.

W. Somerset Maugham

To everything there is a season, and a time to every purpose under the heaven: a time to be born, and a time to die; a time to plant, and a time to pluck up that which is planted; a time to kill, and a time to heal; a time to break down, and a time to build up; a time to weep, and a time to laugh; a time to mourn, and a time to dance; a time to cast away stones, and a time to gather stones together; a time to embrace, and a time to refrain from embracing; a time to get, and a time to lose; a time to keep, and a time to cast away; a time to rend, and a time to sew; a time to keep silence, and a time to speak; a time to love, and a time to hate; a time of war, and a time of peace. What profit hath he that worketh in that wherein he laboreth?

Ecclesiastes 3:1–10

We do not remember days, we remember moments.

Cesare Pavese

We have to do with the past only as we can make it useful to the present and the future.

Frederick Douglass

Applications

1. Write a journal entry responding to the Wilde quote. How might writing in your journal enhance your memories?

2. Discuss the points of view in Perspectives. Then write a one-paragraph analysis about the roles of tradition.

In the Beginning
Bantu Creation Story

African Legend

Here are two different stories about how the world was created. The first is a legend from the Bantu, a diverse black people inhabiting a large part of southern Africa south of the Congo and speaking many languages (including Zulu and Swahili) and dialects. The second is the opening of the Popol Vuh, *the sacred saga of the Quiché, a branch of the great Mayan civilization. The Quiché Maya lived in what is now western Guatemala.*

IN THE BEGINNING, in the dark, there was nothing but water. And Bumba was alone.

One day Bumba was in terrible pain. He retched and strained and vomited up the sun. After that light spread over everything. The heat of the sun dried up the water until the black edges of the world began to show. Black sandbanks and reefs could be seen. But there were no living things.

Bumba vomited up the moon and then the stars, and after that the night had its light also.

Still Bumba was in pain. He strained again and nine living creatures came forth: the leopard named Koy Bumba, and Pongo Bumba the crested eagle, the crocodile, Ganda Bumba, and one little fish named Yo; next, old Kono Bumba, the tortoise, and Tsetse, the lightning, swift, deadly, beautiful like the leopard; then the white heron, Nyanyi Bumba, also one beetle, and the goat named Budi.

Last of all came forth men. There were many men, but only one was white like Bumba. His name was Loko Yima.

The creatures themselves then created all the creatures. The heron created all the birds of the air except the kite. He did not make the kite. The crocodile made serpents and the iguana. The goat produced every beast with horns. Yo, the small fish, brought forth all the fish of all the seas and waters. The beetle created insects.

Then the serpents in their turn made grasshoppers, and the iguana made the creatures without horns.

Then the three sons of Bumba said they would finish the world. The first, Nyonye Ngana, made the white ants; but he was not equal to the task, and died of it. The ants, however, thankful for life and being, went searching for black earth in the depths of the world and covered the barren sands to bury and honour their creator.

Chonganda, the second son, brought forth a marvellous living plant from which all the trees and grasses and flowers and plants in the world have sprung. The third son, Chedi Bumba, wanted something different, but for all his trying made only the bird called the kite.

Of all the creatures, Tsetse, lightning, was the only troublemaker. She stirred up so much trouble that Bumba chased her into the sky. Then mankind was without fire until Bumba showed the people how to draw fire out of trees. "There is fire in every tree," he told them, and showed them how to make the firedrill and liberate it. Sometimes today Tsetse still leaps down and strikes the earth and causes damage.

When at last the work of creation was finished, Bumba walked through the peaceful villages and said to the people, "Behold these wonders. They belong to you." Thus from Bumba, the Creator, the First Ancestor, came forth all the wonders that we see and hold and use, and all the brotherhood of beasts and man.

Quiché-Mayan Creation Story

Quiché-Mayan Legend

BEFORE THE WORLD was created, Calm and Silence were the great kings that ruled. Nothing existed, there was nothing. Things had not yet been drawn together, the face of the earth was unseen. There was only motionless sea, and a great emptiness of sky. There were no men anywhere, or animals, no birds or fish, no crabs. Trees, stones, caves, grass, forests, none of these existed yet. There was nothing that could roar or run, nothing that could tremble or cry in the air. Flatness and emptiness, only the sea, alone and breathless. It was night; silence stood in the dark.

In this darkness the Creators waited, the Maker, Tepeu, Gucumatz, the Forefathers. They were there in this emptiness, hidden under green and blue feathers, alone and surrounded with light. They are the same as wisdom. They are the ones who can conceive and bring forth a child from nothingness. And the time had come. The Creators were bent deep around talk in the darkness. They argued, worried, sighed over what was to be. They planned the growth of the thickets, how things would crawl and jump, the birth of man. They planned the whole creation, arguing each point until their words and thoughts crystallized and became the same thing. Heart of Heaven was there, and in the darkness the creation was planned.

Then let the emptiness fill! they said. Let the water weave its way downward so the earth can show its face! Let the light break on the ridges, let the sky fill up with the yellow light of dawn! Let our glory be a man walking on a path through the trees! "Earth!" the Creators called. They called only once, and it was there, from a mist, from a cloud of dust, the mountains appeared instantly. At this single word the groves of cypresses and pines sent out shoots, rivulets ran freely between the round hills. The Creators were struck by the beauty and exclaimed, "It will be a creation that will mount the darkness!"

Interpretations

1. In the Bantu story "The creatures themselves then created all the creatures": fish produced fish, birds produced birds (except for the predatory kite), and so on. How "scientific" is this explanation?

2. Why is there almost no explanation of Bumba's identity (other than his being white and "the Creator, the First Ancestor") or of his sickness? Are such details better omitted? Can you supply the missing explanation?

3. In the Bantu story what purpose does the retching incident serve? (What tone does it set?)

4. What is the purpose of the Bantu story?

Interpretations

5. How important in the Quiché creation story is language?

6. In the Quiché story what are the creators' main attributes? How are they demonstrated in the story?

7. What seems to be the Creators' main motive in creating "a man" in the Quiché story?

8. Interpret the last sentence of the Quiché story. What explanation does it provide for the Creation?

9. Compare the tones and meanings of the two creation stories.

Correspondences

1. Review the quotation *Ecclesiastes* (pages 3–4). Compare the creation concepts in Ecclesiastes with those in the Bantu and Quiché stories. Which account do you prefer? How do they differ in implication?

2. We are accustomed to thinking of time as segments of past, present, and future. Compare your concept of time with those implied in Ecclesiastes 3:1–10 and the two creation stories.

Applications

1. Discuss the digital watch as a symbol of our preoccupation with time.

2. Write a journal entry on the significance of light and darkness in both creation accounts.

from Morrisonville

Russell Baker

*Russell Baker (b. 1925) was born in Morrisonville, Virginia. He is a regular
columnist for* The New York Times. *He began his career in journalism with
the* Baltimore Sun, *and in 1954 joined the Washington Bureau of the* Times.
His books include An American In Washington *(1961),* All Things Considered *(1965),* Poor Russell's Almanac *(1972), and two autobiographies,*
Growing Up *(1982) and* The Good Times *(1989).*

    In "Morrisonville," a selection from The Good Times, *Baker shares childhood
memories about the delight of growing up nineteenth-century style, but adds that it
was a poor time in which to prepare for the twentieth century. As you read this
selection, focus on what Baker has to say about the memories triggered at his mother's
funeral and about family traditions.*

WHEN MY MOTHER died in 1984 we went back to the Virginia churchyard
where my father and Herb were buried. It was a bitterly cold January day,
and the wind off the Short Hill Mountain scattered the preacher's words
down the valley and made us cling tight to each other against the icy blasts
of winter and death.

    "They'll never get me back up there in those sticks," she used to say in
the bad old Depression days after she had taken Doris and me out of Virginia
and made us city people in New Jersey.

    "Back up there in those sticks." She made it sound so forlorn, such a
Godforsaken backwater out beyond Nowhere. She said it so often—"back
up there in those sticks"—that it became my memory of the place. For years
I never wanted to go back. Sometimes I even told people, "They'll never get
me back up there in those sticks."

    She was talking of Morrisonville, the village where I was born. It lay in
the Loudoun Valley of northern Virginia, a long sweep of fat, rich Piedmont
farmland cradled between mountains that parallel the Blue Ridge into the
Potomac River. Four miles to the north was the New Jerusalem Lutheran
Church where Morrisonville worshiped and buried its dead. I remembered
going there in a long procession of black cars for my father's funeral on a
golden November day in 1930.

    "This is the biggest funeral there's ever been in the Lutheran church,"
an old gentleman told my mother that day, trying to make her feel honored,
I guess.

    A few weeks later my mother, Doris, and I were gone from Morrisonville.

Gone for good, to hear her tell it. "Never get me back up there in those sticks."

She had been brave then. Maybe the bravest of all the brave things she did was giving Audrey, her baby, only ten months old, for adoption by my uncle Tom and aunt Goldie. Uncle Tom, one of my father's brothers, had a good job with the B&O Railroad and could give Audrey a comfortable life, not the kind of adventure my mother was in for as she headed off to New Jersey with Doris and me, off to patching those worn-out smocks in the A&P laundry.

"Never get me back up there in those sticks."

Maybe it was only bravado, which was lost on a boy, but I was in middle age and had seen half the world before I came back to Morrisonville one day and gazed at it in wonder, thinking, *My God, this is one of the most beautiful places I have ever seen.*

Until then, I had never thought of it longingly with love, though it was my birthplace and my father's, too, and had been home to my father's family for two hundred and fifty years. For me it had always been a shabby, mean place "back up there in those sticks" which I had been lucky to escape.

So bringing her back at the end was not a vengeful attempt to have the last word in the lifelong argument between us. It was done out of a sense that a family is many generations closely woven; that though generations die, they endure as part of the fabric of the family; and that a burying ground is a good place to remind the living that they have debts to the past. This churchyard was where she belonged. It was full of her life.

The grave was beside Herb's. He had died in 1962. My father was a short stroll southward down the slope, beside his mother, Ida Rebecca. Ida Rebecca and my mother had once been bitter competitors in the passionate matter of which one would rule my father. A short stroll westward was Uncle Tom, a good and gentle man who had been a loving father to Audrey.

Down the hillside a few yards from Ida Rebecca and my father were Uncle Irvey and his wife, Aunt Orra. Uncle Irvey was Ida Rebecca's oldest boy, the solemn one, the responsible one. My mother never liked Uncle Irvey, although he and Orra had taken her and my father to live with them at Morrisonville when they were first married and too poor to afford their own place, and though I had been born in Uncle Irvey's house. Maybe she could never forgive Uncle Irvey for having once needed his charity; still, she had dearly loved Aunt Orra.

There was far more of Morrisonville in the graveyard than there was in Morrisonville. Here was my uncle Edgar, one of Ida Rebecca's twin boys, who used to manage the Morrisonville baseball team. Here was my father's youngest brother, Uncle Lewis, who used to put me on a board on his barber chair and cut my hair with artistic scissor flourishes, then douse it with Jeris or Lucky Tiger when my father took me to his barbershop.

Nearby were the husband and wife with whom my mother boarded when she first came to Loudoun County as a young schoolteacher in the 1920s. And the preacher whose Sunday sermons she had attended. The teacher who taught the upper grades in the two-room schoolhouse they shared. Students she had taught in the second grade.

That day's ceremony was not among the biggest funerals ever held there. She was in her eighty-seventh year. Except for children, grandchildren, and great-grandchildren, most of her world had passed by. Doris, Audrey, Mary Leslie, and I huddled together under a canvas canopy crackling in the wind. The people we had married stood close behind with some of our children and three or four of our cousins from nearby Lovettsville who remembered her from long ago.

Our sorrow that day was tempered by relief. After six years of the nursing home, of watching her change into somebody else, and then into nobody at all, death seemed not unwelcome. It had been heartbreaking to see her mind run down, fading slowly at first, then swiftly emptying out almost everything but a few old memories that had got wedged in the crevices and the primordial instinct not to give up, not to quit, not to let life beat you, not to die.

"Don't be a quitter, Russell," she used to tell me. "If there's one thing I hate, it's a quitter."

Toward the end, sitting by the bed, holding her hand, I had silently told her, "It's not worth fighting for anymore. Give it up. Let go. It's all right to quit now."

For three days we argued the point in absolute silence. I don't think I won that argument. I don't think she finally quit there at the end. She was just overwhelmed by superior power.

Afterward, I felt bad about having broken the faith. Maybe I had let her down at the end. This was romantic nonsense, of course, because for all practical purposes she had been gone for years, and, in any case, that silent argument over the final three days had not been an argument at all, but only my own mind privately doubting the values she had hammered into me in childhood. Still, even in death, she retained the power to make me dissatisfied with myself by dwelling on the failures.

There was my failure to become the next Edwin James, for instance. Hadn't I disappointed her there? Never mind that I lacked the temperament, the desire, and the talent to run a big bureaucracy like the *Times*'s news operation. Maybe I could have overcome those drawbacks if I hadn't given in to Old Devil Laziness. Or so I told myself when the memory of her battle cries rattled my peace of mind.

"If at first you don't succeed . . ."

"For God's sake, Russell, show a little gumption for once in your life. . . ."

To be sure, the column had been successful enough. I had been writing it nearly twenty-two years by the time she died. It was not a column meant to convey news, but a writer's column commenting on the news by using different literary forms: essay devices, satire, burlesque, sometimes even fiction. It was proof that she had been absolutely right when she sized me up early in life, guessed I'd been born with the word gene, and steered me toward literature, believing that writing might be the way I could make something of myself, could amount to something.

The column had got its share of the medals American newspaper people give themselves, including a Pulitzer Prize in 1979. My mother never knew about that. The circuitry of her brain had collapsed the year before, and she was in the nursing home, out of touch with life forevermore, with the world of ambition, success, prizes, and vanity.

I could only guess how the woman she used to be might have responded to the news of the Pulitzer, but the guessing wasn't hard. I'm pretty sure she would have said, "That's nice, Buddy. It shows if you buckle down and work hard you'll be able to make something of yourself one of these days."

In training me to pass hard judgments on myself, she finally led me to pass hard judgments on the values by which she lived. Long before she died, even before her mind collapsed, I had begun to have a bad conscience about the constant hunger for success that had consumed those good, early years in the business.

Things had come my way too easily. Hadn't I repaid Buck Dorsey shabbily, considering how much he seemed a father to me? I hadn't even been involved in the great stories of my era, as the earlier generation of World War Two reporters had been. Reston, Phil Potter, Bill Lawrence, Price Day, Bill White, Gerry Fay, Eric Sevareid, Harrison Salisbury—tempered by their experience of the war, they all seemed to have a depth of character, a passion for their calling, and a sense that there were things even more important than success, another raise, a promotion, a gaudy title, and a prize citation to hang on the wall.

Well, of course, in my time as a reporter, which was from 1947 to 1962, there were not many great stories to broaden a newsman and deepen the character. Those were the good times, from the summer I started at the *Sun* in 1947 to Dallas in 1963, at least compared to what had gone before and what came afterward. They were especially good times if you were young, ambitious, energetic, and American. Being young makes all times better; being American in that brief moment that was America's golden age of empire made it the best of any time that ever was or will be. Provided you were white.

Good times, though, are not the best times for a reporter. When the country began to pull apart in the 1960s and 1970s, I felt melancholy about being left out as a new bunch of reporters went off to cover the demonstrations, riots, wars, and assassinations; to challenge the integrity of the government my generation had believed in; and, eventually, to change the entire character of American journalism, and change it for the better, too.

Part of the upheaval of that time was an attack on the values my mother had preached and I had lived by. The attack on ambition and striving for success was especially heavy. People who admitted to wanting to amount to something were put down as materialists idiotically wasting their lives in the "rat race." The word "gumption" vanished from the language.

Our children were adolescents now. They brought the fever for change into the house. Not wanting to be the dead hand of the corrupt past, I tried to roll with the new age. I decided not to drive my children as my mother had driven me with those corrupt old demands that they amount to something.

Materialism, ambition, and success were out the window. The new age exalted love, self-gratification, mystical religious experience, and passive Asian philosophies that aimed to help people resign themselves peaceably to the status quo. Much of this seemed preposterous to me, but I conceded that my mother might have turned me into a coarse materialist, so kept my heretical suspicions to myself while trying to go along with the prevalent theory, enunciated best by The Beatles, that "love is all you need."

And then I broke. The trouble was that too many people were not playing the love game. Too many people were still playing my mother's gumption game, and playing it very hard. Gradually I saw that these people were quietly preparing themselves to take over the country. Slowly, I began to fear that our three children—Kathleen, Allen, Michael—were not going to be members of the take-over class. I started preaching the ambition gospel to them.

It was silly, of course. Adolescence is too late to start hearing about gumption. Still, something had to be done. The schools were sending home alarming report cards. Reading that progression of grim report cards, I reached a shameful conclusion: I had failed to fire my children with ambition.

This was a time when, despite the new age, parents talked about getting their children into Harvard the way old folks once talked about getting into Heaven. It was the old rat race. Still going on. And plenty of children not too love-besotted to run the course. Everywhere I saw adults transforming their children into barracuda, pressuring tots for grades that would get them into elite colleges, which would get them elite jobs, where they would eat life's losers.

My children's report cards read like early warning signals. I panicked. Were my lovely children destined to feed the barracuda because I had failed them?

One evening at dinner, when the report cards had been as bad as usual, I heard myself shouting, "Don't you want to amount to something?"

The children looked blank. Amount to something? What a strange expression. The antique idea of life as a challenge to "make something of yourself" meant nothing to them because I had never taught it to them.

I had been at the martinis before dinner.

"Don't you want to make something of yourselves?" I roared.

The children studied their plates with eloquent faces. I could see their thoughts.

That isn't Dad yelling, they were thinking. *That's those martinis.*

They were only partly right. It wasn't the gin that was shouting loudest. It was my mother. The martinis had freed me to preach her old-time religion. The gin only gave me the courage to announce that yes, by God, I had always believed in people trying to make something of themselves, had always believed in success, had always believed that without hard work and self-discipline you could never amount to anything, and didn't deserve to.

In gin's awful grip, I was renouncing the faith of the new age in the power of gentleness, love, and understanding. I was reverting to the primitive faith of my mother. She had embedded it in my marrow, bone, and blood. There, anchored beyond reason's power to crush, it would keep me always restless, discontented, always slightly guilty for not amounting to something a little bit more.

In those days it led me into misunderstanding the children. The bleak report cards did not forebode failure, but a refusal to march to the drumbeat of the ordinary, which should have made me proud. Now they were grown people with children of their own, and we liked each other and had good times when we were together.

One defect of my mother's code was the value it placed on money and position. The children never cared a lot for that. To care, I suppose, you had to have been there with her during the Depression.

The ceremony in the churchyard was briefer than it might have been, because of the icy wind off the mountain, and afterward we went to a house in Morrisonville for food and the warmth of oak logs burning in a stone fireplace.

A house of primitive log construction, it was maybe a hundred and seventy years old, maybe more. Nobody could tell for sure. Some long-dead forebears of mine, names lost to the twentieth century, had probably helped dig the foundation, raise the logs, or mix the chinking. The family had been in those parts since 1730, but they had not been a people who wrote things down, except for an occasional ancient tombstone inscription here and there around the county.

The house was filled with a sense of timelessness that afternoon. Doris, Audrey, Mary Leslie, and I were children of the twentieth century. Up the road a short distance, I had been babied and spoiled by my grandmother, Ida Rebecca, who was born in the time of the Civil War.

My mother, whose death had brought us there, back up there in those sticks, had spent childhood in the age of the horse, buggy, and Teddy Roosevelt.

Two of Audrey's eight children had come down from New England with her, and Mimi's and my three children were also there. These were the children of America in the good times, born in the middle of the twentieth century, destined most likely to know what the twenty-first holds.

And two of our granddaughters were there, Mimi's and mine, born in the 1980s, who would, all going well, reach far into the next century. I was aware of my life stretching across a great expanse of time, of reaching across some two hundred years inside this old house and connecting Ida Rebecca's Civil War America with whatever America might be in the middle of the twenty-first century.

My father's funeral procession had set out from another house just up the road from this one. Thirty-three he was at death. And now my daughter Kathy was thirty-two, my son Allen thirty-one, my son Michael twenty-nine.

Looking at them grouped with Audrey's children around the fireplace, I realized that if my father were mysteriously compelled to join us this day, he would gravitate naturally to my children for the companionship of his own kind. If he noticed me staring too curiously at him, he might turn to Kathy or Allen or Michael and whisper, asking, "Who's the old man in the high-priced suit?"

I was now old enough to be his father.

So it is with a family. We carry the dead generations within us and pass them on to the future aboard our children. This keeps the people of the past alive long after we have taken them to the churchyard.

"If there's one thing I can't stand, Russell, it's a quitter."

Lord, I can hear her still.

Interpretations

1. What purpose(s) does repetition serve? Is Baker's use of it successful? Why or why not?

2. If Morrisonville was, in his mother's view, the hated "sticks," why did Baker bring her body back there for burial?

3. How can funerals serve tradition? Can funerals do so more effectively than weddings or other anniversaries? Why or why not?

4. Baker's grandmother Ida Rebecca and his mother "had once been bitter competitors in the passionate matter of which one would rule [his] father." What is the tone of the phrase "the passionate matter"? Why would Baker now want (or be able) to take an objective second view of this once "passionate matter"?

5. What portrait of Baker's deceased mother emerges? Consider such phrases as "Maybe the bravest of all the brave things she did was giving Audrey,

her baby, only ten months old, for adoption by my uncle Tom and aunt Goldie" and "Maybe she could never forgive Uncle Irvey for having once needed his charity" and, of course, "[They'll] Never get me back up there in those sticks."

6. Does the pervading American culture cause or fuel conflict between mothers and daughters-in-law over who bosses the son/husband, or has it developed some way of establishing harmony? (*Is* there a single dominant culture in such matters?)

Correspondences

Review the Perspectives on pages 3–4.

1. How does the Camus quotation apply to Baker's memories of his mother's struggles, values, and influence on his life? To what extent do his insights about the family tradition go beyond the personal?

2. Review the last section of Baker's essay, beginning with "The ceremony in the churchyard. . . ." What does he experience there? How does the "sense of timelessness" here compare with that in Ecclesiastes 3:1–10?

Applications

1. Write an essay about a grandparent or other older adult who, like Baker's mother, had a clear philosophy of life. Describe this philosophy by recounting a specific event that sharply portrays your subject.

2. Write a journal entry on the significance of or necessity for memoirs, both public and private.

The Way to Rainy Mountain

N. Scott Momaday

N{atachee} Scott Momaday (b. 1934), is a native of Oklahoma and a member
of the Kiowa tribe. His writings include a novel The House Made of Dawn
(1968), a story of a man caught between cultures (for which he won the 1969
Pulitzer) and The Way to Rainy Mountain (1969), a collection of Kiowa
legends and folktales. Recently he has chosen poetry as a vehicle to re-create the often
poignant legends of his people.

   In the following excerpt from The Way to Rainy Mountain, Momaday
traces the migration of his tribe, from their origins in Montana to Oklahoma. He
chronicles alliances of the Kiowas with other tribes (the Comanches and the Crows)
and their subjugation by the U.S. Army. Notice how Momaday uses the memories
of his grandmother's death to evoke the importance of preserving tribal traditions.

   After 1840 the Kiowas, occupying the Arkansas River region of western
Oklahoma, allied with the Comanches and others against Eastern tribes that had
moved west. This provoked the U.S. Army to move against both groups. By 1874
the Kiowa were devastated; their horses had been killed, and their leaders had been
deported to Florida. They surrendered at Fort Sill. By 1879 most of the tribe had
been moved to a reservation in southwest Oklahoma, between Fort Sill and the
Washita River—the very landscape Momaday describes so dramatically here.

A SINGLE KNOLL rises out of the plain in Oklahoma, north and west of the
Wichita Range. For my people, the Kiowas, it is an old landmark, and they
gave it the name Rainy Mountain. The hardest weather in the world is there.
Winter brings blizzards, hot tornadic winds arise in the spring, and in summer
the prairie is an anvil's edge. The grass turns brittle and brown, and it cracks
beneath your feet. There are green belts along the rivers and creeks, linear
groves of hickory and pecan, willow and witch hazel. At a distance in July
or August the steaming foliage seems almost to writhe in fire. Great green-
and-yellow grasshoppers are everywhere in the tall grass, popping up like
corn to sting the flesh, and tortoises crawl about on the red earth, going
nowhere in the plenty of time. Loneliness is an aspect of the land. All things
in the plain are isolate; there is no confusion of objects in the eye, but *one*
hill or *one* tree or *one* man. To look upon that landscape in the early morning,
with the sun at your back, is to lose the sense of proportion. Your imagination
comes to life, and this, you think, is where Creation was begun.

   I returned to Rainy Mountain in July. My grandmother had died in the spring, and I wanted to be at her grave. She had lived to be very old and at last infirm. Her only living daughter was with her when she died, and I was told that in death her face was that of a child.

I like to think of her as a child. When she was born, the Kiowas were living that last great moment of their history. For more than a hundred years they had controlled the open range from the Smoky Hill River to the Red, from the headwaters of the Canadian to the fork of the Arkansas and Cimarron. In alliance with the Comanches, they had ruled the whole of the southern Plains. War was their sacred business, and they were among the finest horsemen the world has ever known. But warfare for the Kiowas was preeminently a matter of disposition rather than of survival, and they never understood the grim, unrelenting advance of the U.S. Cavalry. When at last, divided and ill-provisioned, they were driven onto the Staked Plains in the cold rains of autumn, they fell into panic. In Palo Duro Canyon they abandoned their crucial stores to pillage and had nothing then but their lives. In order to save themselves, they surrendered to the soldiers at Fort Sill and were imprisoned in the old stone corral that now stands as a military museum. My grandmother was spared the humiliation of those high gray walls by eight or ten years, but she must have known from birth the affliction of defeat, the dark brooding of old warriors.

Her name was Aho, and she belonged to the last culture to evolve in North America. Her forebears came down from the high country in western Montana nearly three centuries ago. They were a mountain people, a mysterious tribe of hunters whose language has never been positively classified in any major group. In the late seventeenth century they began a long migration to the south and east. It was a long journey toward the dawn, and it led to a golden age. Along the way the Kiowas were befriended by the Crows, who gave them the culture and religion of the Plains. They acquired horses, and their ancient nomadic spirit was suddenly free of the ground. They acquired Tai-me, the sacred Sun Dance doll, from that moment the object and symbol of their worship, and so shared in the divinity of the sun. Not least, they acquired the sense of destiny, therefore courage and pride. When they entered upon the southern Plains, they had been transformed. No longer were they slaves to the simple necessity of survival; they were a lordly and dangerous society of fighters and thieves, hunters and priests of the sun. According to their origin myth, they entered the world through a hollow log. From one point of view, their migration was the fruit of an old prophecy, for indeed they emerged from a sunless world.

Although my grandmother lived out her long life in the shadow of Rainy Mountain, the immense landscape of the continental interior lay like memory in her blood. She could tell of the Crows, whom she had never seen, and of the Black·Hills, where she had never been. I wanted to see in reality what she had seen more perfectly in the mind's eye, and traveled fifteen hundred miles to begin my pilgrimage.

Yellowstone, it seemed to me, was the top of the world, a region of deep lakes and dark timber, canyons and waterfalls. But, beautiful as it is, one might have the sense of confinement there. The skyline in all directions is close at hand, the high wall of the woods and deep cleavages of shade. There is a perfect freedom in the mountains, but it belongs to the eagle and the elk, the badger and the bear. The Kiowas reckoned their stature by the distance they could see, and they were bent and blind in the wilderness.

Descending eastward, the highland meadows are a stairway to the plain. In July the inland slope of the Rockies is luxuriant with flax and buckwheat, stonecrop and larkspur. The earth unfolds and the limit of the land recedes. Clusters of trees and animals grazing far in the distance cause the vision to reach away and wonder to build upon the mind. The sun follows a longer course in the day, and the sky is immense beyond all comparison. The great billowing clouds that sail upon it are shadows that move upon the grain like water, dividing light. Farther down, in the land of the Crows and Blackfeet, the plain is yellow. Sweet clover takes hold of the hills and bends upon itself to cover and seal the soil. There the Kiowas paused on their way; they had come to the place where they must change their lives. The sun is at home on the plains. Precisely there does it have the certain character of a god. When the Kiowas came to the land of the Crows, they could see the dark lees of the hills at dawn across the Bighorn River, the profusion of light on the grain shelves, the oldest deity ranging after the solstices. Not yet would they veer southward to the caldron of the land that lay below; they must wean their blood from the northern winter and hold the mountains a while longer in their view. They bore Tai-me in procession to the east.

A dark mist lay over the Black Hills, and the land was like iron. At the top of a ridge I caught sight of Devil's Tower upthrust against the gray sky as if in the birth of time the core of the earth had broken through its crust and the motion of the world was begun. There are things in nature that engender an awful quiet in the heart of man; Devil's Tower is one of them. Two centuries ago, because they could not do otherwise, the Kiowas made a legend at the base of the rock. My grandmother said:

> Eight children were there at play, seven sisters and their brother. Suddenly the boy was struck dumb; he trembled and began to run upon his hands and feet. His fingers became claws, and his body was covered with fur. Directly there was a bear where the boy had been. The sisters were terrified; they ran, and the bear after them. They came to the stump of a great tree, and the tree spoke to them. It bade them climb upon it, and as they did so, it began to rise into the air. The bear came to kill them, but they were just beyond its reach. It reared against the tree and scored the bark all around with its claws. The seven sisters were borne into the sky, and they became the stars of the Big Dipper.

From that moment, and so long as the legend lives, the Kiowas have kinsmen in the night sky. Whatever they were in the mountains, they could be no more. However tenuous their well-being, however much they had suffered and would suffer again, they had found a way out of the wilderness.

My grandmother had a reverence for the sun, a holy regard that now is all but gone out of mankind. There was a wariness in her, and an ancient awe. She was a Christian in her later years, but she had come a long way about, and she never forgot her birthright. As a child she had been to the Sun Dances; she had taken part in those annual rites, and by them she had learned the restoration of her people in the presence of Tai-me. She was about seven when the last Kiowa Sun Dance was held in 1887 on the Washita River above Rainy Mountain Creek. The buffalo were gone. In order to consummate the ancient sacrifice—to impale the head of a buffalo bull upon the medicine tree—a delegation of old men journeyed into Texas, there to beg and barter for an animal from the Goodnight herd. She was ten when the Kiowas came together for the last time as a living Sun Dance culture. They could find no buffalo; they had to hang an old hide from the sacred tree. Before the dance could begin, a company of soldiers rode out from Fort Sill under orders to disperse the tribe. Forbidden without cause the essential act of their faith, having seen the wild herds slaughtered and left to rot upon the ground, the Kiowas backed away forever from the medicine tree. That was July 20, 1890, at the great bend of the Washita. My grandmother was there. Without bitterness, and for as long as she lived, she bore a vision of deicide.

Now that I can have her only in memory, I see my grandmother in the several postures that were peculiar to her: standing at the wood stove on a winter morning and turning meat in a great iron skillet; sitting at the south window, bent above her beadwork, and afterwards, when her vision had failed, looking down for a long time into the fold of her hands; going out upon a cane, very slowly as she did when the weight of age came upon her; praying. I remember her most often at prayer. She made long, rambling prayers out of suffering and hope, having seen many things. I was never sure that I had the right to hear, so exclusive were they of all mere custom and company. The last time I saw her she prayed standing by the side of her bed at night, naked to the waist, the light of a kerosene lamp moving upon her dark skin. Her long, black hair, always drawn and braided in the day, lay upon her shoulders and against her breasts like a shawl. I do not speak Kiowa, and I never understood her prayers, but there was something inherently sad in the sound, some merest hesitation upon the syllables of sorrow. She began in a high and descending pitch, exhausting her breath to silence; then again and again—and always the same intensity of effort, of something that is, and is not, like urgency in the human voice. Transported so in the dancing light among the shadows of her room, she seemed beyond the reach of time. But that was illusion; I think I knew then that I should not see her again.

Interpretations

1. According to tribal myth, the Kiowa "entered the world through a hollow log." From what sort of world did they consider themselves to have emerged from? How might this tradition have shaped the Kiowas' attitude toward life and death?

2. Momaday says his grandmother regarded the last Kiowa Sun Dance (1887) as "a vision of deicide," or god-killing. Do you agree? Was it the death of a god or of a people?

3. What portrait of Momaday's grandmother emerges from the essay? How would you describe his relationship to her?

4. What is the significance of Momaday's equating family with tribe?

5. How does Momaday use description of the setting (the mountains and plains, the great spaces of the West) to control the mood or tone of his essay?

Correspondences

1. Memory plays an important role in the selections by Momaday and Baker. What do their memories suggest about the impact of the passage of time on family and tribe?

2. Momaday concludes his essay with a description of his grandmother praying, while Baker organizes his around his mother's funeral. How do these narrative techniques further contribute to the unity and purpose of the selections?

Applications

1. Momaday's vivid memories of his grandmother's house give rise to a sensuous re-creation of it. Describe a place you vividly recall because it played an important part in your life.

2. Discuss what you learned about Kiowa traditions from Momaday's essay.

from Life in the Villages

Jehan Sadat

Jehan Sadat (b. 1934) is the widow of Egyptian president Anwar el-Sadat, who was assassinated in 1981. As you will discover in Chapter 2, she grew up in Cairo as the daughter of an Egyptian civil servant and an English mother. In the selection here entitled "Life in the Villages," from her 1987 autobiography A Woman of Egypt, *Sadat is introduced to rural life by her husband. During her husband's eleven-year presidency, Jehan Sadat was active in social and humanitarian affairs, especially women's rights. Since his assassination in 1981, she has continued to fight for causes she believes in. At the same time, she has pursued an academic career as lecturer in Arabic literature at Cairo University and in the United States. Although she is a practicing Muslim, her efforts to increase Egyptian women's civil rights have met with frequent opposition from Muslim fundamentalists. For example, the decree her husband issued in 1979, popularly known as "Jehan's law" for her perceived influence, was abolished by the Egyptian supreme court in 1985. (This decree had allowed Egyptian women key civil rights: the right to sue for divorce and to retain custody of children if a husband was found to be polygamous. You will read of traditional Muslim child-custody practices in a Chapter 2 selection, Shusha Guppy's "Aunt Batool.")*

One of the oldest and culturally richest civilizations, at a crossroads between East and West, Egypt has been influenced by many invaders, among them the Persians, Greeks, Romans, and Arabs, the last of whom introduced the dominant religion (Islam) and language (Arabic) of Egypt. Egypt is a densely populated but largely barren country. Most of its population hugs the banks of the Nile. A British protectorate from 1914 to 1922, Egypt remained under British domination until 1952, when King Farouk was overthrown. Gamal Abdel Nasser became president in 1956. His protégé Anwar Sadat began his rise in the new government, becoming president in 1970. As the following selection shows, in spite of his revolutionary and reforming sympathies, Sadat retained strong ties with village culture and was able to inspire his city-bred wife with the same feelings.

"UM GAMAL, is your son well?"

"Um Gamal, I feel so sorry for you. You must have more children."

It did not matter to the women in Anwar's village of Mit Abul-Kum that I had three beautiful daughters as well as a son. No. I was known in the village only as Um Gamal, the Mother of Gamal. No matter how much I protested, in the village my daughters—or anyone's daughters—did not count. "You have only one child," the women would chide me even after my youngest daughter, Jehan, was born in 1961.

"I have four," I'd reply.

"But you have only one son. You must try to have another so he won't be all alone."

"He is not alone. He has three sisters and three half sisters as well," I would answer.

But the women would exchange side glances and shake their heads. "You should have more children," they would pronounce gravely. "Otherwise you might lose your husband."

I loved going to Anwar's village with him in the Nile Delta. The two-hour drive from Cairo was beautiful, the road lined with sycamore and eucalyptus trees and passing through miles and miles of cotton fields which were bright green in winter and filled with pale-yellow flowers in summer. As soon as we arrived in Mit Abul-Kum, my husband was transformed. Shedding his city business suit and putting on the long white galabiyya worn by all the men in the village, Anwar would go for long walks with me and the children, laughing while they rolled in the clover like puppies. Often Anwar would sing in his very loud voice the mournful songs of peasants toiling in the fields and I would wait for the neighbors to complain, but they never did. At home he taught the children to bake bread just the way he had loved to as a child, breaking an egg over the dough just before it went into the oven. They practiced and practiced to get it just right.

Anwar had been very nervous when he first brought me to his village. "You cannot go out during the day at all. You must stay inside until evening," he had told me. Not go out?

"Why?" I asked him.

"Because the people in my village will not understand you," he said.

"Anwar, what is it?" I pressed him.

He looked uneasy. "You are a woman used to the ways of the city," he explained. "The people in my village are very conservative. They will not respect you if they see you in your city clothes showing your arms and legs with your head uncovered. Such dress for women is not in our tradition."

Why, then, could I be seen in the evenings?

"That is the time set aside for visiting when the landowners and those with government jobs go out in the villages," Anwar explained. "The people are used to different ways then and accept it."

The next day I went to Tanta where I bought material for a long dress like those of the fellaheen, and a colorful scarf which I fixed to my head, as they did, with a band of flowers. And the next time we went to the village, I went out.

At first Mit Abul-Kum seemed as foreign to me as if we had gone not only to a different country but into a different century. The streets were unpaved, enveloping all who passed in their own little clouds of dust. The houses were made of baked mud and had very few windows; openings in the palm-thatched roofs let smoke out. On most roofs were piled stacks of fuel cakes made from animal dung and straw, drying in the sun. Deeply superstitious, many in the village painted their doors blue to ward off the jinns, the evil spirits described in the Quran.[1] For more insurance against the evil eye and the curses of the envious, villagers also dipped their hands into blue paint and placed their palmprints on the outside walls to evoke the protective symbol of Fatima, the Prophet's daughter. Horseshoes and ceramic hands bearing blue beads were also hung over the doors to the houses, fixed to the harnesses of their farm animals, even hung over the peasants' beds.

The lucky few in the village who had made their pilgrimage to Mecca had painted the story of their sacred journey on the outside walls of their houses as well. If they had crossed the Red Sea to Saudi Arabia by boat, there was a painting of a ship crossing the water. If they had flown, there was a painting of an airplane. Some had gone part of the way by bus or car. All this was depicted colorfully on the house walls, along with a rendition of the Kaaba, the black boxlike structure in the Great Mosque in Mecca which is the most sacred shrine in Islam.

The mud houses were very secure, as there was little rain, but they were very primitive. Before the power plant at the Aswan Dam was completed in 1968, there was no electricity in Mit Abul-Kum, no indoor plumbing or running water. The villagers rose by the sun and went to bed by the moon. Most of the houses were divided into two rooms, one used by the family to cook, sleep and pray in, the other to shelter their water buffaloes, donkeys, cows or even a camel, along with a few geese, ducks and chickens. In between the rooms there was usually an open area where the women hung their *hasiras*, or bamboo mats. Salted yogurt was placed in them to drip until the yogurt turned into cheese.

In the center of the village there was a high tower for the pigeons to roost in, always noisy with the flapping of wings. The beautiful white birds were a food staple to the fellaheen[2] as well as a product to sell on market day. The only building taller than the pigeon tower was the village mosque, built shortly after the Revolution. Anwar had contributed some of its construction costs himself, donating his first paycheck from *el-Gumhuriyya*[3] so that the small mud mosque of Mit Abul-Kum could be replaced by one built with red bricks and a high minaret.

The sight of the village women depressed me at first. Older women over forty dressed always in black from head to toe and the women of all ages worked harder than the men. At dawn the women rose to the voice of the muezzin calling the faithful to the morning prayer, and then prepared the morning meal of white cheese and very sweet black tea for their families. Then there were the dirt floors of their houses to sweep out, the animals to

[1]Or Koran, the sacred scriptures of Islam.

[2]Peasants, farmworkers.

[3]*The Republic*, newspaper started by Anwar Sadat.

feed, the dough to make for fresh bread, water which the women pumped by hand from the village well and carried back in jugs on their heads. Just in time they then hurried to carry lunch to their husbands in the fields, where, after the meal, they joined the men for the remainder of the day, weeding, hoeing and harvesting the crops of cotton, corn, clover and wheat.

The scene in Mit Abul-Kum was always the same, the dawn sky lighting the procession of the men in their galabiyyas toward the fields, followed by the children taking the water buffaloes and the cows out to graze and drink. Flocks of white egrets would fly behind them, settling in the early-morning fields to catch the worms which had come to the surface during the night. The egrets to me made the fields look like green carpets covered with white polka dots. By midmorning the egrets had moved, settling now on the animals, where they enthusiastically picked off the bugs from their backs.

At dusk the procession would be reversed, but it was now of a different shape. The flat horizon would silhouette not only the animals and the men in their robes, but the shapeless profiles of their long-robed wives walking behind, often carrying large loads of produce on their backs. The egrets would follow them home to roost in the trees, turning the branches totally white.

Though this view was always beautiful, I shivered when first I saw it. The women seemed like nothing but beasts of burden—or even less, because the men cared more for their cows than they did for their wives. The cow was the man's livelihood, bringing him milk and cheese and butter to eat and to sell. If his wife died he would be sad, of course. But if his cow died, he would be heartbroken, having lost his life savings and his economic future. It was cheaper, after all, for a man to add another wife than it was for him to buy a new cow.

The women were constantly kept in their place by the men. "Kill your cat on your wedding night," the men would say to each other after they married, stressing their need to be the dominant one in a marriage. The birth of a daughter was joyous, as all Egyptians love children, but it did not come close to the birth of a son. *'Illi taht el-tarha malhash farha"* was a common village expression: "What is under a veil brings no joy." The men hardly referred to their wives by name, always calling out to them "Ya sitt," or "Hey, woman!" A woman could not interrupt her husband while he was talking with his friends, and had to walk behind him rather than beside him as they went to market. How miserable the women must be, I thought. I was wrong.

Why are you looking so pleased, Amina?" one woman asked another at the waterwheel where all gathered to chat and gossip at noon before the women took the midday meal to their husbands in the fields.

"I sold three chickens and fourteen eggs yesterday at the market," Amina replied. "Now I can buy enough sugar and tea for the rest of the winter."

Another woman was also smiling. "Our cow is giving so much milk that I was able to sell ten kilos of cheese. My daughter's wedding will be the most splendid in the village."

Every day I joined the women at the waterwheel to listen to their conversation. And every day, while the yoked donkey or water buffalo drew the water by walking around and around the well, wearing a blindfold so that it wouldn't get dizzy and stop, my perception of these women changed. By modern standards they were disadvantaged, the great majority being illiterate. But compared to many middle-class women in Egypt in the fifties and even the sixties, the women of the village had far more freedom and independence.

What choices did middle-class women have except for those living in Cairo or Alexandria? In the smaller cities women had little education, certainly not enough to get a good job. Their husbands from the same class clung to the old traditions, expecting their wives to stay at home and care only for them and their children. These middle-class women lived in social isolation, sharing nothing of their husbands' lives and having no lives of their own outside the home.

In the rural areas the women worked side by side with the men, sharing in all aspects of their daily lives. Together they irrigated the fields, weeded and harvested the crops, sowed the new seeds. When the time came for a cow to bear a calf, the wife gladly assisted her husband in the delivery, for the birth of a calf was a blessing on any home. Not only would the family have milk to drink, but they would also prosper by having extra milk and cheese to sell. Individually, the women had their own businesses as well. They raised their own chickens and geese, collected the eggs, made their own cheese and sold what they could spare on market day. These were small freedoms, but it is many small things which make a whole. And in a way I envied them. They were certainly participating more in outside activities than I was when my children were small.

I loved the direct way the women talked. They were very bright and full of life, like my friend Hanem whose son was a nurse in the new village clinic. Hanem could neither read nor write, but because she, like many of the other women, listened to her portable radio all day, she was better informed than many of her contemporaries in the cities. Often I felt as though I were listening to a current-affairs professor when I visited with Hanem, she was so knowledgeable about events happening outside Egypt.

Though the men would certainly not admit it, it was the women in the village who made many of the decisions for the family, deciding when to build an extra room on their houses or to buy new animals to raise and sell. "The man is a river and the woman is a dike," went one popular expression in the villages. In Mit Abul-Kum the women had even organized a gam'iyya, a financial cooperative. Every month each woman would pay a small amount of money into a single fund, and each month a different woman would take the whole pot. In that way it was possible even for a very poor woman to get enough money to pay her son's bride-price or to buy a new sofa, straw rugs for her home, or a new dress which she would rush to show us all at the waterwheel.

The women helped each other in many ways. The oldest women in the village looked after the young children while their mothers worked in the fields. When one woman fell sick or had a baby, the other women served food to her family and cleaned her house. If a husband died—or a child—the women took turns bringing food to the poor widow, knowing she probably had little money and was not in the mood to cook anyway.

I had not been in the village long when Um Muhammad lost her son in a military accident. When I went to pay condolences, I had no difficulty locating her house. I simply followed sounds of grief. When I entered Um Muhammad's house, I found at least sixty women all dressed in black surrounding the poor mother, crying as if their own sons had died.

"I remember him as a little boy. I can see him now dressed in his military uniform coming to the village in a Jeep just like a prince," one woman was crying out as I came through the door. Immediately all the women burst into wails, some beating their breasts and tearing at their clothes.

When the crying died down a little, another woman spoke. "I remember sitting at his wedding just five years ago," she cried out. "Never had he looked so beautiful dressed in his white galabiyya and a silk shawl. He looked like an angel." And again the women burst into shrieks of pain.

The atmosphere of loss was palpable. I began to cry myself, to feel the pain of the mother, and to share it. "We are never going to see Muhammad again," another woman sobbed, her arms around Um Muhammad. "Such a wonderful son. I remember when he brought you his first paycheck. 'Mother, this first salary is for you,' he said. 'You have suffered and sacrificed for me. You have been strict with me because you wanted to see me as an officer. Now it is my honor to thank you.' "

For three days the women came to lament with Um Muhammad, from the first rays of dawn until the evening, when they had to go tend to their own families. The village women did not leave their grieving sister for one minute. One third of them would bring lunch for everyone one day, another third the next, and so on. But they did not bring very good food, nor when they poured coffee and tea for those paying condolences did they offer sugar to sweeten it. This was not a time for pleasure. Only the food and drink offered to Um Muhammad, who would not eat, was sweetened.

"Try just this one bite of pigeon and take one swallow of this lemonade," the women urged Um Muhammad.

"Let me die," she cried out again and again. "Can there ever be happiness living without my son, never being able to see him again?" Immediately all the women would wail again.

The lamenting reached new peaks when Um Muhammad's grandchildren, who had been sent to another house during the day, returned at night. "See how small they are," the lament now ran. "It is too early for them to be orphans."

By the end of the three days, everyone, including Um Muhammad, was exhausted. By calling up every measure of grief at the young man's death, the women had helped to cleanse Um Muhammad's pain and to leave behind no hard grief. Nor did they desert her after the three days. Her close friends and neighbors stayed with her after that. And every Thursday afternoon until the fortieth-day ceremony, all the women returned to lament, though more quietly, with Um Muhammad while her grief began to fade. In Cairo we treated death much more privately and kept our sorrow to ourselves. But in the village everyone shared in everything.

Interpretations

1. What made the village of Mit Abul-Kum seem to Jehan Sadat like a visit to "a different century"?

2. "In the village everyone shared in everything." According to Sadat, what are the advantages of such a way of life? the disadvantages?

3. What did Sadat learn about the villagers and about herself as a result of her visit?

4. Most of the women Sadat writes about are illiterate and could never read this essay. How do you think they would react to it if they *could* read it? How would the male villagers react if they read it? For what audience do you think Sadat is writing, Egyptian or non-Egyptian, Muslim or non-Muslim? Support your answer.

5. What purpose does the dialogue in the introduction serve? How effective is it? (Does it present any problems for the general reader? If so, what are they and are they later solved?)

Correspondences

1. "Where there is pain, there are no words, all pain is the same." How is this Toni Morrison quotation borne out in Sadat's description of village mourning rituals?

2. Sadat and Momaday are very aware of their surroundings. Compare Sadat's memories of village landscapes with those of Momaday's in the opening paragraph of "The Way to Rainy Mountain." How does each description contribute to the overall effectiveness of the whole selection?

Applications

1. "The man is a river and the woman is a dike." What examples does Sadat offer to support the village roles implied by this saying? How does this description apply to gender relationships in your culture?

2. According to Sadat, people in large cities like Cairo hold their emotions close and private while people in rural areas are open and public. Write a journal entry analyzing the advantages or disadvantages of publicly sharing highly emotional experiences.

from The Wedding

Shusha Guppy

Shusha Guppy emigrated from Iran in the 1960s and is now a folksinger and the London editor of The Paris Review. *She is the last child of Iran's leading philosopher, born during World War II into a country that occupies a strategic place between the Middle East and South Asia.*

Once a powerful independent empire, Persia, Iran was later conquered by the Turks and then the Mongols. In the nineteenth century, Russia and the British vied for control of the oil-rich country. In 1925 Reza Khan reestablished a native dynasty, being succeeded by his son Reza Pahlavi in 1941. In an effort to modernize Iran, the last shah made great changes in Iran's economy and social and political systems. However, he was intolerant of political opposition and had overlooked the power of the Shiite branch of Islam (which claims over ninety percent of the Iranian population, but a minority in the world of Islam) and its conservative clergy, the mullahs. In January 1979, Pahlavi was driven into exile by revolution.

In the same month that the Pahlavi Dynasty was expelled, the Ayatollah Ruhollah Khomeini returned from exile in France. In the ensuing struggle, an Islamic republic was established that gave supreme power to the Ayatollah. Iran quickly changed from relative liberalism to strict conservatism. Guppy experienced both swings of the political pendulum. She is therefore in a good position to compare the Persia of her childhood and her parents' privileged lives—a Persia then already undergoing great change—with postrevolutionary Iran. The following essay focuses on prerevolutionary times and is understandably nostalgic—in this case, for the traditional wedding customs of the upper classes.

HAJI SEYYED MOHAMMAD and Haji Ali-Baba: two more different men could hardly be imagined, the one intelligent, shrewd, hedonistic, the other imbued with the Northerner's simplicity of mind and heart—the cunning and sophistication of the Bazaar versus the candour and nobility of the land. Ali-Baba wore the white turban of the Sheikh, while Mohammad sported the black one of the Seyyed—the descendants of the Prophet.

Haji Ali-Baba's eldest daughter, Azra, was 17 when Kazem returned to Persia. She had unusual looks: blonde hair, grey-green eyes, high cheekbones and a very fair complexion, "just like a *Farangi* [European]." In reality she looked rather Russian, an impression enhanced by her intensely emotional and fiery temperament. She had had many suitors but her father had refused them all—they were "not good enough for her!"

As soon as the two men met, Ali-Baba fell completely under Kazem's spell; he was impressed by his erudition and captivated by his charm.

"I have found Azra's husband," he declared upon arriving home that evening. The snag was that Kazem had no wish to get married. On the contrary, he planned to lead the life of a celibate, ascetic philosopher and Sufi.

"I'm honoured by your generous interest," he rejoined, when his future father-in-law offered him his daughter's hand, "but I am in no position to marry, as I have no proper job and no money."

"Nonsense!" retorted the Sheikh. "I will give you both!" He was not a man to be contradicted, the offer was tempting and timely, and Kazem's resolve was broken.

"Oh, it was the grandest and loveliest wedding of the year!" recounted Aunt Ashraf. The story of my parents' nuptials was one of my favourites when I was a small child, and I often begged Aunt Ashraf to tell it.

"The preparations took months, at the end of which she had a fantastic trousseau—the finest rugs from Kerman and Kashan, gold-studded leather chests containing her clothes and linen—all finely embroidered—brocade spreads and wrappings, glass from Bohemia, china from France, and a large samovar from Tula (in Russia). She had enough for a whole house, although at first they were going to live at your grandfather, Haji Seyyed Mohammad's house."

"Then what happened?"

"Then came the wedding which lasted three days and three nights. The first day was devoted to the *Aqd* [the marriage ceremony and registration]. At dawn they brought the *Ghoncheh*. Now you probably don't know what that is, because it is going out of fashion among you modern people, but in those days it was part of the festivities. It consisted of two big trays, one containing coloured seeds arranged in decorative abstract patterns, the other a long flat bread, equally decorated with saffron and other vivid colours, and together they symbolised prosperity and fertility. The *Ghoncheh* was ordered from specialists in the Bazaar, and sent over with trays of cakes, biscuits, sweets and fruit arranged on silver dishes. Porters carried the enormous trays, precariously balanced on their heads, in a procession through the streets, followed by crowds of noisy urchins. It was displayed in the drawing room, around the bridal seat. When everything was ready and the guests arrived, they brought in the bride and sat her in the middle of the room on a *soozani* [an embroidered mat] in front of her wedding mirror, flanked by two candelabras and a glass lamp, to give light and happiness to the couple's life together.

"Then the groom's party arrived, headed by Haji Seyyed Mohammad, his secretary, and the mullah who was to perform the ceremony. Your mother sat there reading the Qoran while her younger sisters rubbed two pieces of block sugar above her head on a scarf. The sugar is supposed to make her life sweet ever after. Presently the mullah read the marriage contract from behind the door, and asked the bride if she agreed to it. When she said,

'Yes,' everyone cried, 'God be praised,' and the party began, for the women in the *andaroon* and for the men in the *birooni*. It wasn't like today when men and women are all mixed up together!"

"What happened the next day?"

"The next day was the public feast, when all the poor of the district were invited to a meal. They brought their containers, which were filled with delicious rice and stew, and went away to eat it with their families and pray for the couple's happiness and good health."

"And the third day?"

"Ah, that was the wedding proper! There was a sumptuous dinner for family and friends. Again outside caterers were hired—cooks, assistants, waiters. They arrived with cartloads of huge pots and pans and serving dishes. Smoke from the charcoal braziers drifted high above the roof of Haji Ali-Baba's house, streaked the turquoise-blue firmament, and filled the air with the aromas of barbecued lamb, spicy stews and saffron rice. The whole neighbourhood was abuzz with excitement and shared in the festivities. It was wonderful!"

On the wedding day, the *hammam* [public baths] had been rented exclusively; the women went in the morning and the men in the afternoon. My mother had been taken there, washed, rubbed with rosewater and made up with powder and rouge. She was dressed in white satin and lace, and wrapped in her black *chador*—it was several years before the veil was abolished. Her father had covered her in gold and jewellery, as an investment to be used in emergency or later to buy a house. Bangles jingled on her wrists and forearms; gold necklaces and chains, hung with sovereigns and half-sovereigns covered her chest, and her fingers flashed with rings. Her father ordered the most beautiful four-horse coach from the royal stables, complete with liveried footmen and grooms, and a fleet of lesser vehicles and droshkies for the guests to ride the short journey to the groom's house:

"I can see him standing outside his front door," went on Aunt Ashraf, "tears pouring down his cheeks, throwing fistfuls of *noql* [tiny pieces of almond coated with sugar] and silver coins to the crowds that lined the street. Urchins scrambled to pick up the coins while he showered more and more handfuls on them, until the bag was empty and the cortège had disappeared round the corner."

At its destination, the nuptial room had been prepared with the bride's trousseau. She sat on a brocade mat, ready to receive the groom. One by one the female guests kissed her goodbye:

"May God give you many sons," "May your household be blessed," "May God's shadow never leave your heads," were some of their valedictory blessings.

It was customary for an elderly relative—in this case, the old nanny—to remain outside the nuptial room. Sometime during the night, the door would be opened and the groom would give her a blood-stained handkerchief, proof of his bride's virginity. If, by any chance, the bride had turned out not to be a virgin, she would be sent back to her father's house, the marriage contract would be annulled, and her life thereafter blighted by opprobrium and dishonour. At other times, there would be cover-ups: stories were told of the knightly gallantry of husbands who had cut their own fingers to produce the necessary few drops of blood and save the honour of their wives. Other tales told of bloody battles that had resulted from a girl's dishonour and engulfed whole families for generations. Sometimes the bridegroom would be too nervous, chivvied by the presence of the old woman waiting outside and the rest of the family not far off, and would fail to "perform." His excruciating misery and humiliation the next morning can be imagined. But such customs were already considered barbaric by the educated people and the upper classes, and my father had sent the nanny to bed with a tip before entering the nuptial room, certain of his wife's virtue.

Left alone, Azra began to pray. Presently the door opened and the groom entered. My mother had never seen him, of course, except once, when she had caught a glimpse of him through a window as he was entering the *birooni* to visit her father. She had exclaimed: "Oh but he's so *old!*" Sharp glances had darted towards her like poisoned arrows and put an end to her comments. Nor had she ever been consulted about her wishes as to her future husband. At the wedding ceremony, the mullah had spoken the marriage formula, Will-you-take-this-man-as-your-husband, etc., and she had answered, "Yes," but then no bride in known memory had ever said, "No." There were instances of the bride being quite adamant—if the groom was a relative she had seen and disliked, or if she secretly desired another. But surrounded with threatening parents and relations, the prospect of dishonour and scandal, she had always ended up by saying, "Yes," only to regret it for the rest of her life. Why anyone bothered to ask the bride at all was only because Islam, in fairness to women, had insisted upon their consent, and so consent was duly extracted by hook or crook.

My mother told me the rest of the story herself . . .

"Father came in and greeted me with a *salam* [hello—peace be on you]. I was supposed to say it first, being his wife, but I could not open my mouth with nervousness. He then sat beside me on the mat, and took my hand, kissed it and said:

"Well, young lady, what brings you to our part of the world?"

That made me laugh and the ice was broken. I thought well what if he's a bit old? He *is* kind and charming, so perhaps I will like him . . .

In fact he was 23 years older than her, but she fell in love with him that night and loved him single-heartedly for the rest of her life. He died a few years before her, but she continued communicating with him through dreams and prayers: every night he came to her while she slept, as ever soothing, consoling, guiding her as he had done throughout their lives together.

My mother's old nanny stayed on with her for a few weeks to show her the ropes and give her moral support, then she returned home, leaving her to manage on her own and be absorbed into the *andaroon* life.

Eventually my mother sold her gold and jewellery, and with the proceeds my parents bought their first house. By then no one had separate *andaroon* and *birooni,* just one house divided into two spheres:

"We were so happy then," mother used to reminisce wistfully. "Your father helped me to cook as I learnt by trial and error, before we could afford a proper cook, and he shared the chores. Nowadays you modern people think it is natural for your husbands to help you, but in those days it was unheard of! Everybody was jealous of me, seeing how lovingly he treated me. He taught me everything I know about the world."

Of all the beautiful objects my mother had in her trousseau the finest was a filigree gold and tortoise-shell toilette set—Haji Ali-Baba's personal gift to his son-in-law. It consisted of a gold tray, with three gold bowls of varying sizes fitting into each other, a shaving brush of tortoise-shell decorated with gold, a mirror and a tortoise-shell comb framed with gold, all most delicately made. My mother did not display it, but kept it hidden in a box, and locked in a cupboard with other family documents, photograph albums, and a few objects of sentimental value. She kept the key to the cupboard always in her handbag. Twice she showed me the toilette set, and I remember marvelling, even as a small child, at the beauty of the design and the delicacy of its execution. Of all family heirlooms that disappeared in the events of 1979—stolen, looted or sold for a pittance—it was the loss of that gold and tortoise-shell set that I most regretted, for in my memory it symbolised my parents' union.

On my last visit to Persia in 1977, my mother gave me a few pieces from her trousseau: her French wedding lamp, painted with cherubs whirling among the clouds, a Bohemian glass water-pipe which I have converted into a lamp and which was made specially for the Qojar king, Nasserudin Shah, and her samovar from Tula. Everything else has gone. But it matters not, compared to the loss of innocent life other families have suffered from the revolution. I have often wondered where the filigree gold and tortoise-shell set now is. I was told that, soon after the revolution, Japanese antique dealers came to Persia and bought everything cheaply from those who had looted the houses. So I would like to think that today it is displayed in a Japanese home among other beautiful works of art.

Interpretations

1. What does the existence of separate parts of the house for women and men (*andaroon* and *birooni*) indicate about the relationship between the sexes? Do we have anything analagous to women's quarters and men's quarters (not

counting restrooms)? Where can such relations between the sexes still be found today? How do you feel about such relations?

2. What does the "filigree gold and tortoise-shell toilette set" symbolize for the author's family?

3. Why would the "events of 1979" make the few family "heirlooms" that survived these events even more valuable to Guppy? Why do you suppose she elected to use "Persia" instead of the more current "Iran"?

4. Analyze use of narrative voice in this selection: What is gained by telling most of the story in the words of Aunt Ashraf? by switching at times to her mother's voice? by using "I" directly (that is, without quotation marks) only at the very end?

Correspondences

1. Social class is an important factor in both "The Wedding" and "Life in the Villages." How is social class revealed in the traditions of each culture? What examples attest to its influence on gender relationships? To what extent does it mirror (or not mirror) your own cultural traditions?

2. Attitudes toward personal space and territoriality differ among cultures. How do these affect traditions in the selections by Guppy and Sadat? To what extent have they been modified by the passing of time?

Applications

1. Would you ever consent to an arranged wedding? Why or why not? (In responding, consider the nature of the marriage that evolved in "The Wedding.")

2. Write a journal entry on the significance of wedding rituals in your family.

Footbinding

John King Fairbank

John King Fairbank (b. 1907) was born in South Dakota and received degrees from Harvard and Oxford universities. He was the director emeritus of Harvard's East Asian Research Center and enjoyed a distinguished career in the field of Asian studies. His numerous books on China include Modern China: A Bibliographical Guide to Chinese Works, 1898–1937 *(1950);* The United States and China *(1971); and* Chinabound: A Fifty-Year Memoir *(1983).*

    China, one of the world's oldest civilizations (dating at least to 5000 B.C.) with a fifth of the world's population (about a billion inhabitants), has had a tumultuous history, especially in the last two centuries. For thousands of years, beginning with the Shang Dynasty (about 1500–1000 B.C.), a succession of dynasties ruled China and expanded Chinese political and cultural domination of East Asia. In 1644 a foreign invader, the Manchus, established the Ch'ing Dynasty without destroying the underlying culture. The nineteenth century was a time of increasing stagnation and rebellion. European powers took advantage of internal strife to take control of large parts of the country. The country became a republic in 1912 but lost much of its territory to the Japanese, both before and during World War II. The People's Republic of China was declared in 1949 under the leadership of Mao Zedong by which time footbinding—but not its effects—had vanished. In the excerpt that follows, Fairbank describes the rise of the custom of footbinding in the tenth century, details its mechanics and its influence on domestic life, and advances reasons for its longevity.

OF ALL THE MANY unexplored facets of China's ancient history, the subjection of women has been the least studied. Women were fitted into the social and cosmic order (which were a continuum) by invoking the principles of Yang and Yin. All things bright, warm, active, male, and dominant were Yang while all things dark, cold, passive, female, and yielding were Yin. This dualism, seen in the alternation of night and day or the contrast of the sun and moon, was a ready-made matrix in which women could be confined. The subjection of women was thus a sophisticated and perfected institution like the other Chinese achievements, not a mere accident of male biceps or female childbearing as might be more obviously the case in a primitive tribe. The inequality between the sexes was buttressed with philosophical under-pinnings and long-continued social practices. Symbolic of woman's secondary status was her bridal night: she expected to be deflowered by a stranger, a husband selected by her family whom she had never seen before. Even though the facts may often have been less stark, the theory was hard-boiled.

Out of all this complex of theory and custom by which the Chinese world was given an enduring and stable order, the most neglected aspect is the institution of footbinding. This custom arose at court in the tenth century during the late T'ang and spread gradually among the upper class during the succeeding Sung period. By the Ming and Ch'ing eras after 1368 it had penetrated the mass of the Han Chinese population. It became so widespread that Western observers in the nineteenth century found it almost universal, not only among the upper class but throughout the farming population.

Footbinding spread as a mark of gentility and upper-class status. Small feet became a prestige item to such an extent that a girl without them could not achieve a good marriage arrangement and was subjected to the disrespect and taunts of the community. In short, bound feet became *de rigueur,* the only right-thinking thing to do for a daughter, an obligation on the part of a mother who cared about her daughter's eventual marriage and success in life. The bound foot was a must. Only tribal peoples and exceptional groups like the Manchu conquerors or the Hakka Chinese migrant groups in South China or finally the mean people, that lowest and rather small group who were below the social norms of civility, could avoid binding their daughters' feet.

The small foot was called a "golden lotus" or "golden lily" *(chin-lien)* and was much celebrated in poems and essays by male enthusiasts. Here is the early Sung poet Su Tung-p'o (1036–1101):

Anointed with fragrance, she takes lotus steps;
Though often sad, she steps with swift lightness.
She dances like the wind, leaving no physical trace.
Another stealthily but happily tries on the palace style,
But feels such distress when she tries to walk!
Look at them in the palms of your hands, so wondrously small that
they defy description.

The Sung philosophers stressed women's inferiority as a basic element of the social order. The great Chu Hsi (1130–1200) codified the cosmology of China as magistrally as his near contemporary Thomas Aquinas (d. 1274) codified that of Western Christendom. When he was a magistrate in Fukien province, Chu Hsi promoted footbinding to preserve female chastity and as "a means of spreading Chinese culture and teaching the separation of men and women."

By the Ming period the overwhelming majority of Han Chinese women all over the country had artificially small feet. The Manchu emperors many times inveighed against it in hortatory edicts, but to no avail. Male romanticizing on the subject continued unabated as in this poem of the fourteenth century:

> Lotus blossoms in shoes most tight,
> As if she could stand on autumnal waters!
> Her shoe tips do not peek beyond the skirt,
> Fearful lest the tiny embroideries be seen.[1]

There can be no doubt that footbinding was powered by a sexual fetish. Chinese love manuals are very specific about the use of bound feet as erogenous areas. All the different ways of taking hold of the foot, rubbing it with the hands, and using the mouth, tongue, and lips are explicitly catalogued. Many cases are recorded with the verisimilitude of high-class pornography. Meanwhile, the aesthetic attractiveness of the small shoes with their bright embroidered colors was praised in literature, while the tottering gait of a bound-foot woman was considered very fetching as a symbol of feminine frailty, which indeed it was. In fact, of course, bound feet were a guarantee of chastity because they kept women within the household and unable to venture far abroad. Lily feet, once formed, could not be unlocked like a chastity belt. By leaving only men able-bodied, they ensured male domination in a very concrete way.

Thus the prevalence of footbinding down to the 1920s, while the movement against it began only in the 1890s, vividly index the speed and scope of China's modern social revolution. This may be less comprehensible to white American males than to white women, or especially to black Americans, for Chinese women within the present century have had an emancipation from veritable slavery.

While footbinding is mentioned in so many foreign books about China, it is usually passed by as a curious detail. I don't think it was. It was a major erotic invention, still another achievement in Chinese social engineering. Girls painfully deformed themselves throughout their adolescence in order to attract desirable husbands who, on their part, subscribed to a folklore of self-fulfilling beliefs: for example, that footbinding made a vagina more narrow and muscular and that lotus feet were major foci of erotic sensitivity, true erogenous zones, a net addition of 50 percent to the female equipment. Normal feet, we are now told by purveyors of sexual comfort, are an underdeveloped area sensually, but one must admit they are a bit hard to handle—whereas small lotus feet could be grasped, rubbed, licked, sucked, nibbled, and bitten. The garrulous Jesuit Father Ripa, who spent a decade at the court of K'ang-hsi in the early 1700s, reported that "Their taste is perverted to such an extraordinary degree that I knew a physician who lived with a woman with whom he had no other intercourse but that of viewing and fondling her feet."[2] Having compacted all their nerve endings in a smaller area, golden

---

[1] Howard Levy, *Chinese Footbinding: The History of a Curious Erotic Custom* (New York: Walton Rawls, 1966), p. 47.

[2] Fortunato Prandi, ed. and trans., *Memoirs of Father Ripa* (London: John Murray, 1855), p. 58.

lilies were far more sensitive than, for example, the back of the neck that used to bewitch Japanese samurai. After all, they had been created especially for male appreciation. When every proper girl did it, what bride would say that her sacrifice, suffering, and inconvenience were not worth it? A bride without small feet in the old China was like a new house in today's America without utilities—who would want it? Consequently in the 1930s and '40s one still saw women on farms stumping about on their heels as they worked, victims of this old custom.

A girl's foot was made small, preferably only three inches long, by pressing the four smaller toes under the sole or ball of the foot (plantar) in order to make it narrower. At the same time it was made shorter by forcing the big toe and heel closer together so that the arch rose in a bowed shape. As a result the arch was broken and the foot could bear no weight except on the heel. If this process was begun at age five, the experience was less severe than if a little girl, perhaps in a peasant household, had been left with normal feet until age eight or ten so that she could be of more use in the household.

> When I was seven [said one woman to Ida Pruitt], my mother . . . washed and placed alum on my feet and cut the toenails. She then bent my toes toward the plantar with a binding cloth ten feet long and two inches wide, doing the right foot first and then the left. She . . . ordered me to walk but when I did the pain proved unbearable. That night . . . my feet felt on fire and I couldn't sleep; mother struck me for crying. On the following days, I tried to hide but was forced to walk on my feet . . . after several months all toes but the big one were pressed against the inner surface . . . mother would remove the bindings and wipe the blood and pus which dripped from my feet. She told me that only with removal of the flesh could my feet become slender . . . every two weeks I changed to new shoes. Each new pair was one- to two-tenths of an inch smaller than the previous one. . . . In summer my feet smelled offensively because of pus and blood; in winter my feet felt cold because of lack of circulation . . . four of the toes were curled in like so many dead caterpillars . . . it took two years to achieve the three-inch model . . . my shanks were thin, my feet became humped, ugly and odoriferous.[3]

After the first two years the pain lessened. But constricting the feet to a three-inch size was only the beginning of trouble. By this time they were very private parts indeed and required daily care, washing and manicuring at the same time that they had to be kept constantly bound and shod night and day. Unmanicured nails could cut into the instep, bindings could destroy

---

[3]Ida Pruitt, *A Daughter of Han: The Autobiography of a Chinese Working Woman* (Yale University Press, 1945), p. 22.

circulation, blood poisoning or gangrene could result. Massage and applications of hot and cold water were used to palliate the discomfort, but walking any distance remained difficult. It also produced corns on the bent-under toes, which had to be pared with a knife. Once deformed to taste, bound feet were of little use to stand on. Since weight was carried entirely on the heels, it had to be constantly shifted back and forth. Since the bound foot lacked the resilience of a normal foot, it was a tiring and unsteady support.

Footbinding, in short, had begun as an ostentatious luxury, which made a girl less useful in family work and more dependent on help from others. Yet, once the custom had spread among the populace, lotus feet were considered essential in order to get a good husband. Marriages, of course, were arranged between families and often by professional matchmakers, in whose trade the length of the lily foot was rated more important than beauty of face or person. When the anti-footbinding movement began at the end of the nineteenth century, many mothers and daughters, too, stubbornly clung to it to avoid the public shame of having large feet. The smallness of the foot, in short, was a source of social pride both to the family and to the victim. First and last one may guess that at least a billion Chinese girls during the thousand-year currency of this social custom suffered the agony of footbinding and reaped its rewards of pride and ecstasy, such as they were.

There are three remarkable things about footbinding. First, that it should have been invented at all—it was such a feat of physio-psycho-sociological engineering. Second, that once invented it should have spread so pervasively and lasted so long among a generally humane and practical-minded farming population. We are just at the beginning of understanding this phenomenon. The fact that an upper-class erotic luxury permeated the peasantry of Old China, for whom it could only lower productivity, suggests that the old society was extraordinarily homogeneous.

Finally, it was certainly ingenious how men trapped women into mutilating themselves for an ostensibly sexual purpose that had the effect of perpetuating male domination. Brides left their own homes and entered their husband's family in the lowest status, servants of their mothers-in-law. Husbands were chosen for them sight unseen, and might find romance in extramarital adventures or, if they could afford it, bring in secondary wives. But a woman once betrothed, if her husband-to-be died even as a child, was expected to remain a chaste widow thereafter. Mao remarked that "women hold up half the sky," but in the old China they were not supposed to lift their heads. The talent that one sees in Chinese women today had little chance to grow and express itself. This made a weak foundation for a modern society.

Interpretations

1. What is Fairbank's purpose in describing "the principles of Yang and Yin"? How does this relate to the topic of footbinding? Does the intellectual theory

(Yang-Yin) really explain any important aspects of Chinese behavior? (or is it a rationalization? a pretext? an emblem?)

2. The (non-Chinese) Manchu Dynasty did not practice or condone footbinding; indeed, it tried to eradicate the practice. Why, according to Fairbank, did they fail? How was the end of footbinding like emancipation from slavery?

3. Fairbank estimates that "at least a billion Chinese girls during the thousand-year currency of this social custom suffered the agony of footbinding. . . ." What does this estimate suggest about the need to re-examine custom?

4. What examples can you give of elaborate psychological or other theories in contemporary America that have the aura of science or intellect but really explain very little? Do these theories affect our society for good or for ill, or do they simply remain in the realm of theory? If you find they have practical effects on people's behavior, what effects?

Correspondences

1. Review the Douglass quotation on traditions (page 4). How does it apply to the selection by Fairbank? (To what extent was footbinding "useful" in the culture of its day?)

2. Review the Geiger quotation (page 3). How does it apply to "Footbinding"? To which other selections in this chapter is it also relevant? In what way?

Applications

1. Fairbank describes the process involved in footbinding. Write an essay in which you describe a process that you perform in order to relax. Does the way you relax reveal anything about your philosophy of life, about the things in life that you consider important and valuable?

2. Write a journal entry describing *how* you were taught to write in grade school, in high school, and in college. Were these processes similar and different? Which has been the most valuable? (How has your attitude toward writing been shaped by these teaching styles?)

The Lottery

Shirley Jackson

Shirley Jackson (1919–1965) was born and raised in California. In 1933, she moved with her family to Rochester, New York, where she briefly attended the University of Rochester. Notable publications include the novel Hangsman *(1951), the play* We Have Always Lived in the Castle *(1962). In "The Lottery" (1948), a frequently anthologized piece, Jackson scrutinizes scapegoating.*

THE MORNING of June 27th was clear and sunny, with the fresh warmth of a full-summer day; the flowers were blossoming profusely and the grass was richly green. The people of the village began to gather in the square, between the post office and the bank, around ten o'clock; in some towns there were so many people that the lottery took two days and had to be started on June 26th, but in this village, where there were only about three hundred people, the whole lottery took less than two hours, so it could begin at ten o'clock in the morning and still be through in time to allow the villagers to get home for noon dinner.

The children assembled first, of course. School was recently over for the summer, and the feeling of liberty sat uneasily on most of them; they tended to gather together quietly for a while before they broke into boisterous play, and their talk was still of the classroom and the teacher, of books and reprimands. Bobby Martin had already stuffed his pockets full of stones, and the other boys soon followed his example, selecting the smoothest and round-est stones; Bobby and Harry Jones and Dickie Delacroix—the villagers pronounced this name "Dellacroy"—eventually made a great pile of stones in one corner of the square and guarded it against the raids of the other boys. The girls stood aside, talking among themselves, looking over their shoulders at the boys, and the very small children rolled in the dust or clung to the hands of their older brothers or sisters.

Soon the men began to gather, surveying their own children, speaking of planting and rain, tractors and taxes. They stood together, away from the pile of stones in the corner, and their jokes were quiet and they smiled rather than laughed. The women, wearing faded house dresses and sweaters, came shortly after their menfolk. They greeted one another and exchanged bits of gossip as they went to join their husbands. Soon the women, standing by their husbands, began to call to their children, and the children came re-luctantly, having to be called four or five times. Bobby Martin ducked under his mother's grasping hand and ran, laughing, back to the pile of stones. His father spoke up sharply, and Bobby came quickly and took his place between his father and his oldest brother.

The lottery was conducted—as were the square dances, the teen-age club, the Halloween program—by Mr. Summers, who had time and energy to devote to civic activities. He was a round-faced, jovial man and he ran the coal business, and people were sorry for him, because he had no children and his wife was a scold. When he arrived in the square, carrying the black wooden box, there was a murmur of conversation among the villagers, and he waved and called, "Little late today, folks." The postmaster, Mr. Graves, followed him, carrying a three-legged stool, and the stool was put in the center of the square and Mr. Summers set the black box down on it. The villagers kept their distance, leaving a space between themselves and the stool, and when Mr. Summers said, "Some of you fellows want to give me a hand?" there was a hesitation before two men, Mr. Martin and his oldest son, Baxter, came forward to hold the box steady on the stool while Mr. Summers stirred up the papers inside it.

The original paraphernalia for the lottery had been lost long ago, and the black box now resting on the stool had been put into use even before Old Man Warner, the oldest man in town, was born. Mr. Summers spoke frequently to the villagers about making a new box, but no one liked to upset even as much tradition as was represented by the black box. There was a story that the present box had been made with some pieces of the box that had preceded it, the one that had been constructed when the first people settled down to make a village here. Every year, after the lottery, Mr. Summers began talking again about a new box, but every year the subject was allowed to fade off without anything's being done. The black box grew shabbier each year; by now it was no longer completely black but splintered badly along one side to show the original wood color, and in some places faded or stained.

Mr. Martin and his oldest son, Baxter, held the black box securely on the stool until Mr. Summers had stirred the papers thoroughly with his hand. Because so much of the ritual had been forgotten or discarded, Mr. Summers had been successful in having slips of paper substituted for the chips of wood that had been used for generations. Chips of wood, Mr. Summers had argued, had been all very well when the village was tiny, but now that the population was more than three hundred and likely to keep on growing, it was necessary to use something that would fit more easily into the black box. The night before the lottery, Mr. Summers and Mr. Graves made up the slips of paper and put them in the box, and it was then taken to the safe of Mr. Summers's coal company and locked up until Mr. Summers was ready to take it to the square next morning. The rest of the year, the box was put away, sometimes one place, sometimes another; it had spent one year in Mr. Graves's barn and another year underfoot in the post office, and sometimes it was set on a shelf in the Martin grocery and left there.

There was a great deal of fussing to be done before Mr. Summers declared the lottery open. There were the lists to make up—of heads of families, heads of households in each family, members of each household in each family.

There was the proper swearing-in of Mr. Summers by the postmaster, as the official of the lottery; at one time, some people remembered, there had been a recital of some sort, performed by the official of the lottery, a perfunctory, tuneless chant that had been rattled off duly each year; some people believed that the official of the lottery used to stand just so when he said or sang it, others believed that he was supposed to walk among the people, but years and years ago this part of the ritual had been allowed to lapse. There had been, also, a ritual salute, which the official of the lottery had had to use in addressing each person who came up to draw from the box, but this also had changed with time, until now it was felt necessary only for the official to speak to each person approaching. Mr. Summers was very good at all this; in his clean white shirt and blue jeans, with one hand resting carelessly on the black box, he seemed very proper and important as he talked interminably to Mr. Graves and the Martins.

Just as Mr. Summers finally left off talking and turned to the assembled villagers, Mrs. Hutchinson came hurriedly along the path to the square, her sweater thrown over her shoulders, and slid into place in the back of the crowd. "Clean forgot what day it was," she said to Mrs. Delacroix, who stood next to her, and they both laughed softly. "Thought my old man was out back stacking wood," Mrs. Hutchinson went on, "and then I looked out the window and the kids was gone, and then I remembered it was the twenty-seventh and came a-running." She dried her hands on her apron, and Mrs. Delacroix said, "You're in time, though. They're still talking away up there."

Mrs. Hutchinson craned her neck to see through the crowd and found her husband and children standing near the front. She tapped Mrs. Delacroix on the arm as a farewell and began to make her way through the crowd. The people separated good-humoredly to let her through; two or three people said, in voices just loud enough to be heard across the crowd, "Here comes your Missus, Hutchinson," and "Bill, she made it after all." Mrs. Hutchinson reached her husband, and Mr. Summers, who had been waiting, said cheerfully, "Thought we were going to have to get on without you, Tessie." Mrs. Hutchinson said, grinning, "Wouldn't have me leave m'dishes in the sink, now, would you, Joe?" and soft laughter ran through the crowd as the people stirred back into position after Mrs. Hutchinson's arrival.

"Well, now," Mr. Summers said soberly, "guess we better get started, get this over with, so's we can go back to work. Anybody ain't here?"

"Dunbar," several people said. "Dunbar, Dunbar."

Mr. Summers consulted his list. "Clyde Dunbar," he said. "That's right. He's broke his leg, hasn't he? Who's drawing for him?"

"Me, I guess," a woman said, and Mr. Summers turned to look at her. "Wife draws for her husband," Mr. Summers said. "Don't you have a grown boy to do it for you, Janey?" Although Mr. Summers and everyone else in the village knew the answer perfectly well, it was the business of the official of the lottery to ask such questions formally. Mr. Summers waited with an expression of polite interest while Mrs. Dunbar answered.

"Horace's not but sixteen yet," Mrs. Dunbar said regretfully. "Guess I gotta fill in for the old man this year."

"Right," Mr. Summers said. He made a note on the list he was holding. Then he asked, "Watson boy drawing this year?"

A tall boy in the crowd raised his hand. "Here," he said. "I'm drawing for m'mother and me." He blinked his eyes nervously and ducked his head as several voices in the crowd said things like "Good fellow, Jack," and "Glad to see your mother's got a man to do it."

"Well," Mr. Summers said, "guess that's everyone. Old Man Warner make it?"

"Here," a voice said, and Mr. Summers nodded.

A sudden hush fell on the crowd as Mr. Summers cleared his throat and looked at the list. "All ready?" he called. "Now, I'll read the names—heads of families first—and the men come up and take a paper out of the box. Keep the paper folded in your hand without looking at it until everyone has had a turn. Everything clear?"

The people had done it so many times that they only half listened to the directions; most of them were quiet, wetting their lips, not looking around. Then Mr. Summers raised one hand high and said, "Adams." A man disengaged himself from the crowd and came forward. "Hi, Steve," Mr. Summers said, and Mr. Adams said, "Hi, Joe." They grinned at one another humorlessly and nervously. Then Mr. Adams reached into the black box and took out a folded paper. He held it firmly by one corner as he turned and went hastily back to his place in the crowd, where he stood a little apart from his family, not looking down at his hand.

"Allen," Mr. Summers said, "Anderson. . . . Bentham."

"Seems like there's no time at all between lotteries any more," Mrs. Delacroix said to Mrs. Graves in the back row. "Seems like we got through with the last one only last week."

"Time sure goes fast," Mrs. Graves said.

"Clark. . . . Delacroix."

"There goes my old man," Mrs. Delacroix said. She held her breath while her husband went forward.

"Dunbar," Mr. Summers said, and Mrs. Dunbar went steadily to the box while one of the women said, "Go on, Janey," and another said, "There she goes."

"We're next," Mrs. Graves said. She watched while Mr. Graves came around from the side of the box, greeted Mr. Summers gravely, and selected a slip of paper from the box. By now, all through the crowd there were men holding the small folded papers in their large hands, turning them over and over nervously. Mrs. Dunbar and her two sons stood together, Mrs. Dunbar holding the slip of paper.

"Harburt. . . . Hutchinson."

"Get up there, Bill," Mrs. Hutchinson said, and the people near her laughed.

"Jones."

"They do say," Mr. Adams said to Old Man Warner, who stood next to him, "that over in the north village they're talking of giving up the lottery."

Old Man Warner snorted. "Pack of crazy fools," he said. "Listening to the young folks, nothing's good enough for *them*. Next thing you know, they'll be wanting to go back to living in caves, nobody work any more, live *that* way for a while. Used to be a saying about 'Lottery in June, corn be heavy soon.' First thing you know, we'd all be eating stewed chickweed and acorns. There's *always* been a lottery," he added petulantly. "Bad enough to see young Joe Summers up there joking with everybody."

"Some places have already quit lotteries," Mrs. Adams said.

"Nothing but trouble in *that*," Old Man Warner said stoutly. "Pack of young fools."

"Martin." And Bobby Martin watched his father go forward. "Over-dyke. . . . Percy."

"I wish they'd hurry," Mrs. Dunbar said to her oldest son. "I wish they'd hurry."

"They're almost through," her son said.

"You get ready to run tell Dad," Mrs. Dunbar said.

Mr. Summers called his own name and then stepped forward precisely and selected a slip from the box. Then he called, "Warner."

"Seventy-seventh year I been in the lottery," Old Man Warner said as he went through the crowd. "Seventy-seventh time."

"Watson." The tall boy came awkwardly through the crowd. Someone said, "Don't be nervous, Jack," and Mr. Summers said, "Take your time, son."

"Zanini."

After that, there was a long pause, a breathless pause, until Mr. Summers, holding his slip of paper in the air, said, "All right, fellows." For a minute, no one moved, and then all the slips of paper were opened. Suddenly, all the women began to speak at once, saying, "Who is it?" "Who's got it?" "Is it the Dunbars?" "Is it the Watsons?" Then the voices began to say, "It's Hutchinson. It's Bill." "Bill Hutchinson's got it."

"Go tell your father," Mrs. Dunbar said to her older son.

People began to look around to see the Hutchinsons. Bill Hutchinson was standing quiet, staring down at the paper in his hand. Suddenly, Tessie Hutchinson shouted to Mr. Summers, "You didn't give him time enough to take any paper he wanted. I saw you. It wasn't fair!"

"Be a good sport, Tessie," Mrs. Delacroix called, and Mrs. Graves said, "All of us took the same chance."

"Shut up, Tessie," Bill Hutchinson said.

"Well, everyone," Mr. Summers said, "that was done pretty fast, and now we've got to be hurrying a little more to get done in time." He consulted his next list. "Bill," he said, "you draw for the Hutchinson family. You got any other households in the Hutchinsons?"

"There's Don and Eva," Mrs. Hutchinson yelled. "Make *them* take their chance!"

"Daughters drew with their husbands' families, Tessie," Mr. Summers said gently. "You know that as well as anyone else."

"It wasn't *fair*," Tessie said.

"I guess not, Joe," Bill Hutchinson said regretfully. "My daughter draws with her husband's family, that's only fair. And I've got no other family except the kids."

"Then, as far as drawing for families is concerned, it's you," Mr. Summers said in explanation, "and as far as drawing for households is concerned, that's you, too. Right?"

"Right," Bill Hutchinson said.

"How many kids, Bill?" Mr. Summers asked formally.

"Three," Bill Hutchinson said. "There's Bill, Jr., and Nancy, and little Dave. And Tessie and me."

"All right, then," Mr. Summers said. "Harry, you got their tickets back?"

Mr. Graves nodded and held up the slips of paper. "Put them in the box, then," Mr. Summers directed. "Take Bill's and put it in."

"I think we ought to start over," Mrs. Hutchinson said, as quietly as she could. "I tell you it wasn't *fair*. You didn't give him time enough to choose. *Every*body saw that."

Mr. Graves had selected the five slips and put them in the box, and he dropped all the papers but those onto the ground, where the breeze caught them and lifted them off.

"Listen, everybody," Mrs. Hutchinson was saying to the people around her.

"Ready, Bill?" Mr. Summers asked, and Bill Hutchinson, with one quick glance around at his wife and children, nodded.

"Remember," Mr. Summers said, "take the slips and keep them folded until each person has taken one. Harry, you help little Dave." Mr. Graves took the hand of the little boy, who came willingly with him up to the box. "Take a paper out of the box, Davy," Mr. Summers said. Davy put his hand into the box and laughed. "Take just *one* paper," Mr. Summers said. "Harry, you hold it for him." Mr. Graves took the child's hand and removed the folded paper from the tight fist and held it while little Dave stood next to him and looked up at him wonderingly.

"Nancy next," Mr. Summers said. Nancy was twelve, and her school friends breathed heavily as she went forward, switching her skirt, and took a slip daintily from the box. "Bill, Jr.," Mr. Summers said, and Billy, his face red and his feet overlarge, nearly knocked the box over as he got a paper out. "Tessie," Mr. Summers said. She hesitated for a minute, looking around defiantly, and then set her lips and went up to the box. She snatched a paper out and held it behind her.

"Bill," Mr. Summers said, and Bill Hutchinson reached into the box and felt around, bringing his hand out at last with the slip of paper in it.

The crowd was quiet. A girl whispered, "I hope it's not Nancy," and the sound of the whisper reached the edges of the crowd.

"It's not the way it used to be," Old Man Warner said clearly. "People ain't the way they used to be."

"All right," Mr. Summers said. "Open the papers. Harry, you open little Dave's."

Mr. Graves opened the slip of paper and there was a general sigh through the crowd as he held it up and everyone could see that it was blank. Nancy and Bill, Jr., opened theirs at the same time, and both beamed and laughed, turning around to the crowd and holding their slips of paper above their heads.

"Tessie," Mr. Summers said. There was a pause, and then Mr. Summers looked at Bill Hutchinson, and Bill unfolded his paper and showed it. It was blank.

"It's Tessie," Mr. Summers said, and his voice was hushed. "Show us her paper, Bill."

Bill Hutchinson went over to his wife and forced the slip of paper out of her hand. It had a black spot on it, the black spot Mr. Summers had made the night before with the heavy pencil in the coal-company office. Bill Hutchinson held it up and there was a stir in the crowd.

"All right, folks," Mr. Summers said. "Let's finish quickly."

Although the villagers had forgotten the ritual and lost the original black box, they still remembered to use stones. The pile of stones the boys had made earlier was ready; there were stones on the ground with the blowing scraps of paper that had come out of the box. Mrs. Delacroix selected a stone so large she had to pick it up with both hands and turned to Mrs. Dunbar. "Come on," she said. "Hurry up."

Mrs. Dunbar had small stones in both hands, and she said, gasping for breath, "I can't run at all. You'll have to go ahead and I'll catch up with you."

The children had stones already, and someone gave little Davy Hutchinson a few pebbles.

Tessie Hutchinson was in the center of a cleared space by now, and she held her hands out desperately as the villagers moved in on her. "It isn't fair," she said. A stone hit her on the side of the head.

Old Man Warner was saying, "Come on, come on, everyone." Steve Adams was in the front of the crowd of villagers, with Mrs. Graves beside him.

"It isn't fair, it isn't right," Mrs. Hutchinson screamed and then they were upon her.

Interpretations

1. What do the villagers mean by "fairness"? (What is implied by the fact that the only villager to complain about the lottery's consequences is Tessie Hutchinson?)

2. By showing how familiar the process of the lottery is to the villagers, what does Jackson imply about tradition, mass psychology, and social pressure?

3. Why does Jackson use a flat, reportorial style to describe an event that would normally be headline news? (Consider the role of irony in this story.)

4. How important is it that the story is set in roughly contemporary New England? (How, for example, would its influence differ if the story were set in Aztec Mexico, a culture that routinely practiced human sacrifice?)

5. The tradition here depicted brings summary execution or reprieve. What traditions do we participate in that have life-or-death consequences, in either the short or the long run?

Correspondences

1. Review the Maugham quotation (page 3). What does it mean? How does it apply to "The Lottery"?

2. The selections by Jackson and Fairbank suggest that some traditions might benefit from a reevaluation. Do you agree? What criteria would you suggest?

Applications

1. When Shirley Jackson's story was first published in *The New Yorker* in 1948, she received hundreds of letters from people "who wanted to know where these lotteries were held, and whether they could go there and watch." What does this response suggest about human nature? (What was *your* response to the story?)

2. Consult a dictionary on the origin and meaning of *scapegoat*. Then look up historical examples of it in the *Micropaedia* of the *Encyclopaedia Britannica* (1979 or subsequent editions). What modern examples or uses of scapegoating can you think of? Write a brief essay on the topic.

The Water-Faucet Vision

Gish Jen

Gish Jen lives in Cambridge, Massachusetts. Support for her writing has come from the James Michener/Copernicus Society, the Bunting Institute, the Massachusetts Bay Transportation Authority, and The National Endowment for the Arts. Her fiction has appeared in The New Generation, *an anthology, and her most recent story, "What Means Switch" (1990), set in New York City, features an encounter between a polite Chinese girl and her Japanese boyfriend who knows Judo but not English. Jen was featured in the February 1990 issue of* Atlantic Monthly *as one of four prominent writers of the new generation.*

To PROTECT MY SISTER Mona and me from the pains—or, as they pronounced it, the "pins"—of life, my parents did their fighting in Shanghai dialect, which we didn't understand; and when my father one day pitched a brass vase through the kitchen window, my mother told us he had done it by accident.

"By accident?" said Mona.

My mother chopped the foot off a mushroom.

"By accident?" said Mona. "By *accident*?"

Later I tried to explain to her that she shouldn't have persisted like that, but it was hopeless.

"What's the matter with throwing things?" She shrugged. "He was *mad*."

That was the difference between Mona and me: fighting was just fighting to her. If she worried about anything, it was only that she might turn out too short to become a ballerina, in which case she was going to be a piano player.

I, on the other hand, was going to be a martyr. I was in fifth grade then, and the hyperimaginative sort—the kind of girl who grows morbid in Catholic school, who longs to be chopped or frozen to death but then has nightmares about it from which she wakes up screaming and clutching a stuffed bear. It was not a bear that I clutched, though, but a string of three malachite beads that I had found in the marsh by the old aqueduct one day. Apparently once part of a necklace, they were each wonderfully striated and swirled, and slightly humped toward the center, like a jellyfish; so that if I squeezed one, it would slip smoothly away, with a grace that altogether enthralled and—on those dream-harrowed nights—soothed me, soothed me as nothing had before or has since. Not that I've lacked occasion for soothing:

50

though it's been four months since my mother died, there are still nights when sleep stands away from me, stiff as a well-paid sentry. But that is another story. Back then I had my malachite beads, and if I worried them long and patiently enough, I was sure to start feeling better, more awake, even a little special—imagining, as I liked to, that my nightmares were communications from the Almighty Himself, preparation for my painful destiny. Discussing them with Patty Creamer, who had also promised her life to God, I called them "almost visions"; and Patty, her mouth wadded with the three or four sticks of Doublemint she always seemed to have going at once, said, "I bet you'll be doin' miracleth by seventh grade."

Miracles. Today Patty laughs to think she ever spent good time stewing on such matters, her attention having long turned to rugs, and artwork, and antique Japanese bureaus—things she believes in.

"A good bureau's more than just a bureau," she explained last time we had lunch. "It's a hedge against life. I tell you: if there's one thing I believe, it's that cheap stuff's just money out the window. Nice stuff, on the other hand—now that you can always cash out, if life gets rough. *That* you can count on."

In fifth grade, though, she counted on different things.

"You'll be doing miracles too," I told her, but she shook her shaggy head and looked doleful.

"Na' me," she chomped. "Buzzit's okay. The kin' things I like, prayers work okay on."

"Like?"

"Like you 'member the dreth I liked?"

She meant the yellow one, with the crisscross straps.

"Well gueth what."

"Your mom got it for you."

She smiled. "And I only jutht prayed for it for a week," she said.

As for myself, though, I definitely wanted to be able to perform a wonder or two. Miracle-working! It was the carrot of carrots: it kept me doing my homework, taking the sacraments; it kept me mournfully on key in music hour, while my classmates hiccuped and squealed their carefree hearts away. Yet I couldn't have said what I wanted such powers *for,* exactly. That is, I thought of them the way one might think of, say, an ornamental sword—as a kind of collectible, which also happened to be a means of defense.

But then Patty's father walked out on her mother, and for the first time, there was a miracle I wanted to do. I wanted it so much I could see it: Mr. Creamer made into a spitball; Mr. Creamer shot through a straw into the sky; Mr. Creamer unrolled and replumped, plop back on Patty's doorstep. I would've cleaned out his mind and given him a shave en route. I would've given him a box of peanut fudge, tied up with a ribbon, to present to Patty with a kiss.

But instead all I could do was try to tell her he'd come back.

"He will not, he will not!" she sobbed. "He went on a boat to Rio Deniro. To Rio Deniro!"

I tried to offer her a stick of gum, but she wouldn't take it.

"He said he would rather look at water than at my mom's fat face. He said he would rather look at water than at me." Now she was really wailing, and holding her ribs so tightly that she almost seemed to be hurting herself— so tightly that just looking at her arms wound around her like snakes made my heart feel squeezed.

I patted her on the arm. A one-winged pigeon waddled by.

"He said I wasn't even his kid, he said I came from Uncle Johnny. He said I was garbage, just like my mom and Uncle Johnny. He said I wasn't even his kid, he said I wasn't his Patty, he said I came from Uncle Johnny!"

"From your Uncle Johnny?" I asked stupidly.

"From Uncle Johnny," she cried. "From Uncle Johnny!"

"He said that?" I said. Then, wanting to go on, to say *something,* I said, "Oh Patty, don't cry."

She kept crying.

I tried again. "Oh Patty, don't cry," I said. Then I said, "Your dad was a jerk anyway."

The pigeon produced a large runny dropping.

It was a good twenty minutes before Patty was calm enough for me just to run to the girls' room to get her some toilet paper; and by the time I came back she was sobbing again, saying "to Rio Deniro, to Rio Deniro" over and over again, as though the words had stuck in her and couldn't be gotten out. As we had missed the regular bus home and the late bus too, I had to leave her a second time to go call my mother, who was mad only until she heard what had happened. Then she came and picked us up, and bought us each a Fudgsicle.

Some days later, Patty and I started a program to work on getting her father home. It was a serious business. We said extra prayers, and lit votive candles; I tied my malachite beads to my uniform belt, fondling them as though they were a rosary, I a nun. We even took to walking about the school halls with our hands folded—a sight so ludicrous that our wheeze of a principal personally took us aside one day.

"I must tell you," she said, using her nose as a speaking tube, "that there is really no need for such peee-ity."

But we persisted, promising to marry God and praying to every saint we could think of. We gave up gum, then gum and Slim Jims both, then gum and Slim Jims and ice cream—and when even that didn't work, we started on more innovative things. The first was looking at flowers. We held our hands beside our eyes like blinders as we hurried by the violets by the flagpole, the window box full of tulips outside the nurse's office. Next it was looking at boys: Patty gave up angel-eyed Jamie Halloran and I, gymnastic Anthony Rossi. It was hard, but in the end our efforts paid off. Mr. Creamer came back a month later, and though he brought with him nothing but dysentery, he was at least too sick to have all that much to say.

Then, in the course of a fight with my father, my mother somehow fell out of their bedroom window.

Recently—thinking a mountain vacation might cheer me—I sublet my apartment to a handsome but somber newlywed couple, who turned out to be every bit as responsible as I'd hoped. They cleaned out even the eggshell chips I'd sprinkled around the base of my plants as fertilizer, leaving behind only a shiny silverplate cake server and a list of their hopes and goals for the summer. The list, tacked precariously to the back of the kitchen door, began with a fervent appeal to God to help them get their wedding thank-yous written in three weeks or less. (You could see they had originally written "two weeks" but scratched it out—no miracles being demanded here.) It went on:

> Please help us, Almighty Father in Heaven Above, to get Ann a teaching job within a half-hour drive of here in a nice neighborhood.
>
> Please help us, Almighty Father in Heaven Above, to get John a job doing anything where he won't strain his back and that is within a half-hour drive of here.
>
> Please help us, Almighty Father in Heaven Above, to get us a car.
>
> Please help us, A.F. in H.A., to learn French.
>
> Please help us, A.F. in H.A., to find seven dinner recipes that cost less than 60 cents a serving and can be made in a half-hour. And that don't have tomatoes, since You in Your Heavenly Wisdom made John allergic.
>
> Please help us, A.F. in H.A., to avoid books in this apartment such as You in Your Heavenly Wisdom allowed John, for Your Heavenly Reasons, to find three nights ago (June 2nd).

Et cetera. In the left-hand margin they kept score of how they had fared with their requests, and it was heartening to see that nearly all of them were marked "Yes! Praise the Lord" (sometimes shortened to PTL), with the sole exception of learning French, which was mysteriously marked "No! PTL to the Highest."

That note touched me. Strange and familiar both, it seemed like it had been written by some cousin of mine—some cousin who had stayed home to grow up, say, while I went abroad and learned what I had to, though the learning was painful. This, of course, is just a manner of speaking; in fact I did my growing up at home, like anybody else.

But the learning *was* painful: I never knew exactly how it happened that my mother went hurtling through the air that night years ago, only that the wind had been chopping at the house, and that the argument had started about the state of the roof. Someone had been up to fix it the year before, but it wasn't a roofer, it was some man my father had insisted could do just as good a job for a quarter of the price. And maybe he could have, had he not somehow managed to step through a knot in the wood under the shingles and break his uninsured ankle. Now the shingles were coming loose again, and the attic insulation was mildewing besides, and my father was wanting to sell the house altogether, which he said my mother had wanted to buy so she could send pictures of it home to her family in China.

"The Americans have a saying," he said. "They saying, 'You have to keep up with Jones family,' I'm saying if Jones family in Shanghai, you can send any picture you want, *an-y* picture. Go take picture of those rich guys' house. You want to act like rich guys, right? Go take picture of those rich guys' house."

At that point my mother sent Mona and me to wash up, and started speaking Shanghaiese. They argued for some time in the kitchen while we listened from the top of the stairs, our faces wedged between the bumpy Spanish scrolls of the wrought-iron railing. First my mother ranted, then my father, then they both ranted at once until finally there was a thump, followed by a long quiet.

"Do you think they're kissing now?" said Mona. "I bet they're kissing, like this." She pursed her lips like a fish and was about to put them to the railing when we heard my mother locking the back door. We hightailed it into bed; my parents creaked up the stairs. Everything at that point seemed fine. Once in their bedroom, though, they started up again, first softly, then louder and louder, until my mother turned on a radio to try to disguise the noise. A door slammed; they began shouting at one another; another door slammed; a shoe or something banged the wall behind Mona's bed.

"How're we supposed to *sleep?*" said Mona, sitting up.

There was another thud, more yelling in Shanghaiese, and then my mother's voice pierced the wall, in English. "So what you want I should do? Go to work like Theresa Lee?"

My father rumbled something back.

"You think you're big shot because you have job, right? You're big shot, but you never get promotion, you never get raise. All I do is spend money, right? So what do you do, you tell me. So what do you do!"

Something hit the floor so hard that our room shook.

"So kill me," screamed my mother. "You know what you are? You are failure. Failure! You are failure!"

Then there was a sudden, terrific, bursting crash—and after it, as if on a bungled cue, the serene blare of an a cappella soprano, picking her way down a scale.

By the time Mona and I knew to look out the window, a neighbor's pet beagle was already on the scene, sniffing and barking at my mother's body, his tail crazy with excitement; then he was barking at my stunned and trembling father, at the shrieking ambulance, the police, at crying Mona in her bunnyfooted pajamas, and at me, barefoot in the cold grass, squeezing her shoulder with one hand and clutching my malachite beads with the other.

My mother wasn't dead, only unconscious, the paramedics figured that out right away, but there was blood everywhere, and though they were reassuring about her head wounds as they strapped her to the stretcher, commenting also on how small she was, how delicate, how light, my father kept saying, "I killed her, I killed her" as the ambulance screeched and screeched headlong, forever, to the hospital. I was afraid to touch her, and glad of the metal rail between us, even though its sturdiness made her seem even frailer than she was; I wished she was bigger, somehow, and noticed, with a pang, that the new red slippers we had given her for Mother's Day had been lost somewhere along the way. How much she seemed to be leaving behind as we careened along—still not there, still not there—Mona and Dad and the medic and I taking up the whole ambulance, all the room, so there was no room for anything else; no room even for my mother's real self, the one who should have been pinching the color back to my father's grey face, the one who should have been calming Mona's cowlick—the one who should have been bending over us, to help us to be strong, to help us get through, even as we bent over her.

Then suddenly we were there, the glowing square of the emergency room entrance opening like the gates of heaven; and immediately the talk of miracles began. Alive, a miracle. No bones broken, a miracle. A miracle that the hemlocks cushioned her fall, a miracle that they hadn't been trimmed in a year and a half. It was a miracle that all that blood, the blood that had seemed that night to be everywhere, was from one shard of glass, a single shard, can you imagine, and as for the gash in her head, the scar would be covered by hair. The next day my mother cheerfully described just how she would part it so that nothing would show at all.

"You're a lucky duck-duck," agreed Mona, helping herself, with a little *pirouette,* to the cherry atop my mother's chocolate pudding.

That wasn't enough for me, though. I was relieved, yes, but what I wanted by then was a real miracle, not for her simply to have survived, but for the whole thing never to have happened—for my mother's head never to have had to be shaved and bandaged like that, for her high, proud forehead never to have been swollen down over her eyes, for her face and neck and hands never to have been painted so many shades of blue-black, and violet, and chartreuse. I still want those things—for my parents not to have had to live with this affair like a prickle bush between them, for my father to have been able to look my mother in her swollen eyes and curse the madman, the monster that could have dared do this to the woman he loved. I wanted to be able to touch my mother without shuddering, to be able to console my father, to be able to get that crash out of my head, the sound of that soprano—

so many things that I didn't know how to pray for them, that I wouldn't have known where to start even if I had the power to work miracles, right there, right then.

A week later, when my mother was home, and her head beginning to bristle with new hairs, I lost my malachite beads. I had been carrying them in a white cloth pouch that Patty had given me, and was swinging the pouch on my pinky on my way home from school, when I swung just a bit too hard, and it went sailing in a long arc through the air, whooshing like a perfectly thrown basketball through one of the holes of a nearby sewer. There was no chance of fishing it out: I looked and looked, crouching on the sticky pavement until the asphalt had crazed the skin of my hands and knees, but all I could discern was an evil-smelling musk, glassy and smug and impenetrable.

My loss didn't quite hit me until I was home, but then it produced an agony all out of proportion to my string of pretty beads. I hadn't cried at all during my mother's accident, and now I was crying all afternoon, all through dinner, and then after dinner too, crying past the point where I knew what I was crying for, wishing dimly that I had my beads to hold, wishing dimly that I could pray but refusing, refusing, I didn't know why, until I finally fell into an exhausted sleep on the couch, where my parents left me for the night—glad, no doubt, that one of the more tedious of my childhood crises seemed to be finally winding off the reel of life, onto the reel of memory. They covered me, and somehow grew a pillow under my head, and, with uncharacteristic disregard for the living room rug, left some milk and pecan sandies on the coffee table, in case I woke up hungry. Their thoughtfulness was prescient: I did wake up in the early part of the night; and it was then, amid the unfamiliar sounds and shadows of the living room, that I had what I was sure was a true vision.

Even now what I saw retains an odd clarity: the requisite strange light flooding the room, first orange, and then a bright yellow-green, then a crackling bright burst like a Roman candle going off near the piano. There was a distinct smell of coffee, and a long silence. The room seemed to be getting colder. Nothing. A creak; the light starting to wane, then waxing again, brilliant pink now. Still nothing. Then, as the pink started to go a little purple, a perfectly normal middle-aged man's voice, speaking something very like pig Latin, told me quietly not to despair, not to despair, my beads would be returned to me.

That was all. I sat a moment in the dark, then turned on the light, gobbled down the cookies—and in a happy flash understood I was so good, really, so near to being a saint that my malachite beads would come back through the town water system. All I had to do was turn on all the faucets in the house, which I did, one by one, stealing quietly into the bathroom and kitchen and basement. The old spigot by the washing machine was too gunked up to be coaxed very far open, but that didn't matter. The water didn't have to be full blast, I understood that. Then I gathered together my pillow and blanket and trundled up to my bed to sleep.

By the time I woke up in the morning I knew that my beads hadn't shown up, but when I knew it for certain, I was still disappointed; and as if that weren't enough, I had to face my parents and sister, who were all abuzz with the mystery of the faucets. Not knowing what else to do, I, like a puddlebrain, told them the truth. The results were predictably painful.

"Callie had a *vision*," Mona told everyone at the bus stop. "A vision with lights, and sinks in it!"

Sinks, visions. I got it all day, from my parents, from my classmates, even some sixth and seventh graders. Someone drew a cartoon of me with a halo over my head in one of the girls' room stalls; Anthony Rossi made gurgling noises as he walked on his hands at recess. Only Patty tried not to laugh, though even she was something less than unalloyed understanding.

"I don' think miracles are thupposed to happen in *thewers*," she said.

Such was the end of my saintly ambitions. It wasn't the end of all holiness; the ideas of purity and goodness still tippled my brain, and over the years I came slowly to grasp of what grit true faith was made. Last night, though, when my father called to say that he couldn't go on living in our old house, that he was going to move to a smaller place, another place, maybe a condo— he didn't know how, or where—I found myself still wistful for the time religion seemed all I wanted it to be. Back then the world was a place that could be set right: one had only to direct the hand of the Almighty and say, just here, Lord, we hurt here—and here, and here, and here.

Interpretations

1. What effect does attending a parochial school seem to have had on Callie's dreams and career plans? How are these religious matters connected with later events?

2. What does the list of hopes and goals left behind by the narrator's tenants reveal about them? Are they, in words from the last sentence of the story, attempting to "direct the hand of the Almighty"?

3. Would this list have been better placed at the *end* of the story, to keep the chronology unbroken? Why or why not?

4. When does the meaning of the title become clear?

5. What connection is there between the list the tenants left and Patty's belief that miracles aren't "thupposed to happen in *thewers*"? (Why do you think the author included this incident? What light does it shed on her plight?)

Correspondences

1. Review the Wilde quotation (page 3). How does it apply to "The Water-Faucet Vision?" What rituals and customs does the narrator "carry about with [her]"? What do they reveal about her? What do they contribute to the story?

2. Religious traditions are important in the selections by Gish Jen, Momaday, and Sadat. What role do they play in each narrative? How are the religious traditions of each author similar to or different from yours?

Applications

1. Write a journal entry on your first significant religious memory.

2. Parents and other adults are sometimes viewed by children as perfect people who will always protect them, a viewpoint encouraged by tradition. What do the children in Gish Jen's story discover about adults? If you have a similar recollection, develop it into an essay.

Kissing Customs

Michael T. Kaufman

Michael T. Kaufman (b. 1938) was born in Paris but raised and educated in the United States. He attended the City College of New York and Columbia University. He has worked for The New York Times *as a reporter and as bureau chief in Ottawa and Warsaw. His book about Poland,* Mad Dreams, Saving Graces, *was published in 1991. Here is a general description of that experience: "In the years I lived in Poland, the old order was crumbling, Solidarity had been temporarily driven underground and much of society was organized as a conspiracy. I loved it. Men and women validated themselves not by winning and losing, both of which were impossible, but by seeking honor and avoiding shame. I loved that too." The temporary outlawing of Solidarity that Kaufman refers to took place in 1981. A year earlier, the Polish government had made concessions to the demands of striking workers in the Lenin Shipyard in Gdansk. By 1981, nine million workers had joined Solidarity, the independent trade union. That same year, Lech Walesa and other Solidarity leaders were arrested. An irate United States retaliated with economic sanctions, which were lifted when martial law was suspended in 1982. Free elections, the first in more than forty years, were held on June 4, 1989, and Tadeusz Mazowiecki became the first non-Communist to head an Eastern bloc nation. Throughout this time of tremendous change, Poland's economy has continued to suffer. Housing and food are in chronic short supply, even though the "old order" that Kaufman knew is indeed gone.*

"Kissing Customs" was published in the "About Men" column of The New York Times *(1988).*

I RETURNED not long ago from a three-year assignment in Poland, where men kiss the hands of women as a matter of course when they meet. When I first arrived in Warsaw, I did not think this was such a great idea. At the time I thought of myself as a democratic kid from the streets of New York, and the notion of bending over and brushing my lips over the back of a woman's hand struck me as offensively feudal and hopelessly effete. Each time some perfectly fine woman offered me the back of her hand to kiss, I stammered my apology, saying something like, "Gosh, no offense intended, but where I come from we don't carry on like this, and while I respect you enormously, can't we make do with a simple handshake?"

I was at the time mindful of what my feminist friends back home might have said. I do not think they would have wanted me to kiss the hands of all women simply because they were women. They would have, rightly, seen this as a sexist custom, pointing out that not even in the grip of the most obsequious compulsions would anyone kiss the hand of a man.

But then I began to realize that the Polish custom had one particularly subtle and attractive aspect. After forty years of living under an unpopular Communist Government that sought to restrict society to the proletarian standard of some concocted Soviet model, the Poles were defending themselves with chivalrous customs. Instead of addressing each other with terms like "comrade citizen," as their Government had once urged them to do, Poles intuitively responded by assuming the manners of dukes and barons. In such circumstances it was pleasant and instructive to watch factory workers, mailmen, soldiers, peasants and high-school students kiss the hands held out to them while the Communist Party people, often identifiable by their wide ties and out-of-date suits, maintained stiff though ideologically correct postures.

Under this kind of social pressure, I kissed. At first it was tricky. There was nothing in my Upper West Side of Manhattan public-school education that prepared me for the act. I had to experiment. I think my first attempts were perhaps too noisy. They may also have been too moist. I realized that generally what I was expected to communicate was respect and not ardor, but I didn't want to appear too distant. I had observed some aristocrats take the hands extended to them and swoosh down without making real contact. I was trying for slightly more commitment.

Eventually, I got it right. And, to my surprise, I liked it. Each new encounter became a challenge. I found I needed to make subtle little alterations in technique as the situations demanded. For instance, if the woman was younger, I would bring her hand to my lips. If she was older, I would bring my lips to her hand. When I could not tell if she was younger or older, I went on the premise that she was younger. Sometimes you could play out little dramas. It was nothing serious or marriage-threatening, but you could, by kissing with more than normal pressure, make yourself noticed—and you could notice yourself being noticed. Or you could imagine you were somebody else, which, at least in my case, can be pleasant.

The real advantage of hand-kissing, I came to realize, was that it provided a ritual that enriched the routine of everyday life. Whenever I returned to the West on holidays I was struck by how few such rituals existed in my own society. Hardly anyone shook hands, let alone kissed them. Instead, waiters would tell me their names before taking my order and wish me a good day as they took my money. But I never felt they really cared. I would be called by strangers who wanted to sell me something over the phone, and they would address me as Mike. I would try to squelch them with what I thought was chilling irony and say, "Make that Mr. Mike." No one got it, but some said, "That's cute: Mr. Mike."

In this cultural context, I doubt that the United States is ready for hand-kissing. We seem to lack the self-discipline, or perhaps the confidence, and then too, there is the real danger of insulting feminists and getting your nose broken. And, to our credit, we have limited tolerance for lah-di-dah.

Still, I think it would be good to have some gesture or ritual that signifies at least minimal mutual respect. The idea would be to affirm something less than intimacy but more than passing acquaintance. What I have in mind would be useful for both intersexual and intrasexual contacts. It would replace the exchange of monosyllables like "hi" and "yo."

My suggestion is that we shake hands every day with the people we hold in esteem. The practice, as common in Poland as hand-kissing, is, I realize, not unknown here. But in America it is sporadic and all too casual.

Since returning from Poland, I've renewed many acquaintances. Among them was a person whose actions had once offended my sense of ethics. We chatted civilly enough, talking of our families and our recent experiences, but I did not offer him my hand. I did this as a point of honor—and to send a message. Had I been talking to a Pole, he might have reddened, stammered or walked away. But my old acquaintance didn't even notice. In this country, the symbolism of such a small act is lost. Of course, I could have thrown a rock through one of his windows, or cursed his parentage, or even turned abruptly from him, but all that would have been overkill for the graveness of his offense.

As for kissing the hands of women, my reflex, unfortunately, is waning. Under the social pressures of democracy, the Polish impulses that would have me turn wrists and kiss are growing fainter and fainter. The kid from the streets of New York is reasserting himself on his home ground with authentic and atavistic boorishness. *Tant pis*.[1]

Interpretations

1. For what purpose, according to Kaufman, do Poles use hand-kissing? Do you expect the end of Soviet domination of Poland to affect this custom? Why or why not?

2. What does hand-kissing reveal about the relationship between the sexes in Poland? (Men kiss women's hands, but not vice versa, of course.)

3. Kaufman seems to associate hand-kissing with "dukes and barons." With whom else is hand-kissing associated, and why?

4. Kaufman despairs that North Americans will ever learn hand-kissing. However, he recommends that we restore handshaking—because we need "some gesture or ritual that signifies at least minimal mutual respect." Why is such ritual important? (Why is it important to show, and not just feel, respect? Are there larger implications of such rituals?)

---

[1]French idiom, "So much the worse [for us]"; "[That's] our loss."

Correspondences

1. "The real advantage of hand-kissing, I came to realize, was that it provided a ritual that enriched the routine of everyday life": What examples support this point? What role does social custom play in gender relationships in Sadat's essay? How do they support or contradict Kaufman's thesis?

2. To enhance their narratives, Gish Jen ("The Water-Faucet Vision") uses humor and Kaufman ("Kissing Customs") uses irony. What two examples of each do you find most effective?

Applications

1. Review Kaufman's comment about "the real danger of insulting feminists" in the United States. How "real" is the danger? Is the writer suggesting that Polish women are less liberated? (What is *your* response to the custom of hand-kissing?)

2. Expressions such as "Have a good day," "No problem," and "Take care" are common in conversation. What does their frequency suggest about how Americans relate to one another? Discuss the popularity and significance of these expressions. (Are such sayings to be taken more literally or symbolically? Can such sayings be considered rituals?)

ADDITIONAL WRITING TOPICS

1. Many writers in this chapter recall aspects of their family's traditions—weddings, funerals, and religious customs. Focus on a ritual that you would like to record, and do so from a cross-generational or a cross-cultural perspective. Interview members of your family and extended family on their memories and associations. Write an account of these recollections that illustrates and explains their importance.

2. Past experiences—their own or others—are important to Momaday, Sadat, and Guppy. Does the fact that each essay is about a particular culture and its traditions have any relevance to the writer's purpose? Have you had a similar experience that could be valuable to record? Before writing your essay, decide whether your purpose is to inform or persuade.

3. Review Bellah's statement in the chapter introduction (page 1): "In our forward-facing society, we are more apt to talk about the future than the past . . . yet even in the debate about our future, our cultural tradition, in its several strands, is still very much present." To what extent do the selections in this chapter support or refute Bellah? What is your own point of view?

4. According to Cesare Pavese, "We do not remember days, we remember moments." Freewrite about a moment of special significance for you. Then expand on the memory and its importance in a fully developed essay. (Why do you remember it so vividly? What do you remember? How might you best explain its effects on you?)

5. All cultures observe holidays of national or international importance. What functions do these observances serve? Write an essay about the holidays your family celebrates and the rituals you observe. How "traditional" are these observances—and your role in them?

6. Write a journal entry on what you know about your own roots. (What else would you like to discover about them? Which members of your immediate and extended family might you consult? What sources—letters, journals, family photographs—might be useful?) After compiling information from these various sources, write a narrative essay on what you discovered about your origins.

7. Some traditions, such as the observances on college campuses of African-American history month and women's history month, are fairly recent. What functions do such observances serve? (Are they important only to particular groups?)

8. How might your college involve the community in participating in "new" traditions? In a group, explore ways to broaden community observance of these events.

CHAPTER 2

Relationships

Cross-cultural studies of relationships show incredible variations in social relationships, but one theme remains constant. We are social beings. Not many of us could or would want to live a life of isolation. The variations that exist in courtship, marriage, and family, friendship, and treatment of neighbors have been built on a changeless foundation of need.

The thousand-year-old parable of the Good Samaritan establishes a clear definition of "neighbor," a definition that transcends tribal and even family differences and calls on us to value service to others over our own comfort. Those who accept this definition as an ideal, however, admit that it is very difficult to practice.

Moving from the general "neighbor" to the specific "lover" or "daughter," we encounter few absolute guidelines. When personality, individualism, and sense of identity become all-important, who helps us reconcile self and society, independence and interdependence? The cross-cultural examples in this chapter may suggest some answers.

The most recurrent and controversial aspect of family relationships to be found in Chapter 2 selections is the debate between patriarchs and feminists. Are men rightly in charge of the family and tribe? Shouldn't women be accorded the same personal, political, and economic rights? Perhaps the impact of this debate is most evident in Mead's essay on the American family. Can it survive the challenge to traditionalism in changing personal and economic gender roles? Are women who return to the workplace surrendering their matriarchal role of nurturer of the family and tribe? The ancient idea of male supremacy has left its mark. In some selections it is taken for granted and in others it is vigorously rejected, and intrapersonal and intracultural harmony is shattered.

Some women steer a course between the two extremes: some do it well, but others are torn apart. Jehan Sadat's English mother holds on to her religious principles and her concepts of childraising without challenging or undermining the authority of her Muslim husband. But Shusha Guppy's Aunt Batool is an example of "multitudes of Persian women of her generation and class" who are victims: "abused virgins, long-suffering wives, deprived mothers and desperate spinsters. . . ."

We generally think that romantic male-female relationships are a sign of modern times, but it would be hard to find a more romantic lover than Black Elk's lovesick swain High Horse. In our own not so traditional culture and in that relationship that we now call "a relationship," the battle between the romantics and the realists goes on. Bruce Weber says the realists are winning, and you may agree. Equality of the sexes is taken for granted in Penelope Lively's story about a modern couple troubled by the decision whether to continue living together or to marry. On a lighter note, a modern Ghanaian woman makes a patriarch pay—in more than one sense—for his rampant polygamy.

Immigrant family relationships add different voices to the debate. The patriarchal family described in Julia Alvarez's "El Doctor" is transplanted from Santo Domingo to New York City, but the city hardly intrudes into this intimate portrait. The focus is not on language or generational conflicts, but rather on the continuity of the family across generational and national boundaries.

But immigration may put a heavy strain on family solidarity. Her family's immigration from China to California makes an angry feminist of Maxine Hong Kingston. Cultural differences in the way female children are treated are much greater between China and America than between the Dominican Republic and America. Kingston's Chinese family seems much more patriarchal than Alvarez's, in spite of *machismo*. Kingston must leave her family to find herself. The parent/child relationship is badly strained. The struggle turns Kingston into a "woman warrior."

The basic importance of family whether it be patriarchal, matriarchal or some compromise between the two, is one of the lessons of a cross-cultural study of relationships.

Margaret Mead and Rhoda Metraux also look at a variant of family—friendship. Although styles of friendships vary in America, France, Germany, and England, there is consensus that friendships are yet another reflection of our desire for relatedness. All of the Chapter 2 selections reinforce how much of our personal and cultural identity is deeply rooted in the need for community.

PERSPECTIVES

No people are ever as divided as those of the same blood.

Mavis Gallant

Your children are not your children. They are the sons and daughters of life's longing for itself. They come through you but not from you, and though they are with you, yet they belong not to you.

Kahlil Gibran

"Family" is not just a buzz word for reactionaries; for women, as for men, it is the symbol of the last area where one has any hope of control over one's destiny, of meeting one's most basic human needs, of nourishing that core of personhood, threatened now by vast impersonal institutions and uncontrollable corporate and government bureaucracies.

Betty Friedan

Love will redeem a man and change his entire character and existence; lack of love will literally drive a woman crazy.

Jean Anouilh

The word love *has by no means the same sense for both sexes, and this is one of the serious misunderstandings that divide them.*

Simone de Beauvoir

Friendship is by its very nature freer of deceit than any other relationship we can know because it is the bond least affected by striving for power, physical pleasure, or material profit, most liberated from any oath of duty or constancy.

Francine du Plessix Gray

Marriage is a lottery in which men stake their liberty and women their happiness.

Virginia des Rieux

Woman is woman's natural ally.

Euripides

Hold a true friend with both your hands.

Nigerian Proverb

Govern a family as you would cook a small fish—very gently.

Chinese Proverb

Every man's neighbor is his looking glass.

English Proverb

A good marriage is that in which each appoints the other the guardian of his solitude.

Rainer Maria Rilke

Applications

1. Write a journal entry on *one* of the quotations above.

2. Discuss the Gallant quotation.

Women

Chinese Folk Tale

Milton Rugoff in his A Harvest of World Folk Tales *introduced this old Chinese story this way:*

> *Popular conceptions of China's isolation notwithstanding, Chinese folk-tales have been no more free of international influence than those of Europe or America. Coming mostly from India through the medium of Buddhism, but also from the Near East, many familiar themes, including those of "Cinderella", the Master Thief, and the trapping of a jinni {genie} in a bottle, appear in Chinese folklore. But the national temperament asserts itself in many ways. Ripened by centuries of a religious philosophy that makes for serenity, the Chinese have lent their stories many distinctive qualities: a gentle whimsicality, fantasy, pathos, the uncanny, a quiet resignation to fate.*

AFTER HE WAS MARRIED, Chang the Third no longer wanted to go to work. He sat at home the whole day and played with his wife. He gazed endlessly at her beautiful face, and the longer he looked the less he wanted to go out. Finally he gave up his job and remained night and day with his wife. He went on in this way for six months, and then for a year; but even the largest fortune is soon exhausted if one does nothing, and Chang had merely lived on his earnings. In two years all his wife's jewels, the chairs, the tables, the linen, the clothes, in fact everything they had, was pawned or sold, and they were left without a penny.

His wife was really unusually beautiful, but she thought to herself, "Since his marriage my husband has never left the house. Day and night he sits around doing nothing but eat. In a short while we shall no longer have the wherewithal to live." So she upbraided him, saying, "You really can't stay at home all day. All men must go to work." But Chang saw her beauty and he thought anxiously, "If I went out another man could come and make love to her." And instead of listening to her words he remained at home, preferring to eat the most miserable food.

But eventually their poverty became unbearable. They could no longer live if he did not work. Finally, one morning, he said good-by to his wife and decided to go to a village. On his way he met a fine-looking man of about fifty years, who said to him, "Which is the way to such and such a village?" Chang answered, "I am going there myself, so we can go together."

During their walk Chang told the stranger his story. "I am so unhappy at leaving my wife," he said. "But I must look for work to enable us to live."

The stranger replied, "The simplest thing is to bottle up your wife. I will give you the bottle, and every day, when you leave, you will only need to look at your wife and blow into the bottle, and she will vanish inside at once. As you can always take it with you, you will never lose your wife. I must now take another road, so farewell." Then he handed Chang a large three-inch bottle from his bag and disappeared. Chang dropped the bottle into his bag, noting what the man had said, and set off gaily for the village. The next day he tried the gift. As his wife was combing her hair before the mirror he secretly blew into the bottle. The woman saw in the mirror the reflection of her husband blowing into a bottle, but then she lost consciousness and woke up to find herself inside the bottle. Chang put the bottle in his pocket and went off to his work in the village. He was quite contented, for now no other man could flirt with his wife. In the evening he tipped the bottle, and his beautiful wife stood before him as before.

One day, however, he was forced to leave his wife at home to do the washing. He begged her not to leave the house when the washing was finished, and then set off to the village, forgetting to take the bottle with him.

After her husband's departure the wife went down to the river to wash the clothes. While she was rinsing a shirt she suddenly felt a long, hard thing between her fingers. She took it out and looked at it carefully. "It's a bottle," she said to herself. "Every morning my husband blows into it and I vanish inside. Why has he forgotten it today?" While she was pondering over the matter, a handsome young man passed by on the other bank. She looked up at him, and without thinking what she was doing blew into the bottle, whereupon the young man disappeared. When she had finished the washing she replaced the bottle in her husband's clothes.

When the man arrived home he immediately asked for the bottle he had left behind, and his wife handed it to him without a word. The next day when he went out he blew into the bottle as usual, and his wife disappeared, and again he flattered himself that she was safe from the caresses of other men.

That evening on his return he tipped the bottle, but this time two people appeared, his wife and a handsome young man. He was very much surprised and said to himself, "How strange! I thought my wife was quite safe shut up in the bottle, but now she has got a man with her! How odd it is! And how impossible it is to keep a beautiful wife to oneself."

Interpretations

1. Describe the relationship between Chang and his wife. How does it change in the course of the story?

2. What type of marriage does the bottle symbolize? What does the mirror symbolize?

3. What seems to be the point (moral) of this tale? (Consider that it was the husband himself who bottled up his wife with a potential lover.)

4. Do you think the title works? Why or why not? Would an equally good title be "Men"?

The Good Samaritan

Luke 10:29-37

The parable of the Good Samaritan is one of a number of stories told by Jesus to his followers. The original city of Samaria was the center of a sect whose worship at a separate temple (on Mt. Gerizim) and whose recognition of the authority of only the Pentateuch (the first five books of the Bible) led to continual tension with the Jews of Jerusalem and elsewhere.

THEN ONE of the experts in the Law stood up to test him and said,

"Master, what must I do to be sure of eternal life?"

"What does the Law say and what has your reading taught you?" said Jesus.

"The Law says, 'Thou shalt love the Lord thy God with all thy heart and with all thy soul and with all thy strength and with all thy mind—and thy neighbor as thyself,' " he replied.

"Quite right," said Jesus. "Do that and you will live."

But the man, wanting to justify himself, continued, "But who is my 'neighbor'?"

And Jesus gave him the following reply:

"A man was once on his way down from Jerusalem to Jericho. He fell into the hands of bandits who stripped off his clothes, beat him up, and left him half dead. It so happened that a priest was going down that road, and when he saw him he passed by on the other side. A Levite also came on the scene, and when he saw him he too passed by on the other side. But then a Samaritan traveler came along to the place where the man was lying, and at the sight of him he was touched with pity. He went across to him and bandaged his wounds, pouring on oil and wine. Then he put him on his own mule, brought him to an inn and did what he could for him. Next day he took out two silver coins and gave them to the innkeeper with the words: 'Look after him, will you? I will pay you back whatever more you spend, when I come through here on my return.' Which of these three seems to you to have been a neighbor to the bandits' victim?"

"The man who gave him practical sympathy," he replied.

"Then you go and give the same," returned Jesus.

Interpretations

1. The lawyer wants to "test" Jesus and, after hearing Jesus' first answer, to "vindicate himself." How do you think he feels after hearing the parable and correctly answering Jesus' question? How do you explain the change?

2. Jesus connects salvation (inheriting "eternal life") with kind service to needy people. How important do *you* consider service to needy people? What's the best way to be of service? Can one do wrong in doing right? Do good works also require sensitivity and intelligence? health and wealth? Why or why not?

3. "Love thy neighbor" turns out to be, in this parable, something quite practical. What is *your* idea of love?

4. Jesus answers the lawyer's second question—"And who is my neighbour?"— with a story instead of a definition. What definition does the story imply? Do you agree with the definition? Why or why not? How does Jesus tailor his story to his audience? (Why does he choose a Samaritan as the hero of his story?)

Correspondences

1. "Every man's neighbor is his looking-glass." What point is this English proverb making about behavior? How might that point apply to the parable of the Good Samaritan?

2. Review the Rilke quotation (page 68). To what extent do you agree with his point about solitude in relationships? What might Chang the Third (of "Women") have learned from Rilke?

Applications

1. Consult a dictionary or thesaurus on the word *neighbor*. How has the concept of neighbor changed with time? (How have urbanization, industrialization, the rat race and a "looking out for Number One" mentality affected relationships among neighbors?) Answer these questions in an essay; use cause-and-effect organization.

2. Personal space and its effects on romantic relationships differ among cultures. Using "Women" as a point of departure, compare your ideas on personal space and romance with those of a classmate or friend from another culture.

Can the American Family Survive?

Margaret Mead

Margaret Mead (1901–1978) was among the most widely recognized of American anthropologists. She won early and immediate acclaim for her study of the transition from adolescence to adulthood in Coming of Age in Samoa *(1928). She also taught for many years at Columbia University and wrote more than twenty books, including* Culture and Commitment *(1970) and* Blackberry Winter: A Memoir *(1972). In this essay, she examines the troubled state of the contemporary American family and suggests some stabilizing changes.*

ALL OVER the United States, families are in trouble. It is true that there are many contented homes where parents are living in harmony and raising their children responsibly, and with enjoyment in which the children share. Two out of three American households are homes in which a wife and husband live together, and almost seven out of ten children are born to parents living together in their first marriage.

However, though reassuring, these figures are deceptive. A great many of the married couples have already lived through one divorce. And a very large number of the children in families still intact will have to face the disruption of their parents' marriage in the future. The numbers increase every year.

It is also true that the hazards are much greater for some families than for others. Very young couples, the poorly educated, those with few skills and a low income, Blacks and members of other minority groups—particularly if they live in big cities—all these are in danger of becoming high-risk families for whose children a family breakdown is disastrous.

But no group, whatever its status and resources, is exempt. This in itself poses a threat to all families, especially those with young children. For how can children feel secure when their friends in other families so like their own are conspicuously lost and unhappy? In one way or another we all are drawn into the orbit of families in trouble.

Surely it is time for us to look squarely at the problems that beset families and to ask what must be done to make family life more viable, not only for ourselves now but also in prospect for all the children growing up who will have to take responsibility for the next generation.

The Grim Picture

There are those today—as at various times in the past—who doubt that the family can survive, and some who believe it should not survive. Indeed, the contemporary picture is grim enough.

- Many young marriages entered into with love and high hopes collapse before the first baby is weaned. The very young parents, on whom the whole burden of survival rests, cannot make it entirely on their own, and they give up.

- Families that include several children break up and the children are uprooted from the only security they have known. Some children of divorce, perhaps the majority, will grow up as stepchildren in homes that, however loving, they no longer dare to trust fully. Many—far too many—will grow up in single-parent homes. Still others will be moved, rootless as rolling stones, from foster family to foster family until at last they begin a rootless life on their own.

- In some states a family with a male breadwinner cannot obtain welfare, and some fathers, unable to provide adequately for their children, desert them so that the mothers can apply for public assistance. And growing numbers of mothers, fearful of being deserted, are leaving their young families while, as they hope and believe, they still have a chance to make a different life for themselves.

- As divorce figures have soared—today the proportion of those currently divorced is more than half again as high as in 1960, and it is predicted that one in three young women in this generation will be divorced—Americans have accepted as a truism the myth that from the mistakes made in their first marriage women and men learn how to do it better the second time around. Sometimes it does work. But a large proportion of those who have resorted to divorce once choose this as the easier solution again and again. Easily dashed hopes become more easily dashed.

- At the same time, many working parents, both of whom are trying hard to care for and keep together the family they have chosen to bring into being, find that there is no place at all where their children can be cared for safely and gently and responsibly during the long hours of their own necessary absence at their jobs. They have no relatives nearby and there is neither a day-care center nor afterschool care for their active youngsters. Whatever solution they find, their children are likely to suffer.

The Bitter Consequences

The consequences, direct and indirect, are clear. Thousands of young couples are living together in some arrangement and are wholly dependent on their private, personal commitment to each other for the survival of their relationship. In the years from 1970 to 1975 the number of single persons in the 25-to-34-year age group has increased by half. Some couples living together have repudiated marriage as a binding social relationship and have rejected the family as an institution. Others are delaying marriage because they are not sure of themselves or each other; still others are simply responding to what they have experienced of troubled family life and the effects of divorce.

At the end of the life span there are the ever-growing numbers of women and men, especially women, who have outlived their slender family relationships. They have nowhere to turn, no one to depend on but strangers in public institutions. Unwittingly we have provided the kind of assistance that, particularly in cities, almost guarantees such isolated and helpless old people will become the prey of social vultures.

And at all stages of their adult life, demands are made increasingly on women to earn their living in the working world. Although we prefer to interpret this as an expression of women's wish to fulfill themselves to have the rights that go with money earned and to be valued as persons, the majority of women who work outside their homes do so because they must. It is striking that ever since the 1950s a larger proportion of married women with children than of married but childless women have entered the labor force. According to recent estimates some 14 million women with children—four out of ten mothers of children under six years of age and more than half of all mothers of school-age children—are working, the great majority of them in full-time jobs.

A large proportion of these working women are the sole support of their families. Some 10 million children—more than one in six—are living with only one parent, generally with the mother. This number has doubled since 1960.

The majority of these women and their children live below the poverty level, the level at which the most minimal needs can be met. Too often the women, particularly the younger ones, having little education and few skills, are at the bottom of the paid work force. Though they and their children are in great need, they are among those least able to demand and obtain what they require merely to survive decently, in good health and with some hope for the future.

But the consequences of family trouble are most desperate as they affect children. Every year, all over the country, over 1 million adolescents, nowadays principally girls, run away from home because they have found life with their families insupportable. Some do not run very far and in the end a great many come home again, but by no means all of them. And we hear about only a handful whose terrifying experiences or whose death happens to come into public view.

In homes where there is no one to watch over them, elementary-school children are discovering the obliterating effects of alcohol; a growing number have become hard-case alcoholics in their early teens. Other young girls and boys, wanderers in the streets, have become the victims of corruption and sordid sex. The youngsters who vent their rage and desperation on others by means of violent crimes are no less social victims than are the girls and boys who are mindlessly corrupted by the adults who prey on them.

Perhaps the most alarming symptom of all is the vast increase in child abuse, which, although it goes virtually unreported in some groups, is not limited to any one group in our population. What seems to be happening is that frantic mothers and fathers, stepparents or the temporary mates of parents turn on the children they do not know how to care for, and beat them— often in a desperate, inarticulate hope that someone will hear their cries and somehow bring help. We know this, but although many organizations have been set up to help these children and their parents, many adults do not know what is needed or how to ask for assistance or whom they may expect a response from.

And finally there are the children who end their own lives in absolute despair. Suicide is now third among the causes of death for youngsters 15 to 19 years old.

What Has Gone Wrong?

In recent years, various explanations have been suggested for the breakdown of family life.

Blame has been placed on the vast movement of Americans from rural areas and small towns to the big cities and on the continual, restless surge of people from one part of the country to another, so that millions of families, living in the midst of strangers, lack any continuity in their life-style and any real support for their values and expectations.

Others have emphasized the effects of unemployment and underemployment among Blacks and other minority groups, which make their families peculiarly vulnerable in life crises that are exacerbated by economic uncertainty. This is particularly the case where the policies of welfare agencies penalize the family that is poor but intact in favor of the single-parent family.

There is also the generation gap, particularly acute today, when parents and their adolescent children experience the world in such very different ways. The world in which the parents grew up is vanishing, unknown to their children except by hearsay. The world into which adolescents are growing is in many ways unknown to both generations—and neither can help the other very much to understand it.

Then there is our obvious failure to provide for the children and young people whom we do not succeed in educating, who are in deep trouble and who may be totally abandoned. We have not come to grips with the problems of hard drugs. We allow the courts that deal with juveniles to become so overloaded that little of the social protection they were intended to provide is possible. We consistently underfund and understaff the institutions into which we cram children in need of re-education and physical and psychological rehabilitation, as if all that concerned us was to get them—and keep them— out of our sight.

Other kinds of explanations also have been offered.

There are many people who, knowing little about child development, have placed the principal blame on what they call "permissiveness"—on the relaxing of parental discipline to include the child as a small partner in the process of growing up. Those people say that children are "spoiled," that they lack "respect" for their parents or that they have not learned to obey the religious prohibitions that were taught to their parents, and that all the troubles plaguing family life have followed.

Women's Liberation, too, has come in for a share of the blame. It is said that in seeking self-fulfillment, women are neglecting their homes and children and are undermining men's authority and men's sense of responsibility. The collapse of the family is seen as the inevitable consequence.

Those who attribute the difficulties of troubled families to any single cause, whether or not it is related to reality, also tend to advocate panaceas, each of which—they say—should restore stability to the traditional family or, alternatively, supplant the family. Universal day care from birth, communal living, group marriage, contract marriage and open marriage all have their advocates.

Each such proposal fastens on some trouble point in the modern family— the lack of adequate facilities to care for the children of working mothers, for example, or marital infidelity, which, it is argued, would be eliminated by being institutionalized. Others, realizing the disastrous effects of poverty on family life, have advocated bringing the income of every family up to a level at which decent living is possible. Certainly this must be one of our immediate aims. But it is wholly unrealistic to suppose that all else that has gone wrong will automatically right itself if the one—but very complex— problem of poverty is eliminated.

A Look at Alternatives

Is there, in fact, any viable alternative to the family as a setting in which children can be successfully reared to become capable and responsible adults, relating to one another and a new generation of children as well as to the world around them? Or should we aim at some wholly new social invention?

Revolutionaries have occasionally attempted to abolish the family, or at least to limit its strength by such measures as arranging for marriages without binding force or for rearing children in different kinds of collectives. But as far as we know, in the long run such efforts have never worked out satisfactorily.

The Soviet Union, for instance, long ago turned away from the flexible, impermanent unions and collective child-care ideals of the early revolutionary days and now heavily emphasizes the values of a stable family life. In Israel the kibbutz, with its children's house and carefully planned, limited contact between parents and children, is losing out to social forms in which the family is both stronger and more closely knit. In Scandinavian countries, where the standards of child care are very high, serious efforts have been made to provide a viable situation for unmarried mothers and the children they have chosen to bring up alone; but there are disturbing indices of trouble, expressed, for example, in widespread alcoholism and a high rate of suicide.

Experience suggests that we would do better to look in other directions. Two approaches may be rewarding. First we can look at other kinds of societies—primitive societies, peasant societies and traditional complex but unindustrialized societies (prerevolutionary China, for example)—to discover whether there are ways in which families are organized that occur in all societies. This can give us some idea of needs that must be satisfied for families to survive and prosper.

Second we can ask whether the problems that are besetting American families are unique or are instead characteristic of families wherever modern industrialization, a sophisticated technology and urban living are drawing people into a new kind of civilization. Placing our own difficulties within a wider context can perhaps help us to assess what our priorities must be as we attempt to develop new forms of stability in keeping with contemporary expressions of human needs.

Looking at human behavior with all that we know—and can infer— about the life of our human species from earliest times, we have to realize that the family, as an association between a man and a woman and the children she bears, has been universal. As far as we know, both primitive "group" marriage and primitive matriarchy are daydreams—or nightmares, depending on one's point of view—without basis in historical reality. On the contrary, the evidence indicates that the couple, together with their children, biological or adopted, are everywhere at the core of human societies, even though this "little family" (as the Chinese called the nuclear family) may be embedded in joint families, extended families of great size, clans, manorial systems, courts, harems or other institutions that elaborate on kin and marital relations.

Almost up to the present, women on the whole have kept close to home and domestic tasks because of the demands of pregnancy and the nursing of infants, the rearing of children and the care of the disabled and the elderly. They have been concerned primarily with the conservation of intimate values and human relations from one generation to another over immense reaches of time. In contrast, men have performed tasks that require freer movement over greater distances, more intense physical effort and exposure to greater immediate danger; and everywhere men have developed the formal institutions of public life and the values on which these are based. However differently organized, the tasks of women and men have been complementary, mutually supportive. And where either the family or the wider social institutions have broken down, the society as a whole has been endangered.

In fact, almost everywhere in the world today societies *are* endangered. The difficulties that beset families in the United States are by no means unique. Families are in trouble everywhere in a world in which change— kinds of change that in many cases we ourselves proudly initiated—has been massive and rapid, and innovations have proliferated with only the most superficial concern for their effect on human lives and the earth itself. One difference between the United States and many other countries is that, caring so much about progress, Americans have moved faster. But we may also have arrived sooner at a turning point at which it becomes crucial to redefine what we most value and where we are headed.

Looking to the past does not mean that we should return to the past or that we can undo the experiences that have brought us where we are now. The past can provide us only with a base for judging what threatens sound family life and for considering whether our social planning is realistic and inclusive enough. Looking to the past is not a way of binding ourselves but of increasing our awareness, so that we are freer to find new solutions in keeping with our deepest human needs.

So the question is not whether women should be forced back into their homes or should have an equal say with men in the world's affairs. We urgently need to draw on the talents women have to offer. Nor is there any question whether men should be deprived of a more intimate family role. We have made a small beginning by giving men a larger share in parenting, and I believe that men and children have been enriched by it.

What we need to be sure of is that areas of caretaking associated in the past with families do not simply drop out of our awareness so that basic human needs go unmet. All the evidence indicates that this is where our greatest difficulties lie. The troubles that plague American families and families all over the industrialized world are symptomatic of the breakdown of the responsible relationship between families and the larger communities of which they are part.

For a long time we have worked hard at isolating the individual family. This has increased the mobility of individuals; and by encouraging young families to break away from the older generation and the home community, we have been able to speed up the acceptance of change and the rapid spread of innovative behavior. But at the same time we have burdened every small family with tremendous responsibilities once shared within three generations and among a large number of people—the nurturing of small children, the emergence of adolescents into adulthood, the care of the sick and disabled and the protection of the aged. What we have failed to realize is that even as we have separated the single family from the larger society, we have expected each couple to take on a range of obligations that traditionally have been shared within a larger family and a wider community.

So all over the world there are millions of families left alone, as it were, each in its own box—parents faced with the specter of what may happen if either one gets sick, children fearful that their parents may end their quarrels with divorce, and empty-handed old people without any role in the life of the next generation.

Then, having pared down to almost nothing the relationship between families and the community, when families get into trouble because they cannot accomplish the impossible we turn their problems over to impersonal social agencies, which can act only in a fragmented way because they are limited to patchwork programs that often are too late to accomplish what is most needed.

Individuals and families do get some kind of help, but what they learn and what those who work hard within the framework of social agencies convey, even as they try to help, is that families should be able to care for themselves.

What Can We Do?

Can we restore family stability? Can we establish new bonds between families and communities? Perhaps most important of all, can we move to a firm belief that living in a family is worth a great effort? Can we move to a new expectation that by making the effort, families can endure? Obviously the process is circular. Both optimism and action are needed.

We shall have to distinguish between the things that must be done at once and the relations between families and communities that can be built up only over time. We shall have to accept willingly the cost of what must be done, realizing that whatever we do ultimately will be less costly than our present sorry attempts to cope with breakdown and disaster. And we shall have to care for the failures too.

In the immediate future we shall have to support every piece of Federal legislation through which adequate help can be provided for families, both single-parent families and intact poor families, so that they can live decently and safely and prepare their children for another kind of life.

We shall have to support Federal programs for day care and afterschool care for the children of working mothers and working parents, and for facilities where in a crisis parents can safely leave their small children for brief periods; for centers where the elderly can be cared for without being isolated from the rest of the world; for housing for young families and older people in communities where they can actually interact as friendly grandparents and grandchildren might; and for a national health program that is concerned not with fleecing the Government but with health care. And we must support the plea of Vice-President Walter F. Mondale, who, as chairman of the Senate Subcommittee on Children and Youth, called for "family impact" statements requiring Government agencies to account for what a proposed policy would do for families—make them worse off or better able to take care of their needs.

Government-funded programs need not be patchwork, as likely to destroy as to save. We need to realize that problems related to family and community life—problems besetting education, housing, nutrition, health care, child care, to name just a few—are interlocked. To solve them, we need awareness of detail combined with concern for the whole, and a wise use of tax dollars to accomplish our aims.

A great deal depends on how we see what is done—whether we value it because we are paying for it and because we realize that the protection given families in need is a protection for all families, including our own. Committing ourselves to programs of care—instead of dissociating ourselves from every effort—is one step in the direction of reestablishing family ties with the community. But this will happen only if we accept the idea that each of us, as part of a community, shares in the responsibility for everyone, and thereby benefits from what is done.

The changes that are needed cannot be accomplished by Federal legislation alone. Over a longer time we must support the design and building of communities in which there is housing for three generations, for the fortunate and the unfortunate, and for people of many backgrounds. Such communities can become central in the development of the necessary support system for families. But it will take time to build such communities, and we cannot afford just to wait and hope they will happen.

Meanwhile we must act to interrupt the runaway belief that marriages must fail, that parents and children can't help but be out of communication, that the family as an institution is altogether in disarray. There still are far more marriages that succeed than ones that fail; there are more parents and children who live in trust and learn from one another than ones who are out of touch; there are more people who care about the future than we acknowledge.

What we need, I think, is nationwide discussion—in magazines, in newspapers, on television panel shows and before Congressional committees— of how people who are happily married can help those who are not, how people who are fortunate can help those who are not and how people who have too little to do can help those who are not and how people who have too little to do can help those who are burdened by too much.

Out of such discussions can come a heightened awareness and perhaps some actual help, but above all, fresh thought about what must be done and the determination to begin to do it.

It is true that all over the United States, families are in trouble. Realizing this should not make us cynical about the family. It should start us working for a new version of the family that is appropriate to the contemporary world.

Interpretations

1. Does the section entitled "The Grim Picture" convince you that the American family is indeed in trouble? If so, how serious is the trouble? What evidence do you consider most convincing?

2. Do you agree that a cross-cultural study of the family might suggest ways to improve family life? Can you offer some insights into other family systems?

3. Mead believes that historical studies of the family will teach us how to provide the kind of caretaking that families used to provide. Do you agree with the author that such caretaking can be provided without asking women to leave the workplace and return to their "place" in the home? Cite reasons for your response.

4. Do you agree that the federal government must play a large part in saving the American family? Why or why not?

5. Which purpose does this essay's data, arguments, and tripartite organization (evidence, causes, solutions) serve better—to inform or to persuade? Cite examples to support your answer.

6. Does the author answer her title question? How? (What role do "optimism and action" play?)

Correspondences

1. Review the Friedan quotation (page 67). How does it apply to Mead's essay? To what extent do you share the anthropologist's views on the importance of family?

2. Mead focuses on the fragmentary nature of the American family. How do her portrayals of family life compare with those by Baker and Sadat (Chapter One)? What factors might account for any differences?

Applications

1. "Women's Liberation, too, has come in for a share of the blame. It is said that in seeking self-fulfillment, women are neglecting their homes and children and are undermining men's authority and men's sense of responsibility. The collapse of the family is seen as the inevitable consequence."

To what extent has the feminist movement had adverse effects on the American family? Write an essay attacking or defending the charges in the quotation. Use specific examples to support your point of view.

2. Review the last section of this essay, "What Can We Do?" Write an essay offering your suggestions for "saving" the American family. Focus on specific solutions, as does the author.

The Unromantic Generation

Bruce Weber

Bruce Weber (b. 1953) is an editor of The New York Times Magazine. *He has written articles on such diverse topics as sports, literary figures, and contemporary social life and has published a collection of stories*—Look Who's Talking: An Anthology of American Short Stories (1986). *In "The Unromantic Generation," published in the April 5, 1987, issue of* The New York Times Magazine, *Weber discusses changing attitudes towards gender relationships.*

HERE IS a contemporary love story.

Twenty-four-year-old Clark Wolfsberger, a native of St. Louis, and Kim Wright, twenty-five, who is from Chicago, live in Dallas. They've been going together since they met as students at Southern Methodist University three years ago. They are an attractive pair, trim and athletic, she dark and lissome, he broad-shouldered and square-jawed. They have jobs they took immediately after graduating—Clark works at Talent Sports International, a sports marketing and management company; Kim is an assistant account executive at Tracy-Locke, a large advertising agency—and they are in love.

"We're very compatible," she says.

"We don't need much time together to confirm our relationship," he says.

When they speak about the future, they hit the two-career family notes that are conventional now in the generations ahead of them. "At thirty, I'll probably be married and planning a family," says Kim. "I'll stay in advertising. I'll be a late parent."

"By thirty, I'll definitely be married; either that or water-skiing naked in Monaco," Clark says, and laughs. "No. I'll be married. Well-established in my line of work. Have the home, have the dog. Maybe not a kid yet, but eventually. I'm definitely in favor of kids."

In the month I spent last winter visiting several cities around the country, interviewing recent college graduates about marriage, relationships, modern romance, I heard a lot of this, life equations already written, doubt banished. I undertook the trip because of the impression so many of us have; that in one wavelike rush to business school and Wall Street, young Americans have succumbed to a culture of immediate gratification and gone deep-down elitist on us. I set out to test the image with an informal survey meant to take the

85

emotional temperature of a generation, not far behind my own, that *seems* so cynical, so full of such "material" girls and boys.

The sixty or so people I interviewed, between the ages of twenty-two and twenty-six, were a diverse group. They spoke in distinct voices, testifying to a range of political and social views. Graduate students, lawyers, teachers, entertainers, business people, they are pursuing a variety of interests. What they have in common is that they graduated from college, are living in or around an urban center, and are heterosexual, mirrors of myself when I graduated from college in 1975. And yet as I moved from place to place, beginning with acquaintances of my friends and then randomly pursuing an expanding network of names and phone numbers, another quality emerged to the degree that I'd call it characteristic: they are planners. It was the one thing that surprised me, this looking ahead with certainty. They have priorities. I'd ask about love; they'd give me a graph.

This isn't how I remember it. Twelve years ago, who knew? I was three years away from my first full-time paycheck, six from anything resembling the job I have now. It was all sort of desultory and hopeful, a time of dabbling and waiting around for some event that would sprout a future. Frankly, I had it in mind that meeting a woman would do it.

My cultural prototype was Benjamin Braddock, the character played by Dustin Hoffman in Mike Nichols's 1967 film *The Graduate,* who, returning home after his college triumphs, finds the prospect of life after campus daunting in the extreme, and so plunges into inertia. His refrain "I'm just a little worried about my future," served me nicely as a sort of wryly understated mantra.

What hauls Benjamin from his torpor is love. Wisely or not, he responds to a force beyond logic and turns the world upside down for Elaine Robinson. And though in the end their future together is undetermined, the message of the movie is that love is meant to triumph, that its passion and promise, however naïve, are its strength, and that if we are lucky it will seize us and transform our lives.

Today I'm still single and, chastened by that, I suppose, a little more rational about what to expect from love. Setting out on my trip, I felt as if I'd be plumbing a little of my past. But the people I spoke with reminded me more of the way I am now than the way I was then. I returned thinking that young people are older than they used to be, *The Graduate* is out of date, and for young people just out of college today, the belief that love is all you need no longer obtains.

"Kim's a great girl; I love her," Clark Wolfsberger says. "But she's very career-oriented. I am, too, and with our schedules the way they are, we haven't put any restrictions on each other. I think that's healthy."

"He might want to go back to St. Louis," Kim Wright says. "I want to go back to Chicago. If it works out, great. If not, that's fine, too. I can handle it either way."

They are not heartless, soulless, cold, or unimaginative. They *are* self-preoccupied, but that's a quality, it seems to me, for which youthful generations have always been known. What distinguishes this generation from mine, I think, is that they're aware of it. News-conscious, media-smart, they are sophisticated in a way I was not.

They have come of age, of course, at a time when American social traditions barely survive. Since 1975, there have been more than a million divorces annually, and it is well publicized that nearly half of all marriages now end in divorce. Yet the era of condoned casual promiscuity and sexual experimentation—itself once an undermining of the nation's social fabric—now seems to be drawing to a close with the ever-spreading plague of sexually transmitted disease.

The achievements of feminist activism—particularly the infusion of women into the work force—have altered the expectations that the sexes have for each other and themselves.

And finally, the new college graduates have been weaned on scarifying forecasts of economic gloom. They feel housing problems already; according to *American Demographics* magazine, the proportion of young people living at home with their parents was higher in 1985 than in the last three censuses. They're aware, too, of predictions that however affluent they are themselves, they're probably better off than their children will be.

With all this in mind, today's graduates seem keenly aware that the future is bereft of conventional expectations, that what's ahead is more chaotic than mysterious. I've come to think it ironic that in a youth-minded culture such as ours, one that ostensibly grants greater freedom of choice to young people than it ever has before, those I spoke with seem largely restrained. Concerned with, if not consumed by, narrowing the options down, getting on track, they are aiming already at a distant comfort and security. I spoke, on my travels, with several college counselors and administrators, and they concur that the immediate concerns of today's graduates are more practical than those of their predecessors. "I talk to them about sex," says Gail Short Hanson, dean of students at George Washington University, in Washington. "I talk about careers. And marriage, with women, because of the balancing act they have to perform these days. But love? I can't remember the last conversation I had about love."

Career-minded, fiercely self-reliant, they responded to me, a single man with a good job, with an odd combination of comradeliness and respect. When the interviews were over, I fielded a lot of questions about what it's like to work at *The New York Times.* How did I get my job? Occasionally, someone would ask about my love life. Considering the subject of our discussions, I was surprised it happened so rarely. When it did, I told them I'd come reasonably close to marriage once, but it didn't work out. Nobody asked me why. Nobody asked if I was lonely.

Micah Materre, twenty-five, recently completed an internship at CBS

News in Chicago and is looking for a job in broadcast journalism. Like many of the young people I talked to, she is farsighted in her romantic outlook: "I went out with a guy last fall. He had a good job as a stockbroker. He was nice to me. But then he started telling me about his family. And there were problems. And I thought, 'What happens if I fall in love and we get married? What then?' "

It may be a memory lapse, but I don't recall thinking about marriage much at all until I fell in love. I was twenty-nine; late, that's agreed. But the point is that for me (and for my generation as a whole, I believe, though you hate to make a statement like that), marriage loomed only as an outgrowth of happenstance; you met a person. Today's graduates, however, seem uneasy with that kind of serendipity. All of the married couples I spoke with are delighted to be married, but they do say their friends questioned their judgment. "I heard a lot of reasons why I shouldn't do it," one recent bride told me. "Finally, I just said to myself, 'I feel happier than I've ever felt. Why should I give this up just because I'm young?' "

Most of them too young to remember the assassination of *either* Kennedy, they are old enough to have romantic pasts, to have experienced the trauma of failure in love. What surprised me was how easily so many of them accepted it; it seems a little early to be resigned to the idea that things fall apart. In each interview, I asked about past involvements. Were you ever serious about anyone? Any marital close calls? And virtually everyone had a story. But I heard very little about heartbreak or lingering grief. Instead, with an almost uniform equanimity, they spoke of maturity gained, lessons learned. It isn't disillusionment exactly, and they *are* too young to be weary; rather, it sounds like determination.

Twenty-five-year-old Peter Mundy of San Francisco, for example, says that until six months ago he'd had a series of steady girlfriends. "I'm down on romance," he says. "There's too much pain, too much pressure. There are so many variables, and you can't tell until you're in the middle of it whether it'll be positive. It's only in retrospect that you can see how things went wrong. In the meantime, you end up neglecting other things."

The prevalent notion is that chemistry is untrustworthy; partners need to be up to snuff according to pretty rigorous standards. Ellen Lubin, twenty-six, of Los Angeles, for example, has just gotten engaged to the man she has been living with for two years. When she met him, she says: "I wasn't that attracted to him right away. But there were things about him that made me say, 'This is what I want in a man.' He's bright. He's a go-getter. He was making tons of money at the age of twenty-five. He's well-connected. He was like my mentor in coming to deal with life in the city."

At the end of *The Graduate*, Benjamin Braddock kidnaps his lady love at the altar, an instant after she has sealed her vows to someone else, and they manage to make their escape because Benjamin bolts the church door from the outside with a cross. That was the 1960s, vehement times. When

I graduated, we were less obstreperous. Sacraments we could take or leave. And marriage wasn't much of an issue. If we put it off, it wasn't for the sake of symbolism so much as that it didn't seem necessary. In the last few years, I've been to a number of weddings among my contemporaries, people in their thirties, and that impression of us is still with me. What we did was drift toward marriage, arriving at it eventually, and with some surprise. Some of us are still drifting.

Today's graduates have forged a new attitude entirely. In spite of the high divorce rate, many of those I spoke with have marriage in mind. Overwhelmingly, they see it as not only desirable, but inevitable. Because of the odds, they approach it with wariness and pragmatism. More cautious than their parents (for American men in 1985, the median age at the time of their first marriage was 25.5, the highest since the turn of the century; it was 23.3 for women, a record), they are methodical in comparison with me.

Perhaps that explains why I find the way they speak about marriage so unromantic. Men and women tend to couch their views in different terms, but they seem to share the perception that marriage is necessarily restricting. Nonetheless they trust in its rewards, whatever they are. Overall, it doesn't represent the kind of commitment that seems viable without adequate preparation.

"I've been dating someone for a year and a half," says Tom Grossman, a twenty-four-year-old graduate of the University of Texas. "We don't talk about marriage, and frankly I don't think it'll occur." Currently area sales manager in San Antonio for the John H. Harland Company, a check-printing concern, Grossman says he has professional success in mind first. "I want to be really well-off financially, and I don't want that struggle to interfere with the marriage. There are too many other stress factors involved. I want to be able to enjoy myself right away. And I never want to look back and think that if I hadn't gotten married, I could have accomplished more."

Many young women say they responded with some alarm to last year's [1986] *Newsweek* report on the controversial demographic study conducted at Harvard, which concluded that once past thirty, a woman faces rapidly dwindling chances of marrying. At a time when women graduates often feel it incumbent on them to pursue careers, they worry that the possibility of "having it all" is, in fact, remote.

Janie Russell, twenty-five, graduated from the University of North Carolina in 1983, left a serious boyfriend behind, and moved to Los Angeles to pursue a career in the film industry. Working now as a director of production services at New Visions Inc., like many other young women she believes the independence fostered by a career is necessary, not only for her own self-esteem but as a foundation for a future partnership. "I look forward to marriage," she says. "But this is a very selfish time for me. I have to have my career. I have to say to myself, 'I did this on my own.' It makes me feel more interesting than I would otherwise. Of course, what may happen is that I'll look up one day and say, 'O.K., husband, where are you?' And he won't be there."

About halfway through my trip I stopped interviewing married couples because they tended to say similar things. They consider themselves the lucky ones. As twenty-four-year-old Adam Cooper put it, at dinner with his wife, Melanee, also twenty-four, in their Chicago apartment: "The grass is not greener on the other side."

I came away thinking it is as true as ever: all happy families are the same. But the couples I spoke with seemed to me part of a generation other than their own, older even than mine. Calling the Coopers to arrange an interview, I was invited for "a good, home-cooked meal."

The next day, I met Micah Materre, who expressed the prevailing contemporary stance as well as anyone. Outgoing and self-possessed, she gave me a long list of qualities she's looking for in a man: good looks, sense of humor, old-fashioned values, but also professional success, financial promise, and a solid family background. "Why not?" she said. "I deserve the best." But as I was folding up my notebook, she added a plaintive note: "I'll get married, won't I? It's the American way, right?"

Very early on in my sexual experience I was flattered by a woman who told me she ordinarily wouldn't go to bed with men who were under twenty-six. "Until then," she said, "all they're doing when they're with you is congratulating themselves." For whatever reason, she never returned my calls after that night. Not an untypical encounter, all in all. Congratulations to both of us.

We were a lusty, if callow, bunch, not least because we thought we could afford to be. Encouraged by the expansive social mores spawned by the sexual revolution, fortified by the advent of a widespread availability of birth control, and fundamentally unaware of germs, we interpreted sex, for our convenience, as pure pleasure shared by "consenting parties." If it feels good, do it. Remember that?

It is an attitude that the current generation inherited and put into practice at an early age. Asked about her circle of friends in Los Angeles, Lesley Bracker, twenty-three, puts it nonchalantly: "Oh, yeah, we were all sexually active as teenagers. When we were younger, it was considered O.K. to sleep around."

Now, however, they are reconsidering. In general, on this topic, I found them shy. They hesitate to speak openly about their sex lives, are prone to euphemism ("I'm not exactly out there, you know, mingling"), and say they worry about promiscuity only because they have friends who still practice it. According to Laura Kavesh and Cheryl Lavin, who write a column about single life, "Tales from the Front," for the *Chicago Tribune* that is syndicated in some sixty other papers around the country, a letter from a reader about the virtues of virginity generated more supportive mail than anything that has appeared in the column in its two years of existence. I'm not about to say there's a new celibacy among the young, but my impression is that even if they're having twice as much sex as they say they're having, it's not as much as you would think.

The AIDS scare, of course, is of primary relevance. "I talk about AIDS on first dates," says Jill Rotenberg, twenty-five, publishing manager of a rare-book company in San Francisco. "I talk about it all the time. I've spoken with the guy I'm dating about taking an AIDS test. Neither one of us is thrilled about condoms. But we use them. The first time we had sex, I was the one who had one in my wallet."

Not everyone is so vehement. But seriously or jokingly, in earnest tête-à-tête or idly at dinner parties, they all talk about it. To some, the new concern is merely a source of disappointment. Several of the young people I spoke with express the sense of having been robbed. It's tough to find sex when you want it, tougher than it used to be, is the lament of many, mostly men. As it was put to me at one point, "I wish I'd been born ten years earlier."

Jill Rotenberg says she feels betrayed: "I've had one long relationship in my life. He was my first lover, and for a long time my only one. So I feel I've had an untainted past. Now I feel I'm being punished anyway, even though I've been a good girl."

"I feel like I'm over the hurdle," says Douglas Ertman, twenty-two, of San Francisco, who got engaged last summer. "I'm really lucky to know that I'll have one sexual partner forever."

Most agree that the solution is monogamy, at least on a temporary basis. "It's a coupled-up society," says Alan Forman, twenty-six, a law student of George Washington University who, for the last several months, has been in a monogamous relationship. "Now more than ever. A lot of people I know are feeling the pressure to get hooked up with somebody."

I ask Forman and his girlfriend, twenty-four-year-old Debra Golden, about their future together. They say they don't know ("I'm too insecure to make a decision like that," she says), and I get the sense they never talk about it. Then she turns to him, genuinely curious. "Say you break up with me and go to New York next year," she says.

"I don't know," he says. "If I meet someone and I like her, what do I have to do, ask her to take a blood test?"

A decade ago, one of the privileges that my contemporaries and I inferred from our sexual freedom was more or less to deny that there might be, in the sexual act, an innately implied emotional exchange. It's no longer feasible, however, to explain away sex as frivolity, inconsequential gratification. And that has complicated things for all of us, of course, whatever age, single or not.

But for young people, it's an issue, like marriage, that has been raised early: what does sex mean, if it doesn't mean nothing?

It's clearly a struggle for them. In one of my first interviews, twenty-five-year-old Karl Wright of Chicago told me: "Maybe there's a silver lining in all this. Maybe AIDS will bring back romance." The more I think about that, the more chilling it gets.

Beverly Caro, a twenty-five-year-old associate in the Dallas law firm of Gardere & Wynne, graduated from Drake University, in Des Moines, in 1983, and attended law school there as well. Her office high above the street looks out on the city's jungle of futuristic skyscrapers. She had offers from firms in Denver and her hometown of Kansas City, Missouri, she says, but chose to come to Dallas because "I see upward mobility here; that's what I was looking for."

Ms. Caro has an attractive, thoughtful manner and a soft voice, but like many of her contemporaries, given the chance to discuss her personal goals, she speaks with a certitude that borders on defiance. Currently, she sees two men "somewhat regularly," she says. "I'd like to have a companion. A friend, I guess. But finding a man is not a top priority. I want to travel. I want to establish myself in the community. I don't see any drastic changes in my life by the time I turn thirty. Except that I'll be a property owner."

During my interviews, the theme of getting on track and staying there surfaced again and again. I came to think of it as the currency of self-definition. As a generation, they are not a particularly well-polled group, but certain figures bear out my impression.

According to annual surveys of 300,000 college freshmen conducted by the Higher Education Research Institute at the Graduate School of Education of the University of California at Los Angeles, young people today, by the time they *enter* college, are more inclined to express concrete life objectives than they've been for many years. Of those surveyed last fall, 73.2 percent cited being "very well off financially" as an essential or very important objective. That's up from 63.3 percent in 1980, 49.5 percent in 1975. Other objectives that the survey shows have risen in importance include "obtain recognition from colleagues for contributions to my special field"; "have administrative responsibility for the work of others"; "be successful in my own business"; and "raise a family." At the same time, the percentage of freshmen who consider it important to "develop a meaningful philosophy of life" has declined from 64.2 percent in 1975 to 40.6 percent last year.

Many of the people I spoke to feel the pressure of peer scrutiny. A status thing has evolved, to which many seem to have regretfully succumbed. Several expressed a weariness with meeting someone new and having to present themselves by their credentials. Yet, overwhelmingly, asked what they're looking for in a romantic partner, they responded first with phrases such as "an educated professional" and "someone with direction." They've conceded, more or less consciously, that unenlightened and exclusionary as it is, it's very uncool not to know what you want and not to be already chasing it.

"Seems like everyone in our generation has to be out there achieving," says Scott Birnbaum, twenty-five, who is the chief accountant for TIC United Corp., a holding company in Dallas.

Birnbaum graduated from the University of Texas in 1984, where, he says, "For me, the whole career-oriented thing kicked in." A native Texan with a broad drawl, he lives in the Greenville section of the city, an area populated largely by young singles. His apartment is comfortably roomy, not terribly well appointed. He shakes his head amiably as he points to the television set propped on a beer cooler. "What do I need furniture for?" he says. "Most of my time is taken up going to work."

Confident in himself professionally, Birnbaum was one of very few interviewees who spoke frankly about the personal cost of career success. Many speculated that they'll be worried if, in their thirties, they haven't begun to settle their love lives; this was more true of women than men. But Birnbaum confesses a desire to marry now. "It's kind of lonely being single," he says. "I'd hate to find myself successful at thirty without a family. Maybe once I'm married and have children, that might make being successful careerwise less important."

The problem, he goes on, is the collective outlook he's part and parcel of. "Here's how we think," he says. "Get to this point, move on. Get to that point, move on. Acquire, acquire. Career, career. We're all afraid to slow down for fear of missing out on something. That extends to your social life as well. You go out on a date and you're thinking, 'Hell, is there someone better for me?' I know how terrible that sounds but it seems to be my problem. Most of my peers are in the same position. Men and women. I tell you, it's tough out there right now."

When I returned to New York, I called Alex de Gramont, whom I'd been saving to interview last. I've known Alex for a long time, since he was a gawky and curious high school student and I was his teacher. Handsome now, gentle-looking, he's a literary sort, prone to attractive gloom and a certain lack of perspective. He once told me that his paradigm of a romantic, his role model, was Heathcliff, the mad, doomed passion-monger from Emily Brontë's *Wuthering Heights*.

A year out of Wesleyan University in Middletown, Conn., Alex has reasons to be hopeful. His book-length senior thesis about Albert Camus has been accepted for publication, and on the strength of it, he has applied to four graduate programs in comparative literature. But he's unenthusiastic, and he has applied to law schools, too. In the meantime, he is living with his parents in New Jersey.

He tells me that last summer he went to West Germany in pursuit of a woman he'd met when he was in college. He expected to live there with her, but he was back in this country in a couple of weeks. "Camus has a line," Alex says, " 'Love can burn or love can last. It can't do both.' " Like Benjamin Braddock, Alex is a little worried about his future.

Dustin Hoffman is forty-nine. I'm thirty-three. Both of us are doing pretty well. Alex, at twenty-three, confesses to considerable unease. "Every minute I'm not accomplishing something, I feel is wasted," he says, sort of miserably. "I feel a lot of pressure to decide what to do with my life. I'm a romantic, but these are very unromantic times."

Interpretations

1. The message of *The Graduate* is that love "is all you need." Weber believed that message when he was in college, and now he finds that his interviewees do not. Do you? Why or why not?

2. Can you formulate a definition of love as Weber and his interviewees are using it? Is it the same as sex? Can you define "romantic" as Weber uses it in his title and throughout the essay? Is "romantic" the opposite of "realistic"? Is it possible that there is an intellectual, nonromantic type of love that is not reducible to feelings? If so, frame your definition of love accordingly.

3. "Today's graduates . . . seem uneasy with . . . serendipity." How have divorce statistics, feminism, and "forecasts of economic gloom" converged to make today's graduates careful "planners"? Do you think being a planner and being open to pleasant surprises (serendipity) are mutually exclusive? Why or why not?

4. Most recent graduates, says Weber, accept marriage as "inevitable." What effect might this attitude have on their marriages? Will other factors offset this fatalism? (What effect might the AIDS scare have?) Will AIDS "bring back romance"? How? Do you consider such a return a desirable development?

5. What is the main point of Weber's interview with Alex de Gramont? Why do you think he wanted to save that interview for last and to report on it last?

6. Is Weber's main purpose to inform or to persuade? Cite evidence to support your opinion.

Correspondences

1. Anouilh's quotation on human relationships (page 67) states that love is a powerful emotion. How is his concept similar to (or different from) those expressed by Weber's interviewees? To what extent are their points of view attributable to what Weber terms "self-preoccupation?"

2. "The achievements of feminist activism—particularly the infusion of women into the work force—have altered the expectations that the sexes have for each other and themselves." How have expectations of relationships changed

according to Weber? To what extent has women's liberation also affected the lifestyles of middle-class women in Egypt? (Sadat Chapter 1).

Applications

1. Watch an episode of *Thirtysomething* and write an essay comparing the gender relationships in the television program and among Weber's interviewees.

2. Most of the young people Weber interviewed felt a great pressure to accomplish much in a short time. To what extent does your generation share their ambition and sense of urgency? How do these factors affect your personal relationships? (For example, do you spend time with people who may not further your career?)

High Horse's Courting

Black Elk

Black Elk (1863–1950) was a holy man of the Oglala Sioux of South Dakota. In 1930 he and the poet John G. Neihardt met and established a friendship that soon led to the publication of Black Elk Speaks *(1932). These memoirs paint a bleak picture of Indian life at the turn of the century, but "High Horse's Courting" provides a rare moment of comic relief. It also reveals something of Sioux courting customs "in the old days."*

The Oglala are a sub-branch of one of the seven tribes of Sioux (or Dakota), who in the mid-eighteenth century drove out the Cheyenne and Kiowas from the Black Hills of South Dakota and occupied the northern Great Plains. They sided with the British in the American Revolution and in the War of 1812, but later signed peace treaties with the United States. In 1867 the Sioux gave up a large section of territory and agreed to retire to a reservation in southwest Dakota, but the discovery of gold in the Black Hills and the resultant rush of prospectors brought on warfare led by such famous chiefs as Sitting Bull, Red Cloud, and Crazy Horse, who was Black Elk's second cousin. This was the outbreak that occasioned the famous last stand by General George A. Custer. Today the Sioux live on reservations in Minnesota, Nebraska, the Dakotas, and Montana. Those living on the nine reservations in South Dakota now number about 58,000.

YOU KNOW, in the old days, it was not very easy to get a girl when you wanted to be married. Sometimes it was hard work for a young man and he had to stand a great deal. Say I am a young man and I have seen a young girl who looks so beautiful to me that I feel all sick when I think about her. I cannot just go and tell her about it and then get married if she is willing. I have to be a very sneaky fellow to talk to her at all, and after I have managed to talk to her, that is only the beginning.

Probably for a long time I have been feeling sick about a certain girl because I love her so much, but she will not even look at me, and her parents keep a good watch over her. But I keep feeling worse and worse all the time; so maybe I sneak up to her tepee in the dark and wait until she comes out. Maybe I just wait there all night and don't get any sleep at all and she does not come out. Then I feel sicker than ever about her.

Maybe I hide in the brush by a spring where she sometimes goes to get water, and when she comes by, if nobody is looking, then I jump out and hold her and just make her listen to me. If she likes me too, I can tell that from the way she acts, for she is very bashful and maybe will not say a word or even look at me the first time. So I let her go, and then maybe I sneak around until I can see her father alone, and I tell him how many horses I can give him for his beautiful girl, and by now I am feeling so sick that maybe I would give him all the horses in the world if I had them.

Well, this young man I am telling about was called High Horse, and there was a girl in the village who looked so beautiful to him that he was just sick all over from thinking about her so much and he was getting sicker all the time. The girl was very shy, and her parents thought a great deal of her because they were not young any more and this was the only child they had. So they watched her all day long, and they fixed it so that she would be safe at night too when they were asleep. They thought so much of her that they had made a rawhide bed for her to sleep in, and after they knew that High Horse was sneaking around after her, they took rawhide thongs and tied the girl in bed at night so that nobody could steal her when they were asleep, for they were not sure but that their girl might really want to be stolen.

Well, after High Horse had been sneaking around a good while and hiding and waiting for the girl and getting sicker all the time, he finally caught her alone and made her talk to him. Then he found out that she liked him maybe a little. Of course this did not make him feel well. It made him sicker than ever, but now he felt as brave as a bison bull, so he went right to her father and said he loved the girl so much that he would give two good horses for her—one of them young and the other one not so very old.

But the old man just waved his hand, meaning for High Horse to go away and quit talking foolishness like that.

High Horse was feeling sicker than ever about it; but there was another young fellow who said he would loan High Horse two ponies and when he got some more horses, why, he could just give them back for the ones he had borrowed.

Then High Horse went back to the old man and said he would give four horses for the girl—two of them young and the other two not hardly old at all. But the old man just waved his hand and would not say anything.

So High Horse sneaked around until he could talk to the girl again, and he asked her to run away with him. He told her he thought he would just fall over and die if she did not. But she said she would not do that; she wanted to be bought like a fine woman. You see she thought a great deal of herself too.

That made High Horse feel so sick that he could not eat a bite, and he went around with his head hanging down as though he might just fall down and die any time.

Red Deer was another young fellow, and he and High Horse were great comrades, always doing things together. Red Deer saw how High Horse was acting, and he said: "Cousin, what is the matter? Are you sick in the belly? You look as though you were going to die."

Then High Horse told Red Deer how it was, and said he thought he could not stay alive much longer if he could not marry the girl pretty quick.

Red Deer thought awhile about it, and then he said: "Cousin, I have a plan, and if you are man enough to do as I tell you, then everything will be all right. She will not run away with you; her old man will not take four horses; and four horses are all you can get. You must steal her and run away with her. Then afterwhile you can come back and the old man cannot do anything because she will be your woman. Probably she wants you to steal her anyway."

So they planned what High Horse had to do, and he said he loved the girl so much that he was man enough to do anything Red Deer or anybody else could think up. So this is what they did.

That night late they sneaked up to the girl's tepee and waited until it sounded inside as though the old man and the old woman and the girl were sound asleep. Then High Horse crawled under the tepee with a knife. He had to cut the rawhide thongs first, and then Red Deer, who was pulling up the stakes around that side of the tepee, was going to help drag the girl outside and gag her. After that, High Horse could put her across his pony in front of him and hurry out of there and be happy all the rest of his life.

When High Horse had crawled inside, he felt so nervous that he could hear his heart drumming, and it seemed so loud he felt sure it would waken the old folks. But it did not, and afterwhile he began cutting the thongs. Every time he cut one it made a pop and nearly scared him to death. But he was getting along all right and all the thongs were cut down as far as the girl's thighs, when he became so nervous that his knife slipped and stuck the girl. She gave a big, loud yell. Then the old folks jumped up and yelled too. By this time High Horse was outside, and he and Red Deer were running away like antelope. The old man and some other people chased the young men but they got away in the dark and nobody knew who it was.

Well, if you ever wanted a beautiful girl you will know how sick High Horse was now. It was very bad the way he felt, and it looked as though he would starve even if he did not drop over dead sometime.

Red Deer kept thinking about this, and after a few days he went to High Horse and said: "Cousin, take courage! I have another plan, and I am sure, if you are man enough, we can steal her this time." And High Horse said: "I am man enough to do anything anybody can think up, if I can only get that girl."

So this is what they did.

They went away from the village alone, and Red Deer made High Horse strip naked. Then he painted High Horse solid white all over, and after that he painted black stripes all over the white and put black rings around High Horse's eyes. High Horse looked terrible. He looked so terrible that when Red Deer was through painting and took a good look at what he had done, he said it scared even him a little.

"Now," Red Deer said, "if you get caught again, everybody will be so scared they will think you are a bad spirit and will be afraid to chase you."

So when the night was getting old and everybody was sound asleep, they sneaked back to the girl's tepee. High Horse crawled in with his knife, as before, and Red Deer waited outside, ready to drag the girl out and gag her when High Horse had all the thongs cut.

High Horse crept up by the girl's bed and began cutting at the thongs. But he kept thinking, "If they see me they will shoot me because I look so terrible." The girl was restless and kept squirming around in bed, and when a thong was cut, it popped. So High Horse worked very slowly and carefully.

But he must have made some noise, for suddenly the old woman awoke and said to her old man: "Old Man, wake up! There is somebody in this tepee!" But the old man was sleepy and didn't want to be bothered. He said: "Of course there is somebody in this tepee. Go to sleep and don't bother me." Then he snored some more.

But High Horse was so scared by now that he lay very still and as flat to the ground as he could. Now, you see, he had not been sleeping very well for a long time because he was so sick about the girl. And while he was lying there waiting for the old woman to snore, he just forgot everything, even how beautiful the girl was. Red Deer who was lying outside ready to do his part, wondered and wondered what had happened in there, but he did not dare call out to High Horse.

Afterwhile the day began to break and Red Deer had to leave with the two ponies he had staked there for his comrade and girl, or somebody would see him.

So he left.

Now when it was getting light in the tepee, the girl awoke and the first thing she saw was a terrible animal, all white with black stripes on it, lying asleep beside her bed. So she screamed, and then the old woman screamed and the old man yelled. High Horse jumped up, scared almost to death, and he nearly knocked the tepee down getting out of there.

People were coming running from all over the village with guns and bows and axes, and everybody was yelling.

By now High Horse was running so fast that he hardly touched the ground at all, and he looked so terrible that the people fled from him and let him run. Some braves wanted to shoot at him, but the others said he might be some sacred being and it would bring bad trouble to kill him.

High Horse made for the river that was near, and in among the brush he found a hollow tree and dived into it. Afterwhile some braves came there and he could hear them saying that it was some bad spirit that had come out of the water and gone back in again.

That morning the people were ordered to break camp and move away from there. So they did, while High Horse was hiding in his hollow tree.

Now Red Deer had been watching all this from his own tepee and trying to look as though he were as much surprised and scared as all the others. So when the camp moved, he sneaked back to where he had seen his comrade disappear. When he was down there in the brush, he called, and High Horse answered, because he knew his friend's voice. They washed off the paint from High Horse and sat down on the river bank to talk about their troubles.

High Horse said he never would go back to the village as long as he lived and he did not care what happened to him now. He said he was going to go on the war-path all by himself. Red Deer said: "No, cousin, you are not going on the war-path alone, because I am going with you."

So Red Deer got everything ready, and at night they started out on the war-path all alone. After several days they came to a Crow camp just about sundown, and when it was dark they sneaked up to where the Crow horses were grazing, killed the horse guard, who was not thinking about enemies because he thought all the Lakotas were far away, and drove off about a hundred horses.

They got a big start because all the Crow horses stampeded and it was probably morning before the Crow warriors could catch any horses to ride. Red Deer and High Horse fled with their herd three days and nights before they reached the village of their people. Then they drove the whole herd right into the village and up in front of the girl's tepee. The old man was there, and High Horse called out to him and asked if he thought maybe that would be enough horses for his girl. The old man did not wave him away that time. It was not the horses that he wanted. What he wanted was a son who was a real man and good for something.

So High Horse got his girl after all, and I think he deserved her.

Interpretations

1. Black Elk sets his story "in the old days." How does this setting affect your response to the narrative?

2. What do you think is Black Elk's purpose in telling the story of High Horse's "sickness"?

3. What role does each participant perform in the courtship ritual? Is it significant that the girl is not named? Why or why not?

4. What is the tone of this narrative? Where does Black Elk use humor? What does the humor indicate about Black Elk's attitude toward the subject?

Correspondences

1. Wealth is important in the Black Elk and Weber selections: how does it affect gender relationships? Is economics important in such relationships, regardless of cultural background? Why or why not?

2. High Horse is romantic, while most of the young men Weber interviews are pragmatic. How does this difference influence their behavior, expectations, and relationships? Which term better describes you?

Applications

1. Write a speech for an unsympathetic audience on the following topic: "Traditional gender roles have contributed significantly to the stability and security of marriage." What tone should you adopt? What arguments will be most convincing? Include specific examples as supporting details.

2. How do generational differences affect concepts of romantic love and courtship customs? Interview some older people, asking them to define romantic love. Write a thesis statement based on their responses and plan an essay. (What other evidence will you need to develop your thesis into an essay?)

El Doctor

Julia Alvarez

*Julia Alvarez (b. 1950) was born in New York City but soon moved to the
Dominican Republic, returning to America ten years later. A published essayist,
poet, and writer of short fiction, she has won several fellowships and prizes. She
is currently on the faculty at Middlebury College, Vermont, where she teaches a
course on Hispanic writers in the United States.*

*As you read "El Doctor," pay particular attention to the conversations between
father and daughter. Notice that both are interested in history, and that Dr.
Alvarez is particularly interested in his ancestors' part in the history of the Dominican
Republic.*

*An island nation about the size of Vermont and New Hampshire combined,
the Dominican Republic shares with Haiti the West Indian island of Hispaniola.
It is also the site of Columbus's landfall in 1492 and the capital Santo Domingo,
the oldest settlement by Europeans in the New World. From 1492 to 1863, the
republic remained intermittently under Spanish rule. A constitutionally elected
government was installed in 1924, but President Rafael Trujillo ruled as a dictator
from 1930 until his assassination in 1961, retaining power even when he was
not in office. U.S. Marines intervened to put down a revolt in 1965. The country
has enjoyed representative democracy since the elections of 1966, but low prices for
the main export commodity, sugar, have caused widespread economic problems. These
problems echo in the family tensions of "El Doctor."*

"LIGHTS! At this hour?" my father asks, looking up from his empty dinner
plate at the glowing lamp my mother has just turned on above the table.
"Are we in Plato's cave,[1] Mother?" He winks at me; as the two readers in
the family we show off by making allusions my mother and sisters don't
understand. He leans his chair back and picks up the hem of the curtain. A
dim gray light falls into the room. "See, Mother. It's still light out there!"

"*Ya, ya!*" she snaps, and flips the switch off.

"Your mother is a wonder," he announces, then he adds, "El Doctor is
ready for bed." Dinner is over; every night my father brings the meal to a
close with a third-person goodnight before he leaves the room.

Tonight he lingers, watching her. She says nothing, head bent, intent
on her mashed plantains with oil and onions. "Yessir," he elaborates, "El
Doctor—" The rest is garbled, for he's balled up his napkin and rubbed his

---

[1]See Plato's "Allegory of the Cave," which compares our search for meaning in life to our leaving
the safe, dark but happy cave of illusions for the burning light of the sun of truth.

lips violently as if he meant to erase them from his face. Perhaps he shouldn't have spoken up? She is jabbing at the few bites of beefsteak on her plate. Perhaps he should have just let the issue drop like water down his chest or whatever it is the Americans say. He scrapes his chair back.

Her scowl deepens. "Eduardo, please." And then, because he already knows better, she adds only, "The wax finish."

"*Por supuesto,*"[2] he says, his voice full of false concern as he examines her spotless kitchen floor for damages. Then, carefully, he lifts his chair up and tucks it back in its place. "This old man is ready for bed." He leans over and kisses the scowl off her face. "Mother, this country agrees with you. You look more beautiful every day. Doesn't she, girls?" And with a wink of encouragement to each of us, he leaves us in the dark.

I remember my mother mornings, slapping around in her comfortable slippers, polishing her windows into blinding panes of light. But I remember him mostly at night, moving down the dark halls, undressing as he climbed the dark stairs to bed.

I want to say there were as many buttons on his vest as stairs up to the bedroom: it seemed he unbuttoned a button on each step so that by the time he reached the landing, his vest was off. His armor, I thought, secretly pleased with all I believed I understood about him. But his vest couldn't have had more than six buttons, and the stairs were long and narrow. Of course, I couldn't see well in the dark he insisted on.

"I'm going to take this dollar," he showed me, holding a bill in one hand and a flickering lighter in the other, "and I'm going to set fire to it." He never actually did. He spoke in parables, he complained in metaphor because he had never learned to say things directly. I already knew what he meant, but I had my part to play.

"Why would you want to do something like that?" I asked.

"Exactly! Why burn up my money with all these lights in the house!"

As we grew up, confirmed in our pyromania, he did not bother to teach us to economize, but went through the house, turning off lights in every room, not noticing many times that we were there, reading or writing a letter, and leaving us in the dark, hurt that he had overlooked us.

At the bedroom door he loosened his tie and, craning his neck, undid the top button of his shirt. Then he sat at the edge of the bed and turned on his bedside lamp. Not always; if a little reflected sun dappled the room with shadowy light, if it was late spring or early fall or summertime, he waited until the last moment to turn on the lamp, sometimes reading in the dark until we came in and turned it on for him. "Papi, you're going to ruin your eyes," we scolded.

Once I worked it out for him with the pamphlet the electric company sent me. Were he to leave his bedside light, say, burning for the rest of his

[2]Of course.

evenings—and I allowed him a generous four decades ("I won't need it for that long," he protested; I insisted)—the cost (side by side we multiplied, added, carried over to the next column) would be far less than if he lost his eyesight, was forced to give up his practice, and had to spend the next four decades—

"Like your friend Milton," he said, pleased with the inspired possibilities of blindness.[3] Now that I was turning out to be the family poet, all the greats were my personal friends. " 'When I consider how my light is spent,' " he began. He loved to recite, racing me through poems to see who would be the first one to finish.

" 'How my light is spent,' " I echoed and took the lead. " 'Ere half my days, in this dark world and wide . . .' "

Just as I was rounding the linebreak to the last line, he interjected it, " 'They also serve who only stand and wait.' "

I scowled. How dare he clap the last line on after I had gone through all the trouble of reciting the poem! "Not every blind man is a Milton," I said, and I gave him the smirk I wore all through adolescence.

"Nutrition," he said mysteriously.

"What about nutrition?"

"Good nutrition, we're starting to see the effects: children grow taller; they have better teeth, better bones, better minds than their elders." And he reached for his book on the bedside table.

Actually, the reading came later. First there is the scene that labels him immigrant and shows why I could never call him, sweetly, playfully, *Daddy*. He took from his back pocket a wad of bills so big his hand could not close over it. And he began to count. If at this point we disturbed him, he waved us away. If we called from downstairs, he did not answer. All over the bed he shared with my mother were piles of bills: I do not know the system; no one ever did. Perhaps all the fives were together, all the tens? Perhaps each pile was a specific amount? But this was the one private moment he insisted on. Not even catching him undressing, which I never did, seems as intimate a glimpse of him.

After the counting came the binding and marking: each pile was held together with rubber bands he saved from the rolled-up *New York Times,* and the top bill was scribbled on. He marked them as a reminder of how much was in each pile, I'm sure, but I can't help thinking it was also his way of owning what he had earned, much as ranchers brand their cattle. The Secretary of the Treasury had signed this twenty; there was Andrew Jackson's picture; he had to add his hand to it to make it his—to try to convince himself that it was his, for he never totally believed it was. Even after he was a successful

<hr />

[3]Milton was an English poet (1608–1674) who, on becoming blind, wrote, "When I consider how my light is spent."

doctor in New York with a house in the suburbs and lands at "home," his daughters in boarding schools and summer camps, a second car with enough gadgets to keep him busy in bad traffic, he was turning off lights, frequenting thrift shops for finds in ties, taking the 59th Street bridge even if it was out of his way to avoid paying a toll to cross the river.

He could not afford the good life, he could only pass it on. And he did. Beneath the surface pennypinching, his extravagance might have led him to bankruptcy several times had mother not been there to remind him that the weather was apt to change. "Save for a snowy day," she advised him.

"Julie! Isn't it rainy day?" he enlisted me. He was always happy to catch his wife at an error since she spoke English so much better than he did. "Save it for a rainy day?"

Eager to be an authority on anything, I considered Arbiter of Clichés a compliment to my literary talent. "Save it for a rainy day," I agreed.

"See, Mother."

She defended herself. "Snow is much worse than rain. For one thing, you need to own more clothes in the winter . . ."

Out from his pocket came a ten when we needed small change for the subway. Away at college I opened the envelope, empty but for the money order for fifty, a hundred; typed out in the blank beside *for* was his memo: "Get yourself a little something in my name." It was the sixties and parental money was under heavy suspicion; my friends needed me as a third world person to be a good example of poverty and oppression by the capitalist, military-industrial complex. I put my little somethings quietly in the bank. By the time I graduated from college, I had a small corrupt fortune.

But my rich father lived in the dark, saving string, going the long way. I've analyzed it with my economist friends. Perhaps since his fortune came from the same work which in his country had never earned him enough, he could never believe that his being well-to-do wasn't an I.R.S. oversight. My psychologist friends claim that it is significant that he was the youngest of twenty-five children. Coming after so many, he would always fear that the good things would run out. And indeed he had a taste for leftovers, which made his compliments come a day or two after a special meal. Whenever we had chicken, he insisted on the wings and the neck bone because those had been the portions left by the time the platter got to him, the baby. He liked the pale, bitter center of the lettuce. ("The leaves were gone when I got the salad bowl.") And when we had soup, he was surprised to find a piece of meat bobbing at the surface. "Someone missed this one."

Unlike mother, he saved for a sunny day. Extravaganza! On his birthday, on Christmas, on his saint's day which was never celebrated for anyone else, his presents multiplied before us. Beside the ones we had bought for him, there were always other glossy packages, ribboned boxes which dwarfed ours. The cards were forged: "To my dearest father from his loving daughter."

"Which of you gave me this?" he asked with mock surprise and real delight. Cordelias[4] all, we shook our heads as he unwrapped a silk lounging jacket or a genuine leather passport case. I wish he had allowed someone to give him something.

Perhaps we did on those evenings after the money was counted and put away, and he was ready for company. With an instinct for his rituals, we knew when it was time to come into the bedroom. We heard the bathroom door click shut; he was undressing, putting on his pajamas. The hamper lid clapped on its felt lip. We heard steps. The bed creaked. We found him in the darkening room with a book. "Papi, you're ruining your eyes!" and we turned on the bedside lamp for him since he could not give himself the luxury of that light. "Oh my God, it's gotten dark already," he almost thanked us.

He wanted company, not conversation. He had us turn on the television so we could learn our English. This after years here, after his money had paid for the good private schools which unrolled our r's and softened our accents; after American boyfriends had whispered sweet colloquialisms in our ears. As the television's cowboys and beauty queens and ladies with disappointing stains in their wash droned on in their native English, he read the usual: a history book in Spanish. We sat at the edge of the king-size bed and wondered what he wanted from us. He wanted presences: Walter Cronkite, his children, his wife, the great gods of the past, Napoleon, Caesar, Maximilian.[5] If one of us, bored with his idea of company, got up to leave, he lowered his book. "Did you know that in the campaign of 1808, Napoleon left his General behind to cut off the enemy from the rear, and the two divisions totally missed each other?" That was the only way he knew to ask us to stay, appealing to history and defeat, to wintry campaigns, bloody frost-bitten feet, a field strewn with war dead.

I taste the mints that he gave us, one each. He kept a stash of them in a drawer next to his bed like a schoolboy and ate exactly one each night and gave away four. That was the other way he kept us there if we got up to go after Napoleon's troops had been annihilated. "Don't you want a mint?" He didn't mean right then and there. It was a promise we had to wait for, perhaps until the chapter ended or the Roman empire fell or he was sure we had given up on the evening and decided to stay, talking in code with each other about school, our friends, our wild (for that room) adventures.

We were not fooled into rash confessions there, for at the merest hint of misadventure, the book came down like a coffin lid on Caesar or Claudius.[6] Oh, we confessed, we were just exaggerating! Of course we didn't raid the dorm kitchen at midnight, our friends did. "Tell me who your friends are,"

[4]Cordelia is the daughter of King Lear (in Shakespeare's play) who remains devoted to her father.
[5]Maximilian was the Emperor of Mexico (1864–1867).
[6]Claudius was the Emperor of Rome (41–54 A.D.).

he said in Spanish, "and I'll tell you who *you* are." No, we hadn't gotten help on our math. "The man who reaches the summit following another's trail will not find his way back to his own valley." If he caught us, hurrying, scurrying, here, there, he stopped us mid-flight to tell us what Napoleon had said to his valet, "Dress me slowly, I'm in a hurry."

But why look beyond one's own blood for good examples? "You come from good stock," he bragged when I came home from boarding school, my pride wounded. I'd been called ugly names by some great-great-granddaughters of the American Revolution. "You tell them your great-grandfather was the son of a count." He had paid a lot of money on a trip to Barcelona to find that out from a man who claimed he was licensed to do family trees. The elaborate chart, magnificently framed in curlicued wood, hung in the waiting room of his office in Spanish Brooklyn along with his medical degrees. His patients, I suppose, were meant to be reassured that their ailments would be treated, not only by the valedictorian of the faculty of medicine of La Universidad de Santo Domingo, but also by the descendant of a count. "We were in this hemisphere before they were. In fact, the first group of Puritans—"

"You don't understand, you don't understand," I wailed, hot tears welling in my eyes. And I closed the door of my room, forbidding anyone to enter.

"What's she doing in there, Mother?" I heard him ask her.

"I don't know. Writing poetry or something."

"Are you sure? You think she's all right?"

I had been reading Sylvia Plath and my talk was spiked with suicide.[7]

"These girls are going to drive us crazy!" My mother said. "That's what I'm sure of. One of them has to have straight hair. Straight hair, at this stage of the game! Another wants to spend the weekend at a boy's school. All the other girls get to! This one wants to die young and miserable!" Then she yelled at father. "I'm going to end up in Bellevue![8] And then you're all going to be very sorry!" I heard the rushed steps down the stairs, the bang of the screen door, finally the patter of the hose as she watered the obedient grass in the growing dark.

He knocked first. "Hello?" he asked tentatively, the door ajar. "Hello, hello, Edgar Allan Poe," he teased, entering. He sat at the foot of my bed and told me the story of his life.

"The point is," he concluded, " '*La vida es sueño y los sueños, sueños son.*' "[9] He stood by the window and watched my mother watering her fussy bushes as if she could flush roses out of them. "My father," he turned to me, "used to say that to my mother: Life is a dream, Mauran, and dreams are dreams."

---

[7]Sylvia Plath was an American poet (1932–1963) who committed suicide.

[8]Psychiatric hospital in New York City.

[9]Translated at the end of the paragraph, from *Life Is a Dream* by Spanish playwright Calderon (1600–1681).

He came across the shadowy room as if he did not want anyone to overhear. It was getting late. In the darkening garden she would be winding the hose into drooping coils. "Always, always," he said. "I always wanted to be a poet. *'La vida es sueño,'* 'They also serve who only stand and wait.' 'To be or not to be.' Can you imagine! To say such things! My God! Everyone gets a little something." He cupped his hands towards me. I nodded, too stunned at his flood of words to ask him what he meant. "And some make a building," he made a building with a wave of his hand. "Some," he rubbed his thumb and index finger together, "make money. Some make friends, connections, you know. But some, some make something that can change the thinking of mankind! Oh my God!" He smacked his forehead with his palm in disbelief. "Think of the Bible. Think of your friend Edgar Allan Poe. But then," he mused, "then you grow older, you discover . . ." He looked down at me. I don't know what he saw in my eyes, perhaps how young I still was, perhaps his eyes duplicated in my face. He stopped himself.

"You discover?" I said.

But he was already half way across the room. "Papi?" I tried to call him back.

"Your mother," he explained, letting himself out of the room and the revelation. "I think she is calling for me."

A few days later as I sat in his bedroom after supper, waiting for him to fall asleep, I tried to get him to finish his sentence. He couldn't remember what he was about to say, he said, but speaking of discoveries, "We're descended from the conquistadores, you know? Your grandfather traveled the whole north coast on horseback![10] Now there was a great man!" The supporting evidence was slim. "He looked like an Irishman. Ah, he was big and pink-tinted—what is that word, Julie? *Rowdy?*"

"You mean *ruddy?*" I said, knowing Don José de Jesus was probably ruddy with drink and rowdy with women. He had sired twenty-five children, widowed once, and kept four or five mistresses who raised the figure to thirty-five children. Of course, father never told us that; mother did when she explained how one of our uncles could be born within two months of father's birthday. She cautioned us never ever to mention to father what she had told us.

The youngest did, pretending ignorance, practicing addition. If Teolinda, the first wife, had ten children, and Mauran, the second one, had fifteen, and four of the kids had already died, then how come there were still thirty uncles and aunts left? "They were not hijos de padre y madre,"[11] he explained. "You know where that term came from? *Hijos de padre y madre?* When the Spaniards—"

"Where did the extra uncles and aunts come from?" She was not one to

---

[10]The north coast of the Caribbean island of Hispaniola.

[11]Children of father and mother.

be diverted by a red herring twitching in the sun when a skeleton was rattling in the closet.

So, so he said. The time had come. The uncles and aunts were half brothers and sisters. The mothers *were* wives, yes, in the eyes of God, where it really mattered.

When we raised our eyebrows and pressed the smile out of our lips, he would have none of it. Customs changed. Our grandfather was a patriotic man. There had been a terrible epidemic, the island was underpopulated, the birthrate was low, the best men did what they had to do. "So," he looked pointedly at each of us. "There's a good *ejemplo*[12] for you. Always put in that extra little bit in whatever you do," he said, lifting up the history of Constantinople or Machu Picchu or Rome.

His mother? He sighed. Don't talk to him about his mother! A saint! Sweet, very religious, patience personified, always smiling. They didn't make them like that anymore, with a few exceptions, he winked at me.

But since Mauran knew about the half children, and being very religious, she must have believed her husband and she would spend eternity separated, I imagined her as a dour and dowdy woman alternately saying her rosary when her husband transgressed or having his children when he didn't.

"Does mother remind you of her?" I asked, thinking that leading questions might help him remember what he had been about to say in my room a few nights ago.

"Your mother is a wonder," he said. A good woman, so devoted, so thorough, a little nervous, so giving, a little forceful, a good companion, a little too used to her own way, so generous. "Every garland needs a few thorns," he added.

"I heard that," she said, coming into the room, "What was that about too used to my own way?"

"Did I say that, girls?" father turned to us. "No, Mami, you misheard."

"Then what did I say?"

"What did I say, girls?"

We shrugged, leaving him wide open.

"I said, Mother," he said, unwrapping a rare second mint and putting it in his mouth to buy time. "I said: so used to giving to others. Mother, you're too generous!"

"Ay, put gravy on the chicken." She waved him off, terribly pleased as father winked at our knowing looks.

A few nights later, still on the track of his secret self, I asked him, "Papi, how do you see yourself?" Only I, who had achieved a mild reputation as a deep thinker, could get away with such questions.

"You ask deep questions," he mused, interrupting Napoleon's advance across the Russian steppes. "I like that."

[12]Example.

He offered me my mint and unwrapped his. "I am the rock," he said, nodding.

"Ay, Papi, that's too impersonal. How do you perceive yourself? What kind of man are you?" I was young and thought such definitions could be given and trusted. I was young and ready to tear loose, but making it harder for myself by trying to understand those I was about to wound.

"I am a rock," he repeated, liking his analogy. "Mother, you girls, my sisters, everyone needs my support. I am the strong one!"

That admission put a mermaid on the rock, luring me back with a delicate song about loss and youth's folly and the loneliness of the father. "But, Papi," I whispered as I moved from the armchair to the foot of his bed, "you don't always have to be strong."

That was my mistake. The conversation was over. He hated touching scenes; they confused him. Perhaps as the last child of an older, disappointed woman, he was used to diffuse attention, not intimacy. To take hold of a hand, to graze a cheek and whisper an endearment were beyond him. Tenderness had to be mothered by necessity: he was a good doctor. Under the cover of Hippocrates' oath, with the stethoscope around his neck and the bright examination light flushing out the personal and making any interchange terribly professional, he was amazingly delicate: tapping a bone as if it were the fontenelle of a baby, easing a patient back on a pillow like a lover his sleeping beloved, stroking hair away from a feverish forehead. But now he turned away.

He fell asleep secretly in that room full of presences, my mother beside him. No one knew exactly when it happened. We looked to him during a commercial or when a slip had implicated us in some forbidden adventure, and the book had collapsed like a card house on his chest and his glasses rode the bridge of his nose like a schoolmarm's. Though if we got up to leave and one of us reached for his glasses he woke with a start. "I'm not asleep!" he lied. "Don't go yet, it's early."

He fell asleep in the middle of the Hundred Days while Napoleon marched towards Waterloo or, defeated, was shipped off to St. Helena. We stifled our giggles at his comic-book snores, the sheets pulled over his head, his nose poking out like a periscope. Very quietly, widening our eyes at each other as if that might stop any noise, we rose. One turned off the set and threw a kiss at mother, who put her finger to her lips from her far side of the bed. Another and another kiss traveled across the hushed room. A scolding wave from mother hurried my sisters out.

I liked to be the one who stayed, bending over the bedside table strewn with candy wrappers, slipping a hand under the tassled shade. I turned the switch over, once. The room burst into brighter light, the tassels swung madly, mother signaled to me, crossly, Out! Out at once! I shrugged apologies. Her scowl deepened. Father groaned. I bent closer. I turned again. The room went back into economical dark.

Interpretations

1. Why is it appropriate that Alvarez's father often describes his action in the third person?

2. What do you consider the doctor's outstanding personality trait? Cite two passages that reveal this trait.

3. In her portrayal of her father, Alvarez refers to several incidents that show that she and he shared a special empathy. Cite at least three examples and say how each contributes to your understanding this empathy.

4. "He wanted company, not conversation." Why would one want company without conversation? Is the doctor's desire unreasonable or uncommon? Is it hard to satisfy? Do you sympathize with it?

5. Alvarez tries many times to try to get her father to complete his statement: "But then, . . . then you grow older, you discover . . ." What do you think he might have intended to say?

6. What is the tone of this portrait? Where is it satirical? Where loving? Do you find that the doctor has an honest, healthy relationship with his daughters, especially the narrator, or does he patronize them? Where's the evidence?

Correspondences

1. Alvarez and Momaday (Chapter 1) talk about their ancestral pasts. In what aspects of that past do they take most pride? How has the past influenced their present? (Why is it important to understand one's past?)

2. Review the Gibran quotation on children (page 67). What does it mean? How might Julia's father respond to Gibran's thoughts on this subject? Cite evidence from the story to support your point of view.

Applications

1. Write an essay about your mother, or father or another adult to prove that you understand that person well. Include specific incidents, allusions, or metaphors that exemplify key personality traits.

2. Alvarez's father encouraged her to express her creativity. Write an essay about important encouragement you have received from an adult (parent, teacher, relative). How did this encouragement affect your relationship?

from Growing Up in Cairo

Jehan Sadat

Jehan Sadat (b. 1934) is the widow of Egyptian president Anwar el-Sadat, who was assassinated in 1981. You will discover in the following selection that she grew up in Cairo and was the daughter of an Egyptian civil servant and an English mother.

For a fuller account of Ms. Sadat, see page 22.

I DID NOT KNOW until I was eleven that my name was Jehan, a Persian name picked out by my father which means "the world." My mother, who was English, had nicknamed me Jean, and that was what I was called by my father, an employee at the Ministry of Health, by my teachers at the Christian missionary school I attended, and by my friends. It was not at all strange for me or my classmates to have European names. I had friends named Mimi and Fifi, Helen and Betty. Egyptians had greatly admired European ways since our leader Muhammad Ali had opened Egypt to foreign influence one hundred years before, believing the Europeans to be much more advanced. But it was strange that I did not even know my proper name until I received my primary-school certificate before moving on to secondary school.

"Who is Jehan?" I asked the teacher, seeing it written on my certificate over my address.

"You," she told me.

I ran home to my mother. "What is my name?" I asked her.

"In school now you are Jehan," she told me. "In our family you are Jean." And to this day that is what my sister and brothers call me.

I was born on Roda Island, one of two islands in the Nile linked by bridges to Cairo in the east and Giza to the west. My island of Roda was a lovely area of gardens and gracious peach limestone villas populated by middle-class Egyptian families. The neighboring island of Zamalek was fancier, home to many British families and those of the Egyptian upper class. The Gezira Sporting Club on Zamalek, to which my family did not belong, boasted cricket pitches and polo fields, tennis courts and swimming pools, and a bar at which liquor was served. The Gezira Club was in another world to me as a child, and to many other Egyptians as well. King Farouk was a member there, as were many of the foreign families, but there was a membership quota for Egyptians.

I was the third of four children in my family, and the first girl. A great space of age spread between my brothers and me. Magdi was ten years older, Ali seven. My mother, I was told, had yearned to have a girl, to comb a daughter's hair and embroider her dresses. The day of my birth was a cause of great celebration in our house, compounded by an *'allawa,* a raise in pay my father took that very same day from his government job. From the beginning, I was considered by my parents to be a good omen. Twenty-one months later, my sister Dalia was born and our family was complete.

We were all very light-skinned, a legacy not only from my English mother but on my father's side as well. My father's father was a Sa'idi, an Upper Egyptian from the tall, usually dark-skinned tribe descended from pure Pharaonic stock. Yet my grandfather too had been fair with blue eyes. His children—my father, my uncle and my two Egyptian aunts—were also fair, and, like all Egyptian families, we were all very close.

When I was a baby we lived with our relatives in one house, splitting up when I was five years old. But no one moved very far away. My bachelor Uncle Mustafa lived just one house away with his divorced sister, 'Aziza, it being his responsibility as a brother to look after her and her young daughter, 'Aida. I visited my Auntie 'Aziza, or Auntie Zouzou as she was nicknamed, every afternoon, and often she came to our home in the evenings. She was my favorite aunt and my Egyptian mother, showering me with affection and spoiling me.

After my Uncle Mustafa finally married at thirty-eight, Aunt Zouzou continued to live with him and his new wife, for it was improper then for a woman to live alone. I'm sure she was very lonely, but she continued to refuse many offers of marriage, fearing that her daughter might be mistreated by a stepfather.

My other aunt, Fatima, whom we fondly called Auntie Batta—Auntie "Duck"—lived just outside Cairo on the Pyramids Road. She was not as affectionate as Auntie Zouzou, but she was a very strong woman. After my grandmother died, Auntie Batta effectively took her place. It was to Auntie Batta's house that the whole family went to break the fast on the first day of Ramadan, and to her that they went to seek advice. Auntie Batta was married to Husni Abu Zaid, an official in the Wafd nationalist party who had served as governor of both Munufiyya province and Minia province. Uncle Husni had a government car, quite a symbol of prosperity at the time, and I loved to drive with him around Cairo. With its official license plate and the flag of Munufiyya fluttering on the fender, the car prompted all the soldiers who saw it to salute. As a little girl, I liked to imagine they were saluting me.

"The mother of the world," the historian Ibn el-Khaldun had called Cairo in the fourteenth century. As a child growing up in Roda, it was easy to see why. Everywhere were the signs of Cairo's rich past. Directly across the Nile to the east was Coptic Cairo, which for more than fifteen hundred years had been the center of Egyptian Christian art and religion. On my way to school I could see the spires of the fourth-century Abu Serga Church, built on the spot where it is believed the family of Jesus stayed during their flight into Egypt. Beyond Abu Serga, I could sometimes make out the thin Ottoman minarets of the Alabaster Mosque, built by Muhammad 'Ali in the nineteenth century. Still farther along was the Old City founded by the Fatimids in 973, and el-Azhar Mosque and University. El-Azhar is the oldest university in the world, and attracts more than 100,000 students from countries as far away as Mauritania and Indonesia. All who come are students of Islam, for though el-Azhar is old, our religion is still young and growing.

From the other side of Roda, I could look across the Nile to the west and see the river gardens of the rich merchants who lived in Giza, beyond to the campus of Cairo University, and to the Pyramids Road, which, if followed to the end, terminated at the Farafra Oasis in the Libyan Desert. On a clear day when no dust or sand blew, I could make out the tips of the Great Pyramids themselves. And always in the air, five times a day, I could hear the beautiful voices of the muezzins high up in the minarets of Cairo's thousands of mosques, calling the believers in Islam to prayer.

How lovely and quiet Roda Island was during my childhood. Everyone had green gardens, and between the villas on both sides of the island you could always see the Nile passing. In 1933, the population of Egypt was around 15 million, and the population of Cairo less than one million.

My mother must have been very brave to leave her native land of England to come live in Egypt. My father must have been brave also to have married a foreigner. Such a marriage was not against our religion of Islam, for the children of a Muslim man will always themselves be Muslim. It was forbidden only for a Muslim woman to marry into another religion, for her children would have to bear the religion of their father. No. My grandparents' objection to their marriage was not religious, but one of family tradition.

My father, Safwat Raouf, had met my mother, Gladys Charles Cotrell, in 1923 in Sheffield, England, where he was studying medicine at the University of Sheffield and she was a music teacher. Their love was very strong from the beginning. It had to be, for a marriage had already been arranged in Cairo between my father and his cousin. "No one in our family has ever married a foreigner," my grandfather wrote to my father in England. "I will not give you permission to marry this Englishwoman."

My grandparents were well used to the British, of course, for there were many, many British in Egypt at that time. Since the 1800s more than ten thousand British troops had been stationed in Egypt to "protect" our government. The British High Commissioner, Lord Cromer, was effectively ruling the country. Britain and France controlled Egypt's finances. Even Egypt's shares in the Suez Canal, completed in 1869, had had to be sold to the British by our then debt-ridden Khedive Isma'il. It was certainly not uncommon to see the British and many other foreigners in Cairo. But it was difficult for my conservative grandparents to adjust to new ways.

"If you do not allow this marriage, I will not eat until I am dead," my father wrote back to my grandfather. My grandfather was just as stubborn. "I will not give my permission," he replied. And back and forth the letters went until my grandmother grew worried that my father really might harm himself or, just as bad, not come back to Egypt at all. "You must give your permission," she told my grandfather. "Is it not better to welcome our son and his wife home to Egypt than to force him to live in a country foreign to our ways?"

Reluctantly my grandfather had agreed, and my grandmother had sent my mother the traditional Egyptian engagement present of jewelry, in this case a diamond ring and a diamond-and-sapphire necklace she had inherited from her grandfather, along with money for a honeymoon. My mother and father were married in a civil ceremony in England, and when my father returned home with my mother three years later it was with my brother, who had been born in Liverpool. As was the custom then, my parents moved into my grandparents' house on Roda Island. Quickly, my grandparents grew to love my mother, though it must not have been easy for any of them. Our society was more conservative then. And my mother's ways, indeed, were strange.

She never ate Egyptian food, but insisted on the Sudanese cook making a separate meal for her of boiled meat, boiled vegetables, boiled everything. The rest of the family ate the usual Egyptian fare: grilled pigeon; grilled fish; lamb kebab and *kufta,* spiced patties of minced lamb; *wara einab,* grape leaves stuffed with rice and minced meat; *molokhia,* a thick soup made of a minced green leaf and chicken stock; *bamia,* okra sautéed with butter, onion, garlic and tomato paste in broth, served almost always with rice, and different kinds of beans and salads. But my mother would eat boiled mutton and potatoes with mint sauce.

Breakfast was different for us also. In the morning, and indeed for all meals, Egyptians traditionally eat *ful medammes*—fava beans boiled into a thick paste with spices and topped with a fried egg. At our house we had cornflakes, boiled eggs, and thinly sliced toast instead of 'aish, our flat, unleavened bread, along with jam my mother had made. Tea every afternoon at four was sacred, and she would serve us English tea instead of the sweet mint tea Egyptians drink, and wonderful British cakes, biscuits and sweets she'd made for us to eat. They were delicious, really, especially the lemon curd preserve which we didn't have in Egypt at all.

We shared our house with another family who lived in an apartment upstairs, and, to their wonder and the wonder of our other neighbors, my mother would bring a lovely pine tree into the house at Christmas and decorate it with shiny stars and balls, topping it off with a figure of Father Christmas. Nadia and Tahani, the children who lived upstairs, as well as other children in the neighborhood would rush to see our tree, because very few Egyptian families celebrated Christmas and none had ever seen a Christmas tree. Our friends envied us not only because of our tree and the delicious Christmas pudding my mother made, but because we received gifts as well.

It was difficult for my mother to live so far away from her country. During World War II all communication was cut off between England and Egypt. She heard no news from her family at all and was very worried. One day I found her crying in her room when I returned from school.

"What is wrong with Mummy?" I asked Betty, a friend of my mother's who had been visiting.

"She has just learned that her father passed away," Betty told me. "Her family has sent her some money and his watch." A few months later she lost her mother as well.

I felt so sorry for her. I would never have wanted to be away so long from my family. But she did not want to leave her children or her husband to go for a visit. For thirty years she did not return to England, and when she did she could not recognize the streets or even find her family house in Sheffield. To locate her family, my mother put a notice in the local newspaper, saying what hotel she was staying in. That afternoon her only living sister and other relatives rushed to see her. It was a very moving meeting after such a long separation, and the newspaper in Sheffield published a story about it.

My mother did not raise us to be British. Not at all. At home we all spoke Arabic, which she had learned to speak as well. She was not a proselytizer, so she did not influence us in any way from our Muslim traditions. But still it was a little bit confusing to me as a small child. My mother kept a crucifix of the prophet Jesus over her bed, and sometimes I would see her kneeling before it in prayer, her hands clasped together in the Christian manner. Though as small children we did not yet pray, I knew that the Muslims prayed differently, standing with the arms outstretched and prostrating themselves on the ground. I was confused by this difference between my mother and the rest of the family.

"Why are you Christian while we are all Muslim?" I asked her one afternoon after a classmate questioned me about it.

"Nobody chooses their religion," she explained to me in a very sweet way. "We are all what we are born to be. The important thing to remember is that all religions have just one God. It does not matter how we worship Him so long as we have faith."

But still it bothered me. My mother's Christian ways made me think more deeply about our Muslim traditions which others just took for granted. At the Coptic missionary school that all the children attended, the only primary school on Roda, the Christian teacher read stories to us several times a week from the Bible, stories about all the prophets and about Jesus Christ. Every morning before classes began there was a Christian prayer service, which the teacher had told us we did not have to attend if we did not want to. So I didn't, staying at my desk in the classroom while all the other students went to the service, including my sister, who was too young to understand.

"Why don't you come with me?" my sister said.

"It is for the Christians and we are Muslim," I told her.

"But you will make the teacher angry," she said.

I didn't care. "I am not going to go listen to a priest just to please the teacher," I insisted.

But my sister was right. The teacher became cruel toward me, making me stand in the corner with my face to the wall every day during our recreational period.

"Your sister comes to prayers. So do the other students, both of whose parents are Muslim," the teacher said to me. "Why must you be different?"

"I am not a Christian," I would reply. And back I would go into the corner.

I was only eight at the time, and after three weeks of this I told my father how cruelly I felt the teacher was treating me. The next morning he came to see the British headmistress.

"I do not want either of my daughters to attend the Christian prayer service," he told her. "That is not their religion and the teacher is pressuring them."

The headmistress was evidently shocked when my father told her how severely I was being treated. She must have spoken to my teacher, because after my father's visit she treated me very kindly. From then on both Dalia and I stayed at our desks while the others went to chapel.

My mother never converted to Islam, though many of her British friends who were married to Egyptians did. Conversion was very simple, requiring registration as a Muslim at el-Azhar Mosque with two people as witnesses, and the recitation five times of the profession of faith: "I testify that there is no god but God, and Muhammad is His messenger." Her reluctance to convert perplexed my aunts and uncle. "Why doesn't Gladys change her religion?" my father's family and friends used to ask. But my father loved my mother very much and never wanted to pressure her. Instead, we would follow our tradition and holidays with my father's family. And my mother would share somewhat, even fasting a few days during Ramadan* to encourage us. We were a Muslim family with a Christian mother.

She was not a typical Egyptian mother, protectively hovering over her children. Not at all. When we fell playing games in the garden, our aunts would always rush to pick us up. "Let them get up by themselves," my mother would say. Unlike many Egyptian mothers, who, after washing their children's hair, for example, made their children stay inside until their hair was dry, my mother would say, "Nonsense. Go outside and let the wind and sun dry it."

*The ninth month of the Muslim year spent in fasting from sunrise to sunset.

Many Egyptian mothers sat at night with their children until they fell asleep, then left a light burning for them so that they would not be frightened if they awoke. My mother disapproved of that, thinking it made the children dependent and soft. Instead she went in quite the other direction. Every night before we went to bed she made us go out into the black, black garden alone and find our way around it three times in the dark. That way, she said, we would learn not to be afraid of being alone and not be afraid of the dark. And she was right.

Our home had a very warm, loving atmosphere. Every day my father returned from his office at two, the time all government offices closed for the day, with packets of chocolates, a new French cheese or a present of smoked tongue for us. Our main meal was at midday, after which all Cairenes including us, took naps until four or five. After his nap, my father never went out again the way many other Egyptian men did—going to the cafés to drink coffee, play backgammon or smoke the nargilehs or water pipes. Either we all went out together or he stayed home.

Sometimes on Friday, our Sabbath day, my father would take us to the Old City, marked by the Bab el-Metwalli, or Gate of the Holy Man, named after the Sufi sheikh who reportedly sat there centuries before, performing miracles for passersby. For all that Cairo was my hometown, I never ceased to marvel at the sights and the exotic history that made up my city. The streets of the Old City, far too narrow for automobiles, were choked instead with the traffic of horses, donkeys and even people laden down with loads of fresh vegetables, firesticks, vases of copper and brass to be sold in the bustling Khan el-Khalili bazaar. Cairo had been the greatest trading center in the world for centuries, and it was here in the caravanserai of the Khan el-Khalili that medieval traders from all over the Arab world had unloaded their camel trains. It was near here also that the Fatimid sultans had kept a zoo for the giraffes, ostriches and elephants sent to them as tribute from kingdoms in Africa.

The twelve thousand shops of the Khan el-Khalili were filled with remnants of the past being used in the present. My parents often took us through the dark, winding streets to the silver and gold market, located in the very heart of the bazaar so as to protect it from invaders. There my sister and I could buy silver bracelets for ten cents. While my mother stopped by the spice market to buy mint, thyme and sage for her British sauces, we children would strain to hear the clanking finger cymbals of the roving juice seller as children had for centuries, then pester our father to buy us glasses of the cold black syrupy sweet juice of the *tamarhindy*.

Interpretations

1. In what ways was Sadat's childhood Egyptian? European? What evidence is there that Sadat considers herself more Egyptian than European, or at least wants to establish that her Egyptian "half" is not secondary to her European "half"?

2. Which of Sadat's mother's traits do you think most influenced Sadat? Cite evidence. How did Sadat's Aunt Zouzou, her "Egyptian mother," influence her?

3. "Nobody chooses their religion," said Sadat's mother. How true is this? Do you think Sadat's mother should (or could) have changed to her husband's religion? Why or why not?

4. Compare the reactions of Sadat and her sister to the demands of their Christian school. On what principle did Sadat resist the Christian prayer service? (Which meant more to her, the freedom to be "different" or her Muslim religion?)

5. This essay discusses several kinds of cultural and national differences. What is its tone? (inflammatory? tolerant? arrogant? amused? serious? alarmed?)

Correspondences

1. Review the des Rieux quotation on marriage (page 67) and discuss its relevance to the relationship of Sadat's parents. (How did their different religious beliefs affect their marriage and their children's upbringing?)

2. Sadat and Alvarez vividly convey the inner workings of their families. How did their family life contribute to their personal sense of independence? How did their family customs enhance their sense of belonging.

Applications

1. Perhaps, like Sadat, you were raised by parents from different ethnic backgrounds, or, like Alvarez, by immigrant parents in a new culture. If so, write an essay describing and evaluating that experience.

2. Write an essay about someone in your family you once thought of as rather ordinary but whom you now appreciate and value highly. Focus on one event or experience that was most instrumental in your viewing this person in a new light.

from White Tigers

Maxine Hong Kingston

Maxine Hong Kingston (b. 1940) grew up in the Chinese-American community of Stockton, California, and graduated from the University of California. Her award-winning autobiographies The Woman Warrior *(1976), from which "White Tigers" is taken, and* China Man *(1980) focus on growing up female as a first-generation Chinese-American. In 1988 she published a novel,* Tripmaster Monkey. *As a writer, Kingston often blends myth, history, and autobiography to illustrate the importance of stories in the lives and culture of Chinese Americans.*

For more information on China, see John King Fairbank, "Footbinding," Chapter 1.

MY AMERICAN LIFE has been such a disappointment.

"I got straight A's, Mama."

"Let me tell you a true story about a girl who saved her village."

I could not figure out what was my village. And it was important that I do something big and fine, or else my parents would sell me when we made our way back to China. In China there were solutions for what to do with little girls who ate up food and threw tantrums. You can't eat straight A's.

When one of my parents or the emigrant villagers said, "Feeding girls is feeding cowbirds," I would thrash on the floor and scream so hard I couldn't talk. I couldn't stop.

"What's the matter with her?"

"I don't know. Bad, I guess. You know how girls are. 'There's no profit in raising girls. Better to raise geese than girls.' "

"I would hit her if she were mine. But then there's no use wasting all that discipline on a girl. 'When you raise girls, you're raising children for strangers.' "

"Stop that crying!" my mother would yell. "I'm going to hit you if you don't stop. Bad girl! Stop!" I'm going to remember never to hit or to scold my children for crying, I thought, because then they will only cry more.

"I'm not a bad girl," I would scream. "I'm not a bad girl. I'm not a bad girl." I might as well have said, "I'm not a girl."

"When you were little, all you had to say was 'I'm not a bad girl,' and you could make yourself cry," my mother says, talking-story about my childhood.

I minded that the emigrant villagers shook their heads at my sister and me. "One girl—and another girl," they said, and made our parents ashamed to take us out together. The good part about my brothers being born was that people stopped saying, "All girls," but I learned new grievances. "Did you roll an egg on *my* face like that when *I* was born?" "Did you have a full-month party for *me?*" "Did you turn on all the lights?" "Did you send *my* picture to Grandmother?" "Why not? Because I'm a girl? Is that why not?" "Why didn't you teach me English?" "You like having me beaten up at school, don't you?"

"She is very mean, isn't she?" the emigrant villagers would say.

"Come, children. Hurry. Hurry. Who wants to go out with Great-Uncle?" On Saturday mornings, my great-uncle, the ex-river pirate, did the shopping. "Get your coats, whoever's coming."

"I'm coming. I'm coming. Wait for me."

When he heard girls' voices, he turned on us and roared, "No girls!" and left my sisters and me hanging our coats back up, not looking at one another. The boys came back with candy and new toys. When they walked through Chinatown, the people must have said, "A boy—and another boy—and another boy!" At my great-uncle's funeral I secretly tested out feeling glad that he was dead—the six-foot bearish masculinity of him.

I went away to college—Berkeley in the sixties—and I studied, and I marched to change the world, but I did not turn into a boy. I would have liked to bring myself back as a boy for my parents to welcome with chickens and pigs. That was for my brother, who returned alive from Vietnam.

If I went to Vietnam, I would not come back; females desert families. It was said, "There is an outward tendency in females," which meant that I was getting straight A's for the good of my future husband's family, not my own. I did not plan ever to have a husband. I would show my mother and father and the nosey emigrant villagers that girls have no outward tendency. I stopped getting straight A's.

And all the time I was having to turn myself American-feminine, or no dates.

There is a Chinese word for the female *I*—which is "slave." Break the women with their own tongues!

I refused to cook. When I had to wash dishes, I would crack one or two. "Bad girl," my mother yelled, and sometimes that made me gloat rather than cry. Isn't a bad girl almost a boy?

"What do you want to be when you grow up, little girl?"

"A lumberjack in Oregon."

Even now, unless I'm happy, I burn the food when I cook. I do not feed people. I let the dirty dishes rot. I eat at other people's tables but won't invite them to mine, where the dishes are rotting.

If I could not-eat, perhaps I could make myself a warrior like the swordswoman who drives me. I will—I must—rise and plow the fields as soon as the baby comes out.

Once I get outside the house, what bird might call me; on what horse could I ride away? Marriage and childbirth strengthen the swordswoman, who is not a maid like Joan of Arc. Do the women's work; then do more work, which will become ours too. No husband of mine will say, "I could have been a drummer, but I had to think about the wife and kids. You know how it is." Nobody supports me at the expense of his own adventure. Then I get bitter: no one supports me; I am not loved enough to be supported. That I am not a burden has to compensate for the sad envy when I look at women loved enough to be supported. Even now China wraps double binds around my feet.

When urban renewal tore down my parents' laundry and paved over our slum for a parking lot, I only made up gun and knife fantasies and did nothing useful.

From the fairy tales, I've learned exactly who the enemy are. I easily recognize them—business-suited in their modern American executive guise, each boss two feet taller than I am and impossible to meet eye to eye.

I once worked at an art supply house that sold paints to artists. "Order more of that nigger yellow, willya?" the boss told me. "Bright, isn't it? Nigger yellow."

"I don't like that word," I had to say in my bad, small-person's voice that makes no impact. The boss never deigned to answer.

I also worked at a land developer's association. The building industry was planning a banquet for contractors, real estate dealers, and real estate editors. "Did you know the restaurant you chose for the banquet is being picketed by CORE and the NAACP?" I squeaked.

"Of course I know." The boss laughed. "That's why I chose it."

"I refuse to type these invitations," I whispered, voice unreliable.

He leaned back in his leather chair, his bossy stomach opulent. He picked up his calendar and slowly circled a date. "You will be paid up to here," he said. "We'll mail you the check."

If I took the sword, which my hate must surely have forged out of the air, and gutted him, I would put color and wrinkles into his shirt.

It's not just the stupid racists that I have to do something about, but the tyrants who for whatever reason can deny my family food and work. My job is my own only land.

To avenge my family, I'd have to storm across China to take back our farm from the Communists; I'd have to rage across the United States to take back the laundry in New York and the one in California. Nobody in history has conquered and united both North America and Asia. A descendant of eighty pole fighters, I ought to be able to set out confidently, march straight down our street, get going right now. There's work to do, ground to cover. Surely, the eighty pole fighters, though unseen would follow me and lead me and protect me, as is the wont of ancestors.

Or it may well be that they're resting happily in China, their spirits dispersed among the real Chinese, and not nudging me at all with their poles. I mustn't feel bad that I haven't done as well as the swordswoman did; after all, no bird called me, no wise old people tutored me. I have no magic beads, or water gourd sight, no rabbit that will jump in the fire when I'm hungry. I dislike armies.

I've looked for the bird. I've seen clouds make pointed angel wings that stream past the sunset, but they shred into clouds. Once at a beach after a long hike I saw a seagull, tiny as an insect. But when I jumped up to tell what miracle I saw, before I could get the words out I understood that the bird was insect-size because it was far away. My brain had momentarily lost its depth perception. I was that eager to find an unusual bird.

The news from China has been confusing. It also had something to do with birds. I was nine years old when the letters made my parents, who are rocks, cry. My father screamed in his sleep. My mother wept and crumpled up the letters. She set fire to them page by page in the ashtray, but new letters came almost every day. The only letters they opened without fear were the ones with red borders, the holiday letters that mustn't carry bad news. The other letters said that my uncles were made to kneel on broken glass during their trials and had confessed to being landowners. They were all executed, and the aunt whose thumbs were twisted off drowned herself. Other aunts, mothers-in-law, and cousins disappeared; some suddenly began writing to us again from communes or from Hong Kong. They kept asking for money. The ones in communes got four ounces of fat and one cup of oil a week, they said, and had to work from 4 A.M. to 9 P.M. They had to learn to do dances waving red kerchiefs; they had to sing nonsense syllables. The communists gave axes to the old ladies and said, "Go and kill yourself. You're useless." If we overseas Chinese would just send money to the Communist bank, our relatives said, they might get a percentage of it for themselves. The aunts in Hong Kong said to send money quickly; their children were begging on the sidewalks and mean people put dirt in their bowls.

When I dream that I am wire without flesh, there is a letter on blue airmail paper that floats above the night ocean between here and China. It must arrive safely or else my grandmother and I will lose each other.

My parents felt bad whether or not they sent money. Sometimes they got angry at their brothers and sisters for asking. And they would not simply ask but have to talk-story too. The revolutionaries had taken Fourth Aunt and Uncle's store, house, and lands. They attacked the house and killed the grandfather and oldest daughter. The grandmother escaped with the loose cash and did not return to help. Fourth Aunt picked up her sons, one under each arm, and hid in the pig house, where they slept that night in cotton clothes. The next day she found her husband, who had also miraculously escaped. The two of them collected twigs and yams to sell while their children begged. Each morning they tied the faggots on each other's back. Nobody bought from them. They ate the yams and some of the children's rice. Finally Fourth Aunt saw what was wrong. "We have to shout 'Fuel for sale' and 'Yams for sale'," she said. "We can't just walk unobtrusively up and down the street." "You're right," said my uncle, but he was shy and walked in back of her. "Shout," my aunt ordered, but he could not. "They think we're carrying these sticks home for our own fire," she said. "Shout." They walked about miserably, silently, until sundown, neither of them able to advertise themselves. Fourth Aunt, an orphan since the age of ten, mean as my mother, threw her bundle down at his feet and scolded Fourth Uncle, "Starving to death, his wife and children starving to death, and he's too damned shy to raise his voice." She left him standing by himself and afraid to return empty-handed to her. He sat under a tree to think, when he spotted a pair of nesting doves. Dumping his bag of yams, he climbed up and caught the birds. That was when the Communists trapped him, in the tree. They criticized him for selfishly taking food for his own family and killed him, leaving his body in the tree as an example. They took the birds to a commune kitchen to be shared.

It is confusing that my family was not the poor to be championed. They were executed like the barons in the stories, when they were not barons. It is confusing that birds tricked us.

What fighting and killing I have seen have not been glorious but slum grubby. I fought the most during junior high school and always cried. Fights are confusing as to who has won. The corpses I've seen had been rolled and dumped, sad little dirty bodies covered with a police khaki blanket. My mother locked her children in the house so we couldn't look at dead slum people. But at news of a body, I would find a way to get out; I had to learn about dying if I wanted to become a swordswoman. Once there was an Asian man stabbed next door, word on cloth pinned to his corpse. When the police came around asking questions, my father said, "No read Japanese. Japanese words. Me Chinese."

I've also looked for old people who could be my gurus. A medium with red hair told me that a girl who died in a far country follows me wherever I go. This spirit can help me if I acknowledge her, she said. Between the head line and heart line in my right palm, she said, I have the mystic cross. I could become a medium myself. I don't want to be a medium. I don't want to be a crank taking "offerings" in a wicker plate from the frightened audience, who, one after another, asked the spirits how to raise rent money, how to cure their coughs and skin diseases, how to find a job. And martial arts are for unsure little boys kicking away under fluorescent lights.

I live now where there are Chinese and Japanese, but no emigrants from my own village looking at me as if I had failed them. Living among one's own emigrant villagers can give a good Chinese far from China glory and a place. "That old busboy is really a swordsman," we whisper when he goes by, "He's a swordsman who's killed fifty. He has a tong ax in his closet." But I am useless, one more girl who couldn't be sold. When I visit the family now, I wrap my American successes around me like a private shawl; I *am* worthy of eating the food. From afar I can believe my family loves me fundamentally. They only say, "When fishing for treasures in the flood, be careful not to pull in girls," because that is what one says about daughters. But I watched such words come out of my own mother's and father's mouths; I looked at their ink drawing of poor people snagging their neighbor's flotage with long flood hooks and pushing the girl babies on down the river. And I had to get out of hating range. I read in an anthropology book that Chinese say, "Girls are necessary too"; I have never heard the Chinese I know make this concession. Perhaps it was a saying in another village. I refuse to shy my way anymore through our Chinatown, which tasks me with the old sayings and the stories.

The swordswoman and I are not so dissimilar. May my people understand the resemblance soon so that I can return to them. What we have in common are the words at our backs. The ideographs for *revenge* are "report a crime" and "report to five families." The reporting is the vengeance—not the beheading, not the gutting, but the words. And I have so many words— "chink" words and "gook" words too—that they do not fit on my skin.

Interpretations

1. Much of the "disappointment" Kingston has experienced is the result of an engrained favoritism of sons over daughters. How much of this attitude in these particular parents is traditional and how much is heartfelt? Cite details. Do you believe tradition is powerful enough to make parents truly hate a daughter?

2. How does Kingston react to her parents' treatment of her?

3. What obstacles lie in the way of Kingston making herself a "warrior" or "swordswoman"? What is her attitude toward these obstacles—self-pity, humor, philosophical acceptance? How can you tell?

4. What is the tone of the sentence, "Nobody in history has conquered and united both North America and Asia"? Where do you find other sentences in this same tone?

5. Speaking of marriage, the author says, "Even now China wraps double binds around my feet." What does she mean?

6. "From the fairy tales, I've learned exactly who the enemy are." What fairy-tale elements does the author weave into her narrative? What do these elements contribute to the narrative?

7. Kingston has described *The Woman Warrior* as complex and mosaic-like. For example, within a few paragraphs Kingston is a child being rejected by great-uncle, a college student at Berkeley, an indeterminate secondary-school student, and a "little girl." What is the effect of this multifaceted description?

Correspondences

1. "There's no profit in raising girls. Better to raise geese than girls," writes
    Kingston. "What is under a veil brings no joy," states Sadat (Chapter 1).
    According to these authors, how are female children traditionally regarded
    in China and in Egypt? What are the similarities and differences in their
    responses to this treatment?

2. According to Mead, the American family functions primarily as an individual
    unit. In Kingston's narrative the individual family functions with the clan.
    What examples of this interaction does Kingston cite? How might these
    different concepts of family affect competition among family members?

Applications

1. Prepare a presentation for a Parent Teachers Association meeting on the
    following topic: "Parental expectations of children often produce negative
    effects." (What *tone* should you adopt to best reach your audience?)

2. Review the Chinese proverb on page 68. To what extent does it apply to
    Kingston's family? Is Kingston's concept of parental authority similar to or
    different from yours? How?

On Friendship

Margaret Mead and Rhoda Metraux

Among the most widely recognized of American anthropologists, Margaret Mead (1901–1978) won instant acclaim in 1928 for her study of the transition from adolescence to adulthood in Coming of Age in Samoa. *She also taught for many years at Columbia University and wrote more than twenty books, including* Culture and Commitment *(1970) and* Blackberry Winter: A Memoir *(1972).*

Rhoda Metraux (b. 1914) is also an anthropologist and frequent collaborator with Mead. She has done fieldwork in several countries, including Mexico, Haiti, and New Guinea.

The concept of friendship that Mead and Metraux attribute to the French is what one would expect of an established civilization that has long been in the forefront of intellectual and artistic achievements. France combines a respect for the traditional with verve and curiosity about the new. The French were the American colonists' first allies in the American Revolution. Their own Revolution of 1789 is a watershed in modern intellectual and political history. Under Napoléon Bonaparte (Napoléon I, 1769–1821), France dominated much of Europe and, through its colonies, large parts of the world. About the size of Texas, France is both highly industrialized and staunchly agrarian. Urban sprawl afflicts its countryside less so than in some other industrialized nations; it is the largest food exporter in Western Europe.

For more information on Germany, see "German Space," Chapter 5. For more information on England, see "Grow Old Along with Me" in this chapter.

FEW AMERICANS stay put for a lifetime. We move from town to city to suburb, from high school to college in a different state, from a job in one region to a better job elsewhere, from the home where we raise our children to the home where we plan to live in retirement. With each move we are forever making new friends, who become part of our new life at that time.

For many of us the summer is a special time for forming new friendships. Today millions of Americans vacation abroad, and they go not only to see new sights but also—in those places where they do not feel too strange— with the hope of meeting new people. No one really expects a vacation trip to produce a close friend. But surely the beginning of a friendship is possible? Surely in every country people value friendship?

They do. The difficulty when strangers from two countries meet is not a lack of appreciation of friendship, but different expectations about what constitutes friendship and how it comes into being. In those European countries that Americans are most likely to visit, friendship is quite sharply distinguished from other, more casual relations, and is differently related to family life. For a Frenchman, a German, or an Englishman friendship is usually more particularized and carries a heavier burden of commitment.

But as we use the word, "friend" can be applied to a wide range of relationships—to someone one has known for a few weeks in a new place, to a close business associate, to a childhood playmate, to a man or woman, to a trusted confidant. There are real differences among these relations for Americans—a friendship may be superficial, casual, situational or deep and enduring. But to a European, who sees only our surface behavior, the differences are not clear.

As they see it, people known and accepted temporarily, casually, flow in and out of Americans' homes with little ceremony and often with little personal commitment. They may be parents of the children's friends, house guests of neighbors, members of a committee, business associates from another town or even another country. Coming as a guest into an American home, the European visitor finds no visible landmarks. The atmosphere is relaxed. Most people, old and young, are called by first names.

Who, then, is a friend?

Even simple translation from one language to another is difficult. "You see," a Frenchman explains, "if I were to say to you in France, 'This is my good friend,' that person would not be as close to me as someone about whom I said only, 'This is my friend.' Anyone about whom I have to say *more* is really less."

In France, as in many European countries, friends generally are of the same sex, and friendship is seen as basically a relationship between men. Frenchwomen laugh at the idea that "women can't be friends," but they also admit sometimes that for women "it's a different thing." And many French people doubt the possibility of a friendship between a man and a woman. There is also the kind of relationship within a group—men and women who have worked together for a long time, who may be very close, sharing great loyalty and warmth of feeling. They may call one another *copains*—a word that in English becomes "friends" but has more the feeling of "pals" or "buddies." In French eyes this is not friendship, although two members of such a group may well be friends.

For the French, friendship is a one-to-one relationship that demands a keen awareness of the other person's intellect, temperament and particular interests. A friend is someone who draws out your own best qualities, with whom you sparkle and become more of whatever the friendship draws upon. Your political philosophy assumes more depth, appreciation of a play becomes sharper, taste in food or wine is accentuated, enjoyment of a sport is intensified.

And French friendships are compartmentalized. A man may play chess with a friend for thirty years without knowing his political opinions, or he may talk politics with him for as long a time without knowing about his personal life. Different friends fill different niches in each person's life. These friendships are not made part of family life. A friend is not expected to spend evenings being nice to children or courteous to a deaf grandmother. These duties, also serious and enjoined, are primarily for relatives. Men who are friends may meet in a café. Intellectual friends may meet in larger groups for evenings of conversation. Working people may meet at the little *bistro* where they drink and talk, far from the family. Marriage does not affect such friendships; wives do not have to be taken into account.

In the past in France, friendships of this kind seldom were open to any but intellectual women. Since most women's lives centered on their homes, their warmest relations with other women often went back to their girlhood. The special relationship of friendship is based on what the French value most—on the mind, on compatibility of outlook, on vivid awareness of some chosen area of life.

Friendship heightens the sense of each person's individuality. Other relationships commanding as great loyalty and devotion have a different meaning. In World War II the first resistance groups formed in Paris were built on the foundation of *les copains*. But significantly, as time went on these little groups, whose lives rested in one another's hands, called themselves "families." Where each had a total responsibility for all, it was kinship ties that provided the model. And even today such ties, crossing every line of class and personal interest, remain binding on the survivors of these small, secret bands.

In Germany, in contrast with France, friendship is much more articulately a matter of feeling. Adolescents, boys and girls, form deeply sentimental attachments, walk and talk together—not so much to polish their wits as to share their hopes and fears and dreams, to form a common front against the world of school and family and to join in a kind of mutual discovery of each other's and their own inner life. Within the family, the closest relationship over a lifetime is between brothers and sisters. Outside the family, men and women find in their closest friends of the same sex the devotion of a sister, the loyalty of a brother. Appropriately, in Germany friends usually are brought into the family. Children call their father's and their mother's friends "uncle" and "aunt." Between French friends, who have chosen each other for the congeniality of their point of view, lively disagreement and sharpness of argument are the breath of life. But for Germans, whose friendships are based on mutuality of feeling, deep disagreement on any subject that matters to both is regarded as a tragedy. Like ties of kinship, ties of friendship are meant to be irrevocably binding. Young Germans who come to the United States have great difficulty in establishing such friendships with Americans. We view friendship more tentatively, subject to changes in intensity as people move, change their jobs, marry, or discover new interests.

English friendships follow still a different pattern. Their basis is shared activity. Activities at different stages of life may be of very different kinds—discovering a common interest in school, serving together in the armed forces, taking part in a foreign mission, staying in the same country house during a crisis. In the midst of the activity, whatever it may be, people fall into step—sometimes two men or two women, sometimes two couples, sometimes three people—and find that they walk or play a game or tell stories or serve on a tiresome and exacting committee with the same easy anticipation of what each will do day by day or in some critical situation. Americans who have made English friends comment that, even years later, "you can take up just where you left off." Meeting after a long interval, friends are like a couple who begin to dance again when the orchestra strikes up after a pause. English friendships are formed outside the family circle, but they are not, as in Germany, contrapuntal to the family nor are they, as in France, separated from the family. And a break in an English friendship comes not necessarily as a result of some irreconcilable difference of viewpoint or feeling but instead as a result of misjudgment, where one friend seriously misjudges how the other will think or feel or act, so that suddenly they are out of step.

What, then, is friendship? Looking at these different styles, including our own, each of which is related to a whole way of life, are there common elements? There is the recognition that friendship, in contrast with kinship, invokes freedom of choice. A friend is someone who chooses and is chosen. Related to this is the sense each friend gives the other of being a special individual, on whatever grounds this recognition is based. And between friends there is inevitably a kind of equality of give-and-take. These similarities make the bridge between societies possible, and the American's characteristic openness to different styles of relationship makes it possible for him to find new friends abroad with whom he feels at home.

Interpretations

1. According to this essay, which of the four nationals—the Americans, French, Germans, or English—are most likely to seek out friendship? Why?

2. Why should all people be aware that different concepts of friendship are operating in different places?

3. Consider the first six paragraphs an introduction. In this "introduction," is the authors' attitude one of complete neutrality or does it reveal a preference for one of the four types of friendship? Is this neutrality or preference sustained throughout the essay? Cite evidence for your response.

4. What logical or argumentative techniques do the authors use to try to convince you of these cultural differences? Do you find their techniques convincing? For which country do they make the best case? the worst? Can you add, from your own knowledge or experience, to their arguments?

Correspondences

1. Review the du Plessix Gray's quotation on friendship (page 67). To what extent does it apply to the relationships discussed by Mead and Metraux? How does it apply to your friendships?

2. Mead and Metraux distinguish between friendship and kinship. What is the difference? Why might Americans, according to the authors, be less likely to experience kinship? What other cultural factors might influence concepts of friendships in the four countries discussed?

Applications

1. Consult a dictionary or a thesaurus on the words *comrade, companion* and *confidant*. What connotation does each have? In an essay, discuss any two of these words and clearly illustrate differences in connotation and applicability.

2. Write a one-sentence definition of friendship and compare yours with those of your group. Then consider how gender affects friendship. Can men and women be friends? Analyze group responses and formulate a thesis.

Grow Old Along with Me, The Best Is Yet to Be

Penelope Lively

Penelope Margaret Lively (b. 1933) was born in Cairo but lives in England. She graduated with an Honors Degree in Modern History from Oxford University and is a contributor to a variety of journals and magazines including Good Housekeeping *and* Vogue. *She has also authored numerous books, including* Judgement Day *(1980),* Next to Nature *(1982),* Corruption *(1984, from which the following story is taken) and* A House Inside Out *(1987).*

In "Grow Old Along with Me" you will encounter Sarah and Tony, a liberated British couple who are traveling in Gloucestershire, the county just to the west of Lively's home county of Oxfordshire. Around them are architectural reminders of England's long history, including the eighth-century church the couple reads about in "Pevsner." (Sir Nikolaus Pevsner, an architectural historian, wrote the Buildings of England *series.) By the eighth century, the British Isles had been invaded by the Angles, Saxons, and Jutes. The Danish would soon follow. In the eighth century the church in the story would, of course, have been Roman Catholic. By Sara and Tony's time—in fact in the sixteenth century under Henry VIII— the state church had become the Protestant Church of England. Sects such as the Separatists had begun to proliferate. These English Puritans were to found the Massachusetts Bay Colony in 1620.*

"OH, *I* DON'T KNOW . . . ." SAID SARAH. "Decisions, decisions. I hate them. I mean, one of the things that bothers me is—would I stop being *me?* Would I change. If we did."

She wore dungarees in pale turquoise, and a white T-shirt. She drove the Fiat hunched forward over the steering-wheel. Her face was engulfed by large reflecting sun-glasses across which flew hedges, trees, a passing car. "It's rather gorgeous round here, isn't it? Half-asleep, as though nothing happens in a hundred years."

Tony said, "We both might. It's a significant step in a relationship— that's the point of it, I suppose."

"And the point of waiting. Thinking about it. Not rushing."

"Not that we have."

"Quite. Shall we stop and eat soon?"

"Yes—when there's a reasonable pub."

Gloucestershire unreeled at either side: dark green, straw-coloured, unpopulated. Trees drooped in the fields; a village was still and silent except for a lorry throbbing outside a shop. High summer gripped the landscape; birds twitched from hedge to hedge.

"Half the time," said Sarah, "it doesn't crop up. One sort of puts it out of one's mind—there are too many other things to think of. And then it begins to nag. We've got to either do it or not do it."

"We've been not doing it for three years, darling."

"I know, I know. But all the same, it looms."

"We are actually," he said, "better off, from a tax point of view, un-married. Since your rise. We went into that in the winter—remember?"

"What about this—Free House, Bar Snacks. How much better off, exactly?"

"Oh, lord, I don't know. Hundreds, anyway."

She turned the car into the pub yard. "It's a point, then. Ma keeps saying, what happens if there's a baby? And I say well that would of course put a different complexion on things but *until* we are absolutely free to choose. The trouble is that dear ma thinks I'm on the shelf at twenty-six. I keep saying, there aren't shelves now."

The woman behind the bar watched them come in, a good-looking young couple, in the pink of health, not short of money, the kind of people who know their way around. She served them lagers and chicken salad, and noted Sarah's neat figure, not an ounce in the wrong place, which induced vague discontent. I'm dieting, she thought, as from Monday I am, I swear to God. She observed also Tony's tanned forearms, below the rolled sleeves of an indefinably modish shirt, like blokes in colour supp. ads. Thirtyish, nice voice. He didn't look at her, pocketing the change, turning away with the plates. She watched them settle in the corner by the window, sitting close, talking. In love, presumably, lucky so-and-so's.

"Tax is certainly a point," said Sarah. "Getting dependent on each other is another. Look at Tom and Alison. But one still feels that eventually we're going to have to make some kind of decision. You can have my pickled onion."

"Lots of people don't. Decide, I mean. Look at Blake and Susan."

"I don't want to look at Blake and Susan. Blake's forty-two, did you know that? And anyway he's *been* married. Oh, isn't it all difficult? We decided no baby, barring accidents, at least not yet, and that was one decision. Thank God for the pill, I suppose. I mean, imagine when they just *happened*."

"They still do sometimes. Look at Maggie."

"Oh, Maggie meant to, for goodness sake. That baby was no accident. It was psychological."

They ate, for a while, in silence. At the bar middle-aged men, locals, sporadically conversed, out of kilter like clocks ticking at different speeds. The woman wiped glasses. A commercial traveller came in and ordered a steak and kidney with chips. On the wall, hand-written posters advertised a Bring and Buy, a Darby and Joan Outing. Tony stacked their empty plates. "Not exactly the hub of the universe, this."

"It's rather sweet. Laurie Lee country.[1] I used to adore that book— what's-it-called?—we did it for O-levels. Sex in the hedges and all that. O.K.—I'll find the loo and we'll get moving. Where are we, by the way, I've lost track?"

When she came back he had the map book open on his knee. "Let's have a look, there might be something to go and see. Oh, goodness, there is— we're not far from Deerhurst. Oh, we must see Deerhurst. You know— Saxon church, very special."

"Right you are. Do we have Pevsner?"

"On the back shelf of the car. What luck—I never realised Deerhurst was hereabouts."

"Aren't you a clever girl?" he said, patting her knee. "Knowing about Saxon churches."

The woman behind the bar, watching them, thought, yes, that's how it is when you're like that. Can't keep your hands off each other. Ah well. "How's the back, John?" she said. "That stuff I told you about do any good?" The young couple were getting up now, slinging sweaters about their shoulders, leaving without a backwards glance. People passing through, going off into other lives. Young intense lives. "What? Oh, thanks very much—I'll have a lager and lime. Cheers, John."

"Drive or navigate?" said Sarah, in the car park. "You're better with the map than I am, and it's all side roads to this church. I'll tell you one thing— if we do get married it's not going to be any flipping church business. That's what ma's got her eye on, you realise."

"There'd have to be some sort of do."

"We could have it at the flat. Cheaper. The do, I mean. And registry office. But it's all a bit academic, until we actually decide something. Do I go left or right?"

Signposts fingered toward slothful hinterlands. Cars glittered between the hedges, sparks of colour in a world of green and fawn. On the edge of the village, washing-lines held up stiff shapes of clothes, slumping pink and yellow sheets, a rank of nappies. A man scraped around young cabbages with a hoe.

"Corfu," said Tony, "was livelier."

"I thought we agreed never again a package holiday. Anyway, it's the new car this year instead."

"This is our fourth holiday together, Sarah."

"Cor . . . Hey—you're not directing me. That sign said Deerhurst."

---

[1]English poet and autobiographer born in 1914 in Gloucestershire.

"Sorry. My mind was on other things. Incidentally, what started us off on this marriage discussion? Today, I mean."

"I can't remember. Oh yes I can—it was you talking about this aunt of yours. Will you have to go to the wedding, by the way?"

"I hope not. I'd be the only person there under fifty, I should imagine. No—hearty good wishes over the phone and that kind of thing."

"It's nice for her," said Sarah charitably. "At that age. If a bit kind of fake, if you see what I mean."

"Yes. But for that generation there wouldn't be any alternative."

They nodded, sombrely.

"Here we are," said Sarah. "And this must be where you leave cars. Good—there's no one else there, I hate looking at churches when there's anyone else. Where's Pevsner? We're going to do this place properly—it's supposed to be important."

They advanced into the churchyard. The church, squatting amid yews, seemed almost derisive in its antiquity, tethered to something dark and incomprehensible, uncaring, too far away to be understood. Its stone was blurred, its shapes strange and unlovely. Gravestones drowned in grass. An aeroplane, unseen, rumbled across the milky sky.

" '. . . tall narrow nave of the C8,' " Tony read. "Seven hundred and something. Jesus! That makes you think, doesn't it?"

"There's this famous sculpture thing over the door. An animal head. That's it, I suppose. Goodness, isn't it all sinister?"

They stood in silence. "Things that are so incredibly old," Sarah went on, "just leave you feeling respectful. I mean, that they're there at all."

They went into the church. Tony took a few steps down the nave. "Yes. I know what you mean. Even more so inside. All this stone standing for so long"—he gestured at piers, crossing arch, narrow uncompromising windows. "Read Pevsner," instructed Sarah. "I like to understand what I'm looking at." They toured the building, side by side, heads cocked from book to architectural feature, understanding.

The church door, which they had closed behind them, burst open. The sound made them both jump. Turning, they saw a man who stood framed in the gush of light from without: a tall man in tweed jacket and baggy-kneed trousers, an odd prophetic-looking figure with a mane of white hair, like a more robust version of the aged Bertrand Russell. A memorable person, who stood for a moment staring wildly round the church, at Sarah and Tony for one dismissive instant, and who then strode down the aisle searching, apparently, the pillars, and then back to the entrance and out, slamming the door.

"The vicar?" said Tony, after a moment.

"No. Frankly. That was no vicar. Funny to storm out like that, though. This place *vaut le détour,* as *Michelin*[2] says."

---

[2]Is worth a detour according to the *Michelin* travel guidebooks.

"P'raps he's seen it already."

"Presumably." Sarah turned back to Pevsner. "Apparently there's this other carving outside, round at the back, we'd better go and find it. We've done the rest, I think."

She led the way out of the church and round the side, through the long grass and the leaning grave-stones. And came, thus, upon them first.

In the angle of a buttress, up against the wall of the church. The man, the white-haired tall man, his back now turned. Turned because he was locked in an embrace, a succulent sexual embrace (the sound, just, of mouths— the impression of loins pushed together) with a woman little of whom could be seen as, eyes averted, Sarah scurried past, followed a few paces behind by Tony. Both of them at once seeing, and quickly looking away. Seeing of the man his tweed back and his mane of yellow-white hair and of the woman— well, little except an impression of blue denim skirt and plimsolls. And more white hair: crisp curly grey-white hair.

They achieved the back of the church and stood peering up at the wall.

"I can't see this sculpture," said Sarah (voice firm, ordinary, not lowered, rather loud indeed). "It's supposed to be a Virgin—ah, that must be it. Right up just under the window there."

When they came back past the buttress the couple were gone. The churchyard was quite empty. The whole place, which had briefly rocked, had sunk back into its lethargy. That crackling startling charge of passion had dissipated into the stagnant air of the summer afternoon. It was three o'clock, and felt as if it forever would be. Somewhere beyond the hedge a tractor ground across a field.

"Let's go," said Sarah brightly. "I think I've had Deerhurst."

The car was no longer alone. Two others, now, were parked alongside. Sarah whipped the key into the lock and opened the door. She plumped down into the driving-seat. "You know what? That was an assignation we stumbled into."

"So it would seem."

"Where are they now, do you imagine?"

Tony shrugged.

Sarah started the engine. She said with sudden violence, "You know, it was a bit revolting. They were seventy if they were a day."

Tony nodded. Embarrassment filled the car.

Interpretations

1. As the story opens, why don't Sarah and Tony call by name the subject they are discussing? Are they equally undecided, or is one trying to put pressure on the other?

2. How does Tony's aunt's marriage relate to the scene behind the church? What is Sarah's attitude towards his aunt's decision?

3. How does the white-haired couple's "succulent sexual embrace" affect Tony and Sarah? How does it relate to their own earlier discussion of marriage?

4. What do you think Sarah and Tony will decide about their own marriage? Cite reasons for your answer.

5. What is the tone of this story? Is it serious? objective? ironic?

6. For what audience is Lively writing? Do you think men and women respond differently to the story? (What is *your* response?)

Correspondences

1. Sarah and Tony consider themselves modern. Are they? How liberated are their attitudes? How tolerant? Is their outlook on relationships similar to or different from those of the American couples Weber interviewed?

2. Review the de Beauvoir quotation on love (page 67). To what extent does it apply to Tony and Sarah's relationship? Evaluate their relationship.

Applications

1. Assume you are about to enter a living-together arrangement. Write an essay to your parents explaining your decision. What tone should you adopt? What reasons might they find most convincing? Be sure to present your decision in a logical manner.

2. Write an essay analyzing the implications of the title of Lively's short story. How does it apply to the relationships she presents? What is her attitude towards Sarah and Tony?

Anticipation

Mabel Dove-Danquah

Mabel Dove-Danquah was the first woman to be elected a member of any African legislative assembly, that of Ghana. She has studied in England, traveled in the United States, and was the editor of the Accra Evening News *before devoting her time to writing.*

Located on the southern coast of West Africa, Ghana, formerly known as the Gold Coast, was ruled by the British for more than 100 years. It has a population of about 14 million, of whom about a million live in the capital, Accra. The country became independent in 1957. President Kwame Nkrumah supervised the development of the country, but fiscal problems and threats of corruption led him to deny civil rights to his political opponents and to assume dictatorial powers as head of a one-party socialist system. He was deposed in 1966 and after six other coups, Ghana still has a military government. Although English remains the official language, over fifty tribal languages are spoken. About the same percentage of Ghanaians are Christian or Muslim. Indigenous religions account for a slight majority of believers. It is no surprise, then, that several cultures coexist in the following story. Their interplay gives rise to considerable humor.

NANA ADAKU II, Omanhene of Akwasin, was celebrating the twentieth anniversary of his accession to the stool of Akwasin. The capital, Nkwabi, was thronged with people from the outlying towns and villages.

It was in the height of the cocoa season, money was circulating freely and farmers were spending to their hearts' content. Friends who had not seen one another for a long time were renewing their friendship. They called with gifts of gin, champagne or whiskey, recalled old days with gusto and before departing imbibed most of the drinks they brought as gifts. No one cared, everyone was happy. Few could be seen in European attire; nearly all were in Gold Coast costume. The men had tokota sandals on their feet, and rich multi-colored velvet and gorgeous, hand-woven kente cloths nicely wrapped round their bodies. The women, with golden ear-rings dangling, with golden chains and bracelets, looked dignified in their colorful native attire.

The state drums were beating paeans of joy.

It was four o'clock in the afternoon and people were walking to the state park where the Odwira was to be staged. Enclosures of palm leaves decorated the grounds.

The Omanhene arrived in a palanquin under a brightly-patterned state umbrella, a golden crown on his head, his kente studded with tiny golden beads, rows upon rows of golden necklaces piled high on his chest. He wore bracelets of gold from the wrists right up to the elbows. He held in his right hand a decorated elephant tail which he waved to his enthusiastic, cheering people. In front of him sat his "soul," a young boy of twelve, holding the sword of office.

After the Omanhene came the Adontehene, the next in importance. He was resplendent in rich green and red velvet cloth; his headband was studded with golden bars. Other chiefs came one after the other under their brightly-colored state umbrellas. The procession was long. The crowd raised cheers as each palanquin was lowered, and the drums went on beating resounding joys of jubilation. The Omanhene took his seat on the dais with his Elders. The District Commissioner, Captain Hobbs, was near him. Sasa, the jester, looked ludicrous in his motley pair of trousers and his cap of monkey skin. He made faces at the Omanhene, he leered, did acrobatic stunts; the Omanhene could not laugh; it was against custom for the great Chief to be moved to laughter in public.

The state park presented a scene of barbaric splendor. Chiefs and their retinue sat on native stools under state umbrellas of diverse colors. The golden linguist staves of office gleamed in the sunlight. The women, like tropical butterflies, looked charming in their multi-colored brocaded silk, kente and velvet, and the Oduku headdress, black and shiny, studded with long golden pins and slides. Young men paraded the grounds, their flowing cloths trailing behind them, their silken plaited headbands glittering in the sun.

The drums beat on. . . .

The women are going to perform the celebrated Adowa dance. The decorated calabashes make rhythm. The women run a few steps, move slowly sideways and sway their shoulders. One dancer looks particularly enchanting in her green, blue and red square kente, moving with the simple, charming grace of a wild woodland creature; the Chief is stirred, and throws a handful of loose cash into the crowd of dancers. She smiles as the coins fall on her and tinkle to the ground. There is a rush. She makes no sign but keeps on dancing.

The Omanhene turns to his trusted linguist:

"Who is that beautiful dancer?"

"I am sorry, I do not know her."

"I must have her as a wife."

Nana Adaku II was fifty-five and he had already forty wives, but a new beauty gave him the same new thrill as it did the man who is blessed—or cursed—with only one better half. Desire again burned fiercely in his veins; he was bored with his forty wives. He usually got so mixed up among them that lately he kept calling them by the wrong names. His new wife cried bitterly when he called her Oda, the name of an old, ugly wife.

"This dancer is totally different," thought the Chief; "she will be a joy to the palace." He turned round to the linguist:

"I will pay one hundred pounds for her."

"She might already be married, Nana."

"I shall pay the husband any moneys he demands."

The linguist knew his Omanhene: when he desired a woman he usually had his way.

"Get fifty pounds from the chief treasurer, find the relatives, give them the money and when she is in my palace tonight I shall give her the balance of the fifty pounds. Give the linguist staff to Kojo and begin your investigations now."

Nana Adaku II was a fast worker. He was like men all over the world when they are stirred by feminine charm: a shapely leg, the flash of an eye, the quiver of a nostril, the timbre of a voice, and the male species becomes frenzy personified. Many men go through this sort of mania until they reach their dotage. The cynics among them treat women with a little flattery, bland tolerance, and take fine care not to become seriously entangled for life. Women, on the other hand, use quite a lot of common sense: They are not particularly thrilled by the physical charms of a man; if his pockets are heavy and his income sure, he is a good matrimonial risk. But there is evolving a new type of hardheaded modern woman who insists on the perfect lover as well as an income and other necessaries, or stays forever from the unbliss of marriage.

By 6 P.M. Nana Adaku II was getting bored with the whole assembly and very glad to get into his palanquin. The state umbrellas danced, the chiefs sat again in their palanquins, the crowd cheered wildly, the drums beat. Soon the shadows of evening fell and the enclosures of palm leaves in the state park stood empty and deserted.

The Omanhene had taken his bath after dusk and changed into a gold and green brocaded cloth. Two male servants stood on either side and fanned him with large ostrich feathers as he reclined on a velvet-cushioned settee in his private sitting room. An envelope containing fifty golden sovereigns was near him. He knew his linguist as a man of tact and diplomacy and he was sure that night would bring a wife to help him celebrate the anniversary of his accession to the Akwasin Stool.

He must have dozed. When he woke up the young woman was kneeling by his feet. He raised her onto the settee.

"Were you pleased to come?"

"I was pleased to do Nana's bidding."

"Good girl. What is your name?"

"Effua, my lord and master."

"It is a beautiful name, and you are a beautiful woman too. Here are fifty gold sovereigns, the balance of the marriage dowry. We will marry privately tonight and do the necessary custom afterward." Nana Adaku II is not the first man to use this technique. Civilized, semi-civilized and primitive men all over the world have said the very same thing in nearly the same words.

"I shall give the money to my mother," said the sensible girl. "She is in the corridor. May I?" The Chief nodded assent.

Effua returned.

"Nana, my mother and other relatives want to thank you for the hundred pounds."

"There is no need, my beauty," and he played with the ivory beads lying so snugly on her bosom.

"They think you must have noticed some extraordinary charm in me for you to have spent so much money," she smiled shyly at the Omanhene.

"But, my dear, you are charming. Haven't they eyes?"

"But, Nana, I cannot understand it myself."

"You cannot, you modest woman. Look at yourself in that long mirror over there."

The girl smiled mischievously, went to the mirror, looked at herself. She came back and sat on the settee and leaned her head on his bosom.

"You are a lovely girl, Effua." He caressed her shiny black hair, so artistically plaited.

"But, my master, I have always been like this, haven't I?"

"I suppose so, beautiful, but I only saw you today."

"You only saw me today?"

"Today."

"Have you forgotten?"

"Forgotten what, my love?"

"You paid fifty pounds . . . and married me two years ago."

Interpretations

1. What was diplomatic about the linguist's response, "She might already be married, Nana"?

2. How well does the Chief know his forty wives? Do you suppose there is any connection between how well he knows his wives and his boredom with them? Would you recommend a forty-*first* wife as the solution to boredom with forty wives (setting aside for a moment the fact that Effua is not really No. 41)?

3. But "there is evolving a new type of hardheaded modern woman who insists on the perfect lover as well as an income and other necessaries, or stays forever from the unbliss of marriage." What connection exists between this comment and the events of the story? Is Effua's marriage "unblissful"? If so, in what way? Is Effua "hardheaded" in any way? How?

4. What is the purpose of Dove-Danquah's extensive description of clothing and other objects? What is her attitude toward the main character, Nana Adaku II? What is the first indication of this attitude?

5. What is the prevailing tone of this story?

6. What do you consider the most important source of humor in the story? Cite examples.

Correspondences

1. Dove-Danquah and Black Elk use ritual as background to enhance their narratives. What examples did you find most effective? What role does ritual play in the relationships in each selection?

2. What feminist influences are apparent in "Anticipation" and "Grow Old Along with Me"? What might you conclude about cultural influence on gender roles?

Applications

1. Research the Adowa dance and write an essay explaining its origin and significance.

2. Write an analysis of the title of Dove-Danquah's story. To what and to whom does "anticipation" refer?

Aunt Batool

Shusha Guppy

Shusha Guppy is well acquainted with both entrenched tradition and clashing cultures. In the following selection, she focuses on the life of her Aunt Batool, a woman who "epitomized multitudes of Persian women of her generation and class." See also the introductory material on Guppy on page 30.

MY MOTHER'S younger sisters, Aunt Batool and Aunt Zarry—Pride of the Age and Pride of Kings—had been married off young to unsuitable husbands; but while Zarry, the youngest, a vivacious optimist of irrepressible gaiety, had made the best of a bad thing and created an adequate life for herself and her family, Batool, the most beautiful and gifted of Haji Ali-Baba's children, had been relentlessly pursued by ill luck. Her husband had been imposed on her by her mother and the pressure of a whole social network, and she had found him utterly repellent from the moment she had set eyes on him on her wedding night. Her whole being had rejected him outright and irrevocably. Plain, effeminate and puny, her groom, a Bazaar merchant, was totally dominated by his powerful mother and two spinsterish sisters known as "the Two Old Toads." On her wedding night he had clumsily tried to kiss her, and the touch of his lips had provoked such a violent attack of nausea in her that she had vomitted into the silver chamber-pot by her bed. Nonetheless he had managed to fumble around with her and make her pregnant. Thereafter she refused to be "touched" by him and they lay side by side, "like brother and sister," without the slightest attempt on his part to force the issue, hoping that in time she would accept him and submit to her fate. But she never did: passive resistance was not a conscious scheme on her part to get rid of him but an instinctive reaction.

"Oh, but she's a virgin!" exclaimed the midwife nine months later, when she was called to deliver her baby daughter. Apparently this was a common occurrence—virgin girls often got pregnant without complete penetration. "What a shock! And all the while everyone had assumed that the newly-weds were leading a normal married life!"

A few weeks after the birth of her baby, Haji Ali-Baba died and Aunt Batool went home for her father's funeral and wake ceremonies. She never returned. She requested a divorce, and although women had no right to initiate it and her husband could have refused to grant her one till the end of her days, he was persuaded by Uncle Alem to let her go. He never remarried.

Aunt Batool told me the story of what happened next:

"One day, a few months later, there was a knock on the door—it was the Two Old Toads. They had come to take the baby for a day or two to see her father. I did not even pack any clothes for her, thinking she would be back soon, but when three days passed and there was no sign of the baby, I sent Nanny with the coach to bring her back. The Two Old Toads and their mother refused to hand her over, saying that the baby belonged to her father by law and that nothing could make them part with her. I raged and cried and pleaded and offered bribes, but all in vain. They had hearts of stone and wouldn't relent. It would have meant a lengthy law-suit and in the end they would have won—the law was on their side."

Generation after generation of Persian women lived miserable lives, locked up in hopeless marriages, in order not to lose their children:

"Once you have children you just sit and bear it, whatever *it* is," my mother used to say to my sister and myself. Even after the country was modernised and women were emancipated, the laws relating to marriage and divorce remained biased in favour of men for decades, for fear of popular revolt provoked by the mullahs. Eventually, in 1966, the late Shah introduced a Family Protection Law which enabled women to obtain a divorce under certain circumstances without automatically losing their children. As was expected, of all his reforms this one caused the biggest controversy, as it hit the heart of patriarchal supremacy, but he was then at the height of his power and could defy opposition.

"The tears women have shed over centuries of tyranny and bullying by men would run in rivers! Is it not time that some justice be introduced?" he asked in a television speech. Everyone agreed that it was—no one would have dared do otherwise. Who would have believed that only twelve years later the women on whose behalf he had run the gauntlet of disapproval would pour into the streets and clamour for his abdication! Since then these same women have lived to regret it, but "what is done cannot be undone."

Aunt Batool was 18 when she divorced, before I was born. Many years later, she received an invitation to her daughter's wedding. After some deliberation she decided to go and take lavish presents. From then on, mother and daughter saw each other regularly as two loving friends. But that early brutal deprivation and subsequent unhappiness had left an indelible scar on Aunt Batool's soul which was reflected in her huge, beautiful eyes, her languid allure and wistful expression.

Aunt Batool was too lovely and accomplished to remain unmarried for long, yet she did, for the rest of her life. "The thread of her fortune has been knotted by witchcraft," lamented Grandma, or, "The Two Old Toads have blackened her fate." She knew for certain, having been told by Mirza Saleem, the most reliable and skilful of fortune-tellers and magicians in town. It was a complex tale of dark nights in cemeteries and menstrual blood being burnt in skulls, and a dead monkey procured and buried in an empty grave, and endless other recherché machinations, the details of which I have forgotten. Grandma cursed the Two Old Toads night and day and called the fire of hell upon them, but since their fate was no better than Aunt Batool's, it was not easy to assess the efficacy of her imprecations.

Occasionally it looked as though "the knot" on Aunt Batool's "luck-thread" was getting unravelled of its own accord, and that the evil spell she had been cast was being removed, but always something happened at the last minute which maintained the unhappy *status quo:* her suitors withdrew, or she decided against them, or an unforeseen event occurred to stop the marriage. She once fell in love with a handsome Army officer who had become a friend of her brother's, Uncle Alam, and frequented their house. It looked as though everything would work out and that they would marry and live happily ever after. Then, inevitably, Uncle Alem picked a quarrel with the dashing officer and he withdrew his proposal. He did want to marry her, he let it be known, "but could not cope with her brother's insanity." Another time a middle-aged aristocrat, recently widowed, saw her at a wedding, fell madly in love with her, and asked for her hand immediately.

"I can't find any fault with him—he is perfect!" declared Uncle Alem, adding, "And I've accepted his proposal."

Arrangements for the wedding were made in record time; we were all excited, Grandma was over the moon, Aunt Batool glowed as if a cloud had been lifted from her countenance. But, two days before the marriage cere-mony, her fiancé dropped dead with a massive heart attack.

"You see, when fate is adamant, there's nothing anyone can do," com-mentated Aunt Ashraf, who had submitted to her own unfortunate destiny with serenity, in a spirit of Islamic surrender to the will of God. She quoted the poet:

> When misfortune strikes, what is good turns bad;
> One disaster becomes ten, and ten is followed by a hundred more;
> Fire loses its warmth, the sun its light;
> Philosophy becomes erroneous and Logic a lie.

After the death of her fiancé, Aunt Batool gave up hope; yet she still cared about her looks and spent hours in front of the mirror making up her face, curling her abundant dark hair, adjusting her ornaments. She bought beautiful clothes and European accessories; she plucked her eyebrows pencil-thin and smoked cigarettes in long holders in the manner of the movie-stars of the day; but it was all for the benefit of the mirror and her daydreams . . .

When Uncle Alem died and his three sons went to Europe, Grandma and Aunt Batool moved to our house, and once again our home became the center of our family life, where we converged as often as we could from all over the world and enjoyed the delicious food, the warm, noisy atmosphere and the loving solicitude we could get nowhere else.

Aunt Batool died a couple of years after the events of 1979: suddenly her generous loving heart just gave out—she had used it too much!

To me, as an adolescent, Aunt Batool, with her forlorn beauty, her tall, graceful figure and her dignified resignation, epitomised multitudes of Persian women of her generation and class: abused virgins, long-suffering wives, deprived mothers and desperate spinsters, all victims of iniquitous laws and antiquated customs based on perverted religiosity, whose beauty and gifts were lost between the Charybdis of emancipation and the Scylla* of traditional securities.

Interpretations

1. You probably agree with Guppy that mothers should not automatically be deprived of their children after a divorce. But should they automatically get custody of children after a divorce? Why or why not? What principle(s) should determine custody?

2. The "lost" daughter went to live with her father and his sisters known as "the Two Old Toads," whom Guppy's grandmother blamed for witchcraft. Why do you suppose the grandmother cursed not the husband but the Two Old Toads? For how much of Batool's "bad luck" do you think the grandmother was responsible? How much was Uncle Alem responsible for? Which of them accepted responsibility?

3. Guppy's word for the dominant force behind the relationships she describes here is "patriarchal." How much of Iranian life and life in other cultures is still dominated by patriarchs? What alternatives to patriarchy exist or could be devised? In what societies can it be found?

4. The last paragraph is a summary of the abuses suffered by Batool (and many other Persian women). How effective is this conclusion? How does each part of the story of Batool support this list of abuses?

5. The last sentence summarizes the two poles between which women's lives move: emancipation and traditional security. Do you think it is always necessary for women to choose between freedom and security?

6. What is the tone of this essay? How do you think this tone relates to Guppy's *purpose* in writing the essay?

Correspondences

1. Review the Euripides' quotation (page 67). Do you agree with him? Apply the quotation to the selection by Guppy.

*"Charybdis"—In Greek mythology, a daughter of Poseidon thrown into the sea by Zeus, where she swallows waves and creates a whirlpool. "Scylla"—A nymph turned into a monster who tempts Odysseus and his sailors in the straits of Messina. In other words, between two equally hazardous alternatives.

2. Compare the views of Dove-Danquah and Guppy on patriarchal marriage. Consider the tone of each.

Applications

1. "The thread of her fortune has been knotted by witchcraft. . . . You see, when fate is adamant, there's nothing anyone can do." What role do witchcraft and fate play in Aunt Batool's relationships? What is Guppy's purpose in including them? What cultural insights did you gain?

2. "The tears women have shed over centuries of tyranny and bullying by men would run in rivers! Is it not time that some justice be introduced?" How does Guppy support this statement of the Shah? To what extent does female bonding ease the burden of patriarchal oppression?

ADDITIONAL WRITING TOPICS

1. "A friend is someone who chooses and is chosen": To what extent do you agree with Mead and Metraux? (What do you expect of a friend? Has your idea of friendship undergone change?) Write a journal entry on friendship that responds to these questions.

2. "I'd like to have a companion. A friend, I guess. But finding a man is not a top priority. I want to travel. I want to establish myself in the community. I don't see any drastic changes in my life by the time I turn thirty. Except that I'll be a property owner."
   What factors might have contributed to the expectations of Weber's twenty-five-year-old interviewee? How does her attitude towards forming a primary relationship compare with yours? How might choosing pragmatically rather than romantically affect the longevity of the relationship?

3. Write an essay discussing whether it is realistic to expect marriage to last a lifetime today. (What expectations do most people have about marriage? What expectations should they have?)

4. Alvarez, Sadat, Kingston, and Guppy focus on family members and their influence. Why are families so important? Write an essay answering this question. Use examples from this chapter and your own experience.

5. Does the observance of customs, rituals, or traditions promote unity and continuity within the family? What rituals has your family shared over the years? How have these contributed to family relationships? Write an essay explaining how the observance of rituals helps preserve the family.

6. Are old friends necessarily one's best friends? Write an essay comparing three of your friendships. Choose friendships of varying lengths. (How important is the duration of each relationship? What factors are most important?)

CHAPTER 3

Education

Human beings show a wonderful capacity to learn and unlearn—if it were not so you would not see such diversity in this and all the other chapters of this book. "The greatest happiness of man as a thinking being," said Goethe, "is to know what is knowable and quietly to revere what is unknowable." "What is knowable" is a vast area, as any college or library catalog can show, and just *how* vast is one more thing man—and woman—would like to know. Everything, then, about our varied fellow human beings, and not just their thinking, should interest us.

Perhaps the three selections in this chapter that most clearly support Goethe's notion of the joy of learning are those by Marshall, Kontor, and Soto. "Poets in the Kitchen" is an essay on the almost unconscious absorption of poetic language. "Dear Diary," by a Russian exchange student, is a comparison of American and Russian students and educational systems. "Summer School" is a reminiscence about a pleasurable fifth-grade summer school without cross-cultural complications.

There is a good deal of complaining about schools in the essays of this chapter. Is a school's curriculum to be regarded as a culture's propaganda machine, and the school's mission to conserve the culture's values in some pure form, pass them along to the next generation, and help immigrants to assimilate? How can goals be achieved? Marshall wishes that Barbadians had an institution like the Jewish *schul* so that assimilation into North American life and language did not strip Barbadians of their own culture. Is it desirable and possible for public schools to perform this mission without robbing students of their natal language and culture? Is it possible to achieve biculturalism, as well as bilingualism? Is it possible to tolerate, even respect, other religions, systems of law, forms of art and languages without losing respect for one's own? Is our idea of culture clear and distinct enough to speak of absolute boundaries between cultures? If we accept the concept of cultural differences, even cultural boundaries, is cultural exclusiveness the goal we want to pursue?

Armando Rendón regrets the way his schooling temporarily robbed him of his Hispanic heritage. The title character of Sophronia Liu's essay is a Chinese boy, a sacrifice, really, to his parents' aspirations-through-schooling. Norman Cousins says that he was miseducated: school taught him to look for differences rather than similarities between people.

Is a person educated who knows only his or her own culture as it is at that moment? Anyone who knows the *history* of his or her own culture expects change. But at what price? By what vehicle? Even to look at our *own* language or art or religion or social institutions a century or two ago is like a trip to another country.

PERSPECTIVES

*During formal education, the child learns that life is for testing.
This state lasts twelve years, a period during which the child learns
that success comes from telling testers what they want to hear.*

Russell Baker

*Education is not a product: mark, diploma, job, money—in that
order: it is a process, a never-ending one.*

Bel Kaufman

*The expression "a liberal education" originally meant one worthy of
freemen. Such is education simply in a true and broad sense. But
education ordinarily so called—the learning of trades and professions
which is designed to enable men to earn their living, or to fit them for
a particular station in life—is servile.*

Henry David Thoreau

*Education! Which of the various me's do you propose to educate, and
which do you propose to suppress?*

D. H. Lawrence

*Knowledge without special capacity to teach is not the same as
knowledge and capacity.*

A Sufi Tale

*A child cannot be taught by anyone who despises him, and a child
cannot afford to be fooled.*

James Baldwin

Education is hanging around until you've caught on.

Robert Frost

*America's a hard school, I know, but hard schools make excellent
graduates.*

Oriana Fallaci

By doubting we are led to enquire: By enquiry we perceive the truth.

Abelard

If the word has the potency to revive and make us free, it has also the power to blind, imprison and destroy.

Ralph Ellison

Applications

1. Write a journal entry comparing these perspectives on education with yours.

2. In a group, discuss Baldwin's implied philosophy of education. Write a brief summary of the discussion.

Spider Grandmother and Masauwu

Hopi Tale as told by
Harold Courlander

"Spider Grandmother and Masauwu" is one of a group of creation and migration stories handed down orally from generation to generation by the Hopi Indians, who now live mainly on a reservation in Arizona.

IN THE BEGINNING THERE WAS ONLY TOKPELLA, Endless Space. Nothing stirred because there were no winds, no shadows fell because there was no light, and all was still. Only Tawa, the Sun Spirit, existed, along with some lesser gods. Tawa contemplated on the universe of space without objects or life, and he regretted that it was so barren. He gathered the elements of Endless Space and put some of his own substance into them, and in this way he created the First World. There were no people then, merely insect-like creatures who lived in a dark cave deep in the earth. For a long while Tawa watched them. He was deeply disappointed. He thought, "What I created is imperfect. These creatures do not understand the meaning of life."

So Tawa called his messenger, Gogyeng Sowuhti, Spider Grandmother, and told her to go down and prepare the living creatures for a change. Spider Grandmother went down. She spoke to the insect creatures, saying, "Tawa, the Sun Spirit who made you, is unhappy because you do not understand the meaning of life. He says: 'The creatures are fighting among themselves. They see but they do not comprehend. Therefore I will change things. I will make a new world, and I will perfect all things that have life in them.' This is the message Tawa asked me to bring. Therefore, prepare to leave this place to enter the Second World." The creatures said, "If that is the way it must be, very well, let us depart from here."

Spider Grandmother led them on their journey, taking them to another great cave that lay far above the first one. The journey was long, and between the time they began and the time they finished, Tawa changed them into other forms of living things. When at last they emerged into the Second World they looked quite different. They were animals that somewhat resembled dogs, coyotes and bears. There was fur on their bodies, their fingers were webbed, and they had tails. They lived on in the Second World and were happy at first. But because they did not have any understanding they grew bitter and warred upon one another, even eating one another. Tawa saw how the creatures of his Second World were living. He saw that they did not grasp the meaning of life. And so again he sent Spider Grandmother to lead them on another journey.

While they travelled, Tawa created the Third World. He made the atmosphere a little lighter and gave them water to moisten their fields. When the creatures followed Spider Grandmother into the Third World they discovered that their bodies had changed again. Their fur, their webbed fingers and their tails had disappeared. Spider Grandmother said to them: "Now you are no longer merely creatures. You are people. Tawa has given you this place so that you may live in harmony and forget all evil. Do not injure one another. Remember that Tawa created you out of Endless Space, and try to understand the meaning of things." Then Spider Grandmother left them.

The people made their villages. They planted corn. They lived on. They were in harmony, and they were grateful to the Sun Spirit who had created them and given them a new world to live in. Yet things were not perfect. There was a chill in the air, and the light was only a grayness. Spider Grandmother came and taught people how to weave blankets and cloth to keep their bodies warm. She taught the women how to make pots out of clay so that they could store water and food. But the pots could not be baked and they broke easily. And the corn did not grow very well because warmth was lacking.

Then one day a hummingbird came to where some people were working in their fields. The people asked, "Why are you here?"

The hummingbird answered, "I have been sent by my master."

They said, "Who is your master?"

The bird replied, "He is Masauwu, Ruler of the Upper World, Caretaker of the Place of the Dead and the Owner of Fire. He has observed how you live here, and he says, 'The crops do not grow well because the people do not have warmth.' "

The people said, "Yes, it is true. Warmth is lacking."

The hummingbird said, "I have been sent to teach you the secret of warmth." And he gave them the secret, showing them how to create fire with a fire drill. After that he departed.

Now that the people had the knowledge of fire, they gathered grass and wood and made fires around their fields, and the warmth made their corn grow. But once they became careless and the fire spread to a nearby house and consumed it, including everything that was inside. When the ashes were cool the people found that their clay pots had become hard and did not break so easily. Thus they learned the secret of baking pottery. From this time on the people began to cook their meat instead of eating it raw. Those who had received the secret of fire from Masauwu's messenger became known as the Firewood or Fire People. They said, "Masauwu is our relative." Now things were better in the Third World.

It was the powakas, or sorcerers, who brought disruption and conflict among the people. They made medicine to injure those whom they envied or disliked. Worse yet, they turned the people's minds away from virtuous things. The younger people grew disrespectful of the older. Husbands sought other women, and wives sought other men. Instead of caring for their fields, men spent their time in the kivas gambling. And instead of grinding corn, women went into the kivas to join the men. Children wandered about unclean and uncared for, and babies cried for milk. What a man wanted he would take from another instead of fashioning it for himself. Dissension spread everywhere. Instead of seeking to understand the meaning of life, many began to believe that they had created themselves.

In the beginning, life in the Third World had been good. But because people succumbed to the evil unleashed by the powakas, things began to change. The cornstalks in the fields withered before the ears were formed. The flowing rivers moved more sluggishly and the springs dried up. Clouds drifted over the fields but did not release their rain. Squash and melon vines stopped growing, and sickness came into many houses.

Now, those who had not forgotten that Tawa was their father worried greatly about the way things were going. Night after night they met in the kivas to discuss the corruption that was spreading in the Third World. They encouraged the lazy to work, admonished women for their promiscuous ways, threatened the powakas with punishment and sought to create order, yet nothing changed. There was evil and chaos all around them.

Tawa saw what was happening to the world he had made. He called Gogyeng Sowuhti, Spider Grandmother, and sent her to the people with a message. Spider Grandmother went down. She entered a kiva where the people were gathered. She said: "Tawa, the Sun Spirit, is displeased with what he has created. The powakas have made you forget what you should have remembered. Therefore all people of good heart should go away from this place and leave the evil ones behind."

The people said to one another, "Where can we go? Is there another place?" But they did not know of another place anywhere, and they were troubled.

Then an old man said, "Have we not heard footsteps in the sky, as though someone is walking there?"

And other old men replied, "Yes, there has been someone walking above us up there. We have heard it many times when the air was still."

Other people said, "Let us discover what is there. Let us send a messenger to investigate things."

So the chiefs called for the medicine men to sit with them and consider things. They filled a pipe with tobacco and lighted it. They smoked, passing the pipe from one to another until their minds were tranquil. Then one of the chiefs said, "We must send someone to the place above the sky to see what it is like. If it is good, our messenger will request permission for us to come there. But who can make such a difficult journey?"

The medicine men pondered, and after a while one of them said, "We shall create a messenger who can perform this task." The medicine men gathered some clay and shaped a bird out of it. They placed a kwatskiavu cloth, which is the robe made for brides, on the ground and placed the clay bird on it. They covered the clay bird with an ova cloth. They sat in a circle holding the edges of the upper cloth, singing and moving it gently up and down. They placed their hands underneath, doing what no one could see. When at last they removed the cloth there was a living swallow sitting there.

The swallow asked, "Why have you called me?"

The chiefs answered, "We have called you so that you may go up to discover whether there is another world above the sky. If you find someone living in that place, ask if we may come there and begin our lives again."

The swallow flew up. He circled higher and higher, until the people could no longer see him. His strength began to flow away, but still he went upward. At last he saw an opening in the sky. But he was too tired to go on, and he returned to the place where the chiefs and the medicine men were waiting. He fluttered weakly and settled on the ground. He said, "I went up. I found an opening in the sky. It was as though I were looking up through the entrance of a kiva. But my strength failed and so I had to return."

The medicine men decided to make a stronger bird. They began again, fashioning a figure out of clay and covering it with the cloth. They sang and made medicine, and this time when they removed the cloth a white dove sat there. The chiefs said, "How can the dove do what the swallow could not do?"

The medicine men answered, "It has great strength. Let it try."

The white dove spoke, saying, "Why am I here?"

The chiefs said, "We have called you to go above us to see what kind of a world is up there. Pass through the opening in the sky and tell us what lies beyond. If anyone inhabits that place, ask if we may come to find new homes for ourselves."

The dove went up and passed through the opening. He saw a vast land, but no living things, and he returned. He said, "It is true that there is an opening in the sky, and on the other side is a land that spreads in all directions, but I saw nothing that was alive."

The chiefs and the medicine men discussed the matter, recalling the sounds of footsteps in the sky. They said, "Surely someone lives in that place. We must know who he is."

Once more the medicine men fashioned a bird out of clay and brought it to life under the ova cloth. This time it was a hawk. The hawk also went up through the sky and explored the land above, but he returned without discovering what the people wanted to know.

The medicine men tried again, and this time they created a catbird. When the catbird asked, "Why am I here?" the chiefs replied, "You have been called because the swallow and the dove and the hawk have not been able to discover who it is that walks in the land above us. You, catbird, go up, discover who makes the sound of walking up there. Speak to him. Tell him the people of good heart wish to leave this place. Ask for his permission to enter his land. Go and return. Let us know how things are."

So the catbird flew up and passed through the opening in the sky. He passed the place where the hawk had turned back. He went on. He came to a place of sand and mesas. He saw large fires burning alongside gardens of squash, melons and corn. Beyond the gardens was a single house made of stone. A person was sitting there, his head down, sleeping. The catbird alighted nearby and waited. The person awoke and raised his head. His eyes were sunken in deeply, there was no hair on his head, and his face was seared by burns and encrusted with dried blood. Across the bridge of his nose and his cheekbones two black lines were painted. Around his neck were two heavy necklaces, one made of four strands of turquoise, the other of bones. The catbird recognized him. He was Masauwu, Spirit of Death, the Owner of Fire and Master of the Upper World, assigned to this place by Tawa because he had no other place for him.

Masauwu looked at the catbird, saying, "You, why are you here?"

The catbird said, "I was sent from down below to see whose footsteps are heard in the sky."

Masauwu said, "Yes, now you know that the footsteps are mine. Are you not afraid?"

"No," the catbird answered, "for I am only a bird fashioned out of clay just recently. I don't know enough yet to fear anything. I came because the Lower World is infested with evil, and there are many good people who would like to come here to live. Down below, the rain does not fall, the springs do not flow, the corn dries up in the fields, and there are numerous persons who do not respect the virtues of life. The people of good heart ask your permission to enter the Upper World and build their villages here."

Masauwu said, "You see how it is in this place. There is no light, only a grayness here. There is no warmth, and I must build fires to make my crops grow. But there is land and water. If the people wish to come, let them come."

The catbird left Masauwu and returned to the opening through which he had passed. He went down to where the chiefs and the medicine men were waiting. They asked him, "Did you arrive there and find the one who walks in the sky?"

The catbird answered, "Yes, I found the person who lives there. He is Masauwu, Spirit of Death, Owner of Fire and Master of the Upper World. His face is terrifying to see. But I spoke with him. He said: 'You see how it is. There is no light here and no warmth. But there is plenty of land and water, so if the people want to come, let them come.' "

Hearing this, the chief of the Fire People spoke. He said, "Masauwu is our spirit. We are the ones to whom he sent the secret of fire. He is our relative. Therefore we are willing to go." Others said, "Yes, let all of us who wish to escape from evil go there. The Fire People can lead us and speak for us to Masauwu. Let us prepare for the journey."

It was agreed, then, but the chiefs and medicine men looked upward, saying, "How shall we ever reach the sipapuni, the doorway in the sky?"

While they were thinking about this problem, Gogyeng Sowuhti, Spider Grandmother, appeared in the plaza with her young grandsons, the warrior gods Pokanghoya and Polongahoya. She said, "We are here. We will help you pass through the sipapuni." She sent the young warrior gods to find chipmunk, the planter. Soon they returned bringing the chipmunk with them. Spider Grandmother said to the chipmunk, "It is you who have been chosen to make a path for the people into the sky. For this you will always be remembered." And she explained what had to be done.

The chipmunk planted a sunflower seed in the center of the plaza. By the power of singing the people made it grow. If they stopped to catch their breath, the sunflower stopped growing, and Spider Grandmother called out, "Sing! Sing!" As soon as they started to sing again, the sunflower continued growing. In time the sunflower stalk reached toward the sky, but just as it was about to pass through the sipapuni it bent over from the weight of its blossom.

Spider Grandmother said, "Let us try again." This time the chipmunk planted a spruce seed and gave the people a song to sing. They sang the spruce tree into the sky, but when it had finished growing it was not tall enough. So now the chipmunk planted a pine seed, and by the power of singing they made it grow tall. But the pine, also, failed to reach the sipapuni. Once more the chipmunk planted. This time it was a bamboo. The people sang hard and made the bamboo grow straight and tall. Each time they stopped to catch their breath the growing stopped and a joint formed on the bamboo stalk. And when they resumed singing the bamboo grew again. Spider Grandmother went back and forth exhorting the people to sing the bamboo into the sky. Thus it went on. The people began to fear that they did not have breath enough to do what was required of them. But finally Spider Grandmother called out, "It is done! The bamboo has passed through the sipapuni!"

The road to the Upper World was finished, and the people rested. Spider Grandmother spoke, telling of things to come. She said: "The journey will be long and difficult. When we reach the Upper World, that will be only a beginning. Things there are not like things here. You will discover new ways of doing things. During the journey you must try to discover the meaning of life and learn to distinguish good from evil. Tawa did not intend for you to live in the midst of chaos and dissension. Only those of good heart may depart from the Third World. The powakas and all who perform wicked deeds must stay behind. As we go up the bamboo to the Upper World, see that no one carries evil medicine in his belt. See that no powakas go with us. Leave your pots and grinding stones behind. Up above you will make more of these things. Carry nothing that has to be held in your hands, for you will need your hands for climbing. When we have arrived in the Upper World I will tell you more about what is expected of you. Meanwhile, remember this: In the Upper World you must learn to be true humans." Then Spider Grandmother sent the people home to prepare for the journey, which would begin in four days.

The people prepared, and on the fourth day they gathered at the foot of the bamboo. The chiefs stood in front—the village chief, the crier chief, the singer chief and the war chief. Behind them the people stood waiting for the journey to begin. Spider Grandmother arrived with the boy warrior gods, Pokanghoya and Polongahoya. Pokanghoya, the elder, carried lightning arrows in his right hand and a thunderboard in his left. Polongahoya, the younger, carried a buckskin ball in his left hand, and in his right hand he held a nahoydadatsia playing stick. Spider Grandmother went up the bamboo first, followed by the boy warrior gods. The people moved toward the bamboo to begin their climb. But now the chief of the Fire People protested, saying, "Wait. We are the ones who are entitled to go first, for Masauwu is our special benefactor. We shall take the lead." The others deferred to the Fire People. After the Fire People began their ascent, whoever could get to the bamboo took his turn. The mockingbird fluttered around the bamboo, calling out, "Pashumayani! Pashumayani! Be careful! Be careful!" This is the way the people departed from the Lower World. They moved slowly upward, and in time the entire bamboo stalk was covered with human bodies.

As the first climbers emerged through the sipapuni and stepped into the Upper World, Yawpa the mockingbird stood at Spider Grandmother's side and sorted them out. "You shall be a Hopi and speak the Hopi language," he said to one. "You shall be a Navajo and speak the Navajo language," he said to another. "You shall be an Apache and speak the Apache language," he said to a third. He assigned every person to a tribe and a language, and to each tribe he gave a direction to go in its migrations. He named the Paiutes, the Zunis, the Supais, the Pimas, the Utes, the Comanches, the Sioux, and the White Men. The people began to make camp near the sipapuni. There were a great many of them. The chiefs discussed things and said, "Surely all the people of good heart have now arrived." But more were still coming up. The chiefs said, "All those who chose to depart from evil are here. Therefore, let no more come through the sipapuni." The village chief went to the opening and called down, "You who are still climbing, turn and go back. It is because of you that we chose to leave and come to the Upper World. Do not follow us. You are not wanted here."

But the climbers persisted, saying that they also wanted to be in the Upper World. So the warrior gods, Pokanghoya and Polongahoya, grasped the bamboo stalk and pulled its roots from the ground. They shook it and all those clinging to it fell back into the Lower World like seeds falling from ripe grass. The chiefs said, "Now we are secure from the evil ones. Let us make camp." The people camped near the sipapuni and rested.

Pokanghoya and Polongahoya looked around at the vast Upper World. Pokanghoya said, "Everything has a sameness. Something needs to be done." Polongahoya answered, "Yes, see how it is out there. The ground is soft. It is nothing but mud." So they took their buckskin ball and their playing sticks and began to play nahoydadatsia, following the ball wherever it went, running all the time. Wherever their feet touched the soft earth it became hard. They gathered the mud into great mounds and turned them into mountains. Wherever they passed, grass and trees came into being. They raced far to the north, and in an instant they created Tokonave, meaning Black Mountain, which in later times the White Men called Navajo Mountain. From there they ran far to the south, chasing their ball all the while, and created Neuvatikyao, which the White Men later named San Francisco Peaks. They went eastward then, making hills, mountains and mesas everywhere. They arrived at Muyovi, which the White Men came to call the Rio Grande, and near where the Zunis now live they created salt beds, and they also made salt beds at other places. When at last they had done enough things of this kind they returned to the sipapuni.

Spider Grandmother asked them, "Where have you boys been?"

They said, "We have been playing. We have made the Upper World good to look at. See what we have done."

But the light in the Upper World was a grayness and it was not possible to see very far, so what they had done was not clearly visible.

Pokanghoya said, "We need light in this place."

Polongahoya said, "Yes, and we need warmth also."

Spider Grandmother agreed, saying "It is true, light and warmth are needed."

She assembled the chiefs and the medicine men. She said, "Let us do something now to bring light and warmth to this place." She told the people what to do. They brought out many things that they had carried from the Lower World. They took a piece of buckskin and cut it in the shape of a disk, which they then fastened over a large wooden ring. They painted it with white clay and speckled it with black. When they were finished, they laid the buckskin disk on a kwatskiavu cloth and sang, as Spider Grandmother instructed them. Four chiefs took hold of the kwatskiavu cloth at the corners, and with a fast movement they lifted it and sent the disk soaring into the sky. By the power of singing they kept it moving upward until it disappeared from sight. But after a while they saw a light on the eastern horizon, and the buckskin disk rose from beyond the edge of things and moved slowly overhead.

Now the people could see a little better, but it was not yet light enough, and the earth still was not warm enough to grow corn. Spider Grandmother said, "Let us try again." They made another disk in the same way, but it was larger, and this time they painted it with egg yolks and sprinkled it with golden-colored pollen. They painted a face on the golden disk in black and red, and all around its edges they fastened corn silk. They attached an abalone shell to the forehead, and their work was finished. As before, the disk was placed on the kwatskiavu cloth. Four strong men grasped the corners, and with a quick lifting motion they sent the disk sailing into the sky. The people sang the disk upward until it disappeared. But after a while there was a bright glow on the horizon in the east, and a moment later the disk appeared there, shining brightly and making the whole land visible. Now the people could see the mountains and the other things created by the boy warrior gods. The disk also cast warmth on the earth. The people were glad, for now they had a moon and a sun.

Interpretations

1. What does Gogyeng Sowuhti (Spider Grandmother) teach the first people? How does she show her commitment to and concern for these people? (What practical value do her teachings have? What parallels of her exist in other mythologies?)

2. Another teaching god, Masauwu, reveals the secret of fire. How did the people learn more about the Third World through their misuse of fire? Of what non-Hopi god(s) is Masauwu reminiscent?

3. In this myth, lack of understanding or comprehension is criticized. What is the result of this lack for the first people? What is its remedy?

4. Gogyeng Sowuhti is the intermediary or surrogate for Tawa, the Sun Spirit. What is the releationship between Tawa and Spider Grandmother? What is Tawa's nature? What does he expect of people? What kind of ethic would you expect his worshippers to teach?

Correspondences

1. Review the two creation stories in Chapter 1. How are their perspectives on creation similar to or different from that of the Hopi myth?

2. Review the Abelard quotation on education (page 152). What role does enquiry play in the Hopi myth? What do people learn from Spider Woman and Masauwu?

Applications

1. What is the difference between memorizing something and understanding it? To what extent has your education tested your memory and your ability

to understand? (What have you learned from multiple-choice questions? from essay questions?) Compare your responses with those of your group and write an analysis of your conclusions.

2. Consult a research source on Spider Woman. What does she suggest about the role of women in Hopi culture?

Kiss of Death

Armando Rendón

Armando Rendón (b. 1939) was raised in San Antonio, Texas, and is currently vice-president of ATM Systems, a Chicago counseling firm. He has written a film script, El Chicano in Washington, *and* Chicano Manifesto *(1971). He is a regular contributor to* Civil Rights Digest *and* The Washington Post. *In "Kiss of Death," Rendón presents his views on the importance of ethnic identity.*

For more information on Mexico, see Gary Soto, "Looking for Work," Chapter 4.

I NEARLY FELL VICTIM to the Anglo. My childhood was spent in the West Side barrio of San Antonio. I lived in my grandmother's house on Ruiz Street just below Zarzamora Creek. I did well in the elementary grades and learned English quickly.

Spanish was off-limits in school anyway, and teachers and relatives taught me early that my mother tongue would be of no help in making good grades and becoming a success. Yet Spanish was the language I used in playing and arguing with friends. Spanish was the language I spoke with my *abuelita,* my dear grandmother, as I ate *atole* on those cold mornings when I used to wake at dawn to her clattering dishes in the tiny kitchen; or when I would cringe in mock horror at old folk tales she would tell me late at night.

But the lesson took effect anyway. When, at the age of ten, I went with my mother to California, to the San Francisco Bay Area where she found work during the war years, I had my first real opportunity to strip myself completely of my heritage. In California the schools I attended were all Anglo except for this little mexicanito. At least, I never knew anyone who admitted he was Mexican and I certainly never thought to ask. When my name was accented incorrectly, Réndon instead of Rendón, that was all right; finally I must have gotten tired of correcting people or just didn't bother.

I remember a summertime visit home a few years after living on the West Coast. At an evening gathering of almost the whole family—uncles, aunts, nephews, nieces, my *abuelita*—we sat outdoors through the dusk until the dark had fully settled. Then the lights were turned on; someone brought out a Mexican card game, the Lotería El Diablito, similar to bingo. But instead of rows of numbers on a pasteboard, there were figures of persons, animals, and objects on cards corresponding to figures set in rows on a pasteboard. We used frijoles (pinto beans) to mark each figure on our card as the leader went through the deck one by one. The word for tree was called: *Arbol!* It completed a row; I had won. Then to check my card I had to name each figure again. When I said the word for tree, it didn't come at all as I wanted it to; AR-BOWL with the accent on the last syllable and sounding like an Anglo tourist. There was some all-around kidding of me and good-natured laughter over the incident, and it passed.

But if I had not been speaking much Spanish up until then, I spoke even less afterward. Even when my mother, who speaks both Spanish and English fluently, spoke to me in Spanish, I would respond in English. By the time I graduated from high school and prepared to enter college, the break was nearly complete. Seldom during college did I admit to being a Mexican-American. Only when Latin American students pressed me about my surname did I admit my Spanish descent, or when it proved an asset in meeting coeds from Latin American countries.

My ancestry had become a shadow, fainter and fainter about me. I felt no particular allegiance to it, drew no inspiration from it, and elected generally to let it fade away. I clicked with the Anglo mind-set in college, mastered it, you might say. I even became editor of the campus biweekly newspaper as a junior, and editor of the literary magazine as a senior—not bad, now that I look back, for a tortillas-and-beans Chicano upbringing to beat the Anglo at his own game.

The point of my "success," of course, was that I had been assimilated; I had bought the white man's world. After getting my diploma I was set to launch out into a career in newspaper reporting and writing. There was no thought in my mind of serving my people, telling their story, or making anything right for anybody but myself. Instead I had dreams of Pulitzer Prizes, syndicated columns, foreign correspondent assignments, front-page stories—that was for me. Then something happened.

A Catholic weekly newspaper in Sacramento offered me a position as a reporter and feature writer. I had a job on a Bay Area daily as a copyboy at the time, with the opportunity to become a reporter. But I'd just been married, and there were a number of other reasons to consider: there'd be a variety of assignments, Sacramento was the state capital, it was a good town in which to raise a family, and the other job lacked promise for upward mobility. I decided to take the offer.

My wife and I moved to Sacramento in the fall of 1961, and in a few weeks the radicalization of this Chicano began. It wasn't a book I read or a great leader awakening me, for we had no Chávezes or Tijerinas or Gonzálezes at the time; and it was no revelation from above. It was my own people who rescued me. There is a large Chicano population in Sacramento, today one of the most activist in northern California, but at the time factionalized and still dependent on the social and church organizations for identity. But together we found each other.

My job soon brought me into contact with many Chicanos as well as with the recently immigrated Mexicans, located in the barrios that Sacramento had allocated to the "Mexicans." I found my people striving to survive in an alien environment among foreign people. One of the stories I covered concerned a phenomenon called Cursillos de Cristiandad (Little Courses in Christianity), intense, three-day group-sensitivity sessions whose chief objective is the re-Christianization of Catholics. To cover the story properly I talked my editor into letting me make a Cursillo.

Not only was much revealed to me about the phony gilt lining of religion which I had grown up believing was the Church, but there was an added and highly significant side effect—cultural shock! I rediscovered my own people, or perhaps they redeemed me. Within the social dimension of the Cursillo, for the first time in many years I became reimmersed in a tough, *macho ambiente* (an entirely Mexican male environment). Only Spanish was spoken. The effect was shattering. It was as if my tongue, after being struck dumb as a child, had been loosened.

Because we were located in cramped quarters, with limited facilities, and the cooks, lecturers, priests, and participants were men only, the old sense of *machismo* and *camarada* was revived and given new perspective. I was cast in a spiritual setting which was a perfect background for reviving my Chicano soul. Reborn but imperfectly, I still had a lot to learn about myself and my people. But my understanding deepened and renewed itself as the years went by. I visited bracero camps with teams of Chicanos; sometimes with priests taking the sacraments; sometimes only Chicanos, offering advice or assistance with' badly needed food and clothing, distributed through a bingo-game technique; and on occasion, music for group singing provided by a phonograph or a guitar. Then there were barrio organization work; migrant worker programs; a rural self-help community development project; and confrontation with antipoverty agencies, with the churches, with government officials, and with cautious Chicanos, too.

In a little San Francisco magazine called *Way,* I wrote in a March 1966 article discussing "The Other Mexican-American":

> The Mexican-American must answer at the same time: Who am I? and Who are we? This is to pose then, not merely a dilemma of self-identity; but of self-in-group-identity. . . . Perhaps the answer to developing a total Mexican-American concept must be left in the hands of the artist, the painter, the writer, and the poet, who can abstract the essence of what it is to be Mexican in America. . . . When that understanding comes . . . the Mexican-American will not only have acculturized himself, but he will have acculturized America to him.

If anyone knew what he was talking about when he spoke of the dilemma of who he was and where he belonged, it was this Chicano. I very nearly dropped out, as so many other Mexican-Americans have, under the dragging pressure to be someone else, what most of society wants you to be before it hands out its chrome-plated trophies.

And that mystique—I didn't quite have it at the time, or the right word for it. But no one did until just the last few years when so many of us stopped trying to be someone else and decided that what we want to be and to be called is Chicano.

I owe my life to my Chicano people. They rescued me from the Anglo kiss of death, the monolingual, monocultural, and colorless Gringo society. I no longer face a dilemma of identity or direction. That identity and direction have been charted for me by the Chicano—but to think I came that close to being sucked into the vacuum of the dominant society.

Interpretations

1. How does Rendón now regard his formal education? Do you think school would still have this effect today?

2. What did Rendón feel he still had to learn about his people? What evidence do you see in this essay that Rendón now has a clear understanding of Chicano culture?

3. What does the phrase "Anglo kiss of death" mean to Rendón? Do you think being Chicano means more to Rendón than ancestry, family, education, or culture? If so, what else does it mean?

4. "Monolingual, monocultural, and colorless" are three criticisms of Anglo society. How valid are these criticisms? Instead of becoming bicultural himself, Rendón says he rejected one culture and embraced another as if his life depended on it. Do you think he made the right choice? Why did he have to choose?

5. Do you think it desirable or even possible to value cultures other than your own as much as your own? Why or why not?

6. What is the tone of this essay? Is it constructively or destructively critical? objective or subjective? Has Rendón chosen the best tone to appeal to his (obviously English-speaking) audience? Why or why not?

Correspondences

1. Review the D. H. Lawrence quotation on education (page 151). To what extent does it apply to Rendón's experience as a Mexican-American student in the San Francisco school system?

2. Rendón rediscovers his ethnic identity when he "became reimmersed in a tough, *macho ambiente* (an entirely Mexican male environment)." What new perspectives does he gain? How does his experience with a patriarchal culture compare with those of Kingston and Guppy (Chapter 2)?

Applications

1. Rendón states, "The Mexican-American must answer at the same time: Who am I? and Who are we? This is to pose, then, not merely a dilemma of self-identity, but of self-in-group identity." In an essay, explore this concept further. Focus on both self- and self-in-group identity in equal detail.

2. To what degree should a teacher of students from multicultural backgrounds assume responsibility for making them aware of their cultures? How might a teacher try to accomplish this? Read two or three sources on this subject and prepare a presentation for your English or speech class.

Confessions of a Miseducated Man

Norman Cousins

Norman Cousins was born (1912) in New York City. After his graduation from Teachers College of Columbia University he began his career in journalism. In 1940 he became editor of Saturday Review, *and for the next 29 years he wrote on a wide range of cultural and educational issues. In 1979 he published* Anatomy of an Illness, *an account of his struggle against a degenerative disease, followed by* Human Options: An Autobiographical Notebook *(1981), and* The Healing Heart: Antidotes to Panic and Helplessness *(1983). In* Confessions of a Miseducated Man, *which appeared as an editorial on May 10, 1952, Cousins evaluates his educational experiences.*

THESE NOTES are in the nature of a confession. It is the confession of a miseducated man.

I have become most aware of my lack of a proper education whenever I have had the chance to put it to the test. The test is a simple one: am I prepared to live in and comprehend a world in which there are 3 billion people? Not the world as it was in 1850 or 1900, for which my education might have been adequate, but the world today. And the best place to apply that test is outside the country—especially Asia or Africa.

Not that my education was a complete failure. It prepared me superbly for a bird's-eye view of the world. It taught me how to recognize easily and instantly the things that differentiate one place or one people from another. Geography had instructed me in differences of terrain, resources, and productivity. Comparative culture had instructed me in the differences of background and group interests. Anthropology had instructed me in the differences of facial bone structure, skin pigmentation, and general physical aspect. In short, my education protected me against surprise. I was not surprised at the fact that some people lived in mud huts and others in bamboo cottages on stilts; or that some used peat for fuel and others dung; or that some enjoyed music with a five-note scale and others with twelve; or that some people were vegetarian by religion and others by preference.

In those respects my education had been more than adequate. But what my education failed to do was to teach me that the principal significance of such differences was that they were largely without significance. The differences were all but obliterated by the similarities. My education had bypassed the similarities. It had failed to grasp and define the fact that beyond the differences are realities scarcely comprehended because of their shattering simplicity. And the simplest reality of all was that the human community was one—greater than any of its parts, greater than the separateness imposed by the nations, greater than the divergent faiths and allegiances or the depth and color of varying cultures. This larger unity was the most important central fact of our time—something on which people could build at a time when hope seemed misty, almost unreal.

As I write this, I have the feeling that my words fail to give vitality to the idea they seek to express. Indeed, the idea itself is a truism which all peoples readily acknowledge even if they do not act on it. Let me put it differently, then. In order to be at home anywhere in the world I had to forget the things I had been taught to remember. It turned out that my ability to get along with other peoples depended not so much upon my comprehension of the uniqueness of their way of life as upon my comprehension of the things we had in common. It was important to respect these differences, certainly, but to stop there was like clearing the ground without any idea of what was to be built on it. When you got through comparing notes, you discovered that you were both talking about the same neighborhood, i.e., this planet, and the conditions that made it congenial or hostile to human habitation.

Only a few years ago an education in differences fulfilled a specific if limited need. That was at a time when we thought of other places and peoples largely out of curiosity or in terms of exotic vacations. It was the mark of a rounded man to be well traveled and to know about the fabulous variations of human culture and behavior. But it wasn't the type of knowledge you had to live by and build on.

Then overnight came the great compression. Far-flung areas which had been secure in their remoteness suddenly became jammed together in a single arena. And all at once a new type of education became necessary, an education in liberation from tribalism. For tribalism had persisted from earliest times, though it had taken refined forms. The new education had to teach man the most difficult lesson of all: to look at someone anywhere in the world and be able to recognize the image of himself. It had to be an education in self-recognition. The old emphasis upon superficial differences had to give way to education for mutuality and for citizenship in the human community.

In such an education we begin with the fact that the universe itself does not hold life cheaply. Life is a rare occurrence among the millions of galaxies and solar systems that occupy space. And in this particular solar system life occurs on only one planet. And on that one planet life takes millions of forms. Of all these countless forms of life, only one, the human species, possesses certain faculties in combination that give it supreme advantages over all the others. Among those faculties or gifts is a creative intelligence that enables man to reflect and anticipate, to encompass past experience, and also to visualize future needs. There are endless other wondrous faculties the mechanisms of which are not yet within the understanding of their beneficiaries—the faculties of hope, conscience, appreciation of beauty, kinship, love, faith.

Viewed in planetary perspective, what counts is not that the thoughts of men lead them in different directions but that all men possess the capacity to think; not that they pursue different faiths but that they are capable of spiritual belief; not that they write and read different books but that they are capable of creating print and communicating in it across time and space; not that they enjoy different art and music but that something in them enables them to respond deeply to forms and colors and ordered vibrations of sounds.

These basic lessons, then, would seek to provide a proper respect for man in the universe. Next in order would be instruction in the unity of man's needs. However friendly the universe may be to man, it has left the conditions of human existence precariously balanced. All men need oxygen, water, land, warmth, food. Remove any one of these and the unity of human needs is attacked and man with it. The next lesson would concern the human situation itself—how to use self-understanding in the cause of human welfare; how to control the engines created by man that threaten to alter the precarious balance on which life depends; how to create a peaceful society of the whole.

With such an education, it is possible that some nation or people may come forward not only with vital understanding but with the vital inspiration that men need no less than food. Leadership on this higher level does not require mountains of gold or thundering propaganda. It is concerned with human destiny; human destiny is the issue; people will respond.

Interpretations

1. Cousins never says that we should be *un*aware of (or disrespectful of) differences between cultures and/or peoples, but that awareness of differences is only a first step. Do you agree? What is "miseducation"? Do you think the process of education necessarily increases awareness of differences in people and things? Support your answer with examples.

2. Look at several of the examples of diversity in the third paragraph. Do you agree that "such differences [are] largely without significance"? Why or why not? (How important is the word "largely" here?)

3. Cousins seems glad that his education at least "protected [him] against surprise." Do you agree that such protection is a valuable function of education? Is it a side function or a main goal? (What does Cousins mean by "surprise"? How is it a handicap?)

4. What changed Cousins's mind about his education?

5. Some academic subjects or disciplines emphasize similarities between people while others emphasize differences. Which subjects fall into which group?

6. How effective a title is "Confessions of a Miseducated Man"?

Correspondences

1. Cousins states that his formal education highlighted differences among cultures, whereas Rendón feels that his education whitewashed differences and emphasized similarities. What factors led to these opposite conclusions? (Should an education focus only on what people have in common and ignore their differences? Do you feel as they do that you have been "miseducated"? If so, how?)

2. While Cousins argues that the goal of education should be "to create a peaceful society of the whole," Rendón supports stressing ethnic identification. Is it possible to be assimilated yet preserve ethnic identification? Why or why not?

Applications

1. "The old emphasis upon superficial differences had to give way to education for mutuality and for citizenship in the human community." Write an essay agreeing with Cousin's point of view; assume an unsympathetic audience.

2. Prepare a presentation on "The Advantages or Disadvantages of Assimilation." Since your aim is to persuade, pay particular attention to audience and tone.

from Poets in the Kitchen

Paule Marshall

Paule Marshall was born (1929) in Brooklyn, New York, of West Indian (Barbadian) parents. She received her bachelor's degree from Brooklyn College and in 1959 she published her first novel Brown Girl, Brownstones. *In 1961 she published* Soul Clap Hands and Sing *and in 1969* The Chosen Place, the Timeless People, *a symbolic novel about the refusal of inhabitants of a small, underdeveloped Caribbean country to accept modernization. Her most recent novel is* Praisesong for the Widow *(1983). Marshall defines her work as an attempt "to trace history, because as a people we have not as yet really engaged our past." To what extent does she explore that past in "Poets in the Kitchen"?*

The history of Barbados, the most easterly of the West Indies, begins with the arrival of an English ship in 1605 and with British settlers at the uninhabited island in 1627. Slavery was abolished in 1834. The island, eighty percent of whose population of 256,000 is of African descent, declared its independence from Britain in 1966 but remains within the Commonwealth.

SOME YEARS AGO, when I was teaching a graduate seminar in fiction at Columbia University, a well-known male novelist visited my class to speak on his development as a writer. In discussing his formative years, he didn't realize it but he seriously endangered his life by remarking that women writers are luckier than those of his sex because they usually spend so much time as children around their mothers and their mothers' friends in the kitchen.

What did he say that for? The women students immediately forgot about being in awe of him and began readying their attack for the question and answer period later on. Even I bristled. There again was that awful image of women locked away from the world in the kitchen with only each other to talk to, and their daughters locked in with them.

But my guest wasn't really being sexist or trying to be provocative or even spoiling for a fight. What he meant—when he got around to examining himself more fully—was that, given the way children are (or were) raised in our society, with little girls kept closer to home and their mothers, the woman writer stands a better chance of being exposed, while growing up, to the kind of talk that goes on among women, more often than not in the kitchen; and that this experience gives her an edge over her male counterpart by instilling in her an appreciation for ordinary speech.

It was clear that my guest lecturer attached great importance to this, which is understandable. Common speech and the plain, workaday words that make it up are, after all, the stock in trade of some of the best fiction writers. They are the principal means by which a character in a novel or story reveals himself and gives voice sometimes to profound feelings and complex ideas about himself and the world. Perhaps the proper measure of a writer's talent is his skill in rendering everyday speech—when it is appropriate to his story—as well as his ability to tap, to exploit, the beauty, poetry and wisdom it often contains.

"If you say what's on your mind in the language that comes to you from your parents and your street and friends you'll probably say something beautiful." Grace Paley[1] tells this, she says, to her students at the beginning of every writing course.

It's all a matter of exposure and a training of the ear for the would-be writer in those early years of his or her apprenticeship. And, according to my guest lecturer, this training, the best of it, often takes place in as unglamorous a setting as the kitchen.

He didn't know it, but he was essentially describing my experience as a little girl. I grew up among poets. Now they didn't look like poets— whatever that breed is supposed to look like. Nothing about them suggested that poetry was their calling. They were just a group of ordinary housewives and mothers, my mother included, who dressed in a way (shapeless housedresses, dowdy felt hats and long, dark, solemn coats) that made it impossible for me to imagine they had ever been young.

Nor did they do what poets were supposed to do—spend their days in an attic room writing verses. They never put pen to paper except to write occasionally to their relatives in Barbados. "I take my pen in hand hoping these few lines will find you in health as they leave me fair for the time being," was the way their letters invariably began. Rather, their day was spent "scrubbing floor," as they described the work they did.

Several mornings a week these unknown bards would put an apron and a pair of old house shoes in a shopping bag and take the train or streetcar from our section of Brooklyn out to Flatbush. There, those who didn't have steady jobs would wait on certain designated corners for the white housewives in the neighborhood to come along and bargain with them over pay for a day's work cleaning their houses. This was the ritual even in the winter.

Later, armed with the few dollars they had earned, which in their vocabulary became "a few raw-mouth pennies," they made their way back to our neighborhood, where they would sometimes stop off to have a cup of tea or cocoa together before going home to cook dinner for their husbands and children.

The basement kitchen of the brownstone house where my family lived was the usual gathering place. Once inside the warm safety of its walls the women threw off the drab coats and hats, seated themselves at the large center table, drank their cups of tea or cocoa, and talked. While my sister

[1]Contemporary American fiction writer.

and I sat at a smaller table over in a corner doing our homework, they talked—endlessly, passionately, poetically, and with impressive range. No subject was beyond them. True, they would indulge in the usual gossip: whose husband was running with whom, whose daughter looked slightly "in the way" (pregnant) under her bridal gown as she walked down the aisle. That sort of thing. But they also tackled the great issues of the time. They were always, for example, discussing the state of the economy. It was the mid and late 30s then, and the aftershock of the Depression, with its soup lines and suicides on Wall Street, was still being felt.

Some people, they declared, didn't know how to deal with adversity. They didn't know that you had to "tie up your belly" (hold in the pain, that is) when things got rough and go on with life. They took their image from the bellyband that is tied around the stomach of a newborn baby to keep the navel pressed in.

They talked politics. Roosevelt was their hero. He had come along and rescued the country with relief and jobs, and in gratitude they christened their sons Franklin and Delano and hoped they would live up to the names.

If F.D.R. was their hero, Marcus Garvey was their God. The name of the fiery, Jamaican-born black nationalist of the 20s was constantly invoked around the table. For he had been their leader when they first came to the United States from the West Indies shortly after World War I. They had contributed to his organization, the United Negro Improvement Association (UNIA), out of their meager salaries, bought shares in his ill-fated Black Star Shipping Line, and at the height of the movement they had marched as members of his "nurses' brigade" in their white uniforms on Seventh Avenue in Harlem during the great Garvey Day parades. Garvey: He lived on through the power of their memories.

And their talk was of war and rumors of wars. They raged against World War II when it broke out in Europe, blaming it on the politicians. "It's these politicians. They're the ones always starting up all this lot of war. But what they care? It's the poor people got to suffer and mothers with their sons." If it was *their* sons, they swore they would keep them out of the Army by giving them soap to eat each day to make their hearts sound defective. Hitler? He was for them "the devil incarnate."

Then there was home. They reminisced often and at length about home. The old country, Barbados—or Bimshire, as they affectionately called it. The little Caribbean island in the sun they loved but had to leave. "Poor—poor but sweet" was the way they remembered it.

And naturally they discussed their adopted home. America came in for both good and bad marks. They lashed out at it for the racism they encountered. They took to task some of the people they worked for, especially those who gave them only a hard-boiled egg and a few spoonfuls of cottage cheese for lunch. "As if anybody can scrub floor on an egg and some cheese that don't have no taste to it!"

Yet although they caught H in "this man country," as they called America, it was nonetheless a place where "you could at least see your way to make a dollar." That much they acknowledged. They might even one day accumulate enough dollars, with both them and their husbands working, to buy the brownstone houses which, like my family, they were only leasing at that period. This was their consuming ambition: to "buy house" and to see the children through.

There was no way for me to understand it at the time, but the talk that filled the kitchen those afternoons was highly functional. It served as therapy, the cheapest kind available to my mother and her friends. Not only did it help them recover from the long wait on the corner that morning and the bargaining over their labor, it restored them to a sense of themselves and reaffirmed their self-worth. Through language they were able to overcome the humiliations of the work-day.

But more than therapy, that freewheeling, wide-ranging, exuberant talk functioned as an outlet for the tremendous creative energy they possessed. They were women in whom the need for self-expression was strong, and since language was the only vehicle readily available to them they made of it an art form that—in keeping with the African tradition in which art and life are one—was an integral part of their lives.

And their talk was a refuge. They never really ceased being baffled and overwhelmed by America—its vastness, complexity and power. Its strange customs and laws. At a level beyond words they remained fearful and in awe. Their uneasiness and fear were even reflected in their attitude toward the children they had given birth to in this country. They referred to those like myself, the little Brooklyn-born Bajans (Barbadians), as "these New York children" and complained that they couldn't discipline us properly because of the laws here. "You can't beat these children as you would like, you know, because the authorities in this place will dash you in jail for them. After all, these is New York children." Not only were we different, American, we had, as they saw it, escaped their ultimate authority.

Confronted therefore by a world they could not encompass, which even limited their rights as parents, and at the same time finding themselves permanently separated from the world they had known, they took refuge in language. "Language is the only homeland," Czeslaw Milosz, the emigré Polish writer and Nobel Laureate, has said. This is what it became for the women at the kitchen table.

It served another purpose also, I suspect. My mother and her friends were after all the female counterpart of Ralph Ellison's invisible man.[2] Indeed, you might say they suffered a triple invisibility, being black, female and foreigners. They really didn't count in American society except as a source of cheap labor. But given the kind of women they were, they couldn't tolerate

[2]Title of novel published in 1947 which has become the seminal metaphor for African-Americans.

the fact of their invisibility, their powerlessness. And they fought back, using the only weapon at their command: the spoken word.

Those late afternoon conversations on a wide range of topics were a way for them to feel they exercised some measure of control over their lives and the events that shaped them. "Soully-gal, talk yuh talk!" they were always exhorting each other. "In this man world you got to take yuh mouth and make a gun!" They were in control, if only verbally and if only for the two hours or so that they remained in our house.

For me, sitting over in the corner, being seen but not heard, which was the rule for children in those days, it wasn't only what the women talked about—the content—but the way they put things—their style. The insight, irony, wit, and humor they brought to their stories and discussions and their poet's inventiveness and daring with language—which of course I could only sense but not define back then.

They had taken the standard English taught them in the primary schools of Barbados and transformed it into an idiom, an instrument that more adequately described them—changing around the syntax and imposing their own rhythm and accent so that the sentences were more pleasing to their ears. They added the few African sounds and words that had survived, such as the derisive suck-teeth sound and the word "yam," meaning to eat. And to make it more vivid, more in keeping with their expressive quality, they brought to bear a raft of metaphors, parables, Biblical quotations, sayings and the like:

"The sea ain' got no back door," they would say, meaning that it wasn't like a house where if there was a fire you could run out the back. Meaning that it was not to be trifled with. And meaning perhaps in a larger sense that man should treat all of nature with caution and respect.

"I has read hell by heart and called every generation blessed!" They sometimes went in for hyperbole.

A woman expecting a baby was never said to be pregnant. They never used that word. Rather, she was "in the way" or, better yet, "tumbling big." "Guess who I butt up on in the market the other day tumbling big again!"

And a woman with a reputation of being too free with her sexual favors was known in their book as a "thoroughfare"—the sense of men like a steady stream of cars moving up and down the road of her life. Or she might be dubbed "a free-bee," which was my favorite of the two. I liked the image it conjured up of a woman scandalous perhaps but independent, who flitted from one flower to another in a garden of male beauties, sampling their nectar, taking her pleasure at will, the roles reversed.

And nothing, no matter how beautiful, was ever described as simply beautiful. It was always "beautiful-ugly": the beautiful-ugly dress, the beautiful-ugly house, the beautiful-ugly car. Why the word "ugly," I used to wonder, when the thing they were referring to was beautiful, and they knew it. Why the antonym, the contradiction, the linking of opposites? It used to puzzle me greatly as a child.

There is the theory in linguistics which states that the idiom of a people, the way they use language, reflects not only the most fundamental views they hold of themselves and the world but their very conception of reality. Perhaps in using the term "beautiful-ugly" to describe nearly everything, my mother and her friends were expressing what they believed to be a fundamental dualism in life: the idea that a thing is at the same time its opposite, and that these opposites, these contradictions make up the whole. But theirs was not a Manichaean brand of dualism[3] that sees matter, flesh, the body, as inherently evil, because they constantly addressed each other as "soully-gal"— soul: spirit; gal: the body, flesh, the visible self. And it was clear from their tone that they gave one as much weight and importance as the other. They had never heard of the mind/body split.

As for God, they summed up His essential attitude in a phrase, "God," they would say, "don' love ugly and He ain' stuck on pretty."

Using everyday speech, the simple commonplace words—but always with imagination and skill—they gave voice to the most complex ideas. Flannery O'Connor[4] would have approved of how they made ordinary language work, as she put it, "double-time," stretching, shading, deepening its meaning. Like Joseph Conrad[5] they were always trying to infuse new life in the "old old words worn thin . . . by . . . careless usage." And the goals of their oral art were the same as his: "to make you hear, to make you feel . . . to make you *see*." This was their guiding esthetic.

By the time I was 8 or 9, I graduated from the corner of the kitchen to the neighborhood library, and thus from the spoken to the written word. The Macon Street Branch of the Brooklyn Public Library was an imposing half block long edifice of heavy gray masonry, with glass-paneled doors at the front and two tall metal torches symbolizing the light that comes of learning flanking the wide steps outside.

The inside was just as impressive. More steps—of pale marble with gleaming brass railings at the center and sides—led up to the circulation desk, and a great pendulum clock gazed down from the balcony stacks that faced the entrance. Usually stationed at the top of the steps like the guards outside Buckingham Palace was the custodian, a stern-faced West Indian type who for years, until I was old enough to obtain an adult card, would immediately shoo me with one hand into the Children's Room and with the other threaten me into silence, a finger to his lips. You would have thought

---

[3]Religious sect founded in 276 A.D. in Persia, which teaches the release of the spirit from matter through asceticism.

[4]Flannery O'Connor (1925–1964) American writer.

[5]Joseph Conrad (1857–1924) British fiction writer.

he was the chief librarian and not just someone whose job it was to keep the brass polished and the clock wound. I put him in a story called "Barbados" years later and had terrible things happen to him at the end.

I was sheltered from the storm of adolescence in the Macon Street library, reading voraciously, indiscriminately, everything from Jane Austen to Zane Grey, but with a special passion for the long, full-blown, richly detailed 18th- and 19th-century picaresque tales: *Tom Jones*, *Great Expectations*, *Vanity Fair*.

But although I loved nearly everything I read and would enter fully into the lives of the characters—indeed, would cease being myself and become them—I sensed a lack after a time. Something I couldn't quite define was missing. And then one day, browsing in the poetry section, I came across a book by someone called Paul Laurence Dunbar, and opening it I found the photograph of a wistful, sad-eyed poet who to my surprise was black. I turned to a poem at random. "Little brown-baby wif spa'klin'/eyes/Come to yo'pappy an' set on his knee." Although I had a little difficulty at first with the words in dialect, the poem spoke to me as nothing I had read before of the closeness, the special relationship I had had with my father, who by then had become an ardent believer in Father Divine and gone to live in Father's "kingdom" in Harlem. Reading it helped to ease somewhat the tight knot of sorrow and longing I carried around in my chest that refused to go away. I read another poem, "Lias! Lias! Bless de Lawd!/Don' you know de day's/erbroad?/Ef you don' get up, you scamp/Dey'll be trouble in dis camp." I laughed. It reminded me of the way my mother sometimes yelled at my sister and me to get out of bed in the mornings.

And another: "Seen my lady home las' night/Jump back, honey, jump back./Hel'/huh han'/an'/sque'z it tight . . ." About love between a black man and a black woman. I had never seen that written about before and it roused in me all kinds of delicious feelings and hopes.

And I began to search then for books and stories and poems about "The Race" (as it was put back then), about my people. While not abandoning Thackeray, Fielding, Dickens and the others, I started asking the reference librarian, who was white, for books by Negro writers, although I must admit I did so at first with a feeling of shame—the shame I and many others used to experience in those days whenever the word "Negro" or "colored" came up.

No grade school literature teacher of mine had ever mentioned Dunbar or James Weldon Johnson or Langston Hughes.[6] I didn't know that Zora Neale Hurston[7] existed and was busy writing and being published during those years. Nor was I made aware of people like Frederick Douglass and

[6]Paul Laurence Dunbar (1870–1906), James Weldon Johnson (1871–1938), Langston Hughes (1902–1967)—African-American poets of the Harlem Renaissance.
[7]Zora Neale Hurston (1901–1961)—African-American novelist.

Harriet Tubman[8]—their spirit and example—or the great 19th-century abolitionist and feminist Sojourner Truth. There wasn't even Negro History Week when I attended P.S. 35 on Decatur Street!

What I needed, what all the kids—West Indian and native black American alike—with whom I grew up needed, was an equivalent of the Jewish shul, someplace where we could go after school—the schools that were short-changing us—and read works by those like ourselves and learn about our history.

It was around that time also that I began harboring the dangerous thought of someday trying to write myself. Perhaps a poem about an apple tree, although I had never seen one. Or the story of a girl who could magically transplant herself to wherever she wanted to be in the world—such as Father Divine's kingdom in Harlem. Dunbar—his dark, eloquent face, his large volume of poems—permitted me to dream that I might someday write, and with something of the power with words my mother and her friends possessed.

When people at readings and writers' conferences ask me who my major influences were, they are sometimes a little disappointed when I don't immediately name the usual literary giants. True, I am indebted to those writers, white and black, whom I read during my formative years and still read for instruction and pleasure. But they were preceded in my life by another set of giants whom I always acknowledge before all others: the group of women around the table long ago. They taught me my first lesson in the narrative art. They trained my ear. They set a standard of excellence. This is why the best of my work must be attributed to them; it stands as testimony to the rich legacy of language and culture they so freely passed on to me in the wordshop of the kitchen.

Interpretations

1. What does their choice of such subjects as politics reveal about these women's interests and needs? Why were their conversations so crucial to their survival?

2. Were these "poets of the kitchen" as interesting on paper as in their conversation? Why? What does Marshall think their use of English shows about them? What do you think is the best example of this quality?

3. Marshall—and the "well-known male novelist" who visited her classroom, as well as Grace Paley, another well-known fiction writer—say that the most important language for a novelist is "everyday speech," the language of "your parents and your street and friends." Do you agree? Do you think beginning writers are inclined to resist this lesson? Are they contemptuous of using everyday speech in their stories and novels? Why?

[8]Frederick Douglass (1817–1895), Harriet Tubman (1820–1913)—African-American abolitionists.

Correspondences

1. To what extent do Paule Marshall and Armando Rendón both discover that "language is the only homeland"?

2. Marshall writes, "what I needed, what all kids—West Indian and native black American alike—with whom I grew up needed, was an equivalent of the Jewish shul, someplace where we could go after school—the schools that were shortchanging us—and read works by those like ourselves and learn about our history." How might this also apply to Rendón? Should their educational systems have taught them about their own heritage? Why or why not? What has your education taught you about your cultural heritage?

Applications

1. "In this man world you got to take yuh mouth and make a gun" and "The sea ain' got no back door" are sayings the author heard as a child. Are there proverbs which you heard frequently as you were growing up? Write an essay about two or three proverbs or folk expressions. Demonstrate clearly, as does Marshall, the effects of such sayings on your educational development.

2. Marshall's "unknown bards" used language to combat their sense of powerlessness in a culture in which they experienced the "triple invisibility of being black, female and foreigners." Which expressions best reflect this? Are there other situations in which language might be a source of empowerment? Cite examples.

Discovering Books

Richard Wright

Richard Wright (1906–1960) was born on a plantation near Natchez, Missis-
sippi. He had little formal education and dropped out of school at fifteen. He then
moved to Chicago and worked in the post office. In the 1930s he began writing
fiction. His first collection of short stories, Uncle Tom's Children *(1938), won*
the annual award of Story *magazine. His* Native Son *(1940) was the first*
novel by an African-American writer to enter the mainstream of American literature.
The following selection is from Black Boy, *an autobiographical account of Wright's*
Southern childhood.

ONE MORNING I arrived early at work and went into the bank lobby where
the Negro porter was mopping. I stood at a counter and picked up the
Memphis *Commercial Appeal* and began my free reading of the press. I came
finally to the editorial page and saw an article dealing with one H. L.
Mencken. I knew by hearsay that he was the editor of the *American Mercury,*
but aside from that I knew nothing about him. The article was a furious
denunciation of Mencken, concluding with one, hot, short sentence: Mencken
is a fool.

I wondered what on earth this Mencken had done to call down upon
him the scorn of the South. The only people I had ever heard denounced in
the South were Negroes, and this man was not a Negro. Then what ideas
did Mencken hold that made a newspaper like the *Commercial Appeal* castigate
him publicly? Undoubtedly he must be advocating ideas that the South did
not like. Were there, then, people other than Negroes who criticized the
South? I knew that during the Civil War the South had hated northern
whites, but I had not encountered such hate during my life. Knowing no
more of Mencken than I did at that moment, I felt a vague sympathy for
him. Had not the South, which had assigned me the role of a nonman, cast
at him its hardest words?

Now, how could I find out about this Mencken? There was a huge library
near the riverfront, but I knew that Negroes were not allowed to patronize
its shelves any more than they were the parks and playgrounds of the city.
I had gone into the library several times to get books for the white men on
the job. Which of them would now help me to get books? And how could
I read them without causing concern to the white men with whom I worked?
I had so far been successful in hiding my thoughts and feelings from them,
but I knew that I would create hostility if I went about this business of
reading in a clumsy way.

I weighed the personalities of the men on the job. There was Don, a Jew; but I distrusted him. His position was not much better than mine and I knew that he was uneasy and insecure; he had always treated me in an offhand, bantering way that barely concealed his contempt. I was afraid to ask him to help me to get books; his frantic desire to demonstrate a racial solidarity with the whites against Negroes might make him betray me.

Then how about the boss? No, he was a Baptist and I had the suspicion that he would not be quite able to comprehend why a black boy would want to read Mencken. There were other white men on the job whose attitudes showed clearly that they were Kluxers or sympathizers, and they were out of the question.

There remained only one man whose attitude did not fit into an anti-Negro category, for I had heard the white men refer to him as a "Pope lover." He was an Irish Catholic and was hated by the white Southerners. I knew that he read books, because I had got him volumes from the library several times. Since he, too, was an object of hatred, I felt that he might refuse me but would hardly betray me. I hesitated, weighing and balancing the imponderable realities.

One morning I paused before the Catholic fellow's desk.

"I want to ask you a favor," I whispered to him.

"What is it?"

"I want to read. I can't get books from the library. I wonder if you'd let me use your card?"

He looked at me suspiciously.

"My card is full most of the time," he said.

"I see," I said and waited, posing my question silently.

"You're not trying to get me into trouble, are you, boy?" he asked, staring at me.

"Oh, no, sir."

"What book do you want?"

"A book by H. L. Mencken."

"Which one?"

"I don't know. Has he written more than one?"

"He has written several."

"I didn't know that."

"What makes you want to read Mencken?"

"Oh, I just saw his name in the newspaper," I said.

"It's good of you to want to read," he said. "But you ought to read the right things."

I said nothing. Would he want to supervise my reading?

"Let me think," he said. "I'll figure out something."

I turned from him and he called me back. He stared at me quizzically.

"Richard, don't mention this to the other white men," he said.

"I understand," I said. "I won't say a word."

A few days later he called me to him.

"I've got a card in my wife's name," he said. "Here's mine."

"Thank you, sir."

"Do you think you can manage it?"

"I'll manage fine," I said.

"If they suspect you, you'll get in trouble," he said.

"I'll write the same kind of notes to the library that you wrote when you sent me for books," I told him. "I'll sign your name."

He laughed.

"Go ahead. Let me see what you get," he said.

That afternoon I addressed myself to forging a note. Now, what were the names of books written by H. L. Mencken? I did not know any of them. I finally wrote what I thought would be a foolproof note: *Dear Madam: Will you please let this nigger boy*—I used the word "nigger" to make the librarian feel that I could not possibly be the author of the note—*have some books by H. L. Mencken?* I forged the white man's name.

I entered the library as I had always done when on errands for whites, but I felt that I would somehow slip up and betray myself. I doffed my hat, stood a respectful distance from the desk, looked as unbookish as possible, and waited for the white patrons to be taken care of. When the desk was clear of people, I still waited. The white librarian looked at me.

"What do you want, boy?"

As though I did not possess the power of speech, I stepped forward and simply handed her the forged note, not parting my lips.

"What books by Mencken does he want?" she asked.

"I don't know, ma'am," I said, avoiding her eyes.

"Who gave you this card?"

"Mr. Falk," I said.

"Where is he?"

"He's at work, at the M—— Optical Company," I said. "I've been in here for him before."

"I remember," the woman said. "But he never wrote notes like this."

Oh, God, she's suspicious. Perhaps she would not let me have the books? If she had turned her back at that moment, I would have ducked out the door and never gone back. Then I thought of a bold idea.

"You can call him up, ma'am," I said, my heart pounding.

"You're not using these books, are you?" she asked pointedly.

"Oh, no, ma'am. I can't read."

"I don't know what he wants by Mencken," she said under her breath.

I knew now that I had won; she was thinking of other things and the race question had gone out of her mind. She went to the shelves. Once or twice she looked over her shoulder at me, as though she was still doubtful. Finally she came forward with two books in her hand.

"I'm sending him two books," she said. "But tell Mr. Falk to come in next time, or send me the names of the books he wants. I don't know what he wants to read."

I said nothing. She stamped the card and handed me the books. Not daring to glance at them, I went out of the library, fearing that the woman would call me back for further questioning. A block away from the library I opened one of the books and read a title: *A Book of Prefaces*. I was nearing my nineteenth birthday and I did not know how to pronounce the word *preface*. I thumbed the pages and saw strange words and strange names. I shook my head, disappointed. I looked at the other book; it was called *Prejudices*. I knew what that word meant; I had heard it all my life. And right off I was on guard against Mencken's books. Why would a man want to call a book *Prejudices*? The word was so stained with all my memories of racial hate that I could not conceive of anybody using it for a title. Perhaps I had made a mistake about Mencken? A man who had prejudices must be wrong.

When I showed the books to Mr. Falk, he looked at me and frowned.

"That librarian might telephone you," I warned him.

"That's all right," he said. "But when you're through reading those books, I want you to tell me what you get out of them."

That night in my rented room, while letting the hot water run over my can of pork and beans in the sink, I opened *A Book of Prefaces* and began to read. I was jarred and shocked by the style, the clear, clean, sweeping sentences. Why did he write like that? And how did one write like that? I pictured the man as a raging demon, slashing with his pen, consumed with hate, denouncing everything American, extolling everything European or German, laughing at the weaknesses of people, mocking God, authority. What was this? I stood up, trying to realize what reality lay behind the meaning of the words. . . . Yes, this man was fighting, fighting with words. He was using words as a weapon, using them as one would use a club. Could words be weapons? Well, yes, for here they were. Then, maybe, perhaps, I could use them as a weapon? No. It frightened me. I read on and what amazed me was not what he said, but how on earth anybody had the courage to say it.

Occasionally I glanced up to reassure myself that I was alone in the room. Who were these men about whom Mencken was talking so passionately? Who was Anatole France? Joseph Conrad? Sinclair Lewis, Sherwood Anderson, Dostoevski, George Moore, Gustave Flaubert, Maupassant, Tolstoy, Frank Harris, Mark Twain, Thomas Hardy, Arnold Bennett, Stephen Crane, Zola, Norris, Gorky, Bergson, Ibsen, Balzac, Bernard Shaw, Dumas, Poe, Thomas Mann, O. Henry, Dreiser, H. G. Wells, Gogol, T. S. Eliot, Gide, Baudelaire, Edgar Lee Masters, Stendhal, Turgenev, Huneker, Nietzsche, and scores of others? Were these men real? Did they exist or had they existed? And how did one pronounce their names?

I ran across many words whose meanings I did not know, and I either looked them up in a dictionary or, before I had a chance to do that, encountered the word in a context that made its meaning clear. But what strange world was this? I concluded the book with the conviction that I had somehow overlooked something terribly important in life. I had once tried to write, had once reveled in feeling, had let my crude imagination roam, but the impulse to dream had been slowly beaten out of me by experience. Now it surged up again and I hungered for books, new ways of looking and seeing. It was not a matter of believing or disbelieving what I read, but of feeling something new, of being affected by something that made the look of the world different.

As dawn broke I ate my pork and beans, feeling dopey, sleepy. I went to work, but the mood of the book would not die; it lingered, coloring everything I saw, heard, did. I now felt that I knew what the white men were feeling. Merely because I had read a book that had spoken of how they lived and thought, I identified myself with that book. I felt vaguely guilty. Would I, filled with bookish notions, act in a manner that would make the whites dislike me?

I forged more notes and my trips to the library became more frequent. Reading grew into a passion. My first serious novel was Sinclair Lewis's *Main Street*. It made me see my boss, Mr. Gerald, and identify him as an American type. I would smile when I saw him lugging his golf bags into the office. I had always felt a vast distance separating me from the boss, and now I felt closer to him, though still distant. I felt now that I knew him, that I could feel the very limits of his narrow life. And this had happened because I had read a novel about a mythical man called George F. Babbitt.

The plots and stories in the novels did not interest me so much as the point of view revealed. I gave myself over to each novel without reserve, without trying to criticize it; it was enough for me to see and feel something different. And for me, everything was something different. Reading was like a drug, a dope. The novels created moods in which I lived for days. But I could not conquer my sense of guilt, my feeling that the white men around me knew that I was changing, that I had begun to regard them differently.

Whenever I brought a book to the job, I wrapped it in newspaper—a habit that was to persist for years in other cities and under other circumstances. But some of the white men pried into my packages when I was absent and they questioned me.

"Boy, what are you reading those books for?"

"Oh, I don't know, sir."

"That's deep stuff you're reading, boy."

"I'm just killing time, sir."

"You'll addle your brains if you don't watch out."

I read Dreiser's *Jennie Gerhardt* and *Sister Carrie* and they revived in me a vivid sense of my mother's suffering; I was overwhelmed, I grew silent, wondering about the life around me. It would have been impossible for me to have told anyone what I derived from these novels, for it was nothing less than a sense of life itself. All my life had shaped me for the realism, the naturalism of the modern novel, and I could not read enough of them.

Steeped in new moods and ideas, I bought a ream of paper and tried to write; but nothing would come, or what did come was flat beyond telling. I discovered that more than desire and feeling were necessary to write and I dropped the idea. Yet I still wondered how it was possible to know people sufficiently to write about them? Could I ever learn about life and people? To me, with my vast ignorance, my Jim Crow* station in life, it seemed a task impossible of achievement. I now knew what being a Negro meant. I could endure the hunger. I had learned to live with hate. But to feel that there were feelings denied me, that the very breath of life itself was beyond my reach, that more than anything else hurt, wounded me. I had a new hunger.

In buoying me up, reading also cast me down, made me see what was possible, what I had missed. My tension returned, new, terrible, bitter, surging, almost too great to be contained. I no longer *felt* that the world about me was hostile, killing; I *knew* it. A million times I asked myself what I could do to save myself, and there were no answers. I seemed forever condemned, ringed by walls.

I did not discuss my reading with Mr. Falk, who had lent me his library card; it would have meant talking about myself and that would have been too painful. I smiled each day, fighting desperately to maintain my old behavior, to keep my disposition seemingly sunny. But some of the white men discerned that I had begun to brood.

"Wake up there, boy!" Mr. Olin said one day.

"Sir!" I answered for the lack of a better word.

"You act like you've stolen something," he said.

I laughed in the way I knew he expected me to laugh, but I resolved to be more conscious of myself, to watch my every act, to guard and hide the new knowledge that was dawning within me.

If I went north, would it be possible for me to build a new life then? But how could a man build a life upon vague, unformed yearnings? I wanted to write and I did not even know the English language. I bought English grammars and found them dull. I felt that I was getting a better sense of the language from novels than grammars. I read hard, discarding a writer as soon as I felt that I had grasped his point of view. At night the printed page stood before my eyes in sleep.

Mrs. Moss, my landlady, asked me one Sunday morning:

"Son, what is this you keep on reading?"

"Oh, nothing. Just novels."

---

*Segregation and suppression of African-Americans in public places such as buses, restaurants, and educational institutions.

"What you get out of 'em?"

"I'm just killing time," I said.

"I hope you know your own mind," she said in a tone which implied that she doubted if I had a mind.

I knew of no Negroes who read the books I liked and I wondered if any Negroes ever thought of them. I knew that there were Negro doctors, lawyers, newspapermen, but I never saw any of them. When I read a Negro newspaper I never caught the faintest echo of my preoccupation in its pages. I felt trapped and occasionally, for a few days, I would stop reading. But a vague hunger would come over me for books, books that opened up new avenues of feeling and seeing, and again I would forge another note to the white librarian. Again I would read and wonder as only the naive and unlettered can read and wonder, feeling that I carried a secret, criminal burden about with me each day.

That winter my mother and brother came and we set up housekeeping, buying furniture on the installment plan, being cheated and yet knowing no way to avoid it. I began to eat warm food and to my surprise found the regular meals enabled me to read faster. I may have lived through many illnesses and survived them, never suspecting that I was ill. My brother obtained a job and we began to save toward the trip north, plotting our time, setting tentative dates for departure. I told none of the white men on the job that I was planning to go north; I knew that the moment they felt I was thinking of the North they would change toward me. It would have made them feel that I did not like the life I was living, and because my life was completely conditioned by what they said or did, it would have been tantamount to challenging them.

I could calculate my chances for life in the South as a Negro fairly clearly now.

I could fight the southern whites by organizing with other Negroes, as my grandfather had done. But I knew that I could never win that way; there were many whites and there were but few blacks. They were strong and we were weak. Outright black rebellion could never win. If I fought openly I would die and I did not want to die. News of lynchings were frequent.

I could submit and live the life of a genial slave, but that was impossible. All of my life had shaped me to live by my own feelings and thoughts. I could make up to Bess and marry her and inherit the house. But that, too, would be the life of a slave; if I did that, I would crush to death something within me, and I would hate myself as much as I knew the whites already hated those who had submitted. Neither could I ever willingly present myself to be kicked, as Shorty had done. I would rather have died than do that.

I could drain off my restlessness by fighting with Shorty and Harrison. I had seen many Negroes solve the problem of being black by transferring their hatred of themselves to others with a black skin and fighting them. I would have to be cold to do that, and I was not cold and I could never be.

I could, of course, forget what I had read, thrust the whites out of my mind, forget them; and find release from anxiety and longing in sex and alcohol. But the memory of how my father had conducted himself made that course repugnant. If I did not want others to violate my life, how could I voluntarily violate it myself?

I had no hope whatever of being a professional man. Not only had I been so conditioned that I did not desire it, but the fulfillment of such an ambition was beyond my capabilities. Well-to-do Negroes lived in a world that was almost as alien to me as the world inhabited by whites.

What, then, was there? I held my life in my mind, in my consciousness each day, feeling at times that I would stumble and drop it, spill it forever. My reading had created a vast sense of distance between me and the world in which I lived and tried to make a living, and that sense of distance was increasing each day. My days and nights were one long, quiet, continuously contained dream of terror, tension, and anxiety. I wondered how long I could bear it.

Interpretations

1. What details most vividly bring home Wright's poverty?

2. How did Wright's forged note show an understanding of white racism? What lessons for surviving in a racist society does the young Wright learn?

3. What effect does exposure to Mencken have on Wright?

4. Do you think books and libraries are as important as Wright thinks? Would you, if you had to, go to the same lengths he does to borrow books? Why or why not? Is it possible to be too respectful of the written word? If so, what are the signs of this excessive respect—in young Wright? in others?

5. Wright implies that books and reading are *the* most important means of education. Do you agree? Why or why not? (How have TV and radio affected the role of books in education?)

6. Wright is best known as a writer of fiction, especially of novels. What techniques usually associated with fiction does Wright use here? How do these techniques contribute to the excerpt's effectiveness?

Correspondences

1. Libraries play an important part in the education of both Richard Wright and Paule Marshall. Are their library experiences similar or different?

2.   Review the Ellison quotation (page 152). To what extent does it apply to Wright's essay? (To what extent did Wright's experience with "word . . . potency" influence him to become a writer?)

Applications

1.   Write a journal entry on your first memorable reading experience. How has it affected your subsequent attitude toward books?

2.   Richard Wright's educational experiences were shaped primarily by his awareness of himself as an outsider. Have you ever felt like an outsider to the education establishment? Freewrite about the experience and expand on it for an essay.

Dear Diary

Yekaterina Kontor

Yekaterina Kontor (b. 1969), a Muscovite, spent her 1988–89 academic year at Sarah Lawrence College as one of fifty-six students in one of the first undergraduate exchange programs between the United States and the Soviet Union. She was selected for her knowledge of English, her excellent grades, and her interest in theater and environmental issues. The following excerpts are from her journal.

Kontor's native country, the Union of Soviet Socialist Republics, is geographically nearly 2½ times the size of the United States. Nominally a federation of fifteen republics, the largest of which is the Russian Soviet Socialist Republic, the U.S.S.R. has been dominated by the Communist Party since the 1917 Revolution. Only in 1990, under the influence of Gorbachev, did the party's grip loosen significantly. If the U.S.S.R. continues to welcome capitalist influences, programs such as Kontor's should proliferate.

August 8

I CAN'T BELIEVE THIS. Just two days ago I was in Moscow airport with my parents and friends, and now I'm far, far away. I live in Middlebury Inn together with the other students who came with me. Today is our first day of orientation, and at 8 in the morning we had a lecture where I got acquainted briefly with the I.B.M. and Macintosh computers and some methods of working with them. After that we had two hours of English class. My God! I studied English for five years, but I felt like I never studied English before. Probably, it's because I was taught the British variant back home, and the American variant differs a lot.

I didn't know anyone in our exchange group, so everybody was new to me. We looked around—everything is different—architecture, style, cars, streets. At 4 o'clock I went to a lecture about American education. It has some similarities with the Soviet system: we both have seminars and lectures, have examinations and write papers. But there is the major difference: the education in the Soviet Union is free, we don't pay to study at the university. More than that, we don't have colleges for four years and two years of graduate school, like in America. I must study in the university for five years, the first three of which can be compared to the American college's four years of undergraduate school and the last two, to graduate school.

After dinner, I went to see the movie *Annie Hall,* with Woody Allen.

It was very hard to understand the language—I understood probably 25 percent of it. At the end of the day I was exhausted, but I was happy.

August 24

Every day I find something new about America and Americans. We were distributed by American teachers into three groups: in each group a certain number of students who know the language better than the others, and the majority practically on the same level in terms of language. The English classes were interesting, but I would like them to be more advanced.

This weekend our group, together with the director of the consortium program, Raymond Benson, and his assistant, Kate Brown, went to Albany, saw the New York State Capitol and the Museum of Natural History. It was wonderful. We in the Soviet Union tend to know about the United States as a whole but I, for example, didn't know about New York State history.

During the week we had computer orientation, where we were sending messages to each other. I was excited because I never worked with a computer before. At night I went to the computer center and played different games.

Today we learned in which colleges we are going to study. I was asked, along with all the other students, which college I would prefer to go to, but I didn't know any of them. So with the help of the members of collegiate consortium, I eventually go together with Andrei Artemov, a medical student, to Sarah Lawrence. Tomorrow we fly to New York City. We are full of great expectations.

August 31

This week before school starts, Andrei and I are living in Yonkers in the family of one of the professors of Sarah Lawrence, Paul Josephson. Today for the first time, we went to the college. SLC is one of the smallest schools in the U.S.A., and it was a challenge for me to see a small campus after spending three years in the biggest university in the Soviet Union. At Sarah Lawrence, students don't have a settled curriculum. They choose subjects themselves. A week before classes start they have faculty interviews with the teachers—as many as they want—and decide which courses to take. Eventually, each student has to take three courses, but once in two weeks he or she has individual conferences with the teachers. It was new to me, because in my university, we choose the department we would like to join, but not the subjects.

September 7

I had nice interviews with the professors today, and finally chose three courses: 1) American History: Slavery, Civil War and Reconstruction; 2)

American Literature: The Problem of Realism (1864–1918); and 3) German Language (Intermediate).

September 25

My first 10 days of classes went very well. The workload is very heavy—for example, for each history class I had to read 200 to 300 pages in English and write a response to it. At the end of the day I was tired. I noticed that it's harder for me to speak English in the morning and in the evenings. I never lived in the dormitory before, so I had to get used to living without my own room, without my mother's cooking, doing my own laundry and living with Americans from a different culture.

October 20

In the process of studying with and communicating with American students, I learn how people relate to each other, the way they talk, when they smile, when they don't smile, what the interests of my American friends are, how people like to spend their time, what Americans themselves think about their own country, what dreams do they have.

People in New York City are rushy, they try to look successful, they smile a lot, but sometimes they don't have time for conversation. I spoke with one of the girls in college, and she told me, "Thank you that you listened to me. I appreciate it. You know, people are always busy. They don't have time to listen to each other." On the other hand, I think that my American friends are very enthusiastic, they are very open, and always welcome other people to speak about art, politics, health problems.

It's amazing how many people jog in the morning, quit smoking and watch their weight. It's interesting that people, especially women, tend to marry when they are 27 to 30. In Moscow, it is different. Most of the people marry when they are 23 to 25. It's natural for young people in America to live together in the same apartment, far away from their families. In the Soviet Union, it depends on the region of the country, but even in Moscow many people used to live with their parents before they marry. Americans like to move all over the country. You find, not infrequently, a New Yorker who was born in Kentucky, went to college in Illinois, went to graduate school in Harvard and now works and lives in New York City. In my university, most of the students come from all over the country, but after studying in Moscow, they usually go back to the places where they lived before.

Students in this school form a kind of close-set community. Most of the time they study. SLC is a liberal arts college and it is especially good for theater, literature and film students.

For a freshman, it is not easy in Sarah Lawrence socially. Most of the people who go to this school are from the upper middle class, though some are on financial aid. It took me some time and effort to find friends here. As one of the students, Jonathan Silverblatt, who is originally from Los Angeles, told me: "Sarah Lawrence College is near New York City. There's a lot of assimilation of 'New Yorkness.' This is included in both social circles as well as school events. I'd even say that New York has had its influence on SLC philosophy. SLC requires you to conform to its philosophy (in everything, clothes, manners, behavior) and thus, conform to a New Yorker.

November 15

By now I think that I have adapted to the style of life in the college, although I feel that I am always rushing somewhere. It is interesting to see differences and similarities in the studying process for me in Moscow and in Sarah Lawrence. In the philological faculty in Moscow State University, students of the same year are distributed in groups according to what foreign language they study—there are three English groups, French group, German group, etc. Each group doesn't outnumber 10 to 15 people, when we have seminars, so I was not surprised that in Sarah Lawrence there are only 10 to 15 people in the class, which in the United States is considered a very small class.

More than that, the feeling you get when you study in the big university is very different from the thoughts and experiences you obtain in a small school like SLC, where practically all people know each other. In MSU [Moscow State University], where 25,000 people study, you cannot know everyone. But as far as I'm concerned, I like big schools better because you're not "closed" in a small community. Sometimes because of the size of the school (I mean SLC), you don't have privacy. As one of the students on campus said, students "breathe gossip."

On the other hand, in a small school like SLC, your environment means a lot. People with whom you communicate, afterwards in most cases, become your closest friends. MSU is in the city, you can have a lot of acquaintances but never really get to know people, but you have friends. I think that in MSU there are potentialities to combine the curriculum, which is more rigid as compared to SLC, with the independent studies. The good thing about SLC is that you can plan your own day and your classes.

The question of exams is very controversial. On the one hand, it's good to create your own way of studying, but even for your own sake you have to check your knowledge through exams. I hope that for me, as a student coming from the big university with the system where students have exams twice a year, at the end of each semester, SLC would give a different perspective on education—how educational systems can be different and in which ways.

This school helps me a lot to develop my individual thinking and, in spite of certain giveaways in my English, it gradually becomes better. For me, as a linguist, and maybe a future teacher of English, it is especially important.

Americans are very interested in the Soviet Union and in the changes taking place in my country. I help those students who will go next year to the Soviet Union as exchange students in Russian. Through communication with my American friends, I feel that we help our countries to break down barriers that exist when people don't know one another.

January 30

A week ago the new semester at school began. This time I also take one course in Hunter College in the City University of New York. I wanted to see how American educational system is organized in other schools. What is the difference between education in a small SLC and a big city university? Hunter differs a lot.

In Hunter, you can meet diversity of people. Most of them work during the day and take classes in the evening to educate themselves. Of course, there is no conference work like in SLC, but the teacher tries to help his students as much as he can, and the atmosphere in the class is very friendly. We have a textbook—*The Harper's Anthology of American Literature.* In Hunter you meet many more blacks than in SLC. On the other hand, the level of education appears not to be so high as it is in SLC (at least, I can compare literature courses).

February 15

I have three months left in Sarah Lawrence College and in America as well. I'm still taking the course of American history, Advanced Intermediate German, and I audit one course: "Word and Icon: The Shaping of American Literature 1900–1945," which studies the mutual influences of "serious" literature and "popular" culture (particularly film, photojournalism and radio) in the United States during the first half of the 20th century.

March 14

Today I watched the movie *Annie Hall* for the second time. It was fun to recollect that I saw it in Middlebury at the start of the year. This time I understood practically the whole thing. Only some of the New York jokes presented difficulties. During spring break, which begins Monday, I will do my paper, comparing the writings of Thoreau and Henry Adams. Now that I've been at Hunter longer, I realize that there is less of a difference between the level of teaching between it and Sarah Lawrence, though the methods are different. In SLC we do more literary criticism proper, whereas at Hunter my literature teacher, Neal Tolchin, tries to involve students in the process of responding *personally* to reading we do in class. At Hunter we *learn* how to express our feelings, and thoughts emerged from the reading of the books. We write a journal for each class—our responses to reading—and read them and discuss them in class. It gives me a new perception of how differently literature can be taught in the U.S.

March 30

Sometimes I think about how much did this year gave to me—in all aspects—educational, social, personal. It flashes across my mind how hard this year was, hard but exciting. I learned a lot about American people. I met some good friends, mastered English. Of course, I miss my parents and friends and look forward to coming back, but I feel a little bit sad, because this year went very fast.

Interpretations

1. What do you learn about Sarah Lawrence College from Kontor's diary? Do you think it was a wise choice for an overseas student? Why or why not?

2. Does *Annie Hall* provide foreign students with a good orientation to America and American education? Why or why not?

3. Why is Kontor in favor of student exchange between America and the Soviet Union?

4. Would you like to be an exchange student? What, besides language, do you think would be the greatest obstacle for an exchange student to overcome? What countries do you think would benefit most from an exchange of students?

5. A diary is useful both as a supplement to memory and a prod to writing. Which topics from Kontor's diary would you like to see developed into full-fledged essays? What questions about these topics would you suggest she try to answer?

Correspondences

1. Review the Frost quotation on education (page 151). To what extent does it apply to Kontor's experience as a Russian at an American college? What

are her impressions of American students? How are American students similar to or different from the Russian students she describes?

2. Kontor comments that her American educational experience has encouraged her to develop individual thinking; Wright states that "reading grew into a passion." How does each selection demonstrate the importance of individual curiosity? About what is each writer most curious?

Applications

1. Write an essay on what you expect to get from your education. How are your expectations similar to or different from those of Kontor?

2. If you, like Kontor, have had an educational experience in another country, write an essay about the aspects of the experience you value most. Organize your essay in chronological order.

The Lesson

Toni Cade Bambara

Toni Cade Bambara (b. 1939) grew up in New York City deeply conscious of the inequities of race and class. She graduated from Queens College in 1959 and received her M.A. from City College of New York. Her publications include Gorilla, My Love *(1972),* The Sea Birds Are Still Alive *(1977), and* The Salt Eaters *(1980). This is how she perceives her role as a writer:*

> *Stories are important. They keep us alive. In the ships, in the camps, in the quarters, fields, prisons, on the road, on the run, underground, under siege, in the throes, on the verge—the storyteller snatches us back from the edge to hear the next chapter in which we are the subjects. We, the hero of the tales. Our lives preserved. How it was, how it be. Passing it along in the relay. That is what I work to do, to produce stories that save our lives.*

As you read "The Lesson," set in New York City, pay particular attention to Bambara's use of dialogue.

BACK IN THE DAYS when everyone was old and stupid or young and foolish and me and Sugar were the only ones just right, this lady moved on our block with nappy hair and proper speech and no makeup. And quite naturally we laughed at her, laughed the way we did at the junk man who went about his business like he was some big-time president and his sorry-ass horse his secretary. And we kinda hated her too, hated the way we did the winos who cluttered up our parks and pissed on our handball walls and stank up our hallways and stairs so you couldn't halfway play hide-and-seek without a goddamn gas mask. Miss Moore was her name. The only woman on the block with no first name. And she was black as hell, cept for her feet, which were fish-white and spooky. And she was always planning these boring-ass things for us to do, us being my cousin, mostly, who lived on the block cause we all moved North the same time and to the same apartment then spread out gradual to breathe. And our parents would yank our heads into some kinda shape and crisp up our clothes so we'd be presentable for travel with Miss Moore, who always looked like she was going to church, though she never did. Which is just one of things the grownups talked about when they talked behind her back like a dog. But when she came calling with some sachet she'd sewed up or some gingerbread she'd made or some book, why then they'd all be too embarrassed to turn her down and we'd get handed over all spruced up. She'd been to college and said it was only right that she should take responsibility for the young ones' education, and she not even related by marriage or blood. So they'd go for it. Specially Aunt Gretchen. She was the main gofer in the family. You got some old dumb shit foolishness you want somebody to go for, you send for Aunt Gretchen. She been screwed into the go-along for so long, it's a blood-deep natural thing with her. Which is how she got saddled with me and Sugar and Junior in the first place while our mothers were in a la-de-da apartment up the block having a good ole time.

So this one day Miss Moore rounds us all up at the mailbox and it's puredee hot and she's knockin herself out about arithmetic. And school suppose to let up in the summer I heard, but she don't never let up. And the starch in my pinafore scratching the shit outta me and I'm really hating this nappy-head bitch and her goddamn college degree. I'd much rather go to the pool or to the show where it's cool. So me and Sugar leaning on the mailbox being surly, which is a Miss Moore word. And Flyboy checking out what everybody brought for lunch. And Fat Butt already wasting his peanut-butter-and-jelly sandwich like the pig he is. And Junebug punchin on Q.T.'s arm for potato chips. And Rosie Giraffe shifting from one hip to the other waiting for somebody to step on her foot or ask if she from Georgia so she can kick ass, preferably Mercedes'. And Miss Moore asking us do we know what money is, like we a bunch of retards. I mean real money, she say, like it's only poker chips or monopoly papers we lay on the grocer. So right away I'm tired of this and say so. And would much rather snatch Sugar and go to the Sunset and terrorize the West Indian kids and take their hair ribbons and their money too. And Miss Moore files that remark away for next week's lesson on brotherhood, I can tell. And finally I say we oughta get to the subway cause it's cooler and besides we might meet some cute boys. Sugar done swiped her mama's lipstick, so we ready.

So we heading down the street and she's boring us silly about what things cost and what our parents make and how much goes for rent and how money ain't divided up right in this country. And then she gets to the part about we all poor and live in the slums, which I don't feature. And I'm ready to speak on that, but she steps out in the street and hails two cabs just like that. Then she hustles half the crew in with her and hands me a five-dollar bill and tells me to calculate 10 percent tip for the driver. And we're off. Me and Sugar and Junebug and Flyboy hanging out the window and hollering to everybody, putting lipstick on each other cause Flyboy a faggot anyway, and making farts with our sweaty armpits. But I'm mostly trying to figure how to spend this money. But they all fascinated with the meter ticking and Junebug starts laying bets as to how much it'll read when Flyboy can't hold his breath no more. Then Sugar lay bets as to how much it'll be when we get there. So I'm stuck. Don't nobody want to go for my plan, which is to jump out at the next light and run off to the first bar-b-que we can find.

Then the driver tells us to get the hell out cause we there already. And the meter reads eight-five cents. And I'm stalling to figure out the tip and Sugar say give him a dime. And I decided he don't need it bad as I do, so later for him. But then he tries to take off with Junebug foot still in the door so we talk about his mama something ferocious. Then we check out that we on Fifth Avenue and everybody dressed up in stockings. One lady in a fur coat, hot as it is. White folks crazy.

"This is the place," Miss Moore say, presenting it to us in the voice she uses at the museum. "Let's look in the windows before we go in."

"Can we steal?" Sugar asks very serious like she's getting the ground rules squared away before she plays. "I beg your pardon," say Miss Moore, and we fall out. So she leads us around the windows of the toy store and me and Sugar screamin, "This is mine, that's mine, I gotta have that, that was made for me, I was born for that," till Big Butt drowns us out.

"Hey, I'm goin to buy that there."

"That there? You don't even know what it is, stupid."

"I do so," he say punchin on Rosie Giraffe. "It's a microscope."

"Whatcha gonna do with a microscope, fool?"

"Look at things."

"Like what, Ronald?" ask Miss Moore. And Big Butt ain't got the first notion. So here go Miss Moore gabbing about the thousands of bacteria in a drop of water and the somethinorother in a speck of blood and the million and one living things in the air around us is invisible to the naked eye. And what she say that for? Junebug go to town on that "naked" and we rolling. Then Miss Moore ask what it cost. So we all jam into the window smudgin it up and the price tag say $300. So then she ask how long'd take for Big Butt and Junebug to save up their allowances. "Too long," I say. "Yeh," adds Sugar, "outgrown it by that time." And Miss Moore say no, you never outgrow learning instruments. "Why, even medical students and interns and," blah, blah, blah. And we ready to choke Big Butt for bringing it up in the first damn place.

"This here costs four hundred eighty dollars," say Rosie Giraffe. So we pile up all over her to see what she pointin out. My eyes tell me it's a chunk of glass cracked with something heavy, and different-color inks dripped into the splits, then the whole thing put into a oven or something. But for $480 it don't make sense.

"That's a paperweight made of semi-precious stones fused together under tremendous pressure," she explains slowly, with her hands doing the mining and all the factory work.

"So what's a paperweight?" asks Rosie Giraffe.

"To weigh paper with, dumbbell," say Flyboy, the wise man from the East.

"Not exactly," say Miss Moore, which is what she say when you warm or way off too. "It's to weigh paper down so it won't scatter and make your desk untidy." So right away me and Sugar curtsy to each other and then to Mercedes who is more the tidy type.

"We don't keep paper on top of the desk in my class," say Junebug, figuring Miss Moore crazy or lyin one.

"At home, then," she say. "Don't you have a calendar and a pencil case and a blotter and a letter-opener on your desk at home where you do your homework?" And she know damn well what our homes look like cause she nosys around in them every chance she gets.

"I don't even have a desk," say Junebug. "Do we?"

"No. And I don't get no homework neither," says Big Butt.

"And I don't even have a home," say Flyboy like he do at school to keep the white folks off his back and sorry for him. Send this poor kid to camp posters, is his specialty.

"I do," says Mercedes. "I have a box of stationery on my desk and a picture of my cat. My godmother bought the stationery and the desk. There's a big rose on each sheet and the envelopes smell like roses."

"Who wants to know about your smelly-ass stationery," say Rosie Giraffe fore I can get my two cents in.

"It's important to have a work area all your own so that . . ."

"Will you look at this sailboat, please," say Flyboy, cuttin her off and pointin to the thing like it was his. So once again we tumble all over each other to gaze at this magnificent thing in the toy store which is just big enough to maybe sail two kittens across the pond if you strap them to the posts tight. We all start reciting the price tag like we in assembly. "Hand-crafted sailboat of fiberglass at one thousand one hundred ninety-five dollars."

"Unbelievable," I hear myself say and am really stunned. I read it again for myself just in case the group recitation put me in a trance. Same thing. For some reason this pisses me off. We look at Miss Moore and she lookin at us, waiting for I dunno what.

"Who'd pay all that when you can buy a sailboat set for a quarter at Pop's, a tube of glue for a dime, and a ball of string for eight cents? It must have a motor and a whole lot else besides," I say. "My sailboat cost me about fifty cents."

"But will it take water?" say Mercedes with her smart ass.

"Took mine to Alley Pond Park once," say Flyboy. "String broke. Lost it. Pity."

"Sailed mine in Central Park and it keeled over and sank. Had to ask my father for another dollar."

"And you got the strap," laugh Big Butt. "The jerk didn't even have a string on it. My old man wailed on his behind."

Little Q.T. was staring hard at the sailboat and you could see he wanted it bad. But he too little and somebody'd just take it from him. So what the hell. "This boat for kids, Miss Moore?"

"Parents silly to buy something like that just to get all broke up," say Rosie Giraffe.

"That much money it should last forever," I figure.

"My father'd buy it for me if I wanted it."

"Your father, my ass," say Rosie Giraffe getting a chance to finally push Mercedes.

"Must be rich people shop here," say Q.T.

"You are a very bright boy," say Flyboy. "What was your first clue?" And he rap him on the head with the back of his knuckles, since Q.T. the only one he could get away with. Though Q.T. liable to come up behind you years later and get his licks in when you half expect it.

"What I want to know is," I says to Miss Moore though I never talk to her, I wouldn't give the bitch that satisfaction, "is how much a real boat costs? I figure a thousand'd get you a yacht any day?"

"Why don't you check that out," she says, "and report back to the group?" Which really pains my ass. If you gonna mess up a perfectly good swim day least you could do is have some answers. "Let's go in," she say like she got something up her sleeve. Only she don't lead the way. So me and Sugar turn the corner to where the entrance is, but when we get there I kinda hang back. Not that I'm scared, what's there to be afraid of, just a toy store. But I feel funny, shame. But what I got to be shamed about? Got as much right to go in as anybody. But somehow I can't seem to get hold of the door, so I step away for Sugar to lead. But she hangs back too. And I look at her and she looks at me and this is ridiculous. I mean, damn, I have never ever been shy about doing nothing or going nowhere. But then Mercedes steps up and then Rosie Giraffe and Big Butt crowd in behind and shove, and next thing we all stuffed into the doorway with only Mercedes squeezing past us, smoothing out her jumper and walking right down the aisle. Then the rest of us tumble in like a glued-together jigsaw done all wrong. And people lookin at us. And it's like the time me and Sugar crashed into the Catholic church on a dare. But once we got in there and everything so hushed and holy and the candles and the bowin and the handkerchiefs on all the drooping heads, I just couldn't go through with the plan. Which was for me to run up to the altar and do a tap dance while Sugar played the nose flute and messed around in the holy waters. And Sugar kept givin me the elbow. Then later teased me so bad I tied her up in the shower and turned it on and locked her in. And she'd be there till this day if Aunt Gretchen hadn't finally figured I was lyin about the boarder takin a shower.

Same thing in the store. We all walkin on tiptoe and hardly touchin the games and puzzles and things. And I watched Miss Moore who is steady watchin us like she waiting for a sign. Like Mama Drewery watches the sky and sniffs the air and takes note of just how much slant is in the bird formation. Then me and Sugar bump smack into each other, so busy gazing at the toys, 'specially the sailboat. But we don't laugh and go into our fat-lady bump-stomach routine. We just stare at that price tag. Then Sugar run a finger over the whole boat. And I'm jealous and want to hit her. Maybe not her, but I sure want to punch somebody in the mouth.

"Watcha bring us here for, Miss Moore?"

"You sound angry, Sylvia. Are you mad about something?" Givin me one of them grins like she tellin a grown-up joke that never turns out to be funny. And she's lookin very closely at me like maybe she plannin to do my portrait from memory. I'm mad, but I won't give her that satisfaction. So I slouch around the store bein very bored and say, "Let's go."

Me and Sugar at the back of the train watchin the tracks whizzin by large then small then gettin gobbled up in the dark. I'm thinkin about this tricky toy I saw in the store. A clown that somersaults on a bar then does chin-ups just cause you yank lightly at his leg. Cost $35. I could see me askin my mother for a $35 birthday clown. "You wanna who that costs what?" she'd say, cocking her head to the side to get a better view of the hole in my head. Thirty-five dollars and the whole household could go visit Grandaddy Nelson in the country. Thirty-five dollars would pay for the rent and the piano bill too. Who are these people that spend that much for performing clowns and $1000 for toy sailboats? What kinda work they do and how they live and how come we ain't in on it? Where we are is who we are, Miss Moore always pointin out. But it don't necessarily have to be that way, she always adds then waits for somebody to say that poor people have to wake up and demand their share of the pie and don't none of us know what kind of pie she talkin about in the first damn place. But she ain't so smart cause I still got her four dollars from the taxi and she sure ain't gettin it. Messin up my day with this shit. Sugar nudges me in my pocket and winks.

Miss Moore lines us up in front of the mailbox where we started from, seem like years ago, and I got a headache for thinkin so hard. And we lean all over each other so we can hold up under the draggy-ass lecture she always finishes us off with at the end before we thank her for borin us to tears. But she just looks at us like she readin tea leaves. Finally she say, "Well, what did you think of F.A.O. Schwartz?"

Rosie Giraffe mumbles, "White folks crazy."

"I'd like to go there again when I get my birthday money," says Mercedes, and we shove her out the pack so she has to lean on the mailbox by herself.

"I'd like a shower. Tiring day," say Flyboy.

Then Sugar surprises me by saying, "You know, Miss Moore, I don't think all of us here put together eat in a year what that sailboat costs." And Miss Moore lights up like somebody goosed her. "And?" she say, urging Sugar on. Only I'm standin on her foot so she don't continue.

"Imagine for a minute what kind of society it is in which some people can spend on a toy what it would cost to feed a family of six or seven. What do you think?"

"I think," say Sugar pushing me off her feet like she never done before, cause I whip her ass in a minute, "that this is not much of a democracy if you ask me. Equal chance to pursue happiness means an equal crack at the dough, don't it?" Miss Moore is besides herself and I am disgusted with Sugar's treachery. So I stand on her foot one more time to see if she'll shove me. She shuts up, and Miss Moore looks at me, sorrowfully I'm thinkin. And somethin weird is goin on. I can feel it in my chest.

"Anybody else learn anything today?" lookin dead at me. I walk away and Sugar has to run to catch up and don't even seem to notice when I shrug her arm off my shoulder.

"Well, we got four dollars anyway," she says.

"Uh hunh."

"We could go to Hascombs and get half a chocolate layer and then to the Sunset and still have plenty of money for potato chips and ice cream sodas."

"Uh hunh."

"Race you to Hascombs," she say.

We start down the block and she gets ahead which is O.K. by me cause I'm goin to the West End and then over the Drive to think this day through. She can run if she want to and even run faster. But ain't nobody gonna beat me at nuthin.

Interpretations

1. What does Miss Moore hope to accomplish during the class outing? What lesson does she want to teach? Do you agree that the lesson needs teaching? Why? Has Miss Moore chosen an effective method of teaching?

2. What evidence is there that this outing is only the latest in a series of attempts to teach a lesson and that the children already know what they are expected to "learn"? How does that repetition affect your reaction to Sylvia's irritation at Sugar's "treachery" in saying what Sugar believes to be the lesson: "Equal chance to pursue happiness means an equal crack at the dough, don't it?" Has Sylvia failed to understand the lesson or is she irritated at the repetition?

3. Although Sylvia says "I'm mad," she will not admit her anger to Miss Moore. Why not? Does Sylvia know what has made her angry? Do we know?

4. Is Sylvia a reliable informant? (How does she feel about Miss Moore? Is she cooperative?)

5. Why do you think Miss Moore never demands change due her from the narrator?

6. How would this story be different if Miss Moore were the narrator? Would that be an improvement? Why or why not?

7. What do you consider the more important element of this story, the lesson itself or the personalities and/or attitudes of the three or four main characters? Why?

Correspondences

1. Sylvia in "The Lesson" has mixed emotions towards Miss Moore, the mentor of the neighborhood children. What role does she play in the children's lives? What is her purpose in exposing them to new experiences? To what extent did she contribute positively or negatively to their education? Review the last paragraph of Wright's "Discovering Books." Does Mr. Falk serve as a mentor? Why or why not?

2. "White folks crazy" appears twice in "The Lesson." What situations give rise to this conclusion? What emotions are the children expressing through these words? (What is the significance of Sylvia's resolve that "ain't nobody gonna beat me at nothin"?) How is Sylvia's attitude towards white people similar to or different from that of Rendón?

Applications

1. Write an essay about an adult who has had a positive or negative influence on your education. Include in your portrayal an experience which clearly illustrates that influence.

2. According to fiction writer Grace Paley, "If you say what's on your mind in the language that comes to you from your parents and your street and friends you'll probably say something beautiful." Write an essay showing the extent to which "The Lesson" supports Paley's point of view.

So Tsi-fai

Sophronia Liu

Sophronia Liu (b. 1953) was born in Hong Kong and came to America at age 10. She received her Master's Degree in English from the University of South Dakota and is currently working on her doctorate at the University of Minnesota. These are her reasons for writing "So Tsi-fai": "I wrote "So Tsi-fai" as a response to an assignment in a feminist creative writing course. The assignment was to describe a person who had given me my first inkling about social class. I guess for me, my awareness of social class and of the meaning of colonial oppression happened simultaneously in my sixth-grade classroom."

The events of this narrative occurred in Hong Kong, an island ninety miles south of Canton, China. Hong Kong has been a British colony since 1841 and is scheduled to revert to the People's Republic of China in 1997. Only 20,000 of its 5.7 million inhabitants are British. Hong Kong and its mainland adjunct the New Territories have been the destination of more than a million refugees from China, but since the Chinese crackdown on political dissidents in Tiananmen Square in June 1989, many Hong Kong citizens, fearful that the Chinese Communist government in Beijing will not honor the agreement allowing Hong Kong to retain its capitalist system, are themselves contemplating emigration.

For more information on China, see John King Fairbank, "Footbinding," Chapter 1.

VOICES, IMAGES, scenes from the past—twenty-three years ago, when I was in sixth grade:

"Let us bow our heads in silent prayer for the soul of So Tsi-fai. Let us pray for God's forgiveness for this boy's rash taking of his own life . . ." Sister Marie (Mung Gu-liang). My sixth-grade English teacher. Missionary nun from Paris. Principal of The Little Flower's School. Disciplinarian, perfectionist, authority figure: awesome and awful in my ten-year-old eyes.

"I don't need any supper. I have drunk enough insecticide." So Tsi-fai. My fourteen-year-old classmate. Daredevil; good-for-nothing lazybones (according to Mung Gu-liang). Bright black eyes, disheveled hair, defiant sneer, creased and greasy uniform, dirty hands, careless walk, shuffling feet. Standing in the corner for being late, for forgetting his homework, for talking in class, for using foul language. ("Shame on you! Go wash your mouth with soap!" Mung Gu-liang's sharp command. He did, and came back with a grin.) So Tsi-fai: Sticking his tongue out behind Mung Gu-liang's back, passing secret notes to his friends, kept behind after school, sent to the Principal's office for repeated offense. So Tsi-fai: incorrigible, hopeless, and without hope.

It was a Monday in late November when we heard of his death, returning to school after the weekend with our parents' signatures on our midterm reports. So Tsi-fai also showed his report to his father, we were told later. He flunked three out of the fourteen subjects: English Grammar, Arithmetic, and Chinese Dictation. He missed each one by one to three marks. That wasn't so bad. But he was a hopeless case. Overaged, stubborn, and un-cooperative; a repeated offender of school rules, scourge of all teachers; who was going to give him a lenient passing grade? Besides, being a few months over the maximum age—fourteen—for sixth graders, he wasn't even allowed to sit for the Secondary School Entrance Exam.

All sixth graders in Hong Kong had to pass the SSE before they could obtain a seat in secondary school. In 1964 when I took the exam, there were more than twenty thousand candidates. About seven thousand of us passed: four thousand were sent to government and subsidized schools, the other three thousand to private and grant-in-aid schools. I came in around no. 2000; I was lucky. Without the public exam, there would be no secondary school for So Tsi-fai. His future was sealed.

Looking at the report card with three red marks on it, his father was furious. So Tsi-fai was the oldest son. There were three younger children. His father was a vegetable farmer with a few plots of land in Wong Juk-hang, by the sea. His mother worked in a local factory. So Tsi-fai helped in the fields, cooked for the family, and washed his own clothes. ("Filthy, dirty boy!" gasped Mung Gu-liang. "Grime behind the ears, black rims on the fingernails, dirty collar, crumpled shirt. Why doesn't your mother iron your shirt?") Both his parents were illiterate. So Tsi-fai was their biggest hope: He made it to the sixth grade.

Who woke him up for school every morning and had breakfast waiting for him? Nobody. ("Time for school! Get up! Eat your rice!" Ma nagged and screamed. The aroma of steamed rice and Chinese sausages spread all over the house. "Drink your tea! Eat your oranges! Wash your face! And remember to wash behind your ears!") And who helped So Tsi-fai do his homework? Nobody. Did he have older brothers like mine who knew all about the arithmetic of rowing a boat against the currents or with the currents, how to count the feet of chickens and rabbits in the same cage, the present perfect continuous tense of "to live" and the future perfect tense of "to succeed"? None. Nil. So Tsi-fai was a lost cause.

I came first in both terms that year, the star pupil. So Tsi-fai was one of the last in the class: He was lazy; he didn't care. Or did he?

When his father scolded him, So Tsi-fai left the house. When he showed up again, late for supper, he announced, "I don't need any supper. I have drunk enough insecticide." Just like another one of his practical jokes. The insecticide was stored in the field for his father's vegetables. He was rushed to the hospital; dead upon arrival.

"He gulped for a last breath and was gone," an uncle told us at the funeral. "But his eyes wouldn't shut. So I said in his ear, 'You go now and rest in peace.' And I smoothed my hand over his eyelids. His face was all purple."

His face was still purple when we saw him in his coffin. Eyes shut tight, nostrils dilated and white as if fire and anger might shoot out, any minute.

In class that Monday morning, Sister Marie led us in prayer. "Let us pray that God will forgive him for his sins." We said the Lord's Prayer and the Hail Mary. We bowed our heads. I sat in my chair, frozen and dazed, thinking of the deadly chill in the morgue, the smell of disinfectant, ether, and dead flesh.

"Bang!" went a gust of wind, forcing open a leaf of the double door leading to the back balcony. "Flap, flap, flap." The door swung in the wind. We could see the treetops by the hillside rustling to and fro against a pale blue sky. An imperceptible presence had drifted in with the wind. The same careless walk and shuffling feet, the same daredevil air—except that the eyes were lusterless, dripping blood; the tongue hanging out, gasping for air. As usual, he was late. But he had come back to claim his place.

"I died a tragic death," his voice said. "I have as much right as you to be here. This is my seat." We heard him; we knew he was back.

. . . So Tsi-fai: Standing in the corner for being late, for forgetting his homework, for talking in class, for using foul language. So Tsi-fai: Palm outstretched, chest sticking out, holding his breath: "Tat. Tat. Tat." Down came the teacher's wooden ruler, twenty times on each hand. Never batting an eyelash: then back to facing the wall in the corner by the door. So Tsi-fai: grimy shirt, disheveled hair, defiant sneer. So Tsi-fai. Incorrigible, hopeless, and without hope.

The girls in front gasped and shrank back in their chairs. Mung Guliang went to the door, held the doorknob in one hand, poked her head out, and peered into the empty balcony. Then, with a determined jerk, she pulled the door shut. Quickly crossing herself, she returned to the teacher's desk. Her black cross swung upon the front of her gray habit as she hurried across the room. "Don't be silly!" she scolded the frightened girls in the front row.

What really happened? After all these years, my mind is still haunted by this scene. What happened to So Tsi-fai? What happened to me? What happened to all of us that year in sixth grade, when we were green and young and ready to fling our arms out for the world? All of a sudden, death claimed one of us and he was gone.

Who arbitrates between life and death? Who decides which life is worth preserving and prospering, and which to nip in its bud? How did it happen that I, at ten, turned out to be the star pupil, the lucky one, while my friend, a peasant's son, was shoveled under the heap and lost forever? How could it happen that this world would close off a young boy's life at fourteen just because he was poor, undisciplined, and lacked the training and support to pass his exams? What really happened?

Today, twenty-three years later, So Tsi-fai's ghost still haunts me. "I died a tragic death. I have as much right as you to be here. This is my seat." The voice I heard twenty-three years ago in my sixth-grade classroom follows me in my dreams. Is there anything I can do to lay it to rest?

Interpretations

1. To what extent does So Tsi-fai's family help him realize his aspirations? What relation do you see between these aspirations and So Tsi-fai's suicide?

2. What does the statement, "I don't need any supper. I have drunk enough insecticide" show about So Tsi-fai's personality?

3. In two paragraphs of questions, the author tries to convey her feelings about So Tsi-fai's "ghost." Describe these feelings. (Can you answer any of the story questions?)

4. Specifically, which phrases, sentences, or passages control the tone of the essay and most aptly convey the author's feelings about the events surrounding So Tsi-fai's death?

5. Do the children of poor, uneducated parents indeed have a right to a good education? If so, whose responsibility is it to provide that education? Is this a particularly Chinese problem, or do we face it in America?

6. Sometimes poor and uneducated but ambitious parents are surprised to find their educated children alienated. How do you think such alienation can be avoided so that the whole family benefits from the newly educated generation?

Correspondences

1. Review the Baker perspective on American education (page 151). How does it apply to the educational experience of students in Hong Kong? Should educational systems focus less on testing? Why or why not?

2. Parents play an important role in the education of their children. How did So Tsi-fai's parents affect his? How was their attitude towards education different from that of Kingston's parents (Chapter 2)?

Applications

1. "Voices, images, scenes from the past—twenty-three years ago, when I was in sixth grade." Write an essay about a classmate who, like So Tsi-fai, made a deep impression. Describe the person's effect on your education.

2. In an interview, Kingston (Chapter 2) described her ideal school system as follows: "I picture having a school system where the whole class is a tribe and the children do not compete for their grades or a few prizes." Write a journal entry responding to Kingston's statement.

Summer School

Gary Soto

Gary Soto (b. 1952) is a second-generation Mexican-American from Fresno, California. He graduated from California State University in 1974, and in 1976 earned an advanced degree from the University of California at Berkeley, where he teaches English and Chicano studies.

He has received numerous awards including the Academy of American Poets prize (1975), a Guggenheim fellowship (1979–1980), the Levinson Award (1984), and, for Living up the Street: Narrative Recollections, *the American Book Award (1985). In "Summer School," he recalls enjoying elective courses and his rivalry with Little John, a childhood friend from the barrio.*

THE SUMMER BEFORE I entered sixth grade I decided to go to summer school. I had never gone, and it was either school or mope around the house with a tumbler of Kool-Aid and watch TV, flipping the channels from exercise programs to soap operas to game shows until something looked right.

My sister decided to go to summer school too, so the two of us hopped onto our bikes and rode off to Heaton Elementary, which was three miles away, and asked around until we were pointed to the right rooms. I ran off without saying good-bye to Debra.

These were the home rooms where the teachers would check roll, announce bulletins, and read us a story before we dashed off to other classes. That morning I came in breathing hard, smiling a set of teeth that were fit for an adult, and took a seat behind a fat kid named Yodelman so I couldn't be seen.

The teacher, whose name is forgotten, told us that summer school classes were all electives—that we could choose anything we wanted. She had written them on the blackboard, and from her list I chose science, history, German, and square dancing.

Little John, a friend from our street, sat across the room. I had not seen him at first, which miffed him because he thought I was playing stuck-up for some reason, and so he threw an acorn at me that bounced harmlessly off Yodelman's shoulder. Yodelman turned his head slowly, turtle-like, blinked his small dull eyes, and then turned his head back to the teacher who was telling us that we had to fill out cards. She had two monitors pass out pencils, and we hovered and strained over the card: Date of birth, address, grade, career goals. At the last one I thought for the longest time, pencil poised and somewhat worried, before I raised my hand to ask the teacher how to spell paleontology. Surprised, as if someone had presented her flowers, she opened her mouth, searched the ceiling with her eyes, and gave it a stab: p-a-y-e-n-t-o-l-o-g-y. I wrote it in uneven capitals and then wrote "bone collector" in the margin.

Little John glared at me, made a fist, and wet his lips. When class was dismissed he punched me softly in the arm and together the two of us walked out of class talking loudly, happy that we were together.

While Little John went to typing I went to science class. The teacher stood before us in a white shirt, yardstick in hand, surrounded by jars of animal parts floating in clear liquids. This scared me, as did a replica of a skeleton hanging like a frayed coat in the corner. On the first day we looked carefully at leaves in groups of threes, after which the teacher asked us to describe the differences.

"This one is dried up and this one is not so dried up," one kid offered, a leaf in each hand.

The teacher, who was kind, said that that was a start. He raised his yardstick and pointed to someone else.

From there I went to history, a class I enjoyed immensely because it was the first one ever in which I would earn an A. This resulted from reading thirty books—pamphlets to be more exact. I was a page turner, and my index finger touched each paragraph before the thumb peeled a new page, as I became familiar with Edison, Carnegie, MacArthur, Eli Whitney . . . At the end of the five-week summer school, the teacher would call me to the front of the class to tell about the books I had read. He stood behind the lectern, looking down at his watch now and then, and beamed at me like a flashlight.

"Who was Pike?"

"Oh, he was the guy that liked to go around in the mountains."

"Who was Genghis Khan?"

"He was a real good fighter. In China."

With each answer the teacher smiled and nodded his head at me. He smiled at the class and some of the students turned their heads away, mad that I knew so much. Little John made a fist and wet his lips.

From history we were released to the playground where we played softball, sucked on popsicles, and fooled around on the monkey bars. We returned to our classes sweating like the popsicles we had sucked to a rugged stick. I went to German where, for five weeks, we sang songs we didn't understand, though we loved them and loved our teacher who paraded around the room and closed his eyes on the high notes. On the best days he rolled up his sleeves, undid his tie, and sweated profusely as he belted out songs so loudly that we heard people pounding on the wall for quiet from the adjoining classroom. Still he went on with great vigor:

> Mein Hut der hat drei Ecken
> Drei Ecken hat mein Hut

Und wenn er das nicht hatte
Dan war's auch nicht mein Hut

And we joined in every time, faces pink from a wonderful beauty that
rose effortlessly from the heart.

I left, humming, for square dancing. Debra was in that class with me,
fresh from science class where, she told me, she and a girlfriend had rolled
balls of mercury in their palms to shine nickels, rings, earrings, before they
got bored and hurled them at the boys. The mercury flashed on their shoulders, and they pretended to be shot as they staggered and went down to their
knees.

Even though Debra didn't want to do it, we paired off the first day. We
made ugly faces at each other as we clicked our heels, swished for a few steps,
and clicked again.

It was in that class that I fell in love with my corner gal who looked
like Hayley Mills, except she was not as boyish. I was primed to fall in love
because of the afternoon movies I watched on television, most of which were
stories about women and men coming together, parting with harsh feelings,
and embracing in the end to marry and drive big cars.

Day after day we'd pass through do-si-does, form Texas stars, spin, click
heels, and bounce about the room, released from our rigid school children
lives to let our bodies find their rhythm. As we danced I longed openly for
her, smiling like a lantern and wanting very badly for her eyes to lock onto
mine and think deep feelings. She swung around my arm, happy as the music,
and hooked onto the next kid, oblivious to my yearning.

When I became sick and missed school for three days, my desire for her
didn't sputter out. In bed with a comic book, I became dreamy as a cat and
closed my eyes to the image of her allemanding left to "The Red River
Valley," a favorite of the class's, her long hair flipping about on her precious
shoulders. By Friday I was well, but instead of going to school I stayed home
to play "jump and die" with the neighbor kids—a game in which we'd
repeatedly climb a tree and jump until someone went home crying from a
hurt leg or arm. We played way into the dark.

On Monday I was back at school, stiff as new rope, but once again excited
by science, history, the gutteral sounds of German, and square dancing! By
Sunday I had almost forgotten my gal, so when I walked into class my heart
was sputtering its usual tiny, blue flame. It picked up, however, when I saw
the girls come in, pink from the afternoon heat, and line up against the wall.
When the teacher clapped her hands, announced something or another, and
asked us to pair off, my heart was roaring like a well-stoked fire as I approached
a girl that *looked* like my girlfriend. I searched her face, but it wasn't her. I
looked around as we galloped about the room but I couldn't spot her. Where
is she? Is that her? I asked myself. No, no, my girlfriend has a cute nose.
Well, then, is that her? I wondered girl after girl and, for a moment in the

dizziness of spinning, I even thought my sister was my girlfriend. So it was. All afternoon I searched for *her* by staring openly into the faces of girls with long hair, and when class was dismissed I walked away bewildered that I had forgotten what the love of my life looked like. The next day I was desperate and stared even more boldly, until the teacher pulled me aside to shake a finger and told me to knock it off.

But I recovered from lost love as quickly as I recovered from jumping from trees, especially when it was announced, in the fourth week of classes, that there would be a talent show—that everyone was welcome to join in. I approached Little John to ask if he'd be willing to sing with me—"Michael Row the Boat Ashore," "If I Had a Hammer," or "Sugar Shack"—anything that would bring applause and momentary fame.

"C'mon, I know they'll like it," I whined at him as he stood in center field. He told me to leave him alone, and when a fly ball sailed in his direction he raced for it but missed by several feet. Two runs scored, and he turned angrily at me: "See what you did!"

I thought of square dancing with Debra, but I had the feeling that she would screw up her face into an ugly knot if I should ask. She would tell her friends and they would ride their bikes talking about me. So I decided that I'd just watch the show with my arms crossed.

The talent show was held on the lawn, and we were herded grade by grade into an outline of a horseshoe: The first and second grades sat Indian-style, the third and fourth graders squatted on their haunches, and the fifth and sixth graders stood with their arms across their chests. The first act was two girls—sisters I guessed—singing a song about weather: Their fingers made the shape of falling rain, their arching arms made rainbows, and finally their hands cupped around smiling faces made sunshine. We applauded like rain while some of the kids whistled like wind from a mountain pass.

This was followed with a skit about personal hygiene—bathing and brushing one's teeth. Then there was a juggling act, another singing duo, and then a jazz tap dancer who, because he was performing on the grass, appeared to be stamping mud off his shoes. After each act my eyes drifted to a long table of typewriters. What could they possibly be for? I asked myself. They were such commanding machines, big as boulders lugged from rivers. Finally, just as the tap routine was coming to an end, kids began to show up behind them to fit clean sheets of paper into the rollers. They adjusted their chairs as they looked at one another, whispering. A teacher called our attention to the typewriters and we whistled like mountain wind again.

"All summer we have practiced learning how to type," the teacher said in a clear, deliberate speech. "Not only have we learned to type letters, but also to sing with the typewriters. If you listen carefully, I am sure that you will hear songs that you are familiar with." She turned to the kids, whose hands rested like crabs on the keys, raised a pencil, and then began waving it around. Click—clickclick—click—click—click, and I recognized "The Star Spangled Banner"—and recognized Little John straining over his keyboard. Damn him, I thought, jealous that everyone was looking at him. They then played "Waltzing Matilda," and this made me even angrier because it sounded beautiful and because Little John was enjoying himself. Click-click-click, and they were playing "Michael Row the Boat Ashore," and this made me even more mad. I edged my way in front of Little John and, when he looked up, I made a fist and wet my lips. Smiling, he wet his own lips and shaped a cuss word, which meant we would have a fight afterward, when the music was gone and there were no typewriters to hide behind.

Interpretations

1. Are you surprised at Soto's ability to remember specific details of a day in his eleventh/twelfth year? If not, why not? If so, what are some difficult-to-remember examples? If he is not remembering these details, where did they come from? What difference does it make whether you regard this essay as fiction or nonfiction?

2. Soto says that some of his classmates were "mad that [he] knew so much." How do you react to Soto's answers to the teacher's questions about his reading? Is he advanced, average, or below average for a fifth grader? Why do you say so? What is your impression of the quality of his school and teachers?

3. How do you interpret the phrase "a wonderful beauty that rose effortlessly from the heart"? Where are other passages like this? What is their effect?

4. What is the relationship between Soto and Little John? What caused this relationship? What is the effect of repeating the phrase "made a fist and wet my lips"?

5. To which activity does Soto devote the most time—academic classes, square dancing, or the talent show? Why do you suppose he makes such an allocation of time?

6. Soto is a Mexican-American. Is biculturalism an issue in this essay? If so, how and why? (What do you think is Soto's purpose in this essay?)

Correspondences

1. Compare Soto's friendship with Little John with that of Sylvia and Sugar in "The Lesson." How do their relationships contribute to their "education"?

2. Soto and Rendón share a similar cultural heritage and both attended public schools on the West Coast. Compare their educational experiences. How are they similar and different?

Applications

1. Soto's summer school experience was enhanced by the fact "that summer school classes were all electives—that we could choose anything we wanted." What has been your experience with required courses as opposed to electives? In which have you usually learned more?

2. Brainstorm on a learning experience which gave you a sense of liberation. Write an essay in which you describe the experience and explain its effects.

ADDITIONAL WRITING TOPICS

1. Is community part of the educational experiences of Soto, Rendón, Kontor, Liu or Cousins? How does its presence or absence affect their experiences? To what extent was your educational experience shaped by the presence or absence of a sense of community? Should educational institutions be responsible for fostering a sense of community?

2. Review the Kaufman quotation (page 151). What are the ramifications of viewing education as a process rather than a product? To what extent do the selections in this chapter support or refute Kaufman? Write an essay responding to these questions concluding with your views on this issue.

3. According to the Ellison quotation in "Perspectives" (page 152), language can create or destroy, liberate or imprison. How do the selections by Rendón, Wright, and Marshall attest to Ellison's point of view? To what extent do you agree or disagree with Ellison? What educational experience led to your conclusions about the power of language? Frame your reply in a chronological narrative. Include insights gained from the experience.

4. .Should a teacher serve as a role model for students? How important is it that he or she be a member of the students' ethnic group? Do teachers have too much or too little influence on their students? Write an essay that answers these questions.

5. Review the Bambara headnote. Why does she think stories are important? How have stories that you were told and that you have read contributed to your knowledge of your cultural heritage and to your education? Write a speech for your local school board in which you argue for the inclusion of a storytelling component in each of the elementary grades.

6. Some educational theorists argue that because students have grown up with television they prefer the visual to the linear—the image to the word. For such learners, "a picture is worth a thousand words." To what extent do you agree? How has the visual affected information processing? Should more visual techniques of communication be incorporated into the classroom? Write an essay responding to these questions.

CHAPTER 4

Work

We spend a great deal of our lives choosing, preparing for, and doing our work. "What do you do?" is perhaps the first question we want to ask about a new acquaintance. "Talking shop" is supposed to be taboo everywhere except at the office, factory, or construction site, yet no taboo is more frequently, and more gladly, broken. For many people, the workplace is life. Talk about it ranges from the personal and particular to the abstract, whatever one's culture.

As you will discover, attitudes towards work and its value differ among cultures and exist in a matrix of customs, traditions, education, and class. In the Genesis account, work is viewed as a punishment for human disobedience, while in the Nez Percé selection work is portrayed as interfering with dreams.

In the traditional, pre-industrial economy of Guinea, in western Africa, goldsmithing is highly ritualistic work akin to religious "mysteries." From it the craftsman gains an identity and a social status as well as an income. The identity is particularly satisfying and the status exalted.

The most abstract treatment of work in this chapter is Lance Morrow's consideration of recent developments in the nature and psychological impact of work, mostly on Americans, and the American attitude toward work. Ouchi's "The Competitive Edge" is a sociological treatise on cultural and national traits revealed in work habits. He finds the Japanese more suited by temperament than Americans to industrial work because of the Japanese emphasis on cooperation.

The other selections of the chapter focus on individual workers, mostly blue collar, who experience problems: immigrant conditions

217

and the effects of national, racial, or sexual prejudice. Steve Olson, a construction worker, sees his co-workers, the BCGs (blue-collar guys) as a "much maligned group" who "have been portrayed as beer-drinking, big-bellied, bigoted rednecks who dress badly. . . . While white-collar types are debating the value of reading over watching TV, BCGs are doing stuff." (*Newsweek,* November 6, 1989).

In immigrant families work provides, above all, for education. It serves that end however it can. And workers suffer for it. Mario Puzo's family "did stuff," in addition to raising a son who would become a best-selling novelist. The Puzos exchanged a small farm in Italy for working on the railroad in one of the roughest neighborhoods of New York, Hell's Kitchen. The main character of Ann Petry's story is a black factory worker whose white female boss calls him a "nigger." You will see how Johnson handles the problem in "Like a Winding Sheet." Rachel Jones, a black reporter for a Florida newspaper, and one of the few white-collar workers in this chapter, finds work made almost impossible by racial prejudice when she tries to cover a Ku Klux Klan rally. The title character in Bharati Mukherjee's "Jasmine" will put up with almost any indignity and do almost any work in America to escape her home in Trinidad. Gary Soto, our youngest worker, accepts any job on the block in "Looking for Work," but the consequences are much less serious. Unlike blacks and first-generation immigrants, he is not exploited or foiled.

PERSPECTIVES

Work spares us from three great evils: boredom, vice and need.

Voltaire

*How will you know when you have found work you love? One
symptom is that you will lose track of time. You'll look at your watch
and wonder where the hours have gone, at your calendar and wonder
what happened to the week. And that loss of time sense is a symbol as
well as a symptom. We are time-bound creatures, but meaningful
work can make us forget our mortal limitation—because it helps us
transcend it.*

Lynne V. Cheney

*If people are highly successful in their professions they lose their senses.
Sound goes. They have no time to listen to music. Speech goes. They
have no time for conversation. They lose their sense of proportion—the
relations between one thing and another. Humanity goes.*

Virginia Woolf

Work is a necessity for man. Man invented the alarm clock.

Pablo Picasso

*Life is a continual distraction which does not allow us to reflect on
that from which we are distracted.*

Franz Kafka

*Women feel just as men feel . . . and it is narrowminded in their
more privileged fellow creatures to say that they ought to confine
themselves to making pudding and knitting stockings.*

Charlotte Brontë

*This book, being about work, is, by its very nature, about violence—
to the spirit as well as the body.*

Studs Terkel

*In fact, there is perhaps only one human being in a thousand who is
passionately interested in his job for the job's sake.*

Dorothy Sayers

Applications

1. Write a journal entry comparing the Perspectives on work to your own ideas
    about work.

2. Discuss Picasso's viewpoint with your group and write an analysis of their
    responses.

The Fall

Genesis 3:1–19

The Genesis account of the Fall explains among other things, the origin of work, painful childbirth, and death. This seminal story following immediately after the Genesis account of Creation continues to exert an influence on Western culture out of proportion to its modest length.

THE SERPENT was more crafty than any wild creature that the LORD God had made. He said to the woman, "Is it true that God has forbidden you to eat from any tree in the garden?" The woman answered the serpent, "We may eat the fruit of any tree in the garden, except for the tree in the middle of the garden; God has forbidden us either to eat or to touch the fruit of that; if we do, we shall die." The serpent said, "Of course you will not die. God knows that as soon as you eat it, your eyes will be opened and you will be like gods knowing both good and evil." When the woman saw that the fruit of the tree was good to eat, and that it was pleasing to the eye and tempting to contemplate, she took some and ate it. She also gave her husband some and he ate it. Then the eyes of both of them were opened and they discovered that they were naked; so they stitched fig-leaves together and made themselves loincloths.

The man and his wife heard the sound of the LORD God walking in the garden at the time of the evening breeze and hid from the LORD God among the trees of the garden. But the LORD God called to the man and said to him, "Where are you?" He replied, "I heard the sound as you were walking in the garden, and I was afraid because I was naked, and I hid myself." God answered, "Who told you that you were naked? Have you eaten from the tree which I forbade you?" The man said, "The woman you gave me for a companion, she gave me fruit from the tree and I ate it." Then the LORD God said to the woman, "What is this that you have done?" The woman said, "The serpent tricked me, and I ate." Then the LORD God said to the serpent:

> Because you have done this you are accursed
> more than all cattle and all wild creatures.
> On your belly you shall crawl, and dust you shall eat
> all the days of your life.
> I will put enmity between you and the woman,
> between your brood and hers.

They shall strike at your head,
and you shall strike at their heel.

To the woman he said:

I will increase your labour and your groaning,
and in labour you shall bear children.
You shall be eager for your husband,
and he shall be your master.

And to the man he said:

Because you have listened to your wife
and have eaten from the tree which I forbade you,
accursed shall be the ground on your account.
With labour you shall win your food from it
all the days of your life.
It will grow thorns and thistles for you,
none but wild plants for you to eat.
You shall gain your bread by the sweat of your brow
until you return to the ground;
for from it you were taken.
Dust you are, to dust you shall return.

Interpretations

1. What attitude toward work does the passage reveal?

2. What attitude toward woman does the story reveal? Does the story explain why the serpent chose to speak to the woman, not the man? Of what significance is this choice?

3. What attributes of God does this story reveal? Does God's ban on the knowledge of good and evil (morality?) play into the serpent's evil designs, making the man and woman unnecessarily vulnerable? Is obedience God's main objective, and is this simply a test case to see if the new man and woman can obey orders, no matter what the orders?

4. Whom does the story hold ultimately responsible for the existence of evil?

5. Do you think the punishments in this case fit the crime? Why or why not?

My Young Men Shall Never Work

Chief Smohalla as told by Herbert J. Spinden

The Nez Percé are a tribe of American Indians formerly occupying much of the Pacific Northwest whose reservation is in Idaho.

Because Native Americans resisted giving up their homes and nomadic way of life to become farmers, white people have often called them lazy, stubborn, and impractical. But to Indians, whose homes, land, and hunting were sacred, anything that threatened any one of these, threatened their whole system of beliefs and values, in short, their very life.

MY YOUNG MEN shall never work. Men who work cannot dream and wisdom comes in dreams.

You ask me to plow the ground. Shall I take a knife and tear my mother's breast? Then when I die she will not take me to her bosom to rest.

You ask me to dig for stone. Shall I dig under her skin for bones? Then when I die I cannot enter her body to be born again.

You ask me to cut grass and make hay and sell it and be rich like white men. But how dare I cut off my mother's hair?

It is a bad law and my people cannot obey it. I want my people to stay with me here. All the dead men will come to life again. We must wait here in the house of our fathers and be ready to meet them in the body of our mother.

Interpretations

1. Are the Nez Percé objecting to all work? Would you define work to include hunting?

2. What is the Nez Percé's reason for rejecting what they call "work"? What do they value more than work? How common is it for a culture to place the highest value on something other than work? Is work the highest value of American culture? What's the evidence?

3. To what extent is the misunderstanding between the Nez Percé and the whites a matter of language (definition)? of tradition? What is the Nez Percé attitude towards earth? (What metaphor extends through and is elaborated within the whole passage?)

Correspondences

1. Review the Voltaire quotation (page 219). How does it apply to the Genesis account of the origins of work? Which attitude towards work best reflects your own?

2. Review the Kafka quotation (page 219). What does it mean? To what extent does it reflect the sentiments about work expressed by Smohalla of the Nez Percé?

Applications

1. Write a journal entry on work as punishment.

2. Review the headnote to the Nez Percé selection. To what extent does it justify Smohalla's attitude towards work? What does it suggest about tribal values?

What Is the Point of Working?

Lance Morrow

Lance Morrow is a poet and playwright. He worked as a reporter on the Washington Star *before becoming a contributing editor to* Time *magazine. In 1981 he
won the National Magazine Award for his essays regularly featured in* Time,
and in 1985 he published a book on fatherhood, The Chief: A Memoir of
Fathers and Sons. *In "What Is the Point of Working?" Morrow explores American
attitudes towards the workplace.*

WHEN GOD FORECLOSED on Eden, he condemned Adam and Eve to go to
work. Work has never recovered from that humiliation. From the beginning,
the Lord's word said that work was something bad: a punishment, the great
stone of mortality and toil laid upon a human spirit that might otherwise
soar in the infinite, weightless playfulness of grace.

A perfectly understandable prejudice against work has prevailed ever
since. Most work in the life of the world has been hard, but since it was
grindingly inevitable, it hardly seemed worth complaining about very much.
Work was simply the business of life, as matter-of-fact as sex and breathing.
In recent years, however, the ancient discontent has grown elaborately articulate. The worker's usual old bitching has gone to college. Grim tribes of
sociologists have reported back from office and factory that most workers find
their labor mechanical, boring, imprisoning, stultifying, repetitive, dreary,
heartbreaking. In his 1972 book *Working*, Studs Terkel began: "This book,
being about work, is, by its very nature, about violence—to the spirit as
well as to the body." The historical horrors of industrialization (child labor,
Dickensian squalor, the dark satanic mills) translate into the 20th century's
robotic busywork on the line, tightening the same damned screw on the
Camaro's fire-wall assembly, going nuts to the banging, jangling Chaplin-
esque whirr of modern materialism in labor, bringing forth issue, disgorging
itself upon the market.

The lamentations about how awful work is prompt an answering wail
from the management side of the chasm: nobody wants to work any more.
As American productivity, once the exuberant engine of national wealth, has
dipped to an embarrassingly uncompetitive low, Americans have shaken their
heads: the country's old work ethic is dead. About the only good words for
it now emanate from Ronald Reagan and certain beer commercials. Those
ads are splendidly mythic playlets, romantic idealizations of men in groups

who blast through mountains or pour plumingly molten steel in factories, the work all grit and grin. Then they retire to flip around iced cans of sacramental beer and debrief one another in a warm sundown glow of accomplishment. As for Reagan, in his presidential campaign he enshrined work in his rhetorical "community of values," along with family, neighborhood, peace and freedom. He won by a landslide.

Has the American work ethic really expired? Is some old native eagerness to level wilderness and dig and build and invent now collapsing toward a decadence of dope, narcissism, income transfers and aerobic self-actualization?

The idea of work—work as an ethic, an abstraction—arrived rather late in the history of toil. Whatever edifying and pietistic things may have been said about work over the centuries (Kahlil Gibran called work "love made visible," and the Benedictines say, "To work is to pray"), humankind has always tried to avoid it whenever possible. The philosophical swells of ancient Greece thought work was degrading; they kept an underclass to see to the laundry and other details of basic social maintenance. That prejudice against work persisted down the centuries in other aristocracies. It is supposed, however, to be inherently un-American. Edward Kennedy likes to tell the story of how, during his first campaign for the Senate, his opponent said scornfully in a debate: "This man has never worked a day in his life!" Kennedy says that the next morning as he was shaking hands at a factory gate, one worker leaned toward him and confided, "You ain't missed a goddamned thing."

The Protestant work ethic, which sanctified work and turned it into vocation, arrived only a few centuries ago in the formulations of Martin Luther and John Calvin. In that scheme, the worker collaborates with God to do the work of the universe, the great design. One scholar, Leland Ryken of Illinois' Wheaton College, has pointed out that American politicians and corporate leaders who preach about the work ethic do not understand the Puritans' original, crucial linkage between human labor and God's will.

During the 19th century industrialization of America, the idea of work's inherent virtue may have seemed temporarily implausible to generations who labored in the mines and mills and sweatshops. The century's huge machinery of production punished and stunned those who ran it.

And yet for generations of immigrants, work *was* ultimately availing; the numb toil of an illiterate grandfather got the father a foothold and a high school education, and the son wound up in college or even law school. A woman who died in the Triangle Shirtwaist Co. fire [1911] in lower Manhattan had a niece who made it to the halcyon Bronx, and another generation on, the family went to Westchester County. So for millions of Americans, as they labored through the complexities of generations, work worked, and the immigrant work ethic came at last to merge with the Protestant work ethic.

The motive of work was all. To work for mere survival is desperate. To work for a better life for one's children and grandchildren lends the labor a fierce dignity. That dignity, an unconquerably hopeful energy and aspiration—driving, persisting like a life force—is the American quality that many find missing now.

The work ethic is not dead, but it is weaker now. The psychology of work is much changed in America. The acute, painful memory of the Great Depression used to enforce a disciplined and occasionally docile approach to work—in much the way that older citizens in the Soviet Union do not complain about scarce food and overpopulated apartments, because they remember how much more horrible everything was during the war. But the generation of the Depression is retiring and dying off, and today's younger workers, though sometimes laid off and kicked around by recessions and inflation, still do not keep in dark storage that residual apocalyptic memory of Hoovervilles and the Dust Bowl and banks capsizing.

Today elaborate financial cushions—unemployment insurance, union benefits, welfare payments, food stamps and so on—have made it less catastrophic to be out of a job for a while. Work is still a profoundly respectable thing in America. Most Americans suffer a sense of loss, of diminution, even of worthlessness, if they are thrown out on the street. But the blow seldom carries the life-and-death implications it once had, the sense of personal ruin. Besides, the wild and notorious behavior of the economy takes a certain amount of personal shame out of joblessness; if Ford closes down a plant in New Jersey and throws 3,700 workers into the unemployment lines, the guilt falls less on individuals than on Japanese imports or American car design or an extortionate OPEC.

Because today's workers are better educated than those in the past, their expectations are higher. Many younger Americans have rearranged their ideas about what they want to get out of life. While their fathers and grandfathers and great-grandfathers concentrated hard upon plow and drill press and pressure gauge and tort, some younger workers now ask previously unimaginable questions about the point of knocking themselves out. For the first time in the history of the world, masses of people in industrially advanced countries no longer have to focus their minds upon work as the central concern of their existence.

In the formulation of Psychologist Abraham Maslow, work functions in a hierarchy of needs: first, work provides food and shelter, basic human maintenance. After that, it can address the need for security and then for friendship and "belongingness." Next, the demands of the ego arise, the need for respect. Finally, men and woman assert a larger desire for "self-actualization." That seems a harmless and even worthy enterprise but sometimes degenerates into self-infatuation, a vaporously selfish discontent that dead-ends in isolation, the empty face that gazes back from the mirror.

Of course in patchwork, pluralistic America, different classes and ethnic groups are perched at different stages in the work hierarchy. The immigrants—legal and illegal—who still flock densely to America are fighting for the foothold that the jogging tribes of self-actualizers achieved three generations ago. The zealously ambitious Koreans who run New York City's best vegetable markets, or boat people trying to open a restaurant, or chicanos who struggle to start a small business in the *barrio* are still years away from est and the Sierra Club. Working women, to the extent that they are new at it, now form a powerful source of ambition and energy. Feminism—and financial need—have made them, in effect, a sophisticated-immigrant wave upon the economy.

Having to work to stay alive, to build a future, gives one's exertions a tough moral simplicity. The point of work in that case is so obvious that it need not be discussed. But apart from the sheer necessity of sustaining life, is there some inherent worth in work? Carlyle believed that "all work, even cotton spinning, is noble; work is alone noble." Was he right?

It is seigneurial cant to romanticize work that is truly detestable and destructive to workers. But misery and drudgery are always comparative. Despite the sometimes nostalgic haze around their images, the pre-industrial peasant and the 19th century American farmer did brutish work far harder than the assembly line. The untouchable who sweeps excrement in the streets of Bombay would react with blank incomprehension to the malaise of some $17-an-hour workers on a Chrysler assembly line. The Indian, after all, has passed from "alienation" into a degradation that is almost mystical. In Nicaragua, the average 19-year-old peasant has worked longer and harder than most Americans of middle age. Americans prone to restlessness about the spiritual disappointments of work should consult unemployed young men and women in their own ghettos: they know with painful clarity the importance of the personal dignity that a job brings.

Americans often fall into fallacies of misplaced sympathy. Psychologist Maslow, for example, once wrote that he found it difficult "to conceive of feeling proud of myself, self-loving and self-respecting, if I were working, for example, in some chewing-gum factory . . ." Well, two weeks ago, Warner-Lambert announced that it would close down its gum-manufacturing American Chicle factory in Long Island City, N.Y.; the workers who had spent years there making Dentyne and Chiclets were distraught. "It's a beautiful place to work," one feeder-catcher-packer of chewing gum said sadly. "It's just like home." There is a peculiar elitist arrogance in those who discourse on the brutalizations of work simply because they cannot imagine themselves performing the job. Certainly workers often feel abstracted out, reduced sometimes to dreary robotic functions. But almost everyone commands endlessly subtle systems of adaptation; people can make the work their own and even cherish it against all academic expectations. Such adaptations are often more important than the famous but theoretical alienation from the process and product of labor.

Work is still the complicated and crucial core of most lives, the occupation melded inseparably to the identity; Freud said that the successful psyche is one capable of love and of work. Work is the most thorough and profound organizing principle in American life. If mobility has weakened old blood ties, our co-workers often form our new family, our tribe, our social world; we become almost citizens of our companies, living under the protection of salaries, pensions and health insurance. Sociologist Robert Schrank believes that people like jobs mainly because they need other people; they need to gossip with them, hang out with them, to schmooze. Says Schrank: "The workplace performs the function of community."

Unless it is dishonest or destructive—the labor of a pimp or a hit man, say—all work is intrinsically honorable in ways that are rarely understood as they once were. Only the fortunate toil in ways that express them directly. There is a Renaissance splendor in Leonardo's effusion: "The works that the eye orders the hands to make are infinite." But most of us labor closer to the ground. Even there, all work expresses the laborer in a deeper sense: all life must be worked at, protected, planted, replanted, fashioned, cooked for, coaxed, diapered, formed, sustained. Work is the way that we tend the world, the way that people connect. It is the most vigorous, vivid sign of life—in individuals and in civilizations.

Interpretations

1. What do you consider the most interesting or valuable point Morrow makes about work? Why?

2. Have you ever considered not working at all, just avoiding any kind of work for your whole life? Probably not, but *why* not? Aside from food and shelter, what do you expect to get out of work? What portion of your identity do you expect to derive from your work? If your work is not the "central concern of [your] existence," what else could occupy that position? Are your educational choices (or your choice of friends or of entertainment) shaped wholly by your work plans? If not, by what?

3. "Because today's workers are better educated than those in the past, their expectations are higher." Do you agree that education raises expectations? Expectations of what? If you agree, can you explain how this relationship works? What are the advantages and disadvantages of being governed by "higher" expectations?

4. Is it possible to be a failure in your chosen profession and still be a success in life? Explain.

5. How has Morrow limited his subject and where in the essay does he indicate which aspect of work he intends to cover?

Correspondences

1. Review the Cheney quotation (page 219). To what extent is it applicable to Morrow's essay? Do you agree with Morrow that the work ethic is weaker now in America than it was in the past. Why or why not?

2. Morrow suggests that the hardest workers in the United States are immigrants. How do Weber's essay (Chapter 2) or Marshall's story (Chapter 3) support this? (What attitudes toward work are expressed by those Weber interviewed? How do they compare with those of Marshall's "poets"?)

Applications

1. Write an essay analyzing the difference between a job and a position and between having a job and doing a job.

2. Discuss in your group Schrank's thesis that "the workplace performs the function of community." Have you found that to be true of your working experience? Might Schrank's thesis also apply to the homeless? What is the relationship of homelessness to work?

Choosing a Dream: Italians in Hell's Kitchen

Mario Puzo

Mario Puzo (b. 1920) is from New York City. The son of a railroad trackman, he was educated at the New School for Social Research and Columbia University. He has received numerous awards and honors from the American Academy of Motion Picture Arts and Sciences, the Writers Guild of America, West, Inc., for The Godfather *(1972) and* The Godfather, Part II *(1974). In "Italians in Hell's Kitchen," Puzo explains why his youthful contempt for his Italian parents and relatives changed to awe and admiration.*

A major world power under the Romans, the birthplace of the Renaissance and the site of the mother church of Roman Catholicism, Italy was prevented until 1860 by German, French, Spanish, and Austrian intervention from transforming its city states into a unified modern nation (under King Victor Emmanuel II). Even after unification, economic progress, especially in the south, was slow, sending millions of Italians abroad in search of a better life. In the century and a half before 1988, almost ten percent of immigrants to the United States were Italian, among them Puzo's parents.

AS A CHILD and in my adolescence, living in the heart of New York's Neapolitan ghetto, I never heard an Italian singing. None of the grown-ups I knew were charming or loving or understanding. Rather they seemed coarse, vulgar, and insulting. And so later in my life when I was exposed to all the clichés of lovable Italians, singing Italians, happy-go-lucky Italians, I wondered where the hell the moviemakers and story-writers got all their ideas from.

At a very early age I decided to escape these uncongenial folk by becoming an artist, a writer. It seemed then an impossible dream. My father and mother were illiterate, as were their parents before them. But practicing my art I tried to view the adults with a more charitable eye and so came to the conclusion that their only fault lay in their being foreigners; I was an American. This didn't really help because I was only half right. I was the foreigner. They were already more "American" than I could ever become.

But it did seem then that the Italian immigrants, all the fathers and mothers that I knew, were a grim lot; always shouting, always angry, quicker to quarrel then embrace. I did not understand that their lives were a long labor to earn their daily bread and that physical fatigue does not sweeten human natures.

And so even as a very small child I dreaded growing up to be like the adults around me. I heard them saying too many cruel things about their dearest friends, saw too many of their false embraces with those they had just maligned, observed with horror their paranoiac anger at some small slight or a fancied injury to their pride. They were, always, too unforgiving. In short, they did not have the careless magnanimity of children.

In my youth I was contemptuous of my elders, including a few under thirty. I thought my contempt special to their circumstances. Later when I wrote about these illiterate men and women, when I thought I understood them, I felt a condescending pity. After all, they had suffered, they had labored all the days of their lives. They had never tasted luxury, knew little more economic security than those ancient Roman slaves who might have been their ancestors. And alas, I thought, with new-found artistic insight, they were cut off from their children because of the strange American tongue, alien to them, native to their sons and daughters.

Already an artist but not yet a husband or father, I pondered omnisciently on their tragedy, again thinking it special circumstance rather than a constant in the human condition. I did not yet understand why these men and women were willing to settle for less than they deserved in life and think that "less" quite a bargain. I did not understand that they simply could not afford to dream; I myself had a hundred dreams from which to choose. For I was already sure that I would make my escape, that I was one of the chosen. I would be rich, famous, happy. I would master my destiny. . . .

My family and I grew up together on Tenth Avenue, between Thirtieth and Thirty-first streets, part of the area called Hell's Kitchen. This particular neighborhood could have been a movie set for one of the Dead End Kid flicks or for the social drama of the East Side in which John Garfield played the hero. Our tenements were the western wall of the city. Beneath our windows were the vast black iron gardens of the New York Central Railroad, absolutely blooming with stinking boxcars freshly unloaded of cattle and pigs for the city slaughterhouse. Steers sometimes escaped and loped through the heart of the neighborhood followed by astonished young boys who had never seen a live cow.

The railroad yards stretched down to the Hudson River, beyond whose garbagey waters rose the rocky Palisades of New Jersey. There were railroad tracks running downtown on Tenth Avenue itself to another freight station called St. Johns Park. Because of this, because these trains cut off one side of the street from the other, there was a wooden bridge over Tenth Avenue, a romantic-looking bridge despite the fact that no sparkling water, no silver flying fish darted beneath it; only heavy dray carts drawn by tired horses, some flat-boarded trucks, tin lizzie automobiles and, of course, long strings of freight cars drawn by black, ugly engines. . . .

My father supported his wife and seven children by working as a trackman laborer for the New York Central Railroad. My oldest brother worked for the railroad as a brakeman, another brother was a railroad shipping clerk in the freight office. Eventually I spent some of the worst months of my life as the railroad's worst messenger boy.

My oldest sister was just as unhappy as a dressmaker in the garment industry. She wanted to be a school teacher. At one time or another my other two brothers also worked for the railroad—it got all six males in the family. The two girls and my mother escaped, though my mother felt it her duty to send all our bosses a gallon of homemade wine on Christmas. But everybody hated their jobs except my oldest brother who had a night shift and spent most of his working hours sleeping in freight cars. My father finally got fired because the foreman told him to get a bucket of water for the crew and not to take all day. My father took the bucket and disappeared forever.

Nearly all the Italian men living on Tenth Avenue supported their large families by working on the railroad. Their children also earned pocket money by stealing ice from the refrigerator cars in summer and coal from the open stoking cars in the winter. Sometimes an older lad would break the seal of a freight car and take a look inside. But this usually brought down the "Bulls," the special railroad police. And usually the freight was "heavy" stuff, too much work to cart away and sell, something like fresh produce or boxes of cheap candy that nobody would buy.

The older boys, the ones just approaching voting age, made their easy money by hijacking silk trucks that loaded up at the garment factory on Thirty-first Street. They would then sell the expensive dresses door to door, at bargain prices no discount house could match. From this some graduated into organized crime, whose talent scouts alertly tapped young boys versed in strongarm. Yet despite all this, most of the kids grew up honest, content with fifty bucks a week as truck drivers, deliverymen, and white-collar clerks in the civil service.

I had every desire to go wrong but I never had a chance. The Italian family structure was too formidable.

I never came home to an empty house; there was always the smell of supper cooking. My mother was always there to greet me, sometimes with a policeman's club in her hand (nobody ever knew how she acquired it). But she was always there, or her authorized deputy, my older sister, who preferred throwing empty milk bottles at the heads of her little brothers when they got bad marks on their report cards. During the great Depression of the 1930s, though we were the poorest of the poor, I never remember not dining well. Many years later as a guest of a millionaire's club, I realized that our poor family on home relief ate better than some of the richest people in America.

My mother would never dream of using anything but the finest imported olive oil, the best Italian cheeses. My father had access to the fruits coming off ships, the produce from railroad cars, all before it went through the stale process of middlemen; and my mother, like most Italian women, was a fine cook in the peasant style. . . .

I had to help support my family by working on the railroad. After school hours of course. This was the same railroad that had supplied free coal and free ice to the whole Tenth Avenue when I was young enough to steal with impunity. After school finished at 3 P.M. I went to work in the freight office as a messenger. I also worked Saturdays and Sundays when there was work available.

I hated it. One of my first short stories was about how I hated that job. But of course what I really hated was entering the adult world. To me the adult world was a dark enchantment, unnatural. As unnatural to the human dream as death. And as inevitable. . . .

Then why do I dream of those immigrant Italian peasants as having been happy? I remember how they spoke of their forebears, who spent all their lives farming the arid mountain slopes of Southern Italy. "He died in that house in which he was born," they say enviously. "He was never more than an hour from his village, not in all his life," they sigh. And what would they make of a phrase like "retrospective falsification"?

No, really, we are all happier now. It is a better life. And after all, as my mother always said, "Never mind about being happy. Be glad you're alive."

When I came to my "autobiographical novel," the one every writer does about himself, I planned to make myself the sensitive, misunderstood hero, much put upon by his mother and family. To my astonishment my mother took over the book and instead of my revenge I got another comeuppance. But it is, I think, my best book. And all those old-style grim conservative Italians whom I hated, then pitied so patronizingly, they also turned out to be heroes. Through no desire of mine. I was surprised. The thing that amazed me most was their courage. Where were their Congressional Medals of Honor? Their Distinguished Service Crosses? How did they ever have the balls to get married, have kids, go out to earn a living in a strange land, with no skills, not even knowing the language? They made it without tranquillizers, without sleeping pills, without psychiatrists, without even a dream. Heroes. Heroes all around me. I never saw them.

But how could I? They wore lumpy work clothes and handlebar moustaches, they blew their noses on their fingers and they were so short that their high-school children towered over them. They spoke a laughable broken English and the furthest limit of their horizon was their daily bread. Brave men, brave women, they fought to live their lives without dreams. Bent on survival, they narrowed their minds to the thinnest line of existence.

It is no wonder that in my youth I found them contemptible. And yet they had left Italy and sailed the ocean to come to a new land and leave their sweated bones in America. Illiterate Colombos, they dared to seek the promised land. And so they, too, dreamed a dream.

Interpretations

1. Puzo says of the Italians he knew in his childhood, "[T]heir lives were a long labor to earn their daily bread." To what extent were their lives and personalities shaped by their work? Do you think their work played an unusually large part in their lives? Cite evidence. Are most people so shaped by their jobs?

2. How does Puzo use description to support his thesis on these Italian immigrants? Which images back up his point best?

3. Why does Puzo credit his family with saving him and his brothers from a life of crime?

4. What did Puzo consider these Italians' "tragedy"? What effect did it have on Puzo? What is his final explanation for the "tragedy"?

5. Why doesn't Puzo feel guilty for having misjudged his fellow Italians?

6. How does Puzo use his introduction and his conclusion as organizing devices?

Correspondences

1. Review the comments on work by Smohalla of the Nez Percé. How does it apply to the Italian immigrants in Puzo's essay? How does Puzo's last paragraph contradict the Nez Percé sentiments?

2. Review Morrow's comments about ethnic attitudes towards work. How does "Italians in Hell's Kitchen" support or contradict his point of view? How do Morrow's comments apply to the work habits of your ethnic group?

Applications

1. Puzo writes of the Italian immigrants: "They made it without tranquillizers, without sleeping pills, without psychiatrists, without even a dream." Write an analysis of the implications of their system of values as Puzo interprets them. How do these values compare to those of contemporary Americans?

2. Study dictionary and thesaurus definitions of *work, trade, drudgery,* and *vocation.* How do they differ in meaning and applicability? Which best describe what Puzo's family members did to earn a living?

The Competitive Edge:
Japanese and Americans

William Ouchi

William Ouchi (b. 1943) was born in Honolulu. He is now a professor of management at UCLA and the author of Theory Z: How American Business Can Meet the Japanese Challenge *(1981) and* The M-Form Society: How American Teamwork Can Recapture the Competitive Edge *(1984). In the following essay you will see his interests in business management, competition, the United States and Japan come together.*

A centralized feudal government ruled Japan from 1192 to 1867, with very little contact with Westerners until the American Commodore Matthew Perry opened Japan to U.S. trade with a treaty in 1854. The modernizing Emperor Meiji set Japan on a new course in 1868, and in the century and a half since then, Japan has become increasingly involved in the history of other nations (in wars with Russia, China, Korea, and the United States). Since her defeat in 1945, Japan has become one of the most powerful economies in the world and a leader in technology. Japan's growth rate, the highest in the industrial world, has led writers like Ouchi to examine the causes of her success and to ask which factors might be exportable (record on unemployment? high savings rate?). Analysts usually turn sooner or later to the unusual homogeneity of Japan's population. Less than one percent of the Japanese belong to non-Japanese ethnic groups, and a large majority share religions (Buddhism and Shintoism). The "strong orientation to collective values" Ouchi describes is one of the effects of this homogeneity.

PERHAPS the most difficult aspect of the Japanese for Westerners to comprehend is the strong orientation to collective values, particularly a collective sense of responsibility. Let me illustrate with an anecdote about a visit to a new factory in Japan owned and operated by an American electronics company. The American company, a particularly creative firm, frequently attracts attention within the business community for its novel approaches to planning, organizational design, and management systems. As a consequence of this corporate style, the parent company determined to make a thorough study of Japanese workers and to design a plant that would combine the best of East and West. In their study they discovered that Japanese firms almost never make use of individual work incentives, such as piecework or even individual performance appraisal tied to salary increases. They concluded that rewarding individual achievement and individual ability is always a good thing.

236

In the final assembly area of their new plant, long lines of young Japanese women wired together electronic products on a piece-rate system: the more you wired, the more you got paid. About two months after opening, the head foreladies approached the plant manager. "Honorable plant manager," they said humbly as they bowed, "we are embarrassed to be so forward, but we must speak to you because all of the girls have threatened to quit work this Friday." (To have this happen, of course, would be a great disaster for all concerned.) "Why," they wanted to know, "can't our plant have the same compensation system as other Japanese companies? When you hire a new girl, her starting wage should be fixed by her age. An eighteen-year-old should be paid more than a sixteen-year-old. Every year on her birthday, she should receive an automatic increase in pay. The idea that any of us can be more productive than another must be wrong, because none of us in final assembly could make a thing unless all of the other people in the plant had done their jobs right first. To single one person out as being more productive is wrong and is also personally humiliating to us." The company changed its compensation system to the Japanese model.

Another American company in Japan had installed a suggestion system much as we have in the United States. Individual workers were encouraged to place suggestions to improve productivity into special boxes. For an accepted idea the individual received a bonus amounting to some fraction of the productivity savings realized from his or her suggestion. After a period of six months, not a single suggestion had been submitted. The American managers were puzzled. They had heard many stories of the inventiveness, the commitment, and the loyalty of Japanese workers, yet not one suggestion to improve productivity had appeared.

The managers approached some of the workers and asked why the suggestion system had not been used. The answer: "No one can come up with a work improvement idea alone. We work together, and any ideas that one of us may have are actually developed by watching others and talking to others. If one of us was singled out for being responsible for such an idea, it would embarrass all of us." The company changed to a group suggestion system, in which workers collectively submitted suggestions. Bonuses were paid to groups which would save bonus money until the end of the year for a party at a restaurant or, if there was enough money, for family vacations together. The suggestions and productivity improvements rained down on the plant.

One can interpret these examples in two quite different ways. Perhaps the Japanese commitment to collective values is an anachronism that does not fit with modern industrialism but brings economic success despite that collectivism. Collectivism seems to be inimical to the kind of maverick creativity exemplified in Benjamin Franklin, Thomas Edison, and John D. Rockefeller. Collectivism does not seem to provide the individual incentive to excel which has made a great success of American enterprise. Entirely apart from its economic effects, collectivism implies a loss of individuality, a loss of the freedom to be different, to hold fundamentally different values from others.¹

The second interpretation of the examples is that the Japanese collectivism is economically efficient. It causes people to work well together and to encourage one another to better efforts. Industrial life requires interdependence of one person on another. But a less obvious but far-reaching implication of the Japanese collectivism for economic performance has to do with accountability.

In the Japanese mind, collectivism is neither a corporate or individual goal to strive for nor a slogan to pursue. Rather, the nature of things operates so that nothing of consequence occurs as a result of individual effort. Everything important in life happens as a result of teamwork or collective effort. Therefore, to attempt to assign individual credit or blame to results is unfounded. A Japanese professor of accounting, a brilliant scholar trained at Carnegie-Mellon University who teaches now in Tokyo, remarked that the status of accounting systems in Japanese industry is primitive compared to those in the United States. Profit centers, transfer prices, and computerized information systems are barely known even in the largest Japanese companies, whereas they are a commonplace in even small United States organizations. Though not at all surprised at the difference in accounting systems, I was not at all sure that the Japanese were primitive. In fact, I thought their system a good deal more efficient than ours.

Most American companies have basically two accounting systems. One system summarizes the overall financial state to inform stockholders, bankers, and other outsiders. That system is not of interest here. The other system, called the managerial or cost accounting system, exists for an entirely different reason. It measures in detail all of the particulars of transactions between departments, divisions, and key individuals in the organization, for the purpose of untangling the interdependencies between people. When, for example, two departments share one truck for deliveries, the cost accounting system charges each department for part of the cost of maintaining the truck and driver, so that at the end of the year, the performance of each department can be individually assessed, and the better department's manager can receive a larger raise. Of course, all of this information processing costs money, and furthermore may lead to arguments between the departments over whether the costs charged to each are fair.

In a Japanese company a short-run assessment of individual performance is not wanted, so the company can save the considerable expense of collecting and processing all of that information. Companies still keep track of which department uses a truck how often and for what purposes, but like-minded people can interpret some simple numbers for themselves and adjust their behavior accordingly. Those insisting upon clear and precise measurement for the purpose of advancing individual interests must have an elaborate information system. Industrial life, however, is essentially integrated and interdependent. No one builds an automobile alone, no one carries through a banking transaction alone. In a sense the Japanese value of collectivism fits naturally into an industrial setting, whereas the Western individualism provides constant conflicts. The image that comes to mind is of Chaplin's silent film "Modern Times" in which the apparently insignificant hero played by Chaplin successfully fights against the unfeeling machinery of industry. Modern industrial life can be aggravating, even hostile, or natural: all depends on the fit between our culture and our technology.

The *shinkansen* or "bullet train" speeds across the rural areas of Japan giving a quick view of cluster after cluster of farmhouses surrounded by rice paddies. This particular pattern did not develop purely by chance, but as a consequence of the technology peculiar to the growing of rice, the staple of the Japanese diet. The growing of rice requires the construction and maintenance of an irrigation system, something that takes many hands to build. More importantly, the planting and the harvesting of rice can only be done efficiently with the cooperation of twenty or more people. The "bottom line" is that a single family working alone cannot produce enough rice to survive, but a dozen families working together can produce a surplus. Thus the Japanese have had to develop the capacity to work together in harmony, no matter what the forces of disagreement or social disintegration, in order to survive.

Japan is a nation built entirely on the tips of giant, suboceanic volcanoes. Little of the land is flat and suitable for agriculture. Terraced hillsides make use of every available square foot of arable land. Small homes built very close together further conserve the land. Japan also suffers from natural disasters such as earthquakes and hurricanes. Traditionally homes are made of light construction materials, so a house falling down during a disaster will not crush its occupants and also can be quickly and inexpensively rebuilt. During the feudal period until the Meiji restoration of 1868, each feudal lord sought to restrain his subjects from moving from one village to the next for fear that a neighboring lord might amass enough peasants with which to produce a large agricultural surplus, hire an army and pose a threat. Apparently bridges were not commonly built across rivers and streams until the late nineteenth century, since bridges increased mobility between villages.

Taken all together, this characteristic style of living paints the picture of a nation of people who are homogeneous with respect to race, history, language, religion, and culture. For centuries and generations these people have lived in the same village next door to the same neighbors. Living in close proximity and in dwellings which gave very little privacy, the Japanese survived through their capacity to work together in harmony. In this situation, it was inevitable that the one most central social value which emerged, the one value without which the society could not continue, was that an individual does not matter.

To the Western soul this is a chilling picture of society. Subordinating individual tastes to the harmony of the group and knowing that individual needs can never take precedence over the interests of all is repellent to the Western citizen. But a frequent theme of Western philosophers and sociologists is that individual freedom exists only when people willingly subordinate their self-interests to the social interest. A society composed entirely of self-interested individuals is a society in which each person is at war with the other, a society which has no freedom. This issue, constantly at the heart of understanding society, comes up in every century, and in every society, whether the writer be Plato, Hobbes, or B. F. Skinner.

In order to complete the comparison of Japanese and American living situations, consider flight over the United States. Looking out of the window high over the state of Kansas, we see a pattern of a single farmhouse surrounded by fields, followed by another single homestead surrounded by fields. In the early 1800s in the state of Kansas there were no automobiles. Your nearest neighbor was perhaps two miles distant; the winters were long, and the snow was deep. Inevitably, the central social values were self-reliance and independence. Those were the realities of that place and age that children had to learn to value.

The key to the industrial revolution was discovering that non-human forms of energy substituted for human forms could increase the wealth of a nation beyond anyone's wildest dreams. But there was a catch. To realize this great wealth, non-human energy needed huge complexes called factories with hundreds, even thousands of workers collected into one factory. Moreover, several factories in one central place made the generation of energy more efficient. Almost overnight, the Western world was transformed from a rural and agricultural country to an urban and industrial state. Our technological advance seems to no longer fit our social structure: in a sense, the Japanese can better cope with modern industrialism. While Americans still busily protect our rather extreme form of individualism, the Japanese hold their individualism in check and emphasize cooperation.

Interpretations

1. What is Ouchi's thesis or main idea? Where does he first state it? How does he attempt to support or develop it?

2. What factors does Ouchi think have caused the Japanese preference for cooperation?

3. According to Ouchi, what is the basic difference between Japanese and Western workers? Do you think Westerners could benefit by becoming more like the Japanese?

4. "Industrial life requires interdependence. . . ." Do other areas besides industry require interdependence? Is it possible that we Westerners have taken independence too far? Does collectivism necessarily imply a loss of freedom? (What difference do you see between the Japanese ideal of cooperation and what Westerners call unselfishness?)

5. If, as Ouchi thinks, modern industrialism is better suited to Japan than to the West, why do you think industrialism began in the West?

Correspondences

1. What are the economic and cultural implications of the collective sense of responsibility of the Japanese towards work as opposed to the individual's responsibility advocated in the United States? Compare Ouchi and Morrow.

2. "Collective solidarity" is an important aspect of Japanese ethics. Just what does it mean? How does it apply to the experiences of Sadat, Momaday (Chapter 1), and Kingston (Chapter 2)? To what extent is it part of the American work ethic?

Applications

1. Test Ouchi's thesis on American individualism in the workplace by conducting an informal survey of workers varying in age, occupation, and ethnic background on their views on cooperation in the workplace. What conclusions did you reach? Write an essay supporting or refuting Ouchi's thesis.

2. Using your group experience as a basis, write an analysis of how working collaboratively has affected your ability to learn. How has it changed your attitudes toward learning? Be specific.

Like a Winding Sheet

Ann Petry

Ann Petry (b. 1912) was born and raised in Old Saybrook, Connecticut, but has lived most of her adult life in Harlem. She worked as a journalist with the Amsterdam News *and as an editor of the* People's Voice. *For her first novel,* The Street *(1946), she was awarded a Houghton Mifflin Literary Fellowship. Other publications include* Country Place *(1947),* The Narrows *(1953) and* Miss Muriel and Other Stories *(1971). Her fiction reflects her interest in the naturalist school and many of her stories are set in large cities. In "Like a Winding Sheet," Petry explores some causes and effects of boredom in the workplace.*

HE HAD PLANNED to get up before Mae did and surprise her by fixing breakfast. Instead he went back to sleep and she got out of bed so quietly he didn't know she wasn't there beside him until he woke up and heard the queer soft gurgle of water running out of the sink in the bathroom.

He knew he ought to get up but instead he put his arms across his forehead to shut the afternoon sunlight out of his eyes, pulled his legs up close to his body, testing them to see if the ache was still in them.

Mae had finished in the bathroom. He could tell because she never closed the door when she was in there and now the sweet smell of talcum powder was drifting down the hall and into the bedroom. Then he heard her coming down the hall.

"Hi, babe," she said affectionately.

"Hum," he grunted, and moved his arms away from his head, opened one eye.

"It's a nice morning."

"Yeah." He rolled over and the sheet twisted around him, outlining his thighs, his chest. "You mean afternoon, don't ya?"

Mae looked at the twisted sheet and giggled. "Looks like a winding sheet," she said. "A shroud—" Laughter tangled with her words and she had to pause for a moment before she could continue. "You look like a huckleberry—in a winding sheet—"

"That's no way to talk. Early in the day like this," he protested.

He looked at his arms silhouetted against the white of the sheets. They were inky black by contrast and he had to smile in spite of himself and he lay there smiling and savoring the sweet sound of Mae's giggling.

"Early?" She pointed a finger at the alarm clock on the table near the bed and giggled again. "It's almost four o'clock. And if you don't spring up out of there, you're going to be late again."

242

"What do you mean 'again'?"

"Twice last week. Three times the week before. And once the week before and—"

"I can't get used to sleeping in the daytime," he said fretfully. He pushed his legs out from under the covers experimentally. Some of the ache had gone out of them but they weren't really rested yet. "It's too light for good sleeping. And all that standing beats the hell out of my legs."

"After two years you oughta be used to it," Mae said.

He watched her as she fixed her hair, powdered her face, slipped into a pair of blue denim overalls. She moved quickly and yet she didn't seem to hurry.

"You look like you'd had plenty of sleep," he said lazily. He had to get up but he kept putting the moment off, not wanting to move, yet he didn't dare let his legs go completely limp because if he did he'd go back to sleep. It was getting later and later but the thought of putting his weight on his legs kept him lying there.

When he finally got up he had to hurry, and he gulped his breakfast so fast that he wondered if his stomach could possibly use food thrown at it at such a rate of speed. He was still wondering about it as he and Mae were putting their coats on in the hall.

Mae paused to look at the calendar. "It's the thirteenth," she said. Then a faint excitement in her voice, "Why, it's Friday the thirteenth." She had one arm in her coat sleeve and she held it there while she stared at the calendar. "I oughta stay home," she said. "I shouldn't go outa the house."

"Aw, don't be a fool," he said. "Today's payday. And payday is a good luck day everywhere, any way you look at it." And as she stood hesitating he said, "Aw, come on."

And he was late for work again because they spent fifteen minutes arguing before he could convince her she ought to go to work just the same. He had to talk persuasively, urging her gently, and it took time. But he couldn't bring himself to talk to her roughly or threaten to strike her like a lot of men might have done. He wasn't made that way.

So when he reached the plant he was late and he had to wait to punch the time clock because the day-shift workers were streaming out in long lines, in groups and bunches that impeded his progress.

Even now just starting his workday his legs ached. He had to force himself to struggle past the outgoing workers, punch the time clock, and get the little cart he pushed around all night, because he kept toying with the idea of going home and getting back in bed.

He pushed the cart out on the concrete floor, thinking that if this was his plant he'd make a lot of changes in it. There were too many standing-up jobs for one thing. He'd figure out some way most of 'em could be done sitting down and he'd put a lot more benches around. And this job he had— this job that forced him to walk ten hours a night, pushing this little cart, well, he'd turn it into a sitting-down job. One of those little trucks they used around railroad stations would be good for a job like this. Guys sat on a seat and the thing moved easily, taking up little room and turning in hardly any space at all, like on a dime.

He pushed the cart near the foreman. He never could remember to refer to her as the forelady even in his mind. It was funny to have a white woman for a boss in a plant like this one.

She was sore about something. He could tell by the way her face was red and her eyes were half-shut until they were slits. Probably been out late and didn't get enough sleep. He avoided looking at her and hurried a little, head down, as he passed her though he couldn't resist stealing a glance at her out of the corner of his eyes. He saw the edge of the light-colored slacks she wore and the tip end of a big tan shoe.

"Hey, Johnson!" the woman said.

The machines had started full blast. The whirr and the grinding made the building shake, made it impossible to hear conversations. The men and women at the machines talked to each other but looking at them from just a little distance away, they appeared to be simply moving their lips because you couldn't hear what they were saying. Yet the woman's voice cut across the machine sounds—harsh, angry.

He turned his head slowly. "Good evenin,' Mrs. Scott," he said, and waited.

"You're late again."

"That's right. My legs were bothering me."

The woman's face grew redder, angrier looking. "Half this shift comes in late," she said. "And you're the worst one of all. You're always late. Whatsa matter with ya?"

"It's my legs," he said. "Somehow they don't ever get rested. I don't seem to get used to sleeping days. And I just can't get started."

"Excuses. You guys always got excuses," her anger grew and spread. "Every guy comes in here late always has an excuse. His wife's sick or her grandmother died or somebody in the family had to go to the hospital," she paused, drew a deep breath. "And the niggers is the worse. I don't care what's wrong with your legs. You get in here on time. I'm sick of you niggers—"

"You got the right to get mad," he interrupted softly. "You got the right to cuss me four ways to Sunday but I ain't letting nobody call me a nigger."

He stepped closer to her. His fists were doubled. His lips were drawn back in a thin narrow line. A vein in his forehead stood out swollen, thick.

And the woman backed away from him, not hurriedly but slowly—two, three steps back.

"Aw, forget it," she said. "I didn't mean nothing by it. It slipped out. It was an accident." The red of her face deepened until the small blood vessels in her cheeks were purple. "Go on and get to work," she urged. And she took three more slow backward steps.

He stood motionless for a moment and then turned away from the sight of the red lipstick on her mouth that made him remember that the foreman was a woman. And he couldn't bring himself to hit a woman. He felt a curious tingling in his fingers and he looked down at his hands. They were clenched tight, hard, ready to smash some of those small purple veins in her face.

He pushed the cart ahead of him, walking slowly. When he turned his head, she was staring in his direction, mopping her forehead with a dark blue handkerchief. Their eyes met and then they both looked away.

He didn't glance in her direction again but moved past the long work benches, carefully collecting the finished parts, going slowly and steadily up and down, back and forth the length of the building, and as he walked he forced himself to swallow his anger, get rid of it.

And he succeeded so that he was able to think about what had happened without getting upset about it. An hour went by but the tension stayed in his hands. They were clenched and knotted on the handles of the cart as though ready to aim a blow.

And he thought he should have hit her anyway, smacked her hard in the face, felt the soft flesh of her face give under the hardness of his hands. He tried to make his hands relax by offering them a description of what it would have been like to strike her because he had the queer feeling that his hands were not exactly a part of him anymore—they had developed a separate life of their own over which he had no control. So he dwelt on the pleasure his hands would have felt—both of them cracking at her, first one and then the other. If he had done that his hands would have felt good now—relaxed, rested.

And he decided that even if he'd lost his job for it, he should have let her have it and it would have been a long time, maybe the rest of her life, before she called anybody else a nigger.

The only trouble was he couldn't hit a woman. A woman couldn't hit back the same way a man did. But it would have been a deeply satisfying thing to have cracked her narrow lips wide open with just one blow, beautifully timed and with all his weight in back of it. That way he would have gotten rid of all the energy and tension his anger had created in him. He kept remembering how his heart had started pumping blood so fast he had felt it tingle even in the tips of his fingers.

With the approach of night, fatigue nibbled at him. The corners of his mouth drooped, the frown between his eyes deepened, his shoulders sagged; but his hands stayed tight and tense. As the hours dragged by he noticed that the women workers had started to snap and snarl at each other. He couldn't hear what they said because of the sound of machines but he could see the quick lip movements that sent words tumbling from the sides of their mouths. They gestured irritably with their hands and scowled as their mouths moved.

Their violent jerky motions told him that it was getting close on to quitting time but somehow he felt that the night still stretched ahead of him, composed of endless hours of steady walking on his aching legs. When the whistle finally blew he went on pushing the cart, unable to believe that it had sounded. The whirring of the machines died away to a murmur and he knew then that he'd really heard the whistle. He stood still for a moment, filled with a relief that made him sigh.

Then he moved briskly, putting the cart in the storeroom, hurrying to take his place in the line forming before the paymaster. That was another thing he'd change, he thought. He'd have the pay envelopes handed to the people right at their benches so there wouldn't be ten or fifteen mintues lost waiting for the pay. He always got home about fifteen minutes late on payday. They did it better in the plant where Mae worked, brought the money right to them at their benches.

He stuck his pay envelope in his pants' pocket and followed the line of workers heading for the subway in a slow-moving stream. He glanced up at the sky. It was a nice night, the sky looked packed full to running over with stars. And he thought if he and Mae would go right to bed when they got home from work they'd catch a few hours of darkness for sleeping. But they never did. They fooled around—cooking and eating and listening to the radio and he always stayed in a big chair in the living room and went almost but not quite to sleep and when they finally got to bed it was five or six in the morning and daylight was already seeping around the edges of the sky.

He walked slowly, putting off the moment when he would have to plunge into the crowd hurrying toward the subway. It was a long ride to Harlem and tonight the thought of it appalled him. He paused outside an all-night restaurant to kill time, so that some of the first rush of workers would be gone when he reached the subway.

The lights in the restaurant were brilliant, enticing. There was life and motion inside. And as he looked through the window he thought that everything within range of his eyes gleamed—the long imitation marble counter, the tall stools, the white porcelain-topped tables and especially the big metal coffee urn right near the window. Steam issued from its top and a gas flame flickered under it—a lively, dancing, blue flame.

A lot of the workers from his shift—men and women—were lining up near the coffee urn. He watched them walk to the porcelain-topped tables carrying steaming cups of coffee and he saw that just the smell of the coffee lessened the fatigue lines in their faces. After the first sip their faces softened, they smiled, they began to talk and laugh.

On a sudden impulse he shoved the door open and joined the line in front of the coffee urn. The line moved slowly. And as he stood there the smell of the coffee, the sound of the laughter and of the voices, helped dull the sharp ache in his legs.

He didn't pay any attention to the white girl who was serving the coffee at the urn. He kept looking at the cups in the hands of the men who had been ahead of him. Each time a man stepped out of the line with one of the thick white cups the fragrant steam got in his nostrils. He saw that they walked carefully so as not to spill a single drop. There was a froth of bubbles at the top of each cup and he thought about how he would let the bubbles break against his lips before he actually took a big deep swallow.

Then it was his turn. "A cup of coffee," he said, just as he had heard the others say.

The white girl looked past him, put her hands up to her head and gently lifted her hair away from the back of her neck, tossing her head back a little. "No more coffee for a while," she said.

He wasn't certain he'd heard her correctly and he said, "What?" blankly.

"No more coffee for a while," she repeated.

There was silence behind him and then uneasy movement. He thought someone would say something, ask why or protest, but there was only silence and then a faint shuffling sound as though the men standing behind him had simultaneously shifted their weight from one foot to the other.

He looked at the girl without saying anything. He felt his hands begin to tingle and the tingling went all the way down to his finger tips so that he glanced down at them. They were clenched tight, hard, into fists. Then he looked at the girl again. What he wanted to do was hit her so hard that the scarlet lipstick on her mouth would smear and spread over her nose, her chin, out toward her cheeks, so hard that she would never toss her head again and refuse a man a cup of coffee because he was black.

He estimated the distance across the counter and reached forward, balancing his weight on the balls of his feet, ready to let the blow go. And then his hands fell back down to his sides because he forced himself to lower them, to unclench them and make them dangle loose. The effort took his breath away because his hands fought against him. But he couldn't hit her. He couldn't even now bring himself to hit a woman, not even this one, who had refused him a cup of coffee with a toss of her head. He kept seeing the gesture with which she had lifted the length of her blond hair from the back of her neck as expressive of her contempt for him.

When he went out the door he didn't look back. If he had he would have seen the flickering blue flame under the shiny coffee urn being extinguished. The line of men who had stood behind him lingered a moment to watch the people drinking coffee at the tables and then they left just as he had without having had the coffee they wanted so badly. The girl behind the counter poured water in the urn and swabbed it out and as she waited for the water to run out, she lifted her hair gently from the back of her neck and tossed her head before she began making a fresh lot of coffee.

But he had walked away without a backward look, his head down, his hands in his pockets, raging at himself and whatever it was inside of him that had forced him to stand quiet and still when he wanted to strike out.

The subway was crowded and he had to stand. He tried grasping an overhead strap and his hands were too tense to grip it. So he moved near the train door and stood there swaying back and forth with the rocking of the train. The roar of the train beat inside his head, making it ache and throb, and the pain in his legs clawed up into his groin so that he seemed to be bursting with pain and he told himself that it was due to all that anger-born energy that had piled up in him and not been used and so it had spread through him like a poison—from his feet and legs all the way up to his head.

Mae was in the house before he was. He knew she was home before he put the key in the door of the apartment. The radio was going. She had it tuned up loud and she was singing along with it.

"Hello, babe," she called out, as soon as he opened the door.

He tried to say "hello" and it came out half grunt and half sigh.

"You sure sound cheerful," she said.

She was in the bedroom and he went and leaned against the doorjamb. The denim overalls she wore to work were carefully draped over the back of a chair by the bed. She was standing in front of the dresser, tying the sash of a yellow housecoat around her waist and chewing gum vigorously as she admired her reflection in the mirror over the dresser.

"Whatsa matter?" she said. "You get bawled out by the boss or somep'n?"

"Just tired," he said slowly. "For God's sake, do you have to crack that gum like that?"

"You don't have to lissen to me," she said complacently. She patted a curl in place near the side of her head and then lifted her hair away from the back of her neck, ducking her head forward and then back.

He winced away from the gesture. "What you got to be always fooling with your hair for?" he protested.

"Say, what's the matter with you anyway?" She turned away from the mirror to face him, put her hands on her hips. "You ain't been in the house two minutes and you're picking on me."

He didn't answer her because her eyes were angry and he didn't want to quarrel with her. They'd been married too long and got along too well and so he walked all the way into the room and sat down in the chair by the bed and stretched his legs out in front of him, putting his weight on the heels of his shoes, leaning way back in the chair, not saying anything.

"Lissen," she said sharply. "I've got to wear those overalls again tomorrow. "You're going to get them all wrinkled up leaning against them like that."

He didn't move. He was too tired and his legs were throbbing now that he had sat down. Besides the overalls were already wrinkled and dirty, he thought. They couldn't help but be for she'd worn them all week. He leaned farther back in the chair.

"Come on, get up," she ordered.

"Oh, what the hell," he said wearily, and got up from the chair. "I'd just as soon live in a subway. There'd be just as much place to sit down."

He saw that her sense of humor was struggling with her anger. But her sense of humor won because she giggled.

"Aw, come on and eat," she said. There was a coaxing note in her voice. "You're nothing but an old hungry nigger trying to act tough and—" she paused to giggle and then continued, "You—"

He had always found her giggling pleasant and deliberately said things that might amuse her and then waited, listening for the delicate sound to emerge from her throat. This time he didn't even hear the giggle. He didn't let her finish what she was saying. She was standing close to him and that funny tingling started in his finger tips, went fast up his arms and sent his fist shooting straight for her face.

There was the smacking sound of soft flesh being struck by a hard object and it wasn't until she screamed that he realized he had hit her in the mouth— so hard that the dark red lipstick had blurred and spread over her full lips, reaching up toward the tip of her nose, down toward her chin, out toward her cheeks.

The knowledge that he had struck her seeped through him slowly and he was appalled but he couldn't drag his hands away from her face. He kept striking her and he thought with horror that something inside him was holding him, binding him to this act, wrapping and twisting about him so that he had to continue it. He had lost all control over his hands. And he groped for a phrase, a word, something to describe what this thing was like that was happening to him and he thought it was like being enmeshed in a winding sheet—that was it—like a winding sheet. And even as the thought formed in his mind, his hands reached for her face again and yet again.

Interpretations

1. Explain the meaning of Mae's statement in the beginning of the story, "You look like a huckleberry in a winding sheet." What further significance does the title acquire at the end? Do you think a person like Mae would use this language or the closely related "shroud"? Why or why not? Do you find the dialogue in general to be natural? Support your answer with examples. How important is dialogue to the success or failure of the story? Do you find the story to be a success? Why?

2. What part does their work play in Mae's and Johnson's lives? Would different jobs make them different people? What's the evidence? Do you think sedentary jobs are necessarily better jobs? Why?

3. Johnson's forewoman values punctuality, an attitude which provides much of the momentum for the story. In the world of real work, do you find

punctuality to be a highly valued quality in an employee? What experiences led you to that conclusion? Do you think it *should* be highly valued? If so, why?

4. What role does race play in the relationships between Johnson and Mrs. Scott? Johnson and the girl at the coffee shop? Johnson and Mae?

5. Discuss how traditional restrictions on men's behavior affect Johnson. Why does he finally "hit a lady"?

6. Which is the primary cause of Johnson's behavior—that you can't hit *any* woman but you can hit your wife or that you can't hit a white person but you can hit another black?

7. The story organization is generally chronological. How does Petry keep it moving forward without having the time structure become obtrusive?

Correspondences

1. Review the Terkel quotation (page 219). What does it mean? How does it apply to Petry's story? Cite examples of physical and spiritual violence. Which were worse in your opinion?

2. Ouchi talks about the spirit of cooperation and participation in the Japanese workplace. To what extent were these part of Johnson's experience in the American workplace? How was Johnson interested in participating?

Applications

1. Write an essay on the advantages or disadvantages of competitiveness in the American workplace. Cite supporting examples.

2. Discuss gender, race, and class roles in "The Winding Sheet."

Year of the
Blue-Collar Guy

Steve Olson

*Steve Olson is a construction worker living in Madison, Wisconsin. In the following
selection, he focuses on the contributions and the values of blue-collar workers.*

WHILE THE LEARNED are attaching appropriate labels to the 1980s and spec-
ulating on what the 1990s will bring, I would like to steal 1989 for my own
much maligned group and declare it "the year of the blue-collar guy (BCG)."
BCGs have been portrayed as beer-drinking, big-bellied, bigoted rednecks
who dress badly. Wearing a suit to a cement-finishing job wouldn't be too
bright. Watching my tie go around a motor shaft followed by my neck is
not the last thing I want to see in this world. But, more to the point, our
necks are too big and our arms and shoulders are too awesome to fit suits
well without expensive tailoring. Suits are made for white-collar guys.

But we need big bellies as ballast to stay on the bar stool while we're
drinking beer. And our necks are red from the sun and we are somewhat
bigoted. But aren't we all? At least our bigotry is open and honest and worn
out front like a tattoo. White-collar people are bigoted, too. But it's disguised
as the pat on the back that holds you back: "You're not good enough so you
need affirmative action." BCGs aren't smart enough to be that cynical. I
never met a BCG who didn't respect an honest day's work and a job well
done—no matter who did it.

True enough, BCGs aren't perfect. But, I believe this: we are America's
last true romantic heroes. When some 21st-century Louis L'Amour writes
about this era he won't eulogize the greedy Wall Street insider. He won't
commend the narrow-shouldered, wide-hipped lawyers with six-digit un-
earned incomes doing the same work women can do. His wide-shouldered
heroes will be plucked from the ranks of the blue-collar guy. They are the
last vestige of the manly world where strength, skill and hard work are still
valued.

To some extent our negative ratings are our own fault. While we were
building the world we live in, white-collar types were sitting on their ever-
widening butts redefining the values we live by. One symbol of America's
opulent wealth is the number of people who can sit and ponder and comment
and write without producing a usable product or skill. Hey, get a real job—
make something—then talk. These talkers are the guys we drove from the

playgrounds into the libraries when we were young and now for 20 years or more we have endured the revenge of the nerds.

BCGs fidgeted our way out of the classroom and into jobs where, it seemed, the only limit to our income was the limit of our physical strength and energy. A co-worker described a BCG as "a guy who is always doing things that end in the letter 'n'—you know—huntin', fishin', workin' . . .". My wise friend is talking energy! I have seen men on the job hand-nail 20 square of shingles (that's 6,480 nails) or more a day, day after day, for weeks. At the same time, they were remodeling their houses, raising children, and coaching Little League. I've seen crews frame entire houses in a day—day after day. I've seen guys finish concrete until 11 P.M., go out on a date, then get up at 6 A.M. and do it all over again the next day.

These are amazing feats of strength. There should be stadiums full of screaming fans for these guys. I saw a 40-year-old man neatly fold a 350-pound piece of rubber roofing, put it on his shoulder and, alone, carry it up a ladder and deposit it on a roof. Nobody acknowledged it because the event was too common. One day at noon this same fellow wrestled a 22-year-old college summer worker. In the prime of his life, the college kid was a 6-foot-3, 190-pound body-builder and he was out of his league. He was on his back to stay in 90 seconds flat.

Great Skilled Work Force

Mondays are tough on any job. But in our world this pain is eased by stories of weekend adventure. While white-collar types are debating the value of reading over watching TV, BCGs are doing stuff. I have honest to God heard these things on Monday mornings about BCG weekends: "I tore out a wall and added a room," "I built a garage," "I went walleye fishing Saturday and pheasant hunting Sunday," "I played touch football both days" (in January), "I went skydiving," "I went to the sports show and wrestled the bear." Pack a good novel into these weekends.

My purpose is not so much to put down white-collar people as to stress the importance of blue-collar people to this country. Lawyers, politicians and bureaucrats are necessary parts of the process, but this great skilled work force is so taken for granted it is rarely seen as the luxury it truly is. Our plumbing works, our phones work and repairs are made as quickly as humanly possible. I don't think this is true in all parts of the world. But this blue-collar resource is becoming endangered. Being a tradesman is viewed with such disdain these days that most young people I know treat the trades like a temporary summer job. I've seen young guys take minimum-wage jobs just so they can wear suits. It is as if any job without a dress code is a dead-end job. This is partly our own fault. We even tell our own sons, "Don't be like me, get a job people respect." Blue-collar guys ought to brag more, even swagger a little. We should drive our families past the latest job site and say, "That house was a piece of junk, and now it's the best one on the block. I did that." Nobody will respect us if we don't respect ourselves.

Our work is hard, hot, wet, cold, and always dirty. It is also often very satisfying. Entailing the use of both brain and body there is a product—a physical result of which to be proud. We have fallen from your roofs, died under heavy equipment and been entombed in your dams. We have done honest, dangerous work. Our skills and energy and strength have transformed lines on paper into physical reality. We are this century's Renaissance men. America could do worse than to honor us. We still do things the old-fashioned way, and we have earned the honor.

Interpretations

1. Do you agree with Olson that blue-collar workers deserve more respect? Do you agree with his analysis of how and why they were short-changed on respect and with his prescription for regaining it? Why or why not?

2. Which aspect of his subject does Olson emphasize in the essay, the negative (the low morale of BCGs and its causes) or the positive (BCGs' pleasure in their work, their heroic strength, and their contribution to the country)? Do you think he has chosen an appropriate tone?

3. "Nobody will respect us if we don't respect ourselves." Do you consider Olson's primary audience for this essay to be his fellow BCGs or another group? If another, what group? Cite evidence.

4. Olson says his purpose is "not so much to put down white-collar people as to stress the importance of blue-collar people to this country." To what extent does he fulfill his stated purpose? Cite phrases that white-collar workers might find offensive.

Correspondences

1. "While we were building the world we live in, white-collar types were sitting on their ever-widening butts redefining the values we live by": To what extent does this comment apply to Morrow's essay?

2. "Being a tradesman is viewed with such disdain these days that most young people I know treat the trades like a temporary summer job": What factors have contributed to such disdain? To what extent do you agree with Olson's assertion? How does Puzo regard tradesmen?

Applications

1. Conduct an informal survey on attitudes of college administrators, faculty, and counselors towards blue-collar work. Write an analysis of their responses.

2. Write an essay defending or refuting Olson's claim that blue-collar workers "are the last vestige of the manly world where strength, skill and hard work are still valued."

The Mysteries of My
Father's Workshop

Camara Laye

*Camara Laye (1928-1980) was born in Guinea into a family that combined
tribal culture with the religion of Islam. He is the author of three highly acclaimed
novels,* The Radiance of the King *(1956),* A Dream of Africa *(1966), and*
The Guardian of the Word *(1984). His autobiography* The Dark Child
*(1954), written in French, from which the following selection is excerpted, traces
his life to the time when he left Guinea to study engineering in France. There he
found the differences between African and European cultures overwhelming. His
books, however, succeed in combining these discordant elements into unified wholes.
In "The Mysteries of My Father's Workshop" Laye portrays his father's pride in
his work.*

   *Guinea is located on the Atlantic coast of West Africa. About the size of
Oregon, it was under French control from the middle of the nineteenth century until
1958, when President Sékou Touré demanded immediate French withdrawal.
Within days, the French withdrew all aid, administrators, and technicians. (Laye
was living in Guinea in 1956–1966, working part of this time for the state.)
By the 1970s Touré turned Guinea into a Soviet-aligned, one-party state; his
dictatorship lasted 26 years. Laye spent his last years as a teacher in neighboring
Sénégal, one of only five sub-Saharan countries that now govern themselves under
systems of majority rule. Guinea, on the other hand, has been ruled by a military
government since the death of Touré in 1984. The country has the world's largest
bauxite deposits, as well as other natural resources, although most of the resources
remain undeveloped. French is still the official language. About one quarter of the
population is Malinké, the tribe to which Laye belonged, with the remainder divided
among seventeen other tribes. A large majority of Guineans are Muslim.*

OF ALL THE DIFFERENT kinds of work my father performed, none fascinated
me so much as his skill with gold. No other occupation was so noble, no
other needed such a delicate touch; and, moreover, this sort of work was
always a kind of festival: it was a real festival that broke the monotony of
ordinary working days.

   So if a woman, accompanied by a go-between, crossed the threshold of
the workshop, I would follow her in at once. I knew what she wanted: she
had brought some gold and wanted to ask my father to transform it into a
trinket. The woman would have collected the gold in the placers of Siguiri,
where, for months on end, she would have crouched over the river, washing

255

the mud and patiently extracting from it the grains of gold. These women never came alone: they were well aware that my father had other things to do than to make trinkets for all and sundry; and even if the making of jewellery had been his main occupation, they would have realized that they were not his first or his only customers, and that their wants could not be immediately attended to.

Generally these women required the trinket for a certain date, either for the festival of Ramadan or for the Tabaski; or for some other family festivity, or for a dance ceremony.

Thereupon, to better their chance of being quickly served, and the more easily to persuade my father to interrupt the work he had in hand, they would request the services of an official praise-singer, a go-between, and would arrange with him in advance what fee they would pay for his good offices.

The praise-singer would install himself in the workshop, tune up his cora, which is our harp, and would begin to sing my father's praises. This was always a great event for me. I would hear recalled the lofty deeds of my father's ancestors, and the names of these ancestors from the earliest times; as the couplets were reeled off, it was like watching the growth of a great genealogical tree that spread its branches far and wide and flourished its boughs and twigs before my mind's eye. The harp played an accompaniment to this vast utterance of names, expanding it and punctuating it with notes that were now soft, now shrill. Where did the praise-singer get his information from? He must certainly have developed a very retentive memory stored with facts handed down to him by his predecessors, for this is the basis of all our oral traditions. Did he embellish the truth? It is very likely: flattery is the praise-singer's stock in trade! Nevertheless, he was not allowed to take too many liberties with tradition, for it is part of the praise-singer's task to preserve it. But in those days such considerations did not enter my head, which I would hold high and proud; for I used to feel quite drunk with so much praise, which seemed to reflect some of its effulgence upon my own small person.

I could tell that my father's vanity was being inflamed, and I already knew that after having sipped this milk-and-honey he would lend a favourable ear to the woman's request. But I was not alone in my knowledge; the woman also had seen my father's eyes gleaming with contented pride; and she would hold out her grains of gold as if the whole thing were settled: my father, taking up his scales, would weigh the gold.

"What sort of trinket do you desire?" he would ask.

"I want . . ."

And often it would happen that the woman did not know really what she wanted, because she would be so torn by desire, because she would have liked to have many, many trinkets, all out of the same small quantity of gold: but she would have had to have much more than she had brought with her to satisfy such a desire, and eventually she would have to content herself with some more modest wish.

"When do you want it for?" my father would ask.

And she would always want it at once.

"Why are you in such a hurry? How do you expect me to find the time?"

"It's very urgent, I can assure you," the woman would reply.

"That's what all women say, when they want an ornament. Well, I'll see what I can do. Now are you happy?"

Then he would take the clay pot that was kept specially for the smelting of gold and pour in the grains; thereupon he would cover the gold with powdered charcoal, a charcoal which he obtained by the use of plant juices of exceptional purity; finally he would place a large lump of the same kind of charcoal over the whole thing.

Then, having seen the work duly undertaken, the woman, by now quite satisfied, would go back to her household tasks, leaving her go-between to carry on with the praise-singing which had already proved so advantageous to her.

On a sign from my father, the apprentices would start working the two pairs of sheep-skin bellows which were placed on the ground at each side of the forge and linked to it by earthen pipes. These apprentices remained seated all the time, with crossed legs, in front of the bellows; at least the younger did, for the elder would sometimes be allowed to take part in the craftsmen's work and the younger—in those days it was Sidafa—only had to work the bellows and watch the proceedings while awaiting his turn to be elevated to less rudimentary tasks. For a whole hour they would both be working the levers of the bellows till the fire in the forge leapt into flame, becoming a living thing, a lively and merciless spirit.

Then my father, using long pincers, would lift the clay pot and place it on the flames.

Immediately all work would more or less stop in the workshop: actually while the gold is being melted and while it is cooling all work with copper or aluminum is supposed to stop, for fear that some fraction of these less noble metals might fall among the gold. It is only steel that can still be worked at such times. But workmen who had some piece of steel work in hand would either hasten to finish it or would openly stop work to join the other apprentices gathered round the forge. In fact, there were often so many of them at these times pressing round my father that I, the smallest, would have to get up and push my way in among them, so as not to miss any of the operation.

It might happen that, feeling he had too little room to work in, my father would make his apprentices stand well away from him. He would merely raise his hand in a simple gesture: at that particular moment he would never utter a word, and no one else would, no one was allowed to utter a word, even the go-between's voice would no longer be raised in song; the silence would be broken only by the panting of the bellows and by the faint hissing of the gold. But if my father never used to utter actual words at this time, I know that he was uttering them in his mind; I could see it by his lips that kept working while he bent over the pot and kept stirring the gold and the charcoal with a bit of wood that would keep bursting into flame, and so had to be constantly replaced by a fresh bit.

What were the words my father's lips were forming? I do not know; I do not know for certain: I was never told what they were. But what else could they have been, if not magical incantations? Were they not the spirits of fire and gold, of fire and air, air breathed through the earthen pipes, of fire born of air, of gold married with fire—were not these the spirits he was invoking? Was it not their help and their friendship he was calling upon in this marriage of elemental things? Yes, it was almost certainly those spirits he was calling upon, for they are the most elemental of all spirits, and their presence is essential at the melting of gold.

The operation that was going on before my eyes was simply the smelting of gold; but it was something more than that: a magical operation that the guiding spirits could look upon with favour or disfavour; and that is why there would be all round my father that absolute silence and that anxious expectancy. I could understand, though I was just a child, that there was no craft greater than the goldsmith's. I expected a ceremony, I had come to be present at a ceremony, and it really was one, though very protracted. I was still too young to be able to understand why it was so protracted; nevertheless, I had an inkling, beholding the most religious concentration of all those present as they watched the mixing process.

When finally the gold began to melt, I used to feel like shouting, and perhaps we would all have shouted if we had not been forbidden to make a sound: I would be trembling, and certainly everyone else would be trembling as we sat watching my father stirring the mixture, still a heavy paste in which the charcoal was gradually being consumed. The next stage followed swiftly; the gold now had the fluidity of water. The guiding spirits had smiled on the operation!

"Bring me the brick!" my father would say, thus lifting the ban that until then had kept us all silent.

The brick, which an apprentice would place beside the fire, was hollowed out, generously greased with Galam butter. My father would take the pot off the fire, tilt it carefully, and I would watch the gold flowing into the brick, flowing like liquid fire. True, it was only a very sparse trickle of fire, but oh, how vivid, how brilliant! As the gold flowed into the brick, the grease would splutter and flame and give off a thick smoke that caught in the throat and stung the eyes, leaving us all weeping and coughing.

It occurred to me later on that my father could easily have relinquished all the work of smelting the gold to one or other of his assistants: they were not without experience in these matters; they had taken part hundreds of times in the same preparations and they would certainly have brought the work to a successful conclusion. But as I have told you, my father kept moving his lips! We could not hear those words, those secret words, those incantations which he addressed to powers that we should not, that we could not hear or see: this was essential. Only my father was versed in the science of conjuring the spirits of fire, air and gold, and conjuring evil spirits, and that is why he alone conducted the whole operation.

By now the gold would have cooled in the hollow of the brick, and my father would begin to hammer and stretch it. This was the moment when his work as a goldsmith really began. I noticed that before embarking on it he never failed to stroke stealthily the little snake coiled up under the sheepskin; one can only assume that this was his way of gathering strength for what remained to be done, and which was the most difficult.

But was it not extraordinary, was it not miraculous that on these occasions the little black serpent always coiled up under the sheepskin? He was not always there, he did not visit my father every day, but he was always present whenever there was gold to be worked.

Moreover, it is our custom to keep apart from the working of gold all influences outside those of the jeweller himself. And indeed it is precisely because the jeweller alone possesses the secret of his incantations; but also because the working of gold, besides being a task of the greatest skill, is a matter of confidence, of conscience, a task which is not undertaken excepting after due reflection and experiment. Finally, I do not think that any jeweller would renounce the opportunity of performing such a task—I ought to say, such a spectacle!—in which he can display his abilities with a virtuosity that his work as a blacksmith or a mechanic or even as a sculptor is never invested with; even though in these more humble tasks his skill is no less wonderful, even though the statues which he carves in wood with his adze are not insignificant works!

The snake's presence came as no surprise to me; ever since that evening when my father had talked to me about the guiding spirit of our race, it had ceased to surprise me; it was quite natural that the snake should be there: he had knowledge of the future. Did he impart any of that knowledge to my father? It seemed to me quite obvious that he did: did he not always warn him of what was going to happen? But I had another reason for believing implicitly in the powers of the little snake.

The craftsman who works in gold must first of all purify himself, that is, he must wash himself all over and, of course, abstain from all sexual relationships during the whole time. Great respecter of ceremony as he was, it would have been impossible for my father to ignore these rules. Now I never saw him make these preparations. I would see him address himself to his work without any apparent preliminaries. But from that moment it was obvious that, forewarned by his black guiding spirit in a dream of the task that would await him in the morning, my father must have prepared for it as soon as he arose, and had entered his workshop in a state of purity, his body smeared with the magical substances hidden in his numerous pots full of secret potions. So I believe my father never entered his workshop except in a state of ritual purity; and that is not because I want to make him out as being better than he is—he is a man like any other, and has a man's weaknesses—but always when it was a matter of ritual he was uncompromisingly strict.

The woman for whom the trinket was being made, and who would often have looked in to see how the work was getting on, would come for the final time, not wanting to miss anything of the marvelous sight as the gold wire, which my father had succeeded in spinning, was transformed into a trinket. She was here now, devouring with her eyes the fragile golden wire, following its tranquil and inevitable spirals round the little metal cone which gave the trinket its shape. My father would be watching her out of the corner of his eye, and sometimes I would see the corners of his mouth twitch into a smile: the woman's avid attentiveness amused him.

"Are you trembling?" he would say to her.

"*Am* I trembling?" she would ask.

And we would all burst out laughing at her. For she *was* trembling! She was trembling with covetousness for the spiral pyramid in which my father was inserting, among the convolutions, tiny grains of gold. When finally he terminated the work by placing at the summit the largest grain of gold, the woman would jump excitedly to her feet.

Then, while my father was slowly turning the trinket round in his fingers, smoothing it into perfect shape, no one could have displayed such utter happiness as the native woman, not even the praise-singer, whose trade it was to do so, and who, during the whole process of transformation, had kept on singing his praises, accelerating his rhythm, increasing his flatteries as the trinket took shape, and praising my father's talents to the skies.

Indeed, the praise-singer participated in a curious—I was going to say direct, effective—way in the work. He, too, was intoxicated with the joy of creation; he declaimed his rapture, and plucked his harp like a man inspired; he warmed to the task as if he had been the craftsman himself, as if the trinket had been made by his own hands. He was no longer a paid thurifer; he was no longer just the man whose services each and anyone could hire: he had become a man who creates his song under the influence of some very personal, interior necessity.

When my father, after having soldered the large grain of gold that crowned the summit, held out his work to be admired, the go-between would no longer be able to contain himself, and would intone the douga—the great chant which is only sung for celebrated men, and which is danced to only for them.

But the douga is a tremendous chant, a provocative chant, a chant that the go-between would not venture to sing, and that the man for whom it is sung would not venture to dance to, without certain precautions.

My father, forewarned in a dream, had been able to take these precautions as soon as he got up; the praise-singer had taken them as a matter of course when he had made his bargain with the woman. Just as my father had done, he had smeared his body with magic lotions and so had rendered himself invulnerable to the bad spirits which the douga would undoubtedly stir into activity, invulnerable also even to his fellow praise-singers who, jealous perhaps, were only waiting to hear the chant, the note of exaltation and the loss of control which that exaltation entails, to cast their evil spells upon him.

At the first notes of the douga, my father would rise and utter a cry in which happiness and triumph were equally mingled; and brandishing in his right hand the hammer that was the symbol of his profession, and in his left a ram's horn filled with magic substances, he would dance the glorious dance.

No sooner had he finished than workmen and apprentices, friends and customers in their turn, not forgetting the woman for whom the trinket had been created, would flock round him, congratulating him, showering praises on him, and complimenting at the same time the go-between, who found himself laden with gifts, gifts that are almost the only resources he has in his wandering life, that he leads after the fashion of the troubadours of old. Beaming, aglow with dancing and the praises he had received, my father would offer kola nuts, that small change of Guinean civility.

All that now remained to be done was to redden the trinket in a little water mixed with chlorine and seasalt. I could go now: the ceremony was over! But often, as I was leaving the workshop, my mother, who might be in the yard pounding millet or rice, would call me.

"Where have you been?" she would ask, although she knew very well where I had been.

"In the workshop."

"Oh, yes, your father was making something out of gold. Gold! It's always gold!"

And she would pound furiously the helpless bowl of rice or millet. "Your father's ruining his health! You see what he's doing."

"He's been dancing the douga," I would reply.

"The douga! The douga won't stop him ruining his eyesight! And you would be better off playing here in the yard instead of going and breathing the dust and smoke in the workshop!"

My mother did not like my father to work with gold. She knew how harmful the soldering of gold can be: a jeweller can wear his lungs out, puffing at his blowpipe, and his eyes suffer by being so close to the intense heat of the forge; and even more perhaps from the microscopic delicacy of the work. But even if there had been no danger in it, my mother still would have disliked this work: she held it in suspicion, for you cannot solder gold without the help of other metals, and my mother used to think that it was not strictly honest to keep the gold which was saved by its alloys, although this was the accepted thing; and she, too, was quite prepared, whenever she took cotton to be woven, to receive in return a piece of cloth of only half the original weight.

Interpretations

1. How did Laye's father feel about his work? What were his working conditions? (What were the economic pressures and rewards? the non-economic rewards?) Where are such conditions and rewards still possible in an industrialized country like ours?

2. The praise-singer sang the praises—sometimes exaggerating them—of the ancestors of the person whose favors were sought. Does our culture have the equivalent of a praise-singer (in a perhaps disguised form)? If so, where? Do we still identify with our ancestors to the point of "vanity . . . inflamed" when we hear them praised? If so, give an example.

3. What was the meaning and purpose of the gold-smelting ceremony? How did the snake contribute to the aura? What did the dream contribute? Do you think smelting gold deserves this special attention or aura? Why or why not? What economic and cultural factors in the American workplace make such a mixing of religion and work unlikely? Is any work in our culture such a mixture? What? Why?

4. What is Laye's attitude toward the customs and the people he describes? (Approving, critical, apologetic, impressed, detached, amused?) Cite details to support your answer.

5. At times Laye seems to fear he might be misunderstood. What aspect of Laye's story do you think a general audience would have the most trouble understanding? Where do you find Laye attempting to bridge the gap in understanding between his reading audience and the events he describes?

Correspondences

1. Working with gold allows Laye's father to be both artist and magician. In what particular aspects of the process does he take pride? How does his attitude toward his craft compare to that of Alvarez's father in "El Doctor" (Chapter 2)?

2. Discuss the role tradition plays in Ouchi's essay. How do cultural factors affect attitudes towards work in both selections?

Applications

1. Laye's father was part of an agrarian as opposed to an industrial economy. How are they different? How might these differences affect attitudes towards quality as opposed to quantity of work as well as towards creativity and productivity?

2. What is the evidence that Laye sees a connection between a praise-singer and an author—for example, a poet or dramatist or novelist—or, for that matter an autobiographer like himself? Write a journal entry explaining this connection.

The Price of Hate:
Thoughts on Covering a
Ku Klux Klan Rally

Rachel L. Jones

Rachel Jones (b. 1961) was born in Cairo, Illinois. She attended Northwestern University and Southern Illinois University and held internships at The New York Times *and the* Washington Post *before working as a general assignment reporter with* The Miami Herald.

We think you will be interested in Jones's reasons for choosing journalism as a profession:

> *I decided at a relatively early age that I would use words to make a living. I was fascinated by them and the images they could evoke, how they could make you feel, hear, smell and taste power there, and decided that I would attempt some profession that used words.*
>
> *My approach to reporting was based in practicality; the love of words and writing had to be channeled into a realistic endeavor. I had followed newspapers like* The Chicago Tribune *and* The St. Louis Post-Dispatch *all my life and was curious about the process of putting out a whole paper every day.*
>
> *Ironically, the first newspaper I ever worked at was* The New York Times, *and it was an awe-inspiring way to learn about journalism. But it taught me a respect for the field that remains to this day. I learned that what a reporter does is to translate events—everyday and extraordinary—into digestible bites for the reader at home. We are like walking lightning rods, collecting the information, putting ourselves into someone else's shoes and then writing about it so that even more people can understand. Or, as one editor once told me, we're the guys who have to make John Q. Public believe that the sewage treatment plant really IS important. We have to write the stories that even if they aren't read, will make people aware that their world is growing and changing and they ought to keep up—and that they CAN, if they'll read a newspaper.*

In "The Price of Hate," Jones's dedication to covering an assignment is put to an unusual test.

264

I WAS SITTING at my computer terminal when I overheard someone in the office mention his concern because he thought a black couple was moving into a house on his street.

He was standing only four feet away from me, yet lacked a mechanism that would prevent him from making racist statements in front of a black person. I stopped typing and stared at his back. He froze momentarily, and the woman he was talking to glanced at me.

I didn't confront him. I had to transmit copy to St. Petersburg and then leave to cover a graduation. Besides, my stomach was churning. Just seven days earlier, at a Ku Klux Klan rally in Clearwater, I had stood only four feet away from a Tarpon Springs man who told me he was tired of "the n-----s getting everything."

I'd be lying if I said that the possibility of covering a Ku Klux Klan rally didn't cause me a few moments' concern about my physical well-being. But when another reporter came over to tell me about the May 28th Klan rally in front of Clearwater City Hall, I reasoned, "It's just another assignment. I am a reporter, and I know my life isn't all budget meetings."

I must also admit to a curiosity about the Klan, and it seemed a good opportunity to take a look at that sideshow of human nature. Now, I *could* have asked to be excused from that particular assignment. As a police reporter, my Saturdays are sometimes very busy. Had I approached my editor to delicately decline, we could have both made ourselves believe it was only natural to send a burly young man into the fray. Anything could have happened that day—traffic accidents, drownings, first-degree murders at the jail.

I couldn't be two places at once, could I?

But two days before the event, I turned to my editor and asked, "I AM covering the rally on Saturday, aren't I?"

She didn't miss a beat. Yes, of course. Just a short story, unless the streets were running with blood or something.

I jokingly told her about the only slightly feigned horror of my older sister, who shrieked into the phone, "They're letting a black reporter cover the KLAN?"

At the Klan rally, the man from Tarpon Springs saw my press badge and figured I was a part of something he called the "Black Associated Press," which he swore was denying white journalism graduates jobs. Mr. Tarpon told me that n-----s weren't qualified to get the jobs they were getting through affirmative action, and that America is for white people.

I paused momentarily and asked what he thought should be done about black people. He didn't know or care.

"Send 'em all to hell," he said, while I took notes.

It's funny—it was all so clinical. My voice held an even tone, and while he talked I searched his contorted face for some glimmer of recognition on his part that *I* was a human being, and the words that he spat just might hurt me.

Just as I later waited for Mr. Welcome Wagon to turn around and apologize for his blunder, I waited for the Tarpon Springs man to show some spark of humanity, but he finished his conversation and walked away.

My stomach was still churning hours later as I relived that rally. The whole experience was like being scalded, like having something sharp raked over my flesh until it was raw.

After it was over I went home and drank a shot from the bottle of brandy I'd bought last Christmas. In Harlequin romances, handsome princes always proffered hard liquor to soothe the jangled nerves of a distraught heroine.

But I was alone, and I was no heroine. That night, every noise from the apartment upstairs made me jump, and the pattern of trees against the curtains frightened me as I tossed and turned. I called three of my siblings, but other than offering sympathy, they felt helpless to ease my trauma.

I had been so naive about the whole assignment. The thing is, I never thought it would change me. I figured it would be difficult, but I didn't want it to *change* me.

What you must understand about the Klan is that its members and supporters have been stripped of their humanity. I gained that insight and feel stronger for it. It was easy enough on one level to say, "These people are stupid, so I shouldn't be bothered by what they say."

But that was cold comfort as I walked across the City Hall parking lot, feeling a numbness creep through my arms and legs. I thought I must have been walking like the Scarecrow in *The Wizard of Oz,* but figured if I could just make it to the church across the street, I'd be fine.

At the church, I asked to use the phone and was sent down a hall and to the left. My fingers felt like sausages as I tried to use the rotary dial, muttering curses as I fouled up several times. Finally managing to reach an editor, I was coherent enough to give her information for a brief summary of the rally.

But when the next editor picked up the phone, I dissolved in tears after three words. He was puzzled, and I think unaware of what was wrong at first. I whimpered that I was sorry and didn't know what was wrong, either. I gasped and caught a few breaths before describing in a wavering voice what had happened.

He tried calming me down to discuss the facts. How many people attended? Had there been any clashes? What did police have to say? I planned to write a full story.

The editor said maybe we should just ignore the event. He asked if any of the Klan members had been abusive to me. I mumbled, "Uh hum," and the tears flowed fresh. He told me to get as much police information as I could and to call him back later.

I placed the phone on the hook and buried my face in my hands, letting the sobs come freely. The man who had let me use the church phone brought me a box of tissues and a Coke.

After I splashed my face with cold water and controlled the sobs, I headed back to the rally, just as the Klansmen were loading up to leave. Shouts of "white supremacy" rang through the air as they rolled out, and my photographer walked over to give me the Klansmen's names. I turned away, telling her that I probably wouldn't use them anyway.

"I didn't think it would affect me," I whispered.

"Don't cry. They aren't worth it, Rachel," she said.

But even then, it had started to change me . . .

When you have stared into the twisted face of hate, you *must* change. I remember watching the documentary *Eyes on the Prize*, in particular the segment on the desegregation of Little Rock High School in 1957, and being disturbed by the outpouring of rage against those nine students.

The whites who snarled into the camera back then had no explanation for their vitriol and violence other than that the students were black, and they didn't care who knew it. They weren't going to let those n-----s into the school, no matter what.

I've struggled all my life against a visceral reaction to that kind of racism. I have been mistreated because of my color, but nothing ever came near to what those students went through on a daily basis.

That and countless other examples let me know what I'd been spared, and I decided to choose the path of understanding, realizing that some people are always going to fear or even hate me because of my color alone.

It's a burden blacks must carry no matter how high a level of achievement they reach, and I sought to incorporate that into my own striving. Watching films of what hate turned those people into made me choose to reject it, to deal with people individually and not tarnish all whites with the same obscene images. *I would not hate.*

But as one Klan supporter muttered, "N----- b----," at me as I weaved my way through the crowd, that resolve crumbled. It stung as much as if he *had* slapped me or thrown something.

The leader shouted taunts and epithets at a black woman who was infuriated by the proceedings, and who had even lunged at several people in the small group of supporters.

As the black woman walked away, the leader shouted, "Why don't you go back to Nee-gor Africa where you came from!" I laughed because he sounded foolish, but he saw me and sent a fresh stream of obscenity my way.

A Jewish woman who came to protest was heaped with stinging abuse, and the rabble was ingenious in its varied use of sexual and racial obscenities directed toward her.

Other reporters and photographers eyed me warily throughout the rally, watching for my reactions to the abuse. When the leader started passing out leaflets and avoided my outstretched hand, a photographer asked for two and brought me one.

I said thank you. He said quietly, "You're very, very welcome," and was embarrassed when I caught his eye.

When it was all over, several police officials called me brave. But I felt cold, sick and empty. I felt like such a naive fool. I felt bitter. So this is what it feels like, I thought. Why *shouldn't* I just hate them right back, why couldn't I diffuse this punch in the gut?

What is noble about not flinching in the face of hate? Slavery, lynchings, rape, inequality, was that not enough? If they want to send me to hell, shouldn't I want to take them along for the ride?

But I still couldn't hate. I was glad I had cried, though. It defied their demented logic. It meant I was human.

Interpretations

1. Jones felt that her work did not absolutely require her to jeopardize her "physical well-being" by covering a Klan rally. What would she have lost if she had "delicately" asked her editor "to send a burly young man" to cover the story? Do you think she was right to undertake the assignment? (She admits to extreme naiveté.) If so, why? Do you think she will do it again? Do you think she could have better prepared herself emotionally for the experience? If so, how?

2. What is the tone of the essay? Why do you think she failed to quote the "fresh stream of obscenity" at several points? Do you find any humor?

3. One thing Jones learned from the assignment was how emotionally vulnerable she was. What else did she learn? She mistakenly thought that by remembering how "stupid" Klansmen are, she would be protected. Do you think remembering how stupid one's enemy is can sometimes protect one from that enemy? Why? Under what circumstances?

4. "I planned to write a full story of the rally," says the author. Did she? Would you like to read it? Why?

5. What is Jones's purpose in comparing her experience with that of the students at Little Rock High School in 1957?

6. What *is* the price of hate? Jones says that even after this experience she "still couldn't hate." Is it really possible to "turn the other cheek"? How do you know?

7. What instances of kindness in this hateful scene does Jones report? Why do you think she included them?

Correspondences

1. Review the Ellison quotation (page 152). How does it apply to the people Jones encountered on her assignment? To what extent do you agree with Jones's conclusion that "[they] have been stripped of their humanity"?

2. Jones, a black journalist, covers an assignment in Florida in 1988. How does her experience in the workplace compare with that of Johnson, an unskilled worker in Petry's story in New York in 1945?

Applications

1. Review Jones's biography (page 264). Why did she want to become a journalist? Characterize *your* goals with respect to future work. What criteria will you use? Write an essay defining your career goals.

2. Discuss the Woolf quotation on work (page 219) with your group and write an analysis of their responses.

Looking for Work

Gary Soto

Gary Soto (b. 1952) is a second-generation Mexican-American from Fresno, California. He earned degrees from California State University and from the University of California at Berkeley, where he teaches English and Chicano studies. He has received numerous awards, including the Academy of American Poets prize (1975), a Guggenheim Fellowship (1979–1980), Levinson Award (1984), and American Book Award (1985) for Living Up the Street: Narrative Recollections. *"Looking for Work" shows more of Soto's consciousness of his Mexican-American identity than does his essay in Chapter 3, "Summer School."*

Mexicans can trace their history at least to 21,000 B.C. and can boast of a series of advanced civilizations. The Olmec, Toltec, Mayan, and Aztec cultures flourished variously between 100 and 900. Hernando Cortez, a Spanish conquistador, defeated the Aztecs in 1519–1521, establishing the Spanish rule that would last until independence was declared in 1821.

The California in which Soto grew up, along with much of the present American Southwest, was part of Mexico until the Mexican-American War (1848) stripped Mexico of all its territory north of the Rio Grande. Only 13 percent of Mexico's land is arable. The per capita annual income in 1984 was about $2,000. Some land redistribution and the discovery of oil in the 1970s brightened Mexico's economic prospects somewhat. However, large numbers of Mexicans continue to flow into the United States in search of employment. In the 1970s, fourteen percent of immigrants to the United States, or six million people, came from Mexico. In 1988 alone, almost a million Mexicans came north over the Rio Grande.

ONE JULY, while killing ants on the kitchen sink with a rolled newspaper, I had a nine-year-old's vision of wealth that would save us from ourselves. For weeks I had drunk Kool-Aid and watched morning reruns of *Father Knows Best,* whose family was so uncomplicated in its routine that I very much wanted to imitate it. The first step was to get my brother and sister to wear shoes at dinner.

"Come on, Rick—come on, Deb," I whined. But Rick mimicked me and the same day that I asked him to wear shoes he came to the dinner table in only his swim trunks. My mother didn't notice, nor did my sister, as we sat to eat our beans and tortillas in the stifling heat of our kitchen. We all gleamed like cellophane, wiping the sweat from our brows with the backs of our hands as we talked about the day: Frankie our neighbor was beat up by Faustino; the swimming pool at the playground would be closed for a day because the pump was broken.

Such was our life. So that morning, while doing-in the train of ants which arrived each day, I decided to become wealthy, and right away! After downing a bowl of cereal, I took a rake from the garage and started up the block to look for work.

We lived on an ordinary block of mostly working class people: warehousemen, egg candlers, welders, mechanics, and a union plumber. And there were many retired people who kept their lawns green and the gutters uncluttered of the chewing gum wrappers we dropped as we rode by on our bikes. They bent down to gather our litter, muttering at our evilness.

At the corner house I rapped the screen door and a very large woman in a muu-muu answered. She sized me up and then asked what I could do.

"Rake leaves," I answered, smiling.

"It's summer, and there ain't no leaves," she countered. Her face was pinched with lines; fat jiggled under her chin. She pointed to the lawn, then the flower bed, and said: "You see any leaves there—or there?" I followed her pointing arm, stupidly. But she had a job for me and that was to get her a Coke at the liquor store. She gave me twenty cents, and after ditching my rake in a bush, off I ran. I returned with an unbagged Pepsi, for which she thanked me and gave me a nickel from her apron.

I skipped off her porch, fetched my rake, and crossed the street to the next block where Mrs. Moore, mother of Earl the retarded man, let me weed a flower bed. She handed me a trowel and for a good part of the morning my fingers dipped into the moist dirt, ripping up runners of Bermuda grass. Worms surfaced in my search for deep roots, and I cut them in halves, tossing them to Mrs. Moore's cat who pawed them playfully as they dried in the sun. I made out Earl whose face was pressed to the back window of the house, and although he was calling to me I couldn't understand what he was trying to say. Embarrassed, I worked without looking up, but I imagined his contorted mouth and the ring of keys attached to his belt—keys that jingled with each palsied step. He scared me and I worked quickly to finish the flower bed. When I did finish Mrs. Moore gave me a quarter and two peaches from her tree, which I washed there but ate in the alley behind my house.

I was sucking on the second one, a bit of juice staining the front of my T-shirt, when Little John, my best friend, came walking down the alley with a baseball bat over his shoulder, knocking over trash cans as he made his way toward me.

Little John and I went to St. John's Catholic School, where we sat among the "stupids." Miss Marino, our teacher, alternated the rows of good students with the bad, hoping that by sitting side-by-side with the bright students the stupids might become more intelligent, as though intelligence were contagious. But we didn't progress as she had hoped. She grew frustrated when one day, while dismissing class for recess, Little John couldn't get up because his arms were stuck in the slats of the chair's backrest. She scolded us with a shaking finger when we knocked over the globe, denting the already troubled Africa. She muttered curses when Leroy White, a real stupid but a great softball player with the gift to hit to all fields, openly chewed his host when he made his First Communion; his hands swung at his sides as he returned to the pew looking around with a big smile.

Little John asked what I was doing, and I told him that I was taking a break from work, as I sat comfortably among high weeds. He wanted to join me, but I reminded him that the last time he'd gone door-to-door asking for work his mother had whipped him. I was with him when his mother, a New Jersey Italian who could rise up in anger one moment and love the next, told me in a polite but matter-of-fact voice that I had to leave because she was going to beat her son. She gave me a homemade popsicle, ushered me to the door, and said that I could see Little John the next day. But it was sooner than that. I went around to his bedroom window to suck my popsicle and watch Little John dodge his mother's blows, a few hitting their mark but many whirring air.

It was midday when Little John and I converged in the alley, the sun blazing in the high nineties, and he suggested that we go to Roosevelt High School to swim. He needed five cents to make fifteen, the cost of admission, and I lent him a nickel. We ran home for my bike and when my sister found out that we were going swimming, she started to cry because she didn't have the fifteen cents but only an empty Coke bottle. I waved for her to come and three of us mounted the bike—Debra on the cross bar, Little John on the handle bars and holding the Coke bottle which we would cash for a nickel and make up the difference that would allow all of us to get in, and me pumping up the crooked streets, dodging cars and pot holes. We spent the day swimming under the afternoon sun, so that when we got home our mom asked us what was darker, the floor or us? She feigned a stern posture, her hands on her hips and her mouth puckered. We played along. Looking down, Debbie and I said in unison, "Us."

That evening at dinner we all sat down in our bathing suits to eat our beans, laughing and chewing loudly. Our mom was in a good mood, so I took a risk and asked her if sometime we could have turtle soup. A few days before I had watched a television program in which a Polynesian tribe killed a large turtle, gutted it, and then stewed it over an open fire. The turtle, basted in a sugary sauce, looked delicious as I ate an afternoon bowl of cereal, but my sister, who was watching the program with a glass of Kool-Aid between her knees, said, "Caca."

My mother looked at me in bewilderment. "Boy, are you a crazy Mexican. Where did you get the idea that people eat turtles?"

"On television," I said, explaining the program. Then I took it a step further. "Mom, do you think we could get dressed up for dinner one of these days? David King does."

"Ay, Dios," my mother laughed. She started collecting the dinner plates, but my brother wouldn't let go of his. He was still drawing a picture in the bean sauce. Giggling, he said it was me, but I didn't want to listen because I wanted an answer from Mom. This was the summer when I spent the mornings in front of the television that showed the comfortable lives of white kids. There were no beatings, no rifts in the family. They wore bright clothes; toys tumbled from their closets. They hopped into bed with kisses and woke to glasses of fresh orange juice, and to a father sitting before his morning coffee while the mother buttered his toast. They hurried through the day making friends and gobs of money, returning home to a warmly lit living room, and then dinner. *Leave It To Beaver* was the program I replayed in my mind:

"May I have the mashed potatoes?" asks Beaver with a smile.

"Sure, Beav," replies Wally as he taps the corners of his mouth with a starched napkin.

The father looks on in his suit. The mother, decked out in earrings and a pearl necklace, cuts into her steak and blushes. Their conversation is politely clipped.

"Swell," says Beaver, his cheeks puffed with food.

Our own talk at dinner was loud with belly laughs and marked by our pointing forks at one another. The subjects were commonplace.

"Gary, let's go to the ditch tomorrow," my brother suggests. He explains that he has made a life preserver out of four empty detergent bottles strung together with twine and that he will make me one if I can find more bottles. "No way are we going to drown."

"Yeah, then we could have a dirt clod fight," I reply, so happy to be alive.

Whereas the Beaver's family enjoyed dessert in dishes at the table, our mom sent us outside, and more often than not I went into the alley to peek over the neighbor's fences and spy out fruit, apricots or peaches.

I had asked my mom and again she laughed that I was a crazy *chavalo* as she stood in front of the sink, her arms rising and falling with suds, face glistening from the heat. She sent me outside where my brother and sister were sitting in the shade that the fence threw out like a blanket. They were talking about me when I plopped down next to them. They looked at one another and then Debbie, my eight-year-old sister, started in.

"What's this crap about getting dressed up?"

She had entered her profanity stage. A year later she would give up such words and slip into her Catholic uniform, and into squealing on my brother and me when we "cussed this" and "cussed that."

I tried to convince them that if we improved the way we looked we might get along better in life. White people would like us more. They might invite us to places, like their homes or front yards. They might not hate us so much.

My sister called me a "craphead," and got up to leave with a stalk of grass dangling from her mouth. "They'll never like us."

My brother's mood lightened as he talked about the ditch—the white water, the broken pieces of glass, and the rusted car fenders that awaited our knees. There would be toads, and rocks to smash them.

David King, the only person we knew who resembled the middle class, called from over the fence. David was Catholic, of Armenian and French descent, and his closet was filled with toys. A bear-shaped cookie jar, like the ones on television, sat on the kitchen counter. His mother was remarkably kind while she put up with the racket we made on the street. Evenings, she often watered the front yard and it must have upset her to see us—my brother and I and others—jump from trees laughing, the unkillable kids of the very poor, who got up unshaken, brushed off, and climbed into another one to try again.

David called again. Rick got up and slapped grass from his pants. When I asked if I could come along he said no. David said no. They were two years older so their affairs were different from mine. They greeted one another with foul names and took off down the alley to look for trouble.

I went inside the house, turned on the television, and was about to sit down with a glass of Kool-Aid when Mom shooed me outside.

"It's still light," she said. "Later you'll bug me to let you stay out longer. So go on."

I downed my Kool-Aid and went outside to the front yard. No one was around. The day had cooled and a breeze rustled the trees. Mr. Jackson, the plumber, was watering his lawn and when he saw me he turned away to wash off his front steps. There was more than an hour of light left, so I took advantage of it and decided to look for work. I felt suddenly alive as I skipped down the block in search of an overgrown flower bed and the dime that would end the day right.

Interpretations

1. How does Soto keep the idea of work from getting lost in a welter of detail and digressions? Does he value work more for itself or for what it can bring him? Cite evidence for your response.

2. What are the major character traits of the nine-year-old Soto?

3. It is of course not true that the "kids" of "the very poor" are "unkillable." But why do they sometimes seem so to middle-class people? What is the truth about the health and life expectancy of poor kids vs. that of middle-class or wealthy kids? (Do you think Soto's aspirations for his family and himself are unkillable? Why or why not?)

4. How seriously do you take the nine-year-old Soto's claims that he, alone of his family, had aspirations to rise above the "commonplace" subjects discussed at table and longings for the "wealth that would save [them] from

[themselves]"? What would it mean for the Soto family to be "saved from" itself?

5.   What do you think is Soto's thesis or main point in this essay? Contrast Soto's interests with those of his brother. What is the effect of this discrepancy on the tone of the essay and on the thesis or main point?

6.   How, in general, does the Soto family get along with the other families on the block? Do you think the Sotos feel discriminated against or disliked? What's the evidence? What was the range of income and ethnic groups among the families on the block?

7.   How does the chronology provide unity?

Correspondences

1.   "Little John and I went to St. John's Catholic School, where we sat among the 'stupids.' Miss Marino, our teacher, alternated the rows of good students with the bad, hoping that by sitting side-by-side with the bright students, the stupids might become more intelligent, as though intelligence were contagious." In "So Tsi-Fai" (Chapter 3) Liu's teacher viewed So Tsi-fai as "incorrigible, hopeless and without hope." Do people get tracked for the future as early as grammar school? In a parochial school in Fresno as well as in Hong Kong? How does such stereotyping affect future work choices?

2.   Soto and Bambara (Chapter 3) use a child as narrator. How does that affect their use of dialogue, their portrayals of relationships and your response as reader? Cite examples from both selections.

Applications

1.   In "Looking for Work" Soto compares his working-class way of life with that of middle-class white families exemplified by "Father Knows Best" and "Leave It to Beaver." How are their work habits similar and different?

2.   "One July, while killing ants on the kitchen sink with a rolled newspaper, I had a nine-year-old's vision of wealth that would save us from ourselves." Write a journal entry on your motivation for looking for your first "job."

Jasmine

Bharati Mukherjee

*Bharati Mukherjee (b. 1940) was raised in Calcutta, India, and came to the
United States in 1961. She lived in Canada from 1968 to 1972 before returning
to the United States, where she is now a permanent resident. She received her Ph.D.
from the University of Iowa and has taught at several academic institutions,
including Skidmore College and Columbia University. Her novels include* The
Tiger's Daughter *(1972),* The Wire *(1975), and* Jasmine *(1989), an ex-
pansion of the story "Jasmine." With her husband, she also co-authored* Days and
Nights in Calcutta *(1977), a journal of their impression of a return visit to
India. In "Jasmine," taken from* The Middleman and Other Stories *(1988),
the title character is a young immigrant from Trinidad who becomes infatuated
with Ann Arbor, Michigan.*

*Trinidad and Tobago is an island republic off the eastern coast of Venezuela
about the size of Delaware. Its population of 1,262,000 is forty-three percent
African and forty percent East Indian. Trinidad and Tobago, a parliamentary
democracy, won independence from Britain in 1962 and became a republic in 1976.
One of the most prosperous countries in the Caribbean, much of its prosperity is based
on oil drilling and refining.*

JASMINE came to Detroit from Port-of-Spain, Trinidad, by way of Canada.
She crossed the border at Windsor in the back of a gray van loaded with
mattresses and box springs. The plan was for her to hide in an empty mattress
box if she heard the driver say, "All bad weather seems to come down from
Canada, doesn't it?" to the customs man. But she didn't have to crawl into
a box and hold her breath. The customs man didn't ask to look in.

The driver let her off at a scary intersection on Woodward Avenue and
gave her instructions on how to get to the Plantations Motel in Southfield.
The trick was to keep changing vehicles, he said. That threw off the immigration guys real quick.

Jasmine took money for cab fare out of the pocket of the great big
raincoat that the van driver had given her. The raincoat looked like something
that nuns in Port-of-Spain sold in church bazaars. Jasmine was glad to have
a coat with wool lining, though; and anyway, who would know in Detroit
that she was Dr. Vassanji's daughter?

All the bills in her hand looked the same. She would have to be careful
when she paid the cabdriver. Money in Detroit wasn't pretty the way it was
back home, or even in Canada, but she liked this money better. Why should
money be pretty, like a picture? Pretty money is only good for putting on

your walls maybe. The dollar bills felt businesslike, serious. Back home at work, she used to count out thousands of Trinidad dollars every day and not even think of them as real. Real money was worn and green, American dollars. Holding the bills in her fist on a street corner meant she had made it in okay. She'd outsmarted the guys at the border. Now it was up to her to use her wits to do something with her life. As her Daddy kept saying, "Girl, is opportunity come only once." The girls she'd worked with at the bank in Port-of-Spain had gone green as bananas when she'd walked in with her ticket on Air Canada. Trinidad was too tiny. That was the trouble. Trinidad was an island stuck in the middle of nowhere. What kind of place was that for a girl with ambition?

The Plantations Motel was run by a family of Trinidad Indians who had come from the tuppenny-ha'penny country town, Chaguanas. The Daboos were nobodies back home. They were lucky, that's all. They'd gotten here before the rush and bought up a motel and an ice cream parlor. Jasmine felt very superior when she saw Mr. Daboo in the motel's reception area. He was a pumpkin-shaped man with very black skin and Elvis Presley sideburns turning white. They looked like earmuffs. Mrs. Daboo was a bumpkin, too; short, fat, flapping around in house slippers. The Daboo daughters seemed very American, though. They didn't seem to know that they were nobodies, and kept looking at her and giggling.

She knew she would be short of cash for a great long while. Besides, she wasn't sure she wanted to wear bright leather boots and leotards like Viola and Loretta. The smartest move she could make would be to put a down payment on a husband. Her Daddy had told her to talk to the Daboos first chance. The Daboos ran a service fixing up illegals with islanders who had made it in legally. Daddy had paid three thousand back in Trinidad, with the Daboos and the mattress man getting part of it. They should throw in a good-earning husband for that kind of money.

The Daboos asked her to keep books for them and to clean the rooms in the new wing, and she could stay in 16B as long as she liked. They showed her 16B. They said she could cook her own roti; Mr. Daboo would bring in a stove, two gas rings that you could fold up in a metal box. The room was quite grand, Jasmine thought. It had a double bed, a TV, a pink sink and matching bathtub. Mrs. Daboo said Jasmine wasn't the big-city Port-of-Spain type she'd expected. Mr. Daboo said that he wanted her to stay because it was nice to have a neat, cheerful person around. It wasn't a bad deal, better than stories she'd heard about Trinidad girls in the States.

All day every day except Sundays Jasmine worked. There wasn't just the bookkeeping and the cleaning up. Mr. Daboo had her working on the match-up marriage service. Jasmine's job was to check up on social security cards, call clients' bosses for references, and make sure credit information wasn't false. Dermatologists and engineers living in Bloomfield Hills, store owners on Canfield and Woodward: she treated them all as potential liars. One of the first things she learned was that Ann Arbor was a magic word. A boy goes to Ann Arbor and gets an education, and all the barriers come crashing down. So Ann Arbor was the place to be.

She didn't mind the work. She was learning about Detroit, every side of it. Sunday mornings she helped unload packing crates of Caribbean spices in a shop on the next block. For the first time in her life, she was working for a black man, an African. So what if the boss was black? This was a new life, and she wanted to learn everything. Her Sunday boss, Mr. Anthony, was a courtly, Christian, church-going man, and paid her the only wages she had in her pocket. Viola and Loretta, for all their fancy American ways, wouldn't go out with blacks.

One Friday afternoon she was writing up the credit info on a Guyanese Muslim who worked in an assembly plant when Loretta said that enough was enough and there was no need for Jasmine to be her father's drudge.

"Is time to have fun," Viola said, "We're going to Ann Arbor."

Jasmine filed the sheet on the Guyanese man who probably now would never get a wife and got her raincoat. Loretta's boyfriend had a Cadillac parked out front. It was the longest car Jasmine had ever been in and louder than a country bus. Viola's boyfriend got out of the front seat. "Oh, oh, sweet things," he said to Jasmine. "Get in front." He was a talker. She'd learned that much from working on the matrimonial match-ups. She didn't believe him for a second when he said that there were dudes out there dying to ask her out.

Loretta's boyfriend said, "You have eyes I could leap into, girl."

Jasmine knew he was just talking. They sounded like Port-of-Spain boys of three years ago. It didn't surprise her that these Trinidad country boys in Detroit were still behind the times, even of Port-of-Spain. She sat very stiff between the two men, hands on her purse. The Daboo girls laughed in the back seat.

On the highway the girls told her about the reggae night in Ann Arbor. Kevin and the Krazee Islanders. Malcolm's Lovers. All the big reggae groups in the Midwest were converging for the West Indian Students Association fall bash. The ticket didn't come cheap but Jasmine wouldn't let the fellows pay. She wasn't that kind of girl.

The reggae and steel drums brought out the old Jasmine. The rum punch, the dancing, the dreadlocks, the whole combination. She hadn't heard real music since she got to Detroit, where music was supposed to be so famous. The Daboo girls kept turning on rock stuff in the motel lobby whenever their father left the area. She hadn't danced, really *danced,* since she'd left home. It felt so good to dance. She felt hot and sweaty and sexy. The boys at the dance were more than sweet talkers; they moved with assurance and spoke of their futures in America. The bartender gave her two free drinks and said, "Is ready when you are, girl." She ignored him but she felt all hot and good deep inside. She knew Ann Arbor was a special place.

When it was time to pile back into Loretta's boyfriend's Cadillac, she just couldn't face going back to the Plantations Motel and to the Daboos with their accounting books and messy files.

"I don't know what happen, girl," she said to Loretta. "I feel all crazy inside. Maybe is time for me to pursue higher studies in this town."

"This Ann Arbor, girl, they don't just take you off the street. It *cost* like hell."

She spent the night on a bashed-up sofa in the Student Union. She was a well-dressed, respectable girl, and she didn't expect anyone to question her right to sleep on the furniture. Many others were doing the same thing. In the morning, a boy in an army parka showed her the way to the Placement Office. He was a big, blond, clumsy boy, not bad-looking except for the blond eyelashes. He didn't scare her, as did most Americans. She let him buy her a Coke and a hotdog. That evening she had a job with the Moffitts.

Bill Moffitt taught molecular biology and Lara Hatch-Moffitt, his wife, was a performance artist. A performance artist, said Lara, was very different from being an actress, though Jasmine still didn't understand what the difference might be. The Moffitts had a little girl, Muffin, whom Jasmine was to look after, though for the first few months she might have to help out with the housework and the cooking because Lara said she was deep into performance rehearsals. That was all right with her, Jasmine said, maybe a little too quickly. She explained she came from a big family and was used to heavy-duty cooking and cleaning. This wasn't the time to say anything about Ram, the family servant. Americans like the Moffitts wouldn't understand about keeping servants. Ram and she weren't in similar situations. Here mother's helpers, which is what Lara had called her—Americans were good with words to cover their shame—seemed to be as good as anyone.

Ann Arbor was a huge small town. She couldn't imagine any kind of school the size of the University of Michigan. She meant to sign up for courses in the spring. Bill brought home a catalogue bigger than the phonebook for all of Trinidad. The university had courses in everything. It would be hard to choose; she'd have to get help from Bill. He wasn't like a professor, not the ones back home where even high school teachers called themselves professors and acted like little potentates. He wore blue jeans and thick sweaters with holes in the elbows and used phrases like "in vitro" as he watched her curry up fish. Dr. Parveen back home—he called himself "doctor" when everybody knew he didn't have even a Master's degree—was never seen without his cotton jacket which had gotten really ratty at the cuffs and lapel edges. She hadn't learned anything in the two years she'd put into college. She'd learned more from working in the bank for two months than she had at college. It was the assistant manager, Personal Loans Department, Mr. Singh, who had turned her on to the Daboos and to smooth, bargain-priced emigration.

Jasmine liked Lara. Lara was easygoing. She didn't spend the time she had between rehearsals telling Jasmine how to cook and clean American-style. Mrs. Daboo did that in 16B. Mrs. Daboo would barge in with a plate of stale samosas and snoop around giving free advice on how mainstream Americans did things. As if she were dumb or something! As if she couldn't keep her own eyes open and make her mind up for herself. Sunday mornings she had to share the butcher-block workspace in the kitchen with Bill. He made the Sunday brunch from new recipes in *Gourmet* and *Cuisine.* Jasmine hadn't seen a man cook who didn't have to or wasn't getting paid to do it. Things were topsy-turvy in the Moffitt house. Lara went on two- and three-day road trips and Bill stayed home. But even her Daddy, who'd never poured himself a cup of tea, wouldn't put Bill down as a woman. The mornings Bill tried out something complicated, a Cajun shrimp, sausage, and beans dish, for instance, Jasmine skipped church services. The Moffitts didn't go to church, though they seemed to be good Christians. They just didn't talk church talk, which suited her fine.

Lara showed her the room she would have all to herself in the finished basement. There was a big, old TV, not in color like the motel's and a portable typewriter on a desk which Lara said she would find handy when it came time to turn in her term papers. Jasmine didn't say anything about not being a student. She was a student of life, wasn't she? There was a scary moment after they'd discussed what she could expect as salary, which was three times more than anything Mr. Daboo was supposed to pay her but hadn't. She thought Bill Moffitt was going to ask her about her visa or her green card* number and social security. But all Bill did was smile and smile at her—he had a wide, pink, baby face—and play with a button on his corduroy jacket. The button would need sewing back on, firmly.

Lara said, "I think I'm going to like you, Jasmine. You have a something about you. A something real special. I'll just bet you've acted, haven't you?" The idea amused her, but she merely smiled and accepted Lara's hug. The interview was over.

Then Bill opened a bottle of Soave and told stories about camping in northern Michigan. He'd been raised there. Jasmine didn't see the point in sleeping in tents; the woods sounded cold and wild and creepy. But she said, "Is exactly what I want to try out come summer, man. Campin and huntin."

Lara asked about Port-of-Spain. There was nothing to tell about her hometown that wouldn't shame her in front of nice white American folk like the Moffitts. The place was shabby, the people were grasping and cheating and lying and life was full of despair and drink and wanting. But by the time she finished, the island sounded romantic. Lara said, "It wouldn't surprise me one bit if you were a writer, Jasmine."

Two months passed. Jasmine knew she was lucky to have found a small, clean, friendly family like the Moffitts to build her new life around. "Man!"

---

*Work permit issued only to immigrants who have permanent resident status in the U.S.

she'd exclaim as she vacuumed the wide-plank wood floors or ironed (Lara wore pure silk or pure cotton). "In this country Jesus givin out good luck only!" By this time they knew she wasn't a student, but they didn't care and said they wouldn't report her. They never asked if she was illegal on top of it.

To savor her new sense of being a happy, lucky person, she would put herself through a series of "what ifs": what if Mr. Singh in Port-of-Spain hadn't turned her on to the Daboos and loaned her two thousand! What if she'd been ugly like the Mintoo girl and the manager hadn't even offered! What if the customs man had unlocked the door of the van! Her Daddy liked to say, "You is a helluva girl, Jasmine."

"Thank you, Jesus," Jasmine said, as she carried on.

Christmas Day the Moffitts treated her just like family. They gave her a red cashmere sweater with a V neck so deep it made her blush. If Lara had worn it, her bosom wouldn't hang out like melons. For the holiday weekend Bill drove her to the Daboos in Detroit. "You work too hard," Bill said to her. "Learn to be more selfish. Come on, throw your weight around." She'd rather not have spent time with the Daboos, but that first afternoon of the interview she'd told Bill and Lara that Mr. Daboo was her mother's first cousin. She had thought it shameful in those days to have no papers, no family, no roots. Now Loretta and Viola in tight, bright pants seemed trashy like girls at Two-Johnny Bissoondath's Bar back home. She was stuck with the story of the Daboos being family. Village bumpkins, ha! She would break out. Soon.

Jasmine had Bill drop her off at the RenCen. The Plantations Motel, in fact, the whole Riverfront area, was too seamy. She'd managed to cut herself off mentally from anything too islandy. She loved her Daddy and Mummy, but she didn't think of them that often anymore. Mummy had expected her to be homesick and come flying right back home. "Is blowin sweat-of-brow money is what you doin, Pa," Mummy had scolded. She loved them, but she'd become her own person. That was something that Lara said: "I am my own person."

The Daboos acted thrilled to see her back. "What you drinkin, Jasmine girl?" Mr. Daboo kept asking. "You drinkin sherry or what?" Pouring her little glasses of sherry instead of rum was a sure sign he thought she had become whitefolk-fancy. The Daboo sisters were very friendly, but Jasmine considered them too wild. Both Loretta and Viola had changed boyfriends. Both were seeing black men they'd danced with in Ann Arbor. Each night at bedtime, Mr. Daboo cried. "In Trinidad we stayin we side, they stayin they side. Here, everything mixed up. Is helluva confusion, no?"

On New Year's Eve the Daboo girls and their black friends went to a dance. Mr. and Mrs. Daboo and Jasmine watched TV for a while. Then Mr. Daboo got out a brooch from his pocket and pinned it on Jasmine's red sweater. It was a Christmasy brooch, a miniature sleigh loaded down with snowed-on mistletoe. Before she could pull away, he kissed her on the lips. "Good luck for the New Year!" he said. She lifted her head and saw tears. "Is year for dreams comin true."

Jasmine started to cry, too. There was nothing wrong, but Mr. Daboo, Mrs. Daboo, she, everybody was crying.

What for? This is where she wanted to be. She'd spent some damned uncomfortable times with the assistant manager to get approval for her loan. She thought of Daddy. He would be playing poker and fanning himself with a magazine. Her married sisters would be rolling out the dough for stacks and stacks of roti, and Mummy would be steamed purple from stirring the big pot of goat curry on the stove. She missed them. But. It felt strange to think of anyone celebrating New Year's Eve in summery clothes.

In March Lara and her performing group went on the road. Jasmine knew that the group didn't work from scripts. The group didn't use a stage, either; instead, it took over supermarkets, senior citizens' centers, and school halls, without notice. Jasmine didn't understand the performance world. But she was glad that Lara said, "I'm not going to lay a guilt trip on myself. Muffie's in super hands," before she left.

Muffie didn't need much looking after. She played Trivial Pursuit all day, usually pretending to be two persons, sometimes Jasmine, whose accent she could imitate. Since Jasmine didn't know any of the answers, she couldn't help. Muffie was a quiet, precocious child with see-through blue eyes like her dad's, and red braids. In the early evenings Jasmine cooked supper, something special she hadn't forgotten from her island days. After supper she and Muffie watched some TV, and Bill read. When Muffie went to bed, Bill and she sat together for a bit with their glasses of Soave. Bill, Muffie, and she were a family, almost.

Down in her basement room that late, dark winter, she had trouble sleeping. She wanted to stay awake and think of Bill. Even when she fell asleep it didn't feel like sleep because Bill came barging into her dreams in his funny, loose-jointed, clumsy way. It was mad to think of him all the time, and stupid and sinful; but she couldn't help it. Whenever she put back a book he'd taken off the shelf to read or whenever she put his clothes through the washer and dryer, she felt sick in a giddy, wonderful way. When Lara came back things would get back to normal. Meantime she wanted the performance group miles away.

Lara called in at least twice a week. She said things like, "We've finally obliterated the margin between realspace and performancespace." Jasmine filled her in on Muffie's doings and the mail. Bill always closed with, "I love you. We miss you, hon."

One night after Lara had called—she was in Lincoln, Nebraska—Bill said to Jasmine, "Let's dance."

She hadn't danced since the reggae night she'd had too many rum punches. Her toes began to throb and clench. She untied her apron and the fraying, knotted-up laces of her running shoes.

Bill went around the downstairs rooms turning down lights. "We need atmosphere," he said. He got a small, tidy fire going in the living room grate and pulled the Turkish scatter rug closer to it. Lara didn't like anybody walking on the Turkish rug, but Bill meant to have his way. The hissing logs, the plants in the dimmed light, the thick patterned rug: everything was changed. This wasn't the room she cleaned every day.

He stood close to her. She smoothed her skirt down with both hands.

"I want you to choose the record," he said.

"I don't know your music."

She brought her hand high to his face. His skin was baby smooth.

"I want *you* to pick," he said. "You are your own person now."

"You got island music?"

He laughed, "What do you think?" The stereo was in a cabinet with albums packed tight alphabetically into the bottom three shelves. "Calypso has not been a force in my life."

She couldn't help laughing. "Calypso? Oh, man." She pulled dust jackets out at random. Lara's records. The Flying Lizards. The Violent Femmes. There was so much still to pick up on!

"This one," she said, finally.

He took the record out of her hand. "God!' he laughed. "Lara must have found this in a garage sale!" He laid the old record on the turntable. It was "Music for Lovers," something the nuns had taught her to foxtrot to way back in Port-of-Spain.

They danced so close that she could feel his heart heaving and crashing against her head. She liked it, she liked it very much. She didn't care what happened.

"Come on," Bill whispered. "If it feels right, do it." He began to take her clothes off.

"Don't Bill," she pleaded.

"Come on, baby," he whispered again. "You're a blossom, a flower."

He took off his fisherman's knit pullover, the corduroy pants, the blue shorts. She kept pace. She'd never had such an effect on a man: He nearly flung his socks and Adidas into the fire. "You feel so good," he said. "You smell so good. You're really something, flower of Trinidad."

"Flower of Ann Arbor," she said, "not Trinidad."

She felt so good she was dizzy. She'd never felt this good on the island where men did this all the time, and girls went along with it always for favors. You couldn't feel really good in a nothing place. She was thinking this as they made love on the Turkish carpet in front of the fire: she was a bright, pretty girl with no visa, no papers, and no birth certificate. No nothing other than what she wanted to invent and tell. She was a girl rushing wildly into the future.

His hand moved up her throat and forced her lips apart and it felt so good, so right, that she forgot all the dreariness of her new life and gave herself up to it.

Interpretations

1. Jasmine is "a girl with ambition." Ambition for what? Does she accomplish her ambition? How? What are Jasmine's other outstanding character traits? Where do they appear in the story?

2. What is Jasmine's relation with the Moffitts? How does it change? Why? What makes theirs, at least, a confusing relationship?

3. Jasmine glamourizes her hometown when describing it to Lara because she is ashamed of it. What does this indicate about Jasmine and her motivation for emigrating to Canada and then the United States? Do you feel that you understand Jasmine better than she understands herself? Why?

4. Jasmine thinks what she learned about "bargain-priced emigration" from the assistant bank manager in Trinidad more important than anything she had learned in two years of college. What does this tell us about Jasmine? What is the tone of the phrase "bargain-priced emigration"? How do you interpret the sentence, "She'd spent some damned uncomfortable times with the assistant manager to get approval for her loan"?

5. What do you think Jasmine's future holds for her? What leads you to think so?

6. Stories develop mainly from conflict: between two or more characters, within a character as the result of some psychological force (guilt, jealousy), or between a character and some impersonal force like poverty or disease. What is the main conflict in this story? Between what or whom? Is the struggle resolved?

7. What do you think is the point or thesis of the story?

Correspondences

1. "In this country Jesus givin out good luck only!" Why did Jasmine feel "Ann Arbor was the place to be"? To what extent was she, like Puzo's immigrants, captured by the American dream? Was she lucky to work for the Moffitts? Why or why not?

2. Review the Voltaire quotation (page 219). How does it apply to Jasmine's work experiences in the United States? Had Jasmine entered the country legally, might she have chosen differently? Explain your answer.

Applications

1. "Trinidad was an island stuck in the middle of nowhere. What kind of place was that for a girl with ambition?" What evidence is there of Jasmine's ambition? Compare her experiences in Trinidad with those in Michigan.

2. Compare and contrast the work experiences of Marshall's Caribbean immigrants with those of Jasmine more than fifty years later. What factors might account for differences?

ADDITIONAL WRITING TOPICS

1. Review Sayers's perspective on work (p. 220) and test its validity by interviewing people you know in various occupations on their attitudes towards working and the workplace. What conclusions did you reach? Write an analysis based on their responses.

2. Baker (Chapter 1) writes that "one defect of my mother's code was the value it placed on money and position. The children never cared a lot for that. To care, I suppose, you had to have been there with her during the depression." Compare Baker's mother's ideas of ambition and attitude towards work with those of a parent, teacher, counselor or employer. How do they differ? What cultural and generational factors have influenced them?

3. "Our work is hard, hot, wet, cold and always dirty. It is also very satisfying." Test Olson's thesis by interviewing several BCGs; ask them to what extent they are satisfied with their work. Use their responses to support or refute Olson.

4. Olson and Jones note attitudes toward affirmative action in the workplace. Review their comments. Then conduct an informal survey by interviewing several people affected by affirmative action programs. Summarize your findings.

5. According to Morrow, "Work is the way we tend the world, the way that people connect. It is the most vigorous vivid sign of life—in individuals and in civilizations." Test his thesis by asking several people of varying gender, ages and occupations to write a paragraph responding to Morrow's statement. Analyze their responses in a fully developed essay that clearly refutes or supports Morrow's point of view.

6. Despite the fact that teachers have longer vacations and more autonomy than do people in many other professions, statistics indicate a decline in college graduates choosing teaching as a profession. Conduct an informal survey among classmates on their attitudes towards teaching and teachers to try to determine the causes for this decline. Summarize your findings.

7. Sociologists argue that—despite stress, boredom, and burnout in the workplace—many Americans are unable to enjoy their leisure time in simple pursuits. Do you agree? Why is it difficult for people to relax off the job? (Have leisure activities become more sophisticated, expensive, and complex?) To what extent has leisure become another burden?

CHAPTER 5

Interactions

Peaceful interactions among cultures take many forms: treaties, trade, tourism, art exhibits, drama, movies, dance, student exchanges, exchange of scientific information, world fairs, conferring of awards and honors like the Nobel Prizes, sports events, musical events, conferences, emergency and other aid, cooperation in law enforcement, the United Nations. In general, these interactions please, intrigue, or interest us. Variety enhances—in food, dress, language, religion, art, celebrations, government. However, as the Senegalese folktale that begins this chapter implies, there is another side to human nature, and it is bleak. People may be so fond of their vested arrangements, so afraid that change will be for the worse, that they prefer falsehood to truth. Exposure to other cultures, the sifting of truth, the juxtaposition of another's knowledge and our ignorance, for example, are sometimes more than we can stand: "Better the devil we know than the devil we don't" expresses an enduring attitude that quickly surfaces when cultures compete rather than complement. Such clashes exact a price and take various forms.

Lack of awareness of cultural differences or the assumption of one cultural group that another is inferior results in interactions that are painful power struggles. These struggles run the gamut from personal suffering to temporary feuds to civil war or full-scale war. For example, if we had understood the culture of the Japanese immigrants ("nisei") on the west coast in the 1940's, we would have known that they were loyal U.S. citizens, not spies waiting to betray their adopted country. We would never have committed the injustice of interning them in concentration camps during World War II even as we allowed their sons to fight and die in the U.S. armed forces.

Had we known more about Vietnamese culture, we might not have blundered into the Vietnam War.

On a more personal scale, Edward T. Hall suggests that, if we don't know how people in other cultures feel about privacy and private space," we can spend our time with them in anger and confrontation. Michael Novak thinks that the American majority makes too little effort to understand and include immigrants from Italy, Greece, Poland, and other Eastern European countries. Distress can become internalized. Jim Fusilli struggles to understand and reconcile his Italian and Irish halves. The "Englishwoman" in Jhabvala's story of that name could have spared herself a good deal of unhappiness had she known more about upperclass Indian family life and sexual mores.

The shock of cross-cultural interactions may also occur between members of the same culture, as when an emigrant returns home after a long absence. Time and distance can make an alien of a native. Alastair Reid is such an immigrant; a cosmopolitan world traveler and resident of New York City, he returns to his homeland of Scotland to find a place that has "changed less" than any other he can think of. It has "the air of a museum." Peripatetic Reid is amazed at the kind of rootedness that can develop when a Scotsman makes his "peace with place," with Scottish landscapes and people. Likewise, the culture shock in Matshoba's story occurs, not in the interaction between blacks and whites in apartheid-ridden South Africa, but between blacks united against apartheid and reservists (certain black policemen in the story) who cooperate with the whites to keep blacks in their "place."

In the interactions of this chapter sometimes falsehood prevails and the result is disruptive and destructive. But other interactions are based on a respect for truth and on acceptance of the world's cultural variety.

PERSPECTIVES

Culture is that which binds men together.

Ruth Benedict

We are creatures of outside *influences. We originate* nothing *within. Whenever we take a new line of thought and drift into a new line of belief and action, the impulse is always suggested from the outside.*

Mark Twain

The planet has become an intricate convergence—of acid rains and rain forests burning, of ideas and Reeboks and stock markets that ripple through time zones, of satellite signals and worldwide television, of advance-purchase airfares, fax machines, the miniaturization of the universe by computer, of T-shirts and mutual destinies.

Lance Morrow

As social equality spreads there are more and more people who, though neither rich nor powerful enough to have much hold over others, have gained or kept enough wealth and enough understanding to look after their own needs. Such folk owe no man anything and hardly expect anything from anybody. They form the habit of thinking of themselves in isolation and imagine that their whole destiny is in their own hands.
Thus, not only does democracy make men forget their ancestors, but it also clouds their view of their descendants and isolates them from their contemporaries. Each man is forever thrown back on himself alone, and there is danger that he may be shut in the solitude of his own heart.

Alexis de Tocqueville

The only way to make sure people you agree with can speak is to support the rights of people you don't agree with.

Eleanor Holmes Norton

289

Man is an animal suspended in webs of significance which he himself has created. I take culture to be those webs.

Clifford Geertz

No man is an iland, intire of it selfe; every man is a peece of the Continent, a part of the maine; if a Clod bee washed away by the Sea, Europe is the lesse, as well as if a Promontorie were, as well as if a Mannor of thy friends or of thine owne were; any man's death diminishes me, because I am involved in Mankinde; And therefore never send to know for whom the bell tolls; It tolls for thee.

John Donne

Culture regulates our lives at every turn. From the moment we are born until we die there is, whether we are conscious of it or not, constant pressure upon us to follow certain types of behavior that other men have created for us.

Clyde Kluckhohn

It is a terrible, an inexorable, law that one cannot deny the humanity of another without diminishing one's own; in the face of one's victim one sees oneself.

James Baldwin

Applications

1. Select a perspective on interactions with which you agree or disagree. In your journal, record and analyze the reasons for your point of view.

2. Select two perspectives for discussion in your group. What insights did you gain? Record them in your journal.

The Falsehood of Truth

Senegalese Myth

Senegal is a republic in western Africa, which gained independence from France in 1960.

FENE-FALSEHOOD and Deug-Truth started out on a journey one day.

Fene-Falsehood said, "Everyone says that the Lord loves truth better than falsehood, so I think that you had better do all the talking for us."

Deug-Truth agreed, and when they came to a village, Deug-Truth greeted the first woman they met and asked if they could have a drink. She gave them a filthy bowl full of lukewarm water and then sat down in the doorway of her hut and began to eat a big meal of rice. While the two travelers were still there, the woman's husband came home and asked for his supper.

"It's not ready," replied the woman insolently.

The husband then turned to the two strangers who were watching and asked, "What would you say about a woman like that?"

"I would say that she is the worst wife I have seen in a long time. It's bad enough for her not to be hospitable to strangers, but it is really disgraceful when she doesn't feed her own husband," replied Deug-Truth. Fene-Falsehood didn't say a word.

The woman became furious and began to yell and scream louder than either of the two travelers had ever heard anyone scream before. "Are you going to stand by and let these strangers insult me!" she screamed to her husband. "If so, I will go home to my father and you will have to raise a bride-price for a new wife."

Then the husband, too, became angry and chased the two strangers out of town.

So Deug and Fene continued their travels and next came to a village where they found several children dividing up a bull that had just been slaughtered. They thought that this was rather strange, for it was the custom that meat was always divided by the head-man. While they were still watching, they saw the chief come up and take a very poor share of meat which the children handed him. The chief saw the two strangers and asked, "Who do you think is the leader in this village?"

Fene said nothing but Deug immediately answered, "It seems to me that these children must be the leaders of this village, for they are dividing the meat."

The chief immediately became angry and chased them out of that village.

As they continued to walk along, Fene said to Deug, "It is said that the

291

Lord loves you the best, but I am beginning to wonder if man is not rather different from God. It seems to me that men do not like you very well. I think I will try my luck at the next village."

At the next village, they found that all the people were weeping because the favorite wife of the king had just died. Fene thought for a minute and then said, "Go tell the king that a man is here who can raise people from the dead."

Soon Fene was brought before the king and said, "I will raise your wife from the dead if you will give me half of your fortune."

The king immediately agreed and Fene had a hut built above the family grave. The king and all of the people waited outside and listened to the strange noises. First they heard huffing and panting and strange chants, but then they began to hear Fene talking loudly as if he were arguing. Finally he burst out of the door and slammed it shut—holding it tightly.

"Oh, dear," he said, "you did not tell me that your whole family was buried in there. When I woke your wife up, your father and your grandfather both came out too. I thought I had better check before I let them all out."

The king and his advisers began to look frightened, for the king's father had been a very cruel king and the new king and his friends had given his death a little assistance.

I think you had better leave them all," said the king. "We would have a lot of trouble here with three kings."

"Well, it's not that easy," said Fene slyly. "Your father has offered me half of this property to let him out. I am certainly not going to send him back for nothing."

"I will still give you half of my property," said the desperate king. "Just get rid of them all."

So Fene received half of the king's fortune and concluded that while truth might have the favor of God, falsehood was the best way to get ahead with men.

Interpretations

1. Before you read this story, cover up the last sentence, beginning with "concluded that. . . ." When you reach this point in the story, write your own conclusion. Compare your conclusion and the storyteller's. Do you generally like the point of a story stated outright, or would you rather deduce it for yourself? Why? Do you agree with the stated conclusion? Why or why not? If the conclusion is true, why should the reader, of all people, want to learn this "truth"? Isn't it also a falsehood?

2. Are the incidents along the journey well chosen illustrations of the moral? Are people indeed more apt to prefer falsehood in the areas of marriage and tribal leadership (politics?)? Why or why not? Do you think the husband

and the chief make real choices or merely bow to necessity? What makes you think so?

3. Allegorical stories, whose characters are abstractions (like Falsehood and Truth), are rare in American contemporary literature. Why? (What expectations do characters like this set up?)

4. Is it wise to alert the readers or hearers that the story is didactic—meant to teach a lesson? Why or why not? Would we derive the same point from the story if the names Fene and Deug had not been translated for us? Would the story's mood or tone (and thus its effect) be the same? If not, how would it be different?

5. What cultural interaction do you find in the story?

The Wise Rogue

Jewish Folk Tale as told by Moses Gaster

The editor of A Harvest of World Folk Tales *describes the origins of "The Wise Rogue" as follows:*

> *The keynotes of Jewish folk story are wisdom, humor, and piety, and its favorite form is the parable. It is plainly the product of a society that was in its early days priestly and in its later days persecuted. Rare are the mighty, muscular heroes (Samson was one, of course, but David against Goliath and Judith against Holofernes seem much more characteristic); nor are there any authentic fire-breathing dragons or broom-riding witches. The heroes of the Jews are wise kings, learned rabbis, or rogues who live by their wits; their dragons are the Devil and the Temptations; their witches are those who have historically oppressed them. Even their humor is of a worldly-wise or satiric sort; and their sillies, the Wise Men of Helm, are not so much numskulls as absent-minded philosophers, men whose heads are filled with more than is commonly useful.*

A MAN who was once caught stealing was ordered by the king to be hanged. On the way to the gallows he said to the governor that he knew a wonderful secret, and it would be a pity to allow it to die with him, and he would like to disclose it to the king. He would put a seed of a pomegranate in the ground, and through the secret taught to him by his father he would make it grow and bear fruit overnight. The thief was brought before the king, and on the morrow the king, accompanied by the high officers of state, came to the place where the thief was waiting for them. There the thief dug a hole and said, "This seed must be put in the ground only by a man who has never stolen or taken anything which did not belong to him. I being a thief cannot do it." So he turned to the vizier who, frightened, said that in his younger days he had retained something which did not belong to him. The treasurer said that in dealing with large sums he might have entered too much or too little, and even the king owned that he had kept a necklace of his father's. The thief then said, "You are all mighty and powerful and want nothing, and yet you cannot plant the seed, whilst I who have stolen a little because I was starving am to be hanged." The king, pleased with the ruse of the thief, pardoned him.

Interpretations

1. Did the king do the right thing? Why or why not?

2. "The king, pleased with the ruse of the thief, pardoned him." Usually people do not enjoy being tricked; what was different about this case? How would you have felt if the trick had been played on you?

3. What does this story imply about the relationship between justice and mercy?

4. The laws broken seem insignificant. Are they the tip of the iceberg? If officials commit petty crimes, will they also commit serious ones? How can a society prevent lawless people from administering the law?

5. What is the tone of this story? How does it affect the meaning?

Correspondences

1. Review the Donne quotation (page 290). How does it apply to "The False-hood of Truth?" (What episodes in the folktale contradict it? Do you agree with Fene's conclusion about human interactions? Why or why not?)

2. Review the Geertz quotation (page 290). What does it mean? How does it relate to "The Wise Rogue"? What does the story imply about human interactions?

Applications

1. "Honesty is the best policy." Do you believe so? Should honesty be the basis of all human interactions? Write an essay explaining why it is possible or impossible to be totally honest with your best friend.

2. What do both stories suggest about success? Are rogues likely to achieve success? What examples can you think of? Discuss these questions in your group and record your conclusions.

Does America Still Exist?

Richard Rodriguez

Richard Rodriguez (b. 1944) is a Mexican-American who grew up in California. He has studied at Stanford University, Columbia University, and the University of California at Berkeley—where he teaches. In addition to writing essays, he has published the autobiographical Hunger of Memory: The Education of Richard Rodriguez *(1981). The following essay first appeared in* Harper's *(March 1984) as part of a group of essays written in response to the question "Does America Still Exist?"*

FOR THE CHILDREN of immigrant parents the knowledge comes easier. America exists everywhere in the city—on billboards, frankly in the smell of French fries and popcorn. It exists in the pace: traffic lights, the assertions of neon, the mysterious bong-bong-bong through the atriums of department stores. American exists as the voice of the crowd, a menacing sound—the high nasal accent of American English.

When I was a boy in Sacramento (California, the fifties), people would ask me, "Where you from?" I was born in this country, but I knew the question meant to decipher my darkness, my looks.

My mother once instructed me to say, "I am an American of Mexican descent." By the time I was nine or ten, I wanted to say, but dared not reply, "I am an American."

Immigrants come to America and, against hostility or mere loneliness, they recreate a homeland in the parlor, tacking up postcards or calendars of some impossible blue—lake or sea or sky. Children of immigrant parents are supposed to perch on a hyphen between two countries. Relatives assume the achievement as much as anyone. Relatives are, in any case, surprised when the child begins losing old ways. One day at the family picnic the boy wanders away from their spiced food and faceless stories to watch other boys play baseball in the distance.

There is sorrow in the American memory, guilty sorrow for having left something behind—Portugal, China, Norway. The American story is the story of immigrant children and of their children—children no longer able to speak to grandparents. The memory of exile becomes inarticulate as it passes from generation to generation, along with wedding rings and pocket watches—like some mute stone in a wad of old lace. Europe. Asia. Eden.

But, it needs to be said, if this is a country where one stops being Vietnamese or Italian, this is a country where one begins to be an American. America exists as a culture and a grin, a faith and a shrug. It is clasped in a handshake, called by a first name.

As much as the country is joined in a common culture, however, Americans are reluctant to celebrate the process of assimilation. We pledge allegiance to diversity. America was born Protestant and bred Puritan, and the notion of community we share is derived from a seventeenth-century faith. Presidents and the pages of ninth-grade civics readers yet proclaim the orthodoxy: We are gathered together—but as individuals, with separate pasts, distinct destinies. Our society is as paradoxical as a Puritan congregation: We stand together, alone.

Americans have traditionally defined themselves by what they refused to include. As often, however, Americans have struggled, turned in good conscience at last to assert the great Protestant virtue of tolerance. Despite outbreaks of nativist frenzy, America has remained an immigrant country, open and true to itself.

Against pious emblems of rural America—soda fountain, Elks hall, Protestant church, and now shopping mall—stands the cold-hearted city, crowded with races and ambitions, curious laughter, much that is odd. Nevertheless, it is the city that has most truly represented America. In the city, however, the millions of singular lives have had no richer notion of wholeness to describe them than the idea of pluralism.

"Where you from?" the American asks the immigrant child. "Mexico," the boy learns to say.

Mexico, the country of my blood ancestors, offers formal contrast to the American achievement. If the United States was formed by Protestant individualism, Mexico was shaped by a medieval Catholic dream of one world. The Spanish journeyed to Mexico to plunder, and they may have gone, in God's name, with an arrogance peculiar to those who intend to convert. But through the conversion, the Indian converted the Spaniard. A new race was born, the *mestizo,* wedding European to Indian. José Vasconcelos, the Mexican philosopher, has celebrated this New World creation, proclaiming it the "cosmic race."

Centuries later, in a San Francisco restaurant, a Mexican-American lawyer of my acquaintance says, in English, over *salade niçoise,* that he does not intend to assimilate into gringo society. His claim is echoed by a chorus of others (Italian-Americans, Greeks, Asians) in this era of ethnic pride. The melting pot has been retired, clanking, into the museum of quaint disgrace, alongside Aunt Jemima and the Katzenjammer Kids.* But resistance to assimilation is characteristically American. It only makes clear how inevitable the process of assimilation actually is.

For generations, this has been the pattern. Immigrant parents have sent their children to school (simply, they thought) to acquire the "skills" to survive in the city. The child returned home with a voice his parents barely recognized or understood, couldn't trust, and didn't like.

In Eastern cities—Philadelphia, New York, Boston, Baltimore—class

---

*Aunt Jemima—stereotypical black mammy; Katzenjammer Kids—stereotypical cartoon characters.

after class gathered immigrant children to women (usually women) who stood in front of rooms full of children, changing children. So also for me in the 1950s. Irish-Catholic nuns. California. The old story. The hyphen tipped to the right, away from Mexico and toward a confusing but true American identity.

I speak now in the chromium American accent of my grammar school classmates—Billy Reckers, Mike Bradley, Carol Schmidt, Kathy O'Grady. . . . I believe I became like my classmates, became German, Polish, and (like my teachers) Irish. And because assimilation is always reciprocal, my classmates got something of me. (I mean sad eyes; belief in the Indian Virgin; a taste for sugar skulls on the Feast of the Dead.) In the blending, we became what our parents could never have been, and we carried America one revolution further.

"Does America still exist?" Americans have been asking the question for so long that to ask it again only proves our continuous link. But perhaps the question deserves to be asked with urgency now. Since the black civil rights movement of the 1960s, our tenuous notion of a shared public life has deteriorated notably.

The struggle of black men and women did not eradicate racism, but it became the great moment in the life of America's conscience. Water hoses, bulldogs, blood—the images, rendered black, white, rectangular, passed into living rooms.

It is hard to look at a photograph of a crowd taken, say, in 1890 or in 1930 and not notice the absence of blacks. (It becomes an impertinence to wonder if America *still* exists.)

In the sixties, other groups of Americans learned to champion their rights by analogy to the black civil rights movement. But the heroic vision faded. Dr. Martin Luther King, Jr. had spoken with Pauline eloquence of a nation that would unite Christian and Jew, old and young, rich and poor. Within a decade, the struggles of the 1960s were reduced to a bureaucratic competition for little more than pieces of a representational pie. The quest for a portion of power became an end in itself. The metaphor for the American city of the 1970s was a committee: one black, one woman, one person under thirty . . .

If the small town had sinned against America by too neatly defining who could be an American, the city's sin was a romantic secession. One noticed the romanticism in the antiwar movement—certain demonstrators who demonstrated a lack of tact or desire to persuade and seemed content to play secular protestants. One noticed the romanticism in the competition among members of "minority groups" to claim the status of Primary Victim. To Americans unconfident of their common identity, minority standing became a way of asserting individuality. Middle-class Americans—men and women clearly not the primary victims of social oppression—brandished their suffering with exuberance.

The dream of a single society probably died with *The Ed Sullivan Show*.

The reality of America persists. Teenagers pass through big-city high schools banded in racial groups, their collars turned up to a uniform shrug. But then they graduate to jobs at the phone company or in banks, where they end up working alongside people unlike themselves. Typists and tellers walk out together at lunchtime.

It is easier for us as Americans to believe the obvious fact of our separateness—easier to imagine the black and white Americas prophesied by the Kerner report (broken glass, street fires)—than to recognize the reality of a city street at lunchtime. Americans are wedded by proximity to a common culture. The panhandler at one corner is related to the pamphleteer at the next who is related to the banker who is kin to the Chinese old man wearing an MIT sweatshirt. In any true national history, Thomas Jefferson begets Martin Luther King, Jr., who begets the Gray Panthers. It is because we lack a vision of ourselves entire—the city street is crowded and we are each preoccupied with finding our own way home—that we lack an appropriate hymn.

Under my window now passes a little white girl softly rehearsing to herself a Motown obbligato.

Interpretations

1. In the seventh through ninth paragraphs, Rodriguez comes rather close to defining "American" as diversity, tolerance, and pluralism. Do you agree that Americans "pledge allegiance" to these principles? Why do you think Rodriguez did not explicitly define "American" and organize his essay around such a definition?

2. Why was the question "Where you from?" so unsettling, so important to answer "correctly"? What has the boy learned when he learns to answer "Mexico"?

3. Rodriguez frequently uses specifics to stand for something more general, as in "spiced food" and "baseball." What do these two details stand for? Can you find other examples of this kind of symbolic detail?

4. How, according to Rodriguez, do some people misuse their "minority standing"? What has been the result of such misuse?

5. How do you interpret the last sentence? Which do you consider to be the most important words in this sentence?

Correspondences

1. Review the de Tocqueville quotation on social equality (page 289). What points does he make about democracy? How does Rodriguez's essay support or contradict de Tocqueville's views? With whom do you agree more?

2. "Americans have traditionally defined themselves by what they refused to include." What does Rodriguez mean? Cite examples from Rendón or Bambara (Chapter 3) to support or refute his point of view.

Applications

1. To Rodriguez, "The American story is the story of immigrant children and of their children—children no longer able to speak to their grandparents." Write an analysis of the personal and cultural ramifications of this thesis.

2. To Rodriguez, " . . . resistance to assimilation is characteristically American. It only makes clear how inevitable the process of assimilation actually is." Assume the persona of Rendón and write an essay responding to Rodriguez.

In Ethnic America

Michael Novak

Michael Novak (b. 1933), from Johnstown, Pennsylvania, is an American of Slovak descent. A distinguished scholar, he has earned several degrees, including an M.A. (1966) from Harvard University. His teaching career has spanned a number of prestigious universities, and he is currently a Professor of American Studies at the University of Notre Dame. Mr. Novak has authored numerous books, including Naked I Leave *(1970),* The Rise of the Unmeltable Ethnics *(1972),* Confession of a Catholic *(1983), and* Human Rights and the New Realism *(1986). In this selection from* The Rise of the Unmeltable Ethnics, *Novak examines the difficulties many southern and eastern European immigrants encountered as they attempted cultural assimilation in the United States.*

For information on Poland, see Michael T. Kaufman's "Kissing Customs," Chapter 1.; on Italy, see Mario Puzo's "Italians in Hell's Kitchen," Chapter 4; and on Czechoslovakia, see Hana Wehle's "The Impossible Became No Longer Unthinkable," Chapter 6.

GROWING UP in America has been an assault upon my sense of worthiness. It has also been a kind of liberation and delight.

There must be countless women in America who have known for years that something is peculiarly unfair, yet who only recently have found it possible, because of Women's Liberation, to give tongue to their pain. In recent months I have experienced a similar inner thaw, a gradual relaxation, a willingness to think about feelings heretofore shepherded out of sight.

I am born of PIGS—those Poles, Italians, Greeks, and Slavs, those non-English-speaking immigrants numbered so heavily among the workingmen of this nation. Not particularly liberal or radical; born into a history not white Anglo-Saxon and not Jewish; born outside what, in America, is considered the intellectual mainstream—and thus privy to neither power nor status nor intellectual voice.

Those Poles of Buffalo and Milwaukee—so notoriously taciturn, sullen, nearly speechless. Who has ever understood them? It is not that Poles do not feel emotion—what is their history if not dark passion, romanticism, betrayal, courage, blood? But where in America is there anywhere a language for voicing what a Christian Pole in this nation feels? He has no Polish culture left him, no Polish tongue. Yet Polish feelings do not go easily into the idiom of happy America, the America of the Anglo-Saxons and yes, in the arts, the Jews. (The Jews have long been a culture of the word, accustomed to exile, skilled in scholarship and in reflection. The Christian Poles are largely of peasant origin, free men for hardly more than a hundred years.) Of what shall the young man of Lackawanna think on his way to work in the mills, departing his relatively dreary home and street? What roots does he have? What language of the heart is available to him?

The PIGS are not silent willingly. The silence burns like hidden coals in the chest.

All four of my grandparents, unknown to one another, arrived in America from the same county in Slovakia. My grandfather had a small farm in Pennsylvania; his wife died in a wagon accident. Meanwhile, Johanna, fifteen, arrived on Ellis Island, dizzy from witnessing births and deaths and illnesses aboard the crowded ship. She had a sign around her neck lettered PASSAIC. There an aunt told her of a man who had lost his wife in Pennsylvania. She went. They were married. She inherited his three children.

Each year for five years Grandma had a child of her own. She was among the lucky; only one died. When she was twenty-two and the mother of seven (my father was the last), her husband died. "Grandma Novak," as I came to know her many years later, resumed the work she had begun in Slovakia at the town home of a man known to my father only as "the Professor"; she housecleaned and she laundered.

I heard this story only weeks ago. Strange that I had not asked insistently before. Odd that I should have such shallow knowledge of my roots. Amazing to me that I do not know what my family suffered, endured, learned, and hoped these last six or seven generations. It is as if there were no project in which we all have been involved, as if history in some way began with my father and with me.

The estrangement I have come to feel derives not only from lack of family history. Early in life, I was made to feel a slight uneasiness when I said my name. When I was very young, the "American" kids still made something out of names unlike their own, and their earnest, ambitious mothers thought long thoughts when I introduced myself.

Under challenge in grammar school concerning my nationality, I had been instructed by my father to announce proudly: "American." When my family moved from the Slovak ghetto of Johnstown to the WASP suburb on the hill, my mother impressed upon us how well we must be dressed, and show good manners, and behave—people think of us as "different" and we mustn't give them any cause. "Whatever you do, marry a Slovak girl," was other advice to a similar end: "They cook. They clean. They take good ca e of you. For your own good." I was taught to be proud of being Slovak, but to recognize that others wouldn't know what it meant, or care.

Nowhere in my schooling do I recall any attempt to put me in touch with my own history. The strategy was clearly to make an American of me. English literature, American literature, and even the history books, as I recall them, were peopled mainly by Anglo-Saxons from Boston (where most historians seemed to live). Not even my native Pennsylvania, let alone my Slovak forebears, counted for very many paragraphs. (We did have something called "Pennsylvania History" somewhere; I seem to remember its puffs for industry. It could have been written by a Mellon. I don't remember feeling envy or regret: a feeling, perhaps, of unimportance, of remoteness, of not having heft enough to count.

The fact that I was born a Catholic also complicated life. What is a Catholic but what everybody else is in reaction against? Protestants reformed "the whore of Babylon." Others were "enlightened" from it, and Jews had reason to help Catholicism and the social structure it was rooted in fall apart. The history books and the whole of education hummed in upon that point (for during crucial years I attended a public school): to be modern is decidedly not to be medieval; to be reasonable is not to be dogmatic; to be free is clearly not to live under ecclesiastical authority; to be scientific is not to attend ancient rituals, cherish irrational symbols, indulge in mythic practices. It is hard to grow up Catholic in America without becoming defensive, perhaps a little paranoid, feeling forced to divide the world between "us" and "them."

We had a special language all our own, our own pronunciation for words we shared in common with others (Augústine, contémplative), sights and sounds and smells in which few others participated (incense at Benediction of the Most Blessed Sacrament, Forty Hours, wakes, and altar bells at the silent consecration of the Host); and we had our own politics and slant on world affairs. Since earliest childhood, I have known about a "power elite" that runs America: the boys from the Ivy League in the State Department as opposed to the Catholic boys in Hoover's FBI who (as Daniel Moynihan once put it), keep watch on them. And on a whole host of issues, my people have been, though largely Democratic, conservative: on censorship, on communism, on abortion, on religious schools, etc. "Harvard" and "Yale" long meant "them" to us.

We did not feel this country belonged to us. We felt fierce pride in it, more loyalty than anyone could know. But we felt blocked at every turn. There were not many intellectuals among us, not even very many professional men. Laborers mostly. Small businessmen, agents for corporations perhaps. Content with a little, yes, modest in expectation, and content. But somehow feeling cheated. For a thousand years the Slovaks survived Hungarian hegemony and our strategy here remained the same: endurance and steady work. Slowly, one day, we would overcome.

A special word is required about a complicated symbol: sex. To this day my mother finds it hard to spell the word intact, preferring to write "s--." Not that much was made of sex in our environment. And that's the point: silence. Demonstrative affection, emotive dances, an exuberance Anglo-Saxons seldom seem to share; but on the realities of sex, discretion. Reverence, perhaps; seriousness, surely. On intimacies, it was as though our tongues had been stolen, as though in peasant life for a thousand years—as in the novels of Tolstoi, Sholokhov, and even Kosinski—the context had been otherwise. Passion, certainly; romance, yes; family and children, certainly; but sex rather a minor if explosive part of life.

Imagine, then, the conflict in the generation of my brothers, sister, and myself. Suddenly, what for a thousand years was minor becomes an all-absorbing investigation. Some view it as a drama of "liberation" when the ruling classes (subscribers to the *New Yorker*, I suppose) move progressively, generation by generation since Sigmund Freud, toward concentration upon genital stimulation, and latterly toward consciousness-raising sessions in Clit. Lib. But it is rather a different drama when we stumble suddenly upon mores staggering any expectation our grandparents ever cherished.

Yet more significant in the ethnic experience in America is the intellectual world one meets: the definition of values, ideas, and purposes emanating from universities, books, magazines, radio, and television. One hears one's own voice echoed back neither by spokesmen of "middle America" (so complacent, smug, nativist, and Protestant), nor by the "intellectuals." Almost unavoidably, perhaps, education in America leads the student who entrusts his soul to it in a direction which, lacking a better word, we might call liberal: respect for individual conscience, a sense of social responsibility, trust in the free exchange of ideas and procedures of dissent, a certain confidence in the ability of men to "reason together" and adjudicate their differences, a frank recognition of the vitality of the unconscious, a willingness to protect workers and the poor against the vast economic power of industrial corporations, and the like.

On the other hand, the liberal imagination has appeared to be astonishingly universalist and relentlessly missionary. Perhaps the metaphor "enlightenment" offers a key. One is *initiated into light*. Liberal education tends to separate children from their parents, from their roots, from their history, in the cause of a universal and superior religion.

In particular, I have regretted and keenly felt the absence of that sympathy for PIGS which simple human feeling might have prodded intelligence to muster, that same sympathy which the educated find so easy to conjure up for black culture, Chicano culture, Indian culture, and other cultures of the poor. In such cases one finds the universalist pretensions of liberal culture suspended; some groups, at least, are entitled to be both different and respected. Why do the educated classes find it so difficult to want to understand the man who drives a beer truck, or the fellow with a helmet working on a site across the street with plumbers and electricians, while their sensitivities race easily to Mississippi or even Bedford-Stuyvesant?

There are deep secrets here, no doubt, unvoiced fantasies and scarcely admitted historical resentments. Few persons in describing "middle Americans," "the silent majority," or Scammon and Wattenberg's "typical American voter" distinguish clearly enough between the nativist American and the ethnic American. The first is likely to be Protestant, the second Catholic. Both may be, in various ways, conservative, loyalist, and unenlightened. Each has his own agonies, fears, betrayed expectations. Neither is ready, quite, to become an ally of the other. Neither has the same history behind him here. Neither has the same hopes. Neither lives out the same psychic voyage, shares the same symbols, has the same sense of reality. The rhetoric and metaphors proper to each differ from those of the other.

There is overlap, of course. But country music is not a polka; a successful politician in a Chicago ward needs a very different "common touch" from the one needed by the county clerk in Normal. The urban experience of immigration lacks that mellifluous, optimistic, biblical vision of the good America which springs naturally to the lips of politicians from the Bible Belt. The nativist tends to believe with Richard Nixon that he "knows America, and the American heart is good." The ethnic tends to believe that every American who preceded him has an angle, and that he, by God, will some day find one, too. (Often, ethnics complain that by working hard, obeying the law, trusting their political leaders, and relying upon the American dream, they now have only their own naiveté to blame for rising no higher than they have.)

Unfortunately, it seems, the ethnics erred in attempting to Americanize themselves before clearing the project with the educated classes. They learned to wave the flag and to send their sons to war. They learned to support their President—an easy task, after all, for those accustomed to obeying authority. And where would they have been if Franklin Roosevelt had not sided with them against established interests? They knew a little about communism— the radicals among them in one way, and by far the larger number of conservatives in another. To this day not a few exchange letters with cousins and uncles who did not leave for America when they might have, whose lot is demonstrably harder than their own and less than free.

Finally, the ethnics do not like, or trust, or even understand the intellectuals. It is not easy to feel uncomplicated affection for those who call you "pig," "fascist," "racist." One had not yet grown accustomed to not hearing "hunkie," "Polack," "spic," "mick," "dago," and the rest.

At no little sacrifice, one had apologized for foods that smelled too strong for Anglo-Saxon noses; moderated the wide swings of Slavic and Italian emotion; learned decorum; given oneself to education, American style; tried to learn tolerance and assimilation. Each generation criticized the earlier for its authoritarian and European and old-fashioned ways. "Up-to-date" was a moral lever. And now when the process nears completion, when a generation appears that speaks without accent and goes to college, still you are considered "pigs," "fascists," and "racists." Racists? Our ancestors owned no slaves. Most of us ceased being serfs only in the last two hundred years—the Russians in 1861. . . .

Whereas the Anglo-Saxon model appears to be a system of atomic individuals and high mobility, our model has tended to stress communities of our own, attachment to family and relatives, stability, and roots. Ethnics tend to have a fierce sense of attachment to their homes, having been home-owners for less than three generations: a home is almost fulfillment enough for one man's life. Some groups save arduously in a passion to *own;* others rent. We have most ambivalent feelings about suburban assimilation and mobility. The melting pot is a kind of homogenized soup, and its mores only partly appeal to ethnics: to some, yes, and to others, no.

It must be said that ethnics think they are better people than the blacks. Smarter, tougher, harder working, stronger in their families. But maybe many are not sure. Maybe many are uneasy. Emotions here are delicate; one can understand the immensely more difficult circumstances under which the blacks have suffered; and one is not unaware of peculiar forms of fear, envy, and suspicion across color lines. How much of this we learned in America by being made conscious of our olive skin, brawny backs, accents, names, and cultural quirks is not plain to us. Racism is not our invention; we did not bring it with us; we had prejudices enough and would gladly have been spared new ones. Especially regarding people who suffer more than we.

Interpretations

1. The first two sentences of this essay serve as a striking introduction; they grab the reader's interest. Do they also state the main point (thesis) of the essay? Is each sentence equally important to the thesis?

2. Novak says that his "estrangement" resulted from lack of knowledge of his family's history and from his sense—symbolized in his name—of being different and not understood. Is not knowing one's family history a common condition among immigrants? What else contributed to Novak's sense of alienation?

3. Those who lived through the 1988 Presidential campaign have become very conscious of the word *liberal*. Examine Novak's extended definition of this word and evaluate it. How does it compare to yours?

4. What reasons does Novak give to support his thesis that the educated classes are more likely to sympathize with blacks than with Slovaks, Poles, Italians, or Greeks? If you agree, why do you? Cite supporting evidence.

5. Why do you think Novak wrote this essay? What was his purpose?

Correspondences

1. "Nowhere in my schooling do I recall any attempt to put me in touch with my own history. The strategy was clearly to make an American out of me."

Should such a "strategy" be the purpose of American education? How does Novak's educational experience compare to that of Marshall and Rendón (Chapter 3)? What might each of the three writers have gained emotionally and intellectually from a curriculum that clearly reflected the contribution of their cultures?

2. Looking for work is an integral part of the immigrant experience. Compare the work experiences of Novak's grandmother (paragraphs six and seven) with those of Jasmine in the story of the same name (Chapter 4). Who has the more fortunate interaction? Why do you say so?

Applications

1. "We did not feel this country belonged to us" reflects not only Novak's point of view but that of many other immigrants. To whom, then, does America belong? How might cultural interactions contribute to better communication and a wider sense of belonging?

2. "[T]he ethnics do not like, or trust, or even understand the intellectuals." Why not? What characteristics do the ethnics associate with intellectuals? What is your definition of an intellectual? How does it compare to Novak's? What interactions can you imagine taking place between ethnics and intellectuals that would contribute to better personal and cultural understanding?

Opting for the Light

Jim Fusilli

Jim Fusilli (b. 1954) is a graduate of St. Peter's College in Jersey City. He has published essays in the Wall Street Journal *and the* New York Times Magazine *as well as in other periodicals. Here are his reasons for writing "Opting for the Light," a personal essay about his family's ethnic backgrounds: "I wrote 'Opting for the Light' for several reasons. I wanted to go beyond my customary critical essays. I hoped the experience would be cathartic (it was not), and I wanted to have something by way of explanation to show my Irish relatives and friends so they'd know there were reasons for the way I feel."*

IT IS A TRUTH long held among my family and friends that I hate being half Irish rather than fully Italian. It is not an unspoken truth. "You hate being Irish," a distant Irish relative recently snapped, because I said her granddaughter looked more like the girl's Italian father than her mother. And: "He is?" said the incredulous Italian wife of an Irish friend. "Yeah," replied the friend, "and he hates it."

There is but a morsel of truth in what they say. "Hate" would imply outright disdain for all things Irish, and I count among my favorite things Joyce's *Dubliners* and the evocative work of Van Morrison. I marvel at Shaw, admire the nationalist fervor of the Irish Renaissance, and relish Yeats's transcendental eloquence and his revision of the English romanticists, who, to me, somehow seem to have found their reverence of nature in the impossible beauty of the green Sheeffry Hills of County Mayo.

Nor can it be said that I don't love my mother or enjoy several other members of the Irish side of my family. My Irish grandmother was perhaps my favorite relative, witty and caustic, a lovable curmudgeon. I can hear her gravel voice now, and see the sheen of her silver hair, the pink frame of her eyeglasses. She was my mother's best friend and a friend of mine, ever present, seemingly as much a part of my life as my parents. (I never lived more than a short walk from her until after college; we never took a vacation without her.) So deeply embedded was she in my life that on the way to the funeral home for her wake I paused to help her across the slippery pavement. For the first time, she was not there.

Further, several of my closest friends are Irish-Americans; their importance to me is immeasurable. And as a child, my hero was a family friend named Molloy, who seemed to me larger than life. He had a big black car with leather seats, and took me to see baseball games in Philadelphia. We cheered Jim Maloney and Jim O'Toole when the Reds came to town.

That said, I can't now deny that if there isn't genuine hate there is at least a deep resentment. For years, I refused to acknowledge it; no one likes a bigot, and I had worked hard to reject the bigotry that surrounded me as a child. (I never understood the sense of pride displayed by my aunt when she related how my Irish great-grandfather, a bartender, would shatter a glass after it was used by a black man.) To admit the resentment would have meant, at some point, to fall to a compulsion to further examine it. That, I knew, would be painful; "An intellectual hatred is the worst," Yeats thought. Briefly, I considered my "hate" the product of what I'd begun to see as a characteristic Irish-American self-loathing. It was plausible: Never did I not *know* that I was Irish; what was Irish in me was what in me was *wrong*.

But, no, despite knowing well what Joyce meant when he wrote, "All the indignities of his life enraged him," instead, I clung to a skittish belief that I simply preferred to be Italian, and was claiming a birthright. I want to be solely Italian, I had told myself, because Italians are wonderful: warm, gregarious, loving. I opted for the light.

Like scores of other seaport cities dotting the Northeast, my hometown was a hub for poor immigrants; the flood of Irish preceded the influx of Italians by several decades. By the time my grandfather arrived in 1903 as a little boy from Foggia, a town in Apulia in southern Italy, the city was largely populated by the Irish; the Irish lived uptown in brownstone houses with lace curtains, the Italians in the downtown tenements recently vacated by the Irish. Having suffered the indignities of prejudice—according to Lawrence J. McCaffrey's *The Irish Diaspora in America,* the Catholic Irish were considered by Anglo-Americans "belligerent, animal-like people with strong backs (and) weak minds" best suited for sports—the Irish seemed intent on heaping similar suffering on the new Italians. They ran City Hall and the police; they could do it, despite the teachings of the church to which they claimed allegiance.

Thus, in the late '40s, my mother was chided by her own for dating and then marrying an Italian, despite my father's reputation as a crooner in the Sinatra mold. (And my immigrant grandfather had a piece of his own small business: a barbershop at Twenty-Third and Seventh in the heart of Manhattan's fur district. He was, as he might have said, "no greenhorn.") As a youngster, I felt at odds straddling the two groups, and saw the tension as caused by the Irish. I remember my Italian grandparents as people who adored my mother—perhaps they saw the marriage of their oldest son as a sign of assimilation—and were baffled by her reserve. ("Cold Irish," I'm told, is the expression.) She almost never attended the splendid Sunday afternoon meals made by my grandmother—dubbed by me Nana Popone; I was her little *popone,* her little melon. My Irish uncles thought these meals were somehow comic—"Did you go to Nana Popone's for 'bisgetti'?" they'd mock. Those meals were magnificent. I can still smell the aroma of my grandmother's cooking as my father and I came up the stairs toward her small kitchen; the garlic simmering in olive oil, the fresh, pungent cheese, her remarkable tomato sauce. I can feel her sloppy kisses, and the huge hugs my grandfather—Papa Popone, of course—gave me. They had a one-eyed black bulldog who could eat an olive and leave behind the pit. My grandmother served me Hoffman's Cream Soda; *my* glass was purple, with a silver base. (How my grandmother wanted to please me; she always asked after my mother.) I loved it there; I resent having been made to feel that it was foolish.

I recall my father accepting the jibes of his Irish in-laws with grace; somehow, whether it was lighthearted or sharp-tongued, it *always* came up. The only time I can remember him exploding over a slight was when my red-headed cousin taunted *me*. (I didn't tell my father that while he was out of earshot my aunt also called me "guinea.") As for me, though we lived in an apartment complex uptown, I can recall only one boy who loved to taunt with ethnic slurs, but even as a child he was viewed as troubled. As for the sour mother of a neighbor who spit ethnic invectives at my friend Leonard Minervini at the 1964 New York World's Fair, I then attributed her misbehavior to a miserable disposition rather than a particular prejudice.

Much of the bias I felt was unspoken, and inferred. The prevailing attitude was that uptown was the preferred place to be and that the Irish had made it so; clearly, my Italian grandparents could not have lived comfortably there. Though I didn't mind my neighborhood—there was a black-topped alley behind the complex where my friends and I could play without worrying about cars and such—there was something appealing about the other. Downtown had a lovely aesthetic: the best food, boisterous shopkeepers, the friendliest people; it was loud, *alive*. (For me, a walk down New York's Carmine Street or in Boston's North End is a taste of the past.) Its two Catholic churches throughout the year sponsored a variety of "feasts"; there were oom-pah bands, zeppole, fireworks, green-white-and-red flags, and men in baggy suits carrying statues of saints. I sat on the curb and, surrounded by the crack and sizzle of sausage rings on open grills, ate fresh watermelon down to the rind. Priests in brown, flowing robes tied with rope played with little boys in short pants and scuffed black shoes.

Uptown turned up its nose at such behavior—at best, it was viewed with superior bemusement—there is nothing quite like Irish condescension—but I loved it. It was such a marked contrast. My parish priest, Father Meehan, was an austere man; the lapels of his black suit jacket were military crisp. Revelry was permitted in the alley, thankfully, but I recall a walk around the block required propriety, unless a fire hydrant had been opened, or Mr. Softee had arrived. I assume there was nightlife in my neighborhood— there must have been; there were four taverns at each intersection—but my memory is of looking out the window and seeing silence. A sense of forced dignity permeated us; today, nothing reminds me so much of uptown as a freshly made hotel room. Downtown, I knew, they were wrapped in joy.

As I grew older and expanded my world, I became less concerned with what the Irish thought of me. Most of my Irish family moved away, taking their jibes with them. With the advent of a maturing second generation, Italians became the political force in my town, thus making them less fashionable to openly mock. I went to a Catholic high school in a neighboring city; my peers were mostly Italians and Hispanics. My first steady girlfriend was Italian; her mother's kitchen reminded me of my grandmother's. My stance became one of Italian pride, and I believed I had struck it without rancor toward the Irish. By then, I almost never heard bitter ethnic insults, and no one knew I was half Irish. (Although, to my amazement, at a party with my mother's family, a cousin called *me* "cold Irish.") I didn't think it would ever be an issue again; at least if it was, I was no longer cluttered with confused feelings: Avoiding the mirror, I knew who I was.

After college, long after my steady girl and I had parted, for a brief time I dated a woman who was fiercely Irish; her father belonged to a Hibernia Club, a bar that did not reflect Irish pride so much as an affinity toward bias and intolerance. In their small home, there were musty pictures of saints and needlepoint samplers of Irish prayers on the wall; her father often drank until he fell. He would sleep in the bedroom that separated the tiny living room and kitchen; no one could speak above a whisper for he might awaken abruptly in a foul mood. No one would turn on the TV.

There was always tension between the two of us. I thought it was because I was five years older than his daughter, a college freshman. ("Oh, so you're a *man*," he sneered when we first met.) But he worked weeknights, and I rarely saw him.

One rainy Saturday evening, there was a party at the Hibernia Club: hot dogs, sauerkraut, cabbage, cold salads. The jukebox played buoyant Irish jigs and baleful ballads. Since women were not allowed beyond the club's backroom, my girlfriend asked me to slip inside and fetch her mother and sister a few hot dogs, which sat in a steaming vat across the crowded bar. As I filled a plate, I heard the girl's father shout above the din, "Hey, look at the guinea going at the free food! No extra food for guineas!" There was great laughter; I died. I was seven years old again, and covered in shadows. I was ashamed of my grandmother and grandfather, the oom-pah bands and the gilded statues of saints; I live *uptown,* I wanted to shout.

That night, at that moment, the knot in my chest that had been gone for years returned.

Fifteen years later, it will not go away.

There is a picture of my grandmother and grandfather on my desk. They are holding me.

Interpretations

1. According to Fusilli, *Irish*-Americans, who themselves were once victims of discrimination by Anglo-Americans, tend to discriminate against blacks and later immigrant groups and use labels like "guinea." How common is this

behavior among immigrant groups? How does it qualify the popular concept of America as a melting pot?

2. As he grew up, most of his Irish family moved away, and Fusilli thought he had solved his "Irish problem." How did he react to its resurfacing? (Explain the last line of the essay.)

3. Fusilli's first sentence sounds like a thesis statement. Does it in fact turn out to express his main point? If not, what *is* his thesis? At what point in the essay are you sure of it? What event confirms the thesis?

Correspondences

1. Fusilli focuses on bigotry within his own family. How does that affect his personal interactions? To what extent is his experience a microcosm of the bigotry to which Japanese-Americans (Ota) (pages 313–317) were subjected during World War II?

2. Fusilli and Sadat (Chapter 2) were each raised by parents from different ethnic backgrounds. How did the cultural interactions of their parents affect their sense of ethnic identity and their concept of family?

Applications

1. Review the Fusilli biography (page 308) and his reasons for writing "Opting for the Light." Write an analysis of the personal and cultural implications of his interactions.

2. Consult dictionary and thesaurus *bigotry, prejudice, racism,* and *bias.* How do their connotations differ? To what extent is each the result of cultural conditioning?

Peter Ota

Studs Terkel

Studs Terkel (b. 1912), hosts a daily hour long radio program of interviews, commentary, and music on WFMT, Chicago. Born in New York City, he grew up in Chicago and was nicknamed after James T. Farrell's fictional Chicagoan Studs Lonigan. He has philosophy and law degrees from the University of Chicago, but is perhaps best known as the author of five collections of interviews: Division Street: America *(1967);* Working *(1974);* American Dreams: Lost and Found *(1980);* "The Good War": An Oral History of World War Two *(1984), from which the following interview is taken; and* The Great Divide: Second Thoughts on the American Dream *(1988). Also in 1988, Terkel appeared as an actor in the movie "Eight Men Out" (playing a Chicago reporter in the story of the 1919 Black Sox scandal), narrated a PBS documentary about the Spanish Civil War (*The Good Fight*), and saw his autobiography,* Talking to Myself, *staged in Evanston, Illinois.*

In the following interview with Peter Ota, a second-generation Japanese-American, Terkel applies his signature technique of taping the interview and then editing out himself; The result is a monologue of the interviewee that reads like an essay. Since the Ota interview was taped, the 60,000 survivors of the 112,000 Japanese-Americans who were rounded up in West Coast cities and detained in various camps have received—under the Civil Liberties Act of 1988 and four decades after their internment—an apology and a promise of $20,000 apiece. Unfortunately, Congress appropriated only enough money to pay 1,000 internees and internees are dying at the rate of 200 a month. The money will not cover their losses, internees say, but it is an important symbol of recognition of the violation of their civil rights.

I THINK BACK to what happened—and sometimes I wonder: Where do I come from?

He is a fifty-seven-year-old Nisei. His father had come from Okinawa in 1904, his mother from Japan. He's an accountant. His father had worked on farms and in the coal mines of Mexico. After thirty-seven years building a fruit and vegetable business, he had become a successful and respected merchant in the community. He was a leader in the Japanese Chamber of Commerce of Los Angeles.

On the evening of December 7, 1941, my father was at a wedding. He was dressed in a tuxedo. When the reception was over, the FBI agents were waiting. They rounded up at least a dozen wedding guests and took 'em to county jail.

For a few days we didn't know what happened. We heard nothing. When we found out, my mother, my sister, and myself went to jail. I can still remember waiting in the lobby. When my father walked through the door, my mother was so humiliated. She didn't say anything. She cried. He was in prisoner's clothing, with a denim jacket and a number on the back.

The shame and humiliation just broke her down. She was into Japanese culture. She was a flower arranger and used to play the *biwa,* a Japanese stringed instrument. Shame in her culture is worse than death. Right after that day she got very ill and contracted tuberculosis. She had to be sent to a sanitarium. She stayed behind when we were evacuated. She was too ill to be moved. She was there till she passed away.

My father was transferred to Missoula, Montana. We got letters from him—censored, of course—telling us he was all right. It was just my sister and myself. I was fifteen, she was twelve. In April 1942, we were evacuated to Santa Anita. At the time we didn't know where we were going, how long we'd be gone. We didn't know what to take. A toothbrush, toilet supplies, some clothes. Only what you could carry. We left with a caravan.

Santa Anita is a race track. The horse stables were converted into living quarters. My sister and I were fortunate enough to stay in a barracks. The people in the stables had to live with the stench. Everything was communal. We had absolutely no privacy. When you went to the toilet, it was communal. It was very embarrassing for women especially. The parent actually lost control of the child. I had no parents, so I did as I pleased. When I think back what happened to the Japanese family . . .

We had orders to leave Santa Anita in September of 1942. We had no idea where we were going. Just before we left, my father joined us. He was brought into camp on the back of an army state truck, he and several others who were released from Missoula. I can still picture it to this day: to come in like cattle or sheep being herded in the back of a pickup truck bed. We were near the gate and saw him come in. He saw us. It was a sad, happy moment, because we'd been separated for a year.

He never really expressed what his true inner feelings were. It just amazes me. He was never vindictive about it, never showed any anger. I can't understand that. A man who had worked so hard for what he had and lost it overnight. There is a very strong word in Japanese, *gaman.* It means to persevere. Old people instilled this into the second generation: You persevere. Take what's coming, don't react.

He had been a very outgoing person. Enthusiastic. I was very, very impressed with how he ran things and worked with people. When I saw him at Santa Anita, he was a different person.

We were put on a train, three of us and many trains of others. It was crowded. The shades were drawn. During the ride we were wondering, what are they going to do to us? We Niseis had enough confidence in our government that it wouldn't do anything drastic. My father had put all his faith in this country. This was his land.

Oh, it took days. We arrived in Amache, Colorado. That was an experience in itself. We were right near the Kansas border. It's a desolate, flat, barren area. The barracks was all there was. There were no trees, no kind of landscaping. It was like a prison camp. Coming from our environment, it was just devastating.

School in camp was a joke. Let's say it was loose. If you wanted to study, fine. If you didn't, who cared? There were some teachers who were conscientious and a lot who were not. One of our basic subjects was American history. They talked about freedom all the time. (Laughs.)

After a year, I was sent out to Utah on jobs. I worked on sugar beet farms. You had to have a contract or a job in order to leave camp. The pay was nominal. We would have a labor boss, the farmer would pay us through him. It was piecework. Maybe fifteen of us would work during the harvest season. When it was over, we went back to camp.

If you had a job waiting, you could relocate to a city that was not in the Western Defense Command. I had one in Chicago, as a stock boy in a candy factory. It paid seventy-five cents an hour. I was only in camp for a year. My sister was in until they were dismantled, about three and a half years. My father was in various camps for four years.

I went from job to job for a year. I had turned draft age, so I had to register. It's ironic. Here I am being drafted into the army, and my father and sister are in a concentration camp waiting for the war to end.

I was in the reserve, not yet inducted, in the middle of 1944, when I received a wire from my father saying that my mother was very ill. I immediately left Chicago for Amache, Colorado, to get my clearance from the Western Defense Command. It took several days. While I was waiting, my mother passed away.

Since we wanted her funeral to be at the camp where my father and sister were, I decided to go on to California and pick up her remains. At Needles, California, I was met at the train by an FBI agent. He was assigned to me. He was with me at all times during my stay there. Whether I went to sleep at night or whether I went to the bathroom, he was by my side.

As soon as we stepped off the train at the Union Station in Los Angeles, there was a shore patrol and a military police who met me. They escorted me through the station. It was one of the most . . . (He finds it difficult to talk.) I don't even know how to describe it. Any day now, I'd be serving in the same uniform as these people who were guarding me. The train stations at that time were always filled. When they marched me through, the people recognized me as being Oriental. They knew I was either an escaped prisoner or a spy. Oh, they called out names. I heard "dirty Jap" very distinctly.

After we got to the hotel, the FBI agent convinced the military that it wasn't necessary for them to stay with me. But he had to. He was disgusted with the whole situation. He knew I was in the reserve, that I was an American citizen. He could see no reason for him to be with me. But he was on assignment. We spoke personal things. His wife was having a baby, he couldn't be with her. He thought it was ridiculous.

I was in the armored division at Fort Knox. We were sent to Fort Mead for embarkation when the European war ended. They didn't know what to do with us Japanese Americans. We were in our own units. Should they send us to the Pacific side? They might not be able to tell who was the enemy and who was not. (Laughs.)

The war ended while I was at Fort McDowell on San Francisco Bay. That was the receiving point for Japanese prisoners captured in the war. I went back with a boatload of them. I didn't know how they'd react to me. I was very surprised. The professional soldiers who were captured during the early days of the war in Guadalcanal, Saipan, never believed the war ended. They would always say, when the subject came up, it was propaganda. The civilian soldiers were very different. We could get along with them. They were very young—*boheitai,* boy soldiers. We could relate to them as to children. They were scared. They had nothing to go back to. Okinawa was devastated. A lot of them lost their families.

My furloughs were spent in camp, visiting my father and sister. Going to camp was like going home for me, to see my family. We made the best of what we had. We celebrated Christmas in the American fashion. We tried to make our lives go easy.

We came back to Los Angeles at the end of the war, believing that there was no other way but to be American. We were discouraged with our Japanese culture. My feeling at the time was, I had to prove myself. I don't know why I had to prove myself. Here I am, an ex-GI, born and raised here. Why do I have to prove myself? We all had this feeling. We had to prove that we were Americans, okay?

My mother and father sent me to a Japanese school teaching the culture. My wife and I did nothing with our children in that respect. We moved to a white community near Los Angeles. It was typical American suburban living. We became more American than Americans, very conservative. My wife and I, we talk about this. We thought this was the thing we had to do: to blend into the community and become part of white America.

My children were denied a lot of the history of what happened. If you think of all those forty years of silence, I think this stems from another Japanese characteristic: when shame is put on you, you try to hide it. We were put into camp, we became victims, it was our fault. We hide it.

My oldest daughter, Cathy, in her senior year at college, wanted to write a thesis about the camp experience. She asked if we knew people she might interview. Strange thing is, many people, even now, didn't want to talk about it. Some of the people she did talk to broke down. Because this was the first time they had told this story. This is the same thing I did. When I first went into detail, it just broke me up. When it came out, I personally felt good about it. It was somethin' that was inside of me that I've wanted to say for a long time.

How do the Sansei feel about it—your daughter's generation?

Very angry. They keep saying, "Why did you go? Why didn't you fight back?" They couldn't understand it. They weren't raised in our culture. Today, I would definitely resist. It was a different situation at that time. This is what we tried to explain to our daughter. Today if this happened, I think a majority of the Japanese would resist.

When I think back to my mother and my father, what they went through quietly, it's hard to explain. (Cries.) I think of my father without ever coming up with an angry word. After all those years, having worked his whole life to build a dream—an American dream, mind you—having it all taken away, and not one vindictive word. His business was worth more than a hundred thousand. He sold it for five. When he came out of camp, with what little money he had he put a down payment on an apartment building. It was right in the middle of skid row, an old rooming house. He felt he could survive by taking in a little rent and living there. My sister worked for a family as a domestic. He was afraid for her in this area. He died a very broken man.

My wife and I, we're up on cloud nine right now. Our daughter just passed the California bar. Guess what she's doing? She works for the redress and reparations group in San Diego. How's that?

Interpretations

1. Imagine yourself an American history teacher at a Japanese-American internment camp school; you are teaching the Bill of Rights. Could you do so without turning the lesson into what Ota calls "a joke"? Why or why not?

2. "Shame in [Ota's mother's Japanese] culture is worse than death." Does Ota now approve of the traditional Japanese way of reacting to shame? Why?

3. If this interview were to be rewritten as an essay for a general audience, what revisions would you recommend?

Correspondences

1. Why did Ota spend his adult life proving he was more American than Japanese? How might Rendón (Chapter 3) and Rodriguez respond to his determination to be assimilated? What is your response?

2. Ota's parents felt alienated by their experiences in America. Is alienation an inevitable part of cultural interactions? Compare the experiences of Rodriguez, Novak and Fusilli with those of Ota's parents. What conclusions do you reach?

Applications

1. Ota and his daughter hold conflicting views on ethnic identification. What factors besides generation difference might account for their opposite points of view? How might their views on this issue affect their social interactions?

2. In 1988, the United States Congress passed a bill granting compensation to Japanese-Americans interred during World War II. Research this bill and write an analysis of the cultural forces behind its passage. (Why 1988? Why not in 1958 or 1948?)

from A Life in Contrasts

Russell Howe

Russell Howe (b. 1925) was born in London, attended Cambridge University and the Sorbonne, and now lives in Washington, D.C. He has been foreign correspondent for Reuters and various newspapers, a professor at Dakar University in Sénégal, and a media consultant. His writings include novels, diplomatic history, and travel accounts, of which The Koreans *(1988)—from which the following excerpt is taken—is an example.*

The Korea of which Howe writes is located in northeast Asia between China and Japan. It has played a prominent part in twentieth-century history and economics, and is now celebrated for its surge toward modernization, industrialization, and economic success. It traces its history at least to the first century B.C. *and was a united kingdom by the seventh century. At times a vassal state to the Chinese Empire, it was forcibly annexed by Japan in 1910 and remained a Japanese colony until the end of World War II, when it was divided into North Korea and South Korea by the occupying troops of the Soviet Union and the United States. The Korean War (1950–1953) involved United States, UN, and South Korean troops against invading Chinese and North Koreans, with 157,000 U.S. casualties. College students have played significant roles in recent Korean politics, spearheading the resignation of the first President of the newly formed (1948) Republic of Korea Syngman Rhee in 1960. Korea was a police state under the next two presidents, but in 1987 students and middle-class office workers, shopkeepers, and business executives, following weeks of violence, forced a popular election in which Roh Tae Woo was elected president.*

WHEN I FIRST CAME to Korea two decades ago, my host, the Food and Agriculture Organization of the United Nations, took me around the country to see projects connected with the peasant society which Korea was then still expected to remain. This afforded me a view of Korea which is disappearing and which, for the casual visitor, has disappeared already. Agricultural and fishing projects tend to be in remote places far from towns, places where there were then no modern hotels, in most places no traditional inn—*yŏ-gwan*—and sometimes not even a real *yŏ-in-suk*, or mom-and-pop guest house. My FAO escort and I would sleep on a thin *yo* of artificial sponge or on mats on the wood-heated floor, our heads on tiny *pe-gae* pillows filled with dried beans or barley husks. We would breakfast on a dozen or so minuscule traditional dishes, which nearly always included grasshoppers in a black-bean, sesame, garlic, and chili-pepper sauce. At the projects, the local official on whom we called would receive the visiting reporter with the self-abnegating grace of a West African chief; but instead of tumblers of schnapps he would offer barley tea, a beverage even more bland than American office coffee. Almost everyone wore traditional dress of white cotton.

Sometimes, I would be left to travel on my own, and once when I doubted my driver's ability to hurl a Toyota wagon through a mountain stream two feet deep, he promised to resign if he stalled in mid-current. He did it all in reverse—out of consideration for me, so that getting out of the torrent, if he failed, would be easier than getting in. On the other side, he checked the chassis and found no damage, bowed, and apologized for the discomfort. I bowed and apologized for doubting his skill and obvious experience. Today, the perfume of that sunset afternoon comes back; one surveys Seoul's cityscape conscious that this is a population made for the graces and also for the risks and relaxations of country life, yet inhabiting a megalopolis—not exactly unwillingly, but with reservations.

Other apparent contradictions abound: a high-fashion secretary with a poodle cut and Lancôme makeup waits at a yellow taxi shelter along with some elderly peasant from the countryside in his loose, off-white *chŏ-g'i* waistcoat, white raffia hat and pantaloons, or perhaps a long gray *paji* tied with a bow. Each understands the other more than each cares to admit. Close by, an expensive French restaurant run by Koreans with *cordon bleu* diplomas is neighbor to a noodle stall. A business administration graduate of Seoul National leaves his skyscraper office to prepare for his promotion interview with the boss by going to a *han-yak*, or traditional apothecary's shop, for a concoction that will make him, he hopes, alert or even brilliant. Both he and the high-fashion secretary, as well as the rice farmer in his country clothes, may have postponed everything from the day before—a fourth or thirteenth or twenty-second of the lunar month, therefore an unpropitious day for action. The young executive's boss may even have stayed away from the office the entire day, to avoid being led by his *in-yon*, or karma, into dire misfortune.

To prepare for his meeting, the young man has read W. Edwards Deming, Dale Carnegie, Galbraith and Schumacher (in pirated Korean editions, of course) and has prayed to Buddha and Jesus and conferred with his late father in meditation; and in order to go to a *han-yak*, he has had to resort to a thin subterfuge. Although it is the lunch hour, his immediate supervisor has stayed at his desk, meaning that none of his staff can decently leave their desks either. It is, however, acceptable to do so briefly if you stay behind in spirit, so the young executive has left his gabardine raincoat and umbrella on the office hatstand, even though it has started to rain.

In the *han-yak*, the apothecary takes down a few bottles with labels handwritten in Chinese ideographs, the Latin of traditional Korean medicine. He mixes chrysanthemum seeds with some tree bark and the grated brainbox of a frog. He pestles all this together and pours it into tamarind juice. The drenched young man pays and swills the potion down on the spot. Despite the expense, he also decides to ask for some deer horn gratings. He and his girlfriend are going dancing in a psychedelic disco that night; he has high hopes of what will follow, and wants to be at the peak of his sexual powers. He hurries through the rain shower, back to his office building, and is soon seated once more in front of his Samsung computer, working on the new import contract proposals from Philadelphia and Bombay.

His supervisor finally leaves at eight P.M., and the staff make a dignified rush for the door two minutes, or one elevator run, later. The young executive walks down a narrow street, pausing to watch a traditional cloisonné artist at work in his shabby shop, which bears the official sign that confirms that he is a government-recognized craftsman. The young man's attention has been attracted by the fact that the artisan is using a computer not much different from his own to compose a version of a traditional graphic design for a vase.

Continuing on his way, the young man comes to a street stall where he takes a seat along with other well-dressed businessmen, a housewife with a child, and a couple of van drivers, and orders a bowl of *mae-un-t'ang,* seafood and vegetables in a steaming broth. He drinks a pint of *so-ju* with his dinner, then chews a breath deodorant. Now, it is dark everywhere, but a department store is still open and he goes in to buy a gift for his girl. The store resembles its counterparts in Paris or San Francisco or Tokyo except that, as he steps onto the escalator, a sixteen-year-old maiden in traditional Lyi dynasty *hanbok* dress bows to him, and again to the woman customer behind him, thus completing her 5,137th bow of the day.

You could spend an hour at a Tokyo bus stop in a freak electric storm, and your sole neighbor in the shelter might never say a word to you. Only the British are as covetous of their privacy. There is, however, a logical reason preventing the Japanese from addressing a stranger: he cannot know *how,* because the person *is* a stranger. Koreans share the same necessity to know if you are superior, equal, or inferior; like the Japanese, they would prefer to know what you do and what rank you occupy in your company or profession. And in this, you cannot be too precise. There are, for instance, different words in both languages for *writer,* according to whether you write fiction or nonfiction. There is no word for *broadcaster;* one has to be more specific— radio? television? scriptwriter? anchorperson?

But the Koreans have a solution which few Japanese would attempt. They ask questions. They are curious. They *stare.* Other Asian peoples may appear inscrutable to us, and us to them, but the Koreans are not inscrutable. They dare not be, because they *scrute.* Those of us who had mothers who wisely boxed our ears if we focussed our gaze on a passerby with only one arm, or an oriental face, or who had just fallen facedown in a puddle, are startled by the unabashed inquisitiveness everywhere in Korea, in spite of the general insistence on *mŏt*—manners, taste. Even shy sales assistants will ask about your work, your family situation, your age—the latter being an important determinant in societal rank. All Koreans go up one rank in prestige every year; they even start with a bonus—time in the womb counts as the first year of life, so that you are born at the age of one. Moreover, all birthdays occur on the lunar new year: if you are born in December, you are two almost before you can even gurgle.

Modern Japanese comedy films like *Tampōpo* or *The Family Game* are as daring in their environment as the first erotic photo-essay magazines in America a generation or so ago; but in Korea, humor is endemic. Although the slapstick of television kitchen-sink comedies and soap operas borrows routines from Tinseltown, the genre was always there. However, like most people who love clowning, Koreans are sad and stoical at heart; the vague-à-l'âme courses through every artery of Korean life. If your taxi driver switches on his radio, and you are not forced to listen to outdated Western rhythms, you will hear Korean pop music as sad as Portuguese fado. Understanding the words isn't necessary. The themes are those of American country music: lovers and mistresses are ever unfaithful, absent, or gone forever; and as the voice of the singer breaks with spurious emotion, you usually hear the word *nun-mul* (eye-water). What other language has an onomatopoeic for sobbing? For that matter, in what other tongue do birds or bells weep instead of singing or pealing?

This is, at base, a Confucian society. The most important relationship was always between father and son, followed by ruler and subject, then husband and wife, then elders and youth, then loyalty between friends. The first four are different forms of the same. The second relationship, that of ruler and subject, which successive militaro-republican regimes have sought to exploit in recent times, is increasingly challenged in an era when the taxpayer has ascended the throne and begun to assert that generals are nothing more than armed usurpers.

The quality of loyalty, as important to Koreans as to Turks or Scots, is commanded by more than blood and friendship. As in Africa, there is an automatic kithship involving loyalties between classmates—people of the same age who have gone through high school, military service, university and so on together. In 1987, a great debate emerged as to how President Ch'ŏn Du-hwan, before he retired, would ensure that all his fellow-members of the eleventh graduating class of the Military Academy would have suitable civil posts to take care of their military retirement years.

However, social rank, including rank by age, is primordial. Superiors— or elders—go first. For instance, a husband enters a taxi, bus, or theater ahead of his wife. There are five different ways of saying he and she, according to whether the person is an elder or an employer or, at the other end of the scale, a child or a servant. As in French, the way an officer speaks to a soldier, or a farmer to his laborers, or a policeman to a pimp, is also the way you address a colleague when you finally recognize him as a close friend, or a member of the opposite sex when you want to convey a trembling heart.

For twelve and a half centuries, from 667 to 1905, when Korea became a Japanese protectorate, much of the battle for rank revolved around the annual civil service examinations, prepared for by rote learning, Chinese fashion. These examinations assigned literate Koreans to their rung on the social ladder. This Confucian concept of the *yang-ban* (member of the gentry) has given way to the global ethos of our meritocratic era; but militarism has often replaced Confucianism, and the university or military college entrance examinations are now the master keys of the career gate. Two-thirds of all who take them fail; there is usually only one second chance a year later, and that's it! And even passing successfully doesn't guarantee a place. The old Confucian exams could be taken over and over again, into old age, and people who never passed still pridefully noted their improved scores every year.

Chinese influence also remains in the ideograph, still used alongside the Korean *han-gŭl* alphabet in publications, because ideographs distinguish between different meanings for the same word and also make for briefer headlines and titles. As in Japan, a high school student must learn eighteen hundred Chinese characters to graduate.

These days, of course, he or she must also study English, from middle school on, with its vastly more illogical alphabet than *han-gŭl,* its often confusingly dissimilar "big" and "small" letters, its seven different ways of pronouncing *-ough,* its differences between Standard English and Indian English and American English, its galaxy of geographical accents, and so on. There are also lessons on how to use a knife and fork: Koreans must be the only East Asians who sometimes prefer to eat rice with a spoon instead of *jŏtgarak,* chopsticks.

Interpretations

1. Russell says "apparent contradictions abound" in Korea. Contradictions between what? Would you call them contradictions, cultural crossings, or perhaps just interactions? In the hypothetical day in the life of the young business executive, what are the most obvious "contradictions"?

2. Compare Korean, Japanese, and American interactions with strangers. Why do you think Howe makes the comparison?

3. Why has cultural crossing apparently always been a feature of Korean life? What has been the effect of this crossing on Korea and on her neighbors?

4. What's the evidence that Howe aims to entertain as well as inform? Do you see a plan or organization to his arrangement of detail, or is it random? Do you think he gives enough detail to satisfy his purpose in writing? If not, where would you like to see more detail?

5. What is the tone of this essay? What do you think is Howe's purpose in writing? What is the tone of the concocted word *scrute*? Although he uses

both words, which word better suits Howe's purpose in describing Korean life, *contradictions* or *contrasts?* What is the connotation of each? Is his use of both words confusing? Why or why not?

6. In explaining that Korea is "a Confucian society," Howe describes various relationships and paths to advancement. How different are these relationships and paths from the ones Americans are familiar with? How are they similar?

Correspondences

1. Howe and Jhabvala discuss marriage. What evidence is there of patriarchy in both selections? How does the marriage of the Englishwoman compare to that of Guppy's parents (Chapter 1) in another patriarchal culture?

2. Ota (Terkel) highlights perseverance as a dominant Japanese trait, while Howe emphasizes Korean curiosity. To what extent does each trait make the writers' cultural interactions easier or more difficult? Which trait, if any, do you associate most with your ethnic group?

Applications

1. According to Howe, Korea is currently involved in an interaction between the traditions of the past and the intrusions of the present. What evidence does he offer to support his point of view? Which cultural interactions might prove most difficult to reconcile?

2. Write a journal entry about an interaction in which you were involved that affirmed or contradicted Benedict's perspective that "culture is that which binds men together."

The Englishwoman

Ruth Prawer Jhabvala

Ruth Prawer Jhabvala (b. 1927) was born in Cologne, Germany, emigrated to England in 1939, and became a British citizen in 1948. She married C.S.H. Jhabvala, an architect, in 1951, and currently lives in New York. They have three children. She has published many novels—among them Amrita *(1956),* The Nature of Passion *(1956),* The Householder *(1960), and* Three Continents *(1988)—and many collections of stories. Her screenplays include* A Passage to India *and* Room with a View, *for which she won an Academy Award in 1987. In "The Englishwoman" she returns to a prevalent theme in her writings, being an outsider in an Indian family.*

The India to which Jhabvala moved from England in 1951 had just (in 1947) declared its independence from the British, who had controlled most of India for about 300 years. Colonial India had at the same time been partitioned into Pakistan and India, creating in the same year about 12 million Hindu and Muslim refugees, of whom about 200,000 were killed. Mohandas K. Gandhi (known as the Mahatma), the leader of Indian independence who had advocated nonviolent civil disobedience and abolition of the Untouchable caste, was assassinated the year after independence. The Congress Party dominated Indian politics for forty years (from Independence until late 1989) under Prime Ministers Jawaharlal Nehru, his daughter Indira Gandhi (no relation to Mohandas), and her son Rajiv Gandhi. Indian history, one of the oldest in the world, can be traced to at least 5,000 B.C. The founder of Buddhism lived in 5th-century India. In the 3rd century B.C. Buddhism became the established religion; the native Hinduism revived, however, and eventually prevailed, and now claims well over three-quarters of the Indian population of 800 million.

THE ENGLISHWOMAN—her name is Sadie—was fifty-two years old when she decided to leave India. She could hardly believe it. She felt young and free. At fifty-two! Her bag is packed and she is running away. She is eloping, leaving everything behind her—husband, children, grandchildren, thirty years of married life. Her heart is light and so is her luggage. It is surprising how few things she has to take with her. Most of her clothes are not worth taking. These last years she has been mostly wearing dowdy cotton frocks sewn by a little turbaned tailor. She still has a few saris but she is not taking them with her. She doesn't ever intend to wear those again.

The person who is crying the most at her impending departure is Annapurna, her husband's mistress. Annapurna has a very emotional nature. She looks into the packed bag; like Sadie, she is surprised by its meager contents. "Is that all you are taking with you?" she asks. Sadie answers, "It's all I've got." Annapurna breaks into a new storm of tears.

"But that's good," Sadie urges. "Not to accumulate things, to travel light—what could be better?"

"Oh, you're so spiritual," Annapurna tells her, wiping her eyes on the other's sleeve. "Really you are far more Indian than I am."

"Nonsense," Sadie says, and she means it. What nonsense.

But it is true that if Indian means "spiritual"—as so many people like to believe—then Annapurna is an exception. She is a very, very physical sort of person. She is stout, with a tight glowing skin, and shining eyes and teeth, and hair glossy with black dye. She loves clothes and jewelry and rich food. Although she is about the same age as the Englishwoman, she is far more vigorous, and when she moves, her sari rustles and her bracelets jingle.

"But are you really going?"

Annapurna keeps asking this question. And Sadie keeps asking it of herself too. But they ask it in two very different ways. Annapurna is shocked and grieved (yes, grieved—she loves the Englishwoman). But Sadie is incredulous with happiness. Can it really be true? she keeps asking herself. I'm going? I'm leaving India? Her heart skips with joy and she has difficulty in repressing her smiles. She doesn't want anyone to suspect her feelings. She is ashamed of her own callousness—and yet she goes on smiling, more and more, and happiness wells up in her like a spring.

Last week she went to say goodbye to the children. They are both settled in Bombay now with their families. Dev, her son, has been married for two years and has a baby girl; Monica, the daughter, has three boys. Dev has a fine job with an advertising company; and Monica is working too, for she has too much to drive to be content with just staying at home. She calls herself a go-go girl and that is what she is, charging around town interviewing people for the articles she writes for a women's magazine, talking in the latest slang current in Bombay, throwing parties of which she herself is the life and soul. Monica looks quite Indian—her eyes are black, her skin glows; she is really more like Annapurna than like the Englishwoman, who is gaunt and pale.

Although so gay, Monica also likes to have serious discussions. She attempted to have such a discussion with her mother. She said, "But, Mummy, *why* are you going?" and she looked at her with the special serious face she has for serious moments.

Sadie didn't know what to answer. What could she say? But she had to say something, or Monica would be hurt. So she too became solemn, and she explained to her daughter that when people get older they begin to get very homesick for the place in which they were born and grew up and that this homesickness becomes worse and worse till in the end life becomes almost unbearable. Monica understood what she said and sympathised with it. She made plans how they would all come and visit her in England. She promised that when the boys became bigger, she would send them to her for long holidays. She was now in full agreement with her mother's departure, so Sadie was glad she told her what she did. She was prepared to tell Dev the same thing if he asked her, but he didn't ask. He and his wife were rather worried in those days because there was an outbreak of chicken pox in their apartment building and they were afraid Baby might catch it. But they too promised frequent visits to her in England.

Only Annapurna is still crying. She looks at Sadie's little suitcase and cries, and then she looks at Sadie and cries. She keeps asking, "But why, why?" Sadie tries to tell her what she told Monica, but Annapurna waves her aside; for her it is not a good enough reason and she is right, Sadie herself knows it isn't. She asks wouldn't Sadie miss all of them and their love for her, and wouldn't she miss the life she has lived and the place in which she has lived it, her whole past, everything she has been and done for thirty years? Thirty years! she cries, again and again, appalled—and Sadie too is appalled, it is such a long time. Annapurna says that an Indian wife also yearns for her father's house, and at the beginning of her marriage she is always waiting to go off there to visit; but as the years progress and she becomes deeper and deeper embedded in her husband's home, these early memories fade till they are nothing more than a sweet sensation enshrined in the heart. Sadie knows that what Annapurna is saying is true, but also that it does not in the least apply in her own case because her feelings are not ones of gentle nostalgia.

The Englishwoman doesn't like to remember the early years when she first came to live here. It is as if she wished to disown her happiness then. How she loved everything! She never gave a backward glance to home or England. Her husband's family enjoyed and abetted her attempts to become Indian. A whole lot of them—mother-in-law, sister-in-law, aunts, cousins and friends—would cram into the family car (with blue silk curtains discreetly drawn to shield them from view) and drive to the bazaar to buy saris for Sadie. She was never much consulted about their choice, and when they got home, she was tugged this way and that while they argued with each other about the best way to drape it round her. When they had finished, they stood back to admire, only instead of admiring they often could not help smiling at her appearance. She didn't care. Yes, she knew she was too tall for the sari, and too thin, and too English, but she loved wearing it and to feel herself Indian. She also made attempts to learn Hindi, and this too amused everyone and they never tired of making her repeat certain words, going into peals of laughter at her pronunciation. Everyone, all the ladies of the household, had a lot of fun. They were healthy, rich and gay. They were by no means a tradition-bound family, and although their life in the house did have something of the enclosed, languorous quality of purdah living, the minds flowering within it were full of energy and curiosity. The mother-in-law herself, at that time well over sixty, spent a lot of her time reading vernacular novels, and she also attempted to write some biographical sketches of her own, describing life in a high-caste household in the 1880s. She took to smoking cigarettes quite late in life and liked them so much that she ended up as a chain-smoker. When Sadie thinks of her, she sees her reclining on an embroidered mat spread on the floor, one elbow supported on a bolster, some cushions at her back, reading a brown tattered little volume through her glasses and enveloping herself in clouds of scented cigarette smoke.

Annapurna often speaks about those days. Annapurna was a relative, some sort of cousin. She had run away from her husband (who drank and, it was whispered, went in for unnatural practices) and had come to live with them in the house. When Annapurna speaks about those distant times, she does so as if everyone were still alive and all of them as young and gay as they were then. Often she says, "If only Srilata [or Radhika—or Raksha—or Chandralekha] were here now, how she would laugh!" But Srilata died of typhoid twenty years ago; Raksha married a Nepalese general and has gone to live in Kathmandu; Chandralekha poisoned herself over an unhappy love affair. To Annapurna, however, it is as if everyone is still there and she recalls and brings to life every detail of a distant event so that to Sadie too it begins to appear that she can hear the voices of those days. Till Annapurna returns to the present and with an outstretched hand, her plump palm turned up to heaven, she acknowledges that they are all gone and many of them are dead; and she turns and looks at the Englishwoman and says, "And now you are going too," and her eyes are full of reproach.

It may seem strange that the mistress should reproach the wife, but Annapurna is within her rights to do so. For so many years now it is she who has taken over from the Englishwoman all the duties of a wife. There has never been any bitterness or jealousy between them. On the contrary, Sadie has always been grateful to her. She knows that before her husband became intimate with Annapurna, he used to go to other women. He *had* to go; he was such a healthy man and needed women as strong and healthy as he was. These were often young prostitutes. But for a long time now he has been content with Annapurna. He has put on an enormous amount of weight in these last years. It is Annapurna's fault; she feeds him too well and panders to his passion for good food. His meals are frequent and so heavy that in between them, he is not capable of moving. He lies on a couch arranged for him on a verandah and breathes heavily. Sometimes he puffs at a hookah which stands within easy reach. He lies there for hours while Annapurna sits on the other end of the couch and entertains him with lively gossip. He enjoys that, but doesn't mind at all if she has no time for him. When he feels like talking, he summons one of the servants to come and squat on the carpet near his couch.

When Sadie first knew him, as a student at Oxford, he was a slim boy with burning eyes and a lock of hair on his forehead. He was always smiling and always on the go. He loved being a student, and though he never managed to graduate, got a lot out of it. He gave breakfast parties and had his own wine merchant and a red car in which he drove up to London several times a week; he was always discovering new pleasures, like hampers from Fortnum and Mason's and champagne parties on the river. Sadie had grown up in rather an austere atmosphere. Her family were comfortably off but had high principles of self-restraint and preferred lofty thought to lavish living. Sadie herself—a serious girl, a spare, stringent, high-bred English beauty—thought she had the same principles, but the young Indian made her see another side to her nature. When he went back to India, it was impossible to stay behind. She followed him, married him, and loved him even more than she had in England. He belonged here so completely. Sometimes Sadie didn't see him for days on end—when he went on shooting parties and other expeditions with his friends—but she didn't mind. She stayed at home with the other women and enjoyed life as much as he did. There were summer nights when they all sat out in the garden by the fountain, and Chandralekha, who had a very sweet voice, sang sad songs from the hills while Radhika accompanied her on a lutelike instrument; and the moon shone, and Annapurna cut up mangoes for all of them, and the smell of these mangoes mingled with that exuding from the flowering bushes in a mixture so pungent, so heady, that when the Englishwoman recalls those nights now, it is always by their scent that they become physical and present to her.

Annapurna and Sadie's husband play cards every evening. They play for money and Annapurna usually loses and then she gets cross; she always refuses to pay up, and the next evening they conveniently forget her debt and start again from scratch. But if he loses, then she insists on immediate payment: she laughs in triumph, and holding out her hand, opens and shuts it greedily and shouts, "Come on, pay up!" She also calls to Sadie and the servants to witness his discomfiture; those evenings are always merry. But sooner or later, and often in the middle of a game, she falls asleep. Once Annapurna is asleep, everything is very quiet. The servants turn off the lights and go to their quarters; the husband sits on his couch and looks out into the garden and takes a few puffs at his hookah; Sadie is upstairs in her bedroom. Nothing stirs, there isn't a sound, until the husband gives a loud sigh as he heaves himself up. He wakes Annapurna and they support each other up the stairs to their bedroom, where they sink onto their large, soft bed and are asleep immediately and totally until it is morning. It is a long time before Sadie can get to sleep. She walks up and down the room. She argues with herself to and fro, and her mind heaves in turmoil like a sea in storm. The fact that everything else is calm and sleeping exacerbates her restlessness. She longs for some response, for something or someone other than herself to be affected by what is going on within her. But there is only silence and sleep. She steps out of her room and onto the verandah. The garden is in imperfect darkness, dimly and fitfully lit by the moon. Occasionally—very, very occasionally—a bird wakes up and rustles in a tree.

It was during these hours of solitude that she came to her decision to leave. To others—and at the actual moment of making it, even to herself—it seemed like a sudden decision, but in fact, looking back, she realizes that she has been preparing for it for twenty years. She can even mark the exact day, twenty years ago, when first she knew that she did not want to go on living here. It was when her son was sick with one of those sudden mysterious illnesses that so often attack children in India. He lay burning in the middle of a great bed, with his eyes full of fever; he was very quiet except for an occasional groan. All the women in the house had gathered round his bedside and all were giving advice and different remedies. Some sat on chairs, some on the floor; the mother-in-law squatted crosslegged on the end of his bed; her spectacles on her nose, smoking cigarettes and turning the pages of a novel; from time to time she made soothing noises at Dev and squeezed his ankles. Annapurna sat by his side and rubbed ice on his head. Every time Dev groaned they all said, "Oh, poor Baba, poor Baba." The servants moved in and out; they too said, "Oh, poor Baba," and looked at him pityingly. The Englishwoman remembered the sickbeds of her own childhood, how she lay for hours comfortable and bored with nothing to do except watch the tree outside the window and the fat wet raindrops squashing against and sliding down the window-pane. The only person who ever came in was her mother, when it was time for her medicine. But Dev wouldn't have liked that. He wanted everyone with him, and if one of the aunts was out of the room for too long a time, he would ask for her in a weak voice and someone would have to go and fetch her.

Sadie went out onto the verandah. But it was no better there. The day was one of these murky yellow ones when the sun is stifled in vapours of dust. She felt full of fears, for Dev and for herself, as if they were both being sucked down by—what was it? the heat? the loving women inside? the air thick as a swamp in which fevers breed? She longed to be alone with her sick child in some cool place. But she knew this was not possible and that they belonged here in this house crammed full with relatives and choking under a yellow sky. She could never forget the despair of that moment, though in the succeeding years there were many like it. But that was the first.

As she stood there on the verandah, she saw her husband arrive home. He was a very bright spot in that murky day. He was dressed in a starched white kurta with little jewels for buttons, and his face was raised towards her as she stood up on the verandah, and he was smiling. He was no longer the slim boy she had first known but neither was he as fat as he is today: no, he was in the prime of life then, and what a prime! He came bounding up the outside staircase toward her and said, "How is he?"

"How can he be," she answered, "with all of them in there?"

Surprised at her tone, he stopped smiling and looked at her anxiously. Her anger mounted, and there were other things mixed in with it now: not only the heat and the overcrowded room but also that he was so sleek and smiling and young while she—oh, she felt worn out, wrung out, and knew she looked it. She thought of the prostitutes he went to. It seemed to her that she could see and smell their plump, brown, wriggling young bodies greasy with scented oil.

In a shaking voice she said, "They're stifling that poor boy—they won't let him breathe. No one seems to have the least idea of hygiene."

He knew it was more than she was saying and continued to look at her anxiously. "Are you ill?" he asked and put out his hand to feel her forehead. When she drew back, he asked, "What is it?" full of sympathy.

They had been speaking in low voices, but all the same from inside the crowded room Annapurna had sensed that something was wrong. She left the bedside and came out to join them. She looked enquiringly at Sadie's husband. They were not yet lovers at the time, but there was that instinctive understanding between them there was between all the members of that household.

"She is not well," he said.

"I *am* well! I'm perfectly well!" Sadie burst into tears. She had no control over this. Furiously she wiped the foolish tears from her cheeks.

Both of them melted with tenderness. Annapurna folded her in an embrace; the husband stroked her back. When she struggled to get free, they thought it was a new outbreak of anguish and redoubled their attentions. At last she cried, "It's so *hot!*" and indeed she could hardly breathe and perspiration ran down her in runnels from her being squashed against fat Annapurna. Then Annapurna let her go. They both stood and looked at her, full of anxiety for her; and these two round healthy shining faces looking at her with love, *pitying* her, were so unbearable to her that, to prevent herself from bursting into the tears that she despised but that they, she knew, not only awaited but even expected, she turned and, hurrying along the verandah that ran like a gallery all round the house, she hid herself in her bedroom and locked the door. They followed and knocked urgently and begged to be allowed to enter. She refused to open. She could hear them discussing her outside the door: they were full of understanding; they realized that people did get upset like this and that then it was the duty of others to soothe and help them.

She was always being soothed and helped. She is still being soothed and helped. Annapurna has taken everything out of her suitcase and is repacking it in what she considers is a better way. She has had special shoe bags sewn. As a matter of fact, she would like to have a completely new outfit of clothes made for her. She says how will it look if Sadie arrives with nothing better than those few shabby rags in that little suitcase? Sadie thinks silently to herself: Look to whom? She knows almost no one there. A few distant relatives, one old school friend; she hasn't been there for thirty years, she has no contacts, no correspondence—and yet she is going home! Home! And again happiness rushes over her in waves, and she takes a deep breath to be able to bear it.

"And not a single piece of jewelry," Annapurna grumbles.

Sadie laughs. She has given it all away long ago to Monica and to Dev's wife: and very glad she was to get rid of all those heavy costly gold ornaments. They were her share of the family jewels, but she never knew what to do with them. Certainly she couldn't wear them—she was always too thin and pale to be able to carry off those pieces fit for a barbarian queen; so she had left them lying around for years in a cupboard till Annapurna had taken them away from her to lock up in a safe.

At least *one* piece you could have let me keep for you," Annapurna now says. "Then you would have had something to show them. What will they think of us?"

"What will *who* think?" Sadie asks, and the idea of the distant relatives and her poor school friend (Clare, still unmarried and still teaching) having any thoughts on the subject of what properties she has brought back with her from India makes her laugh again. And there is a lightheartedness in her laughter that hasn't been there for a long time, and Annapurna hears it and is hurt by it.

They are both hurt by her attitude. It has been years since Sadie saw her husband so upset; but then it has been years since anything really upset him. He has led a very calm life lately. Not that his life was not always calm and comfortable, but there were times in his younger days when he, like everyone else in the house, had his outbursts. She particularly remembers one he had with his sister Chandralekha. Actually, at that time, the whole house was in upheaval. Chandralekha had formed an unfortunate attachment to a man nobody approved of. They were not a rigid family that way—there had been several love matches—but it seemed Chandralekha's choice was entirely unsuitable. Sadie had met the man, who struck her as intelligent and of a strong character. In fact, she thought Chandralekha had shown excellent taste. But when she told her husband so, he waved her aside and said she didn't understand. And it was true, she didn't; everything that went on in the house during those days was a mystery to her. Oh, she understood vaguely what it was all about—the man was of *low birth*, and all his virtues of character and self-made position could not wipe that stain away—but the passions that were aroused, the issues that were thought to be at stake, were beyond her comprehension. Yet she could see that all of them were suffering deeply, and Chandralekha was in a torment of inner conflict (indeed, she later committed suicide).

One day Chandralekha came in carrying a dish of sweet rice which she had made herself. She said, "Just wait till you taste this," and she lovingly ladled a spoonfull onto her brother's plate. He began to eat with relish, but quite suddenly he pushed the plate away and began to cry out loud. Everyone at once knew why, of course. The only person who was surprised was Sadie—

both at the suddenness of the outburst and at the lengths to which he went. He banged his head against the wall, flung himself on the ground at Chandralekha's feet, and at one point he snatched up a knife and held it at his own throat and had to have it wrested away from him by all the women there surrounding him. "The children, the children!" he kept crying, and at first Sadie thought he meant their own children, Monica and Dev, and she couldn't understand what was threatening them; but everyone else knew he meant Chandralekha's children who were yet unborn but who would be born, and if she married this man, born with polluted blood. Sadie didn't know how that scene ended; she went away and locked herself up in her bedroom. She covered her ears with her hands to shut out the noise and cries that echoed through the house.

When he learned of her decision to leave, Sadie's husband begged and pleaded with her in the same way he had done with Chandralekha all those years ago. The Englishwoman felt embarrassed and ashamed for him. He looked so ridiculous, being so heavy and fat, with his great bulk heaving, and emitting cries like those of a hysterical woman. No one else found him ridiculous—on the contrary, the servants and Annapurna were deeply affected by his strong emotions and tried to comfort him. But he wouldn't be comforted till in the end his passion spent itself. Then he became resigned and even quite practical and sent for his lawyer to make a settlement. He was very generous toward his wife, and indeed keeps pressing her to accept more and is distressed because she doesn't need it. So now she feels ashamed not of him but of herself and her own lack of feeling.

It is her last night in India. As usual, her husband and Annapurna are playing cards together. When she joins them, they look at her affectionately and treat her like a guest. Annapurna offers tea, sherbet, lime water, and is distressed when she declines all these suggestions. She is always distressed by the fact that Sadie needs less food than she does. She says, "How can you live like that?" After a moment's thought, she adds, "How will you live *there*? Who will look after you and see that you don't starve yourself to death?" When Sadie looks at her, it is as she feared: tears are again flowing down Annapurna's cheeks. A sob also breaks from out of her bosom. It is echoed by another sob: Sadie looks up and sees that tears are also trickling down her husband's face. Neither of them speaks, and in fact they go on playing cards. The Englishwoman lowers her eyes away from them; she sits there, silent, prim, showing no emotion. She hopes they think she *has* no emotion; she does her best to hide it—the happiness that will not be suppressed, even at the sight of their tears.

Annapurna has had enough of playing. She flings down the cards (she has been losing). She wipes her tears away with her forearm like a child, yawns, sighs, says, "Well, time to go to bed," in resignation. He says, "Yes, it's time," with the same sigh and the same resignation. They have accepted the Englishwoman's departure; it grieves them, but they submit to it, as human beings have to submit to everything, such as old age and disease and loss of every kind. They walk upstairs slowly, leaning on each other.

When Sadie goes up to her own room, she is almost running in her excitement. She looks in the mirror and is surprised at the drained face that looks back at her. She doesn't feel like that at all—no, she feels the way she used to do, so that now she expects her bright eyes back again and her pink cheeks. She turns away from the mirror, laughing at her own foolishness; and she can hear her own laughter and it is just the way it used to be. She knows she won't sleep tonight. She doesn't want to sleep. She loves this feeling of excitement and youth and to pace the room with her heart beating and wild thoughts storming in her head. The servants have turned out the lights downstairs and gone to bed. The lights are out in her husband and Annapurna's room too; they must be fast asleep, side by side on their bed.

The Englishwoman can't see the moon, but the garden is lit up by some sort of faint silver light. She can make out the fountain with the stone statue, and the lime trees, and the great flowering bush of Queen of the Night; there is the bench where they used to sit in the evenings when Chandralekha sang in her sweet voice. But as she goes on looking, the moonlit scene brightens until it is no longer that silver garden but English downs spreading as far as the eye can see, yellow on one side, green on another. The green side is being rained upon by mild soft rain coming down like a curtain, and the yellow side is being shone upon by a sun as mild and soft as that rain. On a raised knoll in the foreground there is an oak tree with leaves and acorns, and she is standing by this tree; and as she stands there, on that eminence overlooking the downs, strong winds blow right through her. They are as cold and fresh as the waters of a mountain torrent. They threaten to sweep her off her feet so that she has to plant herself down very firmly and put out her hand to support herself against the trunk of the tree (she can feel the rough texture of its bark). She raises her face, and her hair—not *her* hair but the shining hair of her youth—flies wild and free in that strong wind.

Interpretations

1. Sadie's decision to leave India is connected in her mind with what happened to her son when he was sick twenty years ago. Why does she feel such despair? What aspects of Indian culture does she find most difficult to accept?

2. To what extent does her husband's relationship with Annapurna contribute to the decision?

3. Why does Jhabvala use the generic "The Englishwoman" as a title instead of "Sadie"? What is the difference in implication?

4. Why is Sadie's husband never given a name or allowed to speak, except in one scene?

5. What is Jhabvala's purpose in writing this story?

Correspondences

1. Jhabvala's Englishwoman is ambivalent about India, her adopted country. How does her ambivalence affect her personality, family and choices? Contrast her reaction to India with that of Sadat's mother (Chapter 2), also English, to Egypt, her adopted country. What factors might account for the differences in their reactions?

2. Rank and social class are important in Korean culture (Howe), while the caste system is an integral part of Indian society (Jhabvala). What role does social rank play in the social interactions in each selection?

Applications

1. The Englishwoman felt alienated in India. Have you also ever felt like a stranger in a different environment? How did cultural differences contribute to your alienation? Describe the place, then analyze the experience and its effects.

2. According to the Englishwoman, she and Annapurna had never been jealous of each other. Do you find this plausible? To what extent does the account of their social interactions refute or support her assertion?

German Space

Edward T. Hall

Edward T. Hall (b. 1914) was born in Webster Groves, Missouri, and received his Ph.D. from Columbia University. He has conducted fieldwork in the south-western United States, in Micronesia, and as the following selection shows, in Europe. Hall has reported his findings in numerous anthropological writings, such as The Silent Language *(1954),* The Hidden Dimension *(1966), from which the following essay was taken,* Beyond Culture *(1976), and* The Dance of Life *(1983). He has taught anthropology at Columbia, the University of Denver, Bennington College, and Northwestern University. His research has often been concerned with cross-cultural questions involving body language and particularly proxemics, the study of the distances at which people of different cultures relate, as in conversation. Here, the cultures compared are Germany and the United States.*

Germany was united into a single state only in 1871. SInce World War II, it has been divided into the German Democratic Republic (East Germany) and the Federal Republic of Germany (West Germany). German impact on European and Western culture has been powerful and pervasive. It is the home, for example, of the leader of the Protestant Reformation (1517), Martin Luther, and of many leading scientists, philosophers, and artists, such as Einstein, Hegel, and Beethoven. The economic recovery after World War II of West Germany, which now has a population of about sixty million, is usually called a "miracle," but the country still suffers from the memory of the horrors of Adolph Hitler's Third Reich (1933–1945), which led the world into World War II and instituted genocide against an estimated six million Jews. Out of this war came the division of the world into Communist and non-Communist sectors—the Cold War—which is only now coming to an end with the tearing down of the Berlin Wall (November 1989), the permitting of free travel between East and West Germany, and the breakdown of Communist Party monopolies throughout Eastern Europe. The two Germanys were reunited on October 3, 1990.

I SHALL NEVER FORGET my first experience with German proxemic patterns, which occurred when I was an undergraduate. My manners, my status, and my ego were attacked and crushed by a German in an instance where thirty years' residence in this country and an excellent command of English had not attenuated German definitions of what constitutes an intrusion. In order to understand the various issues that were at stake, it is necessary to refer back to two basic American patterns that are taken for granted in this country and which Americans therefore tend to treat as universal.

First, in the United States there is a commonly accepted, invisible bound-ary around any two or three people in conversation which separates them from others. Distance alone serves to isolate any such group and to endow it with a protective wall of privacy. Normally, voices are kept low to avoid intruding on others and if voices are heard, people will act as though they had not heard. In this way, privacy is granted whether it is actually present or not. The second pattern is somewhat more subtle and has to do with the exact point at which a person is experienced as actually having crossed a boundary and entered a room. Talking through a screen door while standing outside a house is not considered by most Americans as being inside the house or room in any sense of the word. If one is standing on the threshold holding the door open and talking to someone inside, it is still defined informally and experienced as being *outside*. If one is in an office building and just "pokes his head in the door" of an office he's still outside the office. Just holding on to the doorjamb when one's body is inside the room still means a person has one foot "on base" as it were so that he is not quite inside the other fellow's territory. None of these American spatial definitions is valid in northern Germany. In every instance where the American would consider himself *outside* he has already entered the German's territory and by definition would become involved with him. The following experience brought the conflict between these two patterns into focus.

It was a warm spring day of the type one finds only in the high, clean, clear air of Colorado, the kind of day that makes you glad you are alive. I was standing on the doorstep of a converted carriage house talking to a young woman who lived in an apartment upstairs. The first floor had been made into an artist's studio. The arrangement, however, was peculiar because the same entrance served both tenants. The occupants of the apartment used a small entryway and walked along one wall of the studio to reach the stairs to the apartment. You might say that they had an "easement" through the artist's territory. As I stood talking on the doorstep, I glanced to the left and noticed that some fifty to sixty feet away, inside the studio, the Prussian artist and two of his friends were also in conversation. He was facing so that if he glanced to one side he could just see me. I had noted his presence, but not wanting to appear presumptuous or to interrupt his conversation, I unconsciously applied the American rule and assumed that the two activities—my quiet conversation and his conversation—were not involved with each other. As I was soon to learn, this was a mistake, because in less time than it takes to tell, the artist had detached himself from his friends, crossed the intervening space, pushed my friend aside, and with eyes flashing, started shouting at me. By what right had I entered his studio without greeting him? Who had given me permission?

I felt bullied and humiliated, and even after almost thirty years, I can still feel my anger. Later study has given me greater understanding of the German pattern and I have learned that in the German's eyes I really had been intolerably rude. I was already "inside" the building and I intruded when I could *see* inside. For the German, there is no such thing as being inside the room without being inside the zone of intrusion, particularly if one looks at the other party, no matter how far away.

Recently, I obtained an independent check on how Germans feel about visual intrusion while investigating what people look at when they are in intimate, personal, social, and public situations. In the course of my research, I instructed subjects to photograph separately both a man and a woman in each of the above contexts. One of my assistants, who also happened to be German, photographed his subjects out of focus at public distance because, as he said, "You are not really supposed to look at other people at public distances *because it's intruding.*" This may explain the informal custom behind the German laws against photographing strangers in public without their permission.

Germans sense their own space as an extension of the ego. One sees a clue to this feeling in the term "Lebensraum," which is impossible to translate because it summarizes so much. Hitler used it as an effective psychological lever to move the Germans to conquest.

In contrast to the Arab, the German's ego is extraordinarily exposed, and he will go to almost any length to preserve his "private sphere." This was observed during World War II when American soldiers were offered opportunities to observe German prisoners under a variety of circumstances. In one instance in the Midwest, German P.W.s were housed four to a small hut. As soon as materials were available, each prisoner built a partition so that he could have *his own space*. In a less favorable setting in Germany when the *Wehrmacht* was collapsing, it was necessary to use open stockades because German prisoners were arriving faster than they could be accommodated. In this situation each soldier who could find the materials built his own tiny dwelling unit, sometimes no larger than a foxhole. It puzzled the Americans that the Germans did not pool their efforts and their scarce materials to create a larger, more efficient space, particularly in view of the very cold spring nights. Since that time I have observed frequent instances of the use of architectural extensions of this need to screen the ego. German houses with balconies are arranged so that there is visual privacy. Yards tend to be well fenced; but fenced or not, they are sacred.

The American view that space should be shared is particularly troublesome to the German. I cannot document the account of the early days of World War II occupation when Berlin was in ruins but the following situation was reported by an observer and it has the nightmarish quality that is often associated with inadvertent cross-cultural blunders. In Berlin at that time the housing shortage was indescribably acute. To provide relief, occupation authorities in the American zone ordered those Berliners who still had kitchens and baths intact to share them with their neighbors. The order finally had to be rescinded when the already overstressed Germans started killing each other over the shared facilities.

Public and private buildings in Germany often have double doors for soundproofing, as do many hotel rooms. In addition, the door is taken very seriously by Germans. Those Germans who come to America feel that our doors are flimsy and light. The meanings of the open door and the closed door are quite different in the two countries. In offices, Americans keep doors open; Germans keep doors closed. In Germany, the closed door does not mean that the man behind it wants to be alone or undisturbed, or that he is doing something he doesn't want someone else to see. It's simply that Germans think that open doors are sloppy and disorderly. To close the door preserves the integrity of the room and provides a protective boundary between people. Otherwise, they get too involved with each other. One of my German subjects commented, "If our family hadn't had doors, we would have had to change our way of life. Without doors we would have had many, many more fights . . . When you can't talk, you retreat behind a door. . . . If there hadn't been doors, I would always have been within reach of my mother."

Whenever a German warms up to the subject of American enclosed space, he can be counted on to comment on the noise that is transmitted through walls and doors. To many Germans, our doors epitomize American life. They are thin and cheap; they seldom fit; and they lack the substantial quality of German doors. When they close they don't sound and feel solid. The click of the lock is indistinct, it rattles and indeed it may even be absent.

The open-door policy of American business and the closed-door patterns of German business culture cause clashes in the branches and subsidiaries of American firms in Germany. The point seems to be quite simple, yet failure to grasp it has caused considerable friction and misunderstanding between American and German managers overseas. I was once called in to advise a firm that has operations all over the world. One of the first questions asked was, "How do you get the Germans to keep their doors open?" In this company the open doors were making the Germans feel exposed and gave the whole operation an unusually relaxed and unbusinesslike air. Closed doors, on the other hand, gave the Americans the feeling that there was a conspiratorial air about the place and that they were being left out. The point is that whether the door is open or shut, it is not going to mean the same thing in the two countries.

The orderliness and hierarchical quality of German culture are communicated in their handling of space. Germans want to know where they stand and object strenuously to people crashing queues or people who "get out of line" or who do not obey signs such as "Keep out," "Authorized personnel only," and the like. Some of the German attitudes toward ourselves are traceable to our informal attitudes toward boundaries and to authority in general.

However, German anxiety due to American violations of order is nothing compared to that engendered in Germans by the Poles, who see no harm in a little disorder. To them lines and queues stand for regimentation and blind authority. I once saw a Pole crash a cafeteria line just "to stir up those sheep."

Germans get very technical about intrusion distance, as I mentioned earlier. When I once asked my students to describe the distance at which a third party would intrude on two people who were talking, there were no answers from the Americans. Each student knew that he could tell when he was being intruded on but he couldn't define intrusion or tell how he knew when it had occurred. However, a German and an Italian who had worked in Germany were both members of my class and they answered without any hesitation. Both stated that a third party would intrude on two people if he came within seven feet!

Many Americans feels that Germans are overly rigid in their behavior, unbending and formal. Some of this impression is created by differences in the handling of chairs while seated. The American doesn't seem to mind if people hitch their chairs up to adjust the distance to the situation—those that do mind would not think of saying anything, for to comment on the manners of others would be impolite. In Germany, however, it is a violation of the mores to change the position of your chair. An added deterrent for those who don't know better is the weight of most German furniture. Even the great architect Mies van der Rohe, who often rebelled against German tradition in his buildings, made his handsome chairs so heavy that anyone but a strong man would have difficulty in adjusting his seating position. To a German, light furniture is anathema, not only because it seems flimsy but because people move it and thereby destroy the order of things, including intrusions on the "private sphere." In one instance reported to me, a German newspaper editor who had moved to the United States had his visitor's chair bolted to the floor "at the proper distance" because he couldn't tolerate the American habit of adjusting the chair to the situation.

Interpretations

1. Do you accept Hall's description of the two basic American patterns regarding intrusion on private space? If so, cite instances from your own experience. Were you aware of these patterns at the time? What do these patterns imply about American culture?

2. Hall says his American subjects acknowledged the possibility of feeling intruded upon but couldn't specify a numerical measurement. Is that your experience too? Would factors other than distance enter into your definition of intrusion? Can you and the Americans you know find privacy without physical barriers? If so, how?

3. Why do you think it might be important to know about German and American attitudes toward space and intrusion? How could you use this information?

4. Do you know of other nationalities or ethnic groups that reject the two basic American patterns mentioned in Question 1?

Correspondences

1. Hall in "German Space" and Jhabvala in "The Englishwoman" explore German and Indian attitudes towards personal space and social interactions. How do these attitudes affect personal and public communication? To what extent does the Mead and Metraux analysis of German friendships (Chapter 2) substantiate Hall's conclusion about German space?

2. Hall and Howe compare German and Korean corporate styles with that of American executives. How are they similar? different? What cross-cultural influences on corporate styles are apparent?

Applications

1. You have been asked to prepare a manual for executives in the foreign trade department of your company. With what should they be familiar in addition to a particular culture's attitudes towards personal/public space and punctuality? Using the selections of Howe and Hall as your point of departure, prepare a brief but specific manual.

2. Define your concept of private space and describe its effects on your personal interactions. Write for an audience who does *not* share your concept of private space. How can you best present your concept?

Trying on Scotland

Alastair Reid

*Alastair Reid (b. 1926) was born in Scotland and lives in New York and Spain.
He is a poet, translator, essayist, and author of books for children. He has published
several volumes of poetry, including* Weathering: New and Selected Poems
(1978), and contributes frequently to the Atlantic Monthly, Encounter, *and*
The New Yorker. *He comments on being a writer in exile: "I like the state of
being a foreigner. It sharpens the ear and eye, and the kind of alienation it implies
is not a bad wavelength for a writer to work on, as long as his nerve and curiosity
are up to it, and as long as the mails still go through." In the following excerpt
from* Whereabouts: Notes on Being a Foreigner, *Reid recalls his impressions
of a visit to his Scottish birthplace.*

*Scotland, now joined with England and Wales in the United Kingdom of
Great Britain and Northern Ireland, occupies the northern third of the main island.
About 75 percent of the population of five million and most of the industry are
found in a 60-mile-wide belt of land from the Firth of Clyde on the west to the
Firth of Forth on the east. In this belt are the capital Edinburgh and the industrial
center Glasgow; St. Andrews, one of eight Scottish universities, is a few miles north
of the Firth of Forth. The kingdoms of Scotland, founded in 1018, and England
have shared a common monarch since 1603 and a common parliament since 1707.
Monuments to Scotland's Robert Burns, Sir Walter Scott, the Calvinist reformer
John Knox, and Mary, Queen of Scots draw many tourists, as do the "unfailingly
beautiful" land- and seascapes that also draw Reid back from time to time.*

I HAVE A FRIEND in Scotland, a painter, who still lives in the fishing town
he was born in, grew up in, went to school in, was married in, raised his
children in, works in, and clearly intends to die in. I look on him with
uncomprehending awe, for although I had much the same origins that he
had, born and sprouting in rural Scotland, close to the sea, living more by
the agrarian round than by outside time, I had in my head from an early age
the firm notion of leaving, long before I knew why or how. Even less did I
realize then that I would come to restless rest in a whole slew of places,
countries, and languages—the shifting opposite of my rooted friend. Walking
with him through his parish, I am aware that the buildings and trees are as
familiar to him as his own fingernails; that the people he throws a passing
word to he has known, in all their changings, over a span of some fifty years;
that he has surrounding him his own history and the history of the place, in
memory and image, in language and stone; that his past is ever present to
him, whereas my own is lost, shed. He has made his peace with place in a
way that to me is, if not unimaginable, at least by now beyond me.

I spent a part of the summer of 1980 digging up Scotland and to some extent coming to terms with it, for although I have gone back to it at odd intervals since I first left, I have always looked on it more as past than as present. My childhood is enclosed, encapsulated in it somewhere, but the threads that connect me to it have long been ravelled. When I return, however, I realize that the place exists spinally in my life, as a kind of yardstick against which I measure myself through time—a setting against which I can assess more clearly the changes that have taken place in me, and in it. When I go back, I am always trying on the country to see if it still fits, or fits better than it did. In one sense, the place is as comfortable to me as old clothes; in another, it is a suit that did not fit me easily from the beginning.

Still, the landscapes of childhood are irreplaceable, since they have been the backdrops for so many epiphanies, so many realizations. I am acutely aware, in Scotland, of how certain moods of the day will put me suddenly on a sharp edge of attention. They have occurred before, and I experience a time warp, past and present in one, with an intense physicality. That double vision is enough to draw anyone back anywhere, for it is what gives us, acutely, the experience of living *through* time, rather than simply living *in* time. People's faces change when they begin to say, "I once went back to . . ." Something is happening to them, some rich realization, the thrill of retrieval that pervades Nabokov's writing, past and present in one. Places provide these realizations more readily than people do: places have longer lives, for one thing, and they weather in less unpredictable ways. Places are the incarnations of a modus vivendi and the repositories of memory, and so always remain accessible to their own children; but they make very different demands on their inhabitants. In Scotland, the sense of place is strong; when I had left that attachment behind me, I had a loose curiosity about new places, and I still spark up at the notion of going somewhere I have never been to before.

Nevertheless (a favorite Scottish qualification), places embody a consensus of attitudes; and while I lived in a cheerful harmony with the places I grew up in, as places, I did not feel one with them. The natural world and the human world separated early for me. I felt them to be somehow in contradiction, and still do. The Scottish landscape—misty, muted, in constant flux and shift—intrudes its presence in the form of endlessly changing weather; the Scottish character, eroded by a bitter history and a stony morality, and perhaps in reaction to the changing turbulence of weather, subscribes to illusions of permanence, of durability, asking for a kind of submission, an obedience. I felt, from the beginning, exhilarated by the first, fettered by the second. Tramps used to stop at our house, men of the road, begging a cup of tea or an old shirt, and in my mind I was always ready to leave with them, because between Scotland and myself I saw trouble ahead.

When I go back to Scotland, I gravitate mostly to the East Neuk of Fife, that richly farmed promontory jutting into the North Sea to the northeast of Edinburgh, specifically to the town of St. Andrews, a well-worn place that has persisted in my memory from the time I first went there, a very young student at a very ancient university. I have come and gone at intervals over some thirty years, and St. Andrews has changed less in that time than any other place I can think of. It is a singular place, with an aura all its own. For a start, it has a setting unfailingly beautiful to behold in any weather—the curve of St. Andrews Bay sweeping in from the estuary of the River Eden across the washed expanse of the West Sands, backed by the windy green of the golf courses, to the town itself, spired, castled, and cathedraled, punctuated by irregular bells, cloistered and grave, with gray stone roofed in slate or red tile, kempt ruins and a tidy harbor, the town backed by green and gold fields with their stands of ancient trees. If it has the air of a museum, that is no wonder, for it sits placidly on top of a horrendous past. From the twelfth century on, it was in effect the ecclesiastical capital of Scotland, but the Reformation spelled its downfall: its vast cathedral was sacked, and by the seventeen-hundreds the place had gone into a sad decline. Its history looms rather grimly, not just in the carefully tended ruins of castle and cathedral but in the well-walked streets; inset in the cobblestones at the entrance to St. Salvator's College quadrangle are the initials "P.H.," for Patrick Hamilton, who was burned as a martyr on that spot in 1528; students acquire the superstition of never treading on the initials. With such a weighty past so tangibly present, the townspeople assume the air and manner of custodians, making themselves as comfortable and inconspicuous as they can among the ruins, and turning up their noses at the transients—the students, the golfers, the summer visitors. Yet, as in all such situations, it is the transients who sustain the place, who flock into it, year in, year out, to the present-day shrines of the university and the golf courses.

The date of the founding of the University of St. Andrews is given, variously, as 1411 or 1412: the ambiguity arises from the fact that in fifteenth-century Scotland the year began on March 25, and the group of scholars who founded the institution received their charter in February of that dubious year. Such matters are the stuff of serious controversy in St. Andrews. As students, we felt admitted to a venerable presence, even if the curriculum appeared to have undergone only minimal alteration since 1411. A kind of wise mist enveloped the place, and it seemed that we could not help absorbing it, unwittingly. The professors lectured into space, in an academic trance; we took notes, or borrowed them; the year's work culminated in a series of written examinations on set texts, which a couple of weeks of intense immersion, combined with native cunning and a swift pen, could take care of. What that serious, gravid atmosphere did was to make the present shine, in contradistinction to the past. Tacitly and instinctively, we relished the place more than the dead did or could, and we felt something like an obligation to fly in the face of the doleful past. The green woods and the sea surrounded us, the library, and an ocean of time. When I left St. Andrews to go into the Navy in the Second World War, the place, over my shoulder, took on a never-never aura—not simply the never-neverness of college years but as contrast to the troubled state of the times. It appeared to me, in that regard, somewhat unreal.

In its human dimension, St. Andrews embodied the Scotland I chose to leave behind me. The spirit of Calvin, far from dead, stalked the countryside, ever present in a pinched wariness, a wringing of the hands. We were taught to expect the worst—miserable sinners, we could not expect more. A rueful doom ruffles the Scottish spirit. It takes various spoken forms. That summer, a man in Edinburgh said to me, "See you tomorrow, if we're spared," bringing me to a horrified standstill. "Could be worse" is a regular verbal accolade; and that impassioned cry from the Scottish spirit "It's no' right!" declares drastically that *nothing* is right, nothing will ever be right—a cry of doom. Once at an international rugby match between Scotland and England in which the Scots, expected to win comfortably, doggedly snatched defeat from the jaws of victory, a friend of mine noticed two fans unroll a carefully prepared, hand-stitched banner bearing the legend "WE WUZ ROBBED." The wariness is deep-rooted. I prize the encounter I once had with a local woman on the edge of St. Andrews, on a heady spring day. I exclaimed my pleasure in the day, at which she darkened and muttered, "We'll pay for it, we'll pay for it"—a poem in itself.

> It was a day peculiar to this piece of the planet,
> when larks rose on long thin strings of singing
> and the air shifted with the shimmer of actual angels.
> Greenness entered the body. The grasses
> shivered with presences, and sunlight
> stayed like a halo on hair and heather and hills.
> Walking into town, I saw, in a radiant raincoat,
> the woman from the fish-shop. "What a day it is!"
> cried I, like a sunstruck madman.
> And what did she have to say for it?
> Her brow grew bleak, her ancestors raged in their graves
> as she spoke with their ancient misery:
> "We'll pay for it, we'll pay for it, we'll pay for it!"

And my father, who gleefully collected nuggets of utterance, often told of an old parishioner of his who, in the course of a meeting, rose to his feet and declared, "Oh, no, Mr. Reid. We've *tried* change, and we know it doesn't work." I noticed on a bus I caught in St. Andrews on my last visit, a sign that read "PLEASE LOWER YOUR HEAD"—a piece of practical advice that had, for me, immediate Calvinist overtones.

Some of that girn and grumble lingers on in the Scots. The choice is to succumb to it or to struggle energetically against it. Or, of course, to leave it behind—the woe and the drear weather—and begin again in kinder climates. What Calvin ingrained in the Scottish spirit was an enduring dualism. *The Strange Case of Dr. Jekyll and Mr. Hyde* is the quintessential Scottish novel. The mysterious elixir of transformation is simply whisky, which quite often turns soft-spoken Scots into ranting madmen. Mr. Hyde lurks in these silent depths. Virtue had to be achieved at the expense of the flesh and the physical world, in which we were always being judged and found wanting— the world, it seemed, had a vast, invisible scoreboard that gave no marks for virtue but buzzed mercilessly at miscreants. It buzzed for me. It buzzed for me and for Kathleen, one of my sisters, so regularly that we became renegades, outwitting the system when we could. In St. Andrews, that dreich outlook regularly took the form of an audible sniff of disapproval.

Interpretations

1. Reid distinguishes between living *"through* time" and "living *in* time." What does he mean?

2. What elements, according to Reid, created the Scottish character? To what extent does he find this character appealing?

3. What do the teaching methods at St. Andrews University suggest about education philosophy in Scotland? How do they compare with methods at your own college?

4. What cultural clashes or interactions are depicted in this essay?

Correspondences

1. Memory plays an important role in the Reid and Jhabvala narratives. How are their attitudes towards their pasts and presents similar and different? What do they suggest about their responses to the choices they have made?

2. According to Reid, the curriculum at St. Andrews University has changed little since 1411, yet "students felt admitted to a venerable presence." How do you explain their attitude? Might it be due partly to Scotland's homogeneity? Contrast the Scottish students' attitude with that of Novak. Might his dissatisfaction with education be accounted for by America's heterogeneity? What other reasons can you offer?

Applications

1. Reid says of Scotland: "In one sense, the place is as comfortable to me as old clothes; in another, it is a suit that did not fit me easily from the

beginning." Write an essay about a place to which you have a similar paradoxical reaction. Include both what is appealing and unappealing about the place.

2. "A rueful doom muffles the Scottish spirit. It takes various spoken forms." What examples does Reid offer to support this thesis? Which did you find most effective? How do they help explain why Reid became a renegade from his native land?

Call Me Not a Man

Mtutuzeli Matshoba

Mtutuzeli Matshoba (b. 1950) is from Soweto, South Africa, and was educated at the University of Fort Hare. In 1978, reception of his first literary contribution, by the newspaper The Voice, *encouraged him to continue writing. He is the author of* Seeds of War *(1981), a novel, and* Call Me Not a Man *(stories, 1979), which was inspired by his dealings with police reservists, who openly practiced robbery and thievery.*

Apartheid ("apartness") became law in South Africa in 1948. Under the law of segregation, blacks, who comprise over two-thirds of the population, live separately from whites and have been forced into overcrowded and poverty-striken townships. Blacks are severely restricted to certain occupations, and are paid far lower wages than whites for similar work. Only whites may vote or run for public office. Blacks must carry permits or passbooks. In 1948 alone, more than 238,000 blacks were jailed for entering a white area without a passbook.

South African antagonisms are exacerbated by the presence of both black reservists and black policemen. Although black policemen in South Africa are "shunned as quislings {traitors} by some other blacks," more than half of the country's 65,000 policemen and policewomen are nonwhite and their numbers are increasing. "The pay is good by black standards and job security attractive. Many volunteers come from rural areas where unemployment is rampant and political protest minimal." (New York Times, *January 1, 1990)*

Black protests against apartheid have increased in recent years. In retaliation, the government has since 1986 declared a nationwide state of emergency, which gives almost unlimited power to the police. In 1988 two million black workers staged a massive strike to protest new labor laws and the prohibition on political activity by anti-apartheid groups, led, among others, by Nobel Peace Prize-winner Archbishop Desmond Tutu. Nelson Mandela's release from prison in February 1990, is expected to signal the end of apartheid.

For neither am I a man in the eyes of the law,
Nor am I a man in the eyes of my fellow man.

BY DODGING, lying, resisting where it is possible, bolting when I'm already cornered, parting with invaluable money, sometimes calling my sisters into the game to get amorous with my captors, allowing myself to be slapped on the mouth in front of my womenfolk and getting sworn at with my mother's private parts, that component of me which is man has died countless times in one lifetime. Only a shell of me remains to tell you of the other man's plight, which is in fact my own. For what is suffered by another man in view of my eyes is suffered also by me. The grief he knows is a grief I know. Out of the same bitter cup do we drink. To the same chain-gang do we belong.

Friday has always been their chosen day to go plundering, although nowadays they come only occasionally, maybe once a month. Perhaps they have found better pastures elsewhere, where their prey is more predictable than at Mzimhlope, the place which has seen the tragic demise of three of their accomplices who had taken the game a bit too far by entering the hostel on the northern side of our location and fleecing the people right in the midst of their disgusting labour camps. Immediately after this there was a notable abatement in the frequency of their visits to both the location and the adjacent hostel. However the lull was short-lived, lasting only until the storm had died down, because the memory tarnishes quickly in the locations, especially the memory of death. We were beginning to emit sighs of relief and to mutter "good riddance" when they suddenly reappeared and made their presence in our lives felt once again. June 'seventy-six had put them out of the picture for the next year, during which they were scarcely seen. Like a recurring pestilence they refuse to vanish absolutely from the scene.

A person who has spent some time in Soweto will doubtless have guessed by now that the characters I am referring to are none other than some of the so-called police reservists who roam our dirty streets at weekends, robbing every timid, unsuspecting person, while masquerading as peace officers to maintain law and order in the community. There are no greater thieves than these men of the law, men of justice, peace officers and volunteer public protectors in the whole of the slum complex because, unlike others in the same trade of living off the sweat of their victims, they steal out in the open, in front of everybody's eyes. Of course nothing can be done about it because they go out on their pillaging exploits under the banners of the law, and to rise in protest against them is analogous to defiance of the powers that be.

So, on this Friday too we were standing on top of the station bridge at Mzimhlope. It was about five in the afternoon and the sun hung over the western horizon of spectacularly identical coalsmoke-puffing roof-tops like a gigantic, glowing red ball which dyed the foamy clouds with the crimson sheen of its rays. The commuter trains in from the city paused below us every two or three minutes to regurgitate their infinite human cargo, the greater part of whom were hostel-dwellers who hurried up Mohale Street to cook their meagre suppers on primus stoves. The last train we had seen would now be leaving Phefeni, the third station from Mzimhlope. The next train had just emerged from the bridge this side of New Canada, junction to East and West Soweto. The last group of the hostel people from the train now leaving Phefeni had just turned the bend at Mohale Street where it intersects with Elliot. The two-hundred-metre stretch to Elliot was therefore relatively empty, and people coming towards the station could be clearly made out.

As the wheels of the train from New Canada squealed on the iron tracks and it came to a jerking stop, four men, two in overalls and the others in dustcoats, materialized around the Mohale Street bend. There was no doubt who they were, from the way they filled the whole width of the street and walked as if they owned everything and everybody in their sight. When they came to the grannies selling vegetables, fruit and fried mealies along the ragged, unpaved sides of the street, they grabbed what they fancied and munched gluttonously the rest of the way towards us. Again nothing could be done about it, because the poverty-stricken vendors were not licensed to scrape together some crumbs to ease the gnawing stomachs of their fatherless grandchildren at home, which left them wide open for plunder by the indifferent "reserves." "*Awu!* The Hellions," remarked Mandla next to me, "Let's get away from here, my friend."

He was right. They reminded one of the old western film; but I was not moving from where I was simply because the reservists were coming down the street like a bunch of villains. One other thing I knew was that the railway constable who was on guard duty that Friday at the station did not allow the persecution of the people on his premises. I wanted to have my laugh when they were chased off the station.

"Don't worry about them. Just wait and see how they're going to be chased away by this copper. He won't allow them on the station," I answered.

They split into twos when they arrived below us. Two of them, a tall chap with a face corroded by skin-lightening cream and wearing a yellow golf cap on his shaven head, and another stubby, shabbily dressed, middle-aged man with a bald frontal lobe and a drunk face, chewing at a cooked sheep's foot that he had taken from one of the grannies, climbed the stairs on our right-hand side. The younger man took the flight in fours. The other two chose to waylay their unsuspecting victims on the street corner at the base of the left-hand staircase. The first wave of the people who had alighted from the train was in the middle of the bridge when the second man reached the top of the stairs.

Maybe they knew the two reservists by sight, maybe they just smelt cop in the smoggy air, or it being a Friday, they were alert for such possibilities. Three to four of the approaching human wall turned suddenly in their tracks and ran for their dear freedom into the mass behind them. The others were caught unawares by this unexpected movement and they staggered in all directions trying to regain balance. In a split second there was commotion on the station, as if a wild cat had found its way into a fowl-run. Two of those who had not been quick enough were grabbed by their sleeves, and their passes demanded. While they were producing their books the wolves went over their pockets, supposedly feeling for dangerous weapons, *dagga*[1]

---

[1]Marijuana.

and other illegal possessions that might be concealed in the clothes, but really to ascertain whether they had caught the right people for their iniquitous purposes. They were paging through the booklets when the Railway policeman appeared.

"Wha . . .? Don't you fools know that you're not supposed to do that shit here? Get off! Get off and do that away from Railway property. Fuck off!" He screamed at the two reservists so furiously that the veins threatened to burst in his neck.

"Arrest the dogs, *baba!* Give them a chance also to taste jail!" Mandla shouted.

"*Ja,*" I said to Mandla, "you bet, they've never been where they are so prepared to send others."

The other people joined in and we jeered the cowards off the station. They descended the stairs with their tails tucked between their legs and joined their companions below the station. Some of the commuters who had been alerted by the uproar returned to the platform to wait there until the reservists had gone before they would dare venture out of the station.

We remained where we had been and watched the persecution from above. I doubted if they even read the passes (if they could), or whether the victims knew if their books were right or out of order. Most likely the poor hunted men believed what they were told by the licensed thieves. The latter demanded the books, after first judging their prey to be weak propositions, flicked through the pages, put the passes into their own pockets, without which the owners could not continue on their way, and told the dumbfounded hostel men to stand aside while they accosted other victims. Within a very short while there was a group of confused men to one side of the street, screaming at their hostel mates to go to room so-and-so and tell so-and-so that they had been arrested at the station, and to bring money quickly to release them. Few of those who were being sent heard the messages since they were only too eager to leave the danger zone. Those who had money shook hands with their captors, received their books back and ran up Mohale Street. If they were unlucky they came upon another "roadblock" three hundred metres up the street where the process was repeated. Woe unto them who had paid their last money to the first extortionists, for this did not matter. The police station was their next stopover before the Bantu Commissioners, and thence their final destination, Modderbee Prison, where they provided the farmers with ready cheap labour until they had served their terms for breaking the law. The terms vary from a few days to two years for *loaferskap,*[2] which is in fact mere unemployment, for which the unfortunate men are not to blame. The whole arrangement stinks of forced labour.

The large *kwela-kwela*[3] swayed down Mohale Street at breakneck speed.

[2]Vagrancy.

[3]Police van.

The multitudes scattered out of its way and hung on to the sagging fences until it had passed. To be out of sight of the people on the station bridge, it skidded and swerved into the second side street from the station. More reservists poured out of it and went immediately to their dirty job with great zeal. The chain-gang which had been lined up along the fence of the house nearest the station was kicked and shoved to the *kwela-kwela* into which the victims were bundled under a rain of fists and boots, all of them scrambling to go in at the same time through the small door. The driver of the *kwela-kwela,* the only uniformed constable among the group, clanged the door shut and secured it with the locking lever. He went to stand authoritatively near one of the vendors, took a small avocado pear, peeled it and put it whole into a gargantuan mouth, spitting out the large stone later. He did not have to take the trouble of accosting anyone himself. His gangsters would all give him a lion's share of whatever they made, and moreover buy him some beers and brandy. He kept adjusting his polished belt over his potbelly as the .38 police special in its leather holster kept tugging it down. He probably preferred to wear his gun unconventionally, cowboy style.

A boy of about seventeen was caught with a knife in his pocket, a dangerous weapon. They slapped him a few times and let him stand handcuffed against the concrete wall of the station. Ten minutes later his well-rounded sister alighted from the train to find her younger brother among the prisoners. As she was inquiring from him why he had been arrested, and reprimanding him for carrying a knife, one of the younger reservists came to stand next to her and started pawing her. She let him carry on, and three minutes later her brother was free. The reservist was beaming all over his face, glad to have won himself a beautiful woman in the course of his duties and little knowing that he had been given the wrong address. Some of our Black sisters are at times compelled to go all the way to save their menfolk, and, as always, nothing can be done about it.

There was a man coming down Mohale Street, conspicuous amidst the crowd because of the bag and baggage that was loaded on his overall-clad frame. On his right shoulder was a large suitcase with a grey blanket strapped to it with flaxen strings. From his left hand hung a bulging cardboard box, only a few inches from the ground, and tilting him to that side. He walked with the bounce of someone used to walking in gumboots or on uneven ground. There was the urgency of someone who had a long way to travel in his gait. It was doubtless a *goduka* on his way home to his family after many months of work in the city. It might even have been years since he had visited the countryside.

He did not see the hidden *kwela-kwela,* which might have forewarned him of the danger that was lurking at the station. Only when he had stumbled into two reservists, who stepped into his way and ordered him to put down his baggage, did he perhaps remember that it was Friday and raid-day. A baffled expression sprang into his face as he realized what he had walked into. He frantically went through the pockets of his overalls. The worried countenance deepened on his dark face. He tried again to make sure, but he did not find what he was looking for. The men who had stopped him pulled him to one side, each holding him tightly by the sleeve of his overall. He obeyed meekly like a tame animal. They let him lift his arms while they searched him all over the body. Finding nothing hidden on him, they demanded the inevitable book, although they had seen that he did not have it. He gesticulated with his hands as he explained what had caused him not to be carrying his pass with him. A few feet above them, I could hear what was said.

"Strue, *madoda*,"[4] he said imploringly, "I made a mistake. I luggaged the pass with my trunk. It was a jacket that I forgot to search before I packed it into the trunk."

"How do we know that you're not lying?" asked one of the reservists in a querulous voice.

"I'm not lying, *mfowethu*.[5] I swear by my mother, that's what happened," explained the frightened man.

The second reservist had a more evil and uncompromising attitude. "That was your own stupidity, mister. Because of it you're going to jail now; no more to your wife."

"Oh, my brother. Put yourself in my shoes. I've not been home to my people for two years now. It's the first chance I have to go and see my twin daughters who were born while I've been here. Feel for another poor Black man, please, my good brother. Forgive me only for this once."

"What? Forgive you? And don't give us that slush about your children. We've also got our own families, for whom we are at work right now, at this very moment," the obstinate one replied roughly.

"But, *mfo*. Wouldn't you make a mistake too?"

That was a question the cornered man should not have asked. The reply this time was a resounding slap on the face. "You think I'm stupid like you, huh? Bind this man, Mazibuko, put the bloody irons on the dog."

"No, man. Let us talk to the poor bloke. Perhaps he can do something for us in exchange for the favour of letting him proceed on his way home," the less volatile man suggested, and pulled the hostel man away from the rest of the arrested people.

"*Ja*. Speak to him yourself, Mazibuko. I can't bear talking to rural fools like him. I'll kill him with my bare hands if he thinks that I've come to play here in Johannesburg!" The anger in the man's voice was faked, the fury of a coward trying to instil fear in a person who happened to be at his mercy. I doubted if he could face up to a mouse. He accosted two boys and ran his hands over their sides, but he did not ask for their passes.

[4, 5]Terms of respect.

"You see, my friend, you're really in trouble. I'm the only one who can help you. This man who arrested you is not in his best mood today. How much have you got on you? Maybe if you give something he'll let you go. You know what wonders money can do for you. I'll plead for you; but only if I show him something can he understand." The reservist explained the only way out of the predicament for the trapped man, in a smooth voice that sounded rotten through and through with corruption, the sole purpose for which he had joined the "force."

"I haven't got a cent in my pocket. I bought provisions, presents for the people at home and the ticket with all the money they gave me at work. Look, *nkosi,*[6] I have only the ticket and the papers with which I'm going to draw my money when I arrive at home." He took out his papers, pulled the overall off his shoulders and lowered it to his thighs so that the brown trousers he wore underneath were out in the open. He turned the dirty pockets inside out. "There's nothing else in my pockets except these, mister, honestly."

"Man!"

"Yessir?"

"You want to go home to your wife and children?"

"Yes, *please,* good man of my people. Give me a break."

"Then why do you show me these damn papers? They will feed your own children, but not mine. When you get to your home you're going to draw money and your kids will be scratching their tummies and dozing after a hectic meal, while I lose my job for letting you go and my own children join the dogs to scavenge the trashbins. You're mad, *mos.*" He turned to his mate. "Hey, Baloyi. Your man says he hasn't got anything, but he's going to his family which he hasn't seen for two years."

"I told you to put the irons on him. He's probably carrying a little fortune in his underpants. Maybe he's shy to take it out in front of the people. It'll come out at the police station, either at the charge office or in the cells when the small boys shake him down."

"Come on, you. Your hands maan!"

The other man pulled his arms away from the manacles. His voice rose desperately, "*Awu* my people. You mean you're really arresting me? Forgive me! I pray do."

A struggle ensued between the two men.

"You're resisting arrest? You—" and a stream of foul vitriolic words concerning the anatomy of the hostel man's mother gushed out of the reservist's mouth.

"I'm not, I'm not! But please listen!" The hostel man heaved and broke loose from the reservist's grip. The latter was only a lump of fat with nothing underneath. He staggered three steps back and flopped on his rump. When he bounced back to his feet, unexpectedly fast for his bulk, his eyes were

[6]Term of respect.

blazing murder. His companions came running from their own posts and swarmed upon the defenceless man like a pack of hyenas upon a carcase. The other people who had been marooned on the bridge saw a chance to go past while the wolves were still preoccupied. They ran down the stairs and up Mohale like racehorses. Two other young men who were handcuffed together took advantage of the diversion and bolted down the first street in tandem, taking their bracelets with them. They ran awkwardly with their arms bound together, but both were young and fit and they did their best in the circumstances.

We could not stand the sickening beating that the other man was receiving any more.

"Hey! Hey. *Sies,* maan. Stop beating the man like that. Arrest him if you want to arrest him. You're killing him, dogs!" we protested loudly from the station. An angry crowd was gathering.

"Stop it or we'll stop you from doing anything else forever!" someone shouted.

The psychopaths broke their rugger scrum and allowed us to see their gruesome handiwork. The man was groaning at the base of the fence, across the street where the dirt had gathered. He twisted painfully to a sitting position. His face was covered with dirt and blood from where the manacles that were slipped over the knuckles had found their marks, and his features were grotesquely distorted. In spite of that, the fat man was not satisfied. He bent and gathered the whimpering man's wrists with the intention of fastening them to the fence with the handcuffs.

"Hey, hey, hey, Satan! Let him go. Can't you see that you've hurt that man enough?"

The tension was building up to explosion point and the uniformed policeman sensed it.

"Let him go, boys. Forgive him. Let him go," he said, shooting nervous glances in all directions.

Then the beaten-up man did the most unexpected and heart-rending thing. He knelt before the one ordering his release and held his dust-covered hands with the palms together in the prayer position, and still kneeling he said, "Thank you very much, my lord. God bless you. Now I can go and see my twins and my people at home."

He would have done it. Only it never occurred in his mind at that moment of thanksgiving to kiss the red gleaming boots of the policeman.

The miserable man beat the dust off his clothes as best he could, gathered his two parcels and clambered up the stairs, trying to grin his thanks to the crowd that had raised its voice of protest on his behalf. The policeman decided to call it a day. The other unfortunates were shepherded to the waiting *kwela-kwela.*

I tried to imagine how the man would explain his lumps to his wife. In the eye of my mind I saw him throwing his twins into the air and gathering them again and again as he played with them.

"There's still a long way to cover, my friend," I head Mandla saying into my ear.

Interpretations

1. What is the evidence that both the police reservists and their victims are black? How does their blackness affect your response to their behavior? Do you think this point should be made clear earlier in the story? Why?

2. To what extent does the scene with the *avocado* serve as a symbol of the relationship between the reservists and the black citizens of Soweto?

3. The story is told in the first person by an unnamed narrator. What do we know about this narrator? What are his dominant traits? What is his relation to the events he narrates? Would the story be improved if told by the hostel man or by the author in the third person? Why or why not?

4. Does the attitude in the hostel man upon his release strip him of his manhood, as the title suggests? Why or why not?

5. What is the tone of this story? What is implied by the use of three different terms to suggest respect? Is the style appropriate to the subject? Describe the style and give examples to support your description.

Correspondences

1. Review the first paragraph of Matshoba's story. Why does he use the word "man" so often? What is he implying about his own manhood and that of the other members of the symbolic chain gang? Review Jones's essay (Chapter 4) on covering the Klan rally in Florida in 1988. How do whites refer to her? How does this interaction affect her concept of herself?

2. Review the Baldwin quotation (page 290). What does it mean? To what extent do you agree with it? How does it apply to social interactions in "Call Me Not a Man"? *Who* saw himself in the eyes of the victim?

Applications

1. Review the Kluckhohn quotation (page 290). How does it apply to the beaten man's interaction with the policeman who sprayed him? to the last line of the story? How pertinent is it to Wright's interactions with whites (Chapter 3)? What might you conclude about the cost of survival?

2. Write a journal entry for the following: Apartheid prohibits racial interaction. "Call Me Not A Man" is a result.

ADDITIONAL WRITING TOPICS

1. "Growing up in America has been an assault upon my sense of worthiness. It has also been a kind of liberation and delight." What aspects of Novak's' interactions reflect this paradox? To what extent does the paradox also apply to the experiences of Fusilli and Ota?

2. What more did you learn about the political system depicted in Matshoba's story? What can an individual living under apartheid do to end this system? Does he or she have any choice but to support and accept it? What can people living outside the system do?

3. Review the Norton quotation (page 289). Is it easier to support theoretically than practically? To what extent do the interactions presented in the selections in this textbook reflect the kinds of tolerance of individual differences Norton advocates?

4. Review the Morrow quotation (page 289). What does it suggest about interactions? How do the selections by Howe, Hall, and Jhabvala support or refute Morrow's thesis?

5. Write about a group you participated in recently. Analyze how the group members interact with one another. By what means do they communicate with one another? How do they handle disagreement or friction? Write an essay on what you learned about group relations.

6. Bilingual education is a complex and controversial issue. Some theorists, like Rendón, (Chapter 3) believe that immersion in the English language results in alienation from family and culture. Others, like Rodriguez, advocate that all students become part of the educational mainstream. Present these differing viewpoints to several students for whom English is a second language. What are their views? With whom do they agree? for what reasons? Write an essay summarizing your findings. To what extent do their responses alter your views on this issue?

7. What might you contribute to community discussions on such issues as changing ethnic populations and cultural diversity? How have the readings in this and other chapters contributed to your better understanding of these issues.

CHAPTER 6

Choices

Culture, according to anthropologist Bronislaw Malinowski, is the "artificial, secondary environment" that human beings superimpose on nature. We human beings, then, are "in" both nature and culture, and both influence our choices. A diversity of cultures, which the following selections illustrate, makes for great choice and sometimes great difficulty of choice. Cultures are "dramatic conversations about things that matter," says Robert Bellah, (see the introduction to Chapter 1) and those conversations are about choices.

While nature is passively selecting the fittest organisms for survival, we humans are actively, sometimes painfully, choosing, making a variety of choices—ethical, political, economic—for a variety of reasons both rational and emotional. If we make the same choice time after time, such as training ourselves to set the alarm clock and getting up when it rings, it becomes "second" nature, and we are on time for work or school without having to think much about it. Where life runs its traditional course, unconscious habit often replaces conscious choice, but when crises arise, social or personal, habit is useless and all kinds of choices must be made, including painful ones. This is the complex situation in the essays of this chapter.

Is culture, like nature, a limitation on freedom of choice, or does it allow more free play of individual wisdom and imagination? Do we increase our own choices to the degree we free ourselves from culture? The first selection in the chapter poses such a possibility. The young man in the Swahili tale chooses a wife and finds that the choice is involved with such cultural requirements as a bride price. The wife's culture denies her the choice of husband, but her wisdom, which is even greater than her beauty, shows to her subsequent choices which allow her to triumph.

In a crisis, habit cannot necessarily ease the pain of choice. When she decided one December day in 1955 not to sit in the back of the bus in Montgomery, Alabama, Rosa Parks made a painful choice whose effects are still being felt all over the world. She rejected her enslaved grandfather's fierce hatred of whites, but still reads her American history with an eye for hypocrisy. Leonardo, facing a crisis in "A Train Ride," is forced into a painful "dramatic conversation" with himself that leads to a surprising and momentous choice.

It would be hard to imagine more painful choices than those made by Anna in the impossible political situation of Hana Wehle's "The Impossible Became No Longer Unthinkable." Uprooted from her home in Prague and transported with her husband and his parents to the Theresienstadt ghetto (where they were later joined by Anna's mother), the twenty-five-year-old Anna tried to keep together the "little cluster of three broken women" after the two men died.

A change of place may also alter the significance of moral, economic and social choices. Several of the selections in this chapter show immigrants to the United States faced with changing choices. Manuela's early life ("A Tale of Two Moralities") seems to have offered few choices, but once she began to extricate herself from the traditional village, the choices (and problems) increased. Richard Rodriguez in "To the Border" sympathetically, poetically, recreates the emotions and wrenching choices of a boy (Rodriguez's father?) who is one of the lonely "Mexicans without Mexico." And Gloria Bonilla recounts her decision to leave El Salvador for Washington, D.C. "The process was painful and difficult. But I survived."

Marshall Glickman reaches across cultural lines to choose Zen Buddhism. In so doing, he changes his definitions of success and failure and, along with them, his behavior, his health, and his goals. In "Banderillero" we see a bullfighter in Spain struggle with success and failure and make a difficult career choice. And the Afrikaner farmer Marais Van der Vyver in Nadine Gordimer's story makes a series of life-and-death choices. In the following selections nature, culture, and choice—three sometimes incompatible but essential elements—combine in uneasy and interesting ways.

PERSPECTIVES

January 1
Look to this day,
For it is life, the very life of life.
In its brief course lie all the varieties and realities of
*   your existence,*
The bliss of growth, the glory of action, the splendor of
*   beauty;*
For yesterday is but a dream; and tomorrow is only a vision,
But today well lived makes
Every yesterday a dream of happiness
And every tomorrow a vision of hope.

Bhagavad-Gita

People are trapped in history and history is trapped in them.

James Baldwin

Look out how you use proud words.
When you let proud words go, it is
*   not easy to call them back.*
They wear long boots, hard boots; they
*   walk off proud; they can't hear you*
*   calling—*
Look out how you use proud words.

Carl Sandburg

Troubles overcome are good to tell.

Yiddish Proverb

If man's condition is unjust, he has only one alternative, which is to
be just himself.

Albert Camus

One doesn't throw the stick after the snake has gone.

Liberian Proverb

Once to every man and nation comes the moment to decide
In the strife of truth with falsehood, for the good or evil side.

James Russell Lowell

Two roads diverged in a wood, and I—I took the one less traveled
by, and that has made all the difference.

Robert Frost

Every time a man has contributed to the victory of the dignity of the
spirit, every time a man has said no to an attempt to subjugate his
fellows, I have felt solidarity with his act.

Frantz Fanon

Applications

1. Write a journal entry on one of the perspectives on choices. To what extent do you consider yourself free to make choices?

2. Discuss the quotation from the Bhagavad-Gita. What does it imply about time and choice?

The Wise Daughter

Swahili Folk Tale

Swahili is spoken widely in East Africa and is an official language of Kenya and Tanzania.

THERE WAS ONCE a young man whose parents died and left him a hundred cattle. He was lonely after the death of his parents, so he decided to get married. He went to his neighbors and asked them to help him find a wife.

Soon one of the neighbors came to tell him that he had found the most beautiful girl in the country for him to marry. "The girl is very good and wise and beautiful, and her father is very wealthy," he said. "Her father owns six thousand cattle."

The young man became very excited when he heard about this girl. But then he asked, "How much is the bride price?"

"The father wants a hundred cattle," was the reply.

"A hundred cattle! That is all I have. How will we be able to live?" replied the young man.

"Well, make up your mind. I have to take an answer to the father soon," said the neighbor.

The young man thought, "I cannot live without this girl." So he said, "Go and tell the father that I want to marry his daughter."

So the two were married. But after they returned home, they quickly ran out of food, and the young man had to herd cattle for a neighbor to get anything to eat. What he got was not very much for a young lady who was used to eating well and living in style.

One day as the young wife was sitting outside the house, a strange man came by and was struck by her beauty. He decided to try to seduce her and sent a message to her. The young wife told him that she could not make up her mind and he would have to come back later.

Several months later, the girl's father came to visit. She was very upset because she did not have anything to feed him. But on that same day, the seducer came back. So the young wife told the seducer that she would give in to his requests if he would bring her some meat to cook for her father.

Soon the seducer returned with the meat and the girl went inside to cook it. Her husband returned, and he and her father sat down to eat and have a good time. The seducer was standing outside listening. Soon he became angry and went inside to see what was happening. The young husband, who was hospitable, invited him in.

The young wife then brought in the meat and said, "Eat, you three fools."

"Why do you call us fools?" the three men said all together.

"Well, Father," the girl replied. "You are a fool because you sold something precious for something worthless. You had only one daughter and traded her for a hundred cattle when you already had six thousand."

"You are right," said her father. "I was a fool."

"As for you, husband," she went on. "You inherited only a hundred cattle and you went and spent them all on me, leaving us nothing to eat. You could have married another woman for ten or twenty cows. That is why you were a fool."

"And why am I a fool?" asked the seducer.

"You are the biggest fool of all. You thought you could get for one piece of meat what had been bought for a hundred cattle."

At that, the seducer ran away as fast as he could. Then the father said, "You are a wise daughter. When I get home, I will send your husband three hundred cattle so that you shall live in comfort."

Interpretations

1. Is this tale about how *not* to make choices? Explain your answer.

2. In many cultures the bride must provide a dowry, whereas in the East African culture of this story the groom must pay a bride price; how do you feel about these customs? How do you think they affect relations between the sexes? Why?

3. What is the woman's role in the tale? Is she manipulative or wise? Explain your answer.

Correspondences

1. Review the Liberian proverb on page 361. How does it apply to the Swahili tale? What does the latter suggest about making choices based on emotions? Do you agree? Why?

2. In the Swahili tale, the women are described as wise, the men foolish. Compare the woman in this selection with Effua in "Anticipation" (Chapter 2). How are they similar? Are women, as the selections suggest, more logical than men in affairs of the heart? Cite evidence.

Applications

1. Write a journal entry about a choice that you regret having made. What did you learn from the experience?

2. Study a dictionary or thesaurus entry for *wisdom*. Which connotations best express your associations with wisdom? Can wisdom be taught? Do we value wise people? How might wisdom affect choices?

The Zen Master, My Father, and Me

Marshall Glickman

Marshall Glickman (b. 1961) majored in philosophy at Northwestern University and after graduation worked for three years for Shearson Lehman Brothers. Since then he has been traveling, reading, meditating, writing, and spending time with family and friends. This is how he describes his purpose in writing "The Zen Master, My Father, and Me."

After I was beaten with the stick, I spent the night thinking about what had happened and why. I consoled myself that at the very least the experience would make an interesting story. In my mind I saw a catchy opening line for an essay: "A Zen master beat me so hard my back swelled a purple lump the size of a baseball." Then I realized that I was composing an essay as an escape, using it to make a scary event safe. So I dropped the idea.

Years later, I told my girlfriend (now wife) Margaret about my experiences at camp. After I told her, I made a nonverbal connection to my experience at a sesshin. *Writing the essay allowed me to figure out what that connection was.*

THE ZEN MASTER pulled my shoulder forward with one hand and grabbed his stick with the other. "Shout!" he commanded. As I bent over, his wooden stick cracked across my back. "Louder!" he roared. I yelled again. Another sharp slap stung my back. I screamed as loud as I could. He hit me again—and again—until I lost count of the blows and my hoarse screams.

When he rang his bell, indicating the end of our meeting, I was dazed and shaken. I bowed and left the room, resuming my vow of silence.

I was at a *sesshin,* a week-long meditation retreat. Seven days without phones, TV, radio, or showers. Seven days spent meditating eleven hours a day.

I am nine; my brother Joe eleven. We're at a sleepaway sports camp. My father's red and contorted face is inches from mine. His glasses are crooked; his neck strained from yelling.

He's in a rage because we've called home every day for a week, crying, begging mom to bring us home. We hate camp. We hate waking at 6:30 to a recording of reveille and laps around the obstacle course. We hate the drills and swimming lessons. The bathrooms stink; the food is worse. The kids are mean. My first nights were spent wet and cold from midnight water raids.

"THE WORLD IS A TOUGH PLACE!" he screams. "YOU'VE GOT TO BE STRONG. OTHERWISE YOU'LL END UP STARVING IN A CONCENTRATION CAMP. IF SOMEONE PICKS ON YOU, PUNCH THEM IN THE FACE."

I am dazed and shaken—too shocked to speak or cry. Normally, my dad isn't scary. He never hit me. He rarely raised his voice to Mom. He usually only yelled at football games or on the tennis court. Joe and I don't wave as we watch my parents' car disappear past the camp gates.

The next day I got into a fight. I can't remember with who, or why, but I know I didn't cry.

Camp was a distant memory until I saw my bruised back in a bathroom mirror in the monastery. A bright purple lump the size of a baseball swelled from a sea of lavender and blue. I was shocked. Why had I let myself be beaten? I spent a sleepless night wondering if I should leave the *sesshin*.

Zen Buddhism had been my anchor since college. From day one freshman year, I practically lived at the library. My major was philosophy, but my real interest was Harvard Law School. I obsessed over A's and worked hard to stay motivated—even tacking a sign over my bed that read: "WAKE UP ASSHOLE." By my junior year, a persistent tension rash covered my legs.

During a study break in the library, I came across a book about Zen. Its philosophy was much different from the metaphysics I studied in class. Zen wasn't concerned with logic. Its wisdom came from direct experience. And better yet, Zen offered a way to be—a take-life-as-it-comes fluidity that I lacked.

The book said to meditate and concentrate on the present. It also said something that sounded surprising, but somehow felt true: the ego is an illusion. The self does not exist as a separate unchanging entity and we cause ourself needless pain by clinging to the idea of self. What we really want is simply a full deep experience of life—not achievements.

It made sense to me. If I lived in the moment, waking up late wouldn't ruin my day. If I wasn't dominated by my ego, I wouldn't worry about my grades. I read more books about Zen, savoring descriptions of *satori* (enlightenment) like a prisoner dreams of freedom.

I started meditating. For half an hour a day, I tried to sit still in the half-lotus position, letting thoughts pass like clouds in the sky. My mind would calm down for about fifteen minutes, until the only thing I could think about were my aching back and burning thighs and ankles. Yet rather than move my legs, I would scream into a pillow or throw my alarm clock across the room. I was determined to relax. Within a few months, I was meditating two hours a day.

The more I meditated, the more I wanted to be released from my desire to succeed. Happiness shouldn't depend on getting into Harvard or landing a good job. It was more important to learn how to live. Unfortunately, there was a problem: I needed an income.

After graduating, I got a job as a stockbroker. I wanted to save enough money to be freed from a regular job. I disciplined myself even more than I had in college. I woke up at 5:30 in the morning, meditated before work and made calls until nine or ten at night. My savings goal and the words "DO IT" were taped to my phone. I became both the demanding boss and the down-trodden worker. A new rash covered my dialing hand.

Two years later, the lump on my back told me I was doing the same thing with Zen. I had turned *satori* into an accomplishment that demanded sacrifice. I embraced the Zen tradition of yelling and blows to the back because they gave increased energy for concentration. Like volunteering for extra credit, I always asked to be hit when monks prowled the meditation hall with sticks.

But I hadn't asked the Zen master (*roshi*) to hit me during our meeting— and even if I had, he'd gone beyond "extra credit" or a little shot of energy.

The *roshi* seemed to be the consummate wise sage. He spoke carefully and intelligently with an endearing Japanese accent. His movements were measured and graceful; his advice penetrating and funny. I didn't know him intimately, but I idolized him in the way I had my dad as a kid. I wanted his approval; wanted to know what he knew. And I assumed he knew better than I did.

Maybe the *roshi's* austere training as a monk in Japan made him believe that a serious student had to be beaten for insight. Maybe he wanted his students to have *satori* so much that he turned it into a goal too. In college, as I developed what I thought were my own values, I had learned that my father could make mistakes. Now I saw that the *roshi* could too.

The point isn't to blame the *roshi* or my dad; what mattered was the problem in me. For the first time, I clearly saw how I was living for results. I had thought that the West in me pushed for success, while the East tried to let go. But the truth was, I was always pushing, always putting the goal first. Camp had made me tougher. It taught me some discipline. But the real lesson I learned wasn't "stand up for myself"; it was DON'T FAIL.

After realizing this at the *sesshin,* my first reaction was: get rid of goals and discipline because they cause anxiety—I'm going home. But that wasn't the answer; discipline can be a good tool. It had enabled me to save enough money to quit my job. And the discipline of meditating is basically healthy. What I needed to remember is failing isn't a disgrace. Because when failing isn't an option, discipline turns into dictatorship.

I decided to finish the *sesshin* and not push anymore. I didn't ask for the stick. I didn't attend meetings. I just sat still. As hours slipped into days, I found a deeper level of awareness than ever before. I experienced a glimpse of pure boundless energy—life without the ego. Maybe the *roshi* thought that would happen. It's hard to tell.

I haven't attended another *sesshin,* but I still meditate every day—although I don't call it Zen. I just try to sit still, relax, and be aware. My rash has gotten smaller, but it hasn't disappeared. It's a reminder that it may take a lifetime to truly learn that while goals aren't that important, trusting myself and listening are.

Interpretations

1. What is Glickman's purpose in juxtaposing the Zen master and his father in the first two sections of the story? What elements do the scenes share? How are they different?

2. Without having suffered a "persistent tension rash," would Glickman have started studying Zen? Why does he say the lump on his back was "doing the same thing with Zen"?

3. Judging from Glickman's summary of Zen Buddhism, what does it teach about human aspiration? about the "desire to succeed"? Are aspiring and succeeding the same? Why or why not?

4. Right from the beginning of the essay, discipline is an important idea. What are the stages in the development of Glickman's final conception of discipline? To what extent do you agree with his conception? Why is it valuable? Can discipline be developed? If so, how? Is discipline of value only as a "tool," or does it have intrinsic value?

5. How does Glickman change in the course of the story? How does he account for the change? Is it an improvement? Is it a common change? What is Glickman's final attitude toward meditation? Do you share his attitude? Why or why not? What is his final attitude toward Zen?

6. What does Glickman mean by learning to "trust [oneself]"? Why might learning to do so take a lifetime? How does trusting oneself relate to relaxing, meditating, and/or deemphasizing goals?

7. Glickman says that he was first attracted to Zen Buddhism because it "wasn't concerned with logic." Might Zen also have appealed to Glickman simply because it came from another culture?

Correspondences

1. "What I needed to remember is failing isn't a disgrace. Because when failing isn't an option, discipline turns into dictatorship." To what extent do you

agree with Glickman? Can one learn from failure? How might adherence to this same philosophy have altered the destiny of So Tsi-fai (Chapter 3)?

2. "It's a reminder that it may take a lifetime to truly learn that while goals aren't that important, trusting myself and listening are." What brings Glickman to this conclusion? How does it affect his choices? How might Baker's mother (Chapter 1) respond to such a philosophy?

Applications

1. Glickman feels that his preoccupation with success in the future has diminished his enjoyment of the present. To what extent do you agree? Does this insight change your own outlook?

2. Some choices are not clear cut. Is there a choice about which you feel or have felt ambivalent? Write a journal entry analyzing the reason(s) for any ambivalence.

from A Long Way to Go

Rosa Parks

Rosa Parks (b. 1913) from Pine Level, Alabama, became the center of civil rights controversy in 1955 when she was arrested for refusing to give up her seat on a bus to a white man in Montgomery, Alabama. In protest, the blacks of the city, led by 26-year-old Dr. Martin Luther King, Jr., boycotted the segregated buses. One year later the buses were desegregated. The Statue of Liberty is the fitting focal point of "A Long Way to Go," for it reflects Ms. Parks's assessment of complex race relations in the United States, past and present.

WHEN I WAS COMING UP, I went to a one-room country school in Pine Level, Alabama, where all the pupils and the teachers were black. In the sixth grade, my mother sent me to Montgomery, where I went to the Montgomery Industrial School, which was run by Miss Alice White. She was a very proper older woman who ran the school with a group of Northern white ladies who were sympathetic to the plight of Negroes. That's what they called us back then.

In school, we learned all of the civics lessons that children were supposed to learn. We had to memorize Abraham Lincoln's Gettysburg Address and portions of the Constitution. We recited the Pledge of Allegiance. We studied all of the Presidents—Washington, Jefferson, Lincoln—and we knew about all the wars.

I guess for most of us children, the Statue of Liberty was just something we read about in a civics book. We learned that poem about the statue, but it was just another lesson we had to recite, just like the Civil War poem about the Blue and the Gray, or the Gettysburg Address.

The Africans who came over on the slave ships never saw the statue. Of course, they didn't mention that in the history books. The studies we did in our books were based on freedom and equality and the pursuit of happiness and all. But in reality we had to face the fact that we were not as free as the books said. What they taught us in school didn't apply to us as a race. We were being told to be as submissive and as useful as possible to white people, to do their work and see to their comforts and be segregated from them when they saw fit for us not to be around.

Even Miss Alice White, who had all the best intentions in the world, was part of the system. In her lectures, she would tell us how horrible slavery was, but then she would say that at least it brought the Negro out of savagery in Africa. Of course, none of those slave traders ever asked the Africans whether they wanted to come to America. I imagine that if the Africans had come around after the statue was built, they would have had some terrible ideas about what it meant to them. I don't think they would have written any poems.

My family knew the brutality and disillusionment of not being treated like human beings. My grandfather was a slave. He was the son of the plantation owner, so he was very white in appearance. My grandfather used to say that the overseer took an instant dislike to him because he looked so white. He would always tell me how he had to dodge and hide to keep out of trouble with the overseer. Until the day he died, my grandfather had a fierce hatred of white people.

My mother had a mind of her own. She always held to the belief that none of us should be mistreated because of our race. She was pretty outspoken, and of course that didn't endear her to too many whites. It didn't endear her to too many blacks, either, because in those days the general attitude among our people was to go along in silence. If you differed with that, you had to stand pretty much alone.

I remember that one of the first books I read, back when I was 8 years old, was called *Is the Negro a Beast?* That was the kind of attitude that white people had in Alabama in those days. It was so different from what we were reading about in our American history and civics lessons, with all the positive messages about life in this country, and I could see that what we were being taught wasn't so, at least as far as black people were concerned.

It didn't change much when I was working. I encountered all kinds of discrimination. If you were black in the South, it was just something you lived with all the time. I would just meet it in silence, bite my lip, go on. I saw it a lot with the bus drivers. If they thought you were about to make trouble, they would just shut the door on you and drive on off. In fact, the same red-headed driver who arrested me in 1955 [starting the Montgomery bus boycott led by Martin Luther King] had evicted me from a bus in 1943. He didn't want me to walk through the white section of the bus to get to the section for blacks, and I told him I wasn't going to get off the bus while I was already on. He took me by the sleeve of my winter coat and led me off. When I got on his bus again 12 years later, I remembered him very well, but I didn't expect him to disturb me a second time.

I didn't actually get to see the Statue of Liberty until about a year after the boycott. By that time, my attitude was a little different. I thought that saying—"Give me your tired, your poor . . ."—was impressive, that we should help people who come to the United States. This was a better place than where they had been.

I was invited to come to New York by Dr. Ralph Bunche and met him at the United Nations. I stayed with a Quaker couple, Mr. and Mrs. Stuart Meacham, who lived on Franklin D. Roosevelt Drive in Manhattan, right on the East River. Mr. Meacham asked me what was the first thing I wanted to do in New York. I told him, to see the Statue of Liberty. I had always been fascinated by tall buildings and monuments.

We went across the water by ferry about noon. It was just the way I thought it would be, that big arm waving the torch high above everything. We walked up all those stairs to the very top, right in the crown. We looked out from the windows in the crown, and we could see for miles. When we went back down, Mr. Meacham took my picture at the foot of the statue.

I guess the statue should be a symbol of freedom. I would not want our young people to be so disillusioned that they couldn't feel a sense of awe about it. But I can't find myself getting overwhelmed. We are supposed to be loyal and dedicated and committed to what America stands for. But we are still being denied complete equality. We have to struggle to gain a little bit, and as soon as it seems we make some gains for all our sacrifices, there are new obstacles, and people trying to take away what little we have.

Certainly there is a degree of freedom in America that we can celebrate, but as long as a difference in your complexion or your background can be used against you, we still have a long way to go.

Interpretations

1. How was Parks influenced by her family (for example, by choices her mother made and by her grandfather's reaction to slavery)?

2. How do the writer's childhood and adult responses to the Statue of Liberty differ? What accounts for the difference?

3. Do you agree with the writer's assessment of the current "degree of freedom in America" (last two paragraphs)?

4. Explain the significance of the title.

Correspondences

1. Review the Baldwin perspective on choices. How does it apply to "A Long Way to Go"? Does Parks accept "being trapped in history"? Cite evidence for your answer.

2. As a student in sixth grade, Parks concludes that "what they taught us in school didn't apply to us as a race." How might her educational experience, that of Marshall and Rendón (Chapter 3), and that of Rodriguez, Novak, and Ota (Chapter 5) be used to convince educators of the need for a multicultural curriculum in American elementary schools? (Also cite evidence from your own experience.)

Applications

1. Which is the more courageous response to the violence of others, violence or nonviolence? Narrate an incident that illustrates your position. Use the third person.

2. Rosa Parks was arrested for civil disobedience. Is there a cause for which you too would be willing to break the law? Under what circumstances can you imagine making such a choice?

Leaving El Salvador

Gloria Bonilla

Gloria Bonilla (b. 1951) left the country in 1981, following a raid on her home by the military. She had studied sociology in El Salvador and went on to complete her master's degree in the United States. Her studies included a detailed study of Salvadoran immigrants in Washington, D.C., where she works as a legal aide. "Leaving El Salvador" is from You Can't Drown the Fire: Latin American Women Writing in Exile *(1988), a collection of essays, narratives, and poetry by Latinas who have experienced exile, torture, and even death.*

El Salvador, a Central American country of five million people, is about the size of Massachusetts. Since a military coup in 1979, the country has been involved in civil war. Complex politics have been compounded by foreign intervention, both overt and covert. While leftist guerrillas, armed by Cuba and Nicaragua, controlled parts of the country, mostly in the East, and extreme right-wing death squads were held responsible for over a thousand deaths in 1983, the Reagan administration supported the government with military aid. In 1990 the war entered its tenth year. Renewed death-squad activity has resulted in about 50,000 deaths.

January 4, 1988

I saw my friend Alicia this afternoon while I was at the post office waiting in line. We began chatting of things, projects, etc. The book, her deadline. El Salvador. Incredible! It has been almost seven years since I left. I have not been back since.
—Write something, write about your feelings—
It is so difficult to write, to think, to reflect on it. My experience. It is still painful to remember.

I FLED El Salvador, leaving behind my family and friends, my undergraduate studies, a job, and all short- and long-term personal goals, in April of 1981 to escape government persecution. In an effort to remain in the United States more than three months at one time, and map out bits and pieces of an unknown future, I was required to change my tourist visa to a student visa. Because the United States recognized then, and continues to recognize today, the government of El Salvador, I have been unable to enter the United States as a refugee, nor can I realistically expect to receive political asylum.

My story does not differ very much from the stories that most Salvadorans tell. I consider myself more fortunate because I did not have to cross the Mexican border and enter the United States illegally. I was also able to maintain a legal status which allows me to continue my education in the United States.

I think, like my parents, I have learned through life quite a bit. My father used to say that we never stop learning in life. He did not go to college. I remember him very much because most of what he knew he had learned on his own. My first recollections of the history of El Salvador were through my father and mother. That history was not in print.

My trip to the United States was sudden, precipitous. I, like many other Salvadorans, finally realized that El Salvador was no longer a safe place to live.

I arrived in Washington, D.C., in April of 1981. When I arrived, my good friend, John, was waiting for me at the airport, carrying a heavy coat, assuming I would have no winter clothing. I met John in El Salvador back in the seventies when he was a Peace Corps volunteer. After he came back to the United States, he kept in touch with me, until the political conditions in El Salvador reached serious and dangerous proportions. Then he invited me to come to the United States, an invitation which I did not decline, but which I postponed until I could no longer remain in El Salvador. One day, I called John from Guatemala to let him know I was on my way.

I knew no one in Washington except John, who sheltered me until I was able to support myself. John introduced me to his friends, some of whom are my friends still. As insiders, they helped me to become familiar with the United States. I am grateful for all their help.

A lot has happened since that moment on that spring day in 1981, when I arrived in the United States.

I underwent a metamorphosis. I went from a period of mutiny, in which I encapsulated myself like a larva in a cocoon, to a period of awakening and rebirth. The process was painful and difficult. But I survived. Because I left El Salvador so quickly, I hardly had the chance to reflect on what was happening. When I came to the United States, I carried with me my past, which tied me to people and a land that I had to give up.

There is no medicine to take care of heartache and homesickness—not even here in the United States where there are drugs for almost everything, mostly for pain. I believe we unconsciously or consciously develop methods to cope with those ailments. So, I made up a prescription of my own to help me stay sane and survive in my new niche. I filled my hours, my days, without respite, so I had no time to think, cry or break.

I forced myself to learn English. I took intensive English courses from 9:00 A.M. to 2:00 P.M. I worked in the afternoons. Later, I got a full-time job and I enrolled at the university, finished college and went straight for a master's degree in sociology. I did it all in five and a half years.

I did not do it alone, but with the support of friends. I had moments of despair in which I felt lost, with little or no hope. My driving force was that I had no relatives in Washington to look after me. Therefore, I could not afford to lose my most precious commodity, my mind. Some call it pride; for others it is survival instinct. I experienced both.

The United States Immigration and Naturalization Service regulates, controls, and restricts the free access of foreigners to society and subsequently to its benefits. For example, I had a legal status that allowed me to study and remain in the United States as long as I attended school full time. On the other hand, that same status forbade me to work and compete freely for jobs that I thought I was qualified for.

I maintained that legal status as long as I went to school full time. I paid my bills as long as I worked full time. I had no choice. My constant concerns were basic: food, shelter, education, legal status.

A legal status which allows an immigrant to work is an imperative. In my case, the choice was to apply for political asylum or for permanent residence. The best bet was permanent residence.

Political asylum, in the case of Salvadorans, becomes a dead end since U.S. immigration law requires the applicant to provide evidence of a well-founded fear of persecution. A subjective condition, when you think about it. For example, the army did not need any evidence to determine that I was a "suspicious individual," and to break into my home and my parents' home in 1981. Ironically, it is the same subjective reasoning used by a U.S. immigration judge that determines the non-eligibility of a Salvadoran for political asylum. Salvadorans in exile in the United States have been required to all but present a signed affidavit from their persecutors in order to prove their well-founded fear of persecution.

I believe I had good enough reasons to be granted political asylum back in 1981 if I had applied. But a U.S. judge might have disagreed with me, since I did not have concrete evidence of my fear of persecution. Worse, I came from a country whose government is friendly to the United States.

I eliminated the political asylum option from the very beginning. Salvadorans had, back in the early 1980s, little or no chance of having a political asylum application approved; later, it became pointless, since the Reagan administration had invested so much money "democratizing" El Salvador.

I am only an example of what Salvadorans could do if given the chance. In my case, maintaining a student visa gave me access to education, something most Salvadorans have not been able to attain. That is why Salvadorans in the United States hold occupations that require little or no formal education.

I think Salvadorans have tried their best to prove their worth. Our future in the United States does not look promising. Lawmakers had an opportunity to offer better conditions to Salvadorans. The Immigration Reform and Control Act proves it. The United States had a chance to review the law and to review the Central American question, but did not. I believe Salvadorans in the United States have been sentenced without trial. When you think about it, it is not very different from the way our people are treated in El Salvador.

Interpretations

1. Bonilla says she fled El Salvador because the army broke into her home and her parents' home in 1981. Does she tell enough about her situation to convince you that she deserves political asylum? If not, what further information do you need to make this judgment? Can you speculate as to why she didn't provide that information?

2. Characterize Bonilla's experiences since 1981. Does this essay emphasize the advantages or the disadvantages of her choice to flee to the United States? How?

3. Do you agree with Bonilla that the immigration law should be changed to allow immigrants on student visas to work? Why or why not?

4. What is Bonilla's purpose in writing this essay? How well does she achieve it? (If the essay falls short, suggest ways it might be strengthened.)

Correspondences

1. Bonilla chose to leave El Salvador to find greater personal and political freedom in the United States. For similar reasons, Parks chose *not* to leave the bus in Montgomery. What is ironic about their situation? Compare the ramifications of their choices.

2. Bonilla's entry into the United States would have been impossible without the help of her friend John, a former Peace Corps member. Review Mead's and Metraux's comment on American friendship (Chapter 2). To what degree does John fit the profile?

Applications

1. In the last paragraph of her essay, Bonilla states that the "future in the United States does not look promising" for Salvadorans. Do you think her pessimism is warranted? Why do you agree or not agree with her view?

2. "I did not do it alone, but with the support of friends. I had moments of despair in which I felt lost, with little or no hope. My driving force was that I had no relatives in Washington to look after me. Therefore, I could not afford to lose my most precious commodity, my mind. Some call it pride; for others it is survival instinct. I experienced both." Write a journal entry responding to this description by Bonilla of the consequences of her choice.

To the Border

Richard Rodriguez

Richard Rodriguez (b. 1944) is from San Francisco and the child of Spanish-speaking Mexican immigrants. He entered school with little knowledge of English but graduated with a Ph.D. in literature from the University of California at Berkeley. Rodriguez has received critical acclaim for his autobiography Hunger of Memory: The Education of Richard Rodriguez *(1982). In "To the Border," he focuses on the plight and perils of Mexicans who have illegally crossed the Mexican-American border or have been contracted to work as farm workers in the United States.*

For more information on Mexico and Mexican immigration to the United States see Gary Soto, "Looking for Work," Chapter 4.

YOU STAND around. You smoke. You spit. You are wearing your two shirts, two pants, two underpants. Jesús says if they chase you, throw that bag down. Your plastic bag is your mama, all you have left: the yellow cheese she wrapped has formed a transluscent rind; the laminated scapular of the Sacred Heart nestles flame in its cleft. Put it in your pocket. Inside. Put it in your underneath pants' pocket. The last hour of Mexico is twilight, the shuffling of feet. Jesús says they are able to see in the dark. They have X rays and helicopters and searchlights. Jesús says wait, just wait, till he says. Though most of the men have started to move. You feel the hand of Jesús clamp your shoulder, fingers cold as ice. *Venga, corre.*[1] You run. All the rest happens without words. Your feet are tearing dry grass, your heart is lashed like a mare. You trip, you fall. You are now in the United States of America. You are a boy from a Mexican village. You have come into the country on your knees with your head down. You are a man.

Papa, what was it like?

I am his second son, his favorite child, his confidant. After we have polished the De Soto, we sit in the car and talk. I am sixteen years old. I fiddle with the knobs of the radio. He is fifty.

He will never say. He was an orphan there. He had no mother, he remembered none. He lived in a village by the ocean. He wanted books and he had none.

[1]Go, run.

You are lucky, boy.

In the Fifties, Mexican men were contracted to work in America as *braceros*, farm workers. I saw them downtown in Sacramento. I saw men my age drunk in Plaza Park on Sundays, on their backs on the grass. I was a boy at sixteen, but I was an American. At sixteen, I wrote a gossip column, "The Watchful Eye," for my school paper.

Or they would come into town on Monday nights for the wrestling matches or on Tuesdays for boxing. They worked over in Yolo County. They were men without women. They were Mexicans without Mexico.

On Saturdays, they came into town to the Western Union office where they sent money—money turned into humming wire and then turned back into money—all the way down into Mexico. They were husbands, fathers, sons. They kept themselves poor for Mexico.

Much that I would come to think, the best I would think about male Mexico, came as much from those chaste, lonely men as from my own father who made false teeth and who—after thirty years in America—owned a yellow stucco house on the east side of town.

The male is responsible. The male is serious. A man remembers.

Fidel, the janitor at church, lived over the garage at the rectory. Fidel spoke Spanish and was Mexican. He had a wife down there, people said; some said he had grown children. But too many years had passed and he didn't go back. Fidel had to do for himself. Fidel had a clean piece of linoleum on the floor, he had an iron bed, he had a table and a chair. He had a coffeepot and a frying pan and a knife and a fork and a spoon, I guess. And everything else Fidel sent back to Mexico. Sometimes, on summer nights, I would see his head through the bars of the little window over the garage at the rectory.

The migration of Mexico is not only international, south to north. The epic migration of Mexico, and throughout Latin America, is from the village to the city. And throughout Latin America, the city has ripened, swollen with the century. Lima, Caracas, Mexico City. So the journey to Los Angeles is much more than a journey from Spanish to English. It is the journey from *tú*—the familiar, the erotic, the intimate pronoun—to the repellent *usted* of strangers' eyes.

It is 1986 and I am a journalist. I am asking questions of a Mexican women in her East L.A. house. She is watchful and pretty, in her thirties, she wears an apron. Her two boys—Roy and Danny—are playing next door. Her husband is a tailor. He is sewing in a bright bedroom at the back of the house. His feet work the humming treadle of an old Singer machine as he croons Mexican love songs by an open window.

I will send for you or I will come home rich.

Mexico is poor. But my mama says there are no love songs like the love songs of Mexico. She hums a song she can't remember. The ice cream there is creamier than here. Someday we will see. The people are kinder—poor, but kinder to each other.

My mother's favorite record is *"Mariachis de Mexico y Pepe Villa con Orquesta."*

Men sing in Mexico. Men are strong and silent. But in song the Mexican male is granted license he is otherwise denied. The male can admit longing, pain, desire.

HAIII—EEEE—a cry like a comet rises over the song. A cry like mock weeping tickles the refrain of Mexican love songs. The cry is meant to encourage the balladeer—it is the raw edge of his sentiment. HAIII-EEEE. It is the man's sound. A ticklish arching of semen, a node wrung up a guitar string, until it bursts in a descending cascade of mockery. HAI. HAI. HAI. HAI. The cry of a jackal under the moon, the whistle of the phallus, the maniacal song of the skull.

Mexico is on the phone—long-distance.

A crow alights upon a humming wire, bobs up and down, needles the lice within his vest, surveys with clicking eyes the field, the cloud of mites, then dips into the air and flies away.

Juanito killed! My mother shrieks, drops the phone in the dark. She cries for my father. For light.

The earth quakes. The peso flies like chaff in the wind. The police chief purchases his mistress a mansion on the hill.

The door bell rings. I split the blinds to see three nuns standing on our front porch.

Mama. Mama.

Monsignor Lyons has sent three Mexican nuns over to meet my parents. The nuns have come to Sacramento to beg for Mexico at the eleven o'clock Mass. We are the one family in the parish that speaks Spanish. As they file into our living room, the nuns smell pure, not sweet, pure like candles or like laundry.

The nun with a black mustache sighs at the end of each story the other two tell. Orphan. Leper. Crutch. Dry land. One eye. Casket.

¡Que lástima![2]
Tell me, Papa.

---

[2]What a pity!

What?

About Mexico.

I lived with the family of my uncle. I was the orphan in the village. I used to ring the church bells in the morning, many steps up in the dark. When I'd get up to the tower I could see the ocean.

The village, Papa, the houses too . . .

The ocean. He studies the polished hood of our beautiful blue De Soto.

Relatives invited relatives. Entire Mexican villages got re-created in three stories of a single house. In the fall, after the harvest in the Valley, families of Mexican adults and their American children would load up their cars and head back to Mexico in caravans, for weeks, for months. The schoolteacher said to my mother what a shame it was the Mexicans did that—took their children out of school.

Like Wandering Jews. They carried their home with them, back and forth; they had no true home but the tabernacle of memory.

Each year the American kitchen takes on a new appliance.

The children are fed and grow tall. They go off to school with children from Vietnam, from Kansas, from Hong Kong. They get into fights. They come home and they say dirty words.

The city will win. The city will give the children all the village could not—VCRs, hairstyles, drumbeat. The city sings mean songs, dirty songs. But the city will sing the children a great Protestant hymn.

You can be anything you want to be.

Your coming of age. It is early. From your bed you watch your mama moving back and forth under the light. The bells of the church ring in the dark. Mama crosses herself. From your bed you watch her back as she wraps the things you will take.

You are sixteen. Your father has sent for you. That's what it means. He has sent an address in Nevada. He is there with your uncle. You remember your uncle remembering snow with his beer.

You dress in the shadows. You move toward the table, the circle of light. You sit down. You force yourself to eat. Mama stands over you to make the sign of the cross on your forehead with her thumb. You are a man. You smile. She puts the bag of food in your hands. She says she has told *La Virgen.*

Then you are gone. It is gray. You hear a little breeze. It is the rustle of your old black Dueña, the dog, taking her shortcuts through the weeds, crazy Dueña, her pads on the dust. She is following you.

You pass the houses of the village, each window is a proper name. You pass the store. The bar. The lighted window of the clinic where the pale medical student from Monterrey lives alone and reads his book full of sores late into the night.

You want to be a man. You have the directions in your pocket: an address in Tijuana and a map with a yellow line that leads from the highway to an X on a street in Reno. You are afraid, but you have never seen snow.

You are just beyond the cemetery. The breeze has died. You turn and throw a rock back at La Dueña, where you know she is—where you will always know where she is. She will not go past the cemetery. She will turn in circles like a *loca*[3] and bite herself.

The dust takes on gravel, the path becomes a rutted road which leads to the highway. You walk north. The sky has turned white overhead. Insects click in the fields. In time, there will be a bus.

I will send for you or I will come home rich.

Interpretations

1. Who is the "you" in the first (and subsequent) sentence? What choice has been made?

2. What attitude did the sixteen-year-old Rodriguez have toward the Mexican farm workers he saw downtown in Sacramento? How far removed from their situation was his? (How does this account for his attitude?)

3. What attitude toward the United States is revealed by the last line of the essay?

4. The last vignette of this essay describes the beginning of a voyage from the known to the unknown: ". . . each window is a proper name." What are some of the "knowns" the Mexican boy is leaving? Why do you think Rodriguez chose to include each of them? What is their combined impact?

5. Rodriguez avoids a bald statement of his main point or thesis, apparently preferring to create a mood and force his reader to intuit meaning. What is the mood and the point?

Correspondences

1. "So the journey to Los Angeles is much more than a journey from Spanish to English. It is the journey from *tú*—the familiar, the erotic, the intimate pronoun—to the repellant *usted* of strangers' eyes." What is Rodriguez implying about the personal costs involved in "choosing" to cross the border? To what extent did Bonilla's decision to leave El Salvador involve similar costs?

2. "The male is responsible. The male is serious. A man remembers." What did Rodriguez learn from his male role models? How does his experience

---

[3]Crazy woman.

compare to that of Rendón (Chapter 3)? How did their mentors affect their choices?

Applications

1. Rodriguez writes that the Mexican migrant workers are "[l]ike Wandering Jews. They carried their home with them, back and forth; they had no true home but the tabernacle of memory." What is the meaning here of "tabernacle"? In what sense does memory serve as a refuge? At what price does one "choose" to become a migrant worker?

2. *"You can be anything you want to be."* Is this belief a realistic basis on which to choose to emigrate to the United States? Does the United States offer this possibility to all of its citizens? Write an essay stating specific reasons for your point of view.

The Moment Before the Gun Went Off

Nadine Gordimer

Nadine Gordimer (b. 1923) was born in Johannesburg, South Africa, and educated at the University of Witwatersrand. She is the renowned author of nine novels and eight volumes of short stories, the recipient of numerous international awards, and an outspoken critic of South African apartheid policies. Her most recent novel is A Sport of Nature *(1987).*

Apartheid (apartness) became law in South Africa in 1948; under it blacks and those of mixed race (coloreds) live separately from whites and have been forced into overcrowded and poverty-stricken townships.

For more information on South Africa see Mtutuzeli Matshoba, "Call Me Not a Man," in Chapter 5.

MARAIS VAN DER VYVER shot one of his farm laborers, dead. An accident, there are accidents with guns every day of the week—children playing a fatal game with a father's revolver in the cities where guns are domestic objects, nowadays, hunting mishaps like this one, in the country—but these won't be reported all over the world. Van der Vyver knows his will be. He knows that the story of the Afrikaner farmer—regional leader of the National Party and commandant of the local security commando—shooting a black man who worked for him will fit exactly *their* version of South Africa, it's made for them. They'll be able to use it in their boycott and divestment campaigns, it'll be another piece of evidence in their truth about the country. The papers at home will quote the story as it has appeared in the overseas press, and in the back and forth he and the black man will become those crudely drawn figures on anti-apartheid banners, units in statistics of white brutality against blacks quoted at the United Nations—he, whom they will gleefully be able to call "a leading member" of the ruling Party.

People in the farming community understand how he must feel. Bad enough to have killed a man, without helping the Party's, the government's, the country's enemies as well. They see the truth of that. They know, reading the Sunday papers, that when Van der Vyver is quoted saying he is "terribly shocked," he will "look after the wife and children," none of those Americans and English, and none of those people at home who want to destroy the white man's power will believe him. And how they will sneer when he even says of the farm boy (according to one paper, if you can trust any of those reporters), "He was my friend, I always took him hunting with me." Those city and overseas people don't know it's true: farmers usually have one particular black boy they like to take along with them in the lands; you could call it a kind of friend, yes, friends are not only your own white people, like yourself, whom you take into your house, pray with in church, and work with on the Party committee. But how can those others know that? They don't want to know it. They think all blacks are like the bigmouth agitators in town. And Van der Vyver's face in the photographs, strangely opened by distress—everyone in the district remembers Marais Van der Vyver as a little boy who would go away and hide himself if he caught you smiling at him, and everyone knows him now as a man who hides any change of expression round his mouth behind a thick, soft mustache, and in his eyes by always looking at some object in hand, a leaf or a crop fingered, pen or stone picked up, while concentrating on what he is saying, or while listening to you. It just goes to show what shock can do; when you look at the newspaper photographs you feel like apologizing, as if you had stared in on some room where you should not be.

There will be an inquiry; there had better be, to stop the assumption of yet another case of brutality against farm workers, although there's nothing in doubt—an accident, and all the facts fully admitted by Van der Vyver. He made a statement when he arrived at the police station with the dead man in his *bakkie*. Captain Beetge knows him well, of course; he gave him brandy. He was shaking, this big, calm, clever son of Willem Van der Vyver, who inherited the old man's best farm. The black was stone dead, nothing to be done for him. Beetge will not tell anyone that after the brandy Van der Vyver wept. He sobbed, snot running onto his hands, like a dirty kid. The captain was ashamed for him, and walked out to give him a chance to recover himself.

Marais Van der Vyver left his house at three in the afternoon to cull a buck from the family of kudu he protects in the bush areas of his farm. He is interested in wildlife and sees it as the farmers' sacred duty to raise game as well as cattle. As usual, he called at his shed to pick up Lucas, a twenty-year-old farmhand who had shown mechanical aptitude and whom Van der Vyver himself had taught to maintain tractors and other farm machinery. He hooted, and Lucas followed the familiar routine, jumping onto the back of the truck. He liked to travel standing up there, spotting game before his employer did. He would lean forward, bracing against the cab below him.

Van der Vyver had a rifle and .30 caliber ammunition beside him in the cab. The rifle was one of his father's, because his own was at the gunsmith's in town. Since his father died (Beetge's sergeant wrote "passed on") no one had used the rifle, and so when he took it from a cupboard he was sure it was not loaded. His father had never allowed a loaded gun in the house, he himself had been taught since childhood never to ride with a loaded weapon in a vehicle. But this gun was loaded. On a dirt track, Lucas thumped his fist on the cab roof three times to signal: look left. Having seen the white-ripple-marked flank of a kudu, and its fine horns raking through disguising bush, Van der Vyver drove rather fast over a pothole. The jolt fired the rifle. Upright, it was pointing straight through the cab roof at the head of Lucas. The bullet pierced the roof and entered Lucas's brain by way of his throat.

That is the statement of what happened. Although a man of such standing in the district, Van der Vyver had to go through the ritual of swearing that it was the truth. It has gone on record, and will be there in the archive of the local police station as long as Van der Vyver lives, and beyond that, through the lives of his children, Magnus, Helena, and Karel—unless things in the country get worse, the example of black mobs in the town spreads to the rural areas and the place is burned down as many urban police stations have been. Because nothing the government can do will appease the agitators and the whites who encourage them. Nothing satisfies them, in the cities: blacks can sit and drink in white hotels now, the Immorality Act has gone, blacks can sleep with whites . . . It's not even a crime anymore.

Van der Vyver has a high, barbed security fence round his farmhouse and garden which his wife, Alida, thinks spoils completely the effect of her artificial stream with its tree ferns beneath the jacarandas. There is an aerial soaring like a flagpole in the backyard. All his vehicles, including the truck in which the black man died, have aerials that swing their whips when the driver hits a pothole: they are part of the security system the farmers in the district maintain, each farm in touch with every other by radio, twenty-four hours out of twenty-four. It has already happened that infiltrators from over the border have mined remote farm roads, killing white farmers and their families out on their own property for a Sunday picnic. The pothole could have set off a land mine, and Van der Vyver might have died with his farm boy. When neighbors use the communications system to call up and say they are sorry about "that business" with one of Van der Vyver's boys, there goes unsaid: it could have been worse.

It is obvious from the quality and fittings of the coffin that the farmer has provided money for the funeral. And an elaborate funeral means a great deal to blacks; look how they will deprive themselves of the little they have, in their lifetime, keeping up payments to a burial society so they won't go in boxwood to an unmarked grave. The young wife is pregnant (of course) and another little one, a boy wearing red shoes several sizes too large, leans under her jutting belly. He is too young to understand what has happened, what he is witnessing that day, but neither whines nor plays about; he is solemn without knowing why. Blacks expose small children to everything, they don't protect them from the sight of fear and pain the way whites do theirs. It is the young wife who rolls her head and cries like a child, sobbing on the breast of this relative and that. All present work for Van der Vyver or are the families of those who work; in the weeding and harvest seasons, the women and children work for him too, carried at sunrise to the fields, wrapped in their blankets, on a truck, singing. The dead man's mother is a woman who can't be more than in her late thirties (they start bearing children at puberty), but she is heavily mature in a black dress, standing between her own parents, who were already working for old Van der Vyver when Marais, like their daughter, was a child. The parents hold her as if she were a prisoner or a crazy woman to be restrained. But she says nothing, does nothing. She does not look up; she does not look at Van der Vyver, whose gun went off in the truck, she stares at the grave. Nothing will make her look up; there need be no fear that she will look up, at him. His wife, Alida, is beside him. To show the proper respect, as for any white funeral, she is wearing the navy blue and cream hat she wears to church this summer. She is always supportive, although he doesn't seem to notice it; this coldness and reserve— his mother says he didn't mix well as a child—she accepts for herself but regrets that it has prevented him from being nominated, as he should be, to stand as the Party's parliamentary candidate for the district. He does not let her clothing, or that of anyone else gathered closely, make contact with him. He, too, stares at the grave. The dead man's mother and he stare at the grave in communication like that between the black man outside and the white man inside the cab the moment before the gun went off.

The moment before the gun went off was a moment of high excitement shared through the roof of the cab, as the bullet was to pass, between the young black man outside and the white farmer inside the vehicle. There were such moments, without explanation, between them, although often around the farm the farmer would pass the young man without returning a greeting, as if he did not recognize him. When the bullet went off what Van der Vyver saw was the kudu stumble in fright at the report and gallop away. Then he heard the thud behind him, and past the window saw the young man fall out of the vehicle. He was sure he had leapt up and toppled—in fright, like the buck. The farmer was almost laughing with relief, ready to tease, as he opened his door, it did not seem possible that a bullet passing through the roof could have done harm.

The young man did not laugh with him at his own fright. The farmer carried him in his arms, to the truck. He was sure, sure he could not be dead. But the young black man's blood was all over the farmer's clothes, soaking against his flesh as he drove.

How will they ever know, when they file newspaper clippings, evidence, proof, when they look at the photographs and see his face—guilty! guilty! they are right!—how will they know, when the police stations burn with all the evidence of what has happened now, and what the law made a crime in the past? How could they know that *they do not know*. Anything. The young black callously shot through the negligence of the white man was not the farmer's boy; he was his son.

Interpretations

1. From whose point of view is the story told? How and why does the author put the reader in an awkward position?

2. How does Van der Vyver's wife view her husband's emotional state?

3. Why will the captain not tell anyone that Van der Vyver wept? How does his weeping confirm or refute his wife's opinion of him?

4. What is ironic about the statement that "blacks can sleep with whites now"?

5. What important choices has Van der Vyver made in the past? What does he now face as a result?

Correspondences

1. Gordimer's protagonist assumes financial responsibility for the family of the young man he shot accidentally. How did this affect your view of him? (Would he have done this had he not also been his illegitimate son? Why or why not?) What does this story and the essays by Parks and Bonilla suggest about the *consequences* of choices?

2. To what extent is Gordimer's South Africa patriarchal? What is the evidence? How does her portrayal of patriarchy compare to that of Rodriguez in "To the Border"?

Applications

1. Write an essay analyzing the public and private lives of Van der Vyver. To what extent was his public life the result of a personal choice?

2. Study the life and career of one of the following South Africans: Nelson Mandela, Winnie Mandela, Nadine Gordimer, Athol Fugard, Stephen Biko, Bishop Desmond Tutu, or Donald Woods. Then write an analysis of the factors behind your subject's choice to fight apartheid.

A Tale of Two Moralities

Peter Berger

Peter Ludwig Berger (b. 1929) was born in Vienna, Austria, and emigrated to the United States in 1946. He received his Ph.D. in 1954 from the New School for Social Research and has taught at several major universities, among them Brooklyn College of the City University of New York and Rutgers University. His publications include The Homeless Mind: Modernization and Consciousness *(1973),* Pyramids of Sacrifice: Political Ethics and Change *(1974), and* To Empower People: The Role of Mediating Structures in Public Policy *(1977). In the following selection, Berger examines some ethical and cultural dilemmas that commonly confront many Mexican immigrants in the United States.*

For more information about Mexican-Americans see headnote on Rendon page 163.

MANUELA KEEPS DREAMING about the village. She does not think about it very much in the daytime. Even when she thinks about Mexico, it is not usually about the village. In any case, during the day it is the brash, gleaming reality of California that dominates, its loud demand for full attention pushing into the background the old images and feelings. It is at night that the village comes back, reclaiming its power over Manuela. It is then as if she had never left it—or, worse, as if she must inevitably return to it.

It is often very hot in the village, though at night one may freeze. The earth is dry. Time moves very slowly, as the white clouds move through the brightly blue sky over the brown and arid hills. Time moves slowly in the faces of the people, too, and the faces too are brown and arid. Even the faces of the very young seem to hold old memories. The children do not smile easily. The day is measured by the halting motion of shadows over houses and trees. The years are mostly measured by calamities. The past is powerfully present, although there are few words for it. No one in the village speaks an Indian language, though everyone has Indian blood. Can the blood speak, without words? Do the dead speak from the earth? Somewhere in this blue sky and in these brown hills there are very old presences, more threatening than consoling. Some years ago the schoolteacher dug up some Indian artifacts and wanted to take them to the city, to sell them to a museum. Calamity struck at once, all over the village. The dead do not want to be disturbed, and they are dangerous.

The village is distant. Distant from what? Distant from everything, but most importantly distant from the places where time moves quickly and purposefully. There is no paved road, no telephone, no electricity. Even the schoolteacher only comes on two days of the week. He has two other villages to take care of, and he lives somewhere else. To get to the nearest bus station one rides on a donkey for three hours over footpaths of trampled dirt. Time and distance determine the world of the village, in fact and in Manuela's dreams. If she were to put it in one sentence, this world, she would have to say: It is very far away, and life there moves very slowly. On the maps the village is in the state of Guerrero, in a very specific location between Mexico City and the Pacific Ocean. In Manuela's dreams the village is located in the center of her self, deep down inside rather than out there somewhere.

Manuela was born in the village twenty-two years ago. Her mother died shortly afterward. Her father, already married to another woman with seven legitimate children, never acknowledged Manuela. Indeed, he has never spoken with her. She was raised by one of her mother's brothers, a man without land and much of the time without work, with a large family of his own that he barely managed to support. There was never any question about the family obligation to take care of Manuela; the only question at the time, lengthily discussed by her grandfather and the three uncles still living in the area, was which of the three would take the baby in. But this obligation did not greatly exceed supplying the bare necessities of life. There was never the slightest doubt about Manuela's status in her uncle's household as the unwanted bastard who took the food out of the mouths of her more deserving cousins—and she was told so in no uncertain terms on many occasions. If there was little food, she would be the hungriest. If there was hard work, she would be the one to do it. This does not mean that she received no affection. She was a very pretty, winsome child, and often people were kind to her. But she always knew that affection and kindness were not her right, were given to her gratuitously—and, by the same token, could be gratuitously taken away again. As a child Manuela wished for someone who would love her all the time, reliably, "officially." However, she was only dimly unhappy in her uncle's household, since she knew nothing else. She was often hungry, sometimes beaten. She did not have shoes until her tenth birthday, when her grandfather made her a present of a pair. This was also the first occasion when she went outside the village, accompanying her grandfather on a visit to the doctor in the nearest town.

Her grandfather and one of her uncles in the village were *ejidatários*, belonging to the minority that owned parcels of land under the village *ejido* (agricultural cooperative). Most of the time the uncle with whom she stayed worked on this land, too, though he would hire himself out for work elsewhere when there was an opportunity. When she was not working in the house or taking care of her little cousins, Manuela also worked in the fields or with the animals belonging to her family. After her tenth birthday she sometimes worked for outsiders, but she was expected to turn over the money she received for this. Sometimes she succeeded in keeping a few coins for herself, though she knew that she would be beaten if found out. She was allowed to go to school and, being very bright, she learned to read and write well. It was her brightness that attracted her grandfather, who was amused by her and took a liking to her (much to the annoyance of her cousins).

"Bad blood will show." "You will come to no good end, like your mother." Manuela must have heard this hundreds of times during her childhood. The prophecy was fulfilled when she was fifteen and made pregnant by the secretary of the *ejido,* one of the most affluent farmers in the village. When her condition could no longer be concealed, there was a terrible scene and her uncle threw her out of the house. Her grandfather, after slapping her a couple of times rather mildly, gave her the address of an aunt in Acapulco and enough money to pay her busfare there. It was thus that she left the village.

Manuela marveled at Acapulco and its astonishing sights, but, needless to say, she lived there in a world far removed from that experienced by the tourists. Her aunt, a gentle widow with two children and a maid's job in one of the big hotels, took Manuela in very warmly (at least in part because she could use some help in the house). Manuela's baby was born there, a healthy boy whom she named Roberto. Not much later Manuela also started to work outside the house.

A Mexican *campesino,* when he migrates, normally follows an itinerary taken before him by relatives and *compadres.* When he arrives, the latter provide an often intricate network of contacts that are indispensable for his adjustment to the new situation. They will often provide initial housing, they can give information and advice, and, perhaps most important, they serve as an informal labor exchange. Such a network awaited Manuela in Acapulco. In addition to the aunt she was staying with, there were two more aunts and an uncle with their respective families, including some twelve cousins of all ages. This family system, of course, was transposed to the city life from the village, but it took on a quite different character in the new context. Freed from the oppressive constraints of village life, the system, on the whole, was more benign. Manuela experienced it as such. Several of her cousins took turns taking care of little Roberto when Manuela started to work. Her aunt's "fiancé" (a somewhat euphemistic term), who was head clerk in the linen supply department of the hotel, found Manuela a job in his department. The uncle, through a *compadre* who was head waiter in another hotel, helped her get a job there as a waitress. It was this uncle, incidentally, who had gone further than any other member of the Acapulco clan, at least for a brief time. An intelligent and aggressive man, he worked himself up in the municipal sanitation department to the rank of inspector. Through a coup, the details of which were shrouded in mystery but which were safely assumed by everyone to involve illegality of heroic proportions, Uncle Pepe amassed the equivalent of about one thousand U.S. dollars in a few months' time, a staggering sum in this ambience. With this money he set out for Mexico City, ostensibly to look into a business proposition. In fact he checked into one of the capital's finest hotels, made the rounds of nightclubs and luxury brothels, and returned penniless but not overly unhappy a month later. The clan has viewed him with considerable awe ever since.

Manuela now had a fairly steady cash income, modest to be sure, but enough to keep going. This does not mean, however, that she could keep all of it for herself and her child. The family system operated as a social insurance agency as well as a labor exchange, and there was never a shortage of claimants. An aunt required an operation. An older cousin set up business as a mechanic and needed some capital to start off. Another cousin was arrested and a substantial *mordida* was required to bribe his way out of jail. And then there were always new calamities back in the village, requiring emergency transfers of money back there. Not least among them was the chronic calamity of grandfather's kidney ailment, which consumed large quantities of family funds in expensive and generally futile medical treatments.

Sometimes, at the hotel, Manuela did baby-sitting for tourists with children. It was thus that she met the couple from California. They stayed in Acapulco for a whole month, and soon Manuela took care of their little girl almost daily. When they left the woman asked Manuela whether she wanted a job as a maid in the States. "Yes," replied Manuela at once, without thinking. The arrangements were made quickly. Roberto was put up with a cousin. Uncle Pepe, through two trusted intermediaries, arranged for Manuela to cross the border illegally. Within a month she arrived at the couple's address in California.

And now she has been here for over a year. California was even more astonishing than Acapulco had been when she first left the village, but now she had more time to explore this new world. She learned English in a short time and, in the company of a Cuban girl who worked for a neighbor, she started forays into the American universe, in ever-wider circles from her employers' house. She even took bus trips to Hollywood and San Francisco. For the first time in her life she slept in a room all by herself. And, despite her regular payments for Roberto's keep, she started to save money and put it in a bank account. Most important, she started to think about her life in a new way, systematically. "What will become of you when you go back?" asked the American woman one day. Manuela did not know then, but she started to think. Carmelita, the Cuban girl, discussed the matter with her many times—in exchange for equal attention paid to her own planning exercises. Eventually, one project won out over all the alternatives: Manuela would return to go to commercial school, to become a bilingual secretary. She even started a typing course in California. But she would not return to Acapulco. She knew that, to succeed, she would have to remove herself from the family there. She would go to Mexico City, first alone, and then she would send for Roberto.

This last decision was made gradually. It was the letters that did it. Manuela, some months before, had mentioned the amount of money she had saved (a very large amount, by her standards, and enough to keep her and Roberto afloat for the duration of the commercial course). Then the letters started coming from just about everyone in the Acapulco clan. Most of the contents were family gossip, inquiries about Manuela's life in the States, and long expressions of affectionate feelings. There were frequent reminders not to forget her relatives, who took such good care of Roberto. Only gradually did the economic infrastructure emerge from all this: There was to be a *fiesta* at the wedding of a cousin, and could Manuela make a small contribution. The cousin who had been in jail was still to be tried, and there were lawyer's expenses. Uncle Pepe was onto the most promising business opportunity of his "long and distinguished career in financial activities" (his own words), and just three hundred American dollars would make it possible for him to avail himself of this never-to-recur opportunity—needless to say, Manuela would be a full partner upon her return. Finally, there was even a very formal letter from grandfather, all the way from the village, containing an appeal for funds to pay for a trip to the capital so as to take advantage of a new treatment that a famous doctor had developed there. It took a while for Manuela to grasp that every dollar of her savings had already been mentally spent by her relatives.

The choice before Manuela now is sharp and crystal-clear: She must return to Mexico—because she wants to, because of Roberto, and because the American authorities would send her back there sooner or later anyway. She can then return to the welcoming bosom of the family system, surrender her savings, and return to her previous way of life. Or she can carry through her plan in the face of family opposition. The choice is not only between two courses of action, but between two moralities. The first course is dictated by the morality of collective solidarity, the second by the morality of personal autonomy and advancement. Each morality condemns the other—as uncaring selfishness in the former case, as irresponsible disregard of her own potential and the welfare of her son in the latter. Poor Manuela's conscience is divided; by now she is capable of feeling its pangs either way.

She is in America, not in Mexico, and the new morality gets more support from her immediate surroundings. Carmelita is all for the plan, and so are most of the Spanish-speaking girls with whom Manuela has been going out. Only one, another Mexican, expressed doubt: "I don't know. Your grandfather is ill, and your uncle helped you a lot in the past. Can you just forget them? I think that one must always help one's relatives." Manuela once talked about the matter with the American woman. "Nonsense," said the latter, "you should go ahead with your plan. You owe it to yourself and to your son." So this is what Manuela intends to do, very soon now. But she is not at ease with the decision. Every time another letter arrives from Mexico, she hesitates before opening it, and she fortifies herself against the appeals she knows to be there.

Each decision, as dictated by the respective morality, has predictable consequences: If Manuela follows the old morality, she will, in all likelihood, never raise herself or her son above the level she achieved in Acapulco—not quite at the bottom of the social scale, but not very far above it. If, on the other hand, she decides in accordance with the new morality (new for her, that is), she has at least a chance of making it up one important step on that scale. Her son will benefit from this, but probably no other of her relatives will. To take that step she must, literally, hack off all those hands that would hold her back. It is a grim choice indeed.

What will Manuela do? She will probably at least start out on her plan. Perhaps she will succeed. But once she is back in Mexico, the tentacles of the old solidarity will be more powerful. They will pull more strongly. It will be harder to escape that other village, the village of the mind within herself. The outcome of the struggle will decide whether the village will be Manuela's past or also her future. Outside observers should think very carefully indeed before they take sides in this contest.

Interpretations

1. What is Berger's purpose in telling this story?

2. What is your reaction to the main features of life in "the village"? Do you find them appealing? Why or why not?

3. As a result "of telling her relatives how much money she had saved," why is Manuela faced not just with two choices but two moralities. What are they? Have you ever faced these two moralities? Do you think you made the right choice? Why? If Manuela had not mentioned the amount of her savings in her letters, would she still be faced with this dilemma?

4. Berger gives us an opportunity to take sides in this "contest," but warns us too to think carefully beforehand. Which side do you take and why? To what extent do you share Manuela's sense of responsibility to family?

5. "A Tale of Two Moralities" is fiction. How can fiction sometimes be "truer" than nonfiction? Is such the case with this "tale"? How?

Correspondences

1. Manuela must choose between two moralities—her obligation to herself (the newfound morality of the United States) and her obligation to her family (the "old" morality of the Third World). What aspects of her choice are the most difficult? How does her choice compare to that of Bonilla or Glickman?

2. "The outcome of the struggle will decide whether the village will be Manuela's past or also her future." How will Manuela's personal and traditional

associations influence her choice? Might she agree with Reid (Chapter 5) that "The landscapes of childhood are irreplaceable, since they have been the backdrop for so many epiphanies, so many realizations"? What epiphanies (*see* Glossary) and realizations did Manuela experience?

Applications

1. Watch the film *El Norte*. What does it add to your understanding of Manuela's "two moralities" and of the dangers involved in border crossings? What other insights did you gain?

2. Where does responsibility to family end and responsibility to oneself begin? How are your family's needs and expectations similar to or different from those of Manuela? Write an essay comparing family responsibilities in Manuela's culture(s) with those of most families in the United States.

The Impossible Became No Longer Unthinkable

Hana Wehle

Hana Wehle (b. 1917) was born in Czechoslovakia. She is a survivor of the Theresienstadt, Auschwitz, and Stutthof concentration camps. After the defeat of the Nazis in 1945, she returned to Czechoslovakia, where she remarried. In 1951, she and her husband, also a survivor of Auschwitz, emigrated to the United States. She has published several essays about her concentration camp experiences. This is how she describes her purpose in writing "The Impossible Became No Longer Unthinkable":

> *This piece is about choices made in the alien universe of the concentration camp. I feel compelled to bear witness at every possible opportunity, so that such madness as the Holocaust will not occur again. Since the responses of the Free World during that period were either silence or inaction resulting in the death of millions, I want to address especially the generation born after World War II. It is they who will be responsible for choices made in the future.*

Prague, the capital of Czechoslovakia, has been a cultural center of the Holy Roman Empire and then of the Austro-Hungarian Empire at least since the fourteenth century, but the nation of Czechoslovakia was born almost at the same time as Wehle. A provisional government set up during World War I in 1914 proclaimed the new republic in 1918, a month before the end of World War I. It emerged from that war a stable democracy to soon enjoy recognition as an industrial and technological leader. However, in 1939 Hitler overran and dissolved Czechoslovakia, and he began to implement the "Final Solution"—systematic extermination of Jews. Soviet troops entered the country in 1944 and in 1948 Communists seized power. A harsh period of Stalinist rule followed. All political opposition was suppressed except for a brief period of democratization under Alexander Dubček in 1968 known as the "Prague Spring." When Warsaw Pact nations invaded Czechoslovakia seven months later and reimposed a hard-line Communist government, forty thousand Czechs fled. In 1989 a new chapter opened in Czechoslovakia's tumultuous history when street demonstrations and events in neighboring Poland, Hungary, and East Germany brought down the Communist government and chose as head of state Vaclav Havel, a distinguished playwright who had spent several years in prison for his outspoken opposition to the Soviet-dominated government.

IN MAY 1942, Anna, then 25 years old, together with her husband Peter and his elderly parents, was deported by the Germans from her home in Prague to the Ghetto Theresienstadt[1] in the northern part of Bohemia.

With this deportation their old world was demolished and a new, incomprehensible world was thrust upon them which uprooted and completely dislocated them from any habitual way of life.

The "Ghettoization" process of Anna and her family began immediately after their arrival, when they were separated and dispatched to various living quarters throughout the Ghetto. Anna was assigned to work in the Ghetto laundry, while Peter was assigned to the registration of new arrivals. Peter's parents, being over the working age limit, were mostly confined to their living places. After work, Peter, Anna, or both tried to visit them as often as possible. The young couple managed to warm their lonely existence either with some news which at the time was circulating in the Ghetto, or they all would pull out from the recesses of their memories some precious recollections from the past. [At] other times they would satisfy their empty stomachs by talking about the delicious meals they had eaten at home—the place they had loved and lost.

Gradually, life in the Ghetto took on a certain routine of fending off hunger and disease. With the constantly incoming transports, the average population of 35,000 swelled in the summer of 1942 to 50,000. The barracks and houses were filled to overflowing and sanitary conditions worsened every day, causing a dysentery epidemic which added to the already unbearable situation.

In the height of the summer, the streets were dotted with the dead and dying. Soon also Peter's father became one of the victims. The family gathered in the dark, overcrowded room where a small bulb shed a dim pool of light on his body lying on the wooden floor. In spite of the room's stifling air, the skin of this kind man seemed to glow with relief and peace. The mourning scene lost its usual significance or rather assumed a different one. It was only

---

[1]Theresienstadt before the war served as a garrison town with a capacity of about 3,500 soldiers housed in several barracks, scattered amidst some 200 houses. The town was built as a fortress almost three centuries ago by the Austrian Emperor Joseph the Second, who named it after his mother Maria Theresa.

The new history of Theresienstadt began in 1941, when the Nazis transformed the town into a Ghetto for the Jews deported there from the German occupied lands in Europe. By the end of that year, under the label "Resettlement," trains from all over Europe began to converge on the Ghettos and death camps. On the one hand, Jews were deported to Poland, which became a mass execution ground for them, on the other hand, the Nazis established a grotesque "Model Ghetto" in Theresienstadt where they practiced the greatest art of deception. They actually succeeded in keeping alive the concept of "The Settlement of the Jews," as they called it for the visits of foreign observers, in order to conceal from the world their plan of isolation, deportation and finally extermination of the European Jews.

Peter's mother, a tiny, pious woman, clutching in her gnarled fingers a worn-out prayer book, who submerged herself in silent prayer.[2]

Slowly the autumn colors blended into the monotonous landscape of the Ghetto and there was a shiver of the coming winter in the air. The transports, dispatched from Theresienstadt to the East in irregular intervals, became one of the most important and sinister features of the Ghetto life, which soon took on energy of its own only between the incoming and outgoing transports.

In December, Christmas bells were tolling "Peace on Earth" in the Christian world, while in the Jewish world in Theresienstadt, the ever-present threat of deportation to the extermination camps in Poland posed [sic] like a descending pendulum above the pit of the Ghetto. Whenever the summonses for the deportation were distributed, an ominous panic permeated the desperate population. Life almost ceased to exist and began to tick again only for those "lucky" ones who were, for the time being, permitted to still dwell in the misery of Theresienstadt.

When the pale March sun melted the last vestiges of snow, Anna's mother arrived in the Ghetto as well. Now the endless fearful expectation which accompanied every incoming transport was over. Anna met her mother in a dense concentration of bewildered people. Both tried to smile at each other through tears tinted with tenderness and sadness. But there was no time for tears in this merciless place. Soon her mother was led away together with a group of other women and assigned to a dwelling space in a barrack not too far away from Anna's.

The very next day Anna's mother was marched off in a group of working women to a part-time job as a cleaning person for the women's lavatories. Anna thought at first that it was remarkable how her mother, whose husband and son had been deported already in January, 1941, to Riga in Estonia, stoically adapted herself to the new, unfamiliar circumstances. However, within a very short time, Anna noticed with great concern how this once handsome woman who used to return from brisk morning walks in the countryside with gleaming red cheeks, had suddenly aged and how her almost wrinkle-free face had become shrunken and pale. She had loved nature and after her walks she would enthusiastically talk about the rising sun, birds, and flowers which had greeted her on her way. Then, Anna remembered her retreats to the "salon," as she called the room where she surrounded herself with books. Often she would recite poems by Goethe, Schiller, and Heine in German which Anna, to the annoyance of her mother, could not understand. "I hope you will learn German one day," she would say, "so you will be able to enjoy these classics!" It was ironic that for Anna's mother German literature was the source of ethical and moral inspiration which she faithfully

---

[2]Since the death of hundreds of inmates daily occurred in the Ghetto at that time, the event of one death became almost part of everyday life.

transmitted to her children; many of her quotations became engraved in Anna's memory and formed a lasting link to her happy childhood.

It was almost a year since Anna, Peter, and his parents had arrived in Theresienstadt and two months after the arrival of her mother. In the Ghetto, days sank into the past, washing away the hopes they cradled in their hearts. Things turned out very differently from what they expected.

One day in April, Anna was on her way to her mother. The sun was already sliding behind the arches of the courtyard, when she was about to enter the gate of the barrack. Suddenly, an SS man driving a tractor flashed out of the yard—and was gone. After the gray cloud of dust settled behind him, Anna, somewhat perturbed, spotted a group of people in one of the arches. Curiously she turned into the yard and headed toward them. Already from some distance she heard their agitated voices blaming the driver of the tractor for deliberately hitting the stricken man in their midst. With apprehension she joined the group of onlookers.

On the blood-stained cobblestones worn to smoothness by the feet of centuries was a torn leather coat shielding the crushed body of a man. Startled, Anna was about to lean forward when her body froze midway and her eyes signaled something awful, something so dark and chilling. . . . She looked down on the blood-covered body of—her Peter. "He is dead!" she gasped. But it took a while for her numbed senses to grasp the meaning of her words. The whole world sank before her eyes. . . .

In the semi-darkness of her room Peter's mother was waiting. Anna looked into the deeply lined face with a terrifying silence. It took more courage than she could command to produce some reassuring words. "Her only son is dead and his mother still lives," Anna contemplated; "she must be made whole if at all possible." With a great effort Anna produced a faint smile that was rather close to tears. But suddenly there was a new gravity in her face and tears, hot like molten iron brimmed over, and she began to tell the horrible truth. The color drained from Peter's mother's face leaving it as white as her hair. Her eyes looked as if all life had vanished out of them. With both hands she covered her face and muttered: "Dead? Peter dead? He can't be dead! All that can't be true!" Her voice broke, not her words only but the agony in her voice laid bare her torment.

Had the circumstances surrounding Peter's death been less horrifying, Anna might have recovered more quickly. But the nightmarish event of that day was seared deep in her memory. She missed Peter terribly; her mind turned again and again to the incredible fact that he was dead. Despite her own grief Anna also grieved for her mother-in-law. If Peter's dying could do this to her, what must it have done to his mother! With all her will, Anna tried to pour out love toward this devastated woman, even though his going had created a gap so huge that she herself did not know how they could go on without him.

A cluster of three broken women was all that was left. Weeks went by, then months before Anna could begin again to harness her energy toward their survival. She could not permit herself to dwell only on that awful past, since the tide of a new battle was closing in on them. For some reason during the next few months there were no transports leaving Theresienstadt, but on September 1, 1943, the illusion of safety abruptly ended and the deportations to the East resumed. The prisoners of the Ghetto did not know what the destination "East" really meant since information about Auschwitz, crematoria and gas chambers was still a well-guarded German secret.[3] However, even though the official version was that the transports were heading for some labor camps in the East, there was an uneasy foreboding in the air and everyone feared the worst.

In the evening of the first of September, the dreaded summonses were distributed throughout the Ghetto. This time Anna's mother was one of the recipients as well. Troubled, Anna inspected the fateful slip. Then she tried to read her mother's deep-seeing eyes resting intensely upon her. Never had she seen her mother crushed like this; nor could she face her mother-in-law's forsaken look. At that moment more than ever Anna felt that her life was no longer her own. Time was running out and a decision had to be made.

Hoping against hope that she might be able to give some assistance to her mother, Anna murmured more to herself: "I cannot let you go alone!" Then with a sense of guilt she looked at her mother-in-law who was visibly shaken. Her quivering chin produced a slow movement of her colorless lips: "I will go with you wherever you go; just don't leave me here alone," she pleaded with almost childlike fear. Anna blinked to hide her tears and her thoughts turned inward. How could she expose this fragile woman to the terrifying unknown awaiting her mother and her? Through the shadows of Anna's thoughts came the light of Peter's reassuring voice accompanied with a gentle smile. As she examined with tenderness the two solemn faces in front of her, a powerful urgency to struggle on together surged through her. She reached the decision that she herself, together with her mother-in-law, would voluntarily join her mother in the transport . . . And so the lonely group savored their last evening in the Ghetto together, packing, and sharing the last fragile moments of anxiety and love.

In the morning of September 2, a heartbreaking procession of 5,000 deportees burdened with their pathetic belongings, a transport number swinging around their necks, were marched off toward the railroad station. Anna and her mother were among them while Peter's mother, upon Anna's suggestion, was waiting in her room in order to be spared the long hours of waiting in line.

Already in the distance, the loading of the prisoners could be seen and heard. There was pushing and screaming. Everyone was brutally forced into the prepared cattle cars. A cordon formed by gendarmes together with trans-

---

[3]Auschwitz was one of many extermination camps in Poland.

port orderlies forcefully enclosed the swelling crowd. "This is the time I must get my mother-in-law," Anna thought to herself. But suddenly she felt something snap inside her instead. At that moment it became clear to her that she must do something, do it at once and do it quickly, or else. . . .

As if she were someone else, Anna removed the transport number from her and her mother's necks and let them slide to the ground. Then, she seized her mother's hand and urged her to follow her. The next moment a frantic jerk propelled them through the cordon of the guards and in the ensuing confusion, both of them escaped the perilous scene. Any minute they expected to be stopped: a cry, an order, a blow on the head . . . Nothing. In order not to become conspicuous they now walked in slow, measured steps and lost themselves in the turmoil of the Ghetto.

Their wild escape ended in a deserted lumberyard on the periphery of the Ghetto. Terror stricken, they scanned the area around them. Perhaps the aroma of the freshly cut wood agitated their senses; in a frenzy they slipped, like two wild animals, behind a wall of piled up lumber. Still gasping for breath, they set their scanty luggage on the sawdust covered ground. Before long the mother's trembling legs gave way, and she slouched between the lumber behind and the suitcases in front of her.

Anna bent over her mother's recumbent body with an uneasy feeling. Only now did she realize what they had just done. A chill crept down her fingertips as she touched the curve of her mother's shoulder. "Everything will be all right. You just stay here until I come back to get you," she said with tough tenderness. It seemed that only the soothing tone of Anna's voice reached her mother's consciousness which had already succumbed to an irresistible sleep. Anna withdrew cautiously, leaving her mother in the protection of the strip of shade stretching alongside the wall of lumber.

As she moved anxiously off, she watched her mother fade away until she could hardly distinguish the frail shape blending into the wall of lumber behind her. Anna forced herself not to think, not to do anything but hasten forward on the dusty road toward the rampart above the deportation area. Finally, she reached the elevation from where she could follow the scene below, where the process of loading the "cargo" of Jews into the cattle cars was in full swing. There were panic, screams, blows! The cars filled up quickly and each time the heavy sliding doors were shut and the iron bars were pushed down with thuds into their slots. The fate of the victims was sealed. She could hear the frantic cries escaping through the small, barred windows in the upper corner of the cars. Anna agonized over the aching spasms of the travelers who would be spending many hours behind the steel doors of these "rolling coffins." And still, incredible as it might seem, she calculated that the faster the doors were to close, the closer the success of their escape would be. Her nerves overloaded, she was now only waiting for the last wagon to be closed. Entirely absorbed in the process of loading, a sort of callousness began to take hold of her.

At last, some frantic activities on the platform heralded the imminent departure of the train. Anna's hope began to grow and grew with each minute. Finally, the train began crackling and squealing as if panting for breath. The black locomotive was howling mournfully and flurries of furious puffs were rising toward the sky. The train jerked against the rails and crept forward, then the speed increased and finally it became a smoky streak in the distance. It was all over. . . .

Despite the situation, Anna felt a hysterical sensation of triumph. However, it did not last too long; soon the exuberant feeling changed into a nervous tremor. What about her mother in the lumberyard! Terror gripped her throat. So many hours had passed since she left her. Had she panicked? Had the Germans found her? She descended from the rampart as fast as she could.

The Ghetto was enveloped in darkness and silence. Anna looked around, her heart beating violently; at every step she glanced from the corner of her eyes at the shadowy passerby. She walked tightly along the pavement and up the dusty path toward the lumberyard. There she found her mother as she had left her. Anna's sagging courage was up again. "I just woke up a little while ago," her mother said with an angelic smile when she saw her daughter again. With a sigh of relief Anna looked into her shining eyes and full of thankfulness realized how the miracle of sleep had washed away the long hours of her mother's waiting.

Anna helped her mother struggle to her feet and both started on their way back. They eagerly inhaled again the Ghetto's dusty air on their way to Peter's mother's place. They found her still waiting, her prayer book open on her lap. She lifted her tired eyes and a twinkle of a smile passed over her exhausted face. Soon the fear subsided and the exhilaration from their reunion kindled new hope as they huddled in the dark room. That night before sinking into sleep, Anna reflected upon the miracle of prayer and the sleep that had blotted out from both mothers the horrors of that day.

However, on December 15th, and 18th, 1943 two transports, each with 2,500 prisoners, were scheduled to leave from Theresienstadt for Auschwitz. This time both mothers received summonses for the December 18th transport. "There is no way out this time," thought Anna "the September 'miracle' can not be repeated." Anna joined them voluntarily. On that day, the three of them became a part of the group of victims struggling behind the closed doors in one of the cattle cars of a long train heading for Auschwitz.

When Anna faced the peril that awaited them at the end of the arduous journey she began to perceive that Auschwitz was an orderly kingdom of the doomed. With all her remaining strength, she managed somehow to hold on to her two mothers as they were herded with the rest of the prisoners into the so-called "Family Camp" in Birkenau.[4] There they found themselves with

---

[4]"Family Camp" Birkenau was a part of the concentration camp Auschwitz which was known as the

people who came from Theresienstadt on the September, 1943, transport. They all looked debilitated, their gazes distant, their bodies starved.

"How will I be able to preserve the weak flicker of my mothers' lives amid such an inferno?" she asked herself bewildered and full of pain. Nevertheless, she was soon to find that they somehow managed to grapple with their day-to-day numbing existence. In the solitude of night, Anna thought back to the days in Theresienstadt, where she still could orchestrate an escape, while in Auschwitz everything was beyond her power of influence.

But not until the night of March 8th, 1944, could the three women really appreciate the true importance of their escape from the September, 1943, transport. On that dark, moonless night, events beyond any imagination took place: Without any warning, camp curfew was ordered and large commandos of SS guards with leashed dogs at their sides stormed the camp. They rounded up 4,000 of the original 5,000 men, women, and children, survivors of the September 1943, transport, from which Anna and her mothers had run away. They were cremated that same night in the gas chambers of Birkenau.

As long as the hope which could come from deep faith pulsated within the three women, survival still seemed possible. This event, however, shattered their remaining faith. "Faith in what? Was that what was also awaiting the December transport?" they asked themselves with trepidation. Auschwitz—a landscape so alienated from any culture ever known, seemed to be the end of the road for the three of them. They counted months, weeks, days until they too would have to follow the fate of the September transport.

Spring turned into summer. The sky became blue without joy, the sun became hot without pity for the doomed prisoners in Birkenau. On July 15th a wintry hush once again swept over the camp's population. A new selection! This time the old, the sick, and children, some accompanied by their mothers, were brutally forced into prepared trucks and transported to the crematoria, where they were, as the transport before them, destroyed with the Nazi "blitz" efficiency. A work force, formed from the younger and still somewhat able-bodied inmates, was transferred to other labor camps. The "Family Camp" in Birkenau was liquidated and so was Peter's mother. . . .

"Czech Family Camp." Its first inmates were 5,000 Jewish men, women and children who arrived there in September, 1943, from the concentration camp Theresienstadt in Czechoslovakia. Unlike all preceding transports, they were not subjected to the notorious selection upon arrival in which the fit were thumbed to the right and life and the unfit to the left and death in the gas chambers. Instead, under a new scheme ordered by the General Reich Security Authority in Berlin, the inmates were to be kept in this camp in a sort of isolation or quarantine of six months' duration, after which period those who were still able would be liquidated or, as it was called euphemistically, "subject to special treatment." In line with this plan, the night of the 8th of March, 1944, the surviving prisoners from the September transport were gassed, while the December transport from Theresienstadt (including Anna and her mothers) were to be quarantined for another three months before they would be gassed as well. However, when the end of that period arrived, the camp was not liquidated in its entirety, as described in the essay.

Anna, together with her mother, huddled in a cattle car again. They arrived in Stutthof, a desolate concentration camp in Prussia. There hard work, starvation, and disease again became their companions. In a few months Anna's mother aged several years. Even though her physical and mental endurance went beyond all limits given the circumstances, Anna noticed the unmistakable signs of her [mother's] imminent collapse. Helpless and in despair, she watched over her deteriorating state of health until one day in January, 1945, the mother succumbed.

Anna (miraculously) survived and so the impossible became no longer unthinkable.

Interpretations

1. Anna's plan was that all three women would leave the camp together. Instead she accomplished "the September miracle." Are you surprised at this accomplishment? Why? What is the most miraculous thing about it?

2. Explain the title. What was "the impossible"?

3. Most of this story deals with Anna's unsuccessful attempts to save the two older women. Was her own salvation merely a matter of chance? If so, does the account make a point about who may survive the death camps? What point?

4. Although in many ways the Holocaust was "unthinkable," Wehle is asking her readers to think about it. What are some of the conclusions thinking might force on one who reads about the Holocaust?

5. From whose point of view is this story told? How do we know that? Why is this the natural choice of point of view?

Correspondences

1. "At that moment more than ever Anna felt that her life was no longer entirely her own. Time was running out and a decision had to be made." Why did Anna decide that she and her mother would not join the transport? Was her decision premeditated? What role did her mother and mother-in-law play in her choice? To what extent does Anna's choice also involve "two moralities"? How does her choice differ from Manuela's?

2. "The mourning scene lost its usual significance or rather assumed a different one." How did ghetto life change the mourning ritual for Peter's mother? What other *cultural* deprivations were they subjected to? Compare internment experiences in Nazi and in American camps (Chapter 5). How did they differ?

Applications

1. Review Wehle's biography (page 397). Why and for whom did she write "The Impossible Became No Longer Unthinkable"? Write a journal entry analyzing your responses to her essay.

2. One of Anna's mother's favorite quotations (from Goethe's *Faust*) was "A good man, driven by his dim impulses is always conscious of his right way." What does it mean? How does this apply to Wehle's essay?

Banderillero

Barry Newman

Barry Newman is a native of New York City. He attended Union College in Schenectady, N.Y., and has worked for The New York Times *and (since 1970) the* Wall Street Journal. *A collection of his columns, of which "Banderillero" is one, was published in 1980 as* East of the Equator. *As the title implies, his columns often report on travels in Asia and Europe. The following essay, on one aspect of the Spanish sport—or art—of bullfighting, is such a report.*

The Spain Newman visits in his column retains many customs associated with much older Mediterranean civilizations. Bullfighting was probably introduced into Spain by the Moors, Islamic conquerors from North Africa who began their conquest in 711 and were not driven out until 1492. Spain sent out explorers like Columbus (in the same year) and colonizers who spread Spanish culture abroad. One such export was bullfighting, which took an especially firm hold in Mexico and other Latin American countries. Spain retained an extensive empire until the early nineteenth century. She lost the Philippines and Puerto Rico to the United States in the Spanish-American War (1898). Spain was neutral in World War II, but has now joined NATO and is a full member of the Common Market.

Just because your legs is dead don't mean your head is.

Casey Stengel

VILLAMUELAS, Spain—Soldiers don't start out as generals nor politicians as presidents. In business, managers work their way up. Except for a lucky few, the realization slowly and steadily comes to just about everyone that the top is out of reach.

But bullfighting works the other way around. A bullfighter rockets to the top. From first blush, he is a matador—that bold and arrogant swordsman who artfully entices the bull to its moment of truth. A matador monopolizes the spotlight long enough to convince the world of his incompetence. Then his own moment of truth arrives: the shock of failure and the dawning knowledge that he will never be on top again.

The truth came to Ernesto Sabrino thirteen years ago.

"People stopped taking me seriously," he says, driving his old car through a rainstorm on a Sunday morning, heading out of Madrid and across the Castilian tableland to a bullfight in this little town. He is forty. His chestnut hair is all there, but he appears to have a small pillow under his worn blue sweater.

"Life as a matador became a life of pain," he says. "People made fun

407

of me. Promises were never kept. When I was twenty-seven, I faced reality."

A bull gets dragged to the butcher's after its moment of truth. A matador, if he stays alive and retains some spunk, gets to be a banderillero. That's what Ernesto Sabrino is. So is his friend, Paco Dominguez, who is riding in the back seat. His hair is going, but he wears his jacked draped over his shoulders and carries his cigarette with his arm raised, as if acknowledging an ovation.

"The bullfight is a liberation," he says, blowing smoke into the front seat as the car circles the great stone bullring in Aranjuez. "We risk our lives with joy."

Sabrino pulls out a rag and wipes the condensation from the inside of the windshield. "Paco," he says, "you're a romantic. For me, everything is practical. Gambling with life and death is the way I make money. When you are a matador, you can dream. When you are a banderillero, you have to stop."

Banderilleros are the old men of the bullring. Suited up, these bullfighters look like thick-waisted versions of young matadors. The crowd has a chance to take special note of them when they run at the bull with two barbed sticks and try to place them in its hump before the matador moves in for the kill. A hardy banderillero can keep at this until he is past fifty, although his run will inevitably seem longer every year.

Apart from those few seconds when he places the sticks, the old man's job is to make the matador look good. While the matador struts in front of the bull, taunting it, daring it to charge, the banderillero hovers in the background, an experienced eye on the animal's every twitch. When the matador fumbles, a flick of the banderillero's cape can, by distracting the bull, save the matador from a horn through the thigh and, occasionally, from humiliation. All the old man craves in return is some respect and a day's pay.

Villamuelas appears at the base of a slope: half a dozen streets of two-storied buildings. The bullring is just outside town. It is portable, made of corrugated tin and set up in a muddy field. Spain has fewer bullfights than it did before television and the family car. A banderillero takes what he can get.

"It's your legs and your head," Ernesto Sabrino says as he parks his car in front of the bar in the village square. "You need both. I jog. I don't drink or smoke. The crowd doesn't cheer for me. I'm beyond the point where I expect to be a star. But we are the pillars of the bullfight."

The rain has eased off. A woman is washing out a few things at the fountain. A man is selling fried dough. Strung between two balconies, a banner announces today's fiesta. The bar is packed, its floor littered with shrimp shells. The band sprawls on plastic chairs, drinking coffee. Men in berets lean on canes, wine glasses in hand. Sabrino works his way through, orders an anisette, then remembers he doesn't drink.

"Just a little," he says. "It warms my stomach. I haven't smoked for a week now." Paco Dominguez lights up. "Must you?" Sabrino says. But Dominguez ignores him—the matador is coming in: tall and svelte, chin held high, hair jet black, eyes hidden behind dark glasses. He is a novice, perhaps twenty years old and, Sabrino confides, without promise.

"A rich kid," he says.

"He comes from a wealthy family," says Dominguez, turning back toward the bar. "His family is investing in him."

"I never had an investor in my life," Ernesto Sabrino says.

His story is the standard one for bullfighters. He was born in a town like this, left school at eleven, delivered groceries, studied the bullfight newspapers, worshipped Manolete. He walked all night to small-town *capeas*—illegal fights in rings built of boards and parked cars. At fourteen, he stood in front of a bull, At sixteen, he was gored. At eighteen, he was noticed. He dressed as a matador for the first time a year later, in 1961, and killed his first bull.

"I always thought I was good," he says, sitting down under the bar's television, which is showing a bicycle race. "There was one day in Rioja. I had a good bull that day. I mastered it. I was artistic. I cut two ears. For me, this was success. But I don't build sand castles; life proved me wrong."

He sips his anisette, and looks up at the bicycles.

In the bullfight business, the impresario pays the matador, sometimes well. The matador pays his banderilleros, though not always on time and rarely well. Fifty years ago, Ernest Hemingway wrote: "There is no man meaner about money with his inferiors than your matador." The banderilleros suffered on. Not until the start of this season did they finally vent their resentment. They walked out.

Their strike lasted a week in March. When it was over, they had won a pay raise of fourteen percent. Now a banderillero gets at least $400 for fighting in a first-class ring. In Villamuelas today, Sabrino should come away with $150. Crisscrossing Spain all summer, he might hit fifty towns and earn $10,000. The extra money will help. But when a bullfight is called off, a banderillero still gets no pay. Nor does he have much of a future, once those legs go.

"Money isn't all that important to me," Sabrino says as he drains his anisette. "I'm sincere about that. I'm talking about dignity."

Lunch is ready. The bullfighters and their entourage file past the bar into a bare hall at the rear. A movie screen hangs from the far wall, a stack of chairs in front of it. Two long tables have been set up in the middle of the hall. The matador and his family sit at one. The banderilleros and the picadors, who fight on horseback, sit at the other. So do a few of the impresario's functionaries, one of whom goes by the name of Cadenas.

Cadenas is getting old. He has a throaty voice and puffy skin. When Ernesto Sabrino was a matador, Cardenas was already a banderillero.

"For thirty-five years I was a bullfighter," he says spitting out an olive pit. "Now I sell the tickets."

"When I'm through," Sabrino says, "I'd like to be a TV repairman." He takes a sip of wine and looks down at his plate. "The pork is tough," he says.

By late afternoon, when lunch is over, the crowd fills the square. The band plays the *Pasodoble Torero.** The loudspeaker crackles: "The greatest spectacle of bullfighting this afternoon in this wonderful city! Get your tickets now! A sensation!" The bullfighters begin to dress in the bedrooms on the other side of the bar. Then the rain comes down.

The impresario returns from the ring, his shoes muddied. "Impossible," he says. The mayor of Villamuelas steps out onto the balcony of the town hall, overlooking the square, and addresses the townspeople. The spectacular, he announces, is canceled.

Sabrino folds his cape. "A funeral," he says. "We don't get a peseta." He and Paco Dominguez drive back to Madrid to wait for the sun, stopping on the way for another anisette.

Two days later, the sun shines on the fiesta of another Castilian town, San Martin de la Vega. The bullring has been erected right in the square, and the cobbles covered with sand. This ring is dangerous. It has too few places for a bullfighter to hide. Looking less than lithe in his salmon-pink suit, Sabrino is keyed up, his face in a fixed grin.

"Sometimes I suffer so much fear in the ring I don't even see the women," he says, surveying the crowd from behind one of the barriers. As a banderillero, he has twice been seriously gored, both times in the groin. "Every time I get dressed for the fight," he says, "I know it can happen again." He takes a swig from a wineskin and shows his teeth to the fans.

The preliminaries soon end and the fight begins. As each bull charges into the ring, Sabrino hangs behind the barrier, letting the matador who employs him today show off his capework. On his first run, the banderillero plants the sticks perfectly, without the slightest attempt at pizzazz. On his second, the sticks go flying. The bull wheels and gives chase. Sabrino flees, stiff-legged, over the barrier, with a look on his face of crazed concentration.

It is the only moment all afternoon when the crowd pays him any heed. After his young matador gracefully dispatches the day's final bull, the coup de grace is left to Sabrino. He performs it with a sharp jab of a short knife, and cuts two ears for the youngster, just as two ears were cut for him on that day in Rioja. Flowers shower down. Sabrino stoops to collect them and presents a bouquet to another novice in his glory.

---

*Traditionally, the music accompanying the bullfighters' procession into the bullring.

The bullfighters parade in triumph and disappear beneath the stands. As the crowd leaves, someone lets a spindly-horned calf run loose in the ring. The boys of San Martin de la Vega jump down onto the sand to dance circles around it, acting out their fantasies of becoming matadors someday.

Interpretations

1. What are the differences between being a banderillero and being a matador?

2. Why did Sabrino choose to become a banderillero? What factors did he consider in making the choice? Is he now content with his choice? Is he temperamentally well suited to the role?

3. The author compares a matador to a soldier, a politician, and a businessman. How comparable are these four careers?

4. The irony of Sabrino's statement "I don't drink or smoke" is inescapable. Is an earlier statement—"We risk our lives with joy"—also meant to be ironic? What is the prevailing tone, sympathetic or satirical? Defend your opinion.

Correspondences

1. "When you are a matador, you can dream. When you are a banderillero, you have to stop." Has Sabrino, in fact, ceased to dream? What role do dreams play in Rodriguez's "To the Border"? Is hope a factor in the choice to cross the border?

2. Sabrino states that making money is less important to him than living with dignity. How does his choice support that claim? Did Glickman decide to stop living for results for this same reason? What is your evaluation of their choices?

Applications

1. Write an essay about the risks involved in choosing a career in the performing arts.

2. Review the epigraph of Newman's essay. What does it mean? How does it apply to Sabrino's choice?

A Train Ride

Hugo Lindo
Translated by
Elizabeth Gamble Miller

Hugo Lindo (b. 1917) is one of El Salvador's best-known poets and novelists. His concern for the political and sociological situation in his country is revealed in his novels, which include Justicia, señor Gobernador *published in 1960.*

As LEONARDO VILLENA strolled along the station platform toward the second-class cars, he inhaled the air with extraordinary gusto. There was always that special aroma of vapors that smelled of a trip. A small briefcase in his left hand was his only baggage. With his right hand he dug into the pocket of his jacket, and, reassured that his ticket was in place, he boarded the train.

The seats in the second-class car were hard, but that didn't seem to matter. He chose one next to a window and sought to entertain himself by looking out. At the moment there wasn't much scenery, unless that's what you would call the yellowed railroad ties piled high like a wall on either side of the tracks. The landscape would later change into meadows and woods, fields of sugar and corn, and little lakes dotted with coveys of wild ducks.

A heavy-set, bald-headed man took the seat beside him and made it immediately clear that he wanted to talk:

"Is your destination La Alianza?"

"No."

"San Esteban?"

"I'm really not going anywhere in particular."

The man was disconcerted, but only for a moment, and then he charged in again:

"Well, I am. I'm going to La Alianza. I've got a whole day of joggling up and down on this foul train. That's where my in-laws are waiting; they're taking care of my little boy while my wife is gone. She's in Miami picking up a few things (lowering his voice to a confidential tone)—contraband, you know."

Leonardo nodded his assent courteously and then directed his attention to lighting a cigarette and taking a deep, long draw.

"They notified me that he got sick, from one day to the next. He's seriously ill, and I have to go to him. I'm really worried, rather upset, you know. I wish the train was almost there."

Leonardo smiled to himself. Everything about the other passenger seemed to be a contradiction: he discussed his anguish with complete composure. He spoke very slowly while explaining his hurry. The man had piqued his interest. For his part he wouldn't try to be aloof or unsociable or to avoid the contact being offered. On the contrary, it was necessary for him to act naturally and even sympathetically. The fact was, he had started the day with a certain pensive disposition, and it was difficult to become engaged in dialogue. He would have to put forth a conscious effort to break down his own noncommunicative shell.

"You say you're not going anywhere in particular. I don't understand."

"I'm just taking a ride. I'll travel until about noon, get off wherever I am and take the next train going west."

"Oh, now I see!"

The car had been filling up with passengers, who were putting their suitcases up, or down in between the seats, or in the passageway, pushing and cursing under their breaths. An atmosphere of ill humor seemed to permeate the air. However, the bad humor around them didn't affect Leonardo Villena or his companion, for they were apparently in another world.

The train whistled, announcing its departure. The men heard the initial asthmatic chugs of the locomotive; that special odor of trains became stronger. They felt the first jerks, heard the squealing of the wheels, and the piles of railroad ties began to move backward, slowly.

"Do you travel like this very often, for pleasure?"

"Not frequently, but when I can. I like trains. Or I should say, I love trains."

"I don't. They bore me; they wear me out. But in a case like this. Just imagine. The poor child, seriously ill and without his mother or his father, depending on his aunts, and what can they do?"

"How old is the boy?" Leonardo asked, in an effort to appear interested.

"Three years old, and an only child. He looks like his mother."

"So much the better!"

The man caught the joke right away and smiled:

"Absolutely! Much better!"

Leonardo's career successes were due to his innate understanding of psychology. He had studied an average amount since entering the university a few years previously. But he had an unusual gift for sizing up people, guessing their intentions, anticipating their actions, and not being caught by surprise. It seemed an appropriate moment to analyze his traveling companion.

As a matter of fact he was rather young. His weight and his baldness contributed to the impression of his being older. This was emphasized by his loose, careless way of dressing. But his small, sharp eyes belied the first impression: there was something about them, a certain innocence, the sign of a rural upbringing; they displayed no tension or malice.

Little by little, the train had picked up speed. The telephone posts sped by and the wires seemed to be suddenly separated and then again united behind the string of cars.

"Don Horacio!"

The greeting was unexpected and enthusiastic. Entering their coach from the second-class car in front of them was a woman. She would have been pretty if it hadn't been for her pronounced nose. Brunette, black eyes, straight hair, a bit fleshy, her appearance was, generally speaking, attractive, although somewhat common. Her only facial feature out of the ordinary was her nose, which made her uglier; however, it also gave her a certain mark of distinction and intelligence.

"Mariita!"

"Where are you bound for?"

Don Horacio—now Leonardo knew his name—repeated the story: the sick child, the absent mother, the aunts, the long tedious train ride, and above all, the concern for his son. The tremendous worry expressed with a placid face; the uncertain urgency spoken of calmly.

Leonardo Villena again tried to immerse himself in his thoughts, but now the woman had taken the seat directly in front of them and was carrying on a long conversation with Don Horacio. She spoke energetically, affectionately, and with exaggerated gestures. Oh, three-year-olds! So precious! So smart! Something new every minute! So adorable!

Mariita found no lack of expressions of affection for children. One might conclude that she belonged to a society for the protection of children. Villena was engaged in his own thoughts when, without warning, the woman threw a direct question at him:

"And you, sir, have you any children?"

"Yes, I have two."

"Oh, how lovely! How old are they? Are they pretty big now?"

"No. The older one is five. The younger is three."

"Little boys?"

"Yes, they are."

Leonardo thought Mariita was too forward, but his rearing obliged him to answer and not ignore her. Yes, his rearing, a vestige of the bourgeois "teachings" that he had been subjected to by his parents and professors and by the general environment. However, there seemed to be something else involved. It was as if that woman held a strange magnetism for him. She spoke, and he was compelled to pay attention. Besides, her words, though simple enough, carried an undercurrent of emotion that could not be ignored.

He was cognizant of the fact that he should not think about his own children. Certainly not with any emotion. The thought of his boys would of necessity be an inhibiting factor and could jeopardize his mission. No sentimentality, no familial sentimentalism. Nevertheless, it seemed that between them, Mariita and Don Horacio were determined to ruin his plans. He couldn't refrain from thinking of his children. When he had left, they were in bed and he had planted a kiss on each forehead. Fortunately, they were healthy. Because when Leonardito, the older one, caught the measles and was completely covered with bumps, his temperature had risen devilishly high. He had been so worried! Every few minutes he would call the doctor, who could do nothing but prescribe aspirin to lower the fever. Don Horacio, the poor devil, must be feeling the same disquietude, only with his temperament, or perhaps it was just a façade, his anxiety didn't show. But what the devil did he care about Don Horacio and Mariita and the children?

The train made its customary noises as it approached the station: it blew, whistled, screeched, rumbled, and finally pulled to a stop in front of the station shed at Las Palmas, a shed blackened by trains like all the others in the country, identical to the others in the Americas and even in the world.

One advantage, he said to himself: this interruption will cut off that woman's chitchat and put an end to this man's meddling. He noted his watch. It wasn't time to get off yet. The next station would be the one. But, because of the circumstances, perhaps it would be preferable.

He didn't reveal his intentions, but as he was moving toward the step in order to get off the train, the heavy-set man spied him and called out in a rather demanding voice that attracted everyone's attention:

"Mister! Mister! You're forgetting your valise!"

He thought quickly. If he ran, they would surely go through his briefcase and consequently his mission would fail. If on the other hand he stayed, there would still be time to think up something that would work.

"No, Don Horacio, I'm not leaving. I was just going to get a breath of fresh air."

It was difficult for him to hide his rage and frustration. Why had his seatmates turned out to be precisely these people with their inopportune interference that seemed destined to upset his plans? Like the best actor, he adopted the disguise of being pleasant and relaxed while he cursed his bad luck. He again took his seat and thanked the man for his trouble over the little baggage that he had.

So it was that the train renewed its journey with its tedious, isochronal rhythm, that the woman in a like manner resumed her chatter about children, their charms, their illnesses, the unsettling moments that await their elders, and he was forced to pay even closer attention because of the necessity for dissimulation.

And it was through the small door this attention had opened that the woman's words gradually crept in. With their intense power of suggestion, their incomparable emotional force and subjugating pathos, in spite of the simplicity and domesticity of the thoughts being expressed, her words convinced him: "Hypnotism or something of that order," thought Leonardo Villena for a moment. Just for a moment, because that thought couldn't occupy the same space being reclaimed by his home. The warm images emerged from behind that prominent nose through the strange voice of Mariita and those steady, unavoidable, demanding eyes that shone like precious stones. "Absurd," he thought instantly. And then again he saw Leonardito burning up with fever, his little head wet with perspiration lying on the pillow and moving about restlessly, just the way this fat man's son must be doing now in La Alianza—the son of his gentle traveling companion.

"Traveling companion"—something clicked in his memory as the phrase crossed his mind. Possible; he was not sure. He did begin to consider that at least for the moment his mission was inopportune. Rather than the government, its victims would be the anonymous train passengers. Perhaps even more than them, the injury would be to that unknown child, his traveling companion's son—the boy who might be Leonardito's traveling companion at some future date.

Exerting his willpower, he shook his head and succeeded in uttering one word, "foolishness," but the word was swallowed up in a great black tunnel mysteriously taking shape as he saw before him Mariita's eyes and, deep within, like a drop of gleaming water, the flash of innocence. He could not complete his mission.

Old houses with crumbling walls moved slowly across the train window. Cows were mooing. Wire fences etched stripes into the landscape. And then came the school yard with its children, lots of children, noisy children whose cries penetrated the railroad car. The train stopped moving and Leonardo found it the opportune moment to escape that diabolical pair. He grabbed his briefcase, muttering to himself the word "traitor," and made his way off the train.

Interpretations

1. When did you first become aware that Leonardo is no ordinary traveler? Cite the clearest indication of how extraordinary he is.

2. Horacio and Mariita never realize that Leonardo is no ordinary traveler. How does the story attempt to make plausible their lack of awareness?

3. What are Leonardo's outstanding character traits? Cite evidence of them.

4. Leonardo notices something contradictory about Horacio: "the tremendous worry" that Horacio expresses about his son is inconsistent with his "complete composure." What is ironic about Leonardo's observations, and what does this irony contribute to the story?

Correspondences

1. Review the Fanon quotation in "Perspectives" (page 362). How does it apply to Leonardo's choice in "A Train Ride"? What is the main factor behind this choice?

2. "Leonardo thought Mariita was too forward, but his rearing obliged him to answer and not ignore her. Yes, his rearing, a vestige of the bourgeois 'teachings' that he had been subjected to by his parents and professors and by the general environment." What personal and political choices does Lindo's traveler make? How do they compare with those of Matshoba's protagonists?

Applications

1. Leonardo makes what most would consider an honorable choice. Yet he refers to himself as a traitor. Write a journal entry explaining this contradiction.

2. Leonardo is a terrorist who chooses not to carry out his mission. Why? At what possible price? (To what extent is he aware of the possible consequences of his choice?)

ADDITIONAL WRITING TOPICS

1. Review the Frost quotation, (page 362). What does it imply about the nature of choice? Under what circumstances might you make a similar choice? In an essay, analyze your reasons for a choice you would make to take "the road less traveled."

2. Using the selections by Mukherjee (Chapter 4) and by Bonilla, Rodriguez, and Berger (this chapter) as a base, write an analysis of the price of being a refugee, migrant worker, or illegal alien in the United States.

3. According to the Yiddish proverb (page 361), "Troubles overcome are good to tell." How does this proverb apply to the selections by Glickman, Parks, and Wehle? To what extent did cultural factors affect their choices?

4. Paule Marshall (Chapter 3) sees language as both a refuge and a weapon. To what extent do Rendón (Chapter 3), Bonilla, Rodriguez, and Berger agree with her? (How real is the power of language? Does language define and shape people or vice versa?) Cite specific examples from this textbook and your own experience to support your point of view.

5. Each chapter in this textbook begins with a myth, a folktale, or a story that teaches a lesson. Collaborate with members of your group on composing a moralistic tale that, like "The Wise Daughter," teaches a moral lesson about choices.

6. View the videotape *Romero* and analyze the factors involved in this Salvadoran priest's decisions to fight terrorism in his own country.

7. Study the videotape *Au Revoir Les Enfants, Garden of the Finzi-Continis,* or *Weapons of the Spirit.* Analyze the nature of the choices or new choices presented. What do you conclude about the price of survival? The phenomenon of survivor guilt?

CHAPTER 7

Aspirations

If "aspirations" sounds a little too grand for ordinary people on an ordinary day, substitute the word "ambitions" or "desires" or "dreams" or "wishes." Aspiration is perhaps more sustained than desire, for it implies more willingness to wait and to struggle, and it is a little less private than a wish.

Is there any limit to human aspirations? Probably not, but there are both natural and cultural limits to which aspirations can be realized. Some desires (perhaps not to be confused with aspirations) are antisocial and destructive. Law and government would be unnecessary if aspirations were never harmful, were never the results of greed and selfishness and intolerance. And many potentially beneficial aspirations are never realized because of fear or laziness or poor education or blind acceptance of unjust political and social systems.

Are our aspirations affected by our culture? Indeed they are. "The American Dream," for example, is more than a slogan adorning a T-shirt; it is a shorthand expression of a widespread belief among Americans that freedom, social justice, and improvement in material standards are desirable and possible for all. Some cultures may ignore or discourage aspirations. Some religions teach that human desire is the cause of all human suffering and that one's goal should be to eliminate desire. Some cultures encourage group but not individual aspirations; and some actively discourage individual aspirations: "The nail that sticks up gets hammered down," they point out. Americans do not often use that proverb. In the United States there is a widespread belief that aspirations can benefit both the individual and the society. Ralph Lamberti's tribute to Rachel Asrelsky is a case in point. Although Asrelsky's life was cut short, it was fulfilling both to herself and to those around her.

Some voices in this chapter echo the typically American desire for upward mobility (Villarreal). Others plead for respect for other cultures (Ford), and for respect and opportunity for minorities (Reed, Lorde, Villarreal, Greenberg, Johnson) or women (Vicioso).

Most of the hopes and dreams in the selections of this chapter are collective or communal. Hiawatha, who lived in the sixteenth century and whose story now contains legendary elements, had a vision of uniting five warring Iroquois tribes so that against a common enemy they could contribute their strengths to a common multicultural tribe. Four centuries later, Ishmael Reed envisions an America in which "blurring of cultural styles" is accepted and the contributions to civilization of non-European peoples are considered on a par with those of Europe. He asserts that "the United States is unique in the world: The world is here." And for the morale of their whole family, Audre Lorde's immigrant parents aspired to escape confrontation with racism in North America.

The aspirations of Sherezada Vicioso and Jay Ford also evidence a combining of the personal and the social. Vicioso values her freedom because it has allowed her to help the people, especially the women, of her country, the Dominican Republic. Although she has paid a "dreadful" price for this freedom, she uses it to work for others' freedom. Her aspiration is limited and immediate: to create a "market for women's literature." By contrast, in "20/20 Hindsight," Jay Ford recounts the effects of a sojourn in Kenya on his sense of identity and his hope that Americans can learn from Kenyans how better to value simple human relationships.

Mexican-American Richard Rubio's aspirations seem more private. The ambitions of twelve-year-old Richard (in José Antonio Villarreal's novel *Pocho*) are very personal, even rebellious. Nevertheless, they are influenced by a general *norteamericano* attitude toward individualism. Richard learns that "everything had another way to it, if only you looked hard enough," that "what people thought was honorable was not important, because he was the important guy," that "he would never succumb to foolish social pressures again." And although Richard is a "nail" willing to be hammered in the boxing ring on the way to his goals, he is not willing to be relegated to some immigrant limbo.

PERSPECTIVES

Out of poverty, poetry;
Out of suffering, song.

Mexican saying

Civilization progresses at the expense of individual happiness.

Sigmund Freud

The greatest mystery is not that we have been flung at random among the profusion of the earth and the galaxy of the stars, but that in this prison we can fashion images of ourselves sufficiently powerful to deny our nothingness.

André Malraux

Where young boys plan for what they will achieve and attain, young girls plan for whom they will achieve and attain.

Charlotte Perkins Gilman

A little madness in the Spring
Is wholesome even for the king.

Emily Dickinson

Possibility is the oldest American story. Head west for freedom and the chance of inventing a spanking new life for yourself. Our citizens are always leaping the traces when their territory gets too small and cramped.

William Kittredge

Only the liberation of the natural capacity for love in human beings can master their sadistic destructiveness.

William Reich

The greatest use of life is to spend it on something that will outlast it.

William James

I have a dream that my four little children will one day live in a nation where they will not be judged by the color of their skin but by the content of their character.

Martin Luther King, Jr.

I don't know the key to success, but the key to failure is trying to please everybody.

Bill Cosby

Applications

1. Write a journal entry on Dickinson's perspective (p. 421). What does she mean by madness? What does madness have to do with aspirations?

2. What are aspirations? How do they differ from dreams, hopes, goals, or convictions? How do they differ in connotation and applicability? Discuss these words in your group.

Hiawatha, the Great Unifier

Iroquois Myth

Hiawatha (b. about 1570), a member of the Mohawk tribe, is credited with forming the League of Five Nations, also known as the Iroquois Confederacy (the Mohawk, Oneida, Onondaga, Cayuga, and Seneca tribes). After later addition of the Tuscaroras, the confederacy became known as the League of Six Nations. In the seventeenth century—at the height of their power—the Iroquois inhabited a large part of New York state and controlled an area bounded by the Kennebec, the Ottawa, the Illinois, and the Tennessee rivers. Their articles of confederation evoked admiration in their time, in particular by Benjamin Franklin.

THE SLUMBER of Ta-ren-ya-wa-gon, Upholder of Heavens, was disturbed by a great cry of anguish and woe. He looked down from his abode to earth and saw human beings moaning with terror, pursued by horrifying monsters and cruel, man-devouring giants. Turning himself into a mortal, Ta-ren-ya-wa-gon swiftly descended to earth and, taking a small girl by the hand, told the frightened humans to follow him. By trails known only to him, he led the group of shivering refugees to a cave at the mouth of a great river, where he fed them and told them to sleep.

After the people had somewhat recovered under his protection, Ta-ren-ya-wa-gon again took the little girl by the hand and led them toward the rising sun. The band traveled for many days until they came to the confluence of two mighty rivers whose waters, white with spray, cascaded over tremendous rocks. There Ta-ren-ya-wa-gon halted and built a longhouse for himself and his people.

For years they lived there, content and growing fat, their children turning into strong men and handsome women. Then Ta-ren-ya-wa-gon, the Sky Upholder became mortal, gathered the people around him and spoke: "You, my children, must now spread out and become great nations. I will make your numbers like the leaves of a forest in summertime, like pebbles on the shore of the great waters." And again he took one little girl by the hand and walked toward the setting sun, all the people following him.

After a long journey they came to the banks of a beautiful river. Ta-ren-ya-wa-gon separated a few families from the rest and told them to build a longhouse at that spot and found a village. "You shall be known by the name of Te-ha-wro-gah, Those-of-Divided-Speech," he told them, and they grew into the Mohawk tribe. And from the moment he had named them, their language changed and they could no longer understand the rest of the people.

To the Mohawks Ta-ren-ya-wa-gon gave corn, beans, squash, and tobacco, together with dogs to help them hunt game. He taught them how to plant and reap and pound corn into meal. He taught them the ways of the forest and the game, for in that long-ago time, people did not yet know all these things. When he had fully instructed them and given them the necessities of life, Ta-ren-ya-wa-gon again took one little girl by the hand and traveled with the remaining people toward the sunset.

After a long journey they halted in a beautiful well-watered valley surrounded by forests, and he commanded another group to build their village at that spot. He gave them what was necessary for life, taught them what they needed to know, and named them Ne-ha-wre-ta-go, the Big-Tree people, for the great forests surrounding them. And these people, who grew into the Oneida nation, also spoke a tongue of their own as soon as he had named them.

Then once more Ta-ren-ya-wa-gon took a little girl's hand and wandered on, always toward the setting sun, and the rest of the people followed him. They came to a big mountain which he named O-nun-da-ga-o-no-ga. At its foot he commanded some more families to build a longhouse, and he gave them the same gifts and taught them the same things that he had the others. He named them after the mountain towering above them and also gave them a speech of their own. And these people became the Onondaga nation.

Again with a small girl at his side, Ta-ren-ya-wa-gon wandered on, leading the people to the shores of a lake sparkling in the sun. The lake was called Go-yo-gah, and here still another group built their village, and they became the Cayugas.

Now only a handful of people were left, and these Ta-ren-ya-wa-gon led to a lake by a mountain called Ga-nun-da-gwa. There he settled them, giving them the name of Te-ho-ne-noy-hent—Keepers of the Door. They too received a language of their own and grew into the mighty Seneca nation.

There were some among the people who were not satisfied with the places appointed to them by the Upholder of Heavens. These wandered on toward the setting sun until they came to a river greater than all others, a river known as the Mississippi. They crossed it on a wild grapevine that formed a bridge from bank to bank, and after the last of them had crossed over, the vine tore asunder. None could ever return, so that this river divided the western from the eastern human beings.

To each nation the Upholder of Heavens gave a special gift. To the Senecas he gave such swift feet that their hunters could outrun the deer. To the Cayugas he gave the canoe and the skill to guide it through the most turbulent waters. To the Onondagas he gave the knowledge of eternal laws and the gift to fathom the wishes of the Great Creator. To the Oneidas he gave skills in making weapons and weaving baskets, while to the Mohawks he gave bows and arrows and the ability to guide the shafts into the hearts of their game and their enemies.

Ta-ren-ya-wa-gon resolved to live among the people as a human being. Having the power to assume any shape, he chose to be a man and took the name of Hiawatha. He chose to live among the Onondagas and took a beautiful young woman of that tribe for his wife. From their union came a daughter, Mni-haha, who surpassed even her mother in beauty and womanly skills. Hiawatha never ceased to teach and advise, and above all he preached peace and harmony.

Under Hiawatha the Onondagas became the greatest of all tribes, but the other nations founded by the Great Upholder also increased and prospered. Traveling in a magic birchbark canoe of dazzling whiteness, which floated above waters and meadows as if on an invisible bird's wings, Hiawatha went from nation to nation, counseling them and keeping man, animal, and nature in balance according to the eternal laws of the manitous.[1] So all was well and the people lived happily.

But the law of the universe is also that happiness alternates with sorrow, life with death, prosperity with hardship, harmony with disharmony. From out of the north beyond the Great Lakes came wild tribes, fierce, untutored nations who knew nothing of the eternal law; peoples who did not plant or weave baskets or fire clay into cooking vessels. All they knew was how to prey on those who planted and reaped the fruits of their labor. Fierce and pitiless, these strangers ate their meat raw, tearing it apart with their teeth. Warfare and killing were their occupation. They burst upon Hiawatha's people like a flood, spreading devastation wherever they went. Again the people turned to Hiawatha for help. He advised all the nations to assemble and wait his coming.

And so the five tribes came together at the place of the great council fire, by the shores of a large and tranquil lake where the wild men from the north had not yet penetrated. The people waited for Hiawatha one day, two days, three days. On the fourth day his gleaming-white magic canoe appeared, floating, gliding above the mists. Hiawatha sat in the stern guiding the mystery canoe, while in the bow was his only child, his daughter.

The sachems, elders, and wise men of the tribes stood at the water's edge to greet the Great Upholder. Hiawatha and his daughter stepped ashore. He greeted all he met as brothers and spoke to each in his own language.

Suddenly there came an awesome noise, a noise like the rushing of a hundred rivers, like the beating of a thousand giant wings. Fearfully the people looked upward. Out of the clouds, circling lower and lower, flew the great mystery bird of the heavens, a hundred times as big as the largest eagles, and whenever he beat his wings he made the sound of a thousand thunderclaps. While the people cowered, Hiawatha and his daughter stood

[1]In Algonquian (and related) tribes, a personal totem discovered through a dream.

unmoved. Then the Great Upholder laid his hands upon his daughter's head in blessing, after which she said calmly, "Farewell, my father." She seated herself between the wings of the mystery bird, who spiraled upwards and upwards into the clouds and at last disappeared into the great vault of the sky.

The people watched in awe, but Hiawatha, stunned with grief, sank to the ground and covered himself with the robe of a panther. Three days he sat thus in silence, and none dared approach him. The people wondered whether he had given his only child to the manitous above as a sacrifice for the deliverance of his people. But the Great Upholder would never tell them, would never speak of his daughter or of the mystery bird who had carried her away.

After having mourned for three days, Hiawatha rose on the morning of the fourth and purified himself in the cold, clear waters of the lake. Then he asked the great council to assemble. When the sachems,[2] elders, and wise men had seated themselves in a circle around the sacred fire, Hiawatha came before them and said:

> What is past is past; it is the present and the future which concern us. My children, listen well, for these are my last words to you. My time among you is drawing to the end.
>
> My children, war, fear, and disunity have brought you from your villages to this sacred council fire. Facing a common danger, and fearing for the lives of your families, you have yet drifted apart, each tribe thinking and acting only for itself. Remember how I took you from one small band and nursed you up into many nations. You must reunite now and act as one. No tribe alone can withstand our savage enemies, who care nothing about the eternal law, who sweep upon us like the storms of winter, spreading death and destruction everywhere.
>
> My children, listen well. Remember that you are brothers, that the downfall of one means the downfall of all. You must have one fire, one pipe, one war club.

Hiawatha motioned to the five tribal firekeepers to unite their fires with the big sacred council fire, and they did so. Then the Great Upholder sprinkled sacred tobacco upon the glowing embers so that its sweet fragrance enveloped the wise men sitting in the circle. He said:

> Onondagas, you are a tribe of mighty warriors. Your strength is like that of a giant pine tree whose roots spread far and deep so that it can withstand any storm. Be you the protectors. You shall be the first nation.

---

[2]A member of the fifty-member council of the Iroquois league.

Oneida, your men are famous for their wisdom. Be you the counselors of the tribes. You shall be the second nation.

Seneca, you are swift of foot and persuasive in speech. Your men
are the greatest orators among the tribes. Be you the spokesmen. You
shall be the third people.

Cayuga, you are the most cunning. You are the most skilled in
the building and managing of canoes. Be you the guardians of our
rivers. You shall be the fourth nation.

Mohawk, you are foremost in planting corn and beans and in
building longhouses. Be you the nourishers.

You tribes must be like the five fingers of a warrior's hand joined
in gripping the war club. Unite as one, and then your enemies will
recoil before you back into the northern wastes from whence they came.
Let my words sink deep into your hearts and minds. Retire now to take
counsel among yourselves, and come to me tomorrow to tell me whether
you will follow my advice.

On the next morning the sachems and wise men of the five nations came
to Hiawatha with the promise that they would from that day on be as one
nation. Hiawatha rejoiced. He gathered up the dazzling white feathers which
the great mystery bird of the sky had dropped and gave the plumes to the
leaders of the assembled tribes. "By these feathers," he said, "you shall be
known as the Ako-no-shu-ne, the Iroquois." Thus with the help of Hiawatha,
the Great Unifier, the mighty League of the Five Nations was born, and its
tribes held sway undisturbed over all the land between the great river of the
west and the great sea of the east.

The elders begged Hiawatha to become the chief sachem of the united
tribes, but he told them: "This can never be, because I must leave you.
Friends and brothers, choose the wisest women in your tribes to be the future
clan mothers and peacemakers, let them turn any strife arising among you
into friendship. Let your sachems be wise enough to go to such women for
advice when there are disputes. Now I have finished speaking. Farewell."

At that moment there came to those assembled a sweet sound like the
rush of rustling leaves and the song of innumerable birds. Hiawatha stepped
into his white mystery canoe, and instead of gliding away over the waters of
the lake, it rose slowly into the sky and disappeared into the clouds. Hiawatha
was gone, but his teachings survive in the hearts of the people.

Interpretations

1. What is the purpose of this legend? What aspiration does it embody? Was
    the goal achieved in Iroquois history? How do we know?

2. What are Hiawatha's outstanding character traits? How are they best revealed?

3. Why do you think Ta-ren-ya-wa-gon, before he led a migration, always took along a small girl "by the hand"? (What does this act reveal about his character and his purpose? How might she relate to Hiawatha's daughter Mni-haha?)

4. The provocation for unifying the Five Nations is the incursion of "wild" tribes from the North. Why are they considered wild? What is Hiawatha's attitude toward warfare?

5. Why do you think Ta-ren-ya-wa-gon/Hiawatha separated and then united the people instead of leaving them united as they were in the beginning?

The Brahman and the Pot of Rice

Indian Folk Tale

"The Brahman and the Pot of Rice" is an ancient Indian story attributed to Buddha. Milton Rugoff introduces the origins of this fable in his A Harvest of World Folk Tales.

> *India may not have been, as certain scholars once thought, the original fountain of fable, but certainly no civilization of antiquity can boast richer collections of story. Among the richest and oldest collections—scenes from it appear on a monument in Central India that dates back to the third century* B.C.*—is the* Iataka, *a gathering of more than five hundred tales reputed to have been drawn by Buddha from his experiences in previous incarnations, when he was preparing to become Buddha. The tales are intended, as the concluding comment of each insists, to be instructive. Even though the moral sometimes seems farfetched or forced, the stories themselves are usually well and interestingly told, and many of them have become in one form or another among the most popular the world over.*

THERE LIVED in a certain place a Brahman, whose name was Svabhavakripana, which means a born miser. He had collected a quantity of rice by begging, and after having dined off it, he filled a pot with what was left over. He hung the pot on a peg on the wall, placed his couch beneath, and looking intently at it all the night, he thought, "Ah, that pot is indeed brimful of rice. Now if there should be a famine, I should certainly make a hundred rupees by it. With this I shall buy a couple of goats. They will have young ones every six months, and thus I shall have a whole herd of goats. Then with the goats I shall buy cows. As soon as they have calved, I shall sell the calves. Then with the cows I shall buy buffaloes; with the buffaloes, mares. When the mares have foaled, I shall have plenty of horses; and when I sell them, plenty of gold. With that gold I shall get a house with four wings. And then a Brahman will come to my house and will give me his beautiful daughter, with a large dowry. She will have a son, and I shall call him Somasarman. When he is old enough to be danced on his father's knee, I shall sit with a book at the back of the stable, and while I am reading the boy will see me, jump from his mother's lap, and run toward me to be danced on my knee. He will come too near the horse's hoof, and full of anger I shall call to my wife, 'Take the baby, take him!' But she, distracted by some domestic work, does not hear me. Then I get up, and give her such a kick with my foot."

While he thought this, he gave a kick with his foot and broke the pot. All the rice fell over him and made him quite white.

Therefore I say, "He who makes foolish plans for the future will be white all over, like the father of Somasarman."

Interpretations

1. How did you react to the concluding statement? Did you anticipate it or were you surprised? Why do you think the storyteller considers the Brahman "foolish"—because of the quantity or the quality of his wishes? Are all his aspirations foolish? If not, which are?

2. Do you think this "panicked litany" could have been stopped earlier or later, or is it important to end it just at the point where the Brahman aspires to kick his wife? Why?

3. What details or aspects of the fable are most influential in setting its tone?

4. What changes would have to be made in the fable to adapt it to American culture?

Correspondences

1. Review the Gilman quotation (p. 421). Can you think of any examples to support it? Then review the last two paragraphs of Hiawatha's teachings. What do his admonitions suggest about his attitude towards and his aspirations for women? To what extent would Gilman "approve"?

2. Compare Hiawatha's ethics with those of the Brahman. What factors account for differences in their aspirations?

Applications

1. Is it important to have a code of ethics? On what should such a code be based? Write an essay on three moral principles in which you believe.

2. Write a journal entry on your most *painful* choice and its relationship to your aspirations.

America: The Multicultural Society

Ishmael Reed

Ishmael Reed (b. 1938) was raised and educated in Buffalo, New York, and now lives in Oakland, California. He has taught at Yale, Harvard, and Dartmouth, and currently teaches at the University of California at Berkeley. His publications include the novels The Free-Lance Pallbearers *(1967),* Mumbo Jumbo *(1978), and* Reckless Eyeballing *(1986), and two essay collections—* Shrovetide in Old New Orleans *(1979) and* Writin' Is Fightin' *(1988).*

At the annual Lower East Side Jewish Festival yesterday, a Chinese woman ate a pizza slice in front of Ty Thuan Duc's Vietnamese grocery store. Beside her a Spanish-speaking family patronized a cart with two signs: "Italian Ices" and "Kosher by Rabbi Alper." And after the pastrami ran out, everybody ate knishes.

New York Times, June 23, 1983

ON THE DAY BEFORE Memorial Day, 1983, a poet called me to describe a city he had just visited. He said that one section included mosques, built by the Islamic people who dwelled there. Attending his reading, he said, were large numbers of Hispanic people, forty thousand of whom lived in the same city. He was not talking about a fabled city located in some mysterious region of the world. The city he'd visited was Detroit.

A few months before, as I was leaving Houston, Texas, I heard it announced on the radio that Texas's largest minority was Mexican-American, and though a foundation recently issued a report critical of bilingual education, the taped voice used to guide the passengers on the air trams connecting terminals in Dallas Airport is in both Spanish and English. If the trend continues, a day will come when it will be difficult to travel through some sections of the country without hearing commands in both English and Spanish; after all, for some western states, Spanish was the first written language and the Spanish style lives on in the western way of life.

Shortly after my Texas trip, I sat in an auditorium located on the campus of the University of Wisconsin at Milwaukee as a Yale professor—whose original work on the influence of African cultures upon those of the Americas has led to his ostracism from some monocultural intellectual circles—walked up and down the aisle, like an old-time southern evangelist, dancing and drumming the top of the lectern, illustrating his points before some serious Afro-American intellectuals and artists who cheered and applauded his performance and his mastery of information. The professor was "white." After his lecture, he joined a group of Milwaukeeans in a conversation. All of the participants spoke Yoruban, though only the professor had ever traveled to Africa.

One of the artists told me that his paintings, which included African and Afro-American mythological symbols and imagery, were hanging in the local McDonald's restaurant. The next day I went to McDonald's and snapped pictures of smiling youngsters eating hamburgers below paintings that could grace the walls of any of the country's leading museums. The manager of the local McDonald's said, "I don't know what you boys are doing, but I like it," as he commissioned the local painters to exhibit in his restaurant.

Such blurring of cultural styles occurs in everyday life in the United States to a greater extent than anyone can imagine and is probably more prevalent than the sensational conflict between people of different backgrounds that is played up and often encouraged by the media. The result is what the Yale Professor, Robert Thompson, referred to as a cultural bouillabaisse,[1] yet members of the nation's present educational and cultural Elect still cling to the notion that the United States belongs to some vaguely defined entity they refer to as "Western civilization," by which they mean, presumably, a civilization created by the people of Europe, as if Europe can be viewed in monolithic terms. Is Beethoven's Ninth Symphony, which includes Turkish marches, a part of Western civilization, or the late nineteenth- and twentieth-century French paintings, whose creators were influenced by Japanese art? And what of the cubists, through whom the influence of African art changed modern painting, or the surrealists, who were so impressed with the art of the Pacific Northwest Indians that, in their map of North America, Alaska dwarfs the lower forty-eight in size?

Are the Russians, who are often criticized for their adoption of "Western" ways by Tsarist dissidents in exile, members of Western civilization? And what of the millions of Europeans who have black African and Asian ancestry, black Africans having occupied several countries for hundreds of years? Are these "Europeans" members of Western civilization, or the Hungarians, who originated across the Urals[2] in a place called Greater Hungary, or the Irish, who came from the Iberian Peninsula?

Even the notion that North America is part of Western civilization because our "system of government" is derived from Europe is being challenged by Native American historians who say that the founding fathers, Benjamin Franklin especially, were actually influenced by the system of

---

[1]Fish soup.

[2]Mountain system in USSR, traditional boundary between Europe and Asia.

government that had been adopted by the Iroquois hundreds of years prior to the arrival of large numbers of Europeans.

Western civilization, then, becomes another confusing category like Third World, or Judeo-Christian culture, as man attempts to impose his small-screen view of political and cultural reality upon a complex world. Our most publicized novelist recently said that Western civilization was the greatest achievement of mankind, an attitude that flourishes on the street level as scribbles in public restrooms: "White Power," "Niggers and Spics Suck," or "Hitler was a prophet," the latter being the most telling, for wasn't Adolph Hitler the archetypal monoculturalist who, in his pigheaded arrogance, believed that one way and one blood was so pure that it had to be protected from alien strains at all costs? Where did such an attitude, which has caused so much misery and depression in our national life, which has tainted even our noblest achievements, begin? An attitude that caused the incarceration of Japanese-American citizens during World War II, the persecution of Chicanos and Chinese-Americans, the near-extermination of the Indians, and the murder and lynchings of thousands of Afro-Americans.

Virtuous, hardworking, pious, even though they occasionally would wander off after some fancy clothes, or rendezvous in the woods with the town prostitute, the Puritans are idealized in our schoolbooks as "a hardy band" of no-nonsense patriarchs whose discipline razed the forest and brought order to the New World (a term that annoys Native American historians). Industrious, responsible, it was their "Yankee ingenuity" and practicality that created the work ethic. They were simple folk who produced a number of good poets, and they set the tone for the American writing style, of lean and spare lines, long before Hemingway. They worshiped in churches whose colors blended in with the New England snow, churches with simple structures and ornate lecterns.

The Puritans were a daring lot, but they had a mean streak. They hated the theater and banned Christmas. They punished people in a cruel and inhuman manner. They killed children who disobeyed their parents. When they came in contact with those whom they considered heathens or aliens, they behaved in such a bizarre and irrational manner that this chapter in the American history comes down to us as a late-movie horror film. They exterminated the Indians, who taught them how to survive in a world unknown to them, and their encounter with the calypso culture of Barbados resulted in what the tourist guide in Salem's Witches' House refers to as the Witchcraft Hysteria.

The Puritan legacy of hard work and meticulous accounting led to the establishment of a great industrial society; it is no wonder that the American industrial revolution began in Lowell, Massachusetts, but there was the other side, the strange and paranoid attitudes toward those different from the Elect.

The cultural attitudes of that early Elect continue to be voiced in everyday life in the United States: the president of a distinguished university, writing a letter to the *Times*, belittling the study of African civilizations; the television network that promoted its show on the Vatican art with the boast that this art represented "the finest achievements of the human spirit." A modern up-tempo state of complex rhythms that depends upon contacts with an international community can no longer behave as if it dwelled in a "Zion Wilderness"[3] surrounded by beasts and pagans.

When I heard a schoolteacher warn the other night about the invasion of the American educational system by foreign curriculums, I wanted to yell at the television set, "Lady, they're already here." It has already begun because the world is here. The world has been arriving at these shores for at least ten thousand years from Europe, Africa, and Asia. In the late nineteenth and early twentieth centuries, large numbers of Europeans arrived, adding their cultures to those of the European, African, and Asian settlers who were already here, and recently millions have been entering the country from South America and the Caribbean, making Yale professor Bob Thompson's bouillabaisse richer and thicker.

One of our most visionary politicians said that he envisioned a time when the United States could become the brain of the world, by which he meant the repository of all of the latest advanced information systems. I thought of that remark when an enterprising poet friend of mine called to say that he had just sold a poem to a computer magazine and that the editors were delighted to get it because they didn't carry fiction or poetry. Is that the kind of world we desire? A humdrum homogeneous world of all brains and no heart, no fiction, no poetry; a world of robots with human attendants bereft of imagination, of culture? Or does North America deserve a more exciting destiny? To become a place where the cultures of the world crisscross. This is possible because the United States is unique in the world: The world is here.

Interpretations

1. "Such blurring of cultural styles occurs in everyday life in the United States . . ." What do you think Reed means by "blurring"? Do you think Reed would prefer cultural identities to be lost, blurred, or "melted" (as in "melting pot")—or retained and respected? Cite evidence for your position.

2. What is the purpose of this essay? Is it to argue that "Western civilization" is a vague concept or entity? Is it to state that cultural blurring is already occurring in the United States ("Lady, [foreign curricula] are already here")? Is it to argue that such blurring should be encouraged ("a more exciting destiny")? Or is it some other purpose? Where is his purpose most clearly indicated?

[3]Variously, a hill in Jerusalem, the Jewish people or homeland, Judaism.

3. What is your reaction to Reed's depiction of the Puritans? Just how important were the Puritans in establishing American "aspirations"?

4. The last paragraph of this essay contends that the United States should lead the world not only in brains but also in imagination. Is this a new idea or a continuation of an earlier one? How might this type of leadership be accomplished? How effective is this concluding paragraph?

Correspondences

1. Why, according to Reed, are categories like "Western civilization, . . . Third World, or Judeo-Christian culture" reflections of "man's attempts to impose his small-screen view of political and cultural reality upon a complex world"? What evidence from other ethnic groups does Reed offer to support his thesis? Which writers in this anthology can you imagine agreeing with him? Who are most likely to disagree? Offer evidence to support your choices.

2. Review Reed's assessment of the positive and negative aspects of the Puritan legacy. How does it compare with that of Novak (Chapter 5)? To what extent do you agree with the views of either or both?

Applications

1. What is cultural assimilation as opposed to cultural "crisscrossing" (Reed's term)? Define each and cite examples that clearly illustrate how they differ.

2. Yale professor Robert Thompson refers to the blending of cultural styles as a "cultural bouillabaisse". What cultural contribution of your ethnic group(s) do you value most? (How does it enrich the "bouillabaisse"?)

For My Indian Daughter

Lewis P. Johnson

Lewis P. Johnson (b. 1935) was raised in Harbor Springs, Michigan, where his great-grandfather was the last official chief of the Potawatomi Ottawas. A surveyor by profession, Johnson is currently working on a study of the Indian approaches to interpretive dreams. In "For My Indian Daughter," Johnson portrays his personal odyssey towards greater ethnic pride and cultural awareness.

According to tradition, the Ottawas, the Ojibway, and the Potawatomi were originally one tribe living north of the Great Lakes. After the Ottawas separated they were active in the Indian Wars as allies of the French. After joining the Huron at Mackinaw in Michigan (adjacent to the area of Johnson's hometown of Harbor Springs and nearby Burt Lake), the Ottawa dispersed over a wide area. When first encountered by whites (in the seventeenth century), the Potawatomi lived mainly near the mouth of the Green Bay in Wisconsin. By the end of the century, they had settled along both sides of the southern end of Lake Michigan. The majority of the tribe still lives in Michigan.

MY LITTLE GIRL is singing herself to sleep upstairs, her voice mingling with the sounds of the birds outside in the old maple trees. She is two and I am nearly 50, and I am very taken with her. She came along late in my life, unexpected and unbidden, a startling gift.

Today at the beach my chubby-legged, brown-skinned daughter ran laughing into the water as fast as she could. My wife and I laughed watching her, until we heard behind us a low guttural curse and then an unpleasant voice raised in an imitation war whoop.

I turned to see a fat man in a bathing suit, white and soft as a grub, as he covered his mouth and prepared to make the Indian war cry again. He was middle-aged, younger than I, and had three little children lined up next to him, grinning foolishly. My wife suggested we leave the beach, and I agreed.

I knew the man was not unusual in his feelings against Indians. His beach behavior might have been socially unacceptable to more civilized whites, but his basic view of Indians is expressed daily in our small town, frequently on the editorial pages of the county newspaper, as white people speak out against Indian fishing rights and land rights, saying in essence, "Those Indians are taking our fish, our land." It doesn't matter to them that we were here first, that the U.S. Supreme Court has ruled in our favor. It matters to them that we have something they want, and they hate us for it. Backlash is the common explanation of the attacks on Indians, the bumper stickers that say,

"Spear an Indian, Save a Fish," but I know better. The hatred of Indians goes back to the beginning when white people came to this country. For me it goes back to my childhood in Harbor Springs, Michigan.

Theft

Harbor Springs is now a summer resort for the very affluent, but a hundred years ago it was the Indian village of my Ottawa ancestors. My grandmother, Anna Showanessy, and other Indians like her, had their land there taken by treaty, by fraud, by violence, by theft. They remembered how whites had burned down the village at Burt Lake in 1900 and pushed the Indians out. These were the stories in my family.

When I was a boy my mother told me to walk down the alleys in Harbor Springs and not to wear my orange football sweater out of the house. This way I would not stand out, not be noticed, and not be a target.

I wore my orange sweater anyway and deliberately avoided the alleys. I was the biggest person I knew and wasn't really afraid. But I met my comeuppance when I enlisted in the U.S. Army. One night all the men in my barracks gathered together and, gang-fashion, pulled me into the shower and scrubbed me down with rough brushes used for floors, saying, "We won't have any dirty Indians in our outfit." It is a point of irony that I was cleaner than any of them. Later in Korea I learned how to kill, how to bully, how to hate Koreans. I came out of the war tougher than ever and, strangely, white.

I went to college, got married, lived in La Porte, Indiana, worked as a surveyor and raised three boys. I headed Boy Scout groups, never thinking it odd when the Scouts did imitation Indian dances, imitation Indian lore.

One day when I was 35 or thereabouts I heard about an Indian powwow. My father used to attend them and so with great curiosity and a strange joy at discovering a part of my heritage, I decided the thing to do to get ready for this big event was to have my friend make me a spear in his forge. The steel was fine and blue and iridescent. The feathers on the shaft were bright and proud.

In a dusty state fairground in southern Indiana, I found white people dressed as Indians. I learned they were "hobbyists," that is, it was their hobby and leisure pastime to masquerade as Indians on weekends. I felt ridiculous with my spear, and I left.

It was years before I could tell anyone of the embarrassment of this weekend and see any humor in it. But in a way it was that weekend, for all its silliness, that was my awakening. I realized I didn't know who I was. I didn't have an Indian name. I didn't speak the Indian language. I didn't know the Indian customs. Dimly I remembered the Ottawa word for dog, but it was a baby word, *kahgee,* not the full word, *muhkahgee,* which I was later to learn. Even more hazily I remembered a naming ceremony (my own). I remembered legs dancing around me, dust. Where had that been? Who had I been? "Suwaukquat," my mother told me when I asked, "where the tree begins to grow."

That was 1968, and I was not the only Indian in the country who was feeling the need to remember who he or she was. There were others. They had powwows, real ones, and eventually I found them. Together we researched our past, a search that for me culminated in the Longest Walk, a march on Washington in 1978. Maybe because I now know what it means to be Indian, it surprises me that others don't. Of course there aren't very many of us left. The chances of an average person knowing an average Indian in an average lifetime are pretty slim.

Circle

Still, I was amused one day when my small, four-year-old neighbor looked at me as I was hoeing in my garden and said, "You aren't a real Indian, are you?" Scotty is little, talkative, likable. Finally I said, "I'm a real Indian." He looked at me for a moment and then said, squinting into the sun, "Then where's your horse and feathers?" The child was simply a smaller, whiter version of my own ignorant self years before. We'd both seen too much TV, that's all. He was not to be blamed. And so, in a way, the moronic man on the beach today is blameless. We come full circle to realize other people are like ourselves, as discomfiting as that may be sometimes.

As I sit in my old chair on my porch, in a light that is fading so the leaves are barely distinguishable against the sky, I can picture my girl asleep upstairs. I would like to prepare her for what's to come, take her each step of the way saying, there's a place to avoid, here's what I know about this, but much of what's before her she must go through alone. She must pass through pain and joy and solitude and community to discover her own inner self that is unlike any other and come through that passage to the place where she sees all people are one, and in so seeing may live her life in a brighter future.

Interpretations

1. What audience besides his daughter is Johnson writing for? Cite evidence. Why do you suppose he waited until he was nearly fifty and had a daughter—he has three other children, boys—to express these thoughts?

2. "I didn't know who I was." What do we have to know about ourselves before we know who we are? How important is ancestry to a sense of identity? What should be our attitude toward our ancestry—or ancestries?

3. Until he asked his mother, Johnson did not know his Indian name, Suwaukquat. Why do you suppose she withheld it? How do you think you
would feel to discover that you had another name? Why?

4. What was involved in Johnson's "finding himself"? Why must such a search
be conducted with others? How did white society delay the search and make
it difficult?

5. How does the return to the "moronic man on the beach" in the conclusion
sum up what Johnson has to say? How does the tone of the image change
in the conclusion (even though the man is still called "moronic")? How does
the description—in both the introduction and the conclusion—of his daughter, the maples, and the birds affect the tone of the essay as a whole?

Correspondences

1. Review the King quotation (page 422). How does it apply to "For My Indian
Daughter"? What judgment of the United States is implied in each father's
dreams?

2. Who prompts Johnson to explore his cultural heritage? How has that experience affected his aspirations? Which other writers in this chapter undergo
a similar experience? With what effect?

Applications

1. "We come full circle to realize other people are like ourselves, as discomfiting
as that may be sometimes." To what extent do you agree with Johnson?

2. Write a journal entry on a part of your cultural heritage you might someday
want to share with your children.

The Fourth of July

Audre Lorde

Audre Lorde (b. 1934) is from New York City. She was educated at Hunter College and Columbia University, and has taught at various colleges of the City University of New York. She has been a professor of English at Hunter College since 1981. Her publications include Between Ourselves *(1976) and* Chosen Poems *(1982). In the following excerpt from her autobiography* Zami: A New Spelling of My Name *(1982),* Lorde *compares her expectations as an African-American with those of her African-Caribbean immigrant parents.*

THE FIRST TIME I went to Washington, D.C., was on the edge of the summer when I was supposed to stop being a child. At least that's what they said to us all at graduation from the eighth grade. My sister Phyllis graduated at the same time from high school. I don't know what she was supposed to stop being. But as graduation presents for us both, the whole family took a Fourth of July trip to Washington, D.C., the fabled and famous capital of our country.

It was the first time I'd ever been on a railroad train during the day. When I was little, and we used to go to the Connecticut shore, we always went at night on the milk train, because it was cheaper.

Preparations were in the air around our house before school was even over. We packed for a week. There were two very large suitcases that my father carried, and a box filled with food. In fact, my first trip to Washington was a mobile feast; I started eating as soon as we were comfortably ensconced in our seats, and did not stop until somewhere after Philadelphia. I remember it was Philadelphia because I was disappointed not to have passed by the Liberty Bell.

My mother had roasted two chickens and cut them up into dainty bite-size pieces. She packed slices of brown bread and butter and green pepper and carrot sticks. There were little violently yellow iced cakes with scalloped edges called "marigolds," that came from Cushman's Bakery. There was a spice bun and rock-cakes from Newton's, the West Indian bakery across Lenox Avenue from St. Mark's School, and iced tea in a wrapped mayonnaise jar. There were sweet pickles for us and dill pickles for my father, and peaches with the fuzz still on them, individually wrapped to keep them from bruising. And, for neatness, there were piles of napkins and a little tin box with a washcloth dampened with rosewater and glycerine for wiping sticky mouths.

I wanted to eat in the dining car because I had read all about them, but my mother reminded me for the umpteenth time that dining car food always cost too much money and besides, you never could tell whose hands had been playing all over that food, nor where those same hands had been just before. My mother never mentioned that Black people were not allowed into railroad dining cars headed south in 1947. As usual, whatever my mother did not like and could not change, she ignored. Perhaps it would go away, deprived of her attention.

I learned later that Phyllis's high school senior class trip had been to Washington, but the nuns had given her back her deposit in private, explaining to her that the class, all of whom were white, except Phyllis, would be staying in a hotel where Phyllis "would not be happy," meaning, Daddy explained to her, also in private, that they did not rent rooms to Negroes. "We will take among-you to Washington, ourselves," my father had avowed, "and not just for an overnight in some measly fleabag hotel."

American racism was a new and crushing reality that my parents had to deal with every day of their lives once they came to this country. They handled it as a private woe. My mother and father believed that they could best protect their children from the realities of race in america and the fact of american racism by never giving them name, much less discussing their nature. We were told we must never trust white people, but *why* was never explained, nor the nature of their ill will. Like so many other vital pieces of information in my childhood, I was supposed to know without being told. It always seemed like a very strange injunction coming from my mother, who looked so much like one of those people we were never supposed to trust. But something always warned me not to ask my mother why she wasn't white, and why Auntie Lillah and Auntie Etta weren't, even though they were all that same problematic color so different from my father and me, even from my sisters, who were somewhere in-between.

In Washington, D.C., we had one large room with two double beds and an extra cot for me. It was a back-street hotel that belonged to a friend of my father's who was in real estate, and I spent the whole next day after Mass squinting up at the Lincoln Memorial where Marian Anderson had sung after the D.A.R. refused to allow her to sing in their auditorium because she was Black. Or because she was "Colored," my father said as he told us the story. Except that what he probably said was "Negro," because for his times, my father was quite progressive.

I was squinting because I was in that silent agony that characterized all of my childhood summers, from the time school let out in June to the end of July, brought about by my dilated and vulnerable eyes exposed to the summer brightness.

I viewed Julys through an agonizing corolla of dazzling whiteness and I always hated the Fourth of July, even before I came to realize the travesty such a celebration was for Black people in this country.

My parents did not approve of sunglasses, nor of their expense.

I spent the afternoon squinting up at monuments to freedom and past presidencies and democracy, and wondering why the light and heat were both so much stronger in Washington, D.C., than back home in New York City. Even the pavement on the streets was a shade lighter in color than back home.

Late that Washington afternoon my family and I walked back down Pennsylvania Avenue. We were a proper caravan, mother bright and father brown, the three of us girls step-standards in-between. Moved by our historical surroundings and the heat of the early evening, my father decreed yet another treat. He had a great sense of history, a flair for the quietly dramatic and the sense of specialness of an occasion and a trip.

"Shall we stop and have a little something to cool off, Lin?"

Two blocks away from our hotel, the family stopped for a dish of vanilla ice cream at a Breyer's ice cream and soda fountain. Indoors, the soda fountain was dim and fan-cooled, deliciously relieving to my scorched eyes.

Corded and crisp and pinafored, the five of us seated ourselves one by one at the counter. There was I between my mother and father, and my two sisters on the other side of my mother. We settled ourselves along the white mottled marble counter, and when the waitress spoke at first no one understood what she was saying, and so the five of us just sat there.

The waitress moved along the line of us closer to my father and spoke again. "I said I kin give you to take out, but you can't eat here. Sorry." Then she dropped her eyes looking very embarrassed, and suddenly we heard what it was she was saying all at the same time, loud and clear.

Straight-backed and indignant, one by one, my family and I got down from the counter stools and turned around and marched out of the store, quiet and outraged, as if we had never been Black before. No one would answer my emphatic questions with anything other than a guilty silence. "But we hadn't done anything!" This wasn't right or fair! Hadn't I written poems about Bataan and freedom and democracy for all?

My parents wouldn't speak of this injustice, not because they had contributed to it, but because they felt they should have anticipated it and avoided it. This made me even angrier. My fury was not going to be acknowledged by a like fury. Even my two sisters copied my parents' pretense that nothing unusual and anti-american had occurred. I was left to write my angry letter to the president of the united states all by myself, although my father did promise I could type it out on the office typewriter next week, after I showed it to him in my copybook diary.

The waitress was white, and the counter was white, and the ice cream I never ate in Washington, D.C., that summer I left childhood was white, and the white heat and the white pavement and the white stone monuments of my first Washington summer made me sick to my stomach for the whole rest of that trip and it wasn't much of a graduation present after all.

Interpretations

1. How do Lorde's descriptions of elaborate picnic food, the pretexts for avoiding of the dining car, and the story of Phyllis's exclusion from her senior class trip increase the impact of the final event of the essay?

2. Where does Lorde reveal how she feels about her parent's general policy of trying to "anticipate and avoid" racial prejudice? In similar circumstances would you feel the same way as Lorde? Why or why not?

3. The tone of the sentence (in the first paragraph) "I don't know what she was supposed to stop being" is somewhat ironic. Find other passages in a similar tone. Is this also the tone of the last paragraph? What is the essay's prevailing tone?

Correspondences

1. What is ironic about the date of Lorde's graduation trip? What incidents occur that contribute to the irony? Compare the author's experience with that of Parks (Chapter 6).

2. "My mother and father believed that they could best protect their children from the realities of race in america and the fact of american racism by never giving them name, much less discussing their nature." What do you think of their manner of protection? Compare the attitude of Parks's parents towards language and racism with that of Marshall's "poets" (Chapter 3), also Caribbean immigrants.

Applications

1. "As usual, whatever my mother did not like and could not change, she ignored. Perhaps it would go away, deprived of her attention." Is it better to ignore unpleasant realities or to confront them? Which attitude is more likely to nurture aspirations? Explain your answer.

2. View a video of *Born on the Fourth of July* and write an analysis of the importance of that date in Lorde's essay and Stone's film.

Days of Awe

Joanne Greenberg

*Joanne Greenberg (b. 1932) is a native of Brooklyn, New York, and a graduate
of the American University and the University of London. Her highly acclaimed
novel* I Never Promised You a Rose Garden *(1964) was published under
the pseudonym Hannah Green. Under her own name, she has published other
novels and also short stories, including* A Season of Delight *(1981),* The
Far Side of Victory *(1983), and* Summering *(1966). In "Days of Awe,"
she portrays the anguish of a Jewish mother whose children have rejected Judaism.*

I USED TO DISLIKE shopping, the rushing to too many stores, all the details
to remember. Now it's almost pleasant. I shop in the morning when the
stores are uncrowded and the early light gleams off the beige brick and glass
of the storefronts. Since Joshua and Miriam are grown and gone, there's less
to do and I can see the young mothers, some of them harried and embattled,
with a sympathy that will soon, very soon, become nostalgia. I like the silence
and order of the house now that I'm used to it. Adam and I sit close together
at his end of the table. We thought we would have less to talk about when
the children were gone, but it turned out not to be so. The daily happenings
still happen and the greater events also.

Rosh Hashanah, the Jewish New Year, has just passed; these are the
Days of Awe, the days between the New Year and Yom Kippur, the Day of
Atonement. In the old days, people faced this week in terror. They cried
aloud in the synagogues, they ran weeping to their neighbors, pressing unpaid
debts upon them before it should be too late and their measuring by the
Lord be over and the mark against them made and blotted. We don't weep
now. Debt is fashionable and we are decorous, rational, and fearless, but it's
still possible to dream old-fashioned nightmares during the week of Awe. I
am forty-seven and the freedom and wealth of my life here are shadowed
during this week with smoke whispering from the chimneys of camps I have
never seen. My grandparents' villages are gone. This Gilboa is in Pennsylvania
and it is autumn here, a blue and golden day, with the mellow warmth of
late summer still in it. I go in to my shopping.

The stores are in a covered mall but the mall is pleasant, lit by skylights.
Down the long center gallery are places to sit; there are trees and shrubbery
planted under the skylights. The people on the squad know that Thursday
I'm out of service until noon, so my pace is leisurely but not idle. Store to
store, steadily. I have my list. I'm a good housewife.

But when I come out of the grocery store, instead of going directly to

444

the car and home, I go to one of the mall's benches and sit down. It's not so I can remember before I leave the one or two things I've forgotten on my list. I want to think about the holiday a little more—about chimneys and villages I have never seen—to give it its time.

There's a young man approaching the bench. I smile a little, in acknowledgment, and move over. To my surprise, he comes up to me and I see that the basket he is carrying is not for shopping but has flowers and leaflets in it. He takes one of these leaflets and hands it to me. There's a picture of a boy and a girl on it.

"Excuse me, ma'am," he says politely, "but did you know that millions of our children are hooked on drugs?"

My hand almost starts for my purse and the donation I think he wants, but then I remember and my heart sinks.

"You're not the Salvation Army or a drug program," I say, and the words come tired and sad. "You're the Unification Church."

"We do a lot of good," he says. "We have programs in all the major cities for drug addicts and runaways."

"You steal Jews," I say.

He has been taught to answer such things, but he misgauges me.

"We're not anti-Semitic," he says. "I myself had a Jewish background. My parents are Jewish."

We are both surprised and he is mortified when I begin to cry. The tears are so sudden and so overwhelming that they have come up into my eyes and flowed over before I know it, as though they had been waiting in ambush for this boy's arrival. But my voice is still steady, and while I have it, I have him.

"Hitler killed one-third of us. A language, a culture, a way of life. Only our dispersion saved us from complete extinction. Now through that—that wound in our People, more blood is flowing away. You and all the others, to the cults that promise heaven which, if they get the power they hunger for, will revenge their parents with hell."

"We don't seek—"

"*You* don't, you poor sap," I cry, "but *they* do. Somewhere in Illinois my son is dressed in yellow and is chanting someone else's ancestral language. His head is shaved. He and you eat, and don't eat for what you call ritual reasons. You're burlesque artists, parodists!"

"Judaism is a bankrupt faith."

I am suddenly, overwhelmingly tired. "When did you invest a moment of yourself in it?" I say.

It's no good and I see it. He can't see my visions, understand my pain. Free and equal. I know, I know. I am I and you are you. My voice is compromised. I'm crying outright.

Blushing wildly, he leaves me. Like any good American, he is unnerved by the public demonstration of emotion. Except in groups. A Jewish mother weeping is his metaphor for hell, a banality he cannot endure. And I, too, am American. I can't sit blubbering in a shopping center mall at eleven in the morning for no visible reason. I'm back on call at eleven. I blow my nose and dry my eyes and drive home.

No more about the Illinois renunciate, I tell myself. But my mind drifts as I drive. Joshua has given over his name, an ordinary Jewish name by which other Jews can know him and other Christians, too, as one of a people, a line, a tradition, a curse, a sorrow, a glory, a law. His new names are Sanskrit. He doesn't realize it but he comes two generations too late. How popular he might have been in Munich in 1934. He is that one most enviable of forebears, an Aryan. It is an irony I cannot share with him. It occurs to me that it has been three days since I last thought of Joshua-Sanjit. Three days without anguish and now the anguish returns.

Miriam also has gone into a world where Jews disappear. She is liberated from her husband and works at a Women's Center in California. I admire her commitments to battered wives and rape victims and the exploited of the Third World. Sadly for me, none of her commitments involves the continued existence of her own people. The blacks and Chicanos with whom she castigates me multiply in all their variety and rich profusion. The poor of the world are not an endangered species. Her former husband was not Jewish and she laughed at me when I begged her to consider raising Kimberley, who is legally so, as a Jew. It wasn't for me, I said, but for our people, so that Hitler would lose again, would lose forever.

"Everything has to change," she said, "some things have to die out, I guess."

Did I tell her that about Biafra, about the American Indians, that she should say it was about *my* minority? *My* people? I wonder: Is there anyone more lonely than the champion of an unfashionable cause?

Unaccountably, as I ride, the day opens outward. The autumn smells its briny apple-smell, but the sun is still in summer. I have the windows open and though I was angry and sobbing twenty minutes ago, there was a relief in the tears and I feel better for them, close to the day and the center of my life. Adam and I didn't die when Miriam met a man and moved in and married without our presence. I made apologies to the family, to my mother who blames me for the loss, to all the aunts and uncles, and went on living. Joshua quit college and found the tide that carried him so far away, and we didn't die then, either. We only spoke a little more quietly when we sat together at dinner. In our ancestral castle we live like modern nobility. There are rooms shut, to save on heat. We remember those rooms, every inch of them, and everything with which they were furnished, but we don't often unlock them and we try to live warmly in the rest of the house.

When I get home, I back into the driveway so that the car faces out. I go into the house and before I unload my groceries, I check the call box. No red light. I call Rita Neri, our dispatcher. I am home.

"O.K.," she says, and we hang up. I'm in the fire and rescue service of this district. There's a dispatch box in the stairwell, and a red gumball light on the roof of my car. If there's an auto wreck or a fire or a heart attack or a serious fall or a sudden illness in Gilboa or the farms or suburbs around it any time of the day or night, I'll hear about it on the call box and I'll go and help deal with it. I've been on the squad for five years, and the whole district including "The Loop" of the Interstate is heavy with anecdote for me.

I unpack my groceries then and put them away. There's no class today, nothing special for me to do, and although I know I should study or do the windows or write letters, I do none of these things. I sit down at the kitchen table and let the day wash over me.

Last year, our student rabbi spoke about the High Holidays and gave examples of Galut—exile. The harvest festival of Succos, soon to come, would find our evenings too cold to sit, as the celebration decrees, under the stars in magical booths hung with bunches of grapes. It is balmy in this season in Jerusalem, but one does not stay dreaming starward, somnolent and peaceful in these latitudes. Half an hour in a *succah* in this Gilboa and hypothermia would set in. To be unable to celebrate the feast correctly, seasonably, is exile, he said, be we ever so wealthy and at peace, be our neighbors ever so warmly disposed to us.

It was a good sermon and must have been partly true or I wouldn't have remembered it. But God is everywhere and He has arranged recompenses for His exiles. The wine-crisp tang of autumn does not blow through Jerusalem. Halleluiah the hills, but not in Haifa. Haifa has hills enough, but they never blaze with a thousand fires in a hundred tones of rose-gold, flame and orange, yellow, purple, umber. My exile lies in fragrant piles on my doorstep and breaks beneath my feet in the snap-twig woodsmoke mornings of my father's chosen land.

Now, I think, would be a suitable time to cry. The house is clean and in order. Adam isn't due home for hours. I could get the old pictures of Joshua and Miriam out of the boxes in the attic and set them around me and remember the hope and the work and the planning, the new starts, the books we read, the pangs of conscience we suffered. It's too late. I have cried my cry already in front of another woman's fool and it's over. The phone rings. I smile. Had I been crying, whoever it was would have caught me at it.

It's Riva, my mother-in-law. Poor woman; she was never very religious but because she's Adam's mother she feels she owes it to her position to uphold the values of her generation. "Grace, Yom Kippur is tomorrow and I still haven't settled things in my mind. What are we planning to do?"

"I think it will all go pretty much as it did last year," I say. "The service will start at nine-thirty, with one break. Afternoon is one-thirty with one break and four-thirty to sundown. Some people will want to go home and break the fast with their families. For those who want to stay there will be a light meal, dairy. What do you want to do? If you want to stay, we will too. If not, we'll all come back here and eat. In any case, I'm down for a potato pudding and a salad. What do you think?"

"When Elia was alive it was so much nicer. We all stayed then. Now . . . And I wish we didn't have services at the town hall. It's so . . ."

"I know," I say. "But right now there is no other place. We've gotten too big for Bert and Joan's basement."

"It was nice there."

I know what she means. Five years ago, the Jews of Gilboa, Russian Grove, and Tarrant numbered no more than twenty families, and of these only half were observant. For years we met in the Finegolds' rumpus room. "The Sisterhood" was four women, the "Hebrew School" eight kids and a teacher; then a new housing development came in between Tarrant and Gilboa and Jews from the suburbs west of Midlothian found it pleasant to come west on the Interstate to us instead of going to the city. Two years ago we found we had to look for another place. Since then we've been meeting in a corner of the town hall basement. There are cooking facilities there and lots of chairs; there are no religious reminders to distract us, but we are dwarfed in the large hall. The sound we make, even praying all together, doesn't fill half the space. We are conscious as never before of ourselves as a minority, a decimated minority.

"I know, Riva, but what can we do? I'm grateful the town fathers let us meet down there. They could have gotten stuffy and talked about separation of church and state. I wish there were a bigger house or a smaller hall that would have us." She sighs into the phone. My signals go up. "What's the matter—is something wrong?"

"No—no. I suppose it's the end of summer. Whenever I have to put on a heavy sweater in the morning, I remember I'm an old lady. Elia used to say, 'One foot in the grave and the other on a banana peel.' " We talk for a while longer—something she isn't saying, isn't ready to say—and when we hang up I find I'm tense and tired. I put up a cup of tea and have a piece of the cake Adam brought home last night. Food, the Jewish tranquilizer. I should be grateful; it could have been booze. Leaving the kitchen door open, I go out to the little porch in back and sit down.

Adam grew up in Gilboa. It was a small Pennsylvania farm town before Midlothian got big with the heavy industry of World War II. Elia Dowben came here in 1912 and set up a dry goods and clothing store. Over the years, the dry goods business was taken over by chains, but the old man, a Russian Jewish peasant from Shedletz, turned out to have a designer's eye for style and an intuitive sense of the wants of his customers. The clothing store flourished. Three years later, he contacted a marriage broker in New York who supplied him with a wife, Riva, from a village near Shedletz. They and their children were the only Jews in Gilboa until the mid-forties. I was raised in Chicago. I met Adam in college and came to Gilboa, to what my family still considers an exile worse than Babylonian. I like the town and the sense of community that, although changed and diluted by the new populations, still speaks in an older voice, in the fire department and the church and between neighbors. It roots Adam, centers him. Although a Jew, he's less an exile than the people I grew up with.

The Caetanos' teen-age daughter is entertaining her friends and the music drifts across to me mellowed, sweetened by distance. I have a book on trauma that I am studying for a class and I dip into it desultorily. It's more important just now to study exactly how the golden field gets its shadows and how the shadows pull long and then how the sun will go behind the hills on the way to Midlothian. When the sun goes, the shadows are destroyed. Then everything stands in equal light, a glow in which each visible thing is made real, complete, itself. And because the year has turned, there will be a little haunting coolness when the light goes. Because we are a little higher than the town we get the light later, so I sit and wait for the first lights to be lit down there. The District. My Chicago relatives are aghast at my doing fire and rescue work. It seems bizarre to them, although there are middle-aged women doing it all over the country. I like the work for many reasons, one of them being that I am able, by virtue of what we do, to look out over Gilboa and on to the great loop of the Interstate exit by exit and know that all of it is, at this moment, within the widest limits possible, at rest.

I think that I should get myself ready for the holiday, stop thinking about classes or cleaning or rescue, take what advantages there are in the serenity of an empty house, and slow down so that I can overtake the holiday at its pace, walking. Adam will be home at five-thirty. We'll eat and be ready for the evening service, and this time we should leave early and walk slowly. We could even go down over the field while it's still light, the short cut that our kids and the ones who live on these streets take to school.

The alarm, two ululant wails and the sheriff's man: "Attention Gilboa Fire and Rescue. You have a first aid at the Methodist Church, Federal and Larch." The call is repeated. I am in my red rescue coat and out the door before the end of the second call. It's six blocks to the church, but there are as many turns, and even with red light and siren, dangerous at this time of day. When I get to the church, Geri Pines, the squad captain, and some of the others are there. Geri radios to the rest of the squad to stand down; we will not need any more people.

We go inside and a woman motions us down to the basement. Then I remember the day, yes, Wednesday, Altar Guild day, and there they are, around the table at their newest project, the raffle quilt for the repair of the leak on the south wall. We stop for a moment. Who is it? Who among all these old women that we know is the one in pain, the one who is short of breath—I think *no,* but it is. They stand aside, away from her as they never would do for one of their living friends in pain. It's Violet, my friend Violet Cleve, my first friend in Gilboa. She's sitting at her place at rest in her chair.

Her hands are on the quilt the women are making. She looks no different from her usual self. I go over and feel for a pulse. None. She's cold. Her legs have stiffened. I know we could not resuscitate her. I know what it would take to try. I shake my head. Geri comes over and listens, then feels at the legs. "How old a woman was she?" Geri asks. I open my mouth to say "seventy," but Addie Arvis says, "Ninety-five. She was ninety-five." Of course. The years, the years have gone by.

"She's been sitting here quietly dead for half an hour at least," Geri says. It's a statement that tells the squad we will not start work on her. It's something on which we all must agree and we all do. The ladies haven't wanted to move her. They are standing back, murmuring at the suddenness. Geri goes out to call the coroner from Midlothian. Someone must stay until he comes and I ask to let it be me. We ease Violet over on to a bench, and cover her. Since the death was unexpected, state law takes over. There's nothing more to do.

I sit and wait, thinking how satisfying rescue is except when there is nothing to be done—except when the pain and death are those of a friend.

Adam is home. I hear the mailbox slam shut because he knows I sometimes forget the mail. I haven't this time. I smile. There's a silence as he comes up the walk and then there is the sound of his step on the front porch and then the door opening. He's early. This past year he's been taking off for a couple of hours on the days when the store is open until nine. I want him to come out here where I'm sitting. I want to tell him about the young man with the flowers and the Jewish parents. We've been through twenty-five years together: a war, death and birth, hopes blossoming, hopes in blight. I want to tell him this, too, but I'm worried that he'll take it the wrong way. Men have strange ideas about the fragility of women. I don't want him to see my weeping as more than it was. But what it was I don't know myself. Now I hear him moving through the house. It makes me smile again. He'll glance at the mail on the hall table, then come into the kitchen and take the cracked mug, the big one with his name on it that the children gave him one birthday long ago, and he'll pour himself a cup of coffee and soon he'll be out here to sit in his butt-sprung old chair and look out over the field and down the long hill to where Gilboa's main streets, hidden by trees, lift their few spires and building tops. Beyond Gilboa, the bypassing freeway arches. To the east of the fields it comes around to us close on the other side. We hear the traffic as a low, constant hum. It's getting a little cooler. I call to him and as I do I decide I'll wait until I know what my tears are before I burden him with them. Perhaps we'll walk to services the back way to the town hall, down over the field and the hill.

We've been so close for so long that it is only in flashes that I see him aging, and I have one of these as he comes toward me. How gray he is now! There are wrinkles around his eyes. It must be the same with me, although

I don't really see it. In another twenty years, if we are lucky, we will both be old. I ask him about his day.

Interpretations

1. What evidence suggests that Grace's religion is very important to her?

2. To what extent has the decision of both of her children to leave Judaism affected the narrator's relationship with them?

3. Why is it ironic that Grace is "out the door before the end of the second call" and that the alarm takes her to a Methodist church?

4. Grace remarks that her husband Adam worries about her "fragility." Is she in fact fragile? Cite evidence for your viewpoint. (If she is, does she have a way of handling her fragility?)

5. What do you think is the main point of the story? Is it stated directly or found only between the lines?

6. Explain the significance of the title.

Correspondences

1. Lorde's essay is written from a child's point of view; Greenberg's, from a parent's. How does point of view affect reader response? (With whom do you empathize in each case?)

2. What aspects of Jewish culture are discussed in "Days of Awe" and "The Impossible Became No Longer Unthinkable" (Chapter 6)? What is Greenberg's attitude toward her religion? Why have her children rejected Judaism?

Applications

1. To what extent is Greenberg's protagonist a person of conviction? How strong are her convictions and what are they? How have they affected her life and those of her children?

2. "Is there anyone more lonely than the champion of an unfashionable cause?" Do you consider yourself such a champion? If so, to what cause are you committed? Write an essay explaining your reasons to an unsympathetic audience. What tone should you adopt?

Rachel Maria Asrelsky

Ralph J. Lamberti

Ralph J. Lamberti is a former borough president of Staten Island, New York. The selection which follows is his memorial eulogy to Rachel Maria Asrelsky.

IN A FEW MINUTES we'll be hearing "The Trumpet Shall Sound" by Handel. Rachel had said that she wanted that aria performed at her wedding. Not that Rachel was contemplating marriage. She wasn't even engaged. Indeed, marriage, I think, had little to do with it. Rather, her selection of an aria years in advance of her wedding was a function of her energy.

Only Rachel, and that handful of endlessly buoyant people like her, could have requested wedding music long before she accepted someone's hand in matrimony. Her energy required that if she liked a piece of music, it could not be allowed to pass but be held onto and scheduled for use in her boundless future.

Some of us may drift through time and space. Not Rachel. She steamed full throttle, filling every place and every moment she occupied with her energy. And what energy it was.

When God made Rachel, He, or as Rachel might say, She, created a whirlwind.

On the program, you'll note Rachel's middle name. It is not pronounced Maria. She pronounced it More-riah. As in, "Call the Wind Moriah."

It was apt. She had the energy of a full gale.

I first encountered it in 1984 in San Francisco. I was a delegate to the national Democratic Party Convention. My wife, Sue, and I were waiting for a trolley when out of nowhere appeared cousin Rachel. Her energy could knock you over.

In less than 24 hours, I had secured for her a visitor's pass, and she was on the convention floor politiking relentlessly by day, attending political dinners by night. She was only 16, and visiting friends in San Francisco.

But already by that time, travelling and sightseeing had become a passion for her, a passion that only increased through the years.

She was the ultimate sightseer. This past October, she declined a second visit to her beloved Capri because she felt obliged to travel to southern Italy and poke around a Greek temple.

As her host family in Italy said of her: "Most students come to Italy to study art; Rachel came to study Italy."

But she was no idle tourist. Beneath the torrent of energy that was her outward life there was deep inside her, a pool of such stillness and depth that in talking and confiding to her others became calm and derived strength. In her depths, they could see themselves with a fiercer clarity.

From her days at Stuyvesant High School and then at Grinnell College, Rachel was psychiatrist, counsellor, confessor and advisor to many. There was a certitude to her that her energy complemented, and it drew people who sought help from their own insecurities.

And she had help to offer. Her strength and determination were always evident. You experienced them directly as soon as you conversed with her. You inferred them quickly by simply observing her.

No one, I found myself thinking, could go off in so many directions, and achieve so much, unless she was motivated by clear direction and mature understanding.

This clarity and maturity were evident in the small things she did as in the big things.

She had written a research paper for the Grinnell Anthropology Department that was valued so highly by the faculty as a piece of original scholarship, that she was urged to pursue her work and have the paper published. The same zeal left Hope and Arnold just a tiny bit exhausted when Rachel returned to Iowa after a semester break. After she had cooked her way through vacation and urged Hope to change her hairstyle, or buy that new dress, or rearrange the furniture, or read this wonderful book, or see that play, or try this recipe.

Throughout the western world, in the homes of people for whom Rachel cooked—and she loved to cook—there are at this moment dozens of little bottles of obscure spices and herbs. They are part of her legacy.

"How could you," she would ask her hosts with that charming and maddening combination of sweetness and iron determination that were Rachel's, "cook without fresh dill? Let me run out and get some." And she would, leaving her hosts baffled and amused and better educated on the subject of cooking.

Cooking was a passion with her, or rather a manifestation of a deeper passion for life, for experience. She had a wicked sense of humor, which this place and this occasion suggest I do not fully ventilate, but let me say that her humor issued from a life force of such intensity that it was as irrepressible in her as it was hilarious for us. To Rachel, life was great fun. It was not, however, a game.

One summer, she worked at the state office of the Public Employees Federation. During this time, she became appalled at the waste of good food from luncheons.

It was characteristic of Rachel that she contacted Trinity Episcopal Church to see if they'd be interested in taking the uneaten food for their feeding ministry. They were. And she arranged it. And the food that would have been wasted went to feed the hungry.

In between feeding the destitute and writing scholarly papers, she studied ballroom dancing, self defense, photography, drawing, jewelry making . . . the list goes on. When she was a little girl, her father took her to a museum.

At the end of the trip she noted, "Museums are places with little pieces of the world." It was not only an astute comment but almost an inspiration for the rest of her life. Those little pieces she had observed in the museum inspired her to seek the big pieces, to travel, to learn, to experience.

These were not superficial impulses, because they were harnessed by something deep within her, something rare and profound—the capacity of the saints to take the data of experience, transmute it into knowledge and distill the knowledge into wisdom.

And others found that wisdom in her and sought her advice constantly. For she brought to anyone's problems—ranging from their romantic and sexual fears to courses they should take to how they might rearrange their dormitory rooms—a force and commitment, an insight and integrity, which leads us to only one word in describing it: love.

Love is not something like knowledge. It need not first be accumulated to be imparted. It has only to be given. Always it must be given. And the more it is given, the more there is to give.

Rachel knew that in her very depths. Her love was true because it was given so freely and because it still goes on.

She touched many lives in ways that will never end. She uplifted; she inspired; she gave. When thinking about her it is easy to believe in immortality. Rachel's spirit is endless. She is the whirlwind.

God gave her to us, and Rachel gave us her love. We'll certainly go mad thinking about what she might have been, and she wouldn't have liked that.

So for me I shall remember what was, and value the love that she gave and which rolls through our lives now and forever. Handel's "The Trumpet Shall Sound" is Rachel's song.

It is triumph, it is passion, it is love, and it is our great good fortune that in our lives, in our time, she was there to play it for us.

Interpretations

1. What was Rachel's attitude toward other cultures? Why does the author think Rachel had the potential to be a successful student of cultures? (What were her aspirations?)

2. The author introduces humor into his eulogy. Where? How does humor honor the memory of Rachel?

3. How do you interpret Lamberti's statement that life to Rachel was "great fun" but not "a game"? What evidence from the eulogy suggests that this is true? What does the subject of food contribute to this characterization of Rachel?

4. Look up the words to Handel's aria from *The Messiah,* "The Trumpet Shall Sound," the central idea of which is death and resurrection. What attitude toward death does the aria express? How is this attitude in tune with Rachel's approach to life and to marriage?

5. "Rachel's spirit is endless." Of what significance is the author's use of Rachel's middle name and the etymology of the word *spirit* (breath, wind) to embody important aspects of Rachel's personality and unify his composition?

Correspondences

1. Review the James quotation (page 421). How does it apply to the memorial tribute to Rachel Asrelsky? (What kind of legacy did she leave?)

2. "Museums are places with little pieces of the world." Are libraries also "places with little pieces of the world"? Review Marshall and Wright (Chapter 3). How did libraries influence their dreams?

Applications

1. In an essay on a favorite museum or library, explain how it helped shape you.

2. "Love is not something like knowledge. It need not first be accumulated to be imparted. It has only to be given." Write a journal entry on the aspect of Rachel's sharing that impressed you most. What does it convey about her aspirations?

20/20 Hindsight

Jay Ford

Jay Ford (b. 1969) was raised and educated in New York City. He graduated from Wesleyan University, majoring in African-American history. In his junior year, he studied for one semester in Kenya as part of an international exchange program. His essay "20/20 Hindsight" is an account of what he learned there—about himself and Kenyan culture.

Kenya, located on the eastern coast of Africa with a population of twenty-three million, is slightly smaller in area than Texas. Kenya won independence from Great Britain in 1963, has until recently had a relatively free political life, and has shown steady growth in industry and agriculture. The official language is Swahili. The Kikuyu account for twenty-one percent of the population and are the largest of Kenya's many ethnic groups. Thirty-eight percent of Kenyans are Protestant, twenty-six percent Roman Catholic, and six percent Muslim. Tourists and other visitors account for $355 million of Kenya's annual budget of $2 billion.

BORN INTO a middle class African-American family on the upper west side of Manhattan, I have spent most of my life chasing the (white) American dream. Absorbing the rhetoric brewed by the media, school curricula, and, more important, my teachers, I was graduated from high school with the goal of travelling to Europe, achieving a college degree, becoming a corporate lawyer and, eventually, marrying a spouse who would be most likely white or a light-skinned black. We would have two homes and probably three children. This was my rough sketch of my future, one with which I was satisfied. I would be a success and this was very important because I clearly represent what W.E.B. DuBois coined as the "talented tenth." Therefore, I had a responsibility to my people to succeed, to vanquish the disabilities associated with my color and earn my place in white America, my America.

In starting off on my journey to success, I met my first obstacle as I neared the end of my sophomore year in college. The student body had taken over the administration building in hopes of persuading the University to divest monies invested in corporations in South Africa. A meeting between the students and the administration had been arranged during which the administration had thoroughly explained its position on divestment. Now it was the students' turn to respond. As student after student approached the microphone, explaining what he/she believed to be the most important reasons for disinvesting, an unsettling feeling began to overwhelm me. Although all of the explanations were more than legitimate reasons to disinvest, none of them had touched my personal reasons for protesting the University's position on divestment.

When it was my turn, I did not actually know what I wanted to say, but I was determined to say something. "My name is Julius J. Ford. I am an Afro-American. Inherent in my title is the word African, meaning "of Africa." My ancestry is from Africa. Africans are therefore my people, my history. So as long as you continue to oppress my people through violence or investment or silence, you oppress me. And as long as you oppress me, I will fight you! I will fight you!" As I returned to my seat, my friend leaned over, patted me on the back and said, "That was great, I never really knew you felt that way." I turned to him and said, "Neither did I."

It was this event that made me question myself. How could I be satisfied with my sketch of success when it had no background or depth? Why had I not felt this strongly about Africa or Africans before? Why was I more attracted to women who possessed European features (straight hair, light skin, thin nose) than those who possessed African features? Why did I feel that Europe was so great and Africa so primitive? Why did I choose to call myself an African-American when I knew virtually nothing about Africa? These questions would trouble my soul for the remainder of the year. In fact, they would push me to apply to a student exchange program in East Africa, Kenya.

Called "An Experiment in International Living," the program would offer me travel throughout the country, during which time I would live in both rural and urban areas, in both huts and hotels, for approximately four months from February through mid-May, 1989. I would be equipped with two academic directors with numerous university and government contacts and ensured a variety of learning opportunities, as I would stay with native families and be allowed to venture off on my own.

Even though this program seemingly presented an optimum opportunity to find answers to all my pending questions, I was still apprehensive about my decision to go. But, perhaps if there was one specific incident that canceled any wavering on my part, it was that Friday afternoon at drama class. On Fridays, I taught drama to about twenty 9–14-year-old kids from predominantly black families with low incomes at a community center about twenty minutes from my college. On this particular day I had decided to ask the class what they thought about my taking a trip to Africa. They shot off these responses: "Why would you want to go to Africa to get even blacker than you are now?", "Why don't you take a trip somewhere nice like Paris, London, Rome?", "But they say in Africa every one is backwards, they can't teach you anything," "People are so black and ugly there." And, although some of the comments from the children were said specifically to make the other children laugh, many of them were exemplifications of how our educational system and other forms of external social propaganda affect a black child's mind.

When I first arrived in Kenya, we stayed in its capital city, Nairobi. Surprisingly enough, my first impression of Nairobi was that it was just like any American city: skyscrapers, movie theatres, discos, and crime. In fact,

I was a bit disappointed, feeling that I had travelled fifteen hours in a Pan Am jet just to come back to New York City. But upon more detailed observation, I realized that this city was quite different from any other I had visited before. This city was black and, when I say black, I'm not talking your coffee-colored Atlanta, Oakland, Harlem black people. I mean black! I mean when you were small and used to play games and chose to embarrass the darkest kid on the block by calling him "midnight," "shadow," and "teeth black."

But the lesson to be learned in Nairobi was that all shades of black were equally attractive and the small children did not penalize attractiveness according to shade of skin, or length of hair, or size of nose. Furthermore, being in a black city, knowing I was in a mostly black country that sits on a predominantly black continent, enhanced my confidence and hence my actions. For the first time in my life I felt as though I could do anything, fit in anywhere, be welcomed by everyone because of my color. This was the feeling I had often assumed blacks felt during the Twenties, the period of the Harlem Renaissance. It was wonderful! I would go for days without being aware of my color. It did not seem to matter.

It was only a few weeks into the program, however, when I began to notice racial insecurities developing within my peer group (of twenty-four I was the only black). As many as half a dozen of the other students declared that they had begun to view black children as more beautiful than white, that black women and black features were more pleasing to the eye than white ones. Others simply segregated themselves from the black society as much as possible, refusing to stay with families without another white person present. Perhaps, then, inherent in the role of minority come feelings of inferiority, a certain lack of confidence, insecurity.

Because there is much tribalism in Kenya, the first title I had to drop was African-American. When people around me refer to themselves as Masai or Kikuyu as opposed to Kenyan or East African, then how could I refer to myself as an African? Furthermore, the language I spoke, my values, morals and education were not African. So this put me in an awkward position. No one could question my ancestry as African because of my color, so I enjoyed most benefits of majority status. Yet, to many Kenyans, I was much more similar to a white American than an African so there was a wide gap between us.

It was here I realized that to be an accepted descendant of Africa I had a lot of work to do. I needed to learn a new language and a new culture. I needed to assimilate, and I figured that that shouldn't be too hard as I had twenty years of experience in that in the United States. But, the difference between my American and Kenyan assimilations is that in Kenya it seemed to be welcomed if not encouraged by the majority. The more knowledge I attained of Kenya and the more I left my English at home and spoke Swahili or another tribal language, the more cultural doors opened to me. For example, as I became increasingly familiar with Gidiam tribal customs and my use of Kiswahili improved, I was able to travel along the coast for days never worrying about food or lodging. I was often given the opportunity to sit and discuss with elders, and take part in tribal ceremonies and had responsibilities bestowed on me by elder men, *Mzees*, or my temporary *Mama*. In fact, toward the end of my trip, when travelling alone, it was often difficult for me to convince people that I was African-American. They would tell me, *"Una toka Africa qwa sababo una weza kusema Kiswahili na una famhamu Africa life"* (You are from Africa because you are able to speak Kiswahili and you understand African life). The more I learned, the more comfortable I was with the title African-American.

I also took more pride in myself. Here it was important to learn that the black empowerment was not from sheer numbers, it was from the fact that the blacks in Africa possess a communal sense of self, a shared past that is to never be forgotten, that has passed through generations, and is used as a reference for modern-day experiences. An exemplification of this concept is the way in which Kenyans and Africans in general treat their elderly. In Kenya you are told that you never grow to equal your parents' authority or knowledge. Your elders will forever be your elders and respected as such. In Kenya, elderly people are cherished not forgotten.

As we visited small villages in the areas of Kisumu, Nakru, and on the coast, villages which by American standards were far below the poverty line, we were welcomed with feasts of foods, drinks, people and music. To them we were guests paying them the honor of visitation. Even on a more individual level, most Kenyan families were extraordinarily hospitable. To be welcomed into a stranger's home and be offered food, wine, and a bed for an unlimited number of days is shocking to Americans and even more so to a New Yorker.

This humanistic view was very difficult to adapt to because it affected every level of Kenyan society. For example, Kenyans have a very limited concept of personal space (but in a country with a population growth rate of 4.3 percent that is quite understandable). So it was often difficult for me to discover that my four newly acquired brothers were also my newly acquired bedmates, to change money at the bank while the people behind me were looking over my shoulder examining my passport and money exchange papers, and, to learn not to tell your family that you would like to be left alone because crazy people stay by themselves.

Also, Americans are lost outside of a linear society. We are taught from kindergarten to stay in line. Order for us is symbolically represented by the line, and we therefore choose to see all other forms of non-linear collective activity as chaotic. Kenyans, however, do not have this same view of order. They choose to mass together, aggressively seeking out their desires and bringing new meaning to the words "organized chaos." Mobs catch buses, herds are seen at ticket counters, and, unfortunately, until your adjustment period is complete, you stand apart from the chaos, "jaw dropped," staring at the stampede of people. As a result, you do not obtain a ticket or get on the bus.

This conception of order plus the Kenyan view of personal space make for exciting moments in the public sphere. For example, there is a type of Kenyan public transportation called *matatus*. Matatus are small privately owned minivans that serve as buses for local citizens. To ride a matatu is like taking the most crowded New York City subway car during rush hour, placing that car on Broadway, and allowing a taxicab driver to control the wheel. Matatus do not actually stop at designated bus stops; in fact, they do not actually stop at all. Instead, they simply slow down and those who need to get off push and shove their way to the front of the van and jump out. And as for those who wish to board, they simply chase the matatu down and shove and push their way onto the van. As with circus clown cars, there is always room for one more.

Another linear concept I was introduced to was time. In rural areas there would sometimes be days when we would have no activities planned. It was at these moments when I would curse my directors for poor planning. But I was soon to learn that doing nothing was not necessarily wasted time. This time to think, relax, conversationalize was most important for a peaceful state of mind. I finally understood that it is not imperative even in America to eat breakfast, read the paper in the street while you are running to the subway, or to work two jobs just to pay off your life insurance bill. Here there was not "so much to do and so little time"; here there was a great deal to do but also the belief that that which is supposed to get done will get done in time.

For example, during the last month of my stay in Kenya I visited a small farm in Kisumu Kaubu, Uganda, with a woman and her three sons. I was only to stay for a day and one night. I had come to visit just prior to the time the rains were expected, so I had assumed that the family was going to spend very little time relaxing with me because it was imperative that the soil and seeds for the year be prepared for the rains which could come at any moment.

However, once I arrived, we did very little field work. We talked instead—about the history of her people, about America, and about American perceptions of Kenya. Of course this was hard work since their English was very limited and my Swahili is fair at best. And as the day crept on to the night, I asked her how she could afford to give her attentions to me when the threat of the rains could come at any day now. *"Pole Pole, bwana,"* she replied (We have not neglected our work to the fields. We have only delayed our work so to welcome our new son, who by joining us will ease our workload). I then asked her, "But, Mama, it is already 11:00 and I leave tomorrow at 9:00." She replied, "Don't worry, bwana, we start to work the cattle (plow) at 2:00 A.M. Good night."

It seemed as though Kenyan culture chose to be humanistic rather than materialistic. The value placed on human life and interaction is much greater than in the States. To shake hands, to share a meal or even your home with a foreigner is an honor, not a burden. And, for you as a guest to turn down that hand, meal, or bed is an insult. How wonderfully strange to travel to a foreign land where people who can hardly understand what language you speak are ready to take you home and make you part of the family. They wouldn't last too long in New York, I thought.

In most places in Kenya, it was common knowledge for one to know his/her environment. People could name the types of trees along the roads, tell you animals indigenous to the area, and explain which types of soil were best for growing specific crops. They could tell you the staple foods of different parts of Kenya *or* even the U.S. In fact, their world geography was superior to that of most American college students. Access to information, whether at home or in schools, was a privilege to be appreciated by those involved and then passed down to younger generations orally. I wonder why I did not feel this way. My country offers more educational opportunities than any other in the world and yet seldom are these opportunities fully exploited. American students go to school, but they do not go to learn. They go to get A's and move up economically. They go to play the game, the educational game of success that I like to refer to as DT (Diploma Training), a process that verifies one's intelligence by certificate as opposed to action or common sense.

Furthermore, along with this overwhelming appreciation for knowledge, Kenyans show reverence for everyday simplicities which we in America take for granted: the appreciation for candlelight, running water, a toilet with a seat cover, a long hot shower every day. Learning to live is to stay in Kenya and survive with twenty-three other people living mostly off rain water, sleeping in huts, and eating many fruits and vegetables with only the occasional beef meal. I felt as though Kenya taught me a new dimension of life, a rebirth of sorts. It put objectives, time, goals, values into a new perspective. It did not tell me, "Please be aware of how much water you use because a drought warning is in effect." It gave me a gallon of water and told me to drink and bathe for an undetermined period. It did not tell me of the beauties of nature, rather it revealed them to me by greeting me in the morning with the sights of Mt. Kenya, Kilimanjaro, and Lake Victoria. I saw no need for National Geographic or wildlife television, for when it wanted to introduce me to animals, a monkey, leopard, or family of raccoons would become my fellow pedestrians. There was no urge to tell me of the paradox of zoos when it could show me national parks with hundreds of acres of land.

In Kenya I felt more free than I have ever felt before. The only thing holding me captive was the earth which would grow the food, the sky which would quench the earth of its thirst, and the sun which would warm and help all things to grow. But these masters were sure to give back all that you have put in. When you worked hard, your rewards were great and if you chose to relax so would your crop and cattle. And with a give-and-take relationship like this, one learns that it is okay to take time, time for others, for oneself, time to enjoy and appreciate all that life and earth offer. Some choose to call this type of relationship religion, a covenant with the Lord and her divinity (sky, earth, and animals and I will not deny that there was a strong sense of God or Allah or Sa or Buddha).

A forest burning to the ground germinates the soil, allowing new life to grow. The omnipotence of nature—floods, lightning, hurricanes, earthquakes, the beauty of a cheetah or giraffe running, an open field, the sky, the mountains, the sea—is overwhelming and foreign to me living so long in a concrete jungle. When all of this engulfed me and I took the time to embrace it, I became convinced that there exists a master craftsperson of this creation, that there exists a God.

Kenya has more than (just) given me a new perception of the world; Kenya has widened my world view. I now realize that there are other significant cultures in the world besides a western one. I no longer think of the world in First, Second, and Third World terms. There are aspects of Kenyan values which should be regarded as more First World than American: humanistic sentiments, importance of family, pride of ancestry, appreciation and respect for other peoples' differences.

Also, whereas I ventured off to Kenya to learn about a new culture and its new people, I found that most of the more important discoveries and evaluations were about myself. Upon leaving Kenya I feel that I have grown more confident about my African-Americanness, my perceptions of the world around me, and my expectation of 21/21 vision and beyond. I do not believe I could have gone anywhere else on earth and been as personally challenged.

Interpretations

1. Was the author wrong to assume that the aspirations of "white America" should or could also be the aspirations of a black American? Why? To what extent are the aspirations ("rhetoric") he mentions in the first paragraph misguided? Why? How does the speech made before students and administration relate to these aspirations and the identity crisis raised by the label "African-American"?

2. What does the title mean? What is the author scrutinizing with 20/20 hindsight? How successfully does he combine the story of an identity crisis with cultural commentary? Support your conclusion.

3. What did the author's young drama-class students teach him about attitudes of American blacks toward Africa? How does this attitude contrast with what he found among children in Nairobi? How reliable are children's conversation and vocabulary as indicators of widespread but unconscious attitudes?

4. "Perhaps . . . inherent in the role of minority come feelings of inferiority. . . ." Can you offer evidence from your own life that supports or refutes this idea? Does the author's evidence (the white group's behavior in Kenya) convince you? How does this idea relate to Ford's later assertion that "black empowerment [in Africa] was not from sheer numbers" but from long and rich cultural traditions?

Correspondences

1. Review the Cosby quotation (page 422). How does it apply to Ford's essay? How did Ford's education in the United States affect his aspirations? What modifications did he make as a result of his semester in Kenya?

2. Ford's semester in Kenya also changed his cultural perspective: "I no longer think of the world in First, Second, and Third World terms." What evidence does he cite? How does his point of view compare to that of Reed in "America: The Multinational Society"?

Applications

1. "American students go to school, but they do not go to learn. They go to get A's and move up economically." Is this an accurate assessment of the aspirations of American college students? Write an essay attacking or defending Ford's point of view.

2. "In Kenya, elderly people are cherished not forgotten." How might such an attitude affect social and cultural aspirations? How does it compare to prevailing attitudes towards older people in the United States?

Richard's Discovery

José Antonio Villarreal

José Antonio Villarreal (b. 1924), the son of a Mexican immigrant, was born and grew up in California. He received his degree from the University of California in 1950 and spent four years in the U.S. Navy. "Richard's Discovery" is from the novel Pocho *(1959), the first known Chicano novel acquired by a major publisher (Doubleday). His subsequent novels include* The Fifth Horseman *(1974) and* Clemente Chacón *(1984). The main character in "Richard's Discovery" lives in California and, like his creator, is very conscious of his Mexican heritage. For information on Mexico, see the headnote to Gary Soto, Chapter 4.*

THE WORLD of Richard Rubio was becoming too much for him. He felt that time was going by him in an overly accelerated pace, because he was not aware of days but of weeks and, at times, even months. And he lived in dread that suddenly he should find himself old and ready to die before he could get from life the things it owed him. He was approaching his thirteenth year, and thought of his friend Joe Pete Manõel, though not forgotten, did not hurt as much. For the most part, he lost himself in dreams or spent hours reading everything he could find, indiscriminate in his choice through his persevering desire to learn. Now, after work, he was a familiar figure in the town library, and later, when the vacation ended, he continued the practice, for by then the meager library at school provided little for him. Yet he was disturbed by the thought that now, while he was young and strong in body, his wanderings should be physical. Imagination would do only when he became old and incapable of experiencing actual adventure.

At school, Richard was the favorite of his teachers because his old-country manners made him most courteous in contrast to the other students. He was also a good student, and stood near the top of his class without seemingly trying. His teachers encouraged his reading, but unfortunately did not direct it, and he became increasingly complex in his moods.

It was natural that in his frantic hunger for reading he went through books he did not understand. A friend of his father had a few Spanish novels, and he read a simplified "Quixote"[1] and made several attempts at Ibáñez,[2] but for the first time in his life he found reading to be actual work. So he limited his Spanish reading to the newspaper he received in the mail from

---

[1]*Don Quixote*, satirical, chivalric romance by Spanish author Miguel Cervantes (1605–1615).

[2]Vincente Blasco Ibáñez (1867–1928), Spanish novelist, journalist, and politician.

Los Angeles. With determination, he followed Tom Jones and Dr. Pangloss[3] through their various complicated adventures. From *Gone with the Wind*, he emerged with tremendous respect and sympathy for the South and its people. And when the Dust Bowl families who had begun trickling into the valley arrived in increasing numbers, he was sad. They represented the South to him, and he mourned that the once proud could come to such decay.

When the boy fell asleep over a book, his father blew out the coal-oil lamp and tenderly put him to bed. Only when riding out in the country lanes was Richard forbidden to read. Twice his father threw his books out the window of the car. "Look!" he would say. "Look at the world around you, burro!" And the boy would think, What a funny one the old man is!

Indeed, the father was a paradox.

Richard went into the barn that was used to house the town's garbage wagons. Today the barn was empty of equipment and full of young guys and a few older people. Over at one end of the building stood a huge ring. It had two ropes, instead of three, and the posts were big iron pipes wrapped in burlap. There were two kids going at it pretty hard, and suddenly one of them put his hands to his mouth and stood transfixed in the center of the ring. The other one jumped around, throwing punches that either missed his opponent completely or landed on his shoulders or the top of his head. The puncher was too anxious, and the one who couldn't believe his mouth was bleeding got away, and then the bell rang.

Two other guys jumped into the ring then, and started dancing around and flexing like professionals, blowing snot all over the place, and then this local guy who was doing pretty good in the game up in the City jumped in there to do the announcing, and another guy who was already in there was the referee.

He noticed that the announcer's face was a little bumpy already, and he was already talking through his nose from fighting pro. He was a little guy and he moved around funny—real jerky, like the old silent movies—and somebody said there goes the next flyweight champ, which meant he would be the Filipino champion, since they were the only flyweights around. Richard could tell already he would not even be champ of Santa Clara, but he did not say anything, because people in small towns are funny about things like that—they think they have the best of everything.

While the two guys were fighting, Thomas Nakano came over to him. He was wearing only pants, and they were rolled up to his knees and he was barefooted.

"You gonna fight, Thomas?" asked Ricky.

"I can't find nobody who's my size and wants to fight me," Thomas said, sounding disappointed.

---

[3]*Tom Jones*, English novel by Henry Fielding (1707–1754). Dr. Pangloss, character in *Candide*, a novel by Voltaire (1694–1778).

Richard felt his stomach begin to get funny, because he knew what was coming. "Don't look at me, Punchie," he said, trying to make a little joke out of it, but nobody laughed and it was real quiet.

"Aw, come on, Richard." He was begging him to let him hit him. "Come on, you're just my size. I'll fight anybody, only they won't let ya less'n you're the same size as the other guy."

He said no he would not, but he felt sorry for Thomas because he wanted someone to fight with him so bad. And then the guys were finished in the ring, and somebody called Thomas and asked him if he had a partner yet. He said no, but by then even guys Richard didn't know were trying to talk him into fighting him, and the pro came over, and in the end he was up in the ring shaking, because he didn't want any of these people to see him look bad. He thought back to the pictures in *Ring Magazine* and tried to imitate the poses, but before he could really decide which he liked best, Thomas was all over him. He kind of clinched and said, "What the hell you trying to do, you crazy bastard?" And Thomas said, "Don't worry—I'll take it easy," and Richard felt pretty good about then, because Thomas was his buddy and he would take it easy on him. But as they pulled away from each other, Thomas clouted him on the mouth when he wasn't looking, and Richard's head felt suddenly numb. Then Thomas was hitting him all over the place, like nobody's business—in the ribs, the stomach, and even his back sometimes, and the gloves were feeling like great big pillows on Richard's hands. It was the longest round in the history of boxing, and Thomas pissed him off. *My friend—one of the gang!* So he thought and thought, and finally, when they were apart one time, he dropped his hands and moved toward Thomas, looking real sadlike right into his eyes, as if to say, *Go ahead, kill me.* Thomas stopped also, and a funny what-the-hell's-going-on? look came to his face, and when Richard knew he was relaxed good, he brought one up from the next neighborhood and clipped him good right on the ear. Thomas spun clean around and started to walk away; then he walked in a circle and the son of a bitch was smiling, but he walked right past Richard and around the other side again, and all Richard could do was stand there and look at the crooked little legs that were browner than his. Then he heard everybody hollering for him to go after Thomas, and he thought he might as well, so he followed him around, but Thomas wouldn't stand still. So finally he grabbed him and turned him around, and Thomas stood there grinning, and his eyes were almost closed, because his eyelids were almost together anyway. Richard couldn't hit him when he was smiling at him like that. He smiled back at him, and then the bell rang.

Richard couldn't help laughing at Thomas's grin, but suddenly he stopped, because the bell rang again and he knew he was in for it. Right away, Thomas hit him in the stomach, and Richard bent right over, and there it was—he just kept right on going, and landed on his head and took the count there curled up like a fetus. He didn't have to fight any more, and Thomas was very happy as he helped him up, and Thomas kept saying how he was like Fitzsimmons and that his Sunday punch was a right to the solar plexus. "I hit you in the solar plexus, Richard," he said over and over again, but Richard wasn't really listening to him, because he was sneaking looks at the people, and finally decided he had made it look pretty good.

The referee and the professional came over to see him. "Nice faking, kid," said the referee. "How'd ya like to be a fighter?"

"Uh-uh," he said, pulling at the laces with his teeth. The man took his gloves off.

"You don't know how to fight, but you got a punch for a kid and you're smart," he said.

"I not only can't fight, but I'm scared to fight, so you don't want me," he said.

"How old are ya, kid?"

"I'll be thirteen soon."

"I thought you was older," he said. "But, hell, I can teach ya a lot, and in a year I can put you in smokers. Make five or ten bucks a night that way."

"Not me, Mister. I don't need five or ten bucks."

"How about me?" said Thomas. "I'm the guy that won. You saw me hit him in the solar plexus." Now Richard knew why Thomas had been so anxious to fight.

"Yeah, I can use you, too," said the man, "but I want this other kid."

"Oboyoboy!" said Thomas. He had a trade now.

"How about it, kid?" asked the man. "I'm giving ya the chance of your life—it's the only way people of your nationality can get ahead."

"I'm an American," said Richard.

"All right, you know what I mean. Mexicans don't get too much chance to amount to much. You wanna pick prunes the rest of your life?" Richard didn't say anything, and he said, "Look, I'll go talk it over with your old man, and I'll bet he'll agree with me. I'll bet he knows what's good for you."

"You better not do that, Mister. You don't know my old man. He's already been in jail for knifing three guys."

Richard could tell he was dumb, and, like a lot of people, believed that Mexicans and knives went together. He thought he had finished with him, but the man said, "All right, we won't tell 'im anything, and when you start bringing money home, he'll come and see *me*."

"Listen," Richard said. "He'll come and see you all right, but it won't make any difference. My old man don't feel about money the way some people do. So leave me alone, why don't you?"

But the man kept insisting, and said, "I gotta line up a smoker for the Eagles, and if you and the Jap kid here put 'em on, I'll give ya each a fin.[4]

---

[4]Five-dollar bill.

Then, when your old man sees the dough, he'll be in the bag. What do you say?"

"Okay with me," said Thomas, "but don't call me no Jap." Richard was walking away by then, and the man followed him. "I'll give ya seven-fifty and the Jap a fin."

"No, thanks." He kept walking. They would never be able to make him do anything like that. He was sure he could be no more than a punching bag, because, hell, everybody in the neighborhood could beat him, and besides he was afraid.

The guys caught up to him, but he wasn't talking. He thought how funny the guy back there was—the fight manager. He felt that the manager was the kid and he was the grownup. *Amount to something!* Jesus! Everybody was telling him what he should make of himself these days, and they all had the same argument, except that this guy was thinking of himself. At least the little old lady who was so nice and let him read the Horatio Alger books was thinking of him when she told him he should work hard to be a gardener and someday he could work on a rich person's estate; she was sure he would be successful at that because she had known of some Mexicans who held very fine places like that. . . . Funny about her, how the Horatio Alger books meant as much to her as the Bible meant to Protestants. . . . And the adviser in the high school, who had insisted he take automechanics or welding or some shop course, so that he could have a trade and be in a position to be a good citizen, because he was Mexican, and when he had insisted on preparing himself for college, she had smiled knowingly and said he could try those courses for a week or so, and she would make an exception and let him change his program to what she knew was better for him. She'd been eating crow ever since. What the hell makes people like that, anyway? Always worried about his being Mexican and he never even thought about it, except sometimes, when he was alone, he got kinda funnyproud about it.

As he walked toward home with the guys, he thought about the things he had just discovered. He would never really be afraid again. Like with hitting Thomas and ending the fight the way he did; funny he had never thought about that before—the alternative. Everything had another way to it, if only you looked hard enough, and he would never be ashamed again for doing something against the unwritten code of honor. Codes of honor were really stupid—it amazed him that he had just learned this—and what people thought was honorable was not important, because he was the important guy. No matter what he did and who was affected by his actions, in the end it came back to him and his feelings. He was himself, and everything else was there because he was *himself,* and it wouldn't be there if he were not himself, and then, of course, it wouldn't matter to him. He had the feeling that *being* was important, and he *was*—so he knew that he would never succumb to foolish social pressures again. And if he hurt anyone, it would be only if he had no choice, for he did not have it in him to hurt willingly.

He thought of Thomas's face in the ring, and began to laugh at the silliness of his grin, and then he laughed louder and louder, about the fight manager and all the people who tried to tell him how to live the good life, and then laughed about the guys with him, because they were laughing like crazy, too, and the sad bastards did not know what the hell they were laughing about.

Interpretations

1. Richard "mourned" the people of the Dust Bowl. What trait does this reaction to reading show? How does this same trait land him in the ring with Thomas?

2. Take note of all the references to Richard's father. What conclusions can you reach about the kind of man he is and why? How does he influence Richard?

3. "[Boxing's] the only way people of your nationality can get ahead." What's the best evidence that Richard doesn't believe this statement and intends to disprove it?

4. "Codes of honor were really stupid. . . ." What specific rule does Richard break in order to end the fight? Do you agree that he has "just learned" something important? about what? What will happen if Richard goes through life applying this lesson?

5. What is Richard's "discovery"?

Correspondences

1. "Mexicans don't get too much chance to amount to much. You wanna pick prunes the rest of your life?" Who besides the referee tries to stereotype Richard? Who among them should have known better? How does Richard respond to their attempts? Compare his response to that of Wright (Chapter 3). How do you account for the difference?

2. Review Kittredge's quotation (page 421). What does he mean by "possibility"? What possibilities does Richard become aware of in himself?

Applications

1. Richard vows never to "succumb to foolish social pressures again." Are such social pressures usually negative? Is it easy to resist them? Write an essay analyzing how they might affect aspirations.

2. "Only when riding out in the country lanes was Richard forbidden to read. Twice his father threw his books out the window of the car. 'Look!' He would say. Look at the world around you, burro!" What have you learned from "looking at the world around you"? How has such looking influenced your dreams or helped to shape your convictions? Respond to these questions in a journal entry.

An Oral History

Sherezada "Chiqui" Vicioso

Sherezada "Chiqui" Vicioso is a native of the Dominican Republic. She lived in New York City for seventeen years and attended both Brooklyn College and Columbia University. Vicioso is the author of two books of poetry, Viajes desde el agua *(1981) and* Un extraño ulular traia el viento *(1985). She presently resides in Santo Domingo. Her "Testimonio," from which the following selection comes, was published in* Breaking Boundaries: Latina Writings and Critical Readings *(1989).*

For information about the Dominican Republic, see Julia Alvarez, "El Doctor," Chapter 2.

I STARTED WRITING when I was very young and found out that the best way to pass Math was to write a poem to the teacher. . . . I began to become aware of the marginalized people in my country when I was an adolescent and worked in the barrios as part of a Christian youth volunteer group. Basically I am a poet, but I also write criticism about women's literature. I began to write in 1978 and published my first book of poetry, *Viajes desde el agua,* in 1981.

Up until about 1977, I regarded literature as a hobby of the petite bourgeoisie, but when I went to Cuba and spoke there with writers whom I very much admired, they showed me that a writer is also a cultural worker. Whereas I took note of this fact on an intellectual level, I realized it on an emotional one only when I went to Africa in 1978. I started writing criticism from 1982 on and published my second book in 1985 *(Un extraño ulular traía el viento).*

Both my books were written for Dominicans and were published in Santo Domingo. I never thought of publishing in the United States because, as a Latina, I felt unable to deal with the publishing establishment in that country. My first book was presented at the Las Américas bookshop and other places for Latinos in New York. After all, New York is the second most important city for Dominicans. The island has six million inhabitants and half a million live in New York. Economically, it's the most important. I never felt far from Santo Domingo when I lived in New York.

I first came to the United States in April 1967. Initially, I had wanted to be a lay nun and work in the barrios. Marriage repelled me, especially when I looked at my aunts, practically all of whom were divorced. I couldn't stand the idiocy of the whole scene: the danger of getting mixed up with someone when you were thirteen or fourteen, worrying about not having a boyfriend when you were sixteen. To me, becoming a nun was my path to freedom. I also wanted to study medicine. The one year I planned to stay eventually became seventeen.

My mother, who had left a year earlier, said I should go to the States in order to improve my English and to get to know the world before embarking on becoming a nun. I was very angry with her at the time, but she was right.

I come from a very special family with an intellectual background. On my father's side, my grandfather was a journalist and a writer, and my father is a poet and a well-known composer. My mother is a better poet than I am, but has never dared to write. She is the daughter of a peasant woman who worked in a tobacco factory and a Dominican oligarch who owned the factory and literally bought her when she was sixteen. My mother is a hybrid of two very distinct classes. I felt this when I went to school in Santiago.

In spite of having studied English in school, I found out, on my arrival in New York, that I didn't know very much. Like most Dominicans who come to the United States, I went to work in a factory: first a hat, and then a button factory (the acetone in which we had to wash the buttons damaged my eyes so that I have had to wear glasses ever since). I went to night school for a while, and then was accepted into a city-sponsored intensive English program, where I was paid to study.

My next job was as a telephone operator, and I quickly acquired a reputation as being extremely courteous to the customers, as my English still wasn't all that good and I said, "Thank you" to everyone, even if they insulted me. Then Brooklyn College opened its doors to minority students. They responded to a policy, initiated under the Johnson administration, whereby colleges were paid federal funds to admit minorities. I was one of eight Dominican students admitted to Brooklyn College.

Since there were only eight of us, and it was very tough to survive in such a racist atmosphere, we joined up with other minority students, principally Puerto Ricans, Blacks, other people from the Caribbean—we formed a Third World Alliance.

This was a real threshold for me; I had never known the people from Barbados or Trinidad, etc. My concept of the Caribbean, up to that time, had been limited to the Spanish-speaking part, and I discovered my identity as a *caribeña* in New York.

I was also racially classified at Brooklyn College, which was an interesting experience for me. In Santo Domingo, the popular classes have a pretty clear grasp of racial divisions, but the middle and upper-middle classes are very deluded on this point. People straighten their hair and marry "in order to improve the race," etc., etc., and don't realize the racist connotations of their language or their attitude. In the United States, there is no space for fine distinctions of race, and one goes from being "trigüeño" or "indio" to being "mulatto" or "Black" or "Hispanic." This was an excellent experience for me. From that point on, I discovered myself as a Caribbean *mulata* and adopted the Black identity as a gesture of solidarity. At that time, I deeply admired and identified with Angela Davis, and ever since then, I have kept on identifying myself as a Black woman.

This opened another door; I learned about Frantz Fanon and other Caribbean theoreticians, and that finished Europe for me. I learned about the triangular trade and how we had financed Europe's development. I realized that capitalism was an impossible model to follow in our development. For me, this was discovering a universe. I only became a feminist much later.

When I first became more radical I was very much put off by feminism and people like Gloria Steinem and Betty Friedan—to me they were representatives of the white U.S. middle class who were busy telling us how *we* were being screwed by machismo. In a first stage I rejected this and, up to a point, I also had a false sense of solidarity with our men, who were racially oppressed as well. I felt that if we women criticized our men, we were only providing the racists with ammunition. This created a conflict of loyalties for me.

Discovering myself as a woman came much later. First I had to discover that I was part of a certain geographical area, and then, that I was Latin American. The great majority of the Latin American exiles converged on New York at that time—the Argentinians, the Uruguayans, the Chileans (Allende fell during those years)—so that, for me, New York became a kind of great doorway to this Latin American world.

Being in New York was very essential to my development. I would not be the woman I am today had I not gone to New York. I would have been the classic *fracasada* (failure) in my country because I know that I would not have found happiness in marriage and having children. I would have been frustrated, unhappy in a marriage, or divorced several times over because I would not have understood that within me was a woman who needed to express her own truths, articulate her own words. That, in Santo Domingo, would have been impossible.

Nevertheless, for the first ten years that I lived in New York, I was engulfed by a great silence; I could write nothing at all. The only poem I salvaged from this era was one about two young Puerto Ricans, aged sixteen and seventeen, who were shot by a bartender they had robbed of $100. I saw an article about it in the paper and it made me terribly sad. The poem ends with the line, "sadness has never come so cheaply." New York was, for me, a crushing kind of silence.

Still, all these experiences were being stored up inside of me. It's that kind of a process; things go in stages.

It was going to Africa that restored my essence as a *caribeña* for me. I went for three and a half months to work on coordinating the first meeting of ministers of education of the Portuguese-speaking African nations, and discovered Amílcar Cabral, the outstanding African cultural and revolutionary theoretician. Up to that point, I had never understood the important role that culture plays in effecting change. This was a central experience for me.

When I returned to the States, I was a different person; I suffered from severe depressions, which I now realize marked the death of one Chiqui and the birth of another. I figured the only thing that could save me was to return to the university, so I decided, at that point, to get an M.A. in Education from Columbia. I tried to work one more year in New York, but it was no good, and I returned to Santo Domingo.

I was there for four years, until last year, when I returned to the States. Some very difficult things happened during that time. The man with whom I had planned to restructure my life died of cancer. I was working terribly hard in my job as an educational coordinator. Basically, I had a kind of breakdown. I returned to the States to recuperate, and then went back to Santo Domingo. I've been there three months now.

I have really wanted to be a literary critic, yet once again I am denying my condition as a writer. The African experience had awakened me to the terrible problem of illiteracy in my country; 40 percent of the population is totally illiterate, another 40 percent, functionally so. I've always moved in this atmosphere of crisis and tension [between the two drives in my life]. Even now, I am teaching not literature but a course on Dominican education at the university.

I had to go back to Santo Domingo because, after a few years, living in the United States gave me a kind of physical malaise. . . . When you first get here from your country, full of strength and energy, you get involved in a first stage of learning, absorbing, discovering. Then comes a time when you have to go back in order to revitalize yourself. If you stay in New York too long, you begin to get worn down by it. Anyone who is in the least sensitive can't help but feel bruised by the destruction of our people. Really. I saw it all the time in the Dominican community. Even though I had already acquired all sorts of New York rituals—I took perfumed baths in a flowered bathtub, swallowed my B12 vitamins, was into meditation—none of it was doing me any good. I realized I had to leave.

The New York experience, which was so crucial to my discovery of my Caribbean and racial identity, has made me a very, very critical person with respect to my own society. Things I never noticed before, I now see. Like racism, for example. Class differences. Santo Domingo is a very societally structured city. The situation of women is atrocious. I get almost rude about this because I can't stand the kind of sexist behavior that exists in my country. And for that, you pay the price of ostracism. It's really hard. By dint of having lived in the United States, I am considered a "liberated woman," which means that the men feel they have a green light to harass me sexually while the women distrust me. That's the most painful part. You come back to your country with a sense of intimate relationship and find that, for the most part, the principal *machistas* are the women themselves. And that's terrible. You find yourself confronted by an immense hostility that is a product of their own frustration. At first you ask yourself, "What have you done to this woman to have her treat you like this?" And then you realize that you symbolize all the things that she has never been able to do, and perhaps never will: leave the country, study what she wants to. She may find herself tied down by three or four children, a husband that bores her, physical confinement, etc.; and you come along as a woman who can come and go as she wishes, write, be creative and productive, freely elect the man she wants to be with, and you become, for her, an object of hatred. It's really dreadful. And with the men, you represent a challenge to try and get you because you're different, but the real challenge is to dominate you. For the women, you are all they cannot be and that must be destroyed for survival. And you have to understand that so that you don't self-destruct. You can laugh off the first two or three aggressions, but by the fourth time, it really hurts.

As a writer I haven't yet been able to talk about my experiences in the States. At some moment in the future I will. Remember that New York was an experience of great silence for me. I feel that a time will come when I will be able to surmount what happened to me in New York and will be able to write about it. Remember, too, that the things I'm telling you in such a light vein today were wrenching experiences for me, especially discrimination. I still can't talk about it, but because I now have a better understanding of the creative process, I have learned not to push the creative instincts so that they won't become artificial. I know I have to let things come to the surface. The time will come when I'll be able to do it. I've written some sociological essays and some journalistic pieces on New York for a Santo Domingo paper in order to let my people know what's happening there, but in terms of literature I haven't yet been able to draw out what I have inside.

Because so many of my potential readers live in New York, I am definitely moving more and more toward publishing in the United States. I think people on the island would be interested as well. . . . We cannot avoid the "invasion" of the Dominicans from the U.S. The whole country is changing: English is spoken all over—you feel the influence of the Dominicans who come back everywhere. I also think there will be interest in my writing in the States, first of all, because there are so many of us there, and second, because I will approach things with the particular viewpoint of a woman. I have a lot to tell about what New York did to my family. I had to assume a kind of paterfamilias role with respect to my siblings. A lot of it was very traumatic.

However, for the moment I'm more interested in women's issues, and especially in testimonials by Dominican women. I'm working on a book that is a collection of women's testimonials from the four years when I was here earlier. I've collected testimonials from all classes of women: peasants, factory workers, etc. I would like to be the voice of those who have no voice. Later, I'll be able to speak about New York.

In Santo Domingo there is a need to create a market for women's literature. As women, we have not yet discovered our power as consumers of books, but some day, when we discover this, perhaps we'll manifest this power by supporting women who write.

Interpretations

1. How did the author become aware that the middle and upper-middle classes in the Dominican Republic are "deluded" on the subject of "racial divisions"? How does she now identify herself?

2. Why was the author slow to identify herself as a feminist? How did contact with American feminists affect her self-concept?

3. Why was New York a period of "great silence"?

4. What factors account for the hostility of the other Dominican women towards the author? How has the contact with them affected writing aspirations?

5. What is Vicioso's purpose in giving this interview? (For what audience is it intended?)

Correspondences

1. Santo Domingo, Cuba, New York, and Africa. How does each place affect Vicioso's perception of herself as a woman, a teacher, and a writer? Compare her experiences in Africa with those of Ford. How are they similar or different?

2. Vicioso has a deep sense of social commitment. How does this sense affect her personal and professional aspirations? Compare her social commitment to that of Rendón (Chapter 3). How has his commitment affected his aspirations?

Applications

1. What causes Vicioso to modify her view of Dominican men? How do Dominican women respond to her? Write an analysis of the extent to which feminism seems to have shaped her aspirations.

2. Vicioso's months in Africa cause her to realize "the important role that culture plays in effecting change." How does her testimony support that thesis? What cultural interactions affect her aspirations most?

ADDITIONAL WRITING TOPICS

1. As a result of his semester in Africa, Ford writes: "There are aspects of Kenyan values which should be regarded as more First World than American; humanistic sentiments, importance of family, pride of ancestry, appreciation and knowledge of natural surroundings and respect for other peoples' differences." In which other selections in this anthology are these values variously expressed? Are these values, as Ford implies, more characteristic of Third World cultures than of Americans? Write an essay attacking or defending Ford's point of view; use examples from selections in this and other chapters as evidence.

2. Review the Freud quotation (page 421). What does it mean? Cite examples from selections in this or in other chapters to support or refute it. Attack or defend the quotation using evidence from the selections and your own experience.

3. ". . . does North America deserve a more exciting destiny? To become a place where the cultures of the world crisscross. This is possible because the United States is unique in the world: The world is here." Is Reed's wish feasible? Given the history of racism to which African-Americans have been subjected in the United States, how do you account for his optimism? Is it possible to create a United States without bigotry? What factors would have to change? Write an essay responding to these questions. Avoid sentimentality and superficial generalizations.

4. Review the Mexican saying on page 421. What does it mean? How might it affect aspirations? In a 500-word essay, explain its application to any three selections in this chapter.

5. The King quotation in "Perspectives" is taken from his "I Have a Dream" speech, delivered on August 28, 1963 during the now historical civil rights march on Washington. There he describes his dream as "being deeply rooted in the American dream." Read this speech and then write your definition of the American Dream, supporting it with specific examples from experience, observation, and prior knowledge.

6. Several selections in this anthology focus on the experiences of Native Americans. Review these selections and write an analysis of what you learned about Native-American interactions and aspirations.

7. As college campuses become more ethnically diverse, how might administrations, faculty, staff, and students work together to create a climate of inclusiveness that enhances educational and social interactions and personal and cultural aspirations? As a member of a group, interview a cross-section of the college community on this issue. What suggestions did they make? What responsibilities were they willing to assume? Write a summary of your findings for your campus or local newspaper.

RHETORICAL GLOSSARY

Abstract   Without physical, tangible existence in itself; a concept as opposed to an object. A "child" is a concrete object that our senses can perceive, but "childishness" is an abstract quality. *See* "Concrete."

Analogy   A comparison that points out a resemblance between two essentially different things. Sleep and death are analogous, although certainly not identical. Often an analogy is drawn to explain simply and briefly something that is complex or abstract by pointing out one way in which it resembles something that is simpler or more concrete. To explain how the mind processes and stores information in its memory, an analogy might be drawn to the way in which a bank processes and stores deposits.

Antonym   A word of opposite meaning from another word. "Good" is an antonym of "bad." *See* "Synonym."

Argumentation   In persuasive essays, a unit of discourse meant to prove a point or to convince; the process of proving or persuading.

Audience   A work's intended readership, the author's perception of which directly affects style and tone. As a rule, the more limited or detailed the subject matter, the more specific the audience. An author may write more technically if the intended audience is composed of specialists in the field and may write less technically if the writing is for the general public.

Cause and Effect   A type of exposition used primarily to answer the questions "Why did this occur?" and "What will happen next?" The structure of a cause-and-effect essay is a series of events or conditions, the last of which (the effect) cannot occur without the preceding ones (causes). When you write a cause-and-effect essay, it is helpful to keep chronology clearly in mind: remember, causes always create effects and effects are derived from causes.

Cliché   An expression so overused that it has lost its ability to convey a sharp image or fresh idea. Clichés, such as "busy as a bee," diminish clarity and precision. Familiarity reduces them to little more than vague generalizations.

Coherence   The sense of connection and interrelationship present among the parts of a work. In a coherent piece of writing each sentence leads reasonably to the next sentence, and each paragraph follows reasonably from the preceding paragraph. A lack of coherence is evident when gaps are left between parts. The reader of a poorly written essay might begin to ask, "Why does the writer say this here?" or "How did the writer get to this idea from the preceding idea?" *See* "Transition" and "Unity."

Colloquialism   A conversational or folksy word or phrase deemed inappropriate in formal writing. Using colloquialisms ("booze" for "whiskey" or "loosen up" for "relax") imparts a less dignified, less studied quality to one's writing. *See* "Slang."

Comparison and Contrast   A type of exposition that states or suggests similarities and differences between two or more things. Two types of organization for comparison and contrast essays are point by point and subject by subject.

Conclusion   A summing up or restatement of the writer's thesis. A strong conclusion imparts a sense of completion and finality to a piece of writing. The conclusion may be no more than a sentence in a short essay; it may be many paragraphs in a long report. A short conclusion may restate the writer's thesis in a memorable way, place the specific topic being discussed within or against a broader framework, or suggest answers to questions raised in the essay. A summary of the writer's main points may be effective as the conclusion to a long paper, but in a short essay it will seem unnecessarily repetitious.

Concrete   Specific and tangible as opposed to general and abstract. "Wealth" is an abstract concept of which "gold" is a concrete form. The use of concrete details, examples, and illustrations is a key to clear and effective writing. *See* "Abstract."

Connotation   The implication(s) and overtones, qualities, feelings, and ideas a word suggests. Connotation goes beyond literal meaning or dictionary definition. "Sunshine" denotes the light rays of the sun, but connotes warmth, cheer, happiness, and even prosperity. *See* "Denotation."

Definition   A type of exposition that explains the meaning of a word or concept by bringing its characteristics into sharp focus. An **extended definition** explores the feelings and ideas you attach to a word. Extended definitions are suited to words with complex meanings, words that are subject to interpretation, or words that evoke strong reactions. Such definitions are an appropriate basis for organizing exposition. A **dictionary definition** places a word in a class with similar items but also differentiates it from members of the same class.

Denotation   The literal meaning of a word as defined in a dictionary. *See* "Connotation."

Description   A method of paragraph development that conveys sensory experience through one or more of the five senses: sight, hearing, touch, taste, and smell. Description is generally either objective or subjective and can be organized in three broad categories: spatial, chronological, or dramatic. *See* "Mode."

Diction   The writer's choice of words. Writers are said to employ proper diction when the words they choose to express their ideas are accurate and appropriate; that is, when what they write says exactly what they mean. Poor diction stems from choosing words whose denotation does not accurately convey the author's intended meaning or from choosing words regarded as inappropriate because they are nonstandard ("ain't"), colloquial, or obsolete.

Epiphany   A moment of insight for a character, often resulting in a turning point.

Exposition   A mode or form of discourse that conveys information, gives directions, or explains an idea that is difficult to understand.

Figure of Speech   An imaginative phrase and comparison that is not meant to be taken literally. "He ran as fast as the wind" is a figure of speech known as a simile. *See* "Analogy," "Hyperbole," "Metaphor," "Personification," "Simile," and "Understatement."

Generalization   A broad statement, idea, or principle that holds a common truth. Despite many possible exceptions, it is generally true that a soldier's job is to go to war. Writing that relies too much on generalization is likely to be vague and overly abstract. *See* "Specificity."

Hyperbole   Obvious exaggeration, an extravagant statement, intentionally designed to give the reader a memorable image. A fisherman who brags that the one that got away was "big as a whale" almost certainly is speaking hyperbolically. *See* "Understatement."

Image   In writing, an image is a picture drawn with words, a reproduction of persons, objects, or sensations that are perceived through sight, sound, touch, taste, or smell. Often an image is evoked to visually represent an idea. *See* "Symbol."

Impressionistic   Depicting a scene, emotion, or character so that it evokes subjective or sensory impressions. An impression is an effect produced upon the mind or emotions. The more writing emphasizes the effects on the writer of scenes, persons, and ideas, the more impressionistic, and hence the less objective, it will be. *See* "Objectivity" and "Subjectivity."

Induction   The process by which one draws a generalized conclusion from specifics. If it is a fact that a high percentage of people who die from lung cancer each year also smoke cigarettes, one might safely induce that cigarette smoking is a contributing factor in the disease. *See* "Deduction."

Introduction   An introduction sets forth the writer's thesis or major themes and establishes tone (attitude toward one's subject), and—particularly in a long paper—suggests an organizational plan. The introduction, or opening, of an essay should capture the reader's attention and interest. Like the conclusion, it may be no more than a sentence or it may be many paragraphs.

Irony   The undermining or contradicting of someone's expectations. Irony may be either verbal or dramatic. **Verbal irony** arises from a discrepancy, sometimes intentional and sometimes not, between what is said and what is meant, as when a dog jumps forward to bite you, and you say, "What a friendly dog!" **Dramatic irony** arises from a discrepancy between what someone expects to happen and what does happen; for example, if the dog that seemed so unfriendly to you saves your life. *See* "Sarcasm" and "Satire."

Jargon   The specialized language of a trade, profession, or other socioeconomic group. Truck drivers employ a jargon on their citizen's band radios that sounds like gibberish to most people. Writing that employs contextless jargon is inappropriate.

Journal   A daily written record of ideas, memories, experiences, or dreams. A journal can be used for prewriting and as a source for formal writing.

Journalism   The profession of writing for newspapers, magazines, wire services, and radio and television. Journalistic writing emphasizes objectivity and factual reportage; the work of editorial writers, columnists, and feature writers often is a more subjective form of reportage.

Literal   The ordinary or primary meaning of a word or expression. Dwelling on literal meaning can promote erroneous thinking. The sentence "Childhood is a time of sunshine" should be read figuratively, not literally. (The sun does not always shine during childhood; rather, childhood is a happy time.)

Metaphor   A figure of speech in which, through an implied comparison, one object is identified with another and some qualities of the first object are ascribed to the second. *See* "Simile."

Mode   A conventional form or usage. Writing includes four customary modes of discourse: description, narration, exposition, and persuasion (argumentation).

Narration   A narrative essay is a story with a point; narration is the technique used to tell the story. When writing a narrative essay, pay close attention to point of view, pacing, chronology, and transitions.

Objectivity   Freedom from personal bias. A report about a scientific experiment is objective insofar as facts in it are explained without reference to the writer's feelings about the experiment. But not even the most factual piece of writing is completely uncolored by the writer's attitudes and impressions. Objectivity is best thought of as a matter of degree, increasing in direct proportion with the writer's distance from the work. *See* "Subjectivity."

Paradox   A statement that sounds self-contradictory, even absurd, and yet expresses a truth. It is paradoxical, though nonetheless true, to say that one person can simultaneously feel both love and hatred for another person.

Parallel Structure   The association of ideas phrased in parallel ways, thus giving a piece of writing balance and proportion. "He loves wine, women, and singing" lacks parallelism. "He loves wine, women, and song" is parallel; the verbal noun "singing" interrupts the series of nouns.

Personification   A figure of speech in which abstract concepts or inanimate objects are represented as having human qualities or characteristics. To write that "death rides a pale horse," for example, is to personify death.

Persuasion   The art of moving someone else to act in a desired way or to believe in a chosen idea. Logic and reason are important tools of persuasion. Equally effective may be an appeal either to the emotions or to the ethical sensibilities.

Point of View   The vantage point from which an author writes. In expository prose, an author may adopt a first-person or a third-person point of view. *See* "Style" and "Tone."

Sarcasm   An expression of ridicule, contempt, or derision. Sarcastic remarks are nasty or bitter in tone and often characterized by irony that is meant to hurt. You might express your displeasure with those who have given you a hard time by sarcastically thanking them for their help. *See* "Irony."

Satire   A genre of writing that makes various use of irony, sarcasm, ridicule, and broad humor in order to expose, denounce, or reform. Satires dwell on the follies and evils of human beings and institutions. The satirist's tone may range from amusement and gentle mockery to harsh contempt and moral indignation.

Simile   A figure of speech including *like* or *as* and stating a direct, explicit comparison between two things: he ate *like* a pig; her heart felt light *as* a feather. *See* "Metaphor."

Slang   Colloquialisms and jargon are deemed inappropriate in formal writing. Whether a word or phrase is considered colloquial or slang is often a matter of personal taste. Also, slang often gains acceptance in time. A word such as *uptight,* once considered slang by cultivated people, is now an acceptable colloquialism. *See* "Colloquialism" and "Jargon."

Specificity   Precision, particularity, concreteness. Specificity, like generalization, is a matter of degree; the word *horse* is more specific than *animal* but more general than *stallion. See* "Generalization."

Style   The "fingerprint," the identifying mark, of a writer—both as an individual and as a representative of his or her age and culture. An author's style is the product of the diction employed, sentence structure and organization, and the overall form and tone in which thoughts are expressed. Style is variously described, depending on the analyzer's purpose. It may be simple or complex, forthright or subtle, colloquial or formal; modern or classical, romantic or realistic, "logical" or poetic. It may be anything, in short, that reflects the writer's personality, background, and talent. *See* "Point of View" and "Tone."

Subjectivity   The personal element in writing. The more subjective a piece of writing, the more it is likely to be focused on the writer's opinions and feelings. *See* "Objectivity."

Syllogism   A highly formal three-part form of deductive logic. The syllogist argues that if a generalization (major premise) is true and a specific case of the generalization (minor premise) is also true, then any conclusion reached is necessarily true. If the major premise is "smoking causes cancer" and the minor premise is "John Doe smokes," then the conclusion is "John Doe will contract lung cancer." Syllogisms often sound logical, but are not true because one or both premises are faulty. See "Deduction."

Symbol   Something that stands for something else. An eagle is a conventional symbol of the United States. Any word, image, or description, any name, character, or action that has a range of meanings and associations beyond its literal denotation may be symbolic, depending on who is interpreting it and the context in which it appears. The word *eagle*, therefore, may bring to mind different images or ideas; it may connote freedom or power or solitude.

Synonym   One of two or more words having approximately the same meaning. "Happiness" and "joy" are synonyms. See "Antonym."

Tautology   Inherent or pointless repetition. To write that a person was treated with "cruel inhumanity" is tautological: inhumanity is always cruel.

Thesis   The main idea or theme of an essay. In expository prose, the writer usually states the thesis clearly in the introduction. The thesis statement should establish point of view, the primary point(s) intended for discussion, and the writer's attitude toward it.

Tone   Tone of voice; an author's attitude toward his or her subject, and, at times, audience. Tone is caught in the "sound" of a piece of writing. The tone of an essay may be angry, resigned, humorous, serious, sentimental, mocking, ironic, sarcastic, satirical, reasoning, emotional, philosophic—anything, in short, that echoes the voice of the author. One tone may predominate or many tones ("overtones"?) may be heard in any work. See "Style."

Topic Sentence   The sentence in a paragraph that states clearly the main theme or point of the paragraph.

Transition   A bridge between one point or topic or idea and another. The logical movement from sentence to sentence and paragraph to paragraph should be easy to follow if a piece of writing is coherent. This logic is often emphasized by means of transitional expressions such as *therefore, hence, similarly, however, but, furthermore, also,* and *for example.* See "Coherence."

Understatement   An obvious downplaying or underrating of something. It is the opposite of hyperbole, although use of either may create a memorable image or an ironic effect. To say that "after they ate the apple, Adam and Eve found life a bit tougher," is to understate their condition. See "Hyperbole."

Unity   The basic focus or theme that permeates a piece of writing, thus lending the piece a sense of wholeness and completeness. The words and sentences and paragraphs, the images and ideas, the explanations and examples, the characters and actions, the descriptions and arguments—all should be relevant to the overriding purpose or point of a work. See "Coherence."

GEOGRAPHICAL INDEX

UNITED STATES: ETHNIC GROUPS

Pages 296–299 Reprinted by permission of Georges Borchardt, Inc., and the author. Copyright © 1988 by Richard Rodriguez. This essay was first published in the March 1984 issue of *Harper's*.

Pages 301–306 Reprinted by permission of Michael Novak, from *The Rise of the Unmeltable Ethnics*. Copyright © 1972, Macmillan Company.

Pages 308–311 Reprinted with permission of Jim Fusilli.

Pages 313–317 From *"The Good War": An Oral History of World War Two* by Studs Terkel. Copyright © 1984 by Studs Terkel. Reprinted by permission of Pantheon Books, a division of Random House, Inc.

Pages 319–323 From "A Life in Contrasts" in *The Koreans: Passion and Grace*. Copyright © 1988 by Russell Warren Howe. Reprinted by permission of Harcourt Brace Jovanovich, Inc.

Pages 325–334 Reprinted by permission of Harriet Wasserman Literary Agency, as agents of the author. Copyright © 1972 by Ruth Prawer Jhabvala.

Pages 336–340 Excerpts from *The Hidden Dimension* by Edward T. Hall. Copyright © 1966 by Edward T. Hall. Used by permission of Doubleday, a division of Bantam, Doubleday, Dell Publishing Group, Inc.

Pages 342–346 Excerpted from *Whereabouts: Notes on Being a Foreigner*, copyright © 1987 by Alastair Reid. Reprinted by permission of North Point Press. This article first appeared in *The New Yorker*.

Pages 348–356 "Call Me Not a Man," by Mtutuzeli Matshoba © 1979 by Ravan Press.

Pages 366–369 Reprinted with permission of Marshall Glickman.

Pages 371–373 Reprinted by permission of the Rosa Parks Institute, Detroit, Michigan.

Pages 375–377 From *You Can't Drown the Fire: Latin American Women Writing in Exile*, edited by Alicia Portnoy, Cleis Press, 1988.

Pages 379–383 Reprinted by permission of Georges Borchardt, Inc., and the author. Copyright © 1988 by Richard Rodriguez. This essay was first published by Aperture (1988).

Pages 385–388 Reprinted by permission of Russell & Volkening as agents for the author. Copyright © 1988 by Nadine Gordimer. This story was first published in the August 1988 issue of *Harper's*.

Pages 390–395 From *Pyramids of Sacrifice: Political Ethics and Social Change* by Peter L. Berger. Copyright © 1974 by Peter L. Berger. Reprinted by permission of Basic Books, Inc., Publishers.

Pages 397–405 Reprinted with permission of Hana Wehle.

Pages 407–411 Reprinted by permission of Dow Jones & Company, Inc. © Dow Jones & Company, Inc., 1983. All rights reserved.

Pages 412–416 From "A Train Ride" by Hugo Lindo. Translated by Elizabeth Gamble Miller. Copyright © 1968 by City Lights Books. Reprinted by permission of City Lights Books.

Pages 423–427 From *American Indian Myths and Legends*, edited by Richard Erdoes and Alfonso Ortiz. Copyright © 1984 by Richard Erdoes and Alfonso Ortiz. Reprinted by permission of Pantheon Books, a division of Random House, Inc.

Pages 429–430 Introduction and story from *A Harvest of Folk Tales*, edited by Milton Rugoff, The Viking Press, 1949.

Pages 431–434 Reprinted with permission of Atheneum Publishers, an imprint of Macmillan Publishing Company, from *Writin' Is Fightin'*, by Ishmael Reed. Copyright © 1988 by Ishmael Reed.

Pages 436–438 From "My Turn" column by Lewis P. Johnson, *Newsweek* magazine, September 5, 1983. Reprinted by permission of *Newsweek*.